The Norman People and Their Existing Descendants in the British Dominions and the United States of America

Anonymous

THE NORMAN PEOPLE

THE NORMAN PEOPLE

AND THEIR EXISTING DESCENDANTS IN
THE BRITISH DOMINIONS AND THE
UNITED STATES OF AMERICA

'The very concurrence and coincidence of so many evidences
that contribute to the proof, carries a great weight.'

SIR MATTHEW HALE

HENRY S. KING & Co.

65 CORNHILL & 12 PATERNOSTER ROW, LONDON

1874

TO THE MEMORY

OF

PERCY VISCOUNT STRANGFORD

PREFACE.

It is the aim of the following pages to apply genealogy to
the illustration of English ethnology. The former branch
of knowledge has been supposed to lie exclusively within
the domain of the antiquary; but a closer examination
will, it is thought, show that the scientific observer, and
the historian also, may find in it classes of facts which
are not beneath their notice and investigation.

If by placing genealogy on a critical and historical
basis, and applying it to ethnology, we should be enabled
to prove the fallacy of some generally received maxims
as to the composition of the English nation—to show
that the Norman settlement at the Conquest consisted of
something more than a slight infusion of a foreign
element—that it involved the addition of a numerous and
mighty people, equalling probably a moiety of the conquered population—that the people thus introduced has
continued to exist without merger or absorption in any

other race—that, as a race, it is as distinguishable now as it was a thousand years since, and that at this hour its descendants may be counted by tens of millions in this country and in the United States of America; if this be so, then it will be admitted that English ethnology is not uninterested in the progress of critical English genealogy—that it may find there a hitherto neglected series of facts, of incalculable value to English and even to foreign ethnology.

If, in addition to this, it be possible to show on historical grounds, that the earlier Northman or Danish immigration had seated in England a people scarcely inferior in number to the Anglo-Saxons; and, in the absence of all evidence to the contrary, to infer by a process of analogical reasoning from the case of the Normans, that this Danish race also has continued to exist up to the present moment, increasing in like ratio with them and the Anglo-Saxons; and that it consequently now rivals each of them in point of numbers; if this be so, history, which at present usually contemplates ancient events in England exclusively from the Anglo-Saxon point of view, and under the influence of Anglo-Saxon feeling, will acquire greater breadth and impartiality, and will extend to the Scandinavian ancestors of a majority of the English and American people that equitable judgment and that filial interest which are now reserved for the Anglo-Saxon ancestors of a minority.

Such are some of the results which may be anticipated from the application of historical genealogy to ethnology, in which this work is a first essay.

The genealogy of the Norman race leads up to its connexion with the Danish and the Anglo-Saxon, which, with it, form the three great constituents of the English nation. To trace that connexion it has been found necessary to enter on the relationship between the Gothic and Teutonic races, which, as far as the author is aware, has not as yet been treated systematically by English writers. It is hoped, however, that the views here enunciated will be found to harmonise generally with those entertained by the most enlightened enquirers.

The later Scandinavian or Norman immigration into England has formed the subject of the following pages; the earlier Scandinavian or Danish has been very slightly noticed in connexion with it. The extent and difficulty of the latter subject have induced the author to reserve its further consideration for another work.

January, 1874.

CONTENTS.

———·◦○◦·———

ADDITIONAL NOTES.

ADDITIONAL NOTES.

I. ON THE NOMENCLATURE OF RACES.

THE term 'English' in these pages is used to describe the people of England for the last seven centuries, during which it has been thus employed. It is not here applied to the natives of England from the year 500 to the Conquest, because, in the author's opinion, the race termed 'English' prior to 880 formed only a moiety of the race so termed in 1066, and only forms a third of the race now so termed. For distinctness' sake, therefore, he uses 'Saxon' or 'Anglo-Saxon,' 'Dane,' and 'Norman,' to describe the three great and nearly equal constituents of the present 'English' race.

II. ON THE EXTENT OF THE DANISH DOMINION IN 879.

In reference to the remarks on this subject (page 102), it may be said that an extent has been there assigned to the Danish dominion after the treaty between Alfred and Guthrum in 878, which is at variance with received opinions; and Mr. Freeman's and Mr. Pearson's statements may be cited. Those eminent writers have, undoubtedly, taken a different view of the case. The former states (Norman Conquest, i. 48), that 'by the terms of the peace of Wedmore the Northmen were to evacuate Wessex and the part of Mercia south of Watling Street; they, or at least their chiefs, were to submit to baptism, and they were to receive the whole land beyond Watling Street as vassals of the West Saxon king. Guthrum, the Danish king, was accordingly baptised by the name of Æthelstan; he took possession of his new dominions,' &c. In a note the exact boundary of the two states is detailed from the treaty extant in Thorpe's 'Laws and Institutes' (i. 152), which is assumed to be the 'peace of Wedmore.' Mr. Pearson (Hist. England, i. 169) repeats these statements, and expands them by adding that by 'this agreement the whole of Mercia was restored to its former dependent condition to Wessex.'

The author ventures to think that these able writers have not, in this case, exhibited their usual critical discrimination. He is unable to divine their reason for terming the treaty of 878 the 'peace' or 'treaty' of 'Wedmore.' The treaty was actually concluded at Chippenham, and Wedmore is only mentioned by the earliest chroniclers as the scene of a ceremony (the chrism-loosing) some weeks later, consequent on Guthrum's baptism. They know nothing of a 'treaty of Wedmore.' The contemporary writers are equally silent as to Guthrum and the Danes holding the north of Mercia as 'vassals' of Alfred; or as to Guthrum's obtaining 'new dominions' in East Anglia by gift of that Prince. These stories were invented at a later date to glorify King Alfred, and ought not to be accepted merely on the authority of the later chroniclers.

Again, the author cannot but wonder that the treaty of 878 between Guthrum and Alfred should be confused by these writers with that between Guthrum and Alfred which is still extant. A very slight examination would have shown that the two treaties are wholly different. We learn from Asser, the contemporary and friend of King Alfred, that the treaty of Chippenham in 878 comprised, after the agreement for peace, two articles— the speedy evacuation of Alfred's dominions by the Danes, and an undertaking by Guthrum to become Christian, and to receive baptism under Alfred's sponsorship. 'Juraverunt se citissimè de suo regno exituros, nec non et Godrum rex eorum Christianitatem subire, et baptismum sub manu Ælfredi regis accipere promisit' (Asser, de reb. gestis Ælfredi Ann. 878). The Saxon Chronicle also states that by the treaty the Danes undertook to leave Alfred's kingdom (thæt hie of his rice woldon), and that their king should receive baptism (Chron. Sax., ed. Petrie, p. 357). Neither of the conditions here mentioned are to be found in the extant treaty; but instead of them we find an article defining the boundaries of the two kingdoms, which is not alluded to by the early writers as forming any part of the treaty of 878. Nor is this all that can be said. The very terms of the extant treaty show that it ought not to be confused with the treaty of 878. It is entitled ' the Peace that King Alfred and King Guthrum and the Witan of all the English nation, and all the people that are in East Anglia, have ordained.' A treaty made by the Danes at Chippenham in Wilts, could not well be said to be made by 'the people that are in East Anglia.'

It is evident from the use of those terms that the treaty in which they were introduced must have been made subsequently to the Danish settlement in East Anglia; but the Danes did not become seated in East Anglia till 880, according to Asser and the Saxon-Chronicle, that is, not till two years after the treaty of Chippenham. Consequently, the treaty we now possess must have been later than the treaty of Chippenham; and the agreement as to the boundaries passing along the Lea, Ouse, and Watling Street, was not made in 878, but at a later date.

In addition to this, Mercia, south of Watling Street, is further proved to have been the territory of the Danes after the treaty of 878, by the statement of the Anglo-Saxon writers, that the Danes fully 'executed' the conditions of that treaty—'quæ omnia ille et sui ut promiserunt impleverunt' (Asser), and 'hie thæt gelæston' (Sax. Chron.), coupled with their statement immediately after, that the Danes, 'according to their promise,' 'departed in 879 from Chippenham to Cirencester, and there remained for one year.' Cirencester was in the south of Mercia, and yet the residence of the Danes there for a year was a fulfilment of their promise under the treaty to evacuate Alfred's 'kingdom.' Therefore South Mercia under the treaty of 878 was not a part of that kingdom. Hence we see at once that Alfred was not in possession of South Mercia in 879, nor was he in possession of any territory north of the Thames till the year 886, when we find him besieging and taking London. 'Interim obsidetur a rege Ælfredo urbs Lundonia. . . . Etiam post manus catervæ confirmatas ibi constituitur dux Æthered a rege præfato custodiendi arcem' (Ethelward Chron. iv. p. 517, Ed. Petrie). Here, then, commenced the acquisition of a part of the Danish dominion north of the Thames by conquest from the Danes, afterwards ratified by treaty.

Mr. Pearson has quoted (i. 170) a charter from the Codex Diplomaticus (311) to prove that Ethelred was appointed duke of Mercia immediately after the treaty of 878. This charter undoubtedly is dated 880, and is witnessed by Alfred and by his daughter Ethelfleda (apparently as wife of Ethelred); and the latter is styled 'duke of Mercia;' but Mr. Kemble has remarked (Cod. Dipl. ii. Preface), that a large proportion of Alfred's charters are forgeries; and it seems, either that the charter under consideration is one of these, or else that its date is an error; for in 880 Ethelfleda was, at the outside, eleven years old (Alfred having married in 868 at nineteen years of age), and could not then have been married, nor is it likely that she should have witnessed a charter at such an age. Mr. Pearson also produces a charter stating that Wulphere's estates were, immediately after

878, confiscated by the Witan of Wessex 'and Mercia;' but there is no evidence whatever of the date of this transaction; it no doubt took place at a date long subsequent to 878, after Alfred had acquired a part of Mercia by conquest.

III. ON THE FAMILY OF HASTINGS.

In p. 280 the author has identified the family of Hastings with that of Le Mareschal de Venoix. A different view has been taken in an elaborate paper on the Hastings Family (Archæological Journal, vol. xxvi.), the general value of which the author desires to acknowledge. Its identification, however, of the house of Hastings with that of Mascarel appears to rest on an unsound inference. It is argued that because William, son of Robert, t. Henry II., and his son Ralph de Hastings, were possessed of estates formerly the property of the Mascarels, and because Alexander Mascarel is expressly stated to have been 'uncle' of William, son of Robert, therefore Robert must have been a Mascarel, and brother of Alexander. But this does not follow: Robert may have married the sister of Alexander Mascarel, in which case the latter would be 'uncle' of William Fitz-Robert; and such, no doubt, was the fact, for Robert was a Hastings, and is mentioned t. Henry I. as 'De Venoix,' the latter being the Norman, and Hastings the English name of the family. It is needless to go into the question of chronology, which appears to be also adverse to this theory. The author hopes, therefore, that he may be excused for not admitting the identity of the Mascarel and the Hastings families as proved.

THE NORMAN PEOPLE.

CHAPTER I.

DISCOVERY OF THE DESCENDANTS OF THE NORMAN NOBILITY IN ENGLAND.

THE Normans were one of those few races of men whose extraordinary mental and physical energies have exercised a profound and enduring influence over the world. They were a race of the same class as the Greek, the Roman, or the Saracen, whose actions fill the pages of history, and will remain engraved on the memory of man as long as humanity itself endures.

Seven centuries have elapsed since the world has known the Normans in England under the form of a separate and distinct nationality. They have been for that space of time inextricably blended with other races in England, and the modern inhabitants of this country are unable to determine the early nationality to which they individually owe their origin. Let it then be permitted to direct closer attention to the Normans, as the most conspicuous amongst the early races of England, and in the first place to their character and exploits in the tenth and eleventh centuries. It is here proposed to quote the testimony of some of our most eminent historians in relation to the Norman character, because it possesses far more value and authority than any other evidence that might be collected from other sources, representing as it does the matured opinions of men perfectly conversant with the subject on which they have written, and whose testimony may be considered to be free from bias or prejudice.

The first whose description of the Norman character deserves attention is Lord Macaulay, who was himself of Celtic origin.

'The Normans,' says Lord Macaulay, 'were then the foremost race of Christendom. Their valour and ferocity had made them conspicuous amongst the rovers whom Scandinavia had sent forth to ravage Western Europe . . . At length one of the feeble heirs of Charlemagne ceded to the strangers a fertile province . . . In that province they founded a mighty state, which gradually extended its influence over the neighbouring principalities of Brittany and Maine. Without laying aside the dauntless valour which had been the terror of every land from the Elbe to the Pyrenees, the Normans rapidly acquired all, and more than all, the knowledge and refinement which they found in the country where they settled. Their courage secured their territory against foreign invasion.

They established internal order, such as had been long unknown in the Frank Empire. They embraced Christianity, and with Christianity they learned a great part of what the clergy had to teach. They abandoned their native speech and adopted the French tongue, in which the Latin was the predominant element. They speedily raised their new language to a dignity and importance which it had never possessed. They found it a barbarous jargon, they fixed it in writing, and they employed it in legislation, in poetry, and in romance. They renounced that brutal intemperance to which all the other branches of the great German family were too much inclined . . . That chivalrous spirit which has exercised so powerful an influence on the politics, the morals, and manners of the European nations was found in the highest exaltation amongst the Norman nobles. These nobles were distinguished by their graceful bearing and insinuating address. They were distinguished also by their skill in negotiation and by a natural eloquence, which they assiduously cultivated . . . But their chief fame was derived from their military exploits. Every country, from the Atlantic Ocean to the Red Sea, witnessed the prodigies of their discipline and valour. One Norman knight, at the head of a handful of warriors, scattered the Celts of Connaught. Another founded the monarchy of the Two Sicilies, and saw the Emperors of the East and West fly before his arms. A third, the Ulysses of the first Crusade, was invested by his fellow-soldiers with the sovereignty of

Antioch; and a fourth, whose name lives in the great poem of Tasso, was celebrated throughout Christendom as the bravest and most generous of the champions of the Holy Sepulchre.'[1]

'The Normans,' says Mr. Freeman, ' were the Saracens of Christendom, spreading themselves over every corner of the world, and appearing in almost every character . . . None knew better how to hold their own against pope and prelate : the especial children of the Church were as little disposed to unconditional obedience as the most stiff-necked of Ghibilines.'

'To free England,' he continues, ' the Norman gave a race of tyrants : to enslaved Sicily he gave a line of beneficent rulers.   But to England he gave also a conquering nobility, which, in a few generations, became as truly English in England as it had become French in Normandy.   If he overthrew our Harolds and our Waltheofs, he gave a Fitz-Walter and a Bigod to win back the rights for which Harold and Waltheof had fallen. . . . Art, under his auspices, produced alike the stern grandeur of Caen and Ely, and the brilliant gorgeousness of Palermo and Monreale.   In a word, the indomitable vigour of the Scandinavian, joined to the buoyant vivacity of the Gaul, produced the conquering and ruling race of Europe.'[2]

The destinies of this imperial race are thus described by a great historian:

---

[1] Lord Macaulay, History of England, i. 11.
[2] Freeman, History of the Norman Conquest, i. 170.

'The Normans,' says Froude, 'in occupying both England and Ireland, were but fulfilling the work for which they were especially qualified and gifted. . . . They were born rulers of men, and were forced by the same necessity which has brought the decrepit kingdoms of Asia under the authority of England and Russia to take the management, eight centuries ago, of the anarchic nations of Western Europe.'[1]

In contemplating the Norman race, then, which became seated in England in the eleventh century, we are to recognise in it one of the most extraordinary manifestations of human intellect and power that the history of the world affords; and we are hence impelled at once to demand further details of the actual life and attendant conditions of a race so singular and remarkable. We are led to enquire, What was the real character and nature of the settlement of the Normans in England? Was it merely the migration of a small body of nobles? Was it, on the other hand, an immigration as truly national as that of the Saxons had been? What was to be the destiny of this new race? Was it, like some mere military aristocracies, predestined to speedy decay, and to ultimate extinction? Was it to be irretrievably lost amidst the masses of the nations whom it had subdued? Was its empire to fall into the hands of an alien nationality? Are those Norman laws, institutions, language, and national attributes, which in England and America bear

[1] Froude, The English in Ireland, i. 16, 17.

such potent testimony to a common origin, merely the memorials of a race that has long passed away, and to which the actual inhabitants of these countries bear as remote a relation as they do to the unknown races which fabricated stone implements or were contemporary with the mammoth?

Or is the reverse of this the truth? Is the Norman race still living—still presenting its essential characteristics—still great, prosperous, progressive, and more than ever multitudinous? Is it still producing new nations? Is it still in the van of human progress, yet still advancing with firm, practical, deliberate, and masculine intelligence?

Such are some of the questions which suggest themselves on perusing the narrative of the adventurous exploits of the Normans; and they are questions which, with all the respect due to the eminent writers who have recorded those exploits, have not as yet received from them the attention to which their interest and their importance are entitled.

Mr. Freeman gives expression to the views most prevalent on this subject. 'The indomitable vigour of the Scandinavian, joined to the buoyant vivacity of the Gaul, produced the conquering and ruling race of Europe. And yet that race, as a race, has vanished. It has everywhere been absorbed by the races which it had conquered.' 'In Old England,' continues the same accomplished writer, 'the Norman race has sunk beneath the influence of a race less brilliant, but more enduring than his own. The Norman has vanished from the world, but he has indeed left a name behind him.'[1] So, too, Gibbon has said, 'The adventurous Normans who had raised so many trophies in France, England and Ireland, in Apulia, Sicily, and the East, were lost in victory or servitude among the vanquished nations.'[2]

These opinions are grounded on the phenomena which meet the eye and appear on the surface of society.

Historians have not as yet sufficiently considered the Normans as a whole. They have adopted as their basis chronicles and records which describe chiefly the actions of the higher classes, and whose allusions to the middle and lower classes are slight and transient, and hence we find the ablest English historians at variance on questions of importance. To some the Norman settlement at the Conquest presents itself in the aspect of the migration of a few thousands of knights and nobles, while others recognise in it the immigration of Normans of all classes. Yet it is obviously of the greatest importance, in an historical point of view, to determine whether the Normans were an aristocracy or a nation. It is evident that a nation cannot be dealt with as if it were an aristocracy without risk of serious error; and it may be said with deference that if our historians had from circumstances been enabled to devote more time and attention to leading questions of

[1] Freeman, History of the Norman Conquest, i. 169, 170.
[2] Gibbon, Decline and Fall, vii. 145. Ed. 1855.

this nature, their views of history might have been in some important respects modified.

History throws very little light on the fate of the Normans after the twelfth century. It does not enable us to resolve satisfactorily the problem of their later existence. It is not, in fact, conversant with those minuter and more detailed enquiries which would alone enable it to determine such questions of fact. From the twelfth century distinctions of race in England entirely disappear from the surface of history, and the continuance and position of the Norman race are merely subjects of conjecture.

The desirableness of a fresh enquiry into the later condition of a race so renowned will perhaps be generally admitted. The uncertainty in which its fate remains involved subsequently to the twelfth century, and the contradictory opinions which prevail on the subject, will constitute a sufficient apology for an attempt to ascertain questions of fact. But the enquiry is surrounded by difficulties so numerous that the reluctance of authors to venture upon it is easily to be accounted for. It demands a special study of subjects not particularly inviting—an examination in detail of facts and circumstances apparently too trivial to claim notice, and yet so numerous as to demand sedulous application, and a considerable expenditure of time. It may disturb opinions very generally received—may create offence in many cases—and may interfere with the most cherished convictions of numerous .

families. And there has been also, till recently, a moral impossibility that almost any amount of leisure could suffice for the elucidation of these questions. They have only come within the reach of solution within the present generation. In the preceding generation the materials for enquiry still remained almost inaccessible in manuscripts; and had not the present writer been enabled to refer to the Great Rolls of the Norman Exchequer in print, as edited by Mr. Stapleton for the Society of Antiquaries about thirty years since, and to realize the valuable results of that publication, by the aid of the Index which at a later period was compiled under direction of the Société des Antiquaires de la Normandie, and which appears in their excellent edition of the same record, it would have been totally impossible to write the present work; and even these materials, valuable as they are, would have been comparatively useless in the author's hands had he not, by the merest accident, brought the Exchequer Rolls of Normandy into juxtaposition with the English records of the twelfth century.

The English and Norman records furnish, in truth, a singular and perhaps unique instance in Europe of the preservation and publication of records of two different countries, of seven hundred years standing, relating to different branches of the same race, and so minutely detailed as to enable us to trace the identity of families, and even individuals, in two countries. Had we possessed either of these classes of records singly, without the other, it would have been impossible to trace the connexion of races ; and so remarkable is the light which they throw on each other, and on the race to which they relate, in its two divisions, that it may be said that in all probability there is no parallel instance in the world. Certainly there is nothing to correspond to it in the case of the Anglo-Saxon and Danish nationalities in England, for there are no records, either in Scandinavia, or in North Germany and Holland, which could throw light on the great masses of the English branches of their race.

A statement of the circumstances in which the present enquiry originated may, perhaps, be the most appropriate mode of conveying to the reader a general notion of the chain of reasoning which gradually resulted in the conclusions hereafter to be detailed.

Some years since a relative expressed to the writer a wish that some of his leisure hours might be given to investigations on the origin of families in which they were mutually interested by descent. In compliance with that desire some attention was given to the subject in question ; and the writer very speedily discovered that the enquiry was not without its attendant difficulties. He found himself immersed in thorny questions of all descriptions, the age and authenticity of manuscripts and records, the precise chronology of events not noticed by ordinary history, the descent of estates and their changes of denomination, the identity or diversity of contemporary individuals bearing the same name, the obsolete forms of existing languages, the force and meaning of forgotten habits, usages, laws, and institutions, the changes in European geography and topography, the correct reading and interpretation of records relating to an order of things that has passed away.

These investigations continued at intervals for years, and in their course familiarity with the sources of knowledge was gradually attained. At length the task was ended, and the results were—the complete establishment of the fact that certain families, supposed to be English, were originally Norman, the recovery of their original Norman names after a disuse of six centuries, and with those names the recovery of their early history, both in Normandy and England, and the overset of sundry received heraldic pedigrees.

The particular cases which led to these results could only be interesting to a very limited circle, but the results themselves appeared to deserve more attentive consideration. When they were carefully studied it was perceived that there must be in England many families which, under English surnames, preserve a Norman descent. It was concluded, further, that the same system of enquiry which had been found successful in some cases might prove equally successful in others; that additional discoveries might be anticipated; and that this result might be attained with comparative facility in consequence of the experience which had been gained. Curiosity being excited, it was resolved to make an excursion into the *terra incognita*, not perhaps without some faint spark of the same interest which led the adventurer of old to launch forth on voyages of discovery.

All that now remained to be done was to choose the point from which investigation should commence. The first selection (as is often the case in new undertakings) proved a failure, and operated as a discouragement. It was attempted to trace the descendants of the Barons of the Conqueror mentioned in Domesday Book; but, after great and not altogether unfruitful research, it was at length realised that families may be traced upwards, but can scarcely be traced downwards, and the attempt had to be abandoned.

This failure, however, did not in any degree affect the principles which had been previously established by experiment. They continued intact. It only remained, therefore, to adopt another field of enquiry. The subject which was chosen was the origin of the peerage families of the kingdom, amounting to from 500 to 600. The extent and the importance of this undertaking rendered it a matter of indispensable necessity that a preliminary survey of the records should be taken, and a critical and historical apparatus be provided, commensurate with the magnitude of the work, and affording facility for prompt reference at every point of the enquiry.

The author accordingly employed several months in the collection and alphabetical arrangement of all facts of importance regarding Norman and native English families,

possessed of land in England from the Conquest to the
fourteenth century. The *Monasticon Anglicanum*, *Domesday Book*, the *Liber Niger*, the *Testa de Neville*, and
other works published under the auspices of the Record
Commissioners and the Government, the *Gallia Christiana*,
the publications of the Society of Antiquaries of Normandy,
the works of Des Bois and Anselme, and many others,
furnished tens of thousands of facts regarding the early
landed aristocracy of England. On the completion of this
apparatus the author found himself in the possession of
details regarding more than 3,000 different Anglo-
Norman families, the ancient lords of the soil in this
country. These families usually consisted of several
branches, and were widely disseminated in all parts of the
kingdom; and their succession remained uninterruptedly
from the Conquest to the fourteenth century. Could the
author place the details before the reader, nothing more
would be requisite to demonstrate the long continuance
of the Norman landed aristocracy.

It may be here observed that the longest list of the
companions of the Conqueror ever published—the Battle
Abbey Roll—includes not much more than 600 names
of Norman families. The list as now collected from the
records exceeded 3,000, or was five times the length of
the Battle Abbey Roll; and long as it was, was not
perfect. The Battle Abbey Roll mentions a certain part
of the Norman aristocracy which was existing in the time

of Edward I., but its compiler was not in a position to enumerate all the families then extant.[1]

Thus provided with a tolerably ample critical apparatus, the author proceeded to undertake the enquiry into the origin of the peerage families of the kingdom. That task involved in the first place the examination of the earlier parts of all the pedigrees which had been accumulating since the sixteenth century, and which had been detailed, and watered down, and abridged in the various works on the peerage. In many cases these pedigrees were of very limited extent; the heralds or others, their compilers, apparently being of opinion, that when any family was so fortunate as to descend from an alderman or a lord-mayor that dignified origin precluded all necessity for further investigation. Even a Turkey merchant, a goldsmith, or an iron manufacturer appeared to satiate the appetite for ancestry; and descent from these honoured personages was sufficient to establish the superfluousness of all remoter history. But so different are tastes, that in other cases families were desirous of attaining the honours of long descent, and the heralds and genealogists of the sixteenth and seventeenth centuries accordingly were set to work to provide pedigrees.

Generally speaking, these documents may be regarded

---

[1] This document, from the Norman-French orthography of its names, and the families which it introduces, cannot be earlier than the time of Edward I. The orthography is that of other documents of that period. Its existence from the Conquest at Battle Abbey is a mere myth, depending on the authority of some unknown herald of the sixteenth century.

as fairly authentic in their account of families as far back
as the fourteenth century; but when they touch on remoter
times they require to be viewed with a discriminative eye.
The genealogical history of England from the eleventh to
the fourteenth century was (except in the case of some
very remarkable families) a *terra incognita* to the mass of
the writers of the sixteenth and seventeenth centuries to
whom the existing pedigrees are due. The consequences
may be anticipated. The author, being aware of the facts
of the case generally, felt satisfied that in examining the
earlier parts of the received pedigrees nothing ought to be
accepted on the mere authority of the heralds or
genealogists of the sixteenth or seventeenth century, or of
the pedigrees then compiled. The statements were in all
cases deserving of consideration; but they required to be
supported by evidence. They were therefore submitted
throughout to the test of record and fact. They were
examined with the aid of common sense, history, chronology, armorial bearings, public or private records, and
with a due regard to the laws of probability and fair
historical inference. By pursuing this course throughout,
wherever it was applicable, the earlier English pedigrees
became to a large extent disintegrated and dissolved.
Mistakes and fabrications came to light; blunders, impossibilities, and absurdities were strewn around. The
older English pedigrees were thus materially affected;
while the Welsh, Irish, and Scottish pedigrees of Celtic
families were almost untouched, simply because the

absence of records in a great degree precluded the possibility either of accepting or rejecting them. They remained in doubt.[1]

The ground having been thus cleared from the rubbish which had been permitted to accumulate, the work of reconstruction of the older pedigrees, and of the completion of the more recent pedigrees, commenced.

A close examination was immediately instituted into the earliest authentic accounts which we possess of the ancestors of each family. The ascertained facts were compared in each case with contemporary history and the records. At the proper point the extensive collections regarding the early aristocracy of England which had been formed came into play, and proved to be of incalculable utility. The course of proceeding was regulated throughout on that which had already been found successful—principles and rules established by practice were systematically carried out. Family after family was traced historically to the Conquest and beyond it; they were reinvested with their early names, once famous in

[1] It is not here intended to make any general or sweeping assertion. There are instances in which Celtic pedigrees can be historically traced; and when it is possible to do so, there is no class of descent in the kingdom which is of deeper interest. This only causes the more regret that the materials for enquiry are so scanty. Why are not the ancient manuscripts which contain the original Irish pedigrees of the eleventh or twelfth century properly edited? And why does Wales retain in manuscript works of a similar nature dating from the fifteenth century or earlier? Why are not the monastic chartularies of Wales, and Cornwall, and Ireland published in detail? In the absence of these essential materials it is impossible to attempt the authentication or elucidation (except in very rare instances) of the Celtic family history of the kingdom.

history and in song. The progress made warranted the expectation that results of importance might be anticipated. It is desirable to pause for a moment, and to consider the results as they actually came out in the end.

The popular peerages ascribe (more or less dubiously) a Norman origin to a score or two of peerage families. In many cases that origin is apocryphal or erroneous; it may be doubted whether a dozen families in the peerages are correctly identified in these works as Norman. The great mass of peerage families are not traced to any particular nationality; but from the circumstance of their being generally endowed with brief pedigrees the impression is left that they have sprung from the masses; and as the latter are (according to received opinion) Anglo-Saxon, the natural inference is that the body of the peerage is also of that race. Hence we have heard noble lords disclaiming for the House of Lords any descent from the Norman invaders of England; and it would appear that at present Anglo-Saxon descent is in especial favour, and that the peers themselves are anxious to claim it wherever practicable, for there are even many noble families which announce themselves as Anglo-Saxon without the slightest right to that distinction, such as it is.

Such being the popular view of peerage families, let it be permitted for a moment to contrast it with the state of things as disclosed by an unbiassed and independent inquiry.

The peerage families which formed the subject of this

*C

inquiry corresponded to the number of peers, about 550 in number.[1]   Of these about twenty were ascertained to be foreign families naturalized in England within the last three centuries.   Eighty, or thereabouts, were found to be Celtic families from Wales, Scotland, and Ireland.   Twenty (about) were determined to be Anglo-Saxon and Danish.   About 110 (many from Scotland), though in most cases ancient, could not be assigned to any particular nationality, but were doubtless either Norman, Danish, Saxon, or Celtic.   The remainder, being about 320, were ascertained to be Norman.   As it may be inferred with probability that the families of unascertained races (about 110) belonged to some of these native races, and might be divided amongst them, in proportion to their respective numbers, it seemed that on this principle the Norman limb of the peerage would rise to 400 out of 550, the Anglo-Saxon and Danish peerage rising at the same time to the number of twenty-five, so that the Norman would be to the Anglo-Saxon and Danish peerage as about sixteen to one.

Facts like these are not altogether without importance. It has been thought advisable to disclaim for the House of Lords any connection with the old feudal and Norman aristocracy: popular ethnological theories no doubt are in harmony with that view.   If, however, as a matter of fact, the peerage of England is not Anglo-Saxon, but

[1] The number of distinct families was less, as some families are represented by more than one peer.

almost entirely Norman, and if the Scottish, Irish, and Welsh peerage only help to lessen the Norman majority by adding Celts, we must make the best we can of the circumstance.

As far as it appears, the Normans have at least as much preponderance in the peerage at the present moment as they had in the time of William the Conqueror and in the following century. The proportions remain nearly the same. And it may here be added that, contrary to what we might have supposed, it is rather in the peerages of modern creation than in those of ancient standing that we find the lineal male descendants of the early baronage. If we were asked to point out those families which are of the highest Norman descent, and whose past is most identified with the history of England, we should have to pass over many of the oldest peerages now existing, and to turn to families which have been considered to be of modern and inferior origin. It is, however, a fact deserving of notice that so great a proportion of the peerage appears to be of Norman blood, and that this observation especially applies to pecrages of modern date. On this some remarks will presently be offered.

Thierry, in his history of the Conquest, has endeavoured to throw contempt on the Anglo-Norman baronage of the Conquest, on the ground that it had in general sprung from the lowest classes in Normandy—a mode of disparagement which in the mouth of so strong an opponent

of the aristocratic principle seems peculiarly inconsistent, as it involves those very distinctions of race which
are most objected to. Few will be inclined, in the
present day, to deny that, if obscurity of birth formed
no obstacle amongst the Normans to the reward of public
services and distinguished merit, it only proves their
superior enlightenment; nor is it a matter of much
importance to refute the imputations of Thierry on the
lineage of the Norman baronage. As simple matter of
fact, however, such imputations are unfounded. As a
whole, the native Norman nobility who were transferred
in a body to England were not inferior in birth to those
of any country in Europe. The greater barons, as well
as the Conqueror himself, were known in the eleventh
century to be of Norwegian blood. They were of princely
birth, representatives of the dispossessed royal families of
the twenty-two ancient kingdoms of Norway, who had
been deprived of their dominions by the conquests of
Harold Harfager. In addition to this, many of the most
illustrious Gothic and Frank houses joined in the invasion,
and their descendants in many cases have remained in
England. In fact, if we look for the descendants of the
early kings of the North, and the Merovingian barons of
France, they will be found at present amongst the Norman
people of England and America.

But it is time to revert to the subject of the existing
peerage families of England. Great numbers of these
families have risen from the middle classes, by commerce,

trade, professions, and successful marriages. Now these Normans of the peerage do not seem, as far as can be noticed, to have had any special advantages in the way of hereditary position and wealth over the Anglo-Saxon, Danish, and Celtic families ; yet in the race of life they have completely distanced them. How is this? Why is it that the peerage of England, which is continually recruited from the middle and lower classes, nevertheless remains essentially Norman, and not only Norman, but in a great degree lineally descended from the Norman nobility of the Conquest?

The Norman families of the peerage will be found noticed in detail in the alphabetical portion of this work under their respective family names. Taken as a class they present another illustration, in addition to the many which already exist, of the long continuance of English society and English institutions. That continuity has been well and eloquently impressed upon us by great living historians. It meets us in a thousand forms—in material fabrics, manners, laws, language, and territorial denominations. The peerage families are, as a class, another evidence of continuity. The same Norman nobility which surrounded the throne of the Conqueror, continues, in its remote posterity, to occupy the same place in the reign of the Conqueror's latest descendant, our present Sovereign—continues to occupy its baronial place in parliament—continues to preside on the judicial bench—continues to lead our armies and navies in battle, and continues generally to control and to direct the affairs of the English empire.

It would be easy to adduce many cases of this description, to enumerate the male representatives of Bigods, De Toesnis, Beauchamps, De Clares, Tankervilles, Braoses, Montfichets, and many others whose names of pride and power once filled the trumpet of fame, and whose posterity still remain seated amidst the peers of England. But a theme on which history and poetry might love to dwell must not here distract attention from our immediate subject. As it has been already observed, the Norman families of the peerage will be found mentioned in the alphabetical series of this work, under their present names.

On the completion of this extensive undertaking (the origin of the peerage families of the kingdom), the author still remained unsatisfied. Others might, perhaps, have supposed that the subject had been pushed sufficiently in advance; but the author could not help feeling distrust in his own conclusions, notwithstanding the care and diligence of his inquiries. He was unable to comprehend the vast disparity in point of numbers between the Normans and the Anglo-Saxon or Danish families in the peerage. However, he resolved to extend the range of the inquiry, and accordingly proceeded to examine numbers of the older families amongst the baronets, many of the older families of landed gentry, and many other families which were no longer in possession of their ancient patrimonies. He discovered in the course of these inquiries the descendants of early baronial families which had no representatives in the peerage, as well as others which occur there. Anglo-Saxon or Danish families he very rarely encountered. In some cases he failed to ascertain the national origin of families; but wherever he was enabled to determine that origin it was usually Norman. The Normans were in a great majority; the Anglo-Saxons and Danes in an insignificant minority. Numerous instances of the results of these inquiries will present themselves in the alphabetical series of names.

The author was next brought into contact with a new class of English families, taken indiscriminately from all ranks. He was led by circumstances to investigate the origin of many of the leading names in English history; the great captains, statesmen, poets, philosophers, jurists, divines, men of science, mechanists, inventors, merchant princes, and others who have gained celebrity in the national annals. That inquiry was laborious, and its length compelled the author eventually to desist from its prosecution. But so far as it proceeded, the facts elicited entirely corresponded with those brought out by preceding inquiries. The ancestry of the intellectual aristocracy of England was generally Norman. The Anglo-Saxon and the Dane were in a hopeless minority; they were considerably outnumbered by the Celt. The Normans far exceeded in number the whole of the other races put together.

A question at length here presented itself—Has race anything to do with mental capacity ? The author does not pretend to deal with that question; but few, he apprehends, will deny the descent of national characteristics to a considerable extent, and the remarkable preponderance of the Normans amongst the most eminent names in English history seems to show that they are an instance of the transmission of hereditary intelligence. The Normans were certainly the most practically intelligent and energetic race of their age. Their descendants would seem to have inherited those high qualities ; and if it be so, their success in life is sufficiently accounted for, and it might even be conjectured that under other circumstances—even if society should break loose from its old moorings and go to pieces—the Normans would still be found in the ascendant. And (as it were to supply food for thought) even now, agricultural labourers and coal-miners cannot combine for objects which demand the exercise of practical ability without finding themselves led by those who, though in humble stations, bear names of undoubted Norman origin.[1]

The author feels himself under a disadvantage in being precluded, by the extent of the evidence on which

---

[1] 'Arch' (whence Thorpe-Arch in Yorkshire) is derived from De Arches, or De Arques, Viscounts of Arques and Rouen. *See* ARCH, and SAVILLE in the alphabetical list. 'Normansell' is a corruption of Normanville, the elder branch of the Bassets, barons of Normanville in the Caux. *See* NORMANVILLE – formerly a great Yorkshire family.

he states these facts, from producing examples which would strengthen his position. He can only refer to the alphabetical series of Norman names which forms the bulk of this work. It would embarrass his argument to adduce here hundreds of instances in proof of what he has stated. Nor can it be pretended that the inquiries which have been instituted have done more than open the subject. They have touched on a very small part of it. The labour of three lives would scarcely suffice to carry out the inquiry completely. There are great numbers of noble Norman houses whose existing descendants have not yet been discovered; vast numbers of others which involve mysteries which may in many cases be inscrutable, and in most would require much expenditure of time and labour to elucidate. Nevertheless, the inquiries of the author, imperfect as they are, and limited as their range may be, will go far to establish the fact that the Norman nobility continues to exist as a whole in England at this day, and that it is still amply represented in the male line—that, in short, if the Normans (as some think) were merely an aristocracy, that aristocracy exists in vastly increased numbers at the present hour.

The result of the inquiry so far satisfied the author that the identification of the whole Norman aristocracy, as still existing in England, was simply a question of time; but at this point the inquiry assumed a new shape, which requires consideration in a separate chapter.

CHAPTER II.

DISCOVERY OF THE DESCENDANTS OF THE NORMAN COMMONALTY IN ENGLAND.

It has been already noticed that the collections which had been formed disclosed the existence of above 3,000 different families of Norman nobility in England, which had become seated here at the Conquest. The inquiries which had subsequently been instituted had showed that several hundred of these families were still in existence, bearing either their original surnames, or English names adopted in lieu thereof at a remote period. It became necessary, however, at length, to consider the rate of progress which had been attained, and the chance that it would be possible to bring the inquiry to any satisfactory conclusion. On a survey of progress made, it appeared that the course hitherto adopted (namely that of tracing individual families to their origin), however satisfactory in itself, involved so great an expenditure of time that the advance made was necessarily but slow. It is true that in some cases it was a matter of facility to connect existing families with their Norman or Saxon ancestors, thanks to the extensive collections above referred to.

But frequently it would require days or weeks to arrive at the desired identification of a single family. Sometimes every English record and every memorial of local history might be searched in vain, until the inquiry in that particular case had to be abandoned as hopeless, and so to remain until, perhaps months afterwards, the information long sought for in vain would accidentally occur in some foreign charter, or elsewhere, where least expected. In many cases, too, where success was at last attained, it was only the result of inquiries of a laborious and complicated nature. It had been necessary, perhaps, to investigate throughout a long series of records the descent and inheritance of family estates; to trace them through changes of orthography and of denomination of a perplexing nature; to examine the history of the various families which had possessed those estates; and to inquire into the earliest forms of the armorial bearings of those families. It had perhaps been found impossible to obtain sufficient information on these points. It had become necessary to examine wholesale the history and the armorial bearings of all families within extensive districts, and thence to gather remote hints leading to the requisite clue.

However interesting might be the attempt to solve the difficulties which presented themselves in these inquiries, it became evident that to identify even a few hundred families would demand a serious expenditure of time— that it would be hopeless to expect, within any definable period, the complete identification of all the early Norman families still extant. Yet it seemed to be undesirable to leave the inquiry altogether unfinished when results so interesting and so satisfactory had been attained in its progress. It therefore became necessary to consider whether any mode of inquiry was practicable by which, without abandoning the historical character of the investigation, a material abridgment of the time consumed in it might be effected. It was at this crisis of the inquiry that a mode of proceeding presented itself which will be presently explained.

When we seek for remains of antiquity in London there is no necessity to make a pilgrimage to Westminster Abbey or the Tower, or to inspect the treasures of the British Museum, or the Record Office. Monuments of equal, or of greater, though unrecognised, antiquity present themselves on every side. The historian or the archæologist need only lift up his eyes and peruse the names which present themselves on shops and warehouses, and on the carts and waggons that roll by. Those names are strangely suggestive to one who is familiar with English history. Their present position tells of strange revolutions in past times. Those names seem to assort but ill with their present places. They once belonged to the mighty nobles and chiefs who conquered England, and whose descendants were renowned in Palestine and France. Those names are now borne by the merchant, the shop-keeper, the artisan, the labourer.

Whence come these memorials of the eleventh century, these resurrections of what was once so famous in history, these names of the past, formerly surrounded by all the attributes of splendour, and power, and chivalry, and almost kingly dominion? Are we to suppose those names to be mere impostures, fraudulent assumptions, forgeries? Or are they not, rather, silent witnesses of the vast changes which time introduces into society? It was not the custom in England to change hereditary surnames without necessity, and from mere fancy or caprice. Nor is there any record in England of the system of clan names by which in Scotland and Ireland the adherents of the patriarchal chieftains distinguished themselves. Clans did not exist in this country, and the adherents of the barons did not adopt the names of their feudal suzerains. The surnames of England have descended lineally in families from remote ages; and those which are found in the middle and lower classes, and which originally belonged to illustrious houses, are, with very few exceptions, beyond doubt genuine. The writer expresses this opinion after careful and lengthened inquiry, and is entirely satisfied that these names have not been adopted in modern times; for the families from which they are derived have been so long forgotten that nothing would have been gained by the assumption of their names. And besides this, a person who wished to obtain the credit of belonging to one of those ancient stocks would at least have been careful, in adopting the name, to preserve its correct orthography; whereas the mass of these old names occur in corrupt forms, and under every conceivable variation of spelling, which clearly indicates the undesigned nature of the changes themselves, and the remoteness of an origin which, in the course of time, had been the source of so many variations.

Setting aside, therefore, any objection to the genuineness of these masses of ancient names as altogether unfounded, we may consider the real causes of the position which they occupy in the middle, and even in the labouring classes.

The decadence of ancient and the rise of new families in England are facts which are well known, and which are evidenced by what is daily passing before our eyes. There is a perpetual ebb and flow in the fortunes of families; and more especially has this been the case for the last three centuries and a half, when the old feudal institutions, which rendered the transfer of estates difficult, and which impeded the creation of large rentals, have come to an end. Landed property has long ceased to be destined to the maintenance of a great national army: it has become an article of commerce—has been thrown open to the monied classes—has become capable of being treated as a source of pecuniary profit. The ancient Norman landholder lived without the aids and appliances of modern luxury. His grandeur consisted, not in the length of his rent-roll, the brilliancy of his equipages, or the beauty of his palaces and parks, but in the strength of his fortresses, and the numbers of armed and disciplined retainers and feudal tenants who followed his standard. His splendour consisted in his power. All this has long since passed away, and land, from the middle of the sixteenth century, began to fall into the position of other marketable property. The result was that, as commercial enterprise created wealth, the old landed aristocracy was gradually replaced by new families. If we compare the landed proprietary of any one county in the present day with the lists of its gentry in the reign of Elizabeth, it would seem at first sight as if the whole of the old proprietary had died out. Rare indeed are the cases in which the same estates have descended in the same name for three centuries. Mr. Shirley, in his interesting work on the 'Gentle and Noble' families of England who have held their estates from A.D. 1500 and previously, is unable to enumerate more than about four hundred altogether, including peers, baronets, and landed gentry—a mere insignificant fraction of the landowners of England. The mass of the old proprietors have either died out or transferred their estates by heiresses to new families; or they have migrated to other parts of England, to Ireland, to Scotland, or to the colonies. Numbers have taken up their abode in America, and their descendants remain there at the present day. They have in the majority of cases ceased to be possessed of landed property, and have engaged in commercial or industrial employments.

In former ages, as now, professions and trade were frequently the resource of the younger sons of good families, for the family estate passing to the elder son, the junior branches had to seek their own fortunes Nor were their undertakings always fortunate : branches of aristocratic families gradually fell lower in the world, and became impoverished. The leading branches of these families, whose importance in some degree upheld the position of these remote kinsmen, gradually died out; the estates passed away by heiresses to new families, or were lost by extravagance, misfortunes, and embarrassments ; the old names were forgotten by the world ; the scions of these ancient families fell lower and lower, till, in some cases, at length nothing remained to them except family names, of whose ancient importance they were no longer conscious. All traces of their descent had been lost and obliterated ; and when rising once more to renewed prosperity, after the lapse of ages, they rose as new families, without antecedents, and without ancestry.

Such have been the variations of society in England, where, notwithstanding an unparalleled stability of institutions, everything is, like the ocean, in a state of perpetual flux and reflux, the old disappearing before the new, and the new superseded in its turn by the old—the nobility, the gentry, the middle classes, and the lower, gradually changing places, and gradually resuming their original positions. In a few generations the noble families of the present will have descended to the ranks of the gentry or the commercial community. The tradesmen of to-day will be the forefathers of the peers of to-morrow ; and we perhaps ourselves have tenants or servants whose blood may be better than our own.

The author had at various times been struck by finding such names as Percy, Mortimer, Basset, Vipont, Fitzwater, amongst the middle and lower classes, but he had not given any particular attention to the fact, or attempted to found any inferences upon it. He had also been led by curiosity from time to time to turn to the Post Office Directory of London, as containing the largest printed list of English surnames, with a view to ascertain whether some of the Norman surnames which are to be found in the ancient records were still in existence, and he had occasionally discovered them there. These casual and transient references conveyed a very imperfect notion of the amount of information actually comprised in that vast repository of surnames.

When, however, it became necessary (as has been explained) to discover a summary mode of completing the lists of existing Norman families, the surnames of the London Directory at once occurred to recollection as the means of determining with increased speed whether the ancient Norman families still survive. Up to that moment the notion that there ever had been originally any class of Normans in England except that of the landholders had not presented itself. Every one habitually regards the Normans of England as an aristocracy. To say that a family is Norman is nearly equivalent to saying that it is amongst the oldest of the old and the noblest of the noble. The current notion appears to be that the people of England after the Conquest were Anglo-Saxon, while the aristocracy was Norman; and the author up to this point remained entirely under the influence of this persuasion, notwithstanding his preceding inquiries. He did not entertain any doubt that the extensive list of Norman names which had been compiled included the whole or nearly the whole of the ancient Norman families which had settled in England, and to ascertain that the names included in that list still subsisted in England would, in his then opinion, have been equivalent to a complete recovery of the Anglo-Norman race.

With such sentiments the author commenced a new task which he prescribed to himself—the examination of all the surnames of the London Directory, in the hope of completing his lists of extant Norman names. Every surname was to be examined : they amounted to nearly 80,000 in number. For the examination of these names he had before him : 1. The London Post Office Directory for 1870 ; 2. The *Rotuli Hundredorum*, 2 vols. folio ; 3. The *Testa de Neville*, 1 vol. folio ; 4. The *Proceedings of the Curia Regis*, from 1194 to 1200, 2 vols. 8vo. ; 5. The *Pipe Rolls, temp.* Henry I. and II., published by the Record Commission ; 6. The *Rotuli de Libertate*, of the time of King John, edited by Sir T. D. Hardy ; 7. The extensive manuscript collections previously made, containing above 3,000 names ; 8. Robson's *British Herald*, 2 vols. 4to. ; 9. The *Patronymica Britannica*, of Mr. Mark Anthony Lower, M.A.

The author avails himself of this opportunity to record his obligations to the last-named work for suggestions regarding particular names, which are duly noticed in their places in the ensuing pages, and also for many identifications of local names, which saved much useless inquiry.

Thus provided with the means of immediate reference on all points, the author proceeded systematically to investigate all the surnames in the London Directory. He found some of these to be Hebrew; others French, Spanish, Greek, Portuguese, Dutch, &c., &c. He came upon plenty of Celtic names from Scotland and Ireland, and the usual Welsh names. These various classes of surnames were all put aside. He then came to great numbers of names derived from localities in England, and some from Scottish localities. These also he put aside as a general rule. It is almost incredible what different forms these local names assume in the London Directory. We may trace a dozen different readings of the same name, and in many cases so strangely disguised that we marvel at the ingenuity of the spelling. Sometimes, too, these names of localities retain the old spelling and form, which has been corrected in the localities themselves, in favour of more modern orthography, for several centuries. We have to look to the very oldest records to discover the types of these existing surnames. The forms of these local names are frequently so singular, from their truncation, their ingenious substitutions of one letter for another, their phonetic spelling, &c., that it is almost impossible to imagine whether they are local names, or patronymics, or Celtic names, or Hebrew, or Norman.

They are to the last degree perplexing. However, with the aid of Mr. Lower's *Patronymica*, where many of these nondescripts are shown to be local names, and by considerable research, this class of names was gradually eliminated from the inquiry.

There remained then a large class of surnames which might probably include the existing Norman families. Nor was this expectation disappointed. These surnames contributed a considerable addition to the number of those Norman names which had already been ascertained to be actually extant, or to be concealed under English names. So far the inquiry was all that had been anticipated. It did not by any means exhaust the list of above 3,000 names which were included in the collections. Numbers of those names still remained not identified as still existing. Yet an advance had been made ; the Norman aristocracy had been more extensively recovered, and it might fairly be expected that, if the whole body of surnames in England could be examined, the remainder of the aristocratic names would make their appearance.

But while this branch of the inquiry was making gradual progress, a phenomenon began to present itself which at first attracted no particular attention. Names came to light in the London Directory which were at once identified as Norman, for various reasons, and more especially because they are actually found in the Norman records of the Exchequer, 1180–1200. But those names were not included in the author's long lists of Norman names of English landowners. He presumed at first, as a matter of course, that these were merely exceptional cases, in which he had omitted to enter any particulars in the collections through some accidental oversight. But he gradually became surprised to find what numbers of these names had been passed over. The numbers that came pouring in began to be an embarrassment. It was impossible to account for this fact. The writer became at length perfectly astonished. The new names came in by masses. His long lists became comparatively useless; they were stranded, like a ship left high and dry by the receding tide. The author felt that they threw the most serious doubts on the value of his lists and collections, which he had been almost inclined to regard as complete and exhaustive. Were those lists which had been so laboriously formed, and which were five or six times the length of any known list of Norman names, a mere failure? Did they, after all, contain a mere fraction of the Norman surnames? Reflection on all that had passed in the compilation of those lists led to the conviction that very little in the shape of Norman names in the old English records could have escaped from the inquiries that had been instituted. The best sources of information had been carefully examined; no name apparently foreign had been wittingly passed over. It seemed that there could have been no material omission of facts bearing on the early landed aristocracy of England. The

writer remained satisfied, after full consideration, that his
lists and collections could not have been materially added
to, even if he had undertaken again to go through the
whole mass of ancient records.

How was it then possible to account for the contradictory fact that the names of his lists were so greatly
outnumbered by Norman names entirely new ?

An explanation of the fact presented itself. Those
new and unaccountable Norman names must have been
transplanted to England in the course of the emigration
of the Huguenots in the reign of Elizabeth, or at the
revocation of the Edict of Nantes, or at the period of the
French revolution. This seemed a possible solution of
the difficulty. It was immediately tested : but it was found
that the names in question could be traced in England
long before the dates above mentioned. They occurred
in the English records of the twelfth and thirteenth
centuries. They were then apparently as old and as much
settled as any other Norman names in this country.
They were also clearly traced in Normandy itself to a
period of undefined antiquity. The inference was that
they had come over from Normandy at the Conquest.

It was then, at length, that the author opened his
eyes to the fact that there must have been another class
of Normans in England besides the Norman aristocracy.
His lists had contained a true list of the Norman landowners or feudal aristocracy. But there had evidently
been a more numerous body of Normans in England than

the landowners, and that body was the Norman middle and lower classes. The Normans, then, had consisted not only of an aristocracy, but of a people : they had come as a nation to England. Not only had the barons and knights of Normandy accompanied King William, but their feudal tenantry, and the free classes of Normandy generally, had accompanied the barons and settled here.

On submitting this view to practical tests, it was confirmed. When those English records which are the first to detail the names of the middle classes were examined, these new Norman names were found there, not amongst the barons and landowners, but amongst the petty landowners, free tenants, villeins, cottiers, and burgesses of towns. They represented the classes of copyholders of manors, petty freeholders, farmers, tradesmen, and merchants. They were to be found in England in much the same position which they occupied in Normandy—not amongst the aristocracy, but amongst the middle, labouring, and industrial classes—the classes of the Norman freemen, who were all of Norman blood. In addition, an unexpected fact was brought to light. The writer had been under the impression that hereditary surnames, like armorial bearings, were in early times peculiar to the higher classes, and that it was not till two or three centuries after the Conquest that their example was followed by the middle and lower classes. But it now became evident that hereditary surnames were in use by all classes in Normandy in the middle of the eleventh century. They descended from that date both in Norman and English branches of the same families: and it may well be conjectured that these names may have been preserved more frequently by the descendants of the middle classes than by those of the aristocracy, for the latter continually exchanged their Norman names for those of their manors, whereas the former had no such inducement to change.

A close inspection of the names of the tenantry in English manors and in English towns in the thirteenth century (being the earliest date at which we become acquainted with the details) was instituted; and it proved that in some cases the Norman names of the tenantry amounted to above, and in others to less than a moiety of the whole, and generally to about a moiety. Instances of these researches will be found further on in this work.[1] Similar cases of Norman names of the middle class presented themselves in cities and boroughs in similar abundance.[2]

These facts necessarily led to a re-examination of history, and of the facts which it records bearing on the Norman race and its migration to England, and it then further appeared that, considering the condition, both of Normandy and of England, before and after the Conquest, there was a moral certainty that the migration to England must have been that of a people, and not (as had been supposed) merely that of an aristocracy. The details of

[1] *See* Chapter V.　　　　[2] Ibid.

this argument will appear further on :[1] they are here omitted in order not to interrupt the course of the narrative.

The inquiry was pursued throughout the whole list of names of the mercantile and trading classes of London in the Directory, amounting, as nearly as can be estimated, to 29,000. Of these about one-tenth appear to be Hebrew, modern-foreign, and Celtic surnames, leaving the properly English surnames about 26,000.

The result of the inquiry into the Norman surnames in the Directory (including those previously ascertained to be existing) showed a total number of about 6,900, besides those English local names which cover Norman descent, and the details of these names and families will be found stated in the alphabetical part of this work. The Norman names, therefore, being about 6,900, and the total of English names 26,000, it appeared that the Norman names constituted about a quarter of the whole.

The surnames of the London Directory, however, form only a small part of the surnames of the United Kingdom. The Registrar-General estimates the sum total at more than 100,000 distinct surnames, of which we may assume that one-tenth are Hebrew, foreign, and Celtic, leaving 90,000 as the corrected number of surnames properly English. If we are entitled to infer that the London Directory is not more Norman in character than the Directory of all England would be, but that the same

[1] *See* Chapter V.

proportion prevails throughout the kingdom, we are to infer further that about 22,500 surnames in England are at this moment Norman.

Feeling the necessity, then, of testing in some way the relation between the London Directory and that of all England as regarded their respective proportions of Norman names, the author obtained (through the courtesy of the Registrar-General) a copy of part of the general list of surnames in all England preserved at Somerset House. On examining the names comprised therein it appeared that, after deducting Hebrew, foreign, and Celtic names, about one-fourth of the residue were Norman.[1]

The results of the inquiry will be found in the Appendix. This experiment showed that the London Directory furnishes a fair specimen of the entire body of English surnames.

The author has stated the above numbers on the assumption that his mode of identifying Norman surnames in the following alphabetical lists will, on the whole, prove to be correct. He cannot pretend to hope that in the process of identifying so many thousands of names he has not fallen into occasional error. He does trust, however, that his errors have not been frequent, and that where they exist they will be found to lie quite as much in the way of omitting names which might have been

---

[1] The total number of distinct names in the London Directory to 'All' was 258, and to the same point in the Somerset House lists about 780. The Norman names in the former case amounted to 70, in the latter to above 200. *See* APPENDIX.

introduced, as of inserting others without sufficient reason.
He trusts, also, that the main principles on which the
inquiry has proceeded, and which will be separately considered,[1] will be admitted to be sound.

It is now necessary to consider another class of names
which were not included in the preceding inquiry. That
inquiry was (as has been said) restricted entirely to
surnames of a purely Norman origin still remaining in
England. But names derived from English localities
were put aside altogether,[2] except the comparatively small
number which had been shown by previous inquiries to
cover Norman descent.

It is, however, here advisable to give some little
attention to the subject of the English names borne by
Norman families. The author is not aware that anyone
has hitherto attempted on system, and to any extent, to
disinter the long-lost aboriginal surnames of families now
bearing English local names. According to his impressions genealogists have been in general satisfied when
they have ascertained the remotest era at which present
surnames can be found recorded; and their authentic
histories commence from that point, whatever is related
by them of earlier times, origin, &c., being founded on
legend or imagination. The author, from the commencement of his inquiries, was enabled to carry the history of

---

[1] *See* Chapters iii., iv.

[2] The names derived from localities seem to amount to about 40 per
cent. of the whole body of surnames.

families to times preceding the dates when their present surnames commenced. His subsequent inquiries have disclosed
numerous cases in which the later English local surname
was merely the substitute for an earlier Norman name.

The writer has, therefore, his own experience, and
nothing but his own experience, to guide him in forming
an estimate of the numbers of those existing local surnames
which may conceal Norman families. That estimate
may be, perhaps, supposed to be founded on too limited
an induction. He admits that the investigation of
something like two hundred and fifty local surnames is a
somewhat narrow basis on which to found an inference,
and he can, therefore, only say, *valeat quantum*.

His experience, however (whatever it may be worth),
is this. In seven cases out of eight (when the origin
can be ascertained) it is Norman : in the eighth it is
Celtic, Saxon, or Danish.[1] The author does not pretend
to say that the same English names borne by Norman
families may not have been equally borne by other
families that were not Norman. It would be difficult to
determine in any way the number of families of the

[1] The Peerage includes about 123 families (i.e. so many peerages) bearing names of English localities. Of these 82 are Norman families, 12
Danish or Saxon, and 29 undetermined. Of the latter, 12 at least bear
strong indications of Norman descent; the remainder are not mentioned at
a sufficiently early date to warrant inferences. This class of names is in
Scotland far more generally of unascertainable origin than in England, from
the defective nature of the early Scottish records. Two-thirds of the
Scottish local names of peers cannot be traced to any definite nationality,
while only one quarter of the corresponding class of names in England are
untraceable.

latter class in relation to that of Norman families bearing the same names. Doubtless, these local names were in many cases borne simultaneously by families of different origin. The names of localities themselves were occasionally found identical in different districts; and therefore, on the whole, notwithstanding the fact that wherever it is possible to trace the origin of locally named families the preponderance lies with the Normans, it would be difficult to estimate the actual proportion of such surnames which should be assigned to the Normans, and to the native races respectively.

What does, however, seem to come out distinctly as the result of the whole inquiry, so far as it has advanced, is this, that the Norman race in England is of very great magnitude. After making allowance for the occurrence of error in the process of identification, it yet seems clear that about a quarter of the whole mass of existing old English surnames are of purely Norman origin, and that a large proportion of the remainder are in all probability borne by families of Norman descent. Many of the Norman names are exceedingly common, being borne by many hundreds of families; and, as far as the writer has been able to ascertain, it seems that on an average the distinctly Norman names are borne by as many families as those which are not distinctly Norman, even including amongst the latter names ending in 'son,' some of the most common of which are probably indicative of Danish origin.

The consequence is that we may fairly assume that the Norman population bears the same ratio to the entire population of England as the Norman names do to the English names generally; and that if a quarter or a third of our names are Norman, the Normans themselves amount to a quarter or a third of the English nation. With these facts before us, it is simply impossible to uphold the notion that the Normans constituted a mere aristocracy in England. We have to deal with the fact that, according to all appearance, a third or more of the English population is Norman; that the Normans amongst us are not to be numbered by units or tens, as some persons suppose, but by millions. All theories as to the extinction of the Normans, or their absorption by the Saxons, are swept away by the weight of facts. It is clear that the Norman Conquest involved the migration of a nation. We cannot conceive that the Normans, who now probably form a third or more of the population of England in the nineteenth century, could have formed less than a third in the eleventh and twelfth centuries. The Norman race remains in England. It has struck its roots deeply into every rank and class of society. It is found throughout, leavening the entire English community, and constituting, we may say, the most important element in the whole. It has been well and nobly said by a great living historian that the Norman became as truly English in England as he had become French in Normandy. The national life is bound up with the existence of this great race.

These pages are perhaps the first which have attempted to trace in detail the connexion of the Norman race with general society in England; to show that the Norman blood pervades all classes and orders alike; that the vigorous life of ancient Scandinavia, which has its counterpart in modern England and in America, has been transmitted through thirty generations to the existing people of these countries.

One or two circumstances may be here mentioned in illustration of the continuance of the Norman blood in various classes of society in England, and its wide national diffusion.

In the southern counties of England there lies a remote and secluded district, where the population has remained in unchanged and unbroken descent for many ages. The same family names of farmers, copyholders, petty tenants, tradesmen, and labourers, may be traced in the parish register from age to age since the commencement of the reign of Elizabeth. The births, marriages, and deaths of this community are recorded with a regularity which might cause envy to some man of brief pedigree and long purse, anxious to extend the list of his ancestry. In the midst of this district rise the grey and massive ruins of a baronial *donjon*, surrounded by extensive trenches, the ancient seat of the lords of the soil. That time-worn castle owes its origin to a mighty baron of the Conqueror, who accompanied him from Normandy, and, obtaining vast territory in England, became the progenitor of a powerful line of peers and chieftains, once famous in English history, and long since forgotten. The titles of that great baronial house have been extinct for many ages; its estates have been transferred to other families; family after family of nobility has held them in succession; they have passed into possession of the Crown, and have been granted afresh. All the long series of owners have departed: the Norman, the Plantagenet, the Tudor, the Stuart, the Hanoverian dynasties have come to an end successively. The ruined *donjon* has outlasted them all; and, strange to say, the Norman tenantry, whose ancestors once paid suit and homage at that ancient fortress, are there still. The whole vicinity abounds in purely Norman names. The ancestors of those who bear those names came from Normandy, and settled around the castle as feudal retainers of its lords at the era of the Conquest. There the Norman race still continues; an independent and manly race of men, not without traces of the Norman beauty and the Norman character. The writer happened for some time to come much into contact with that race; and he has found amongst them men whose humble position was dignified by the highest honour, integrity, and worth. To the best of his recollection, every second name in that district is Norman. He had frequently remarked the peculiar character of the surnames there; but greater knowledge than he then possessed of Norman names now enables him to recal the numbers which in that district are still purely Norman.

Another circumstance may be mentioned in connection with the above, which clearly shows how extensively the Norman element pervades all classes of English society, even to the very humblest—how truly and thoroughly national it now is. In 1872 a vessel was lying in the Thames, about to take its departure for Tasmania. It conveyed as passengers 300 navvies, who had been engaged to proceed to the Colonies, to complete an intended railway. The passengers were all on board, when a fatal collision at night sent the vessel and every human being on board to the bottom.

The list of the drowned passengers appeared in the public journals. It included a large number of purely Norman names. Several names were there recognised as formerly baronial and historical; and one baronial name the writer there discovered, the existence of which in England in the present age he had never before ascertained.

Having now stated the circumstances out of which arose the discovery of the Norman people as now existing in England, it becomes the office of the author to unfold the principles which have directed him in the present inquiry, to point out the corroborative evidence which he has to adduce, and to prepare the way for that exposition of details which will be found in the alphabetical portion of this work.

E

CHAPTER III.

CRITICISM OF FAMILY HISTORY.

IT may be supposed, perhaps, that any revision or re-examination of the existing family history of England is superfluous and presumptuous—that large classes of facts which have been long accepted as authentic, on the authority of eminent heralds, backed by the testimony of the families to which they relate, ought to be exempt from criticism. Such an opinion, however, can only be held where the real condition of the English pedigrees is not understood. Historical truth compels the rejection of much that is to be found in those documents; and as the present work frequently passes over the older pedigrees, and presents facts altogether new, it is necessary to produce evidence to show that such procedure is warranted by the present state of English family history.

To those who are aware of the real state of things this chapter will be a mere repetition of that with which they are already familiar; and they will accordingly pass on to the following chapter; but those who are of opinion that existing pedigrees of old date may be relied on may be induced to adopt a somewhat different opinion on considering the following statements.

In the preceding pages, then, it has been observed that English family history is, as regards its ancient portion, open to much criticism. This ought not to cause surprise when it is considered that even the general history of the nation presents many points on which learned men have come to different conclusions, and in which long established views have been abandoned; and if even in questions of historical importance much uncertainty is occasionally found, how vastly greater must be the uncertainty which in many cases surrounds questions of mere family descent! There are, indeed, cases, such as the inheritance of kingdoms, where the great importance of the subject ensures such an amount of publicity and discussion as to render the task of inquiry comparatively easy, because it places us in possession at least of the materials for forming an opinion. But in the case of family history, taken as a whole, we have no such aids. A family has to be connected with the past under every conceivable difficulty. Its position may not have been conspicuous. Its name may have changed so as scarcely to be recognisable. Ancient records may know of it only under a form altogether strange to us. The transient mention of it in those records may convey different ideas to different minds. There is danger of confusion between different individuals of the same name.

These, and other difficulties which present themselves

to the *bonâ fide* inquirer, are not, perhaps, those which raise any difficulty in the minds of others. It seems to be supposed that heralds and genealogists have some mysterious and recondite power, which enables them with comparative ease and certainty to reproduce the history of families; and there have been times when their recorded statements and pedigrees have been generally accepted with profound and implicit faith. Pedigrees, when they have been adopted by families, become the authentic exposition of their claims. They are transmitted from generation to generation with jealous care, and yet they may be all the time founded on invention. The compilers of pedigrees were, like others, not exempt from error; and it must be added with regret that in many cases their anxiety to gratify their employers has led them to neglect the ordinary laws of historical inquiry, and to put forth hasty statements, which have done much to discredit a branch of knowledge which is capable of affording results of real value.

With a view to convey some notion of the difficulties which the historical inquirer encounters when he attempts to investigate the origin of English families, it may be desirable to notice some instances of those faults and defects which continually present themselves in the existing family history, and which either deter many persons from the study, or stand in the way of *bonâ fide* inquiry.

1. Impossibilities.

We are, for example, informed by one of the peerages that Herveius Walter, father of Theobald Walter, Butler of Ireland, in the reign of Henry II., and ancestor of the Dukes and Marquises of Ormond, was 'a companion of the Conqueror,' *i.e.* that he had in 1066 accompanied him from Normandy. This, no doubt, carries back the family of Butler to the era of the Conquest. But when we look into the facts of the case we find that this Herveius Walter, father of Theobald,[1] was in the time of Henry II. a considerable benefactor to Butley Priory, Suffolk ;[2] and this being a century after the Conquest, it is impossible that he could have been 'a companion of the Conqueror ;' while in addition, as his son Theobald Walter was certainly contemporary with Henry II., Herveius Walter was himself evidently a contemporary of King Stephen and of the Empress Matilda, grand-daughter of the Conqueror. It would seem that the slightest consideration would have precluded the possibility of such a chronological error.

2. Inventions.

The peerages inform us that 'Adam de Aldithley,' ancestor of the Earls of Derby, attended Duke William to England in 1066, 'accompanied, from Aldithley in

---

[1] The filiation is ascertained by means of charters of Theobald Walter, founding Cockersand Abbey, Lancashire, and Wotheny Abbey, Limerick, from which we learn that Herveius Walter was his father, Hubert Walter, Archbishop of Canterbury, his brother, and Ranulph de Glanville his friend. (*Mon. Angl.* ii. 631, 1034.) *See* BUTLER in the alphabetical series.

[2] *Mon. Angl.* ii. 245.

Normandy,' by his sons 'Lydulph and Adam de Aldithley,' and obtained large possessions by gift of the Conqueror. We have here a minuteness of detail which wears all the appearance of authenticity. 'Aldithley' (the origin of the name Audley) was, it appears, in 'Normandy.' Nevertheless, when we come to examine where Aldithley really was, it is ascertained, not merely that there is not the slightest trace of such a place in Normandy (as we might indeed have anticipated from its Gothic etymology), but that the real Aldithley from which the family derived its name of Audley was in Staffordshire. A mistake of this nature, so obvious on the slightest inquiry, forcibly shows the carelessness of which the history of families in England has been unfortunately the subject.

The same account of the Stanleys, Earls of Derby, is further instructive. 'Adam de Aldithley' and his two sons 'Lydulph and Adam de Aldithley,' who are said to have accompanied the Conqueror, are purely imaginary personages. There is no trace of their existence in the records; nor has any one ever attempted to establish their reality by evidence. They owe their origin to the ingenious process of making two persons out of one, assigning the names of one generation to imaginary ancestors in another. Amongst other faults this pedigree invents a Henry de Stonley or Stanley, a maternal ancestor (as alleged) of this family. His imaginary son-in-law lived in the reign of Henry I.,[1] so that he himself must

[1] The son-in-law was Adam de Aldithley, who, according to the state-

have lived in that of the Conqueror; and yet not only is
Domesday silent as to his existence, but Stonley or
Stanley itself does not appear to have existed in 1086,
for Domesday takes no notice of it. ¯ The name of Stanley
appears for the first time in the year 1130,[1] when it was
borne by Robert de Stanley, Viscount of Stafford.[2]
Henry de Stonley is a pure myth. Nothing can be more
instructive than this example of the mode of treating
English pedigrees. If imagination is allowed to exercise
such strange influence even in the case of the most illustrious families in England, what must have been the fate
of others of less eminence.

3. Contradiction to facts.

The history of the Ashburnhams, Earls of Ashburnham, furnishes an instance of the legendary character
of much of the early family history of England, and
of its inconsistency with matter of fact. This pedigree is
one which is usually announced with a confidence and an
apparent authority which are truly imposing, and which
have doubtless brought conviction to the minds of most

---

ment, was son of Lydulph, who came from Normandy with the Conqueror
at the same time as his father Adam. Lydulph was therefore living at the
Conquest, and his son Adam, in the time of Henry I., and Henry de Stanley,
the imaginary father-in-law of the latter, must have been contemporary
with the Conqueror. This personage appears from the peerage statements
to have been owner of Stanley and Balterley, while Domesday shows that
Balterley, together with Aldithley and Talc, belonged in the Conqueror's
reign to Gamel, a native thane (Domesday, Stafford, p. 251.) Stanley in
Stafford is not mentioned.

[1] *Rot. Pip.* 31, Henry I.
[2] *See* STANLEY in the alphabetical series.

readers, as they did to that of honest Thomas Fuller, who was aghast at the antiquity of the Ashburnham family. According to the tale told by the peerages, this family derives from ' Bertram de Ashburnham' (' son of Anchitel, son of Piers, Lord of Ashburnham '), who was ' Sheriff of Surrey, Sussex, and Kent, and Constable of Dover Castle,' in the reign of King Harold, and who, having bravely defended Dover Castle against King William, in 1066, was thereupon, together with his sons, most cruelly put to death by the infuriated Conqueror. Certainly, after a result so tragic, the Ashburnhams seem bound in honour to cherish feelings of hostility to the Norman race.   But this tale, pathetic as it is, is unfortunately of too modern a date to attain credence as a matter of fact.   It rests on the sole and exclusive authority of Francis Thyn, a herald who wrote in 1586, five centuries after the events supposed to have occurred.   There is no trace of this history, or of those Ashburnhams who are its subjects, in any earlier document. The entire story, therefore, on historical principles, falls to the ground, as resting on no adequate authority.   But besides this, the narrative and the whole pedigree founded on it are inconsistent with matter of fact. The Anglo-Saxon Lord of Ashburnham is mentioned in Domesday Book. His name was Sewardus, which is neither that of the pretended Bertram de Ashburnham, nor of either of his sons ; and Domesday further informs us that after this Anglo-Saxon thane had ceased to be owner the estate had passed, amongst many other estates, to the Count of Eu ; and that he had enfeoffed there a foreign knight named Robert de Cruel.[1] It further appears, from a series of records, that the descendants of Robert de Cruel (or Criol) were thenceforth lords of Ashburnham, that for five or six generations they bore the names of Cruel, Crieul, or Criol, and Ashburnham conjointly, and that the Earls of Ashburnham are the lineal descendants of this Norman house,[2] which appears to have been a branch of the Counts of Eu.   Such is fact as opposed to fiction ; and such are the species of statements which have so long passed current as the history of the English aristocracy.

4. Incredibilities.

The family of Burke or Burgh (Earls and Marquises of Clanricarde) furnishes a striking example of the careless inventions of the compilers of pedigrees and peerages. According to the received accounts, this family is of imperial Carlovingian descent in the male line, and is thus of more dignified origin than those of Bourbon, Hanover, Saxony, Savoy, or Stuart. In fact, no family in Europe could pretend to vie in splendour of origin with the Burkes if this pedigree were well-founded.   It unfortunately, however, labours under this disadvantage—the whole of the early pedigree on which such vast pretensions are founded is only of a century's standing, having appeared for the first time in an Irish peerage about the middle of the eighteenth century.   The alleged descent was unknown

[1] Domesday, Sussex.
[2] *See* ASHBURNHAM in the alphabetical series.

to Dugdale, and to all other genealogists of eminence, prior to the date referred to; and yet the family of Burgh had long been of such high rank and eminence that it could not fail to attract the attention of genealogical writers. This pedigree does not pretend to produce a single proof or evidence in its support from any ancient record or from history. It mentions various facts which are said to have occurred in the tenth, eleventh, and twelfth centuries, six, seven, and eight hundred years before its appearance. Of course the whole falls to the ground as unsupported by historical evidence.

It is, however, worth while to dwell for a little on the assertions of the author of this pedigree. William Fitz Adelm, the real ancestor of the family, and Chief Governor of Ireland, lived in the reign of Henry II. His name supplies that of his father, Adelm. The compiler of the pedigree was not aware who this Adelm was, but by a wave of the magician's wand he was transformed into the son and heir of the attainted and dispossessed William, Earl of Cornwall and Mortaine, son of Robert, the Conqueror's half-brother, and consequently nephew of that sovereign. The compiler of this pedigree was probably unconscious that Dugdale, Anselm, and everyone else who had examined the subject, were unable to discover that Earl William ever married or left any posterity; nor did it occur to him that neither Adelm nor William Fitz Adelm his son ever claimed any restoration of the Earldoms of Cornwall and Mortaine, and that history is entirely silent as to the existence of any claimant whatever.

Another wave of the wand converts Herluin de Conteville, grandfather of Earl William, into 'Harlowen de Burgh,' and gives him a father, 'John de Burgh, Earl of Tonsburgh,' a lineal descendant of Charlemagne. It so happens that Herluin's father and ancestry are entirely unknown to history; and John, Earl of Tonsburgh, is an individual of whose existence there is not the slightest trace except in this pedigree. Had he been a reality he could not have failed to be mentioned at an era when the house of Charlemagne was still claiming the throne of France in opposition to the family of Hugh Capet; nor could the name of so illustrious a personage, and the father of Herluin de Conteville, have escaped notice, as it has done, in the pages of Ordericus Vitalis. The real descent of the Burghs, though not imperial, is (if the writer be correct in his view) one of considerable interest, and connects them with some of the names most eminent in the history of England. It is to be regretted that in the case of so eminent a house due inquiry has been superseded by ill-considered guess, and actual fabrication.[1]

5. Inconsistency with history.

The descent of the family of Clifford, so conspicuous in English history, is traced with certainty to Richard Fitz Ponce, who lived in the reign of the Conqueror;[2] but peerage writers, unsatisfied with this ancestry, have exerted their ingenuity to make the pedigree terminate in a more

[1] See BURGH in the alphabetical series of names.
[2] See CLIFFORD in the alphabetical series.

brilliant apex.   According to them, 'Ponce,' the father of Richard, was none other than 'William, Earl of Arques and Toulouse' [meaning Talou], paternal uncle of the Conqueror, who, it is added, 'came into England with his victorious nephew, Duke William.'

Criticism here interposes the inconvenient question, How do we know that Ponce the father of Richard was the same person as William, Count of Arques?   There is no reply except the statement of the peerage—no other authority in support of that statement is vouchsafed; nor is there any evidence that William Earl of Arques ever came to England, or that he left any sons.   What we do know is this—that he rebelled against Duke William and endeavoured to dethrone him—that he was compelled to fly from Normandy—that he spent the rest of his life supported by the bounty of the Count of Boulogne—and that King William on his death-bed spoke with anger of his hostile conduct.   These are matters which are known to all students of the Norman historians, and especially of Ordericus Vitalis; and how, in the face of these well-known facts, it can be imagined that William of Arques and his sons were provided for in England by King William does indeed seem strange.   There was a William of Arques whose family was seated in England; but this family had no connexion with the Count of Arques.[1]

6. Anachronisms.

Cases of this nature are frequent, and one may be here

---

[1] *See* ARCH, SAVILLE, in the alphabetical series of names.

cited from Collins's account of the family of Hotham (Lords Hotham), which was written, according to his statement, in reliance on 'our genealogists'—a discreet reference, which commits no one in particular. According to the story, Sir John de Trehouse was 'Lord of Kilkenny' in Ireland before the Conquest; and, in reward of brilliant services at Hastings, obtained from the king Hotham in Yorkshire, and other estates in England. From him descended the family of De Trehouse, which in the reign of Henry II. or later assumed the name of Hotham. No authority is cited in support of this tale. Its author had not the least difficulty in placing an English or foreign knight in possession of territories in a part of Ireland which was then entirely occupied by the native Celtic population. He seems to have entertained very vague impressions as to the date of the English conquest of Ireland, which he probably assigned to the ninth or tenth century, and had consequently as little difficulty in seating an English lord at Kilkenny in the eleventh as in the thirteenth century. It is needless to add that a circumstance so incredible ought to have been supported by the strongest evidence in order to obtain credence; but there is no evidence whatever. Yet, when statements of this nature, so precise and definite, are advanced, it is very difficult to disbelieve them; and nothing but long experience of the utter recklessness with which statements of this kind have been put forward would enable one to set them aside as unsupported by evidence.

7. Mistranslations.

The popular view of the origin of the family of Fitz-Gerald, Duke of Leinster, is supported only by a misconception of the meaning of the word ' antecessor' in Domesday Book. We are informed by the peerages that Other (whose name they change into ' Otho '), the father of Walter Fitz Other, Castellan of Windsor,[1] and ancestor of the Fitz-Geralds, was a baron of England in the reign of Edward the Confessor, and was the owner of all the estates which, in 1086, were in possession of his son Walter Fitz-Other. On examining Domesday Book it appears that the estates thus held by Walter, had, in the reign of the Confessor, belonged to several different proprietors, whose names are recorded. The name of Other does not occur amongst them. The only ground for the assertion to the contrary is that Cheneteberie, one of these estates, had been held on certain conditions by the ' antecessor' of Walter. This term is rendered ' ancestor,' and it is at once inferred that Other, father of Walter, must have been the ancestor referred to; but the term is usually in Domesday employed in the sense of ' predecessor,' or ' former owner,' and thus is of no value towards establishing relationship. Domesday Book knows nothing of Other ; and there is every reason to conclude that he,

---

[1] ' Walter Fitz Oter, Castellan of Wildesore ' [Windsor], is mentioned in a charter of Abingdon Abbey (Harl. MS. 294, No. 3324), where it is stated that he restored to the Abbey, in the time of the Abbot Faritius, woods named Virdelæ and Backseat, at Winkefield.

like the fathers of the great mass of the Anglo-Norman barons of the Conquest, was a foreigner.[1]

8. Unsupported statements.

We have a remarkable instance of the credence attained by unsupported statements of the elder heralds in the case of the house of Percy, Earls and Dukes of Northumberland. The whole early pedigree of this historical family depends upon the unauthenticated statement of a herald of considerable eminence in the reign of Elizabeth, named Glover. He was a man of attainments, and of great industry, and in general his statements are deserving of credit. But in this particular case, whether it was that the temptation of gratifying the ancestral aspirations of so powerful a family as that of Northumberland overcame his usual discretion, or whether he may have derived his information from some foreign and untrustworthy source, it were impossible now to determine. Suffice it to say, that he derives this family from Mainfred de Percy, a Danish chief, who is said to have lived before the time of Rollo; and whose descendants, named alternately Geoffry and William de Percy, continued in succession Lords of Percy, until the last William de Percy of Normandy went to England, temp. William I., and founded the English house of Percy. On examining this statement, the first difficulty which causes hesitation is the alternate repetition of the names of Geoffry and William, which was inconsistent with the usual system of nomen-

[1] See FITZGERALD in the alphabetical series of names.

clature in those ages ; but what presents a far more
serious difficulty is this. Percy did not belong to any
private family, but was part of the ducal demesne;[1]
consequently it is difficult to suppose that the name of
De Percy could have existed, as the estate did not belong
to a private family, and, in point of fact, the name is not
mentioned in any record till shortly before the English
Conquest, and, it had probably been assumed not long
previously, for in 1026 the estate of Percy was still part
of the demesne of the Duke.[2] We are, therefore, obliged
to come to the conclusion that the whole early pedigree
produced by Glover must be rejected.[3]

These few examples of the difficulties which are to be
found in the pedigrees of the sixteenth, seventeenth, and
eighteenth centuries will suffice to indicate the necessity,
in the interest of truth, of examining carefully the statements of the genealogists of former times before they are
adopted as reliable.

The state of the English pedigrees generally, indeed,
appears to be such as to demand a careful re-examination
with the additional light thrown on such topics by the
intelligent criticism of the present century, and the greatly
increased knowledge of the sources of mediæval history.

[1] Duke Richard, by charter dated 1026, granted to his spouse, in dowry,
Coutances and its county, with the castles of Carusburc, Holm, and Bruot,
the court of Ver, and the court of Cerisy-sur-Seine, Agons-on-the-Sea,
Valengias (Valognes?), the abbey of Portail, the town and port of Sarnes,
the town and port of Hage, the town of Balteis, and Egglandes, the courts
of Percy and of Moyon, and the town of Cathim in the county of Bayeux.
Bouquet, x. 270.

[2] *See* preceding note.

[3] *See* PERCY in the alphabetical series of names.

CHAPTER IV.

CONSTRUCTIVE PRINCIPLES OF THE PRESENT WORK.

IT now becomes necessary to offer some explanation of
the principles which have been held in view in the compilation of the following series of above seven thousand
five hundred names of existing Norman families, traceable
in the London Directory. It has been already observed
that these names are borne by the commercial and trading
classes. In a few cases it has been found necessary to add
some from the peerage, which do not occur amongst those
of the commercial classes of London.

From what has been previously stated, it will be understood that the alphabetical series in question, which
forms the great mass of this work, consists of names of
two classes.

First, those names and families whose origin has been
traced through successive generations in the ordinary
way, by records of all descriptions. These represent the
earlier stages of the inquiry, and are to a considerable
extent additions to, or corrections of, existing family
history. They are presented in the most condensed form
with a view to economise space, and they comprise, con-

*F

sequently, a very small portion of what might in each case have been said on their respective subjects. It is very possible that this condensation may have rendered the force of the argument in some cases less perceptible. It is hoped, however, that, brief as these pedigrees may be, they will afford suggestions as to the true line of research, which may facilitate the inquiries of others. Amongst them will be found notices of the origin of some of those names which the whole world combines to honour.

Secondly, the great mass of the names in the following alphabetical series are those which have been identified without any attempt to trace the lineal descent of families. These names, which are probably unnoticed in other works as Norman, represent the later stage of the inquiry. The names of this class which occur in the London Directory have been identified as Norman by the fact of their occurrence in the records of Normandy of the twelfth and eleventh centuries. In most cases the reference is to the great Rolls of the Exchequer of Normandy, 1180-1200. Their occurrence in England at an early date is shown by references to the English records of the eleventh, twelfth, and thirteenth centuries, especially to those of the *Curia Regis* from 1194 to 1200, to the *Testa de Neville*, 1200–1320, and to the *Rotuli Hundredorum*, c. 1272. Occasionally there are references to records of later date. The inference in each case is that the name, as appearing at an early period both in

Normandy and England, was originally Norman, and passed into England at the Conquest.

It may be objected that such an inference is not sound, because the name in question may have originated simultaneously in both countries, being of Norman origin in Normandy, and of Saxon origin in England. It is not pretended that particular instances of this kind may not have occurred; but as a whole the objection is not applicable to these names, for the great mass of them are not of native but of foreign type. It is the concurrent testimony furnished by so many thousands of instances which will bring conviction to the reader's mind. Assuredly the legal maxim, *Identitas colligitur ex multitudine signorum*, may well be applied to this case. Nor can the objection above referred to have any weight against the broad facts of the case, as may be illustrated by an example in point.

When we examine in detail the surnames of the American people, they are found to be throughout English. Almost every name we meet [1] is evidently and unmistakably English. It may occur under various forms— corresponding varieties of form occur in this country—but it is decidedly English; it cannot be confounded with the surnames of other nationalities. Moreover, the people

[1] The American Directories are in many instances so filled with English names that we are almost unconscious that they belong to a different country. In the case of the recent New York Directories, the Irish-Celtic element is very large; but it is known that the Irish settle chiefly in that city. Elsewhere in America, the Irish element is not larger than it is in this kingdom.

who bear these names speak the English language, and
their jurisprudence is based on the Common Law of
England, and their institutions bear evidences throughout
of an English origin.   Now, even if the pages of history
were closed, could there be a shadow of doubt that, as a
whole, these names and the families that bear them originally came from England?   It makes no difference
whether those families can or cannot trace the line of
their ancestors to the first who landed from England on
the American shores. They are clearly and unmistakably
identified as English; and history comes in at this point
and tells us that the earlier inhabitants of America
actually did come from England, and archæology adds
that these names which we now find in America were
known in England for ages before the foundation of
the English colonies—that they appear in the whole series
of English records.   *Mutatis mutandis*, we are entitled
equally to infer the Norman origin of the Norman names
which appear in the old English records.   The families
which bear them are, as a general rule, unable to trace
their descent; and perhaps have not the remotest con-
ception that their names were Norman; but they are not
the less distinctly identified by those hereditary surnames;
memorials of race which can never be obliterated.

But it must here be observed that, in order to connect
surnames as at present existing with their prototypes, it is
essential to call in the aid of experience, grounded on
acquaintance with the same classes of facts which present

themselves in philology. Surnames, it must be remembered, are merely parts of general language, and they are consequently subject to all those influences which affect language itself so materially, and which issue in the creation of new dialects. Surnames, like other terms, are liable to dialectical variation, and to changes of every description. All alike, from the moment of their formation, are subject to continued alteration. Their vowels gradually change from broad to slender, and the reverse. Their consonants become replaced by other consonants. Sometimes pronunciation abbreviates them, at others it reverses the process, and adds letters, or even syllables. Alterations of this description can be traced to the remotest historical epochs. The tribes which first made their appearance within historical times bore names which assumed different forms; and in the early mediæval history of Europe, before hereditary surnames came into use, so great were the variations in the orthography of names, as we find them recorded in contemporary chronicles and charters, that it involves considerable experience and industry to identify the persons who bore them. The same may be said of the names of localities. They have changed on the Continent and in England to such a degree that the student needs a glossary to enable him to connect the old denominations of localities with the present forms of the same names. It is true that when the original has been pointed out there is little difficulty in understanding the process of alteration which has produced the modern form; but in the absence of such a key the inquirer may altogether fail to recognise names in their original shape.

The truth of this is known to everyone who has attempted to find in Domesday Book the names of the present English localities. Britton, for instance, one of the most industrious of our topographers, attempted in his account of Devonshire to ascertain the modern names of the manors of that county which are mentioned in Domesday Book. In a considerable number of cases he entirely failed, in others he produced instances of extensive alteration—such, for instance, as 'Shirwell' instead of the old form 'Aiscirewell;' 'Axminster' instead of 'Alseministre;' 'Brixton' instead of 'Bretricestane;' 'Dawlish' instead of 'Doelis,' &c.[1] In the same way Collins, in his Peerage, identifies the local name 'Tufton' as having been originally 'Toketon;' 'Onslow' as 'Andislaw,' 'Wyndham' as 'Wimondham.'

Alterations of this description are strictly analogous to those which in the course of ages have converted Latin into French, and Danish and Saxon into English; and which have constituted, and are still forming, new dialects and new languages. Names have the same tendency to abbreviation which has divested nouns and verbs of their grammatical inflexions, and has continually removed from terms all their peculiar and salient points. They are under the operation of the same law of substi-

---

[1] Britton, *Magna Brittania*, vi. Part I. p. liii. &c.

tution which is so familiar to the philologist, and under which *Caballus* has become *Cheval*; *liber* has been converted into *livre*; *infans* into *enfant*; *Salvator* into *Sauveur*.

Subjected to these influences, Norman names long since became as it were hieroglyphics, the key to whose meaning had been lost. They served to distinguish families, but they revealed nothing as to their origin. Yet, when these names are studied with the aid of the new lights which philology has disclosed, they furnish conclusive evidence of the ultimate nationality of the families to which they belong. The progenitors of these families have for centuries borne these names without any consciousness of their origin, or any notion that they were transmitting to their posterity a record of their descent which was destined to be at length interpreted.

In pursuing the process of identification of names, and in removing the accumulated deteriorations, corruptions, or alterations of ages, and restoring names to their earliest forms, most important aid has been derived from the independent and most satisfactory testimony supplied by examination of the evidence furnished by armorial bearings. This branch of archæology was formerly of considerably greater importance than it now is, and the use of arms was guarded with a jealousy unknown in later times. The monuments of the ancient armorial are numerous and authentic. They consist of engraved seals and stone monuments of the twelfth century, and of manuscript records of the thirteenth and subsequent centuries, and are known to all archæologists. This ancient armorial of England, with the addition of arms granted or recorded in modern times, has been published by various writers, and amongst others by Robson, whose work, entitled 'The British Herald,' has been employed in the compilation of the present work.

Now the fact appears to have been hitherto insufficiently recognised—but its importance is obvious—that in numerous instances families have preserved their armorial under all the changes which their names have undergone in the course of ages; and hence a means presents itself of identifying names and families which would not at first sight be supposed to be in any way connected. An instance or two may illustrate what is meant.

The name 'Fidler' presented itself for examination. It might be supposed that this name was merely that of an humble occupation. These very easy and simple identifications are seldom to be trusted; disparaging or contemptuous names are very ordinarily the modern corruptions of the old names; and many are the noble Norman names which in the course of time have assumed vulgar and ludicrous forms. The writer, on examination, was of opinion that the name 'Fidler' was merely a form of the name 'Fidelow,' produced by one of the ordinary laws of corruption. On referring to Robson, it was found that the arms of 'Fidelow' were three wolves' heads. Afterwards it was ascertained that 'Videlow' bore the same arms. It next appeared that 'Vis-de-low' bore the same three wolves' heads; and thus it was at length ascertained that Fidler, Fidelow, Videlow, and Vis-de-low were one and the same name, the earlier form of which was De Visdelu, or Vis-de-loup, probably from a place so named in Normandy, and to which the wolves' heads of the arms bore allusion.

Another instance of the utility of the comparison of armorial is afforded by the name of Toler. The writer for a long time could not discover the origin of this name or family. He formed several theories, all of which he was eventually obliged to relinquish. At length no clue remained except the arms. Those arms consisted of a cross fleury, surmounted by another cross, between four leaves erect. These arms were at first presumed to be of no great antiquity, as in their actual shape they do not present the simplicity which is characteristic of the ancient armorial. It appeared, however, on further inquiry, that the leaves had not originally been included in the arms, for families of 'Toller' and 'Towlers' were ascertained to have borne the same arms without any leaves, so that it was clear that the leaves were merely the emblem of a particular branch of the family. The inquiry was continued with the aid of this armorial, and the family was traced in different parts of England, in former ages, under a name continually varying in form—sometimes Towlers, then Tolers, then Towlowes, Towlons, Tolouse, until at length it appeared clearly that the latter form, which was coeval

with the Conquest, was the original. This pointed to
Toulouse in France as the place from which the family had
originally come ; and desirous to ascertain whether any
trace could be found of a family named from a city so
large as Toulouse (of which there seemed very little
hope), the author directed his attention to works containing information as to the early history of that city.
He turned to Anselme's great work on the peers and
nobles of France, in the hopes of finding under his account
of the Sovereign Counts of Toulouse some references to
works which might enable him to pursue the inquiry.
The volume was accordingly opened which contains the
history of the Counts of Toulouse, when, to his extreme
astonishment, the author recognised the arms of the
English Tolers and Towlers at the head of the history
of that great house! Their arms were the hereditary
emblems of that almost kingly race in all its branches—
the well-known 'Cross of Toulouse,' being a cross fleury
voided (i.e. in skeleton), which English heralds had
described as a cross fleury surmounted by another cross.
Of course all these various families of Toler, Toller, and
others, bearing the Cross of Toulouse, were identified as
one in origin, and as, no doubt, descendants of the
princely house whose name and arms they have borne
from the eleventh century.

The circumstance that an existing family bears a name
which may, with the aid of philological considerations,
be identified with one borne by some ancient Norman

house, and also bears the arms which are attributed to that house, might possibly be considered a mere coincidence; but the occurrence of such circumstances in hundreds of cases is altogether inconsistent with the notion of casual coincidence, and the evidence of consanguinity becomes morally certain. So too, when philology tells us that several families bear names which are cognate forms of a single name, and when it also appears that they all bear the same arms, their consanguinity is well established.

It is of importance, in order to remove any further difficulty from the question of identification, to classify the Norman and English names, with a view to trace the character of the alterations which have brought them to their present form. By so doing we shall be enabled to trace through large classes of names the influences which have removed, changed, or added initial letters; which have altered terminations; which have introduced consonants and omitted them; which have transmuted consonants and vowels; have altered aspirates; and generally have changed, Anglicised, and abbreviated names of foreign origin. Let it not be understood that these changes are always considerable in amount. It will be found in the alphabetical series of names that numerous Norman names are still very accurately preserved—that others are very slightly changed—that others may be recognised with little difficulty. But there are still many cases which require for their interpretation the aid of examples. It is, therefore, proposed to exhibit in a tabular form a series of illustrative examples, presenting those phenomena which are most frequently observable.

The abbreviation of names will be first exemplified:

NAMES ARMORIALLY IDENTIFIED.	NAMES OTHERWISE IDENTIFIED.
Bohun, Boon, Bowne	Cahaignes, Caines, Keynes
Somery, Somers	Kenobel, Knobel
Dakeny, Deacon, Dakins	Canot, Knot
Argentine, Argent	Escatot, Catot, Cato
Cayley, Calley	Rumilly, Rumley
Wayte, Watt	Roiale, Royle, Ryle
Berners, Barnes, Bernes	Bavant, Bavin
Barrey, Barre	Oiseleur, Osler
Jermyn, Jermy	Canivet, Knyvet
Derwentwater, Drinkwater	Noyon, Nunn, Noon

There are numerous instances in which the termination of names has become greatly changed by time. Thus we have:

NAMES ARMORIALLY IDENTIFIED.	NAMES OTHERWISE IDENTIFIED.
Granville, Greenfield	Somerville, Somerfield
Scruteville, Scurfield	Wateville, Waterfield
Fauville, Fallowfield	Estréeville, Streatfield
Frescheville, Freshfield	D'Angerville, Dangerfield
Blonville, Bloomfield	Woodville, Woodfield
Bosville, Boswell	Flamville, Flemwell
Mundeville, Monderel	Fierville, Fairfield
Blundell, Blunden	Rochelle, Rockall
Normanville, Normansell	Huielrat, Wheelwright
Ashburnham, Ashburner	Vitenc, Whiting
Damarel, Daumerle	Walleys, Walhouse
Boyvell, Boynell	Wellebo, Welbore
Russell, Rowswell	Turnebu, Turnbull

As there are many cases in which letters are omitted, there are also many others in which additions have been made by consonants, vowels, and aspirates ; for instance :

NAMES ARMORIALLY IDENTIFIED.	NAMES OTHERWISE IDENTIFIED.
Akeny, Dakins	Amblie, Hamley
Angers, Hanger	Allibone, Hallibone
Habington, Abingdon	Alis, Halys
Hasherst, Ashurst	Alvers, Halver
Ingham, Hingham	Osler, Hostler, Hustler
Hokeley, Okeley	St. Omer, Homer
Filmer, Phillimore	Lamare, Lachmare
Carsack, Caralacke	Kenebel, Kenechbol
Albin, Allibone	Lisle, Lidle,
Bard, Beard	Grelley, Gredley, Gridley
Busse, Bushe	Brand, Braund
Westcott, Wescott	Gage, Gadge
Paris, Parish	Esterling, Stradling
Helliar, Hildyard	Boteville, Butterfield

The commutation or substitution of letters by which different forms of the same name have been created, are analogous to those which are to be found in every language, and which even constitute in a great degree the distinctive differences in vocabulary. The same words can be recognised in many languages, notwithstanding frequent alterations of vowels. Thus, *hook* in English becomes *hoc* in Saxon, *haak* in Dutch, *haken* in German. *Earth* is *erde* in German, *aarde* in Dutch, *jord* in Swedish. *Seek* becomes *secan* in Saxon, *suchen* in German, *sequor* in Latin. In the same mode the changes of vowels are frequent in Norman and English names. Thus we have :

NAMES ARMORIALLY IDENTIFIED.	NAMES OTHERWISE IDENTIFIED.
Goodge, Gooche	Jovene, Young
Sacre, Secker	Bliss, Bleys, Blois
Farrer, Ferrar	Cabbal, Kebbel
Galpin, Gilpin	Audé, Ady
Dakeny, Dickins	Aldrey, Oldrey
Helliard, Hillier	Quentin, Quintin
Imrie, Emery	Welbore, Wildbore
Hussey, House	Wastell, Westall
Havenell, Hovell	Percy, Parsey, Piercey
Darrell, Dorrell	Peatt, Pitt
St. Laud, St. Lo	Punchardon, Pinkerton
Bohun, Boon	Putman, Pitman
Damarel, Daumerle	Ribald, Raybould

Labials and other letters are frequently exchanged. Thus the English word *bear* corresponds to the Latin *fero*; *gouverner* in French is from *guberno*; *volo* is related to *boulomai*; and the German *wollen* and English *will* are cognate forms. In the same way we have such names as the following :

NAMES ARMORIALLY IDENTIFIED.	NAMES OTHERWISE IDENTIFIED.
Paganel, Bagnall	Beckett, Pickett
Bastoyle, Wastoyle	Abadam, Apadam
Bastoyle, Vastoyle	Ballance, Vallance
Valtort, Watort	Bigot, Wigot
Beckering, Pickering	Banks, Panks
Waugh, Baugh	Bastable, Wastable
Bipont, Vipont	Postal, Bostel
Planke, Blanke	Vitot, Witot, Bitot
Bygot, Vigod	Farrow, Pharaoh
Videlow, Fidelow	Vescy, Pheysey
Vene, Fenn	Vicques, Fick
Phillimore, Filmer	Vallery, Fillary
Felton, Phelton	Willy, Villy

The letters G and W are frequently interchanged and

sometimes the former is commuted for J, or *vice versâ*.
Thus the French *guerre* corresponds to the Dutch *jaar*,
and the English *war* : *garenne* again and *warren* are
forms of the same word. We have instances of this in
names, thus :

NAMES ARMORIALLY IDENTIFIED.	NAMES OTHERWISE IDENTIFIED.
Genet, Jennet	Gasceline, Wascelyn
Germaine, Jermyn	Guet, Jewett
Jarrett, Garratt	Gast, West
Giles, Wiles	Geary, Werry

Other modes by which names become altered may
be here mentioned, without reference to armorial identification. Some forms have arisen from the influence of
French pronunciation, as

Bellowe from Belleau	Ganney from Canet
Galley „ Galet	Gallow „ Galot
Goosey „ Goucet	Ferry „ Feret
Mockler „ Mauclerc	Forey „ Foret

Others have arisen from dropping initial letters, as

Sart from Essart	Scures from Escures
Speke „ Espec	Stamp „ Estampes
Sparling „ Esparlen	Scholefield „ Escoville

In other cases *eau* has been changed to *ea* or *ee* :

Beamont from Beaumont	Beacham from Beauchamp
Beevor „ Beauver	Beavis „ Beaufiz
Beavoir „ Beauvoir	Beamish „ Beaumez

In many cases, also, the names are not to be found
until the thirteenth century, the older form of the name
being Latin or French, and the English translation not

appearing till the reign of Henry III. or Edward I. For instance:

Le Blanc, White	Le Cerf, Hart
Faber, Smith	Le Brun, Brown
De Pratis, Meadows	Bonenfant, Goodchild
Ami, Frend	Serviens, Serjeant
Lorimer, Sadler	Teste, Head
De Ariete, Ram	Le Venur, Hunter
Oiseleur, Fowler	Le Gantier, Glover
le Mounier, Milner	Porcus, Pigge
le Lorimer, Sadler	Blancpain, Whitbread
De Fonte, Spring	Le Fevre, Smith
Dulcis, Sweet	Espée, Sword
Citharista, Harper	Le Comte, Earle
Mercator, Marchant	Vulpis, Fox
Chevalier, Knight	Le Cornier, Horner
Rigidus, Stiff	Le Moin, Monk
Esperon, Spurr	Le Fort, Strong
Groceteste, Greathead	Aurifaber, Goldsmith
Le Petit, Little	Accipitrarius, Hawker

These instances may suffice to indicate some of the changes which have passed over English names in the course of the last eight centuries, and some of the rules of alteration in which they have originated. They will at the same time convey some notion of the difficulties experienced by those who attempt to trace names now existing to their sources and original forms. It is impossible to say at once in what direction a given name may have been altered; and it is only by close attention that serious mistakes can be avoided. It may be further explained that each of the ancient names appears in the present day, not merely under one form of alteration, but under several different forms more or less changed from the original. . Sometimes these forms in the case of a single name are numerous; but each of them now constitutes a distinct surname—a unit in the whole mass of English surnames—and represents on the average perhaps 80 families, or 400 individuals. These forms are frequently of great antiquity. They have been handed down from ages when orthography was in a very unsettled state, when names were frequently spelt phonetically—when the knowledge of writing was not possessed even by persons of high rank.

In the following alphabetical series great numbers of names will be found which are referred to other names as their cognates or their prototypes. In most cases it is trusted that the propriety of the reference will commend itself to the reader; but in cases which are less clear the author can only refer to the examples of similar changes contained in the present chapter, for it would evidently be an impossibility for him in so many cases to state the reasons which have led to his reference of each name to its cognate or prototype. Mr. Lower's valuable book, the *Patronymica Britannica*, affords numerous examples of identifications which present the same features as those which will be found in these pages.

One or two remarks must here be offered in further explanation.

The author has omitted several hundreds of names which are apparently or evidently foreign, because he has been unable to identify them in the Norman records.

G

Those names are ancient in England. In all probability they came from parts of the Continent external to Normandy at the Conquest, but there is at present no means of proving that they did so, because the records of France and the Low Countries have not been as yet published (if indeed they exist) on the same extensive scale as those of Normandy and England. Had we the same materials for comparison with the early names in Bretagne, Flanders, Maine, and Poitou, as we have in regard to Normandy, the list of foreign families which is to follow would have no doubt been augmented. As it is, the author has omitted hundreds of such names, which he believes to be foreign and as old as the Conquest, and has merely introduced a few specimens here and there to illustrate his meaning.

The author is also conscious that there are many names which ought to have been here inserted, but which have been inadvertently passed over. He has so often discovered instances of such accidental oversights that he is convinced there have been many more.

These facts should be borne in mind if it be in any cases supposed that the actual identification of a family as Norman is not satisfactory. It is the persuasion of the writer that he has understated the amount of the Norman or early foreign element, rather than overstated it.

CHAPTER V.

NATIONAL CHARACTER OF THE NORMAN SETTLEMENT IN ENGLAND.

IT seems to be received as a species of axiom by many persons that the Norman race has long since perished in England; and the continual use of the term 'Anglo-Saxon,' as synonymous with 'English,' is a sign of the prevalence of this view. Yet writers have seldom attempted to establish the alleged fact by any evidence, and seem to have relied upon mere popular opinion as a sufficient ground-work for belief. A recent historian, however, has abandoned this system of reticence, and has endeavoured to explain the alleged extinction of the Normans by showing that from seven to ten thousand would probably be a large estimate of the numerical force of the Norman settlers.[1] Nor is this all. He proceeds further to allege reasons which render the subsequent extinction of the race a matter of moral necessity—demanded by retributive justice. 'As the Normans were few in number,' observes this writer, 'they were also, like every military aristocracy, especially liable to decay. The curse that follows

[1] Pearson, History of England, i. 387.

G 2

bloodshed and money-getting followed them inexorably, and their sons perished in rebellions or made childless marriages for inheritances.'[1] Such an instance of retribution, were it supported by fact, would, no doubt, be very edifying; but the difficulty which suggests itself is this. Retribution in this sense appears in England to have been singularly one-sided, for it spared the Danes and the Anglo-Saxons, whose ferocity and sanguinary propensities stand in strong contrast to the conduct of the Normans. The Normans did not burn churches, monasteries, and cities, and plunder and murder a defenceless people, as the Danes had done. Still less did they, like the Anglo-Saxons, extirpate an entire nation by the edge of the sword, and take possession of its goods and lands. The Normans permitted the mass of the earlier population to remain; they even allotted to them no inconsiderable portion of the soil of England as owners; and they freely permitted them to occupy perhaps the greater portion of it as tenants and cottiers. Why, then, are the Normans supposed to have been victims of Divine vengeance, while the far more guilty Danes and Saxons are supposed to have escaped? Such theories as these only tend to show the influence which preconceived notions are capable of exerting on the strongest minds.

We must here consider the cardinal error on which the entire theory of the extinction of the Normans depends. That radical and fundamental error consists in assuming

[1] Pearson, History of England, i. 388.

that the Normans who settled in England at the Conquest were not a nation but an aristocracy. Doubtless, if we should assume that the population of England at the present moment is made up entirely of the Peers of the Realm, astonishing conclusions might be drawn. But let us consider the question in a common-sense point of view. It is impossible to suppose that the vast armies of Danes or Normans who overran England and France in the ninth century were composed exclusively of nobles and princes. It is obvious that the numbers of the latter must have been small, and that the masses of these armies consisted of private soldiers. The thirty or forty thousand North-men who in A.D. 886 besieged Paris, must have consisted of common soldiers as well as captains and generals. The Norman army which was subsequently led by Rollo was so strong that it proved to be more than a match for the united forces of France, and could endure the loss of nearly seven thousand men slain in one battle[1] without any apparent diminution of strength, for not long after-wards it dictated the terms of peace, and under them took possession of a great part of Neustria. Undoubtedly, this great army of Normans was not exclusively composed of nobles. It was an important section of the Scandinavian nation, and, like it, consisted of chiefs and of their followers. This army was continually recruited and reinforced by fresh migrations of Scandinavians from Denmark and the North, and Neustria or Normandy became the abode of

[1] Palgrave, History of Normandy and England, i. 677.

a great Scandinavian people, the Normans or Northmen of history. It is probable that this nation may have amounted to nearly a million at the Norman Conquest, or half the estimated number of the then population of England. It may possibly have been somewhat smaller in point of number, but it must have approximated to what has been stated.

The Norman population, thus numbering perhaps a million, or nearly so, consisted of upper and lower classes: the former included barons and knights. We have an official statement of the number of knights' fees held in Normandy in the reign of Henry II.[1] They amounted to twelve hundred altogether, exclusive of knights' fees belonging to the Church, which may have been three or four hundred more. Amongst the principal of those who held fees were the barons of Normandy, whose number in the reign of Philip Augustus was fifty-eight,[2] and this was probably a larger number than that of the baronage in the reign of the Conqueror. The number of distinct noble families in Normandy seems not to have very greatly exceeded the number of knights' fees.[3] It is true

[1] *See* the *Feoda Normanniæ* published by Duchesne in his *Historiæ Norm. Scriptores.—Paris* 1619, p. 1037.

[2] Ibid.

[3] It is clear that many junior branches of the Norman houses obtained fiefs, from whence they assumed new names, and ere long became new families. Thus the Tessons appear to have had junior branches named Marmion, Percy, and Beuron. There were certainly many subenfeoffments in Normandy which created noble families not mentioned specifically in the *Feoda Normanniæ*; but the total number was, after all, very limited. There was no sort of resemblance between the ancient nobility of Normandy,

that three thousand families appear to have become seated in England at the Conquest: but many of these were not purely Norman, but came from adjoining provinces. The Norman aristocracy may have numbered 2,500 families, of which 1,500 were seigneurs and lesser barons, and fifty greater barons; the nobility and gentry, in short, bore pretty much the same proportion to the population of the Duchy as the corresponding classes do to the masses of the English population at this moment. Such was the position of society in Normandy before the Conquest. The great masses of the Normans were tenants of the nobility and gentry, and copyholders, free tenants, retainers, farmers, artizans, tradesmen, mariners, burgesses, and merchants.

The Norman state was so ably administered, and was inhabited by a race of such vitality and energy, that it became developed with extraordinary rapidity. In the course of a hundred and fifty years its population had expanded so greatly that it was no longer sufficient to maintain such multitudes. It had become necessary to find outlets in Apulia and Spain for the teeming military population of Neustria; but these outlets were altogether insufficient, and the masses of Normans, pent up within a narrow territory (only one-quarter of the size of England),

which derived its rank from high ancestral sources and from the possession of feudal domains, and the later noblesse of France, which sprang by scores of thousands from the purchase of petty offices in the Royal household. It was computed at the French revolution that of the 100,000 families of French noblesse, only 4,000 were of old standing. The rest had recently sprung by purchase from the lower ranks.

threatened to overflow their frontiers or to perish from
want of sustenance. Sir Francis Palgrave has thus por-
trayed the condition of Normandy before the English
Conquest:

'As in frozen Iceland, so in fertile Neustria, the land
everywhere was unable to house her children. Normandy
was overflowing with the unemployed, increasing—according to the formula which has become technical in the
science of political economy—beyond the means of sub-
sistence. Large families gathered around the hearth, for
whose keep the father could not provide. The land was
cut up into quillets; not a *mete home*, a feeding-farm, as
it was called in old English, to be had upon which a man
and his family could live—universal unease therefore
prevailing.'[1]

It had become a matter of imperative necessity for
Normandy to find some new outlet for its excessive population. That population was probably twice as dense as
the population of England at the same epoch, for in
England there is no trace of over-population: the inhabitants were sparsely settled over the face of the
country, and enormous forests occupied the greater part
of the soil. The fertile plains of Normandy, however,
were assiduously cultivated by a superabundant people.

The outlet so necessary for Normandy was found in
the conquest of England; and thither accordingly rushed,
in one vast tide of emigration, gentle and simple, baron

[1] Palgrave, History of Normandy and England, iii. 140.

and feudal tenant. The lord and the knight migrated to acquire great feudal domains; the peasant and the peasant's son came to obtain new copyholds and farms, and the means of living, which had been denied to them at home; the tradesman and merchant came to find new markets for their goods, and to introduce new fashions and new wares in exchange for Saxon commodities. The natives of England were at first anxious to be Norman; they became clean-shaven and assumed an air of Norman civilisation; their garments no longer trailed upon the ground; the Norman tailor and cloth-merchant supplied the native with a jaunty cloak of the proper degree of brevity. On all sides were Norman gentlemen who set the fashion, and Norman farmers, soldiers, huntsmen, tradesmen, who laughed at everything else. The native was subdued, not only by the Norman's arms, but by his jests; but between jest and earnest he, before long, lost his temper and became sullen, indignant, and revengeful.

The position of a Norman proprietor was, from the first, no bed of roses. He was surrounded by a native tenantry and population which was willing (if the opportunity had been afforded) to rend him limb from limb, and to assassinate his wife and family. He had to attend the call of his feudal superior with a body of disciplined soldiers,[1] and that call might occur at any moment; he

[1] The usual retinue of the Norman knight consisted of one or two men-at-arms, clad in full armour, and several archers. The whole force, including the knight himself, consisted of six men at least. When, therefore, we read in the chronicles of the eleventh and twelfth centuries of the extra-

could not trust his tenantry or the other natives. If armed they would have taken his life. What, then, was the remedy? There was but one—the settlement of a body of Norman retainers on his estate.

If there be any point in English history on which all historians concur it is the extreme and bitter enmity with which the native races of England regarded the Normans in the time of William the Conqueror. That fact demonstrates at once the necessity which was incumbent on Norman proprietors to surround themselves by foreign military tenants, and the certainty that the king himself, on political and military grounds, and looking even to the safety of his throne, must have encouraged that policy to the utmost of his power. The king and the nobles then in England were as much urged by the necessities of their case to encourage Norman immigration on a large scale, as the Normans themselves were obliged by the wants of an enormous population to avail themselves of it. Moreover, the restless spirit of adventure, so peculiar to the Norman character, impelled the natives to enter on new fields, just as it drives the English race at this moment to embark in new enterprises and to settle in new countries.

England, then, was settled by all classes of Normans, high and low, and not merely by an aristocracy. The

---

ordinary military achievements accomplished by small bodies of Norman knights, it is to be remembered that the number should in each case be multiplied by six, in order to determine the real amount of the force engaged.

aristocracy undoubtedly did migrate to England, and so completely that ultimately the whole Norman nobility became English, and very few relics of it remained to later times in Normandy itself. But that aristocracy must have been driven into the sea by the native English, if it had not been supported by a Norman commonalty well able to keep the native English in due order and submission.

History and legal records rarely accord to the masses more than a transiént allusion; they are entirely conversant with the actions of the few great men whose lives, actions, and possessions are described. The people are too multitudinous and too obscure to merit notice; hence, of course, in the History of England, the history of the Normans is the history of kings and barons, and those who look on the surface of history see Normans only in the character of barons. Even in the records the barons and other great landed proprietors are those who chiefly appear. Those records owe their origin to the action of the Crown, which directed inquiries from time to time to be made with a view to ascertain the possessions and feudal services of its great tenants, or to proceedings in the courts of law, which generally arose out of disputes amongst the landed aristocracy, so that the early records do not relate to the middle classes, except to a limited extent, but to the aristocracy. And it is not till the thirteenth century that we find, for the first time, distinct and detailed notices of the state of the non-aristocratic classes, although many of their names are mentioned long before in various ways, particularly in the ecclesiastical records.

There are writers of eminence who maintain that the Normans died out in a century after the Conquest.[1] The records are in open opposition to such a notion. From the era of the Conquest the monastic charters (in the *Monasticon Anglicanum*) present a vast and unbroken series of evidence relating to the continuance and increase of the Norman race in England. We see them, generation after generation, in the presence of their numerous families and friends, conferring grants for religious uses. Thousands of families appear in their successive generations.

A century after the Conquest an account was taken by royal command of the landed aristocracy of England, above 3,000 in number. (It is preserved in the *Liber Niger*.) Three hundred and twenty-one were barons bearing purely Norman names, except in about twenty-six cases, in which, however, the families can almost all be proved Norman. Of the mesne lords or knights, 1,600 bore directly Norman surnames, 850 bore patronymics also Norman, and 400 or 500 bore English local names without any indications of Anglo-Saxon descent. Scarcely a trace is to be found throughout the whole list of any Christian name that is not foreign, or of anything indicating Anglo-Saxon origin. The 'Proceedings of the

---

[1] *E.g.* Pearson, History of England, i. 888.

Curia Regis,' 1194–1200, reveal a vast Norman aristocracy in England, and abound in every page in Norman names, and the proceedings of those who bore them. As we advance, the 'Parliamentary writs' prove the existence of these names and families in thousands upon thousands, up to the reign of Edward III. They appear again in the lists of gentry of the date of Henry VI., preserved by Fuller; they still appear in the 'State Papers' of the time of Henry VIII., as published officially. They are found in quantities in the 'Chancery Proceedings of the reign of Elizabeth,' and they still appear in thousands at this hour in England. What are we then to say of the imaginary extinction of the Normans? A more unsubstantial vision never passed before the mental eye. It is difficult to understand how any one can hold such a doctrine, except through want of acquaintance with the connected testimony of the national records. The historian is here, however, at a disadvantage, compared with the diplomatist, the archæologist, and the genealogist. He studies general history in chronicles, treatises, and correspondence, and he can speak authoritatively on his proper subject; but he has no leisure to examine genealogies, lists of knights' fees, Parliamentary writs, and monastic chartularies; hence he is liable to overlook facts regarding the population which are perceptible to humbler classes of students.

But we now come to the branch of the subject which has been least investigated by historians, namely, to the non-aristocratic classes of the Normans, the freemen, whose ancestors had followed Rollo and the other North-man princes from Scandinavia to Neustria, and who had become settlers in England.

It has been already shown that these classes, as well as the nobles, must have emigrated to this country, and it hence follows that the middle classes of England (all above the condition of slaves) must have been largely composed of Normans. This is distinctly recognised by one of the principal historians of England, who thus notices the theories of Thierry :—'The whole evidence seems to show that the wide distinction and hostility of the two races, supposed by Thierry and his school to have remained as late as the date of Henry II., is a mere imagination. The probability is, that though the upper classes were mainly Norman—the lower of old English descent—the distinction had then become one of class and not of nation. In the middle class, Thomas's [Becket] own class, the two races must have been much mixed up together. The real phenomenon of the age is, not the struggle between the two races in England, but the fusing together of the two races. . . . This silent gradual fusing of Saxons and Normans . . . was the great work of the twelfth century.'[1]

The classes, then, which were not servile, nor yet noble, were greatly mixed, and consisted of Normans as

[1] Freeman, Essays, 1871, p. 101.

well as Saxons. Thomas Becket himself sprang from these classes, and was of Norman origin.

We find in the proceedings of the Curia Regis, 1194-1200, mention made of names which belong to this middle class. We find earlier and later mention of these names in the *Monasticon* and elsewhere; but those allusions, as a general rule, do not enable us to determine the social status of the persons mentioned. It is, however, different when we come to the more detailed statistics of the thirteenth century. Then, for the first time, we obtain a clear insight into the composition of the middle classes in England, the petty landholders, copyholders, freeholders, free tenants, villeins, cottiers, tradesmen, shopkeepers, and merchants.

There is here a necessity to enter into some dry details, in order to show that in the thirteenth century about a moiety of these non-aristocratic classes above the position of slaves were Normans, the descendants of those who had come over at the Conquest and had settled in this country.

A few instances of the composition of the population in particular manors in different parts of England will show the state of things.

Cloppam, in Bedfordshire, was possessed (c. 1272) by five Lords of Manors, viz. John le Brun, John de Burneby, Ralph de Wedon, Walter Burdon, and Simon de Bayeux, three names being Norman and two local English (probably covering Norman descent). Then come the tenants, sixty-nine in number, and it appears from their names that more than a moiety of these were probably Norman.[1]

Akle, in the same county, next occurs. It was held by the Norman Robert de Borard. The whole number of tenants mentioned is twenty-five, of whom about one-half appear to have been Normans,[2] besides those who bore local English surnames.

Schenley, in Buckinghamshire, belonged to Richard de la Vache, a Norman; and eleven tenants are mentioned, of whom seven appear from their names to have been Normans.[3]

Wesbury, in the same county, was held by Turric Alemannicus (or De Allemagne), a Norman. The

[1] The names of Norman character are—Walter Præpositus (le Prevost), Richard Fitz Adam, Robert Gotyme? Henry Warin, Henry Wygeyn? Gilbert Quadrunss, Richard le Despencer, Ralph Fitz Robert, Walter de Monte, John le Ku, Sabina Burgeys, William Fitz John, John Pont, Henry Fitz Prevost, Richard Burnthard? Adam West, Walter Bertram, Robert Pikel, John de Cisenne, Walter de Monte, Richard Brese, Reginald Waryn, Walter Bretfel? Robert Brese, Robert Waryn, Emma de Bayeux, Henry de Bayeux, John de Eisenne, William Fitz John, John West, Richard West, Juliana Peket, William Fitz John, Henry Est, John Fitz Richard, Roger and Robert West, Richard Yngus? Ralph Fitz Robert, John de Bayeux, Gilbert de Riperia, Ralph Est, Henry Abel, Henry de Bayeux, Richard Maneypeny. Total 45, or, omitting names marked with queries, 40.— *Rotuli Hundr.* ii. 321.

[2] The names probably, or certainly, Norman were, Roger le Chanceler, John Mareschal, Hugo Caunceller, Thomas Coterel, Henry Messor, John Coterel, Simon Udeline, Walter Bercar, Gilbert le Prevost, Richard Fitz Ralph, William Thurstan, Alicia Brok. Total 12.—*Rot. Hundr. Ibid.*

[3] Viz. Gaffrid Bacon, Agnes Pincheon, Juliana Galiun, Matilda Barre, Roger le Clerc, William le Despencer, Hugh le Notte. Total 7.—*Rot. Hundr.* ii. 334.

tenants of all classes were thirteen in number, of whom seven were Norman.[1]

Passing next into Huntingdonshire, we come to Saltrey-Moyne, of which Sir William le Moyne, a Norman, was lord. The total number of tenants was 68, of whom about 32 bore names apparently Norman,[2] and 28 others bore names several of which were local English, and might cover Norman descent.

Thence passing into Oxfordshire, we come to Stoken-church, of which William de Gardino and William de Merifield were lords. Here the tenants were 26 in number, of whom about 15 were probably Norman,[3] besides those who bore English local names.

These cases have been taken as the first that turned up by chance, and they go to prove that probably not less than a moiety of the free classes in England continued to be Norman in the reign of Edward I.

We have next to consider the composition of the town and city population at the same period. There is no

---

[1] William Forest, William le Kene, Joanna Borre, Henry Fitz John, William de Jarpenville, Richard Poynaunt, Thomas le Clerc. Total 7.—*Rot. Hundr.* ii. 334.

[2] The names were Mowyn, Pinel, Oliver, le Fonlere, le Woodwarde, Pinel, Fitz John, Fitz Robert, Fitz Geroan, Gougemont, Fitz William, Berenger, de Stabulo, Fitz Philip, Norreys, Fitz Matthew, Fitz Jordan, Fitz Geoffry, Mastres, Borchier, Frevif, Soliere, Faber (2), Crisp, le Haie, le Parkere, Molendinar, Man, Crane, Thorston, le Bonde. Total 32.—*Rot. Hundr.* ii. 659.

[3] Viz. De Gardino, De la Rokele, La Vine, Malet, Bacon, De Aqua, De Fonte, Champion, Fitz Ralph, Rodelane, Pick, Fitz Auger, Randulf, Delamore, Copdemere. Total 15.—*Rot. Hundr.* ii. 785.

reason to suppose that this class of the population had much varied in its composition from the Conquest. The mercantile and trading families in those times remained stationary, for they had no facility for becoming landed proprietors, or for exacting rents which could reimburse them for the loss of their mercantile gains. The feudal system interposed barriers to the transfer of land or to the creation of rentals. The tenantry usually paid trifling rents or none, and held their tenements by services, military and otherwise. The town population consequently was very stationary, like the rural.

We take, then, the case of the borough of Cambridge in the time of Edward I, c. 1272. There is a full list of the house-owners there, many of whom held several houses each. The total number of persons mentioned is 241, of whom about 106 appear to bear Norman names,[1] besides families concealed under English local names.[2]

---

[1] The names are Le Longe, Le Berchar (3), Norman (2), Botte, André (2), Bangernon, Fitz Wymond (3), Le Cupere, Fitz Norman, Le Mire, Le Tailur (2), Norman, Le Sunr, Fitz Jordan, Warin, Le Barbur, Faber, Warin, Le Chapeler, Le Coteler, Laurence, Mareschal, Porthors, Le Rus, But, Pult, Plumbe (2), St. Alban, Toylet, Huberd, De Arda, Le Cun, Laurence, Le Tanur, Bainard, Perin, Gogging, Hardi, Le Barbur, De Gaunt, Bercarius, De Braci (5), Fitz Ranulph, Morice, Martin, Sabyn, Le Mouner, Gogging, Ercheband, Le Corder, De Ferrur, Chapellan, Le Comber (2), De Cayleys, Beaupain, De Braci, Gregory, Burges, Lucke, Le Blunt, Fitz Morice, De Pax, Fitz Nicholas, Scutard, Le Fraunceys, Le Barbur (2), Le Mouner, Karun, Aurifaber, Le Mercer (2), Abiçon, Crayon, Le Hunte, Le Ferrur (2), Le Coteler, Matelasc, Malerbe, Le Plomer, Le Lorimer, Fitz Robert, Paternoster, Blome, Castelein, Toylet, Le Ber, De Bouden, Bruere, Constable de Holdernesse (see CONSTABLE, Alph. Series), De Walpole. Total 106.—*Rot. Hundr.* ii. 356.

[2] Eighty-three in number.

Passing on from Cambridge to London itself, we come to the official catalogue of the mayor, sheriffs, chamberlains, and coroners of the City, extracted from the '*Liber Custumarum*,' and extending from 1245 to 1320. 239 persons are enumerated in this list of civil magnates—men no doubt engaged in every description of trade and commerce. Amongst them are 105 bearing Norman names,[1] besides those which are probably concealed under English denominations.

There is an account of a meeting of the mayor, aldermen, and sheriffs of the City of London in 1327. Thirteen persons were present, and of these eight (viz. De Bethune, De Chenduit, De Leyre, De Constantine (2), De Gisors, Poyntel, and Chauntecler) were Norman.[2]

These few facts will have shown, however briefly, the nature of the proof which exists for the continuance of the Norman middle classes in vast numbers in England in the thirteenth and fourteenth centuries, and will lend weight to the opinion that their descendants still exist, which this work aims to establish by an induction of facts.

---

[1] The Norman names, many of which are frequently repeated, were—Le Blount, De Arras, Le Fevre, Adrien, Le Engleys, De Columbieres, La Maselinier, Le Walleys, De Gisors, De Betteville, Maserier, Cros, Hauteyn, De Betune, Le Cotiller, Romayn, De Leyre, De Vinetria, Russel, Le Breton, Le Galleys, De Sely, De Armentieres, Le Callere, De Pourte, De Paris, Cosin, De Chenduit, Bolet, Drury, De Say, De Waldechief, Corp, Lambin, Burdeyn, Le Balauncer, Furneys, Pointel. — See *Liber Custumarum Munimenta Gildhallæ*, ed. Riley, ii. part i. p. 239.

[2] *Munimenta Gildhallæ*, ed. Riley, iii. 418.

If, as these pages have already shown, the Norman race in England now amounts to at least a quarter of the English population, and probably to a third or more, we see that the state of the population of England six centuries since was in perfect harmony with that fact.

CHAPTER VI.

THE DANISH SETTLEMENT IN ENGLAND.

IT is generally admitted that the Danish invaders of England in the ninth and following centuries were of the same race as the Northmen who invaded France at the same time, and were afterwards known as Normans. English history sufficiently attests the power of the Danes in England; but present opinion, anxious to believe in the prevalence and ascendancy of the Saxons, is inclined to underrate the importance of the Danish invasion and occupation of England. It is imagined that the effect of the Danish invasion was slight and transient, and that the Danes became extinct or merged in the vast masses of the Anglo-Saxons. Such views are grounded on modern theories, rather than on historical fact. In perusing the 'Saxon Chronicle' and the other contemporary records of the date of the Danish invasions, it is impossible to avoid seeing in the latter all the characters of a national migration. The Anglo-Saxons were astounded at the hosts of the invaders, which seemed absolutely inexhaustible. Fresh armies of Danes appeared as soon as preceding ones had been destroyed. The Saxons sank at length, overwhelmed, not only by the ferocity, but by the numbers of the Northmen; and it was only by a most fortunate combination of circumstances that Alfred (when it appeared least likely) was enabled to recover from the Southern Danes, and their king Guthrum, the southern counties of England, bounded by the Thames. The remainder of England (three times the size of the Saxon territory), extending from the Thames to the Frith of Forth, remained under the Danish dominion. Had this great territory been united in one kingdom, the Anglo-Saxon part of England would have been inevitably conquered in a generation or two. As it was, the Danes established themselves everywhere throughout their territory as lords of the soil and occupiers. The Angles were slain, expelled, enslaved, or compelled to take refuge in exile. From that time, Northumbria and East Anglia and Mercia were generally ruled by Danish kings and jarls. Even when internal divisions had enabled the Saxon kings to advance their sovereignty northwards, the Danes always retained native rulers; and the contest between them and the Saxons continued till fresh invasions of Danes reduced England entirely under the Danish dominion, to revert for a few years to the Saxon, and then to fall again permanently under the Danish (in the shape of the Norman) sway. The Scandinavians have ruled in England since 870.

The Danes came to England as a people. In the pages of Ingulphus we read of eight Danish kings and nineteen jarls, who headed the Danish forces when they invaded Lincolnshire; and the general history of the time mentions several kings of the Danes who simultaneously led their nations to the invasion of England. The movement was national.

The result was that the population of the eastern, midland, and northern counties became chiefly Danish or Norman; and there the Danish population remained [1] and has so remained up to the present day; and the energy and intelligence of the northern English and lowland Scots come from their Danish forefathers. Worsae has very clearly shown the evidences of Danish descent which remain in many parts of the north, where language, manners, customs, and even physical characteristics contribute to establish it. In accordance with the laws of natural reproduction, the continuance of the Danish race in districts where they originally settled in vast numbers must be assumed, unless there is clear proof to the contrary.

The English language (in so far as it is not derived from Latin sources) is in itself sufficient to show the continued existence of a population of Danes fully equal to that of the Saxons.[2] What remains of the Gothic

---

[1] Dr. Dasent says (Jest and Earnest, ii. 10), 'At the Conquest England was more than half Scandinavian. Besides the great district of Northumbria, which reached, it must be remembered, far across the borders into Scotland, and the province of East Anglia, where the Scandinavian stock was fast settled, their nationality reached as far south as Derby and Rugby, in the very heart of Mercia.' Dr. Dasent here underrates the extent of the Scandinavian occupation: it reached to the Thames, as appears by the names of Scandinavian settlements down to its very banks.

[2] It has been remarked by Mr. Cardale, in a note prefixed to his edition of Boethius, that before the Conquest 'pure Anglo-Saxon and Dano-Saxon

element in English is derived as much from Scandinavian or Danish sources as from Saxon—perhaps more so. 'The English language,' says one of our ablest philologists, 'both in conjugation, construction, accent, and pronunciation, is more nearly allied to the Northumbrian or Danish dialect than to that of Wessex.'[1]   What remains of the old Saxon dialect (i.e. that of Wessex), appears in the writings of king Alfred, Ælfric, Cædmon, &c., and is usually styled 'Anglo-Saxon.'   This language is almost purely Gothic, as is elsewhere observed.   The Scandinavian or Danish is another dialect of the Gothic, and that dialect has largely contributed to the formation of modern English.   If we take indifferently a number of words from the English dictionary and compare them with the corresponding terms in the Anglo-Saxon (or West Saxon) and the Scandinavian under its different types of Norse, Swedish, and Danish, it will be found that in most cases the words are nearly identical in English, Saxon, and Scandinavian, but where there is a difference, the third named is more frequently followed in English than the second.   A comparison in tabular form may illustrate what is meant:

were the two great dialects of the language,' and that 'these two dialects of the Anglo-Saxon continued substantially distinct as long as the language itself was in use.'

[1] G. W. Dasent, D.C.L., Jest and Earnest, a Collection of Essays and Reviews, ii. 12, 13.

ANGLO-SAXON.	ENGLISH.	SWEDISH or DANISH.	NORSE.
bringan	bring	bringe	
seld	seat	säte	sit
sencan	sink	sænke	
sendan	send	sende	senda
sioc	sick	syg	
breod	bread		braid
breost	breast	bryst	
byrnan	burn	brinna	
selan	soil	söla	
sylfor	silver	silfwer	silfr
tang	tongs	tång	taung
tellan	tell	tælle	tala
tredan	tread	træde	
trepas	troop	tropp	
wif	wife	vif	
sceanca	shank	shank	
onginnan	begin	begynna	
brecan	break	brække	

Mr. Marsh, in his important work on the English language, observes that 'the remarkable coincidences between the pronunciation of the languages of the Scandinavian countries and of England are an evidence that the former had upon the latter an influence powerful enough to introduce into it some new phonological elements, and to preserve others probably once common to all the Gothic tongues, but which have disappeared from the articulation of the Teutonic dialects.'[1] Professor Max Müller indicates grammatical forms in English derived from Scandinavian sources. All this goes to show that the Scandinavian element of population was, throughout, as strong in England as the Saxon; that

[1] G. P. Marsh, Origin and History of the English Language, 1862, p. 62.

the English races which did not derive their origin from Neustria were about equally divided in point of numbers.

The extent of the Danish dominion and occupation has not been fully realised. Archæologists and historians are agreed that from Northumbria to the midland counties the Danelagh prevailed; and they usually determine its limits by tracing the local names terminating in ' by.' This is, no doubt, a Scandinavian termination, and wherever it occurs sufficiently ascertains the fact of a Scandinavian settlement; but there are other Scandinavian local terminations which are also found in many parts of England north of the Thames, and which considerably extend the area of the Danish settlements. Such terminations are 'thorpe,' 'trop,' 'stad' or 'stead,' 'beck,' 'holm,' 'berg,' 'borg' or 'burgh,' 'dal' or 'dale,' 'toft,' 'see,' 'ness,' 'wik,' 'hoe,' &c., all of which are Scandinavian, and indicate Scandinavian settlements in more parts of England than is generally imagined. Nor are these terminations derived from Denmark alone. It would be a mistake to suppose that the ancient Daci or Dani came merely from within the limits of the modern kingdom of Denmark. They came also from Norway, and, to a very large extent, from Sweden. It almost appears as if the Swedish element was the strongest amongst the English Northmen; for there are evidences of Swedish settlements in this country, and in all parts of it, to a very remarkable extent.

It seems that the Northmen, in settling in England,[1] introduced very largely a class of local names altogether different from the former Anglic names; and that the new names were not merely Scandinavian in form, but in many cases directly Scandinavian—the names of villages and places in Denmark, Sweden, and Norway. The settlers transferred the names of their native villages to England, just as the English of America, in after times, gave to their new settlements the names of old English localities. Hence we find the Anglo-Saxon 'Strenaeshalch,' transformed into 'Whitby' by the Danes, the latter name being transferred from 'Witbé' in Denmark. It may be useful to place in juxtaposition some names of the original Scandinavian localities and their counterparts in this country; and it may be convenient also to arrange the places under English counties.

Essex	Fairstead	from	Farjestad	Sweden
	Hallingoury	„	Hallingeberg	Sweden
	Harwich	„	Arvika	Sweden
	Dunmow	„	Dannemore	Sweden
	Gidea	„	Gidea	Sweden
	Easthorpe	„	Ustrup	Denmark
	Hadham	„	Aadam	Denmark
	Roding	„	Rodding	Denmark
	Bocking	„	Bucking	Denmark
	Halstead	„	Ollestad	Norway

[1] The Northmen also introduced Scandinavian local names in Neustria, though far more sparingly than in England. Valoines from Vallinge, Vesci from Gessie, Tuit from Tveta, Torp from Torpa, Douvres from Dover, are Swedish; Arel from Arle, Goer from Goher, are Danish; and Houlme from Holme, Norwegian.

MIDDLESEX	Kingsbury	from	Kingsbro	Sweden
	Hidland	,,	Hightband	Sweden
	Notting	,,	Notting	Denmark
	Bow	,,	Baw	Denmark
	Harrow	,,	Hanrow	Denmark
HERTFORD	Tewing	,,	Tying	Sweden
BUCKS	Soulsbury	,,	Solvitsborg	Sweden
	Horwood	,,	Horred	Sweden
	Burnham	,,	Bjornholm	Sweden
	Borstall	,,	Borstel	Denmark
OXFORD	Iffley or Gefley[1]	,,	Geflé or Yefflé	Sweden
	Handborough	,,	Hundborg	Denmark
	Adderbury	,,	Haddeburg	Denmark
GLOUCESTER	Burderop	,,	Burdrup	Denmark
	Hatherop	,,	Haderup	Denmark
WORCESTER	Dodderhill	,,	Dodderhull	Sweden
	Salwarp	,,	Skiwarp	Sweden
NORTHAMPTON	Ashby	,,	Asby	Sweden
	Wadenhoe	,,	Wadho	Sweden
	Astrop	,,	Astorp	Sweden
BEDFORD	Hill	,,	Hille	Sweden
HUNTINGDON	Somersham	,,	Cimbrishamn	Sweden
CAMBRIDGE	Elm	,,	Hellum	Denmark
SUFFOLK	Layham	,,	Layholm	Sweden
	Bergholt	,,	Biorkshult	Sweden
	Sotterley	,,	Sodertelgé	Sweden
	Giselham	,,	Grisselhamm	Sweden
	Dalham	,,	Dalhem	Sweden
	Sudbury	,,	Soodberg	Denmark
	Worsted	,,	Gierestad	Denmark
	Bealing	,,	Balinge	Sweden
NORFOLK	Ingoldsthorpe	,,	Ingatorp	Sweden
	Maltby	,,	Mallby	Sweden
	Sall	,,	Sala	Sweden
	Rising	,,	Risinge	Sweden
	Gissing	,,	Gissling	Sweden
	Oxburgh	,,	Oxberg	Sweden
	Gresham	,,	Gresholm	Denmark

[1] The Northman origin of this name is a fact of importance, because it shows that down to the very banks of the Thames the Northmen had settlements.

NORFOLK	Westwich	from	Vestervig	Denmark
	Hilborough	,,	Hulgeberg	Denmark
	Ashill	,,	Osle	Denmark
	Northwold	,,	Northald	Denmark
	Brumstead	,,	Bramsted	Denmark
	Keling	,,	Kelling	Norway
LINCOLN	Aby	,,	Aby	Sweden
	Holland	,,	Oland	Sweden
	Fleet	,,	Flata	Sweden
	Westborough	,,	Ovistbro	Sweden
	Gonnerby	,,	Gunilbo	Sweden
	Sutterby	,,	Soderby	Sweden
	Gunby	,,	Gunneby	Sweden
	Orby	,,	Harby	Sweden
	Axholm	,,	Oxholm	Denmark
	Strubby	,,	Strautby	Denmark
	Silkwilloughby	,,	Silke	Denmark
	Willoughby	,,	Wilbé	Denmark
	Lound	,,	Lunde	Denmark
NOTTINGHAM	Hickling	,,	Hicklinge	Sweden
	Hareby	,,	Arby	Sweden
	Stokeham	,,	Stockholm	Sweden
	Granby	,,	Granbyn	Sweden
LEICESTER	Dalby	,,	Dalby	Sweden
	Hoby	,,	Hoby	Sweden
	Stonsby	,,	Stensbek	Denmark
	Oadby	,,	Otby	Denmark
STAFFORD	Haracles	,,	Harakra	Sweden
	Harwood	,,	Horred	Sweden
	Rowley	,,	Rulley	Sweden
	Stubby	,,	Stiby	Sweden
	Talk	,,	Tolck	Denmark
SALOP	Barrow	,,	Baro	Sweden
	Ness	,,	Nees	Norway
CHESTER	Hassall	,,	Hasala	Sweden
	Norley	,,	Nortelge	Sweden
DERBY	Thorpe	,,	Torp	Sweden
	Foremark	,,	Forsmark	Sweden
	Tunstead	,,	Tonstad	Norway
LANCASHIRE	Wray	,,	Vra	Sweden

LANCASHIRE	Holm	from	Holm	Norway
	Urswick	„	Erwick	Sweden
	Hoker	„	Haker	Denmark
	Hale	„	Hale	Denmark
	Bigland	„	Bygland	Norway
YORKSHIRE	Risby	„	Rysby	Sweden
	Aske	„	Aske	Sweden
	Monkthorp	„	Mukerp	Sweden
	Howden	„	Hudinge	Sweden
	Wike	„	Wikes	Sweden
	Lowthorp	„	Loderup	Sweden
	Byland	„	Bielland	Norway
	Howland	„	Hovland	Norway
	Lee	„	Lie	Norway
	Selby	„	Seby	Denmark
	Nehthorpe	„	Nilstrup	Denmark
	Elland	„	Oeland	Denmark
	Whitby	„	Witbé	Denmark
	Hallam	„	Allum	Denmark
	Bowling	„	Bolling	Denmark
DURHAM	Westwick	„	Westervick	Sweden
	Raby	„	Raby	Sweden
	Newbiggen	„	Nebiggen	Sweden
NORTHUMBER-LAND	Eland	„	Haland	Sweden
	Shaftoe	„	Skafto	Sweden
	Rock	„	Roke	Sweden
BERWICK	Hutton	„	Hutten	Denmark
CUMBERLAND	Ousby	„	Ousby	Sweden
	Holme	„	Holme	Sweden
	Gamelsby	„	Gamelby	Sweden
WESTMORELAND	Swindall	„	Svindal	Norway
SCOTLAND	Edsell	„	Edsele	Sweden
	Turing	„	Turinge	Sweden
	Monkland	„	Mokland	Norway
	Nithsdale	„	Nissedal	Norway
	Gordon	„	Gording	Denmark

This list has been compiled after a brief and cursory
examination of the Scandinavian names of localities; and

there can be little doubt that if the enquiry were followed out, considerable light would be thrown on the Danish settlements in England; but the author has not either time or space to do more. It must be borne in mind that the diversity of orthography has arisen from time. The principal object of introducing the list has been to show, not only the wide diffusion of the Danes over England, and to confirm the fact of their occupying the whole territory to the north of the Thames, but also the fact that, although usually styled 'Daci' or 'Dani,' they might be (as they sometimes were) with more propriety entitled Northmen or Normans, being composed, as the Neustrian Normans were, of nations from different parts of the north.

The comparison of English with Scandinavian names of localities would require for its development a special study. It would involve the examination of Scandinavian geography and topography in their earliest authentic sources, and a comparison of the names of localities with their counterparts in the early English charters, and in Domesday Book. It would hold out, however, to the Scandinavian archæologist almost a greater reward than to the English; for it would probably enable him to restore, to a considerable extent, the topography of Scandinavia in the ninth century, since every local name, identified both in England and Scandinavia, would furnish a proof (and in most cases a unique proof) of the existence before 870 of the present towns and villages of

Sweden, Denmark, and Norway—a date so remote that even the general history of those countries is at that time involved in obscurity.

To establish the continuance of the Danish race in England no weightier authority than that of Sir Francis Palgrave can be cited. His profound knowledge of English history and of the English records entitles his opinion on such a question to the highest consideration. 'The distinctive energy of the Scandinavian races has continued in full vigour amongst us, and still remains unexhausted. No country testifies to the potent influence of Scandinavian blood more than our own. However mingled our population, each emigrant ship steaming from our shores bears away a large proportion of passengers who may claim real Danish ancestry. Many are the Danish Havelocks in our ranks, undistinguished by that heroic name.'[1]

The author regrets that the object and purpose of this work precludes him from entering on the subject of Danish families now existing. It would be easy to name some whose Danish origin is little suspected, and whose history is of surpassing interest; but space forbids any attempt to do justice to the theme; and Danish families, collectively, have not been included in the author's enquiries so far.

It must, however, be here added, that to identify the Danish families of England would be a far more difficult

---

[1] Palgrave, History of Normandy and England, iii. 189.

task than that of recovering the Norman families. The reason is, that in the case of the Danes of England we have no means of instituting a comparison such as we have in the case of the Normans. Family surnames did not exist in England before the Conquest, nor in Scandinavia; consequently, the surnames of the Danes of England cannot be traced in Scandinavia; and there are no records in England of an earlier date than the Conquest, or coeval with it, which could in any degree supply the materials for investigation which are provided in the case of the Normans by the Exchequer Rolls of Normandy, and the contemporary records of England.

CHAPTER VII.

GOTHIC ORIGIN OF THE NORMANS, DANES, AND ANGLO-
SAXONS. PRESENT DIFFUSION AND NUMBERS
OF THE GOTHIC RACE.

WE now come to a different branch of the subject
England was inhabited by the three races of Anglo-
Saxons, Danes, and Normans, and those three races have
for seven centuries become blended into one, long known
as the English race. We have seen the error of the
supposition that either of those races has become extinct,
though all three have abandoned their original names for
one that is common to them all. We have now to consider the original relations of these three races before
their migration to England, and more especially in connection with the origin of the Normans.

What, we ask with natural interest, was the origin of
this mighty race, on which history cannot dwell without
rising to the level of poetry? Whence came these giants
of the Middle Ages—these rivals of the ˙Saracen, the
Roman, and the Macedonian Conquerors?

Their forefathers had, in the ninth century, issued
forth from Scandinavia to conquer new homes for themselves in the south; to obtain an asylum for that deeply-

cherished freedom which northern revolutions had endangered. Like the pilgrim fathers of New England, they had traversed the ocean to preserve their liberties. A branch of them had, with the same object, migrated to Iceland, where they had established a flourishing aristocratic republic, one of the earliest in Europe. The internal wars of its kindred Gothic nations, the severity of its inhospitable climate, and the sterility of its frozen soil, had gradually created in Scandinavia a maritime population of unrivalled enterprise, vigour, and courage. Honour was awarded to bravery alone; the Scandinavian maid disdained the addresses of the man who had not won fame in battle: a peaceful death was considered to be a deep disgrace, and rather than endure it the North-man precipitated himself from a cliff into the surge beneath. If he was made a prisoner, he preferred death to submission; the proud heart broke; or the captive dashed himself to pieces against the walls of his prison. These heathens, whose stern heroism recalls that of the Spartans or the early Romans, were the progenitors of the Normans.

And whence, it may be asked, did these nations of the north—the lineal forefathers of the Normans—derive their origin? Were they indigenous to that soil, and had their abode there been without commencement? The evidence afforded by language and institutions shows that they had formed part of a great family of nations—the GOTHS or GETAE; that they were the advanced guard, or the remotest branch of a race which had extended itself to the shores of the Northern Ocean from the steppes of Central Asia.

The Getae or Goths[1] are first heard of in the East, where one of their branches, the Massa-Getae, in the seventh century B.C., expelled the Scythians from their territories, and in the sixth, defeated and slew Cyrus king of the Persians and his army.[2] This great nation, which was so jealous of its liberties and able so potently to maintain them, was seated in the neighbourhood of the Sea of Aral, and in those territories which now intervene between the dominions of England and of Russia. The Sacae or Saxones,[3] and Dahae or Daci, were neighbouring

---

[1] Rawlinson, in his edition of Herodotus (iii. 84), says: 'The identity of the Getae with the Goths of later times is more than a plausible conjecture. It may be regarded as historically certain. Moreover, the compounds Massa-Getae, Thyssa-Getae, Tyri-Getae, have a striking analogy to the later name of Visi-Goths, and Ostro-Goths.' On Herod., v. 219, he observes, 'It is almost certain that the Getae—one of the principal Thracian tribes, according to Herodotus—are the Gothi or Gothones of the Romans, who are the old German Guthai or Guthones, and are Goths (see Grimm's Geschichte der Deutschensprache, vol. i. pp. 178-184). The one name superseded the other in the same country, and there are not wanting ancient writers who expressly identify the two forms (Philostorgius, Hist. Eccl., ii. 5; Ennodius, p. 52, etc.). Grimm has shown that the change from Γέτης to Goth is according to the analogy of the Teutonic and Græco-Roman form of speech.' Donaldson (Varronianus, 3rd ed. p. 51) speaks of 'the Getae, whether called by this name, or designated as Goths, Guddas, Jutes, and Vites.' The Jutes or Goths in England were styled 'Geata' or 'Getae.' King Alfred's translation of 'Jutis' in Bede, i. 15, is 'Geatum' and 'Geata.' Asser 'looked on the Jutes and Goths as the same people,' says Mr. Freeman.

[2] Herodotus, i. 292.

[3] See Donaldson (Varronianus, p. 49), who connects them with the Saxons in Europe. They are mentioned by Herodotus (i. 153) as a great nation in the time of Cyrus.

nations, probably of the same race, as we find them
equally associated with the Getae in the West and the
East.

These nations of Massa-Getae, Sacae, and Dahae, seem
to have been the rear-guard of the Getic nations, who
migrated from the East from about 1,500 to 2,000 years
B.C., and spread themselves gradually over Europe. We
can form a notion of their route by tracing the various
nations which they established in their course westwards,
and which continued until the time when classical history
and geography take notice of them. The Tyssa-Getae (one
of these branches) were left on the banks of the Volga or
Rha. The Roxolani branched off further on, between the
Tanais (Don) and the Borysthenes (Dnieper). Then the
Tyri-Getac were left to occupy the banks of the Tyras
(Dniester); and when the migration reached the Danube,
the Getae, Daci, Triballi, and Thracians were left behind
to take possession of those regions. Thence turning to
the north-west, the Getic or Gothic migration ascended
the Tyras till it struck the head-waters of the Vistula.
On its route were detached the tribes of the Pien-Getae,
and the Ars-Getae, and the nations of the Bastarnae, who
occupied south Poland ; and here also commenced the
great migration westward, from which sprang the Germanic nations.

I. The GERMAN or TEUTONIC race (which alone with
propriety bears those denominations) was undoubtedly of
the same origin as the Getic, Gothic, and Scandinavian, as

its language sufficiently proves. It consisted of the tribes of Quadi, Marcomanni, Hermanduri, Chatti, Cherusci, Sycambri or Cimbri, and others, which gradually took possession of the centre of modern Germany from the Lippe southwards,[1] and from the Carpathians to the Rhine. These tribes were confederate from an early period. The most ancient known name of the confederation was 'Teutones;' a term which occurs in the fourth century B.C.; that of 'Germans' was given by the Romans. It arose from the guttural pronunciation of 'Hermiones'—then the federal name; and the Romans incorrectly applied this name to all nations east of the Rhine, instead of to the central race, to which alone it properly belonged. The Germans were afterwards confederated under the name of 'Franks,' and were conquerors of northern Gaul.[2] In later times they became again 'Teutones' or Dutch, and 'Germans,' and so continue to the present day. This race, whose language is a harsh and guttural dialect of the original Gothic or Getic, is aboriginal in Germany, having occupied its proper territories, and maintained a distinct federative nationality, for more than 3,000 years.

II. THE GOTHS.—While the German migration of the Getic nations proceeded westwards, the main body of

---

[1] Donaldson (Varronianus, p. 76) observes that the 'strong, but narrow stream,' of high-German conquest disturbed the southern and low-German [i.e. Gothic] tribes.'

[2] For some time Germany was called 'East France.' *See* Freeman, Essays, 1871, pp. 220, 221.

those tribes advanced northwards along the Vistula, to its mouth, under the name of Getae or Goths. To the east of the Vistula, the Samo-Getae were despatched to settle Lithuania.[1] The Goths seated themselves all along the Vistula; the Phrugundiones, one of their branches, to the east, were the same as the Burgundiones, who were seated to the west of the Vistula. Then, as the nation expanded itself along the south shores of the Baltic[2] and the adjacent provinces (while the Germans advanced in parallel columns further south,) the various denominations of Vindals, or Vandals, Lombards, Varini, Suevi arose, and in later times became known in history. Thence the Gothic migration still continually pressed on towards the west, and left the races of Saxones, Chauci, Angli, Frisians, and others, established from the Elbe to the mouths of the Rhine, and beyond them in modern Belgium. These territories of the Goths included the north of the mediæval kingdom of Poland, and the countries we know as Prussia Proper, Brandenburgh, Mecklenburgh, Holstein, Sleswig, Hanover, the Free Cities, Westphalia, Brunswick, Oldenburgh, Holland, and Flanders. It was this wing of the Goths that overthrew the Roman Empire and divided its territories; and from this wing also sprang

---

[1] Donaldson, Varronianus, p. 51.

[2] The inhabitants of the southern shores of the Baltic, extending 6,000 stadia or 750 miles in length, were in common styled Guttones or Goths in the fourth century B.C., according to Pytheas (see Pliny, Hist. Nat., xxxvii. 11). It is stated by Pytheas that the Guttones sold the amber which they found on the shores of the Baltic to their [inland] neighbours the Teutones.

the ANGLO-SAXONS, who were originally tribes of Frisians, Saxons, or Chauci, Angles, and Jutes,[1] or Goths, from the various Gothic provinces extending from the Rhine to the Elbe, and into Jutland.

The Anglo-Saxons were entirely Gothic in origin, and their language was purely Gothic—so much so that modern philologists can re-construct its original inflexions and grammar, wherever defective, merely by inferences from those of the Mœso-Gothic.[2] It is even held by philologists of eminence[3] that the Gothic and the Anglo-Saxon present the normal type of the language, and that in forming a comparison of this family of language with those of the remainder of the Indo-European race it is advisable not to take the German or Teutonic into account, as it appears to be a peculiar and incorrect dialect, harsh and guttural in its form, and differing materially from the softer and more genuine Gothic.

III. THE SCANDINAVIANS.—Setting aside mere speculations as to the migration of the Goths into Sweden and Norway through Russia, and round the north of the

---

[1] The Jutes, Vithes, Goths, or 'Geata,' come from Jutland, or, as it is styled, 'Vithe's-Læth' (Varronianus, 51). It is curious to find the Jutic or Gothic 'Lathe' in Kent, the original settlement of the Jutes, and to notice the Jutic or Jutland local names of Hyem, Hellum, Hobro, Bouling, Soodberg, Sydling, Hemme, Breston, Himstead, Colding, Capel, and Breadstadt, as represented in the Kentish topography by Higham, Elham, Holborough, Bowling, Southborough, Sellinge, Ham, Preston, Hemstead, Cowling, Capel, and Brastead. These names were transferred from Jutland to Kent in the fifth century probably.

[2] *See* Max Müller, Lectures on the Science of Language, p. 236.

[3] Burnouf, cited by Pritchard, Natural History of Man, iii. 347,

Baltic, it seems that the natural course of the Gothic migration into Scandinavia was from the southern shores of the Baltic and the Danish waters. As the Goths spread along the Baltic they came to Jutland, thence passed into the Danish Islands, thence across the Sound into Sweden, and thence throughout the whole of Sweden and Norway. It is conceived that they were the earliest occupants of these countries, and that the Lapps and Finns (a branch of the Tchudi) came afterwards from Asia. From the Goths thus settled in Scandinavia sprang the Goths of Sweden, the Jutes, Getae, or Goths of Denmark, the Daci or Dani[1] of Denmark, and other tribes, all alike of Getic or Gothic origin.

From these tribes sprang the DACI or DANES of England, and the Northmen or NORMANS, who were of the same race, and were indifferently styled by either name. The Danes in England were equally styled Normans, and the Normans were equally entitled Danes. It is pretty certain that of the so-called Danes in England great numbers were from Sweden,[2] and no doubt many Danes

---

[1] The use of 'Daci' instead of 'Dani' is so general amongst mediæval writers, that it appears probable that the latter term is only a corruption of the former. There were Dahae or Dacae, seated near the Getae, in the East, who left their name to Daghestan. They again appear as a branch of the Getae on the Danube. And they also appear with the Getae in Scandinavia.

[2] Mr. F. S. Prideaux remarks, in the Transactions of the Ethnological Society, 1863, pp. 412, 413, on the presence of the English physical type of man in Sweden and Denmark, its absence in German Prussia, and its recurrence in Gothic Brunswick and Hanover.

from Denmark were settled in Normandy besides Norwegians; but the origin of these races was the same—purely Gothic.

The early Russian race was beyond doubt Gothic; but whether Ruric and his people sprang from a direct migration from Sweden, as usually held, or whether they were descendants of the early Roxolani, as held by some, is a point which the author has not time or space to examine, and which appears to have no material bearing on the objects of this work.

From what has been above said, it appears that there is an historical solecism in styling the Scandinavian, Anglo-Saxon, and Gothic nations and their languages 'Teutonic,' or 'Low-German,' as is frequently done from a want of due consideration. We might as well term the 'German' 'Low Scandinavian,' or the 'French' 'Low Spanish,' as style the Gothic races and their dialects 'Low-German.' The Scandinavians, the Hollanders, the Sleswig-Holsteiners, the Dutch, the Hanoverians, the English, and the Americans, cannot with propriety be styled Germans; the Germans and they are descended from coeval ancestors. The Teutons are as much a branch of the English as the English are a branch of the Teutons, and both assertions are equally incorrect. Both nations are descendants of the aboriginal Getae, the greatest of all the families that sprang from Japhet.

It seems desirable to notice the incorrectness of this popular nomenclature of races (which arises from adoption of the German practice), because the question of race has passed out of the category of abstract theory, and has become one of serious reality. 'Nations and languages against dynasties and treaties,' says Professor Max Müller. 'This is what has re-modelled, and will re-model still more, the map of Europe.' The question of 'German' and 'Non-German' is no longer an indifferent theme, since Germany has evinced so strong a disposition to convert theory into fact, and to reduce by force to Germanic unity all nations which it is possible to identify as of Germanic race. It is not wise in the nineteenth century to adopt theories as to the origin of races which might have been prudently indulged in, in the eighteenth.

The English dominions at the present day contain a vast population of Gothic origin. Taking the European races of the Empire at forty millions (setting aside all races of African or Oriental birth) it may be stated generally, that the properly English race comprises thirty millions out of forty millions, the remainder being composed of Celts, foreigners, and Hebrews. These thirty millions, are the descendants of the Gothic race in its threefold form of Saxon, Dane and Norman. In all probability the Danish element is about equal to the Saxon, and the Saxon about equal to the Norman; there is no evidence that any great disparity exists between the respective members of these three races. It seems probable that the mass of the Saxon population remains amongst the less influential and wealthy part of the community, because there is reason to suppose that the superior energy and enterprise of the Danish and Norman character have in general determined the relative position of races in England. It is, however, impossible to suppose a rule which is not liable to many exceptions, and it would be in vain to attempt to apply it in any way to individual cases, or to affirm that Norman and Danish blood always implies energy and intellect, and Saxon descent the reverse; we have too many instances to the contrary. What may be safely affirmed is, that the English nation is homogeneous in a high degree, perhaps more so than any Continental nation of equal importance; and that its origin is not Teutonic, but Gothic.

What has been here remarked of the European population of the English empire may be equally said of that of the United States of America. Different in some respects as may be the political arrangements of the two countries, the same nation constitutes the population of both. In England we have retained those ancient Gothic institutions whose origin ascends not merely to Norman or Anglo-Saxon times, but to the commencement of society in modern Europe, and to an era far more remote than the downfall of the Roman Empire. This country furnishes a unique example of the uninterrupted continuance of those free institutions which characterised the Gothic tribes of the first century, and which had descended from pre-historic times. America has lost the Gothic principle of hereditary suzerainty, founded originally on seniority of descent; and like the early

German and Gothic Confederations, has made its generals or rulers elective; but the nation has continued
to preserve its essential characteristics. There are un-
questionably distinctions between the English and American temperament: on these it would be impossible here to
dwell. The peculiar circumstances of each country may
account for these differences; and perhaps it may arise
in part from the greater preponderance of the Scandinavian
element of population in America than in England, for
it may be supposed that the English emigration to America
was, until recently, confined to those classes which were
not merely of an adventurous and enterprising character,
but which were possessed of some amount of means, and
were not amongst the poorest and most depressed part of
our population.

Setting aside these differences as unimportant, we may
say that England exists in America as well as here. We
have another England on the other side of the Atlantic.
It was not without reason that 'New England' was so
termed; and 'New England' might be the denomination of
the whole of that magnificent empire at the present day.
The population is essentially English in blood and in
name. If every family surname in England were to
become extinct to-morrow, it would be preserved in
America. The identity in blood of the English and the
American people can only be thoroughly appreciated
after comparing the local directories of the two countries.
The names are throughout identical; there are millions

of families there which two centuries since were branches
of our own, and which even now are not removed from us
by a more distant relationship than that which in this
country is still often recognised as connecting families
by the ties of consanguinity. We may ourselves have in
early youth conversed with individuals whose fathers or
grandfathers were living soon after the early emigrants
sailed for America. Tradition may have conveyed to us
the names of our own ancestors who shared in that
emigration, or were contemporary with it—so nearly
related is the English race in America to ourselves.

The numbers of the English in the United States may
be stated as amounting to thirty millions out of the forty
which inhabit that vast dominion.

This is said after considering the aggregate numbers
of other races in the United States. The entire Gothic
or English race of the two countries amounts to sixty
millions. May that race, in remembrance of its intimate
alliance in blood, ever stand united in mutual offices of
friendship and good-will! May every cloud of distrust
and every sentiment of international jealousy be dispelled
by a generous and noble confidence; and may each
branch of this great and memorable race rejoice in the
honour, the power, and the prosperity of the other.

The Goths of the western world are still migrating as
their forefathers were doing four thousand years since, and
they still retain the same indomitable vigour, the same
spirit of enterprise, the same love of liberty, the same

generosity of sentiment, and the same sense of national honour which their Scandinavian and Gothic progenitors always evinced.

To the sixty millions of English race we must add eight millions of the descendants of the illustrious Scandinavian nations in Sweden, Norway, and Denmark, our near and honoured kinsmen and relations in blood; and it is satisfactory to add a fact, which is not generally known, that the country of Gustavus Vasa, of Gustavus Adolphus, and of Charles XII.—the land of Harold Harfagr and Rollo—are presided over by a Northman dynasty—the descendants of the aboriginal Gothic race—the race of the Vikings.[1]

[1] The French surname 'Bernadotte' is one of those corruptions of names which are as common in France as in England. The original form was 'Bernetôt.' That name came from Normandy, where there was a place near Yvetot so styled, and which, in the tenth century, derived its appellation from 'Biorn' or 'Bern,' a Swedish or Norwegian viking; the termination 'tôt' or 'toft' also indicating Scandinavian origin. The descendants of this Scandinavian viking bore the name of De Bernetôt. Geoffry de Bernetôt accompanied the Conqueror to England in 1066, and was succeeded by Geoffry, whose son, Robert Fitz Geoffry, was, in 1165, owner of fiefs in the north of England held from the barony of Hanseline by 'ancient enfeoffment,' i.e. dating before the death of Henry I. (Liber Niger). These possessions were in York, and perhaps in Northumberland, where the name frequently occurs in the records of the thirteenth and fourteenth centuries under the form of 'De Burnetoft' or 'De Bruntofte,' and where it is not yet entirely extinct. The family also remained in Normandy; for John de Bernetôt, with others of the same name, held Peletôt or Peltôt in the Pays de Caux, not far from Bernetôt, in the reign of Philip Augustus, by serjeanty or special service (Mem. Soc. Ant. Norm. xv. 172). From this Norman branch, which was numerous, descended the Bernetots or Bernatots, who are afterwards found seated in the south of France under the name of Bernadotte, and employed in the legal profession, in which the hereditary astuteness of the Northmen has always found a congenial occupation.

To the south of Scandinavia remain our kindred Saxon races, the brethren of the Anglo-Saxons and our own. From Mecklenburg to the borders of Holland, and from the ocean to the Lippe, still remain four millions of Goths—the race of Witekind—now reduced under the German sway, on the pretext of 'German unity.' In Holland, under the heirs of the heroic patriot William of Nassau, and in Belgium eight millions of Goths still retain national independence; and in Normandy proper two millions of Scandinavian race remain, but subject to the dominion of the Franco-Celtic race.

The descendants of the Goths, and of their branch, the Lombards, and of the Normans (also Goths) must be vastly numerous in Italy. They superseded, in a great degree, the ancient population, which had been exhausted and drained off by the corrupt policy of imperial Rome. Probably far more than a moiety of the inhabitants of that renowned country are of Gothic race; and from this Gothic nation sprang the free republics of the Middle Ages, the mercantile enterprise of Genoa and Venice, the genius of Italian poetry, and the high patriotism of Savonarola and Garibaldi.

We find again the descendants of the Goths in France south of the Loire, and in Spain, but mingled with the Celts. The Burgundians (also Goths) have left their posterity in the east of France from Burgundy to the mouths of the Rhone. England was more closely allied in blood to these races than were the Celtic and Frank

(German) races which predominate in France; and while England may have derived incidental advantages from the separation of its kindred races in Aquitaine, it may still be a matter of question whether Aquitaine itself was benefited by the exchange of Gothic freedom, under English protection, for Frank centralisation and Bourbon absolutism.

The Gothic race in the west, then, may probably exceed a hundred millions at present, of which the English race furnishes sixty. Its remote branch, the Teutonic or German race, may number thirty millions. Switzerland sheds its highest splendour on this German branch, and adds to its numbers two or three millions.

What may be the amount of the still remoter branches of the Goths in Russia—what has been the destiny of the Roxolani and of the race of Ruric, it were impossible here to discuss; but that there are still considerable numbers of the descendants of the Goths in Russia is in the highest degree probable.

The sum total of this vast family of Getic nations may perhaps now amount to a hundred and fifty millions in Europe and America, or nearly a seventh part of the human race.

A tabular view of the progress and connection of these nations may be convenient; it is therefore here subjoined.

K

GENEALOGY OF THE GOTHIC NATIONS.

Gothi or Getae of Asia, B.C. 1800–2000.

Gothi or Getae, B.C. 1800	Massa-Getae, Asia	Sacae or Saxones, Asia	Dahae or Daci, Asia

Getae, Europe, B.C. 1700	Roxolani of the Don and Dnieper, B.C. 1700	Tyssi-Getae of the Volga

Getae, Europe B.C. 1600	Tyri-Getae of the Dniester B.C. 1600	Getae, Daci, of the Danube	Triballi, Thracians

Getae or Gothi, Europe B.C. 1500	Bastarnae, Poland	Pien-Getae	Ars-Getae	Teutons or Germans, B.C. 1400

Gothi, Poland B.C. 1400	Lombards (Prussia)	Burgundians (Prussia, Poland)	Vandals (Prussia)	Samo-Getae (Lithuania)	Scandinavians B.C. 1300	Frisians, Angles, Saxons	Germans

Franks

Ostrogoths, Italy	Visigoths South France, Spain	Lombards Italy	Burgundians East France	Vandals, Africa	Danes	Normans		Anglo-Saxons		Franks North France	Germans

ITALIANS		ITALIANS	Swiss, Savoy		English, Americans	English, Americans	Danes, Swedes, Norwegians	English, Americans	Dutch, Hanoverians, Flemings		Germans, Swiss

ALPHABETICAL SERIES

OF

NORMAN NAMES AND FAMILIES FROM THE LONDON POST-OFFICE DIRECTORY.

LIST OF ABBREVIATIONS FREQUENTLY EMPLOYED IN THE ALPHABETICAL SERIES.

Des Bois .	Aubert Des Bois, Dict. de la Noblesse.
Eyton . .	Eyton's History of Salop.
Fuller . .	Fuller, Worthies of England.
Lib. Nig. .	Liber Niger, Ed. Hearne.
Mon. . .	Monasticon Anglicanum (First Ed.)
M. R. S. .	'Magn. Rotul. Scaccarii Normanniæ in the Mémoires de la Société des Antiquaires de la Normandie, t. 15-17.
M. S. A. N.	Mémoires de la Soc. des Antiquaires de la Normandie.
P. P. W. .	Palgrave, Parliamentary Writs (Record Publication).
R. H. . .	Rotuli Hundredorum (Record Publication).
R. C. R. .	Palgrave, Rotuli Curiæ Regis (Record Publication).
Rot. Canc. .	Rotulus Cancellarii (Record Publication).
Testa . .	Testa de Neville (Record Publication).

A

Abbay, a form of Abbé. *See* ABBOTT.

Abbee, a form of ABBEY.

Abbess. Raimond de labisse. Normandy 1198, (MRS). *See* ABBISS.

Abbett, a form of ABBOTT.

Abbey, for l'Abbé, the French form of Abbas. *See* ABBOTT.

Abbiss, or Abice. Jocelin de Abbacia and Richard de A. were of Normandy, 1198 (MRS); Robert de Abbacia was of England, c. 1272 (RH).

Abbitt, a form of ABBOTT.

Abbot. *See* ABBOTT.

Abbott, Roger, Osbert, Radulphus Abbas were of Normandy, 1180–95 (MRS); William A., 1198 (Ib.); N. Abbas or Aba held lands, Northants, 1086 (Domesd.); Galfridus Abbas in Rutland, 1158 (Rot. Pip.). His son in Worcester, 1165 (Lib. Nig.), Gaufrid. l'Abba, witnessed a charter of Robert Earl of Leicester, 12th century (Mon. i. 519). The name changes to Abbot and Abbet in the 13th century. The Lords Colchester descend from Ralph Ab-

bas (mentioned in Normandy), who held half a fee in the honour of Plympton, Devon, t. Henry II. (Testa). William l'Abbe, his grandson, was living 1242 (Testa), and Ralph l'Abbe was also seated in Devon. Nicholas l'A. paid a fine in Devon, 1260 (Roberts, Excerpta); Walter l'A. was of Plympton, 1353 (Pole's Devon). From him descended Robert Abbot, one of the gentry of Dorset, 1443 (Fuller), whose descendant William was of the same county t. Eliz. The representative of the family was of Todbere and Linbury, Dorset, and was an adherent of Charles I. His grandson, John Abbot of Shaftesbury, Esq. was grandfather of Charles A. Lord Colchester.

Abbs, or Abbes. *See* ABBISS.

Abel. John de Aubeale was security in Normandy, 1200, for Roger de Plomes (Mém. Soc. Ant. Norm. v. 104); N. Abel held lands from Lanfranc in Kent, 1086 (Domesd.); Sir John Abel of Kent occurs 1313 (Mon. Angl. i. 358).

133

Abelon. Richard de Abelon of Normandy, 1180 (MRS). Robson preserves the arms of the English branch.

Aberdeen, or Abadain, from Abadon. Rainald de Abadon occurs in Normandy, 1180 (MRS). The arms of Abadain or Abaudain are preserved by Robson.

Aberdein. *See* ABERDEEN.

Ablett. William de Abelot, apparently of foreign origin, occurs in Cambridge, c. 1274 (RH).

Abley, the Norman-French pronunciation of Abelot or Abelet. *See* ABLETT.

Ablitt. *See* ABLETT.

Ablard. William Abillard witnessed, 1196, a charter in Normandy (Mém. Soc. Ant. Norm. v. 201).

Abra, for Abrey or AUBREY.

Absalom, for ABSALON.

Absalon, foreign, stated to be from Flanders (Robson). John Absolon or Abselon occurs in England, c. 1272 (RH).

Absolon. *See* ABSALON.

Abselom. *See* ABSALON.

Acoulon, from Agullon, or Aiguillon, near Alençon. William de Aiguillon, Sire de Trie, defended Pont Audemer against Henry I., 1123 (Ord. Vitalis). He was son-in-law of Theobald Paganus (De Montmorenci), seneschal of Gisors, and died in Palestine, 1147. For the subsequent barons of Aguillon, *see* COLLEY-WELLESLEY. Isabella de Agellion was lady of Scroteby, Norfolk, 1316.

A'Court. Covert or Couert, Normandy, was held by the service of 1 fee of the barony of Braiose. The Coverts held lands in Sussex from Braiose from the Conquest. In 1107 William de Cuvert witnessed

the foundation charter of Barnstaple (Mon. Angl. i. 684). In 1165 William Gubert (Cuvert) held a fee of ancient enfeoffment from William de Courcy, Somerset (Lib. Nig.). About 1480, John Couert or Covert was of Stoke-Courcy (Harl. MS. 1385). Third in descent was Edward Couert, living 1583, whose son William Court of Frome was ancestor of Lord Heytesbury (Hoare, Wilts., H. Heytesbury, 120, 129).

Achard. In 725 the Achards of Angoumois aided in the expulsion of the Saracens (Des-Bois). Achard was Castellan of Domfront, Normandy, 1020. The family was seated in the Passais, Normandy, and Achard, Castellan of Ambrières, accompanied William in 1066. William A., his son, was Constable of Domfront, 1091-1102, and had grants in Berks from Henry I. (D'Anisy et St. Marie, sur le Domesd.). In 1238 Sire Robert Achard witnessed a charter of Bisham Abbey, Berks. (Mon. ii. 355).

Ackew, for ASCUE.

Ackland. *See* ACLAND.

Acland, or De Vautort, from Vautort in Mayenne. Reginald de Valletort or Vautort accompanied Geoffry de Mayenne and other barons of Maine, and received extensive grants in Cornwall from Robert Count of Mortaine, 1066. Roger de Valletort, baron of Hurberton, Devon, his grandson, was ancestor of the Valletorts of North Tawton and those of Acland, who bore a bend. Richard de Vautort, son of Roger, owned Separton, Middlesex, and had issue Hugh de Acland or Vautort, who had a grant of Hetlumbe or Hidland, Middlesex, from William de Say, t. Henry II. He had issue Baldwin de Acland (ancestor of the Aclands), and Simon de Vautort and John de V. It appears from a suit c. 1200 (Palgr. Rot. Car. Regis, ii. 189), that Hugh was son of Richard and father of Simon, whose son was the heir of Seperton, but that John de Vautort, his uncle, had taken possession. The family of Acland, after the reign of Richard II., abandoned their early arms, a bend (with two lions as a difference), and adopted other arms: hence the baronets Acland.

Acrell, for Hockrell. Walter Hockerel, Normandy, 1180 (MRS).

Acton, or Burnell. Ranulph, John, Richard, Gilbert, Hugo, Henry, Robert, Clement, Roger Burnel, of Normandy, 1180–95 (MRS). Roger Burnel, who is mentioned in the Chartulary of Buildwas, held Acton from Roger Corbet in 1086. Ingelram B. was living 1165, and William B. 1170, attested a charter of Wenlock Abbey (Eyton). In 13th century there were two branches of the Burnells at Acton (Ib.). Robert de Acton or Burnel (13th century) was Chancellor of England. One branch adopted the name of Acton, and from it descends Lord Acton.

Adderley, from Adderley, Salop, the caput baroniæ of Alan de Dunstanville, t. Henry I. The name was derived from Doussainville, between Paris and Orleans. This family of De D. continued barons of Adderley in 1255. Henry de Adderley, a younger son, occurs in Staffordshire, 13th century (Testa), and 1310 Robert de Adderle is mentioned (Palgr. Parl. Writs). The usage of those ages restricted the

name of the barony to the family of its lords.

Addington, or De Abernon. Abernon, near Orbec, Normandy, was the seat of this family. Roger de A. in 1086 held lands from Richard Fitz-Gilbert in Surrey and Suffolk (Domesd.). Eguerrand de A. witnessed the Charter of Savigny, Normandy, 1112 (D'Anisy et St. Marie, sur le Domesd.). He occurs in Surrey, 1130 (Rot. Pip.). In 1165 Ingelram de A. held four fees of the Honour of Clare, and was a benefactor to Stoke-Clare, Suffolk (Mon. Angl. i. 1007). Sire John D'A. of Surrey, c. 1300, bore Azure a chevron or (Palgr. Parl. Writs). Reginald, brother of Ingelram, had a grant of Addington, Surrey, t. Henry II. He was patron of Church of Addington, and bore the name (Manning and Bray, iii. 564). His descendants, the Addingtons, bore the arms of Abernon, with different tinctures, as they still do. This branch became seated in Somerset and Devon, 13th century, where Walter de Abernon occurs, 1259 (Roberts, Excerpt.), and Gilbert de Edington in 1324. Thomas Addington of Leigh, Devon, and Essex, 1535, bore the arms now used by his descendant, Viscount Sidmouth (Harl. MS. 1080).

Adlard, for ALLARD.

Adrain. Roger Hadrin occurs in Normandy, 1180–95 (MRS); John Adrien in England, c. 1272 (RH).

Adron. *See* ADRAIN.

Agace, from AGGISS.

Agate, a form of HAGGETT or Hacket.

Agg, armorially identified with Auge or Eu. William de Augo

135

occurs in Normandy, 1195 (MRS); Geoffry de Augo, 1200 (Mém. Soc. Ant. Norm. v. 101); Thomas de Augo in England, 1199 (RCR); and William de Augo, Oxfordshire, in 1249.

Aggas, from AGGS.

Aggiss, from AGGS.

Agland. *See* ACLAND.

Agnew, or Aigneaux, from that lordship near Bayeux, held from the Viscount of St. Sauveur t. Henry I., a tenant of the Church of Bayeux. In 1074 Herbert de Agnellis and Corbin his son sold lands to Odo of Bayeux. Peter de Agnellis was of Winchester, 1148 (Wint. Domesd.). Fulco de A. went to the Crusade, 1096. The name occurs in England, 12th century (Mon. Angl. i. 489, 760). A branch was early seated in Scotland, and held the hereditary Viscounty of Wigton, and from it descend the baronets Agnew.

Agnis. *See* AINS.

Aggs, from AGG.

Ague. William Agote was of Normandy, 1180 (MRS); Stephen Agot, 1818, was M.P. for Wycombe; William de Agou occurs in Warwick and Leicester, 1203 (Rot. Canc.). The name occurs in the Battle Abbey Roll.

Aikin, from DAKIN.

Aingell. *See* ANGELL.

Ainger. *See* Aungier.

Ains, from Aignes, near Angoulême. Ralph de Agnis, 12th century, witnessed a charter of Stamford Priory (Mon. i. 489).

Airel. *See* DARRELL.

Airey, from the Castle of Airey or Arrey, Normandy. Anscher, Ansketel, and Goisbert de Arreio of Normandy, 1198 (MRS).

186

Airy. *See* AIREY. Of this name is the celebrated astronomer.

Alabaster, or Arbalister. Haimard and Serlo Arbalistarius of Normandy, 1180 (MRS); Robert, Berner, Ralph A. possessed baronies in Norfolk, 1086 (Domesd.); Nicholas A. in Devon; Odo A. in York; Warin A. in Wilts. In Devon the baronial family remained till the time of Edward III. All these families came with the Conqueror. The name means 'General of Cross-bowmen.'

Alan, sometimes for Fitz-Alan, a Breton family. *See* STUART.

Alason. *See* ALISON.

Albert. Walter and Peter Albert of Normandy 1180 (MRS). William Fitz Albert, England 1199 (RCR).

Albin, armorially identified with **Albon**.

Albon, armorially identified with St. Albine, or ST. AUBYN (Robson).

Alby, from Auby, near Douay. Everard de Albé, 12th cent., witnessed a charter of Studley, Oxford (Mon. Angl. i. 486). This is a different family from that of Dalby, as appears by the arms. Robert de Albi was of Normandy 1180 (MRS).

Alden. Robert Alden occurs in Normandy 1195 (MRS).

Aldworth, or De La Mare. Alworth or Ayleworth, Gloucester (whence the name), belonged to the house of De la Mare (which was named from the Castle of La Mare near Pont Audemer). (*See* MAUDE.) This line descends from William de la Mare of Herts and Wilts 1086. His grandson Henry De L. M. paid a fine for his father's office (grand-huntsman) and lands, Oxford (Rot. Pip.), and acquired great estates in

Gloucester and Hereford from the Earl of Gloucester. In 1165 Robert De L. M., his son, held 10 knights' fees from that Earl (Liber Niger). This estate was divided amongst his descendants, of whom John De L.M. held Rendcombe from the earl, t. Henry III. Aylworth, a dependance of Rendcombe, passed to his widow Petronilla (Fosbroke, Gloucester), who d. 1262, when Rendcombe, &c. passed to John De L. M., her eldest son (Roberts, Exc. ii. 399). A younger son of John obtained Aylworth, and his descendants bore the arms of De la Mare differenced by billets. His grandson Henry de Aylworth m. the heiress of De Gulafre of Oxfordshire, where he was seated c. 1400 (Visit. Oxford 1556). His son John A. was one of the gentry of Oxford 1433 (Fuller). In 1468 John A. settled Aylworth and other lands in Gloucester on his son John (Fosbroke, Gloucester). The latter was grandfather of Peter, living 1575, and Paul. The latter was father of Richard Aldworth of Berks t. Eliz., ancestor of the Viscounts Doneraile (now St. Leger). Peter was ancestor of the A.'s of Aylworth, Gloucester, and the Aldworths of Stanlake, Oxford, ancestors of the Lords Braybrooke (now Neville).

Of the Oxfordshire line of De la Mare was John De la Mare, who was summoned to parliament as a baron, 1298–1313.

Aleman. *See* ALLMAN.

Alet, from Alet or St. Malo, Bretagne.

Alfrey, Robert Alveré, paid an amerciament at Caen 1195, and Benedict Alvaré in the Bessin(MRS). The name was a patronymic derived

from Alvered or Auvré. Robert Aufré or Alfré was a juror in Sussex 1284. (Suss. Arch. Coll. xx. 4.) Thomas Averay was M.P. for Mere 1307.

Alice, for Alis, or ELLIS.

Alison. Bernard de Alençon who held several lordships from Hervey de Bourges, Suffolk (Domesd. 442, 442 b), belonged to the family of the Counts of Alençon, descended from Ivo de Belesme, c. 940. He was probably brother of Geoffry, Lord of Mortagne, son of Rotrou, son of Geoffry Viscount of Chateaudun, Mortagne, and Nogent, nephew of William I., Count of Alençon. The descendants of Bernard (who bore three eagles on a fesse, which nearly resembled the arms of the Montgomerys, Earls of Alençon, and also three fleur-delys, equally borne by the Montgomerys), were seated 13th cent. in York, where Richard de Alençon or Alazun held two fees of the honour of Lincoln (Testa, 365). He was living 1235 (Ib. 349). From Yorkshire a branch extended to Scotland, from which descend the baronets Alison. Of this name was the eminent historian Sir Archibald Alison.

Allan, for ALAN.

Allanson. *See* ALISON.

Allard. Michael Aelart, and Turold Fitz-Aelard of Normandy 12th cent. (MRS). Hugh and William A. in 1198. (Ib.) This family flourished at Winchilsea from the Conquest.

Allason. *See* ALISON.

Allden. *See* ALDEN.

Allebone, armorially identified with ALBON.

Alleeson. *See* ALISON.

187

Allen, sometimes for Fitz-Alan, a foreign name. *See* ALAN.

Allert, for ALLARD.

Alley. 1. from Ailly near Falaise. William and Roger de Aillio witnessed a charter in Normandy 1082 (Gall. Christ. xi. 69). Walter D'Aile occurs in England 1224 (Hardy, Rot. Claus.) Richard D'Aly was of Kent 1274 (RH).

2. A form of ALLET or HALLETT.

Alleyne. *See* ALLEN.

Allibone. *See* ALBON.

Allies. *See* ALICE.

Allison. *See* ALISON.

Allman, from Allemagne, near Caen. Ernebald, Ansketil, and Ivo de Allemania occur in Normandy 1180 (MRS). John Alemanicus 12th cent. witnessed a charter of Fountains Abbey, York (Mon. i. 758). Henry de A. subscribed a charter of Vale Royal, 13th cent. Many others of the family are mentioned at early dates.

Allott. *See* HALLOWS.

Almaine. *See* ALLMAN.

Alpe, for Helpe, or HELPS. Hugo de Helpe occurs in Normandy 1183. (MRS.) Matilda Alpe in Norfolk c. 1272 (RH).

Alson, for ALLISON.

Alvery. *See* ALFREY.

Alvers, from A. near Coutances, Normandy. Robert de Alvers possessed estates Northants 1086 (Domesd.). Ayleric de Halver was living t. Henry I. (Mon. A. i. 424). Fulk de Auvers held lands of the Honour of Breteuil, Normandy, t. Philip Augustus. In 1327 William Halver possessed estates Suffolk (Palgr. Parl. Writs).

Alves, a form of ALVERS.

Amand, or St. Amand, from St. Amand in the Cotentin, Normandy.

138

Almaric de St. A. witnessed a charter of Henry II. 1172 (Mon. i. 516). Ralph de St. A. held offices in Normandy 1195 (MRS). Almaric de St. A. witnessed a charter of Henry III, 1235 (Mon. i. 841). Almaric de St. A. was summoned to Parliament as a baron 1299; and his descendants were barons till 1508. Younger branches survived.

Amber, from Ambrières. Thomas de Ambrières occurs in Normandy 1195 (MRS).

Ambler, from Ampliers or Aumliers, near Arras. Bartholomew de Aumliers (13th cent.) held lands in Norfolk by serjeantry (Testa).

Amblie. *See* HAMLEY.

Ambrose, armorially identified with Amberas, or Ambreres. *See* AMBER.

Amery, from Hamare near Caen. *See* DORMER.

Ames, from Hiesmes or Exmes, Normandy. The family of De Hiesmes is supposed to descend from the ancient Viscounts of Hiesmes, of whom Amfrid le Danois, 978, was ancestor of the Viscounts of Avranches. Ernald de Aiemis witnessed a charter of Walton Priory, York, t. Stephen (Mon. Angl.). Richard Amias was a benefactor to the Hospitallers (12th cent.). Robert de Amias was of Berks 13th century (Testa). In 1290 William de Ame was Constable of Tickhill Castle. Many other notices occur.

Amherst, or Henhurst, probably a branch of Lanvalai of Bretagne. Henhurst bore a fesse with 5 foils; Lanvalai a fesse. Lanvalai was near Dinant. Ivo de L. was living 1082, and another Ivo de L. was Seneschal of Dol, t. Henry I. In 1154 William de L. possessed estates, Essex

(Rot. Pip.). The Lordship of Henhurst, Kent, was probably subenfeoffed to a younger branch before 1160; for in 1194 Walter and Osbert de Henhurst occur. Gilbert de H. (13th cent.) and Roger H.,' 1278, are mentioned. A branch settled at Pembury, and from it descend the Earls Amherst.

Amias. *See* AMES.

Amies. *See* AMES.

Amis, for AMES.

Ammon, armorially identified with AMAND.

Amond, armorially identified with St. Amand. *See* AMAND.

Amory. *See* DORMER.

Amos. *See* AMES.

Amoss, for AMOS.

Amphlett, from Amflete, near Boulogne (Lower).

Amy. Radulphus Amé, and Robert Amé, of Normandy 1180–90 (MRS). Richard Amy, 13th century, held from Henry de la Pomeray, Cornwall (Testa).

Amyas. *See* AMES.

Ancell. Goisfrid Alseline, or Asceline, held a barony in Lincoln 1086. He appears to have been of the house of Dinant, Bretagne (D'Anisy et St. Marie). His brother was Robert Pincerna (Ib.). In 1165 William Hansel held 2 fees Lincoln from Ralph Alselin or Hansell, his kinsman. From him descended the Ancells, who bore the arms of Alseline.

Ancill. *See* ANCELL.

Anders, from Andres, near Guisnes and Boulogne. Geoffry and John Andre occur in England c. 1272 (RH).

Anderson-Pelham, or De Lisle, from the Castle of Lisle, Normandy. Burcharde Insula witnessed a char-

ter Normandy c. 1066 (Gall. Christ. xi. 61, Instr.). Robert, his son, granted lands to Cerisy Abbey, Normandy, t. William I. (Mon. ii. 961). His descendants were chiefly seated in the North of England. Ralph, John, and Robert de Insula occur in Yorkshire 1130, Otui or Otwer de L in Northumberland 1165; from whom descended Sir John de Lisle of Woodburn, M.P. for that county 1824, whose descendants long continued there. Robert de Lisle of this family t. Henry IV. m. the dau. and heir of Anderson of Lincoln, and assumed that name. His descendant Sire Edmund Anderson was Chief Justice t. Elizabeth, and was ancestor of the Earls of Yarborough.

Andrew, from St. André, near Evreux, a branch of the De Quincys, Earls of Winchester, armorially identified. Alexander de St. Andrew (12th cent.) witnessed a charter of Wetheral Priory (Mon. i. 399). Saher de St. A. gave lands to Sandleford Priory for the soul of his uncle the Earl of Winchester, his own son Robert de Quincy, and others (Mon. i. 482). The family has always borne the mascles of De Quincy.

Andrews. Geoffry and Walter Andreas 1180, William Andreas 1195, of Normandy (MRS). William Fitz-Andreas, Thomas F. A., and others in England 1199 (RCR.) In 13th cent. the name became Fitz Andrée, or André.

Angell, or De L'Angle, from Les Angles, near Evreux. Gilbert de l'Angle 1172, obtained from Hugh de Lacy a barony in Meath. Hamelin de Angelo occurs in Normandy, 1195 MRS, Ranulph de Angles, and Gilbert de Angulis 1198 (Ib.).

Anger, from Angers, Anjou. Osmond Angevinus 1086, possessed estates in Essex (Domesd.). He and Wido A. were ancestors of a family which continued in 1202 (Rot. Canc.). In 1165 many members are mentioned in Oxford, Surrey, York, Essex, and Norfolk (Lib. Nig.). Joscelin D'Aunger 1169 witnessed the charter of Lanercost (Mon. ii. 131). Ralph de Angers (13th cent.) held lands in Wilts (Testa). The Aungiers Earls of Longford, and the Hangers Lords Coleraine, descended from this family.

Angier. See ANGER.

Angle. See ANGELL.

Angwin, for Angevin. See ANGER.

Ankers, for Anceres. See DANCER.

Anley or ANDLEY, from Andely, near Rouen. Richer de Andely held in capite in the West of England 1083 (Exon. Domesd.). The family held Hermanville in the Caux, Normandy. Roger de Andely was made governor of Lavarchier Castle by K. John. Geoffry de A. witnessed the foundation charter of Andover Priory, t. William I. (Mon. i. 553). In 1148 Walter de A. held a tenement at Winchester from the bishop (Wint. Domesd.). Geoffry de A. held three fees from the same See, t. Henry I. (Lib. Niger), which Walter, his son, held 1165; also Thomas de A. held four fees Northants at the same time (Liber Niger).

Annable, or Annabell, from Anneboult, in the Cotentin. The family of D'Annebolt or Dennebaud was of consequence in Somerset and South Wales.

Anne or Anna, from L'Asne, near Argentan, Normandy. Hugo Asinus or De L'Asne witnessed 1066 a charter of Lire Abbey, Normandy (Gall. Christ.

140

xi. 125, Instr.). In 1086 he held a barony in England, and witnessed a charter of St. Evroult, Normandy (Ord. Vit. v.). The barony was lost t. Henry I., but the family continued. Durand de Asnes occurs in the Duchy 1195 (MRS), and Geoffry de A. 1205 had a fief there (Hardy, Obl. et Fin.). Dudo de L'A. 1165 had a barony in Essex. Everard de Adnes held two fees in Lincoln. 1316–19 John, Michael, Philip, and William de Aune or Anne occur.

Annesley, or Le Breton. Richard Brito, or the Breton, accompanied Ralph Fitz-Hubert, Viscount of Maine, 1066, and held from him Annesley, Notts, 1086; his son Ralph de Annesley or Brito, with Reginald de Annesley, his son, founded Felley Abbey, Notts, 1152 (Mon. Angl. ii. 56). Reginald granted the church of Annesley to Felley. Ralph de A. joined the barons t. John. Sire Reginald de Annesley (13th cent.) held two fees in Annesley from Ralph de Fressonville. From him descended Francis Annesley, first Viscount Valentia, temp. James I.; and the Earls of Anglesey, Mountnorris, and Annesley.

Ansell. See ANCELL.

Anstruther, or Malherbe. This family descends from William de Candel or Candela, who obtained grants in Fife, Scotland, c. 1110, and d. 1153. William de Candel, his son, was a benefactor to Balmerinoch Abbey after 1165. His son assumed the title de Anstruther. The name of Candel was from that place in Dorset, which was held in capite (from the Conquest) by the ancestors of Thomas Fitz-Robert, and Robert Malherbe, 13th cent. (Testa). Of those ancestors, Nigel de Chandel occurs 1120 (Mon. Angl.). Malherbe was, no doubt, the original name; and it was borne in Scotland by several persons (probably connected with the Anstruthers) in the 12th and 13th cent. The family of Morham, Haddingtonshire, was a branch of the Malherbes (Chalmers, Caledonia, ii. 537). The name of Malherbe was Norman. William de Mala Herba, Ralph, Hugh, Robert, Adam de M. Norm. 1180-95 MRS; Oliver and Robert Malherbe, Engl. 1189 (Rot. Pip.).

Anthony, or St. Anthony. Robert de St. Antonio of Normandy, 1180-95 MRS. St. Antoine, near Bolbec, gave name to this family. The name of St. Antonis occurs in England, c. 1272 (RH), also that of Antony.

Anvers, or Danvers, from Anvers or Antwerp. Richard de Anvers (12th cent.) witnessed a charter of Roger de Molbrai, York (Mon. ii. 395). Ralph de A. held two fees (13th cent.) of the Honour of Wallingford (Testa). The name occurs soon after in Berks, Hants, Leicester, Oxford, Bucks, and Suffolk.

Anvill, or Hanwell, from Andeville, near Valognes. Samson de A. was sent by Duke William to defend Jersey (De Gerville). William de A. (12th cent.) witnessed a charter of Ranulph Meschin in Cheshire (Mon. i. 592). In 1165 Thomas de A. held six fees of the barony of Eudo Dapifer (Lib. Nig.). Jordan de A. was of Essex, 1203; Richard de A. (13th cent.) had estates in seven counties (Testa). Alexander de A. had a writ of military summons 1263. The family of Andeville or Handville was seated in Kent 17th cent. (Hasted, Kent).

Apadam, or Abadam, probably a form of Abadon. See ABERDEEN. Of this name were the Barons Apadam.

Apear. Hugh Asfagard 1061 witnessed the foundation charter of Bolbec Abbey (Neustria Pia, 402). Apegard was near Dieppe and Bolbec. Richard Affagard witnessed the foundation charter of Combe Abbey, Warwick (Mon. i. 882), and Masilia de Apegard possessed part of Corsham and Culington, Leicester, t. Henry II. (Ib. ii. 605). Ralph de Apegart in Normandy, 1180-95 MRS, Lambert de Apengart, 1198 (Ib.), Ralph le Appelgart in England, c. 1272, RH.

Aplin, for Ablyn, or ABELON.

Arblaster. See ALABASTER.

Arch, or De Arques, from the Castle of Arques, near Dieppe. Osborne Giffard, Sire de Bolbec, m. c. 960 Ameline, sister of Gunnora, wife of Richard I. of Normandy, and had Walter, ancestor of the Earls of Bucks; and Geoffry, Viscount of Arches or Arques, afterwards Viscount of Rouen, and founder of Trinity du Mont, Rouen. William de Arcis, his son, in 1086 held estates from Odo of Bayeux and Lanfranc in Kent, and in Suffolk from Bernard de St. Audoen, and Robert Malet (Archæologia, 1846, 216, &c.; Des Bois, Dict. de la Noblesse; La Roque, Mais. Harcourt, i. 174). Osborne de Archis, his son, made grants to St. Mary, York; and from him descended the family of Saville. Hubert de Arches occurs in Scotland 1165-1214 (Chart. Mailros).

Archdeacon. Stephen Archidiaconus, Robert Fitz-Bernard A., John A. occur in Normandy 1180-95 (MRS). Hubert A. in 1198 (Ib.).

141

Anchetil A. held lands in Kent, 1086 (Domesd.). Walter A. in 1130 was of Oxford (Rot. Pip.), and 1165 held lands of ancient enfeoffment, Berks (Lib. Nig.), as did Roger A. in Norfolk, and Robert A. in York. Stephen A. of Normandy witnessed the charter of Henry II. to Dunbrody Abbey (Mon. ii. 1028). Sir Thomas le Ercedekne was c. 1300 of Cornwall and Devon.

Arcedeckne. *See* ARCHDEACON.

Archer or De Bois of Essex, armorially identified with Boys or De Bosco.

Archer. William Arcuarius (general of bowmen) was a tenant in capite, Hants, 1086 (Domesd.). Fulbert Sagittarius or L'Archer, his son, witnessed t. Henry I. a charter of Geoffry de Clinton (Mon. i. 465). Herbert A. of Warwick (12th cent.) occurs in a charter of Henry II. (Mon. i. 519). Richard Sagittarius occurs in Normandy 1195 (MRS). Stephen S. gave lands to Tristernagh, Meath, c. 1200 (Mon. ii. 1047).

Archard, a form of ACHARD, armorially identified.

Arden, or Ardern. *See* BRACE-BRIDGE.

Ardes or Hards, from Arda or Ardres, near Guisnes and Boulogne. Hubert de Furnes, a descendant of the house of Flanders, m. the heiress of Ardes, and was ancestor of Ernulf de Arda, who accompanied Count Eustace of Boulogne, 1066; and 1086 held fiefs from him in Cambridge and Bedford (D'Anisy et St. Marie). The descendants continued to possess the principality of Ardres till 1293. King John confirmed the grant of Baldwin de Arda to Harewold Priory, Bedford

(Mon. ii. 203). The name is sometimes written Ardagh.

Ardiss. *See* ARDES.

Argles. Wymarc Harcle occurs in Normandy 1198 (MRS). The arms of Harcle and Hargle are mentioned by Robson.

Argent, armorially identified with De Argentine or De Argentan, from Argentan, Berri, where, and in Poitou, the family were seated. Geoffry Sire de A. lived 1082. David de A., his brother, held Wymondley, Cambridge, by grand serjeantry. Giles de Argentine had a writ of military summons 1243, and Reginald de A. a writ of summons as a Baron 1296. The English line substituted covered cups for torteaux, as borne in Poitou, in allusion to their tenure by presenting a cup at the coronation.

Aris, a form of Heris or HARRIS.

Arle or Airel. *See* DARRELL (Lower).

Arliss, a form of ARLE.

Armes. Geoffry Arme or Armatus occurs in Normandy 1180–95 (MRS). The arms of this family are preserved by Robson. Guido de Arm occurs 13th cent. RH.

Armit. Robert Heremita of Normandy 1198 (MRS); Gerard Heremite of England, c. 1272, RH.

Arnald. *See* ARNOLD.

Arnes. *See* ARMES.

Arnold. Robert Ernaldus, or Ernaut, and William Ernaut occur in Normandy 1180–98 (MRS). Peter Fitz-Ernald, William, and Osbert in England 1199 (RCR), several of the name in England 1272 (RH).

Arrah. *See* BETHUNE.

Arrend, from Arenes. Aeliza de Arenes and William de A. occur in Normandy, 12th cent. (MRS).

Arrow. *See* ARRAH.

Arundel. Richard Hirendale, Normandy, 1198, may have been of the family of A.

Arundel. Roger de Arundel held a barony in England, 1086. He was probably Castellan of Arundel under Roger de Montgomery, Earl of Salop, and a relative of his. The Lords Arundel of Wardour and Earls Onslow descend from this family. *See* ONSLOW.

Arundell. *See* ARUNDEL.

Arundle. *See* ARUNDEL.

Ascough. *See* ASKEW.

Ashburnham, or De Criol. In the time of Edward the Confessor Esseborne belonged to Sewardus (Domesd.). In 1086 it belonged to Robert, Count of Eu, from whom it was held by Robert de Cruel (Domesd. 18). The same Robert held salt-works there, and lands in Boxhill and Hou (Ib.). Simon de Criol, his son, had, Reginald de Esseburnham, who held two fees of the Earl of Eu, 1165 (Lib. Nig.), and whose son, Stephen de Ashburnham, confirmed to Battle Abbey the gift of lands at Hou and Denne, and of the salt-works granted by Reginald, his father (Mon. Angl.), and sold lands, as Stephen de Cuell, to Robertsbridge Abbey (Mon. i. 916). The name frequently occurs in the 12th cent. in connection with this family as Cruel, Crieul, and other forms; and was the same as Criol or Kyriel, a Norman baronial family in Kent. It derived from Robert, Count of Eu, whose younger son, Robert, obtained from his father part of Criol, or Crieul, near Eu. His father had been in possession of Criol previously, as appears by one of his charters to the Abbey of Treport (Gall. Christ. xi. col. 13 Instr.). The Ashburn-

hams bore the arms of Criol next their own. Some branches of the house of Criol in England bore the arms of Eu, viz., bendy; and one of their coats is very similar to that of Ashburnham; viz., on a fesse, three mullets, between three fleur-de-lys. The Earls of Ashburnham are of this Norman race.

Ashburner, a corruption of ASHBURNHAM, as appears from the arms (Robson).

Ashley. Walter de Esseleia was of Normandy, 1198 (MRS). He was also of Gloucestershire, 1198 (Rot. Pip.).

Ashley-Cooper, or De Columbers, a baronial family, from Columbières, Normandy, near Bayeux, on which 17 fees were dependent (Des Bois). William de C. is mentioned as a baron, 1082 (Gall. Christ. xi. 71). Ranulph de C., his son, held lands in Kent and elsewhere in capite, 1086 (Domesd.). Philip de C. in 1165 held a barony of 11 fees in Somerset, Wilts, Berks, Dorset, &c. (Lib. Nig.). His son, Philip, d. 1216, from whom descended the Lords Columbers, summoned by writ as barons, 1314.

A branch was seated in Hants, of which Thomas de Columbers was living, 1194 (RCR). Robert de C., his brother or nephew, paid a fine in Hants 1202, and 1231 had a suit there with the family of Le Gros. He was also styled Coparius (i.e. Cupbearer), or Le Cupere, being probably cupbearer to the king (Rot. Canc.; Roberts, Excerpta). His descendants bore the arms of Columbers (a bend), differenced by six lioncels. Richard le Copenore, or Copere (13th cent.), paid a fine for lands in Wilts, and held a knight's

143

tee in Devon, where the Lords Co-lumbers also had estates (Testa, Roberts, Excerpta, ii. 507). In 1275 John le Copere was on an inquisition in Hants (Rot. Hund.). The family possessed estates in Sussex as well as Hants, and resided in the former county, where it was divided into two branches, of whom Henry le Cupere was on an inquisition at Iping, and William at Tortington, 1340 (Non. Inq. 363, 368). From one of these descended the Earls Cowper, who bore the Norman arms of De Columbers. From the Cow-pers of Harting, Sussex, who were seated there before the time of Henry VI., descended the Earls of Shaftesbury, of whom the first earl, t. Charles II., was renowned in the history of his time.

Askew, Eschescol, or Ascough, was granted after 1086 by Alan, Earl of Richmond, to Bardolf, his brother, father of Akaris, ances-tor of the Barons Fitz-Hugh of Ravensworth. Henry Fitz-Akaris granted the tithes of Askew to Marrig (Burton, Mon. Ebor. 269). Randolph, his grandson, had Henry and Adam, between whom Askew was divided. Adam assumed the name of De Askew or Ascough, and Richard de A. possessed eight manors in the vicinity,1270(Whittaker,Rich-mond, ii. 5). William Ascough was Bishop of Salisbury (14th cent.). Of this family was Anne Ascue, the martyr.

Askie, a form of ASKEW.

Aspenlon, from Aspilon or Espilon, the arms of which are pre-served by Robson, evidently foreign.

Asplin. See ASPENLON.

Aspray, probably from Esperraye, Normandy.

144

Asprey. See ASPRAY.

Aster. See EASTER.

Astin. Walter and Ralph d'Astin gave, 1087, the church of Vezins to Culture Abbey, Normandy (Gall. Christ. xi. 107, Instr.). Geoffry Astyn occurs in England, c. 1272 (RH).

Astley, or De Neuburgh. Henry de N., Earl of Warwick, 1068 (a descendant of Bernard the Dane, 936), had issue Roger, his successor, Rotrou, Robert, Geoffry, and Henry, the latter of whom, t. Henry I., ob-tained Estleia, &c., held by the ser-vice of three knights. It was so held by Philip de Estleia, his son, 1165, from the Earl of Warwick. This family bore the arms of the Earls of Leicester and Mellent, the elder line of Newburgh. From it descended the Lords Astley and Hastings, and the Baronets Astley.

Astor. Willielmus Fitz-Estur or Estor, and Robert Estur, of Nor-mandy, 1180; Andreas Estor, 1198 (MRS); Richard, William, and Juliana Astor, of England, c. 1272 (RH).

Athy. See ATTY.

Atty, from Athiés, near Amiens. Gerard de Atie, and Engelard, his nephew, were chief supporters of King John (Roger Wend. iii. 237; Hardy, Lit. Pat. i. 33). Edward II., 1311, committed to John de Athy the custody of Limerick (Rot. Orig. Abbrev. 189).

Aubery. See AUBREY.

Aubrey. Sir Reginald Aubrey, 1088, was granted lands in Breck-nock by Bernard de Newmarché. The Norman origin of this family is admitted. It may be the same as the family of Alvery, or ALFREY. Osmond de Alebrai and Samson de

A. occur in Normandy, 1198 (MRS). Hence the Baronets Aubrey.

Auriol. Matthew de l'Oriel, or L'Oriel. Robert L'Orle, Norm. 1180-95 (MRS).

Austin. William Augustinus occurs in Normandy, 12th cent. (MRS), and in 1198 (Ib.); Geoffry and William Austin, and others, in England, c. 1272 (RH).

Aveling, or Aveline. *See* EVELYN.

Avenell. In 1035 Herveius Avenell, Baron of Biars, confirmed a grant to Marmoutiers Abbey, and 1067 Herveius de Biars and Sigebert, his son, are mentioned. William A. de Biars was seneschal to Robert, Earl of Mortaine, and is mentioned by Wace as present at Hastings. Numerous branches of the family settled in England and Scotland. *See* PIGOT, SAY.

Avens, from Avesnes, in Normandy. Guy de Avesnes and Hubert de Avesnes occur in the Duchy, 1180-95 (MRS). Richard, son of Payne de Avenes, in England, 1194 (RCR).

Averance, from Avranches, Normandy. Turstan Goz, chamberlain to Duke Robert, had issue Richard, Viscount of Avranches, father of Hugh Lupus. His younger son, William de Abrincis, came to England, and was Baron of Folkstone. His sons Robert, Gilbert, Turgis, and Ruallo were living 1130 (Rot. Pip.). Their descendants became widely spread. In 1316 William de Averenges possessed estates in York, when, 1319, Richard de A. was a banneret and commissioner of array.

Averell. Hugo Avril, Norm. 1198 (MRS); Guido de Avrilla held

a fief from Philip Augustus (Mém. Soc. Ant. Norm. v. 186).

Avill, for Aiville or Eyville. *See* CRAVEN.

Avory. *See* EVERY.

Awdry, from Audrieu or Aldrey, near Caen. It was held from the See of Bayeux. In 1083 William de Aldreio had lands in England (Exon. Domesd.). Roger de A., 1183, held lands in Durham (Bolden Book, 580), and William de A., 1165-1214, witnessed a charter in Scotland (Chron. Mailros). In 1194 Hugh de A., of Gloucester, occurs (RCR). In 1318 Peter de Audrey was pardoned as an adherent of the Earl of Lancaster (PPW).

Ayers. *See* AYRES.

Aylard. *See* ALLARD.

Ayre. *See* EYRE.

Ayres. *See* AYRE.

Ayrton, or Flandrensis. Ayrton t. Henry I. was part of the Barony of Skipton, and was subenfeoffed to Walter Flandrensis, or Le Fleming, son of Walter, Baron of Woodhall, or Wahul, Bedford, 1086, descended from the Castellans of Tournay, Flanders. Walter F. in 1120 witnessed a charter of De Romelli (Mon. ii. 10). John Flandrensis granted a mill at Ayrton to Fountains Abbey. His heir, Richard F., paid a fine in York, 1272 (Roberts, Excerpt.). In 1304 Hugh, son of Henry de A., died, and the manor was seized by the escheator, but restored to Henry de A., the heir. In 1437 Richard A. was elected Abbot of Gisborne. John Ayrton, t. Elizabeth, had property in Hertfordshire (Proc. Chanc. t. Eliz.). *See* WENTWORTH.

Ayscough. *See* ASKEW. Hence the Baronets Ayscough.

B

Babington. In 1180 Bartholomew Battayle was a royal officer in Normandy, and William B. also occurs there (MRS). The name continually appears in England 13th cent. (Testa), and Robert Battayle with Bernard de Babington (or Battayle) held Little Babington, Northumberland, by ancient enfeoffment (Ibid.). They were probably brothers or cousins.

Babot. Nicholas Babo of Normandy occurs 1195 (MRS).

Bachelor. Gilbert Bachelor paid taillage in Normandy, 1195 (MRS).

Back. *See* BECK. This name is that of an enterprising navigator of the Polar seas, Sir George Back.

Backs, for BACK.

Bacon. This Norman family, of which the famous Roger Bacon and Francis Bacon, Viscount of St. Albans, the great philosophers, were members, derived its name from that of an ancestor. We find that name Bacon or Bacoo 11th cent. in Maine, but this family was Northman. Anchetil Bacon before the Conquest made grants at his lordship of Molay to St. Barbe en Auge (Des Bois); William B., Lord of Molay, 1082, founded Holy Trinity, Caen; Richard B. occurs later; and 1154 Roger Bacon (who is mentioned 1154 as of Vieux Molay) held estates in Wilts (Rot. Pip.). In 1165 Robert, William, and Alexander B. held four knights' fees of ancient enfeoffment in Essex

146

from the Barony of Montfichet (Lib. Nig.). The further descent of the English family is well known; of it are the Baronets Bacon.

Bagehot, for BAGOT.

Baggett, for BAGOT.

Baggott, for BAGOT.

Bagnall, in some cases armorially identified with Paganel, whose chevron it bears.

Bagot. A baronial family, descended from the Carlovingian Counts of Artois, whose descendants were advocates of Arras, Lords of Bethune, and Castellans of St. Omer, and were amongst the greatest nobles of Flanders; Ivrard d'Arras occurs 975 (Des Bois, art. Gherbode); Robert de Bethune, Advocate of Arras, succeeded; John de Arras was advocate 1038 (Bouquet, Hist. Franc. x. 442); and in 1075 died Robert, Sire de Bethune or Wethune, Advocate of Arras, who had issue, 1, Robert, ancestor of the Advocates of Arras, Earls of Albemarle, and Dukes of Sully; and 2, Wago, Bago, or Bagod de Arras, who in 1075 witnessed a charter in Flanders (Bouquet, xi. 106), and came to England at the Conquest, where his descendants of the line of Bagod and Stafford (Dukes of Buckingham) bore the arms also borne by De Arras in England and France, viz. a chevron gules (or azure). Bago or Bagod d'Arras in 1086 held Bromley in Stafford from Robert de Toesni, Baron of Stafford, and had Rodbert Bagod, who, c. 1140 witnessed a charter of Geva, dau. of Hugh Lupus, founding Canwell Priory (Mon. i. 440). Henry, his son, held three fees from Robert de Stafford (Lib. Nig.). Richard, his son, t. Henry II., had, 1, Simon Bagod, lord of Bromley, lineal ancestor of the Lords Bagot, and 2, Henry Bagod, who became Baron of Stafford by m. with Milicent de Toesni, and was ancestor of the great house of Stafford, Earls and Dukes of Buckingham, so renowned in the history of England.

Bailey. See BAILLIE.

Baillie, from the Norman office of Le Bailli, a species of Viscount or Sheriff. The name occurs as Bailof in Battle Abbey roll. The office, being one of importance, was usually held by Normans of rank. The Baillies of Scotland are a branch of the De Quincys, Earls of Winchester. Richard de Quincy came to England at the Conquest from Quincy in Maine, and had Robert Fitz-Richard, who m. Matilda de Senlis (Mon. ii. 75). Saher, his son (Mon. ii. 78), was father of Saher (the first of the family known to Dugdale), who in 1165 held lands in Bedford and Northants (Lib. Nig.), and in 1180 was Bailli of Nonancourt and Loye, Normandy (MRS). Hence the name of ' Le Bailli.' He m. Maude de Senlis, and had, 1, Robert, who invaded Ireland with Earl Strongbow, and was Seneschal of Leinster; 1174 witnessed in Scotland a charter of King William the Lion for Kelso; had a grant of the barony of Tranent, in Scotland; and was Justiciary of Scotland. He d. s. p., and was succeeded by his brother, 2, Saher, Earl of Winchester, whose son Roger, Earl of W. and

Constable of Scotland, d. 1264, leaving coheiresses. 3. Simon de Quincy, third son of Saher ' Le Bailli,' was ancestor of a line which took that name. He witnessed a charter of Earl Saher, 1214–1219 (Registr. de Newbattle). David de Quincy, his son, appears, c. 1230 (Ib.). Sir John de Quincy, or ' Le Bailli,' his son, witnessed a charter of David Marischall (Chart. S. Crucis), and 1292 was one of those who consented to leave the determination of the succession question to Edward I. Sir William Bailli, his son, Lord of Hoprig (part of the De Quincy barony of Tranent), m. the dau. of the heroic Wallace, Regent of Scotland; and from him descended the Baillies of Lamington and their various branches.

Bailley. See BAILLIE.

Maine, for BAYNE.

Maines, for BAYNES.

Baird. Before the Conquest Ralph Baiart granted lands at Fontenay le Tesson to the Abbey of Barberie, Normandy (MSAN vii. 144). The grant was confirmed by Robert Fitz-Erneis, a Tesson, and probably an ancestor of the Marmions or Percys. The latter houses and the Tessons bore a fesse, and so also did the descendants of Ralph Baiart, with a difference of three mullets. Thomas Bard and Rohais his wife granted the church of Burnonville to the Abbey of Bec (Mon. ii. 983). Jordan Bard occurs in Essex and Herts, 1130 (Rot. Pip.), from whom descended William B., who held two fees in 1165 from the See of London (Lib. Nig.). He was probably ancestor of Bard, Viscount Bellamont, a faithful follower of Charles I. Godfrey Baiard in 1165 held a barony in Northumberland, and from this line descended the great WASHINGTON; and from a branch which passed into Scotland 12th cent. (Chart. Kelso; Raine, North Durham, App. 32) descended the gallant Sir David Baird, the renowned Peninsular general, and the Baronets Baird. This family originally bore the same arms as Bard and Washington, a fesse with three mullets (Baird's *House of Baird*).

Baker, derived 1, from the feudal office of Pistor Regis; 2, from the tenure of lands; 3, in later times from trade. Osmond Pistor Regis (Domesd.), who held Windestorte and Galton, 1086, was ancestor of the Bakers of Dorset. Those of Devon descended from Erchanger Pistor, a Norman, who held lands in Somerset and Cambridge, 1086 (Domesd.); those of Kent from Radulphus Pistor, who possessed estates, Surrey, 1130 (Rot. Pip.). Geoffry, Richard, William, and Peter Pistor occur in Normandy, 1180 (MRS).

Balladen, from Baladon, a castle in Anjou. Drogo de Baladon held a barony in the Welsh Marches, 1086, and from him descended the De Baladuns, or Balaons, Barons of Monmouth. From a younger branch descends the existing family of HUNTLEY.

Ballance, for Valence. William de Ver held Valence, Normandy, from Philip Augustus, c. 1210. *See* VALLANCE.

Baldry. The Haia or Castle of Baldry is mentioned in Normandy, 1180, as is Anchetil Baldrie (MRS).

Baldwin. William Balduinus paid a fine in Normandy, 1180; Robert B. in 1183; Ralph in 1195 (MRS). Alicia Bawdewyne was

148

of Cambridge, 1316. Others occur in York, Hants, and Norfolk (Palgr. Parl. Writs). The family was also seated in the Welsh Marches.

Bally, for BALY or BALLIE.

Balster, from Balister or Balistarius. *See* ALABASTER.

Bambrough. In 1125 William de Bambrough witnessed a charter of Walter de Gand (Mon. ii. 848). In 1201 William Fitz-Odo held Bambrough by tenure from the Conquest (Hardy, Obl. et fin. 114). This was evidently a Norman race.

Bamfield, armorially identified with BAMPFYLD.

Bampfyld, from Baionville, now Banneville, near Caen. In 1093 Fulco de B. witnessed a charter of Robert Fitz-Hugh to Chester Abbey (Mon. i. 101). About 1160 William and Robert de Baionville witnessed a charter of Plympton Abbey, Devon (Mon. ii. 9). In 1165 Osbert de B. held part of a fee, Somerset, from William Malet, and Hugh de B. had lands in Normandy. Walter de B. (13th cent.) held lands of the Honour of Wallingford; and 1316 John de Bamfield was Lord of Weston, Somerset, and of Poltimore and other estates, Devon (Palgr. Parl. Writs). The Lords Poltimore are of this race.

Banard, for Bainard. *See* BANYARD.

Bancroft, from Bancroft, near Warrington, Cheshire, probably a branch of the Lords Boteler of Warrington, whose arms the Bancrofts bore, with a mark of distinction. They held from the Duchy of Lancaster. *See* BUTLER.

Bangs, for BANKS.

Banks, from Banc, near Honfleur. William de Banc was of Cambridge, 1130 (Rot. Pip.); William de Bancs of Cambridge and Hants, 1203 (Rot. Canc.); Geoffry de B. (13th cent.) held three fees of the Barony of Peché, Cambridge (Testa). From this family descended the family of Bankes of Dorset, and Sir Joseph Banks, K.B., so long eminent in the scientific world.

Banner. Robert le Baneor, Normandy, 1180 (MRS).

Bannester, from Banastre, now Benetez, near Estampes. Warin Banastre was Baron of Newton, Lancashire, t. William I. (Baines, Lancashire, i. 115). Alard and John B. possessed lands, Berks, t. Henry I. (Lib. Nig.). The lands of Ralph B. were confirmed to the Church of Bayeux, 1144, by Eugenius III. (Mon.); Adam B. was Viscount of Berks, 1169; Alard, 1173; Thomas, 1204. Robert B. held one fee in capite in Lancaster, 13th cent. (Testa). From him descend the Banastres of Bank. *See* also NELSON, MAUDSLEY.

Bannistre, for BANESTER.

Banyard, armorially identified with Baynard. *See* BEAUMONT, MARSHAM, TOWNSHEND. The Barons Baynard were a branch of the Viscounts of Beaumont and Maine.

Barbe. William, Herbert, and Ralph Barbe occur in Normandy, 1180-95 (MRS). Robert de Barbes was possessed of estates in Kent, and Bernard Barb in Hereford, 1086 (Domesd.).

Barbot. William and Robert Barbot, of Normandy, 1180-95 (MRS). William Barbot witnessed a charter of Richard de Bully for Roche Abbey, 1147 (Mon. i. 836),

and Robert B. one for Hugh de Lacy, Yorkshire (ii. 554).

Bardo, for BARDOLPH.

Bardolph. In 1165 Robert Bardolph held baronial estates in Lincoln and Kent, and also held lands in Normandy of the Honour of Montfort. The name frequently occurs (12th cent.) in the Duchy (MRS). The Bardolphs were Barons of Parliament in England.

Barefoot. Radulphus Barfot occurs in Normandy, 1180 (MRS). The name occurs in England soon after (RH).

Barker. Radulphus Bercarius of Normandy, 1180 (MRS). Le Bercher occurs soon after in England. The Baronets Barker were of this family.

Barne, armorially identified with BARNES.

Barnes, armorially identified as a form of Berners, from Bernieres, near Falaise. Hugo de Bernieres had estates in Essex and Middlesex, 1086 (Domesd.). In 1165 Ralph de Bernieres held six knights' fees, and Richard de B. seven. The Barons Berners descended from this family.

Barnewall, descended from the Norman family of De Barneval. The Viscounts Barnewall, Lords Trimleston, Baronets Barnwall, and several English families are of this house, which is too well known to need proof.

Barney, armorially identified with BERNEY.

Barold. *See* BARRELL.

Baron, from Baron, near Caen. William de Baron, son of Aiulph de Foro, was an early benefactor to Ardennes Abbey, Normandy; and William de B., t. Rich. I., confirmed his ancestor's gifts (Mém. Soc. Ant. Norm.). Richard le (de) Baron held one and a half fee in Devon, 1165. The Barons of Ireland claim descent from FITZGERALD.

Barough, armorially identified with BARROW.

Barr, from La Barre in the Cotentin. Gerard, Geoffry, Peter, Ralph, and Tiger de Barra of Normandy, 1180–95 (MRS). Ralph Barre was of England, 1153 (Mon. ii. 599), Geoffry, Peter, Richard Barre or De la Barre, 13th cent. The De la Barres or De la Beres held Southam, Gloucester.

Barrable, for Barbel. John Barbel occurs in Normandy, 1180–95 (MRS).

Barre, armorially identified with BARRY.

Barrell. Richard Barel occurs in Normandy, 1180 (MRS); Gilbert Barril in Surrey, 1130; Paganus B. in Suffolk, 1165 (holding from the Honour of Clare); Terric B. (13th cent.) in Dorset. The name is mentioned in the roll of Battle Abbey.

Barrey, armorially identified with BARRY.

Barrington, or De Barenton, from B., near Caudebec, Normandy. Humphry de B. witnessed a charter of Henry II. in Essex (Mon. ii. 294), and made a grant to Waltham Abbey (ii. 16). Nicholas de Barentin witnessed a charter of Richard de Montfichet of Essex (ii. 23). From this family descended the Baronets Barrington of Essex, and of Ireland.

Barrow. The celebrated mathematician and divine, Isaac Barrow, was grandson of Isaac B. of Spinney Abbey, Cambridge, Esq., of a family long seated in Suffolk and Norfolk,

which had originally come from Lincoln, where it was seated t. Edward IV. (Harl. MS. 1560, f. 244). Roger de Barowe of Lincoln was deceased before 1271 (Rot. Hundr. i. 368). In 1194 William de Barewe had a suit in the same county (RCR). In 1165 Robert de Jouvigny held a fief at Barrou, Normandy, of the Honour of Grent-Mesnil (Feod. Norm. apud Duchesne). In 1130 Adelaid de Barou occurs in Lincoln (Rot. Pip.), and in 1093 Walleran de Baro witnessed a charter of Chester Abbey (Mon. i. 1202). Barou was near Falaise in Normandy. There is a place named Barrow in Lincoln, which belonged to the Norman families of Quatremars, Le Despencer, Crespin, and Dives; but it is not practicable to connect with it the family of Barrow.

Barry, armorially identified with BARR. Sir Philip de Barre, t. John, witnessed the charter of Fermoy Abbey (Mon. ii. 1046). He was ancestor of the Viscounts Buttevant, Earls of Barrymore.

Bartellot. The name as Bertelot occurs in Normandy 1180 (MRS), and in England 1194 (RCR); and in various parts of England c. 1272 (RH). A branch acquired Stopham, Sussex, t. Rich. II., by m. with the coheiress of Stopham, and holds it under the name of Bartelot.

Bartleet, a form of BARTELOT.

Bartram, armorially identified with BERTRAM.

Bartrum. *See* BARTRAM.

Barwell, for Berville, from B., near Pont Audemer, Normandy. Nigel de Berville held in capite Berks, 1086 (Domesd.). Amabel de B., t. Henry II., m. Hugh de Keynes

(Lipscomb, Bucks, iv. 24). In 1165 William and Hugh de B. held lands in York (Lib. Nig.). The former, as William Malmains, held Berville, Normandy, 1165 (Feod. Norm. Duchesne). The name is also found as ' Burvilla.'

Baskerville, from Bacqueville, near Rouen. Baldwin Teutonicus, c. 990, was ancestor of this family, and of D'Aunou, Courcy, Beaugency, and Neville. In 1109 Robert de Baskerville, on his return from Palestine, granted lands to Gloucester Abbey (Mon. i. 115). Several branches of the family still remain.

Baskett. Walter Pesket, Norm. 1180–95 (MRS).

Baskitt. *See* BASKETT.

Bass. Richard le Bas, and Geoffry, Norm. 1180–98 (MRS). Freret, Hugh, John Basse, Engl. c. 1272 (RH).

Basset, from its ancestor Bathet, or Baset, Duke of the Normans of the Loire 895, 905 (Bouquet, vii. 360; viii. 317). He acquired Ouilly Basset, and Normanville in 912, and had issue Norman, father of Osmond, Viscount of Vernon, c. 960, whose elder son, Hugh Basset, was Baron of Chateau Basset, held from the Abbey of St. Denis, t. Hugh Capet, which barony passed by his widow to the house of Montmorency, c. 990. His brother, Fulco De Alneto, was father of 1, Osmond; 2, Robert D'Ouilly, ancestor of the DOYLEYS; 3, William de Lisures, ancestor of the house of Lisores; 4, Fulco or Fulcelin D'Alnet, ancestor of the DAWNAYS.

Osmond Basset accompanied the Conqueror 1066, and had issue, 1, Hugh Fitz-Osmond, ancestor of the family of NORMANVILLE, and Basset

of Normandy; 2, Norman, Sire de Montrevel, d. s. p.; 3, Anchetil Fitz-Osmond, ancestor of the PALMERS; 4, Ralph Fitz-Osmond, ancestor of the Lords Bassets of Drayton, &c.; 5. Richard Basset, ancestor of the Bassets of ' Devon; 6, William, ancestor of the Bassets of Essex and Wales.

Bassil, armorially identified with Bezilles, from Biszeilles, near Lille, Flanders. Besselsleigh, Berks, derives its name from this family, its ancient lords.

Bastable. N. Wasteble, Norm. 1180–95 (MRS). This name is supposed by Lower to be derived from Barnstaple; but it appears to have been a Norman family.

Bastard, descended from Robert Bastard, a baron in Devon, 1086 (Domesd.), son of William the Conqueror. The name was also written Baisterd and Bestard.

Baswell, for BOSWELL.

Batcheller. *See* BACHELOR.

Batcheler. *See* BACHELOR.

Batell, armorially identified with Battayle. *See* BABINGTON.

Bateman, from Baudemont in the Norman Vexin. Goel de Baudemont held a fief, 1165 (Feod. Norm. Duchesne). Andrew de Baldemont occurs in London, Devon, &c. 1130 (Rot. Pip.). Roger de Battemound held part of the Barony of Hephal, Northumberland, 13th cent. (Testa).

Bath. Rainier, afterwards named De Bada, held three lordships, Wilts, from Robert Fitz-Girold, 1086. He was a foreigner by his name, and was raised to dignity by Henry I. Adelard de Bada was living 1130 (Rot. Pip.). Richard de B. witnessed a charter of King Stephen. From the names it seems probable that this family originally came from Poitou or Aquitaine. The Baronets De Bathe are a branch.

Bathurst, or Bateste. The family of Bateste, Sires de Haubeville and Francoville, Normandy, held from the Abbey of St. Denis. Philip B. accompanied Duke Robert to Palestine, 1096 (Mém. Soc. Ant. Norm. x. 146). William B. in 1170, John B. 1180, witnessed charters of St. Denis. The Norman line bore two bars, in chief three bezants, which the English exchanged for crosses (La Roque, Mais. Harcourt, ii. 2001). The English branch acquired Wasingate, afterwards Badhestgate, Sussex, from Battle Abbey; and in 1203 John Bateste occurs in England (Rot. Canc.). In the 13th cent. and later, the names became Bodhurst, Bodhurstgate, or Badhestgate in the Battle Abbey charters (Burke). Laurence Bathurst of this family settled at Cranbrook, Kent, in the 15th cent., and was ancestor of the Earls Bathurst.

Batley. 1, an English local name; 2, from Batilly, near Alençon, Normandy. William de B., or Batilly, of Stoke, in England, frequently occurs, t. John.

Batten, said to have been Flemish (Lower). Beteyn and Batyn occur t. Edw. I. (Ib.). Joel Batin is mentioned in England, c. 1272 (RH).

Battin. *See* BATTEN.

Battle. *See* BATELL.

Batty, from La Bathie, Maine. Ralph Baty (13th cent.) held a knight's fee of the Earl of Devon in that county (Testa).

Baud, from Calvus or Le Baud. The name often occurs in Normandy 1180-95 (MRS). Almaldus Calvus

held lands in Somerset from Turstan Fitz-Rolf, 1083, and Roger Calvus was a tenant in capite (Ex. Domesd.). Magnus C., 1103, witnessed the agreement between Philip de Braiosa and the Abbot of Fescamp. The name was of importance in Middlesex, Northants, Chester, Hertford, Essex, &c. Sire William Baud was Viscount of Essex t. Edw. I.

Baugh, or De Baa, from Bahaia, near Coutances. Reginald de Ba gave lands to Sempringham, Linc. (Mon. ii. 791). Gilbert de Baa to the Knights Hospitallers of the same co. (ii. 536). In 1165 John de Baha, Gloucester, held one fee from Payn de Mundoublel (Lib. Nig.). Sir Nicholas de Ba was M.P. for Gloucestershire, 1307 (PPW). Sir Walter de Baa was summoned to attend a council at Westminster, 1324 (PPW).

Bavin, or Bavant (Lower), from Bavant, near Caen. The name frequently occurs in Normandy, 1180-95 (MRS). Hubert de Baduent, t. Henry I., held two and a half fees from Hubert de Rie, Norfolk (Lib. Nig.). Roger Bavant was summoned from Sussex to the Coronation of Edward II. (Palgr. Parl. Writs). This family held baronial rank in England.

Bax, or BACKS.

Bayes, for BOYES.

Bayley. *See* BAILLIE.

Bayley-Paget. *See* BAILLIE. Lewis Bayley, Bishop of Bangor, t. James I., who had accompanied that monarch from Scotland, was a scion of the Baillies of Lamington; and one of his descendants marrying the heiress of the Lords Paget, Earls of Uxbridge, this family inherited the Barony of Paget and assumed the name. Hence the Marquises of Anglesey, the first of whom was a celebrated commander under Wellington in the Peninsula and at Waterloo.

Baylly. *See* BAILLIE.

Bayne. *See* BAYNES.

Baynes, from Baynes, near Bayeux, Normandy. Eustace de Bauns, t. William I., witnessed a charter of William Peveril of Dover (Mon. i. 247). Lucas de Bans, or Bayons, was of Lincoln (Mon. ii.), Suspirius de Baynes, t. Edward I., of Lincoln (Inq. p. mort.). Others of the name occur in Lincoln, c. 1272 (R.H).

Bazin. Radulphus and William Bazin, 1180–95, were of Normandy, (MRS); Walter de Beyssin of England 14th cent.

Beach, armorially identified with Beche, or De la Beche, which is also armorially identified with Bech, Bec, or Beke of Eresby, a foreign family (Dugdale, Bar.). Robert de Beche, c. 1100, witnessed a charter of William Peveril of Dover (Mon. i. 347). Goisfrid de Bech was a tenant in capite, Hertford, 1086; Eborard de Becha held one and a half fee from Hamon Peché, Cambridge, 1165. Notwithstanding Dugdale's statement, which gives a Flemish origin to this family, it is believed to have been from Bec in Normandy, which name is frequently written Bech, and Beche in England. *See* PELHAM.

Beacham, for BEAUCHAMP (Lower).

Beachim, for BEACHAM.

Beaumont, or Baynard. Of this family two lines existed in England, one descended from Hubert Fitz-Ralph, Viscount of Maine, Beaumont and St. Suzanne in Maine; the other from Geoffry Baynard, or

De Beaumont, Viscount of Beaumont, his brother. From the latter descend the MARSHAMS, Baynards, Kerdestons or KERRISONS, Townshends, and others in East Anglia, and the Beaumonts of Yorkshire. From the former (Hubert Fitz-Ralph) descend the Beaumonts of Devon and Leicester, Barons and Viscounts Beaumont, and baronets.

The descent is probably from Abbo, Count of Poitiers, 778, ancestor of Bernard Fitz-Adelelm, father of Eminon and Bernard, joint Counts of Poitiers, c. 814 (*See* L'Art de Vérif. les Dates, x. 87, &c.). The latter, who m. the dau. of Roricon, Count of Mans, is styled 'Count' of Mans by Bouquet (Hist. Franc. viii. 101); but probably his title was 'Viscount,' as Roricon had a son who succeeded as Count. This Bernard, Viscount of Mans, or Maine, lost his Earldom of Poitou, which his son Bernard recovered, whose son Ranulph, or Radulphus, became Duke of Aquitaine, and was deposed for assuming the title of King. He appears to have retired to Maine, where Radulphus (his son probably) occurs in 950. He was a benefactor to the Abbey of Marmoutiers 994 (Gall. Christ.; Anselm). He seems to have had a son, Bernard or Bénard, whose son, Radulphus, was living 1056, and whose sons were named Bénard or Bainard. They were, 1, Hubert Fitz-Ralph; 2, Ralph Bainard, Viscount of Lude, whose son lost the vast barony of Baynard's Castle in England; 3, Geoffry Bainard, or De Beaumont.

Hubert Fitz-Ralph, Viscount of Maine, was celebrated for his resistance for two years to the Conqueror and his army, who besieged him in his Castle of St. Suzanne. He was at length victorious, and recovered his territories in Maine and England. Ralph, his son, was living 1109. His son Roscelin, Viscount of Beaumont, m. Constance, a dau. of Hen. I., and had with her Shirwell and other estates, Devon, where the family of Beaumont long continued, and from which sprang the Viscounts and Barons Beaumont, and the Baronets Beaumont.

Beadel. The name occurs in Normandy, 1180-95 (MRS). Godwin Bedel held lands in Bucks, 1086. The name frequently occurs in the 13th cent. (RH). Bishop Bedell was descended from a family seated in Suffolk, in that century.

Beadle, for BEADELL.

Beaden, from Bidon, in Burgundy. John Bidon, 1165, held seven fees in barony Northants; Halenald de Bidon, one from the Honour of Wallingford, and seven from Bigod in Norfolk (Lib. Nig.). Walter Bidon was Chancellor of Scotland, c. 1165. In the 13th cent. this family had estates in Bucks, Bedford, and Northants (Testa).

Beale, or Le Bele, a form of BELL.

Beamis, formerly Beaumis, Beaumeys, or Beaumetz, from Beaumetz, near Abbeville. Roger de Beaumez witnessed a charter of Henry I., 1124 (Gall. Christ. xi. 158). Richard de Belmiz, Viscount of Salop, witnessed, 1087, the charter of Salop Abbey (Mon. i. 376). Hugh Castellan of Beaumitz, m. Beatrice, dau. of Arnold de Gand, Count of Guianes, and was living, 1172. Richard de Belmiz was Bishop of London, 1107; Hugh de B. Lord of Dunnington, Salop, 1316, &c.

Beamish, for BEAMIS.

Beament, armorially identified with BEAUMONT of Yorkshire.

Beamand, armorially identified with BEAUMONT.

Bean, for BENE.

Beard, armorially identified with Bard, a form of BAIRD.

Beards, for BEARD.

Bearfield, or De Berville, from Berville, near Caen, held from Duke Richard, 1024, by Osbern and Anfrid de Bertreville, who granted lands there to Fontenelle Abbey (Neustria Pia, 166). William de Bareville occurs in Normandy 1180-95 (MRS), and Robert de B. in Wilts, c. 1272 (RH).

Boase, for BISSE.

Beaton, for BEATON.

Beaton, or Bethune, from the house of B., Barons of Bethune in Artois, Advocates or Protectors of Arras. This family was descended from the Carlovingian Counts of Artois, and ranked amongst the most potent and illustrious houses in Europe. The great Duke of Sully was one of its descendants. The Advocates of Arras possessed a barony in England from the Conquest, and left numerous descendants here. From the line of St. Omer, a branch of the same house, descended the Bagots, and Staffords, Duke of Buckingham in England, and many branches bearing the names of St. Omer and Arras.

Beauchamp, from Beauchamp, in the Cotentin, part of the Barony of St. Denis le Gaste (De Gerville, Anc. Chateaux). This family was a branch of the Barons of St. Denis, and of the same race as the Meurdracs, Montagues, and Grenvilles, which were armorially identified.

The history of the Beauchamps, Barons of Bedford, Earls and Dukes of Warwick, &c., is too well known to be dwelt on. Hence the Baronets Beauchamp,

Beaufoy, from Beaufay, near Alençon. Ranulph de Belfai occurs in Normandy, 1180 (MRS). Emma de Beaufoy was of Notts (13th cent.), and Ralph, of Hereford (Testa). John de Beaufoy was M.P. for Derby, 1320, and Viscount of Lincoln, 1349.

Beaver, for BEVER.

Beavill, or Beville, from Beuville, near Caen. William de Beevilla held lands in Suffolk, 1086 (Domesd.). Matthew de Beyvill witnessed a charter of Henry II. (Mon. ii. 247). Richard de Bevill was seneschal of the Archbishop of York, 1301 (Mon. ii. 415).

Beavis, armorially identified with Beaufiz. Henry Beaufiz, Lord of Clipston, York, 1316. Henry B. returned from Kent and Wilts to attend the great Council at Westminster, 1324 (Palgr. Parl. Writs).

Becket. See BECKETT.

Beckett. In 1180 Malger Bechet held lands in the Viscounty of Rouen (MRS). John and William Beket, or Bekeit, also occur (Ib.), and Humfrid and William Beket, 1198 (Ib.). Thomas Beket's father was of Caen. Ralph de Beket was of England, c. 1272 (RH.). From hence derived the Baronets Becket, and the famous Becket, Archbishop of Canterbury. William Becket, t. Stephen, witnessed the charter of Bolingbroke Priory, Linc. (Mon. ii. 795). John B. gave lands to Tupholme, Linc., t. John (Mon. ii. 596).

Becketts. See BECKETT.

Beeks, for Beck. See BEACH.

Beckitt. See BECKETT.

Beckwith, stated to have been adopted in lieu of the original Norman name of Malbisse (Lower).

Bedell. See BEADELL.

Bedding, or Bedin. William Betin occurs in Normandy, 1195 (MRS); Philip Bedin in Oxfordshire, c. 1272 (RH).

Bedingfield, stated to be descended from Ogerus de Pugeys (possibly Puchay, near Evreux), who came to England, t. William I., with William Malet, Baron of Eye (Lower).

Beech, a form of BEACH.

Beecham, for BEAUCHAMP.

Beecher, armorially identified with BEACH, of which it is a corruption. Hence the Baronets Wrixon-Beecher.

Beeden. See BEADON.

Beek, armorially identified with Beck or Bec. See BEACH, PELHAM.

Beeman, for BEAUMONT (Lower).

Beerill, for BERRELL.

Beeson, from Beisin, Normandy. Almeric de Beisin occurs in Salop 13th cent. (Testa, 46, 61).

Beeton, for BEATON.

Beever, for BEEVOR.

Beevers. See BEEVOR.

Beevers, or Belvers. See BEEVOR.

Beevor, or De Toesni, descending from Berenger de Belver or Bevor, son of Ralph de Toesni, Baron of Belvoir or Bevor, 1086. Ralph, son of Berenger, witnessed various charters of Roger de Mowbray, York. Thurstan, his son, was a benefactor to Newburgh Priory, York, and John de Beauvor, his son, held from Mowbray, 13th cent. This family long flourished in York and Lincoln, and thence removed to Norfolk. The Baronets Beevor are its descendants.

Belcher. See BELSHES. Richard

Belchere occurs in Gloucester, c. 1272 (RH).

Bell, from Le Bel, a surname which frequently occurs in Normandy, 1180–98 (MRS).

Bellamy, or Bellameys, from Belmeys or Beaumits. *See* BEAMIS.

Bellany, from Belaunay, Normandy. Robert de Bello Alneto (13th cent.) held lands by knight service from William Mauduit at Haneslape, Bucks (Testa, 231, 252).

Bellaers, for Beller, from Bellières, near Alençon. The name frequently occurs in Normandy, 1180–98 (MRS). Hamon Beler (12th cent.) witnessed a charter of Roger de Mowbray (Mon. i. 562). He granted lands to Vaudry Abbey, Lincoln (i. 833). Roger Beler founded Kirby-Beler, Leicester, for the souls of William, Roger, and Ralph, his ancestors (ii. 344). Ralph Beler, 1325, was M.P. for Leicestershire.

Bellars. *See* BELLAERS.

Bellairs. *See* BELLAERS.

Bellas, a form of BELLOWES.

Bellchamber, for Bellencombre or De Warrenne, from Bellencombre Castle, near Dieppe, the baronial seat of the Earls Warrenne and Surrey. Bernard de Bellencombre held lands in Suffolk, 1086. William de Bellecombre paid in Normandy 145*l.*, due by his father (MRS). John and Robert Bellencombre occur in Essex, c. 1272 (RH). In t. Elizabeth, William Belconger occurs in Norfolk, and at length the name changed to Bellchamber.

Bellet. Belet continually occurs as a surname in Normandy, 1180–98 (MRS). William Belet held lands in capite Hants and Dorset, 1086 (Domesd.). William B. was a baron in Dorset, 1165 (Lib. Nig.). Michael

156

B. was grand justiciary to Henry II. (Hov. i. 515). Robert B. (13th cent.) was of Dorset. The Bellets were hereditary butlers to the king.

Bellew, from Belleau or Bella Aqua, in Normandy. William, Osmelin, Guido, and Joseph de Bella Aqua occur in Normandy, 1180–95 (MRS). In 1165 this family held knights' fees in Kent, Berks, and York. Gilbert de Bellu witnessed a charter of the Archbishop of York, c. 1140 (Mon. i. 476). Sire John de Bella Aqua m. Laderina, dau. and coh. of Peter de Brus, Baron of Skelton (Mon. ii. 149). The Lords Bellew of Ireland are of this family.

Bellier. *See* BELLAERS.

Bellis, armorially identified with BELLEW of Cheshire.

Bellot, armorially identified with BELLET.

Bellowes, armorially identified with BELLEW.

Bellows, armorially identified with Bellowe, and Bellewe or BELLEW.

Belshes, a corruption of Bellassize (Seton). Bellassize was near Coulommières. The name is armorially identified with BELCHER.

Belville, from Belville or Bellavilla, near Dieppe, Normandy. Ranulph de Bellaville gave lands in Yorkshire to Vaudry Abbey, Lincoln (Mon. i. 833).

Belward, a form of Belwar, Belver, or Belvoir. *See* BEEVOR, CHOLMONDELEY, EGERTON.

Beman, for BEAMAN.

Bemand, for BEAMAND.

Bemes, for BEAMIS.

Bence. Robert and William Bence occur in Normandy, 1180–98 (MRS); and the same name occurs in England, c. 1272 (RH).

Bene. Hubert de Bene paid a fine in Normandy, 1180 (MRS). Stephen de Bene, 1298, was bailsman for a M.P. for Appleby, as was Peter Bene, 1311 (Palgr. Parl. Writs). From this family descend the Benns, now Benn-Walsh, Lords Ormathwaite.

Benivell, for Beneville, formerly of Devon, from Beneville, near Havre. The name occurs in Normandy, 1180-98 (MRS). Alvared de Benneville (12th cent.) witnessed a charter of Alberic de Ver (Mon. i. 1008). William de Bendeville witnessed a charter for Walden, Essex, in the same century (Mon. i. 643).

Benn. *See* BENE.

Bennet, or Beneyt. William, Robert, and Hugh Benedictus occur in Normandy, 1180-95, and others of the name, 1198 (MRS).

Bennett, Beneyt, or Benedictus, a Norman family. *See* BENNET. Robert Benet (above mentioned in Normandy) occurs, t. Henry II., in Wilts, whose son, Adam, c. 1200, held estates in Wilts (Hardy, Rot. Claus. i. 179, Testa 137). Asceline Beneyt was in the service of King John (Hardy, Rot. Claus. i. 114). From this house descended the Bennets, Earls of Arlington, and of Tankerville.

Berrell, for BARRELL.

Berey, for Barrey or BARRY.

Beringer. Roger de Berenger occurs in Normandy, 1195 (MRS). Robert, William, and John Berenger, c. 1272 in Hants (RH).

Berks, for PERKS or PARKS.

Bernard, a name frequently mentioned in Normandy, 1180-91 (MRS). Hugo Bernardus occurs in Lincoln, 1130 (Rot. Pip.). He witnessed the charter of Roger of Poitou in Lancaster, c. 1100. About 1200 Robert Fitz-Bernard, of Lancashire, granted lands at Howath to the Knights Hospitallers, and mentions Bernard, his son (Mon. i. 507).

From this line descend the Bernards, Earls of Bandon, and probably the family of Howath or Howarth.

Bernes, from Bernes, near Beauvais. Nicholas de Bernes, 1167, was a benefactor to Beauvais Abbey. Adam, his son, lived 1221; and from him descended the Sires de Bernes, Castellans of Longvillers (Des Bois). Agnes de Bernes occurs in Oxford, and Robert de B. in Wilts, c. 1272 (RH).

Berney, 1, from Berney, Norfolk; 2, from Bernai, near Lisieux. Ralph de Bernai, of Worcester and Hereford, witnessed a charter of Malmsbury Abbey, t. William I. (Mon. i. 53), and was a tenant of William Fitz-Osborne, Earl of Hereford (i. 129). In 1096 Robert de Bernay witnessed a charter of Stephen, Count of Aumerle, for the monks of Beauvais (Mon.). The Baronets Berney derive their name from the English locality.

Bernwell, or Barnwell. William de Burnavilla held lands in Norfolk and Suffolk, 1086 (Domesd.). Robert and William de Bernwell in 1165 (Lib. Nig.). The former, t. Stephen, witnessed a charter of Briset Abbey, Suffolk (Mon. ii. 871). John de Burnaville, of Suffolk, 1316, was at the battle of Boroughbridge, 1322 (Palgr. Parl. Writs). This family, which bore a saltire, was different from that of Barnewal, ancestors of Lord Trimleston, &c.

Berrett, for BARRETT.

Berry, armorially identified with BARRY.

Bertie, a form of Bertin, which

occurs in Battle Abbey roll. Roger Bertin paid a fine in Normandy, 1195 (MRS). Helto B. occurs at the same time, and was bailiff of Falaise (Ib.), and in 1203 had remission of a fine at Caen (Rot. Canc.). Helias and Thomas Bertin were benefactors to St. Andrew Gouffern, Normandy. In 1165 Alexander de Bertona held lands in Kent (Lib. Nig.). The family was seated at Berstead, Kent, t. Henry II. (Hasted, ii. 488), and sometimes bore the name of De Berstead. Walter de Bersted, 1257, was Viscount of Kent (Roberts, Excerpt.), and in 1266 was a justiciary. Hamo de Berstede occurs 1305. In 1433 William Bertyn was one of the Kentish gentry. Simon Bertyn, who d. 1530, devised lands at Bersted. Another branch, seated at Bersted also, altered the name to Berty and Bertie. Thomas B. of this line was captain of Hurst Castle t. Henry VIII., and from him descended the Duke of Ancaster, Earls of Lindsey, and of Abingdon.

Bertin. *See* BERTIE.

Bertram, an illustrious Norman name. *See* MITFORD.

Berwell. *See* BARWELL.

Bessett, armorially identified with BISSETT.

Best, an abbreviation of BESSETT. From this house derive the Lords Wynford.

Bever, or Beever, armorially identified with Belvoir or Bevor of Leicestershire, otherwise De Toesni. *See* BERVOR.

Beverel. Richard de Beverel is frequently mentioned in Normandy, c. 1180 (MRS).

Bevington. *See* BOVINGTON.

Beville. *See* BEAVILL.

Bevir, for BEVER.

Bevis, for BEAVIS.

Bevis, armorially identified with Beaufais or Beauvais. Duke Richard II., 1027, confirmed the gift of Ansgot de Belvai of land at Belvai to Fescamp Abbey (Neustria Pia, 212). Goisbert de Beauvais held a barony in Herts, 1082 (Domesd.). John Beauveys was bailsman for a M.P. for Yorkshire, 1313 (Palgr. Parl. Writs).

Bew. *See* BEWS.

Bewley, for Beaulieu. *See* BOWLEY.

Bews, for BAYEUX. Ranulph de Bayeux was one of the Proceres of Normandy, 1050, in rebellion against Duke William (Ord. Vitalis). His descendants were great barons in Lincoln. Hugh de Bayeux, 1165, held two knights' fees in that county. The name continued long as Bayouse, Beyouse, and at last Bews.

Bewsay, for BUSSEY or De Busci.

Bewshea, for BEWSAY.

Bick, a form of Bec. *See* BEACH.

Biddle, for BIDELL.

Bidell, from Bidellus or Bedellus. *See* BEADLE.

Biden, for BIDUN. *See* BEADON.

Biggers. Durand le Bigre, Normandy, 1180–95 (MRS). Ranulph de Bigars, 1198 (Ib.).

Bigot. Richard le Bigot and Robert, Normandy, 1180–95 (MRS). *See* WIGGETT.

Biles, a form of BYLES.

Bill, armorially identified with Byle or Byles, a form of BOYLE.

Billes. *See* BILL, a form of BOYLE.

Billett, armorially identified with BELLET.

Bing. *See* BYNG.

Binge. *See* BYNG.

Bingham, or De Buisli, from Buisli or Builly, near Neûchatel,

Normandy (often supposed to be of Saxon origin). Roger de Busliaco held 149 lordships in barony 1086, chiefly in York and Notts, which were entitled the Honour of Tickhill. He also held Sutton, Somerset, from Roger de Arundel. One of his lordships was Bingham, Notts, an estate of great value and importance. Dugdale confuses this baron with his son and grandson, who bore the same name. The latter suffered forfeiture t. Stephen, and his Honour of Tickhill was, in 1156 and 1165, in the hands of the King (Rot. Pip.; Lib. Niger). Jordan and John de Buiali were then his next heirs. The former had issue Richard de B., who held 6 fees in 1165, and whose dau. carried that estate to Robert de Vipont. The male representation then vested in the descendants of Richard de B., younger son of Roger I., who founded Roche Abbey, York, 1147 (Mon. i. 836). He had issue Richard and William de B. (Ib.). John de B., son of the latter, granted lands to Roche (Ib.). The former paid a fine in Bucks 1158 (Rot. Pip.), and possessing Bingham, was thence named, and, c. 1166, as John de Bingham, witnessed charters in favour of Ellesham Hospital, Lincoln (Mon. ii. 422). His son Clement was father of Hugh de Bingham, living 1199, who was enfeoffed in his lands at Bingham by Hugh Paganel (Testa). The lordship was soon after forfeited. Robert, brother of Clement, and, in 1205, Richard, his son, obtained livery of his lands at Bingham (Hardy, Obl. et fin. 258). He was brother of Robert, Bishop of Salisbury, and had issue William and Robert. The former possessed Sutton, Somerset, which had descended from his ancestor Roger de Buiali (Collinson, vol. ii. 350). From Robert, who m. the heiress of Turberville, descend the Binghams of Dorset, the Earls of Lucan, and Barons Clanmorris.

Birbeck, from Brabant. Henry de Birbeka witnessed a charter of Godfrey Barbatus 1134; and William de B. a charter of Godfrey Duke of Brabant 1179 (Albert. Miræi Oper. Diplomat. i. 107, 174).

Birmingham, or Paynel. The barony of Birmingham was granted by Fulco Paynel, t. Henry I., to Peter (whose family were armorially identified with the Painels, each bearing a bend), by the service of 9 knights. About 1150 William Fitz-Peter witnessed a charter of Gervase Paynel (Mon. ii. 907), and his son Peter Dapifer held 9 fees 1165, and 1187 witnessed a charter of Gervase Paynel (Mon. ii. 911). He had William, Baron of Birmingham (Dugd. War. 897, 8), and Peter de Birmingham, who went to Ireland, and was ancestor of the barons of Athenry, Earls of Louth. *See* PAYNEL.

Biron. *See* BYRON.

Birt. *See* BURT.

Bishop. Radulphus Episcopus, or l'Évêque, paid a fine in Normandy 1180, and Ricardus Episcopus in 1184 (MRS). John Bishop witnessed a charter of Robert Fitz-Harding, t. Henry II. (Mon. ii.). In 1246 Matilda, dau. of Richard le Evesk, paid a fine, Wilts (Roberts, Excerpt.). Sir John Bisshopp was M.P. for Wilts 1315. Of this name were the Bishopps, Baronets, Lords de la Zouche.

Bishopp, armorially identified with BISHOP.

Bisse, armorially identified with a branch of BISSETT bearing 3 escallops in bend, instead of in pale, as borne by Bisse.

Bisse, from La Bisse, Normandy. Richard de la Bisse occurs in 1180 in the Duchy (MRS), and his estate is mentioned (Ib.). William de Bisa witnessed in 1115 a charter of Stephen, Earl of Albemarle, for Alcey Abbey, Normandy (Mon. ii. 999).

Bissell, armorially identified with BISSETT.

Bissett. Ralph and Henry Biset occur in Normandy 1180–98 (MRS). William Biset had possessions in Notts and Derby 1130 (Rot. Pip.). Manasser Biset occurs in Essex 1156 (Ib.), and 1165 he held a fee in Chaucy in the bailifry of Coutances, Normandy (Duchesne, Feod. Norm.), as did Henry Biset from the honour of Montfort. Sire John Byset, of Worcestershire, lived 1300 (Palgr. Parl. Writs). *See* BEST.

Blagrave, or le Breton. B. in Berks was held (13th cent.) by William le Breton and another. The former is armorially identified with Blagrave; both bearing a bend. In 13th cent. Alicia de Blackgrave held Bockhampton, Berks (Testa); and lands in Blagrave were held from William Fitz-Humphry (le Breton) by Nicholas Fitz-Hugh, which Henry III. in 1247 confirmed to Poghele Priory, Berks (Mon. ii. 207). The name le Breton indicates a Breton origin.

Black. Odo, Robert, Matthew, Umfrid, and William Niger (black) occur in Normandy 1180–98 (MRS). Roger Niger occurs 1124 in a charter of Henry I. to Dive Abbey (Gall. Christ. xi. 159). Robertus Niger held 100

lands in Kent 1086 (Domesd.). In 1130 Godehart le Blac occurs at Carmarthen, Nicholas Blac in Warwick 1158 (Rot. Pip.), whose son Geoffry Blache 1165 held from Pershore Abbey. In 1165 Hamo Niger held a fee from Hamo Fitz-Meinfelin, Bucks (Lib. Niger). Some native English families may be included under the name.

Blackett, an abbreviation of BLANCHETT. Hence the baronets Blackett.

Blackstone, or le Breton. Blackstone, Devon, was held 1086 by Alured le Breton (from Bretagne), who appears to have been succeeded by his grandson Payne Fitz-Serlo, who granted the church of B. to Plympton Priory (Mon. ii. 8). In 13th cent. William Blackston, with William de Cleville, held lands at Stanes of the Honour of Wallingford (Testa).

Blake, Admiral Robert, the great Naval Commander t. Cromwell, was of Somerset, in which county Walter Blache occurs 1273 (Rot. Hundr. ii. 121), and Gilbert Niger in 1203 (Rot. Canc.). The latter was then deceased. Roger Niger occurs in a charter to Dive Abbey, Normandy, 1124 (Gall. Christ. xi. 159, instr.). *See* BLACK.

Blakey, the French pronunciation of Blaket. *See* BLACKETT.

Blanchard. Ralph and William Blanchart were of Normandy, 1180–95 (MRS). Richard Blanchard, 12th century, witnessed a charter of Roger de Montbegon, York (Mon. ii. 602). Ponce B. held twelve fees in Hants, granted by Richard I., and Gilbert and William B. had estates, Lincoln (Testa).

Blancheville, from the estate

and forest of B., Normandy. Richard de Blancheville witnessed a charter of Castle Acre Priory, Norfolk (Mon. i. 628). This family had branches in Ireland.

Blanch. William Blanc and Robert and John Blanche occur in Normandy, 1180-95 (MRS); Eleanor Blanche in Cambridge; Henry B. in Oxford, c. 1272 (RH).

Blanchet. Robert and Ralph Blanchet, Blanquet, or Blanket occur in Normandy, 1180-95 (MRS). In England the name appears as Blachet or Blaket.

Blashfield, an Anglicised form of BLANCHEVILLE.

Blaxton, for BLACKSTONE.

Blay, for BLEAY.

Bleakey, for BLAKEY.

Bleay. Unfredus de Ble paid a fine, Normandy, 1180 (MRS); Robert de Blee occurs in Stafford, 1199; Galfridus de Blie in Leicester (RCR).

Blennerhasset, or De Tilliol, from Tilliol, near Rouen. Richard de T., lord of Blennerhasset, Cumberland, t. Henry I., was father of Simon, ancestor of Sire Piers Tilliol of Blennerhasset t. Henry VIII. (Nicholson and Burns, 121, 451). The younger branches bore the name of De Blennerhasset.

Blessett, for BLISSETT.

Blewett, armorially identified with BLUETT.

Blewitt, armorially identified with BLUETT.

Bley, for BLEAY.

Bligh, or De Bloin, from Bretagne, variously written Bloy, Bly, Bloyne, Bloe, Blue, Bloyo, Blohin, Bloihowe, &c. In 1212-22 Jelduin de Bloe or Blew was an envoy from the Viscount of Thouars to Henry III.

Hardy, Rot. Claus. i. 468, 487, 129, 484. The name in Bretagne is mentioned by Lobineau (Hist. Bret. Index). In 1086 Kelin the Christian name omitted) held five ked-ships, making seven fees, in Cornwall. Grallon de Brithon lived t. Stephen; Geoffry, his son, held seven fees, 1165 (Lib. Niger); Alan Bundus, his son, is mentioned 1201 (Hardy, Obl. et fin. 160). Sire Ralph De Brithon had a writ of military summons, 1350; and Alan B., 1401, held fees of the Honour of Mortaine, Cornwall (Carew, Cornw. 39, 43). Of a collateral branch was John Birch or Bloye, 1410, who granted to his son lands in Cornwall. His wife inherited lands in Botadon, Devon, where the family remained seated in the sixteenth century. The earls of Darnley descend from this line, whose arms they bear.

Blundell, for BLUNDELL.

Bliss, for Bleys or Bloya, i.e. Blois. William de Bleys occurs in Worcester, c. 1272 (RH); and Ralph de Blees held Neen-Sollars, Salop, t. Henry VI. (Inq. p. m.). The family is armorially identified with BLOIS.

Blissett, for BLIZARD, or Blizart.

Blizard, or Blizart, perhaps from Blesum, Blois, meaning a native of Blois. The name is evidently foreign.

Blockey, the French pronunciation of Bloquet or Ploquet. See DENMAN.

Bloice, for BLOIS.

Blois, from Blois or Blesum, France. Theobald, count of Blois (whose ancestry is disputed), had Eudes II., who m. Bertha, dau. of Conrad, king of Burgundy, by a dau. of Louis D'Outremer, king of

France, and succeeding 996, acquired Champagne by conquest, of which he assumed the title of Count Palatine. He had issue, 1. Theobald, ancestor of the counts of Champagne, so renowned in the Crusades, and afterwards kings of Navarre. 2. Henry, surnamed Stephen, count of Troyes and Meaux, who refused homage to Henry I., king of France, and was banished, 1041. His son Odo or Eudes de Champagne or Blois, being despoiled of his estates by his uncle, the Count of C., retired to Normandy, and obtained from John, archbishop of Rouen, the lordship of Albemarle, held by ten knights' service. He m. Adelais de Conteville, half sister to the Conqueror, and acquired vast baronies in England, held by his descendants the earls of Albemarle, barons of Holderness. He probably had brothers, from one of whom descended the family of De Blois, who bore the bend of the counts of Blois and Champagne and of the earls of Albemarle. In 1165 Ernald de Bloi held lands of ancient enfeoffment from Earl Alberic de Ver (Lib. Nig.). In 1201 Robert de B. was party to a suit, Essex (RCR), and 1220 again. William de Bloys was bishop of Winchester, 1226; and 1250 Alexander Bleys is mentioned in Gloucester. Thomas Blois, living at Norton, Suffolk, 1470, was ancestor of the baronets Blois.

Blomefield. See BLOOMFIELD. Hence the baronets Blomefield.

Blomfield. See BLOOMFIELD. Hence the late eminent J. C. Blomfield, bishop of London.

Bloomfield, armorially identified with Blomville, from the lordship

so named near Caen and Touques. The name occurs as Blundeville, Blosmeville, Blumville, &c. Richard de Blumville was a benefactor, t. Rich. I., to Bliburg Abbey, Suffolk (Mon. ii. 594). Thomas de B. had custody of the estates of Earl Bigod in Norfolk and Suffolk (Roberts, Excerpt. i. 125), and 1230 Thomas de B. was bishop of Norwich. In 1316 Catherine and William de B. were possessed of six manors in Norfolk (Palgr. Parl. Writs). Hence the lords Bloomfield.

Blossett. The Blossetts of Normandy were barons of Esneval, and Vidames. The last was Eguerrand Baron D'Esneval, c. 1477 (La Roque, Mais. Harc. ii. 1183).

Blount, Le Blund, or Blundus. Gervase, Fromund, Robert, Wymund Blundus of Normandy, 1180-98 (MRS). Gilbert and Robert Blundus (said to be of the family of the counts of Guisnes) held baronies in the Eastern Counties, 1086. There are frequent notices of the name, 12th cent., in Essex, Suffolk, Wilts, Notts, &c. In 1300 three families of Le Blund bore different arms, and were probably of different foreign origins. Hence derive the baronets Blount.

Blow, for Blue or Bloy. See BLIGH.

Blue. See BLEWS.

Bluett. In 1084 Richard and William Bloet occur in Normandy (Gall. Christ. xi. 228 Instr.). Robert Bloiet was bishop of Winchester, t. William I. (Ord. Vit. 703). Briqueville la Blouette was the seat of this family in Normandy (La Roque, Mais. Harc. ii. 1834). Robert Bloet witnessed a charter of William I. (Mon. i. 49), and Ralph B.

at the same time was a benefactor of Gloucester Abbey (Ib. i. 118). William Bluet was summoned with other barons to march against the Welsh, 1256. The name long remained of eminence in the West of England.

Blumfield. *See* BLOOMFIELD.

Blundell. *See* BLUNDEN.

Blunden, armorially identified with Blundell or Blondel. Wastin or Gastin Blondel occurs in Normandy, 1180 (MRS). This family came to England with William Malet, and William B. in 1165 held three fees of the Honour of the Malets of Eye (Lib. Nig.), and Robert de Crek held two more fees from Blondel. In Salop this family was seated before 1250 (Eyton). Sire Robert Blundell witnessed a charter of Abberbury Abbey, Salop (Mon. i. 606). A branch became seated at Ince, Lancashire, and another in Ireland as barons of Edenderry, viscounts Blundell. The baronets Blunden lost the ancient orthography of their name, but retained their original family arms, those of the Blundells, which suffice for their identification.

Blundsfield, for Blundeville (Lower). *See* BLOOMFIELD.

Blunt. Radulf, Roger, Robert le Blont, Norm. 1180–05 (MRS). Hence the baronets Blunt.

Blews, a form of Blew or Blue. Etard de Bleu occurs in Kent, 1199, and Robert de Bloi in Essex (RCR). This name was a form of Bloi, Bloin, or Blohin of Bretagne, often written Blue. *See* BLIGH.

Bly, for Bloi. *See* BLIGH.

Boag, for BOGUE.

Boase, for BOWES (Lower).

Boat, for Buat, from the Castle

of Buat near Falaise. The family of De Buat or Boat long remained in Normandy (Des Bois). Sexus de Bue occurs in Surrey, 1130 (Rot. Pip.). *See* BOWETT.

Boax, for BOASE.

Boas, for BOASE.

Bobart. N. Popart, Normandy, 1180–95 (MRS).

Bockerfield, from Bocherville or Bucheville, Normandy. Hubert de Bucherville (12th cent.) witnessed the charter of Isabella de Say to Wenlock Abbey (Mon. i. 614).

Bockett, originally Boquet (Lower). Robert Bouquet occurs in Normandy, 1198 (MRS).

Bodel, for BUDELL.

Bodger. Adam, Arnulph, Boschier, Norm. 1180–95 (MRS); W. le Boghier, Engl. c. 1272 (RII).

Bodelly, for Botelly or Batelly. *See* BATLEY.

Boffay, from Beaufay near Alençon, Normandy. Eguerrand de Boffei occurs in Normandy, 1195 (MRS). It sometimes now takes the form of Bophey.

Boggis. William de Bogis occurs in Normandy, 1180 and 1195 (MRS). The name De Boges occurs elsewhere in 1182 (Gallia Christ. xvi. 301).

Boggs. *See* BOGGIS.

Bois, from Normandy, several families, viz. :—

1. De Bois-Arnaud, hereditary stewards of the counts of Breteuil, sires of Poilly. Their signatures appear in the charter of William Fitz-Osborne to Lire Abbey, t. William I. They long flourished in Leicester and Northants.

2. De Bois-Guillaume, of the bailifry of Caux, of whom William de B. was seated in Essex, 1086.

They long flourished in the Eastern Counties.

3. De Bois-Herbert, barons of Halberton, Devon; Roger Faitel, baron of B. Herbert, occurs 1050 (Ord. Vit. 466); Hugo de Bosco H. occurs, 1083, in England (Exon. Domesd.). They long flourished in Dorset, and the barons of Halberton, Devon, were a branch.

4. De Bois-Robert or Roard, of whom Robert de B. and his brother held estates in Bucks, 1086. Sire Nicholas de Bois of this family lived 14th century.

5. De Bois, descended from a companion of Bernard de Neumarché, to whom he granted a barony, Brecknock, 1088, named after him Trebois.

Bole, or BOELS.

Boles, a form of BOELS. *See* BOYLE.

Boleyn. Queen Anna Boleyn was great-granddaughter of Sir Geoffry Boleyn, Lord Mayor of London temp. Henry VI., who accumulated a large fortune. The family had formerly been of great consequence. Sir Thomas B. of Blickling, Norfolk, grandfather of Sir Geoffry, lived c. 1400, and was lineally descended from John de Boleyne of Sall, living 1283, whose father Simon purchased lands in Norfolk by fine 1252. The father of the latter m. the sister and heir of Robert Malet (Blomefield), and possessed estates at Walpole, &c. In 1165 Herebert de Buliun held half a knight's fee from Roger Bigod, E. of Norfolk (Lib. Niger). At the same time William de Bolein held 1 fee in York and 1 in Lincoln; which shows that there were then two branches of the family in England. Accordingly, in the preceding generation, Eustace and Simon de Bologne, brothers of Pharamus de B., are mentioned in a charter of the latter (Mon. Ang. i. 583).

It appears from this charter that Pharamus (who had estates in England) was son of William de Bolonia, the son of Geoffry de Bolonia, son of Eustace, Count of Bologne (Ibid.). Pharamus held estates in England from the Count of Bologne, his kinsman, whose English barony consisted of 112 knights' fees.

The Counts of Bologne descended from Angilbert, a Frank noble, who m. Bertha, dau. of the Emperor Charlemagne, and before 790 was created Duke of the maritime territory afterwards styled Ponthieu (Art de Vérif. les Dates, xii. 318). Count Nithard, his son, rendered eminent services to his uncles Lewis and Charles the Bald. Seventh in descent from him was William I., who succeeded before 957. His great grandson was Eustace I., who had issue Eustace II., Goisfrid, Bishop of Paris, Lambert, and Godfrid, or Geoffry, ancestor of the Boleyns.

Bolland. Richard de la Boillante, Norm. 1198, MRS.

Bollen, armorially identified with BOLEYN.

Bolleng, for Boulogne, or BOLEYNE.

Bellowe, for Bellewe, or BELLEW.

Bolster, for Balster or Balistar. *See* ALABASTER.

Bolt, from Bolt or Bout, near Bayeux. Tescelinus de Boalt paid a fine in Normandy 1180, in the bailifry of William Duredent, MRS. Reginald and Richard Bolt occur in Oxford, c. 1272, RH.

Bolton-Nelson, or De Montfichet,

Earls Nelson. Alured Gernon, brother of William Gernon, Baron of Montfichet (*see* CAVENDISH), was father of Matthew, who had 3 sons—1, Ralph, living 1165, ancestor of the Gernons and Cavendishes; 2, Richard, father of Osbert de Gladisfen; 3, Hugh Gernon or De Bolton. The Lordships of Bolton, Bradwell, Gapton, and Hopland, Suffolk, were exchanged, t. Henry I. or Stephen, by their then owner, with the Gernons, for Gyl in Normandy (Test. 295). Matthew G. was probably the grantee of Bolton, &c. He gave them to his sons Ralph, Richard, and Hugh; and Bartholomew de Bolton, son of Hugh, held these estates on condition of paying to Ralph Gernon (son of Ralph) and Osbert de Gladisfen (son of Richard) eight shillings annually (Suckling, Suff. i. 301, 303, 323; Testa, 295). Bartholomew de B. was father of Joceus or Jocelin de B., who is mentioned in the Testa de Neville (103) as king's bailiff of the district where Bolton was situate. After him Robert de B. occurs (Ib.), and in 1286 Thomas de Hopland, brother of the owner of Bolton, &c., occurs (Suckling, Suff. i. 323). The family of Bolton continued in Suffolk till t. James I.; but a branch settled in Norfolk, of which was William B. (probably a younger son of the Suffolk line), who m., c. 1430, an heiress in Norfolk; and from him descended the Lords of Brisingham and Heywood, who continued till the time of · Elizabeth. From a younger branch of these descend the Earls Nelson, who obtained that title as the nearest heirs in blood of the renowned Nelson.

The arms of the Boltons, or Boul-tons (on a bend argent, 3 leopards' heads), were probably originally 3 escallops instead of leopards' heads, an ancient coat of the Gernons being on a bend 3 escallops (Robson). Escallops were frequently exchanged by mistake for leopards' heads.

Bompas, from Bonpas near Perpignan, a Visigoth family. Gilbert, son of William Bonpas, paid a fine, 1265, for an assize, Gloucestershire (Roberts, Excerpt. ii. 418).

Bonamy. Radulphus de Bono Amico occurs in Normandy 1180, MRS, and Robert and William Bon Ami in 1198 (Ib.).

Bone, armorially identified with Bohun of Midhurst, or De Fulgeres. *See* FOULGER.

Bonell, or Bunel, Lords of Tissy near Caen (Des Bois). In 1165 Roger Bunel and Robert Fitz-Julian held 2 fees in Lincoln from Richard de la Haye (Lib. Niger).

Boner. Bartholomew Bonaire party to a suit Hants 1200, RCR. This name appears foreign.

Bonest, from Banaste, or Banastre. *See* BANNISTER.

Boney, for BONNEY.

Bonfield, for Bonville, from the Castle of Bonneville or Bondeville, Normandy. William de Bonville occurs 1124 (Gall. Christ. xi. 159). In 1165 the son of Robert de Bonavilla held lands in York (Lib. Niger). The Barons Bonville were of this house (*See* Dugdale, Baronage).

Bonham. Humphry and William Bonhomme occur in Cambridge c. 1272, R.H. The name is obviously foreign. One family may have derived its name from Bonham, Norfolk. Hence the Baronets Bonham.

Bonhote, or Bonnot, a form of

Bonnett, with which it is armorially identified.

Bonnett. Roger Bonitus witnessed 1075 a charter of William de Braiose, Sussex (Mon. i. 581). The family seat was near Alençon. The name occurs in the Battle Abbey roll. Robert Bonat (13th cent.) held 1½ knights' fees from the Barons Braiose at Wappingthorn, Sussex (Testa).

Bonney. Gaufridus Bonie, Nicholas, and Richard Bonie occur in Normandy 1189–95, MRS; Agnes and Alicia Bonye in Oxfordshire, c. 1272, RH.

Bonnivell, for Bonville. See Bonfield.

Bonom, for Bonham.

Bonus, armorially identified with Bonest.

Boodle, for Budell.

Boog, for Bogue.

Booker. Walter Bochier is mentioned in Normandy 1180, MRS. The name in England is armorially identified with Boocher.

Boole, or Boyle. Ralph Buelles or Buels occurs in Normandy 1195, MRS. See Boyle.

Boolen, for Bullen, or Boleyn.

Bools. See Boole.

Boon, or Boone, armorially identified with Bohun. There were two families of the name, 1 Norman, 2 Breton.

The former descended from Humphry de Bohun, who accompanied the Conqueror, and was ancestor of the Bohuns, Earls of Hereford, Constables of England.

The latter was a branch of the Barons of Fougeres or Filgeres in Bretagne, whose ancestry reaches to the year 900 (Herald and Genealogist). See Foulger.

166

Boone, armorially identified with Bohun. See Boon.

Booser, for Bowser.

Boosey. Alexander de la Buzeia, Normandy 1180, MRS; Ralph Buse, Eng. 1104, CR; William B., Engl. c. 1272, RH.

Boot, perhaps from Boat. The fief of Hugo Boot, however, is mentioned t. Philip Augustus, as held from Walter Tirel in the Vexin, Normandy (Mém. Soc. Ant. Norm. v. 184).

Boothby, a younger branch of the Barons de Tateshall, descended from Eudo, a foreign noble, living 1086 (Domesd.). Boothby was held 13th cent. by Robert de Tateshall, the ancestor of this family (Testa). Sir Alexander de Boothby had a writ of summons, 1296, to march against the Scots. From this family descend the Baronets Boothby.

Borne. Ansold, Anselm, Walter le Borne, Normandy 1180–95, MRS.

Borough, or De Burgh, otherwise Tusard. Hubert de B., the great Earl of Kent t. Henry III., was descended from a family which held Burgh, Causton, &c., in Norfolk, by the service of finding a mounted cross-bow-man for the king's army for 40 days, and had so held those estates from the time of Henry I. These estates being divided between the family of Tusard and that of De Burgh, it appears that the former was the original Norman name, retained by one branch (See Testa de Neville, 293). William Tusard, t. William I., had issue Robert de Burgh and Gerard Tusard, to whom the above lands seem to have been granted by Henry I. (Testa, 293). The latter was a benefactor to Castle Acre, and left descendants named Tusard. The former's lands passed to his brother Rainald de B., father of William de B., whose son Rainier was father of. Hubert de Burgh, the great Earl of Kent. All these persons are mentioned in Blomefield's Norfolk. From this house descended the Lords Burgh or Borough of Gainsborough.

Borrow, armorially identified with BOROUGH and BURGH.

Borrell, armorially identified with BURRELL.

Borrett. John Buret occurs in Normandy 1195, and Radulph de Burettes, MRS. Walter de la Burette in Devon, c. 1272, RH.

Borroughs. See BURROUGH.

Borrowes. See BURROUGH or Burgh. Hence the baronets of the name.

Bose, for Boss.

Boshell, for BUSHELL.

Bosher, a form of BOURCHIER (Lower).

Bosquet. See BOCKETT.

Boss. Radulphus Bos or Bose occurs in Normandy 1180, Durand and Richard B. 1198, MRS. Radulphus B. also occurs in Bucks 1104, RCR., as Rad. Buse.

Bossard, or Bussard. Baldwin, Ranulph, and William Buscart or Buschart occur in Normandy 1198, MRS; Henry Boscard in Salop 1203 (Rot. Canc.). Leighton-Buzzard derives its name from this family.

Bossey. See BOOSEY.

Bossy, for BUSSEY.

Bostel, for Postel. Richard, Robert, Alexander, Ralph, and Eustace Postel of Normandy 1180–95, MRS.

Bostfield, for BOSVILLE.

Bosville, from B. near Caudebec, Normandy. William de Boseville,

with Engelger de Bohun, witnessed the charter of Kenilworth t. Henry I (Mon. ii. 114). Helias de Boseville granted lands to Nostell, York, confirmed by Henry II. (Ib. ii. 37). In 1165 William de B. held lands in Essex, Robert de B. in Suffolk (Lib. Nig.). In Normandy Gaufrid de B. held t. Hen. I., two fees from Hugh de Montfort and the church of Bayeux.

Boswell, armorially identified with BOSVILLE.

Boterill. Geoffry Boterel, brother of Alan, Count of Penthièvre and Richmond, occurs in a Breton charter, 1080 (Morice, Hist. Bret. Preuves, ii. 455). His son Hamon was father of William Botterill, mentioned in England, 1130 (Rot. Pip.). He m. Alice, co-heir of Robert Corbet, sister of Annora, mother of Reginald, Earl of Cornwall by Henry I. This marriage accounts for the settlement of this family in Cornwall, ancestors of the Barons Botreaux.

Bott. William Bot occurs in Normandy 1195–8 (MRS); Walter Botte in Oxfordshire, 1189 (Rot. Pip.).

Bottin. Stephen, Gilbert, and William Botin occur in Normandy, 1180–95 (MRS). Alicia, widow of Thomas Buting or Boting, paid a fine in Lincoln (Roberts, Excerpt. ii. 363).

Botting, for BOTTIN.

Bottle. Roger Botel occurs in Normandy, 1195 (MRS).

Bottrell or Botterel, or De Botereaux, from Bottereaux, near Evreux. This family is frequently mentioned in the 12th cent., in England, as De Boterillis, and bore different arms from that of Botreaux of Cornwall. *See* BOTERILL.

Botevyle, from Bouteville near Carentan, Normandy. The name occurs in Battle Abbey Roll. Robert de Buteville held two fees in Bedford, 1165, and Robert de B. held in Norfolk (Lib. Niger). In 1316 John de Buteville was possessed of the lordship of Cheddingstone, Bucks (Palgr. Parl. Writs). The name of Butterfield is probably a form.

Bouche, from Buces, now Bucels, near Caen. Hugo de Bucis occurs in Normandy, 1180 (MRS); Gilbert de Buche in Surrey, 1190, RCR; and Roger Buche in Norfolk. John de Bucis had a suit in England t. John (Placit. Abbreviatio.).

Boucher, armorially identified with BOURCHIER.

Bouchett, a form of BOCKETT.

Bouffer, from Bouflers, near Abbeville. James Beauflour or Beaufleur was collector in the Port of London, 1322 (Palgr. Parl. Writs).

Boughey, armorially identified with BOWETT. The baronets Boughey are paternally descended from FLETCHER.

Boughton or Boveton, for Boventon, with which it was originally armorially identified, bearing three crescents or (Robson, arms of Boughton of Lawford). *See* BOYNTON. The baronets Boughton descend from hence.

Boulder, from Baudre, near St. Lo, in the Cotentin. Walter Bulder occurs in York, c. 1272, R.H.

Boully. *See* BULLEY.

Boult, armorially identified with BOLT.

Boum, armorially identified with Bohun of Midhurst. *See* BOON.

Boun, armorially identified with Bohun of Midhurst. *See* BOON.

Bound, the same as BOWNE (Lower).

Boundy, from Bondy, near St. Denis, Isle of France. Ralph de Bondé occurs in England, 1199, RCR. Walter Bonde in York, 1216 (Roberts, Excerpta).

Bour, armorially identified with Boun or Bohun. *See* BOON.

Bourchier, a form of Bousser or Bousseres, from Boursières, in Burgundy. Urso de Berseres held Senley, Bucks, 1086 (Domesd.). Sylvester de Bursers in 1165 held lands in Suffolk, of the honour of Clare (Lib. Niger). John de Busser was a justice in Essex and Hertford 1317, 1318; in 1321 a justice of the Common Pleas, and in 1324 Robert de Bousser was summoned from Essex to the Great Council, Westminster. The Lords Bourchier, Earls of Essex and Eu, descended from this family.

Bourdon. Geoffry, John, Arnald, Sylvester, Osbert, Ranulph Bordon, and others in Normandy, 1180–95 (MRS); William B. in Northants, Reginald and Roger in Gloucester 1199, RCR.

Bourke, for Burke or BURGH. The Earls of Mayo are of this name.

Bourlet or Borlet. *See* BARLETT.

Bourner or Burner, a form of Berner or BERNERS.

Bousfield, from Bousville or Bouville, near Pavilly, Normandy. Viger, Walter, Andrew, Serlo de Buesvilla or Buevilla, occur 1180–95 (MRS). In 1244 William de Boevill, son and heir of Ranulph de B., did homage for his lands in the bailifry of Newcastle-under-Line (Roberts, Excerpta, i. 417).

Boutcher, for BOUCHER.

Boutell. *See* BULTELL, and BOTTLE.

Boutroy. Alvaredus, John, and Roger Boteri occur in Normandy, 1180-95 (MRS); William Buteri or Butery in England t. John (Hardy, Rot. De Libertate).

Bouvier. Hugo Bouvier and John Bovier of Normandy, 1180-95 (MRS). *See* BOWYER.

Bouts. *See* BOOT.

Bovay, for BEAUVAIS.

Boville, a baronial family from Booville or Boeville, Normandy. William de B. had possessions in Suffolk, 1086 (Domesd.). Another William de B. occurs in Essex and Herts, 1130 (Rot. Pip.), and 1165 John de B. returned the fees of his barony in Suffolk as four, at which time Otuel de B. held in Essex from the honours of Mandeville and De Thame, and William de B. in Bucks from the Earl (Lib. Niger). William de B. of Norfolk and Suffolk had writs of military summons 1296 and 1300. The family was widely spread through England, and in 1165 held sixteen knights' fees. An eminent chief-justice bore the name.

Bovington or Boventon. *See* BOYNTON.

Bovington. *See* BOYNTON.

Bowack, for BOAG.

Bowcher, for BOURCHIER.

Bowden, from Bodin (Lower). Petrus Bodin occurs in Normandy, 12th cent. (Mém. Soc. Ant. Norm. v. 90).

Bowdler (from whom Hope-Bowdler and other places, Salop), a form of De Bollers or Budlers of Flanders. *See* BULLER.

Bowes, from Boves, Normandy. John de Bowes or Boves occurs in Normandy 1180 (MRS). Hugh de Boves, t. William I., had grants in Notts (Wiffen, Mem. Russell). Hugh

de Boves commanded in Poitou and Flanders for King John (Roger Wendover, iii. 287). William de Boves, of Notts, was dead 1219 (Roberts, Excerpta).

Bowett. Alexander and Unfrid Bouet occur in Normandy 1180-98 (MRS); Richard Bowet, one of the followers of John de Mowbray in pursuit of the Spencers, had pardon 1321 (Palgr. Parl. Writs).

Bowker. *See* BOOKER. There is an armorial relationship between the names.

Bowles or Buelles. *See* BOYLE. Hence W. Lisle Bowles the poet.

Bowless, for BOWLES.

Bowley, for Beaulieu (Lower). Simon de Bello Loco of Normandy 1180, Froger and Nicholas de B. 1198 (MRS). Alexander de Bello Loco paid a fine, Bedfordshire 1255 (Roberts, Excerpt.).

Bown, armorially identified with Bohun of Midhurst. *See* BOON.

Bowne. *See* BOWN.

Bowran, for Beaurain. *See* BOWRING.

Bowring, from Beaurain, near Cambrai, Flanders. Wybert de Beaurain occurs 1180-98 in Normandy (MRS). Hence the able writer Sir John Bowring. *See* BOWRAN.

Bowry. *See* BURY.

Bowser, armorially identified with BOURCHIER.

Bowtell, for BOUTELL.

Bowton, for BOUGHTON.

Bowyer, baronets. This family has been derived from the B.s of Knippersley, Stafford, but erroneously; for the arms entirely differ, nor is there any evidence of descent. The name, as appears by the arms, was originally Bouvier (Robson).

Hugo Bouvier and John B. were of Normandy, 1180-95 (MRS). Galfrid le Boyer occurs in Kent 1250 (Roberts, Excerpt.). In 1273 William B. was of Sussex (Plac. de quo War.). Ralph B. was M.P. for Arundel 1555, and John M.P. for Steyning 1547.

Bowyn, armorially identified with Bohun. *See* BOON.

Boyall, a form of BOYLE (Lower).

Boyce, a form of BOIS.

Boyd, a branch of the Breton family of Dinant. *See* STUART. It descends from a brother of Walter, first high steward of Scotland, and the Earls of Arran, Kilmarnock, and Errol were of the name.

Boydell, descended from Osborne Fitz-Tezzo, Baron of Dodelston, Cheshire, 1086, who appears to have been Norman, as the Church of Boisdel was given to St. Stephen's, Caen, 1082 by Serlo de Lingeure (Gall. Christ. xi. 74). Helto Fitz-Hugh, grandson of Osborne, had issue Hugh Boydel, ancestor of this family (Ormerod, Cheshire).

Boyes, for BOIS.

Boyle, from Boile, otherwise Boelles or Builles, now La Buille, near Rouen. Fulcher Budellus or de Buelles witnessed a charter of Odo of Bayeux 1074 (Mém. Soc. Ant. Norm. viii. 436). Bartholomew de Boel, Vidame of Chartres, was a leader in Palestine 1096 (Ord. Vitalis). William de Boel or Boeles, and Gilbert, occur in Normandy, 1180 (MRS). Osbert de Boel was of Lincoln, 1138 (Mon. ii. 326). Osbert de Boelles, 1165, held lands in Devon (Lib. Nig.), Lambert de B. in the eastern counties (Ib.). The family afterwards appears in Bedford, Warwick, Southants, Stafford, Rutland, Salop. In the latter, William de Buels (descended from Helias de Buel, living t. John) sold estates 1290 to Robert Burnel, Bishop of Bath (Eyton, Salop, iii. 203). His son William and his family settled in Hereford, and hence sprang Ludovic Buel or Boyle of Hereford (Harl. MS. 1545), ancestor of the Earls of Cork, Burlington, Orrery, Shannon, and other great houses.

Boyle, of Scotland, from Boyville of Normandy, otherwise Boeville (*See* BOUSFIELD). Many of the name occur in Normandy, 12th cent. William de Boeville (Bocville) was of Suffolk, 1086, William de Boeville of Essex and Herts, 1130, Helias de Boyvill and William de Buiville of Gloucester and Bucks, 1165 (Lib. Nig.). David de Boyvill of Scotland (12th cent.) witnessed a charter of William the Lion (Chart. Mailros.). Richard, the king's marshal, granted a fishery in the Tweed, held from David De Bouvele, his uncle (Ib.). The Earls of Glasgow of this line have adopted the arms of the English Boyles, as arms of affection, in addition to their own.

Boyles, for Buelles or BOYLE.

Boyls, for BOYLE.

Bogue, for Boges or BOGGIS.

Boynell, armorially identified with Boyville. *See* BOYLE of Scotland.

Boys, for BOIS.

Boyse, for BOIS.

Boyson. William, Ernald, Richard, Amfrid Buisson of Normandy lived 1180-95 (MRS). Roger Buzun occurs in Norfolk 1258 (Roberts, Excerpta).

Boynton, or De Brus, abbreviated from Boventon. *See* BRUCE. Robert

Fitz-Norman Bruis or Bruce of Boventon witnessed a charter of Ranulph de Merlai for St. Mary's, York, 1129 (Mon. ii. 1024). Norman, his father, was son of Robert de Brus, living 1086. The family of De Boventon or Boynton in the 12th and 13th centuries held a leading position in York, and from it descend the baronets Boynton.

Brabant, from the Netherlands. Arnold Braban (Brabant) of Stamford occurs 1297 (Palgr. Parl. Writs).

Brabazon, originally from Brabant. In 1198 Thomas Brabençon paid a fine of 50l. in Normandy, and Roger lent 15l. to the king (MRS). The family continued in Normandy (La Roque, Mais. Harcourt, i. 604). John Brabazon paid a fine Oxfordshire 1247 (Roberts, Excerpt.). Roger le Brabazon was a justiciary 1294–1316, and William de B. was M.P. for Leicestershire 1313, and in 1325 had a writ of military summons to pass into Gascoigne. From this family descended the Earls of Meath and the Baronets Brabazon.

Bracebridge or De Ardern. Ralph, son of William de Ardern, was Lord of Bracebridge, Lincoln, 13th cent. (Testa, 324). The family of Ardern or Arden was Norman, and came to England 1060. The Bracebridge family bear the arms of Arden or Ardern, being a fesse gules, with different tinctures of the field. In 1165 William de Arden held a fief Kent, Helias de Ardern Somerset, Thomas de Arden Essex (Lib. Nig.). In 13th cent. Ralph de A. of Essex held a fee from the honour of Peverill of London (Testa, 364). He was probably the same who held Bracebridge. That this family was connected with the Eastern Counties

appears from the marriage of William de Criketot, Baron of Ixworth, Suffolk, to the dau. of John Bracebrigge (Mon. ii. 184). The latter was living 1305 (Mon. ii. 327).

Brace, from BRACEY.

Bracey, from Brécy, near Caen. Henry and Hamelin de Brecie occur in Normandy 1180-95 (MRS.). Radulphus de Braceio occurs in a Norman charter 1082 (Gall. Christ. xi. 86). William, his son, held Wisteston, Cheshire, and Robert de Bracy, the grandson, held 8 knights' fees in that county from Robert Malbanc, his uncle (Ormerod, iii. 177). This Cheshire family had many branches, from one of which descend the Brasseys now existing, and Brassey the eminent engineer.

Bracher. Alan, Emma, Richard, and Alexander Bracheor occur in Normandy 1180–95 (MRS). *See* BRASIER.

Brack, for Brac. *See* BRAKE.

Bragge, for Brac. *See* BRAKE.

Brain, from Brain, Anjou. Matthew de Brain occurs in Yorkshire 1199 (RCR).

Braines, for BRAIN.

Brake. Eudo and Evain de Bras occur in Normandy 1180–96 (MRS). Richard de la Brache in Bedford 1199 (RCR).

Bran, for BRAND.

Branch, from St. Denis de Branche, Normandy. Roger Branche was a benefactor to Marrig Priory, York (Mon. i. 485). Richard B. witnessed a charter of Galfrid de Saukeville (ii. 637). William B. was of Suffolk 1219 (Roberts, Excerpt.), and Sir William B. of Somerset 1316 (Palgr. Parl. Writs).

Brand. Walter Brandus held lands by knight service in the Viscounty of Caen 1165 (Feod. Norm.

Ducheane). William Brant had estates Norfolk 1086. Matthew Brand 1223 had custody of the heir of Hugo de Bixe (Roberts, Excerpt.). Robert B. (13th cent.) possessed estates in Oxford (Testa). Simon Brand was of Hertfordshire 1325, from whom descended the Lords Dacre of this name.

Brandram. William Brandram occurs in Normandy 1198 (MRS).

Brant. See BRAND.

Brasier. William Braisier paid a fine Normandy 1180, and soon after William de Neelfa was a fugitive for slaying him (MRS). The same name occurs as 'Bracheor.' See BRACHER.

Brasil, from Bresles near Beauvais. Agemund de Bresel paid an amercement in Hants 1203 (Rot. Canc.). .

Brass, for BRACE.

Brassey. See BRACEY.

Bratt, armorially identified with BRETT.

Braund, for BRAND.

Brawn, for BRAUND.

Bray, from Bray, near Evreux, Normandy. William de Bray occurs 1189–95 (MRS). Milo de Brai, father of Hugh Trussel, m., c. 1070, Litheuil, Viscountess of Troyes, and, c. 1064, founded Longport Abbey, Normandy (Ord. Vit., transl. by Forester, iii. 78). Milo de B., his son, was a crusader 1096 (Ord. Vit.). In 1148 Richard de Braio held lands at Winchester from the Bishop (Wint. Domesd.). The De Brais possessed estates in Cambridge and Bedford 1165 (Lib. Nig.). A branch was seated in Devon 13th cent. The Lords Bray descended from this house, and Sir Reginald Bray, the eminent architect, temp. Henry VII.

172

Brayne. See BRAIN.

Brasier. See BRASIER.

Brasill, for BRASILL.

Breache. See BRACHE.

Breary, or De Brereto, from Breuery, near Vesoul, France. The arms are preserved (Robson).

Breeks, for BRAKE.

Brees. See BREESE.

Breese, a form of BRICE, being the Norman-French pronunciation.

Breeze. See BREESE.

Brunker, armorially identified with BROUNKER.

Bren, armorially identified with BREND.

Brench, for BRANCH.

Brend, armorially identified with BRAND.

Brennard, for BURNARD.

Breton, from Bretagne. Many families bore the name; of which were the baronial families of Breton of Devon, of Gloucester, of Bucks, of Lincoln, and of Essex, respectively. Sire John Breton, of Sporle, Essex, sat in Parliament as a baron, 1298.

Brett, from Brette in Maine, or possibly short for Breton. Thurstan Bret witnessed a charter of Roger Earl of Hereford t. Henry II. (Mon. i. 321). Ranulph le Bret witnessed a charter t. Stephen (i. 440). Sire John and Sire Richard B. witnessed (13th cent.) charters of Brecknock Priory. In 1309–17 Geoffry le Bret was one of the barons of Ireland, and Sir John le Bret 1321 had pardon as a follower of the Mortimers (Palgr. Parl. Writs).

Brettell. Gaufrid de Braitells witnessed a Norman charter in 1126 (MSAN. v. 197).

Brettell, lords of Gremonville in Normandy (Des Bois). Robert de

Bretel occurs in Kent, 1130 (Rot. Pip.), and Maurice de Britell was Lord of Stapleton and other lands in Dorset 1316 (Palgr. Parl. Writs). Bretel is near Alençon.

Brettle, for BRETTELL.

Breun, or Brewn, for Brun. *See* BROWN.

Brew, one of the forms of Breux, Brews, or Braiose. *See* BREWIS.

Brewer. 1. from Brovera or Brueria, now Breviare near Caen; a family seated in Devon at the Conquest, and from which descended Henry de Briwere, t. Stephen; Henry B., who held five fees in Devon 1165; and William Briwere, a great baron temp. John. William B. in 1165 was a baron in Notts, and Ralph B. had estates Leicester. 2. from the English translation of Braceator or Braceor. *See* BRAZIER, BRACHER.

Brewhouse, for BREWIS, or De Braiose.

Brewis, or De Braiose, a baronial family, from Braiose, near Argentan, Normandy. The name is frequently mentioned 1180–98 in Normandy (MRS). William de Braiose founded the Abbey of Braiose t. William I. (Mém. Soc. Ant. Norm. xxii. 81, &c.) He was at the battle of Hastings, and made grants to St: Florent, Saumur. Gunnora, his mother, 1082 held lands from Hugo Pincerna and Roger de Cuilli (Gall. Christ. xi. 71). Philip, his son, a powerful baron in Normandy, supported Rufus (Ord. Vit.). From him descended the great house of Braose, barons of Bramber, Brecknock, Gower, Totness, and Limerick in Ireland, and numerous branches of which existed in Sussex, Bedford, Hants, Norfolk, Suffolk, Wales, and elsewhere. The name was frequently written Breose,

Brewes, and Brewis, and is totally different from that of Bruce or Brus, with which it has often been confounded.

Brewn. *See* BREUN.

Brewse. *See* BREWIS.

Brian, armorially identified with BRYAN.

Briant, for Breaunt, Breant, or Breauté, near Havre. The family remained in Normandy 16th cent. (La Roque, Mais. Harc. ii. 1583–4) as Viscounts of Holot. Fulco de Breauté or de Brent was of great power temp. Henry III. (Roger Wendover).

Brice, from St. Brice, near Avranches, Normandy. Robert de St. Brice and the fief of St. Brice are mentioned in Normandy 1180 (MRS). William de St. Bricio took the oaths of allegiance in Normandy to Philip Augustus.

Brickdale, from Briquedale, Normandy, held by Sire Robert de Piessi, t. Philip Augustus. The English family is said to take its name from Brickdale, Lancashire, but I have been unable to ascertain the existence of such a place in England.

Bride, or St. Bride, or St. Bridget. *See* BRIDGETT.

Bridge, or de Ponte. Numerous families of the name occur in Normandy 1180–98 (MRS), and also in England about the same time (RCR).

Bridges, or De Pontibus, or Des Ponts, from Ponts in the Cotentin, Normandy. John de Pontibus occurs in Normandy 1180–95 (MRS); Richard de Puns in Middlesex c. 1272 (RH), and Richard de P. as Viscount of Middlesex 1328 (Palgr. Parl. Writs). The name in **the**

173

13th cent. was usually translated into Bridges.

Bridgett, for Brichet. *See* BRIETT.

Brient, for Brent, or BRIANT.

Brier. *See* BRYER.

Briett. Wimond Brichet occurs in Normandy 1180 (MRS); Ralph de Brecet in England c. 1272 (RH). Of the family of Briset or Bricet were Ralph Briset t. William I., and Jordan B., a great baron, who founded St. John's, Clerkenwell, 1100, and d. 1110, leaving two daughters, his heirs.

Briley, from Broilly near Valognes, Normandy. William de Broilleio occurs in the Duchy 1180-95 (MRS). Osbern de Broily held lands in Bedford 1086, Waleran de Bruellio in Normandy 1165, Robert de Bruilli in 1178 witnessed the charter of Lindores, Scotland (Mon. ii. 1052), Simon de B. held lands in Warwick (Testa), and John de Bruilly, 1324, was summoned to a great council, Westminster.

Brind, armorially identified with BREND.

Brine, for Broyne, Brun, or BROWNE.

Brinson, or De Briançon, from the place so named in Dauphiné. Thomas de Briançon occurs in London and Middlesex 1189 (Rot. Pip.). Giles de Brianzon was returned for Essex and Sussex to the great Council 1324, and had a writ of summons to pass into Guienne 1325, under command of Earl Warrenne, and was commissioner of array in Surrey and Sussex (Palgr. Parl. Writs).

Britain, for Breton (Lower).

Brittain, for BRITAIN.

Brittan, for BRITAIN.

174

Britten, for BRITAIN.

Britton, for BRETON.

Brixey, from Brézé, Anjou. Richard de Brexes is mentioned in Lancashire 1199, RCR.

Brize, for BRICE.

Broach, for BROCK.

Brock, from Broc, Anjou. Nigel, Ranulph, and Robert de Broc are mentioned in England 1189 (Rot. Pip.), and thenceforward the name frequently occurs.

Brookes, for BROCK or Broc (Lower).

Broke, for BROCK or BROC (Lower).

Brond, for BRAND.

Brounker, from Broncort, near Langres, France. Roger Bruncort occurs in Normandy 1199, in the household of King John; Robert Bruncorte in 1180, MRS. This may be the same name as Bruencort and Brucort, which repeatedly occurs 1180-96 in Normandy. The Viscounts Brounker, in Ireland, were of this family.

Brontoft, from Bernetôt, near Yvetot. John de Bernetôt held lands in Normandy, t. Phil. Augustus, MSAN, xv. 172. Robert de B. had a fief Notts 1165 (Lib. Nig.). Richard de Barneton in Essex, 13th cent. (Testa). Nicholas de Burnetoft was appointed to collect customs Hartlepool, 1329 (Rot. Orig. ii. 43). In 1347 Henry Bernetoft was a benefactor to Tinmouth (Inq. p. m. ii. 146). The name of Bernetot in Normandy at length changed to Bernadotte. Hence the royal family of Sweden.

Brook, for BROKE (Lower).

Brooks, for BROCK (Lower).

Brookes, for BROKE (Lower).

Broughton, a branch of VERNON

(Lower). Robert Fitz-Adam and Walter Turstain held Brocton, Stafford (13th cent.), from the see of Chester (Testa). The arms concur with the descent from Vernon.

Broun. *See* BROWN, BROWNE.

Brown. Gilbert le Brun, and William, Normandy 1180–95, MRS. The name Brunus, or le Brun, frequently occurs in Normandy 1180–98, MRS; but it was so frequent in England in the next century (RH), that it probably included other families besides Norman, which it would be difficult to discriminate without extensive research. Some will be noticed under BROWNE.

Browne, a family evidently of foreign descent, one of whom, Hamo le Brun, was Lord of Stapleford and Tarvin, Cheshire, t. Henry II. This line is armorially connected with an Irish line, of whom William Brone witnessed the charter of Dunbrody 1178 (Mon. ii. 1027). Nigel le Brun had a writ of military summons 1309, and Fremond Bruyn was one of the Barons of Ireland 1315–17 (Palgr. Parl. Writs). From this line descend the Lords Oranmore.

Browne. Turulph, a companion of Rollo, obtained, 912, the barony of La Ferté (Firmitas), near Evreux, now la Ferté-Fresnel. His grandson of the same name lived t. Rich. I. (La Roque). Radulphus de la Ferté lived before 1000. William, his son, gave the forest of Notre Dame des Bois to St. Evroult Abbey. Hugh de la Ferté is mentioned by Wace at Hastings. Richard de la F. accompanied Robert of Normandy to Palestine 1096, and had eight sons, the youngest of whom, Gamel de la Ferté, surnamed le Brun, settled in Cumberland, where he had baronial

grants from Waldeve Fitz-Gospatric, t. Henry I. The family of De La Ferté, also called le Brun, long flourished in Cumberland, and its name gradually changed to Broyne, Broun, and Browne. Anthony, younger son of Robert le Broune, M.P. for Cumberland 1317–1339, was father of Robert, from whom descended the Marquises of Sligo, Barons Kilmaine, and Viscounts Montague.

Brownlow. 1. *See* CUST. 2. The Brownlows, Lords Lurgan (originally 'Chamberlain'), bear the arms of the De Tankervilles, Chamberlains of Normandy. *See* CHAMBERLAIN.

Brownett. Robert Brunet occurs in the Duchy of Normandy 1209.

Bruce, from the Castle of Brus or Bruis, now Brix, near Cherbourg, where remain the ruins of an extensive fortress built by Adam de Brus in the 11th cent. (De Gerville, Anc. Chateaux). Hence the Kings of Scotland, the Earls of Elgin, Barons Burleigh, Baronets Bruce, &c. The Castle of Brix was part of the ducal demesne 1026, when it formed part of the dowry granted to Judith, consort of Duke Richard III. (Stapleton, Mag. Rog. Scac. Norm.); and therefore the name of Bruce must have arisen later.

Brudenell, or De Bretignolles, from B. near Alençon, Normandy, which was held by the service of castle-guard at Gisors or Alençon (MSAN, xv. 178). Hugo de Bretinolles, t. Henry I., held a knight's fee in Berks, which he still held 1165 (Lib. Niger). Gilbert de Bretinolles, 1218, held Sandon, Berks, from the honour of Gloucester (Roberts, Excerpta, i. 22). William de B. held from Simon de Montfort,

Earl of Leicester, the same fee (Testa), and another at Colethorp, in the same county (Ib.); and in 1203 had a writ of summons to attend with his military array at Oxford. From this family descended Sire Robert Brudenell, Chief Justice of the Common Pleas 1520, ancestor of the Earls of Cardigan and Marquises of Ailesbury. The change of the name from Bretignolles to Bredenell, Bredenhill, and Brudenel, appears from the records, but space forbids insertion of the particulars.

Bruen, armorially identified with BRUIN.

Bruin, armorially identified with Brun, le Brun, or Browne, of Cheshire.

Brunes, for Brun, now BROWN.

Bruns. *See* BRUNES.

Brus. *See* BRUCE.

Brush. Robert Bros occurs in Normandy 1180, Richard Broche 1198 (MRS).

Brushett. Chapon Broste occurs in Normandy 1198 (MRS); William Bruast in England 1199 (RCR).

Bryan, or Brionne, from Brionne, Normandy, a branch of the Counts of Brionne, and the Earls of Clare and Hertford, descended from Gilbert, Count of Brionne, son of Richard I. of Normandy. Wido de Brionne, an ancestor of this branch, acquired a seigneury in Wales, c. 1090. Baldwin de B. was Viscount of Devon t. Will. I., and Wido de Brionne, of the Welsh line, held five fees of the barony of Oakhampton, Devon, 1165. Wido de Brionne had a military writ of summons, 1259. The name then changed to Bryan, and the Barons Bryan inherited it.

Bryan, for BRYER.

Bryant, for BRIANT.

Bryce, armorially identified with BRUCE or Bruse.

Bryon, armorially identified with BRYAN.

Bryer, for BREWER (Lower).

Bryer. *See* BRIAR.

Bryett. *See* BRIETT.

Bryson. *See* BRISON.

Buck. Radulphus de Bucca occurs in Normandy 1180 (MRS); Ursell, Ranulph, and Racinus de Buc in England 1199 (RCR). Hence the Baronets Buck, now Stukely.

Buck. Walter le Boc, Normandy, 1198 (MRS).

Buckett. *See* BOCKETT.

Buckland, or De Dinan, a branch of the house of Dinant, Lords of Buckland, Devon. Also a family of uncertain, but foreign origin, raised to baronial dignity by Henry I. Of the former probably was the celebrated geologist Buckland.

Buckle, or Buckell, identified by its arms, a chevron, with BUSHELL. Hence the able writer Buckle.

Buckquett. *See* BUCKETT.

Buckroll, or De Berkerolles, from Boquerelles or Bouqueroles, Normandy, held from the Honour of Breteuil, t. Philip-Augustus, by William de Boqueroles.

Budden, for Bodin. *See* BOWDEN.

Buddle, for BUDELL.

Budell, armorially identified with BOYDEL. Reginald Budell occurs in Salop, c. 1272 (RH).

Budgell, for BUSHELL.

Budgen, or De Bouchain, from Bouchaine, near Douay. Andreas de Bucca uncta in 1130 had lands valued at 20*l.*, probably in Middlesex (Rot. Pip.).

Budgett, for BUCKETT.

Buels. *See* BOYLE.

Buffrey, or Beaupré (with which it is armorially identified), or Beaupreau, from Anjóu. This family long remained in Norfolk and Devon.

Buggins. Herebertus Bogin occurs in Normandy 1180 (MRS), Robert Bogun in Derby 1270. (Roberts, Excerpt.).

Bugler. Walter and Waldin le Bugle, Norm. 1180–98 (MRS); Odo le Bouglier, Norm. 1198 (MRS).

Buist. Ernaud and Roger Boiste (or Buiste) occur in Normandy 1198 (MRS).

Bulbic, from Bolbec near Dieppe, a baronial family. Osborne Giffard, baron of Bolbec, m. c. 960 Ameline, sister of the Duchess Gunnora of Normandy, and had 1, Walter; 2, Geoffry, ancestor of the viscounts of Arques and Rouen. *See* SAVILLE, ARCH.

Walter was ancestor of Walter Giffard, who came to England 1066, and became Earl of Buckingham. His brother, Hugh de Bolbec, was a baron in Bucks, &c., 1086 (Domesd.). This barony is said by Dugdale (Bar. i. 452) to have passed to Isabel, d. of Walter, son of Hugh; but two generations have been omitted, for Isabel was living t. Henry III. Hugh de Bolbec possessed a barony in Northumberland by gift of Henry I. From him descended Walter de B., who held the barony 1165 (Lib. Niger). Walter, his son or grandson, d. c. 1205, leaving Hugh his brother and heir, whose son John d. 1262, leaving coheiresses (Dugd.; Hodgson, Northumberland). The Northumberland branch appears also to have possessed the barony in Bucks, &c.

Buley, or Bewley, from Beaulieu. *See* BOWLEY.

Bulgin, a form of BUDGEN.

Bullard, a form of Pullard, or POLLARD.

Bullas, for Bullers or BULLER.

Bullen, armorially identified with BOLEYN.

Buller, or De Bollers. The barony of Boulers or Boularia was one of the principal fiefs of Flanders, and belonged to a powerful race of nobles. Stephen de Boularia, 1096, witnessed a charter of Manasses, bishop of Cambray, and joined in the First Crusade (Alb. Miræi, Opera Diplom. i. 166). Baldwin de Bollers, his son, received from Henry I. the barony of Montgomery with the hand of Sybil de Falaise, his niece (Dugd. Bar.). He had 1, Baldwin, with whose descendants the barony remained till the 13th cent.; 2, Stephen de Bullers, father of Robert de Bullers, who appears to have had possessions in Somerset, and 1194 had a suit with the Abbot of Ford (RCR i.). His son or grandson was seated at Wood, Somerset, t. Edw. III., and was ancestor of the Bullers of Wood (Visitation, Somerset, 1623). From this family descended the Bullers of Devon and Cornwall, and the Lords Churston.

Bullet. Berenger and Radulphus Bulete occur in Normandy, 1180, (MRS); Josceline Bolet, 1207, held lands at Cauquenville, Normandy.

Bullions, for Bulloigne or Boleyne.

Bulley, for Builly. *See* BINGHAM.

Bullis, for Buelles. *See* BOYLE.

Bullivant, or Bonenfant. John, William, Robert, Geoffry Bonenfant occur in Normandy, t. Henry V.,

Stephen Bonenfant in Cambridge, 1253 (Roberts, Excerpta).

Bullon, a form of Bullen or Bo-LEYN.

Bult, for BOLT.

Bulteel, or Buletel, for BUTELL. Beatrix and Michael Buletel possessed lands in Essex, t. Henry III. (Placit. Abbrev.), as did Agnes Buletel in Cambridge, c. 1272 (RH).

Bulwer. *See* WIGGETT.

Bumpus, from Boneboz, Normandy, held from the Earls of Mellent. Reginald, Robert, William de Boneboz occur in Normandy, 1198 (MRS). Gilbert de B. was a benefactor to Dunstable Priory; Waleran, Earl of Mellent, witnessing the charter (Mon. ii. 134).

Bumpus, for BOMPAS.

Bunbury, a well known branch of the family of De St. Pierre of Normandy (Ormerod, Cheshire). Hence the Baronets Bunbury.

Bunce, for BENCE.

Bunche, for BENCE.

Bunge, for BYNG.

Bunker, for Boncœur (Lower). In 1259 the King granted to William Boncuor thirty librates of land (Roberts, Excerpta).

Bunn, from Le Bon (Lower).

Bunyard. *See* BANYARD.

Burbury, from Barbery, Normandy. The abbey of Barbery was in that Duchy, and Robert Barbery occurs there, t. Henry V.

Burchael, armorially identified with BURCHELL.

Burchell. This family, probably foreign, descends from Sir Humphry Burghill or Burchell, a companion of Bernard de Neumarché in the conquest of Brecknock, 1088 (Jones, Brecknock, i. 92). About 1150

178

William de Burchall was witness to a gift to Hereford Abbey; and later, David de Burchall. *See* Jones (Brecknock, ii. 439-442).

Burd, for BURT.

Burden. *See* BURDON.

Burdett. This family descends from the Bordets, Lords of Cuilly, Normandy, of whom Robert Bordet I., with his son Robert II., witnessed a charter of the Count of Anjou before the Norman Conquest. Robert II. and his brother Hugh were seated in England at the Conquest. From the former descended the house of De Cuilly (*see* COLLEY-WELLESLEY), and from the latter the Burdetts Baronets and Baroness Burdett-Coutts.

Burdge, for BURGE.

Burdon. Petrus Burdonius witnessed a Norman charter, 1126 (MSAN, v. 197). Galfrid, John, Ernald, Sylvester Bordon and others occur in Normandy, 1180-98 (MRS). Arnulph Burdin held a mansion at Winchester, 1148 (Wint. Domesd.). Ralph Bourdon paid a fine in Lincoln, 1203 (Rot. Canc.). In 1255 Robert Borden was of Yorkshire (Roberts, Excerpta).

Burfield, or De Bereville. William de Bareville occurs in Normandy, 1183; Robert and Simon de Bereville in England, 1199 (MRS and RCR). The name changes sometimes to Berewell.

Burge, armorially identified with BURGES.

Burges. Simon de Borgeis occurs in Normandy, 1195; Ralph, Roger, William Burgensis, 1198 (MRS).

Burgess. *See* BURGES.

Burgh, or De Burgh. William Fitz-Adelm or Adeline, t. Henry II., the ancestor of this house, was son of Adelelm, Adeline, Adelm, or Alelm of Aldfield in Yorkshire, younger brother of Eustace Fitz-John, Baron of Alnwick, and son of John Fitz-Ponce, brother of Serlo de Burgh, who was of the house of Fitz-Ponce or De Pons. (*See* CLIF-FORD, VESCI.) Adelm of Aldfield probably bore the name of De Burgh. He with Ralph his son gave lands at Fountains to the Abbey, which gift was confirmed by Roger de Mowbray (Burton, Mon. Ebor. 166). Ralph Fitz-Adelin held one fee in Yorkshire from Mowbray, 1165 (Lib. Niger), and witnessed a charter of his brother William Fitz-Adeline or Adelm to the Knights Hospitallers (Mon. i. 510); and as Ralph de Burgo, t. Henry II., witnessed a charter of Trentham Priory (Mon. ii. 261). From him descended Sir Alan de Aldfield, who confirmed his gifts to Fountains (Burton, Mon. Ebor. 166). William Fitz-Adelm, the brother of Ralph de Aldfield, appears first in 1152 as witness to a charter of Henry de Lacy, Baron of Pontefract, York, and in 1165 as holding one fee from Lacy of Pontefract (Lib. Niger), and a barony of three fees in Hants and Essex, with the office of marshal to the king, which he had obtained by m. with the dau. of Robert Doisnell (Ibid.). This family adopted the arms borne by the elder line De Vesci, descended from Eustace Fitz-John, viz., a cross. From it descended the Earls of Ulster, Earls and Marquises of Clanricarde, Earls of Mayo, &c.

Burghes. *See* BURGES.

Burgin. *See* BURGOYNE.

Burgon. *See* BURGOYNE.

Burgoyne, or De Bourgogne, probably a Gothic family from Burgundy. In 1083 Walter Burgundiensis or Borgoin held lands in Devon (Ex. Domesd. 361). Hugh de Burgon of Essex, from whom Woodham Priory held lands, 1198 (Mon. i. 889), was one of twelve knights summoned for a trial in Norfolk, 1200 (RCR.) In 1318 Bartholomew de Burgoyne was of Norfolk (PPW). The Bedfordshire Baronets Burgoyne were probably a branch of the Norfolk line.

Burke. *See* BURGH.

Burl, for Borel. Ralph, Ranulph, Renauld Borel, and others of the name, occur in Normandy, 1180-98 (MRS). *See* BURRELL.

Burley. Roger de Burlie occurs in Normandy, 1198 (MRS).

Burls, for BURL.

Burnall, or Burnell. *See* ACTON.

Burnand, a form of BURNARD.

Burnard. In 1086 Burnard (the Christian name omitted) held lands in Bedford from William, Count of Eu. This family long remained of importance. Roger Burnard (13th cent.) held four knights' fees in Bedford (Testa).

Burnett, the Scottish form of BURNARD. The family descends from Roger de Burnard, who witnessed the foundation charter of Kelso, 1128. The name continued Burnard till 1409, when Robert bore the name of Burnet (Douglas, Baronage, Scotl., i. 41). Hence the Baronets Burnet, and the celebrated writer and politician Bishop Burnet of Salisbury.

Burney, a form of Bernay (Lower). *See* BERNEY.

Burr. Robert, Roger, and Peter Burre occur in Normandy, 1180-98

Stephen Bonenfant in Cambridge, 1253 (Roberts, Excerpta).

Bullon, a form of Bullen or Boleyn.

Bult, for Bolt.

Bulteel, or Buletel, for Butell. Beatrix and Michael Buletel possessed lands in Essex, t. Henry III. (Placit. Abbrev.), as did Agnes Buletel in Cambridge, c. 1272 (RH).

Bulwer. *See* Wiggett.

Bumpus, from Boneboz, Normandy, held from the Earls of Mellent. Reginald, Robert, William de Boneboz occur in Normandy, 1ꞌ (MRS). Gilbert de B. was a ꞌ factor to Dunstable Priory; W Earl of Mellent, witne charter (Mon. ii. 134).

Bumpus, for Bomp

Bunbury, a weꞌ   the of the family of   ulloughby Normandy (ꞌ .ae Baronets Bur-
Hence the P

Bunce.

Bun for Burrell.

Bu for Burrell.

7 for Beaurain. *See* Bow-

J   1, for Burgh; 2, for

Burir.

Burroughs. *See* Burrough.

Burrowes. *See* Burrough.

Burry, armorially identified with Burye.

Bursell, or Burahell, armorially identified with Bushell.

Bursill, for Bursell.

Burt. William Berte paid a fine in the bailifry of Mortaine, Normandy, 1203 (MRS). John Berte occurs in Wilts, Richard and Roger B. in Suffolk and Oxford, c. 1272 (RH).

Burton, or De Richmond. This is a branch of the Musards, Barons

William de Burchall was wit a gift to Hereford Abbey; ꞌ David de Burchall. (Brecknock, ii. 439-44ꞌ

Burd, for Burt.

Burden. *See* ꞋT

Burdett. T꜔ . from the BꞋ Normandy L, with ꞌ a chꞋ befꞋ h

ꞋI Ꞌ
          n, near ꞌ
-          .dson, Roald ꞌ.,
          Priory, 1152 (Mon.
          ꞏs son Alan, Constable
          .ꞏond, witnessed a charter of
          ꞏe Conan of Bretagne, t. Henry
ꞏI. (Mon. ii. 883, 903). From him descended Roald III, Constable of R., t. Henry III., whose son Roald IV., De Richmond or De Burton, performed military service for the Archbishop of York in the Welsh war, 1282 (PPW). Sir Thomas de Richmond, 1300, was returned as holding above 40l. per ann., and was summoned by writ for the Scottish war. His son Thomas de Burton, Constable of Richmond, t. Edw. III., sold his estates to Lord Scrope of Bolton (Gale, Registr. Appendix). From his brothers descended the families of Burton and Richmond, in Yorkshire, who bore a cross between four roses or mullets. Sylvan, one brother, was father of Thomas de Burton, who gave lands to Fountains (Burton, Mon. Ebor. 183). His grandson Sir Edward Burton acquired Longnor, Salop, t. Edward IV., and from him descended the Burtons of Longnor, and their branches

...on bore the same name,
the feudal dignity of
...e Butlers of Corn-
...descended from
...of Mortaine
...m I.; the
...m Hugo
... Eudo
... ...;

...ma...
...This famil...
...d with that of
...arleville.

...n Bures, near Rouen.
...nulph, Jordan de Bures,
...ue Lordship of Bures occur in
...ormandy, 1180-95 (MRS). Sire
John de Bures, 1316-26, possessed
four manors in Berks, four in
Gloucester, six in Somerset; and
was chief commissioner of array in
Gloucester, Oxford, and Berks (Palgr.
Parl. Writs).

Busain, from Buisson, in the
Cotentin. William, Arnold, Amfrid
de Buisson occur in Normandy,
1180-95 (MRS). Roger Buzun
gave his tithes to Thetford Priory,
1103 (Mon. i. 665). William B. in
1165 held nine knights' fees, Devon,
of the honour of Totness. The name
long continued of great eminence.

Busfield, a form of BOSVILLE.

Buscall, for BUSHELL.

Bushe. Hugh de Bucis occurs
in Normandy 1180 (MRS); Aluric
de Busch in Hertford 1086 (Domesd.). William de la Bosche
held a knight's fee, Dorset, of
the honour of Mortaine, 13th cent.
(Testa). Robert Bouche in 1311
M.P. for Wiltshire.

Salop 1199 (RCR). The family
gave its name to Leighton Buzzard,
Bedfordshire.

Byars. See BYERS.

Byard, for Biars. See AVENEL.

Byass, for BYARS.

Byatt, for BYARD.

Byers or De Biars (Lower). See
AVENEL. The gallant General Sir
William Byers was of this name.

Byles, armorially identified with
...LE. A distinguished judge bears
...me.

...from Binge-Gerault, Nor-
...ntioned in a charter of
...Henry de Ferrers (Mém.
...v. 129). In 1191
The nam... ...nessed a charter
Normandy 110... ...ayeux, execu-
cent., Leicester 13th... ...t Reginald
In 1300, Sir Hugh de ... ...obert B.
Lincoln, bore arg. three ba... ... In

Butcher, for BOURCHIER... ...in

Butfield, for BOUTWYLE.

Butieux, for Botreaux. See BOT-
TERELL.

Butler, or De Glanville. This
family derives its name from Theobald Walter,' the first butler of
Ireland, to whom that dignity and
vast estates were granted by Henry
II. He also possessed the barony of
Amounderness, Lancashire, which
he held 1165 by service of one
knight (Lib. Nig.). By his charters
to Cokersand, Lancashire, and
Wotheny, Limerick, it appears that
Hervey Walter was his father;
Hubert W., Archbishop of Canterbury, his brother; and Ranulph de
Glanville, the justiciary, his dear
friend (Mon. ii. 631, 1054).

Hervey Walter, his father, 1171
granted lands to Butley Priory, Suffolk (founded by Ranulph de Glanville, at the chief seat of the G.s),
for the souls of 'our ancestors,' i.e.,

of Ranulph and himself (Mon. Angl. ii. 245); and he is a witness, as Hervey de Glanville, to the foundation charter (Ib.). In the reign of Stephen he witnessed a charter of Bartholomew de Glanville for Bromholm Priory. T.|Henry III. a noble granted lands to St. Osyth's, Essex, for the soul of Hervey de Glanville, his wife's grandfather (Mon. ii. 183); and in 1155 Hervey de Glanville and Ranulph de G. witnessed the foundation charter of Snapes, Essex (Mon. ii. 894).

Hervey Walter, or De Glanville, had relinquished his barony of Amounderness to his son Theobald before 1165; at which time as Hervey de Glanville he held one fee in Suffolk from the See of Ely (Lib. Nig.).

He was son of another Herveius Walter, who granted lands in Rouchcliffe, Thistleton, Greenhale, Lancashire, to Ormus, son of Magnus (Testa, 403), which Ormus witnessed a charter of Richard Bussel, baron of Penwortham (Mon. i. 301). He appears as Hervey de Glanville in the foundation charter of Eye by Robert Malet, early t. Henry I. (Mon. i. 357).

Walter (de Glanville), his father, appears 1086 as owner of estates in Lailand, Lancashire (Domesd.). He is styled in a charter of Warin Bussel, baron of Penwortham, granted to Evesham Abbey, 'his knight' (Mon. Angl.); and no doubt held from him Rouchcliffe, Weeton, &c., which descended to his posterity (Baines, Lanc. i. 117; Testa, 411).

Walter's descendants, the Butlers, bore the arms of De Glanville: a chief indented; merely varying the tinctures. This family was of Glan-

182

ville, near Caen. About 1064 Rainald de Glanville witnessed a charter of Roger de Mowbray in favour of Holy Trinity, Caen (Gall. Christ. xi. 60, Instr.), and had issue, 1, Robert de Glanville, who, in 1086, had great possessions in Suffolk, and was ancestor of William de G., whose barony in Suffolk, 1165, consisted of nine and a half fees; 2, Walter, ancestor of the Butlers.

Hence spring the Marquises of Ormond, Earls of Carrick, Viscounts Mountgarret, Barons Dunboyne, &c.

Butler, Earls of Lanesborough, descended from Hugo Pincerna, feudal Butler of the Counts of Mellent, who accompanied the Count of Mellent 1066, and in 1086 was a baron in Bedford (Domesd.). The family were hereditary butlers of the Earls of Leicester and Mellent. Ralph Pincerna, son of Hugo, in 1130 had custody of the E. of Mellent's estates (Rot. Pip.). Henry I. confirmed his gifts to Kenilworth Priory (Mon. ii. 115, 118, 134). Ralph, his son, was baron of Oversley, and from him descended the barons of Wemme. John, son of Robert Pincerna, son of Ralph (Mon. Angl. ii. 309), held lands in Bedford 1165. Ralph le Botiler, of Bedford, c. 1300, m. Hawisia Gobiun, of the same county (Roberts, Cal. Gen.). In 1376 John B. m. Isolda Gobiun, heiress of Wareesley, Hunts, where he resided.(Lodge, Irish Peerage). From him descended the B.s of Wareesley; one of whom, George B., of Fen Drayton, Cambridge, was lineal ancestor of the Earls of Lanesborough. The arms of this family in various branches are those of the B.s of Wemme.

Butler. Several other families

of distinction bore the same name, derived from the feudal dignity of Pincerna, viz., the Butlers of Cornwall and Kent, descended from Alured, feudal butler of Mortaine and Cornwall, t. William I.; the Butlers of Essex, derived from Hugo Pincerna, feudal butler of Eudo Dapifer, a great baron t. William I.; the Butlers, Barons of Warrington, feudal butlers of Chester, and probably a branch of the houses of Venables and Grosvenor; the Butlers of Bramfield, a branch of the Barons of Wemme, and others; the particulars of which families would occupy too much space.

Butlin, for Butvilein or Boutvileyn (Lower). Ralph, Herbert, Robert, and William Botevilain occur in Normandy 1180-98 (MRS); Robert B. in Bedford 1199 (RCR). This family was long of great consequence in England.

Butt, for BOTT. Roger But was Viscount of Southampton 1203 (Hardy, Obl. et Fin. 405).

Butter. Ralph and Sylvester Butor occur in Normandy 1198 (MRS).

Butterfield, for BOTEVYLE.

Butters, for BUTTER.

Buttery. See BOUTROY.

Buttery. Roger de Boteri, Alvered, John, and Roger occur in Normandy 1180-98 (MRS); William Boter in Gloucester c. 1272 (RH).

Buttle, for BOTTLE.

Buttress, for Botreaux (Lower). See BOTTERELL.

Butts. See BOOT, BOTT.

Butwell, for BOTEVYLE.

Buxar, for BUZZARD.

Buzzard. Hugo, Ranulph, and William Buscart occur in Normandy 1198 (MRS); Henry Boscard in

Salop 1190 (RCR). The family gave its name to Leighton Buzzard, Bedfordshire.

Byars. See BYERS.

Byard, for Biars. See AVENEL.

Byass, for BYARS.

Byatt, for BYARD.

Byers or De Biars (Lower). See AVENEL. The gallant General Sir William Byers was of this name.

Byles, armorially identified with BOYLE. A distinguished judge bears the name.

Byng, from Binge-Gerault, Normandy, mentioned in a charter of King John to Henry de Ferrers (Mém. Soc. Ant. Norm., v. 129). In 1191 Robert de Binga witnessed a charter of Henry, Bishop of Bayeux, executed at Rouen. In 1274 Reginald Binge was of Oxfordshire, Robert B. of Devon (RH. i. 695, ii. 76). In 1340 Thomas Bynge was a juror in Kent (Non. Inq. 399). Reginald Binge was one of the gentry of Essex 1433 (Fuller); and c. 1550 the family of Byng was possessed of Wrotham, Kent. From this Norman family descended the Viscounts Torrington, and the celebrated Sir John Byng, General in the Peninsular War, and Earl of Strafford.

Byron or De Buron, from Beuron, near Mantes, Normandy, which seems to have been the appanage of a younger branch of the Tessons. A brother probably of Ralph Tesson (see PERCY) was Lord of Beuron, and had Ernegis and Ralph de Buron, who in 1086 held considerable baronies in England, the former in York and Lincoln, the latter in Derby and Notts. It appears that the whole of this in the next generation vested in Ralph Tesson (heir of one of the brothers), who in 1130 paid a fine for estates in the four counties (Rot. Pip.). In 1165 Roger de Burun, his son, returned his barony in Notts as 10 fees. Hugh de B. occurs later, whose son Roger forfeited his barony t. John, who granted it to William Briwere. Sir Richard Byron, descended from this baron, m., t. Henry IV., the dau. and heir of Colwick of Notts; and from him descended Lord Byron the poet, and the Barons Byron.

C

Cabban, or Cadban, from Cabane or Chabannes in Perigord. William, Count of Poitou, m. a dau. of the Count of Toulouse, and had issue Hugh de Poitiers, Baron or Prince of Chabannes, who m., 1098, a dau. of the Count of La Marche, and was father of William and Louis de Chabannes, from whom descended the Marquises of that name. A branch of this house came to England, of which was Bartholomew Caban of Berks, living 1322.

Cabbell. Galfridus Cabal paid a fine in Normandy, 1184 (Mag. Rot. Scac.); Walter Cabal had estates in Bucks, t. Richard I. (Hunter, Fines, i. 169); Adam C. (13th cent.) held a knight's fee, Kent, from the Earl of Gloucester (Testa). The name frequently occurs as Kebbel. In 1195 Gilbert de Caable occurs in the bailifry of Pont Audemer, Normandy (Mag. Rot. Scac.).

Cabell, a form of CABBELL.

Cabespine, a corruption of Curbespine, from that lordship in Normandy, near Bernay and Lisieux, which was granted to the See of Lisieux by Henry II. It had belonged to the family of Mamignot.

Cable, a corruption of CABBELL.

Cadd, or Cade. Arnulf Cades, 1184, paid a fine in Normandy for disseisin (Mag. Rot. Scac.); and occurs again, 1198 (Ib.). Eustace Cade was of Lincolnshire, 1189 (Rot. Pip.). Various families of the name formerly bore arms in England (Robson).

Cadenhead, or Cadned, probably a form of De Cadneto or Caisneto. See CHEYNEY.

Cafe, or Chaff, from chauve, bald (Lower). Henry, Nicholas, Robert, Ranulph le Chauve, or Calvus, 1180-95, in Normandy (Mag. Rot. Scac.). These names frequently occur in England, 13th cent. and later.

Caffel, a corruption of CAVELL or Caville.

Caffin, a form of Caufyn or Calvin (Lower). Herbert and Roger Calvin or Cauvin occur in Normandy, 1180 (Mag. Rot. Scac.). The name Chaffin is another form (Lower). It was frequently written Cauvin in Normandy in the 12th cent.

Caffyn. See CAFFIN.

Cage, armorially identified with Gage or De Gaugy, a Norman family (Robson). The latter used indifferently C and G as their initial letter (Rot. Pip., 1189).

184

Cain, sometimes of Hiberno-Celtic origin, generally, however, a corruption of Caen or De Cadomo. Mauritius de Cadomo held lands in Barony, Devonshire, in 1083 (Exon. Domesd.). William de C. occurs in Norfolk, Walter de C. in Norfolk, holding great estates, 1086. Renebald de C. occurs in 1130 (Rot. Pip.). The family of De Caen, Caan, &c., is often mentioned later. In Normandy it occurs in the 12th cent. very frequently.

Caines, from the lordship of Cahaignes, near Vire, Normandy. In 1086 William de C. held a barony, Northants and Cambridge (Domesd.), also in Sussex and Bucks. The chief seat was at Tarrant-Kaines, Dorset, granted by Henry I. (Dugd. Bar. i. 427). The name also occurs as Keynes, and is frequent in Normandy in the 12th cent. (Mag. Rot. Scac.).

Cains. *See* CAINES.

Cakebread, probably a corruption of Calcebued or Caucebued. Radulphus Calcebued was of Normandy, 1180 (Mag. Rot. Scac.).

Calcott, a form of CALDECOTE, armorially identified (Robson).

Calcut, a form of CALDECOTE.

Calcutt. *See* CALCOTT.

Caldecote, a Norman family, though bearing an English surname. Geoffry, Eimont, and Richard de Caldecote occur in Normandy, 1180, as paying fines to the Crown (Mag. Rot. Scac.). Stephen de Caldecote is mentioned in England, 1199 (Palgr. Rot. Cur. Regis).

Caldercourt, probably a form of CALDECOTE.

Caldicott. *See* CALDECOTE.

Cale, a form of Kael, a Breton name. *See* CALL.

Caley, from the lordship of Cailly, Normandy, armorially identified with Calley and CAYLEY.

Calf, an English form of the Norman name Calvus or Le Chauve (*see* CAFE). Hugo Calf occurs in Hants, 1203 (Rot. Canc.); Robert C., Hants, 1313; and William C. in Ireland, 1322.

Call, or De Kael, from Bretagne or Poitou, where the name existed as late as 13th cent., when Walter Cael was envoy to England from the Viscount of Thouars (Hardy, Lit. Claus. i. 525). Edward de Cail was of Cornwall, t. William I., and with his nephew, Oliver de C., occurs in Cornwall, 1130 (Rot. Pip.). Ralph Kail (13th cent.) held lands in C. (Testa). In 1290 Humphry de Kael was M.P. for Somerset, and in 1316 had large estates there and in Devon. The family continued, and the name changed to Kaull, and then Call; and from it descend the Baronets Call.

Callard, from the Norman name Caillart. Walter Caillart occurs in the Duchy, 1180 (Mag. Rot. Scac.). The name in England was Calliard or Callard (Robson), and the family was seated in Norfolk.

Callass, a corruption of Caleys, from the town so named in Picardy. This family occurs in Normandy, 12th cent. (Mag. Rot. Scac.). In England William de Caleis occurs c. 1086 (Inq. Eliensis, p. 497). In 1188 William de Kales witnessed a charter in Lincoln (Mon. i. 530). Robert de C. gave lands to the Templars (Mon. ii. 545). The name occurs later in Kent and Surrey (Testa, and Palgr. Parl. Writs).

Callcott. *See* CALCUT.

Callcott. *See* CALCOTT.

Calley, armorially identified with CAYLEY.

Callf. *See* CALF.!

Callis. *See* CALLASS. This and Cales were the usual forms of the name Calais in the 16th cent.

Callow, from Calot or Galot. Raymond, Peter, and Eustace Calot or Galot occur in Normandy, 12th and 13th cent.

Callut, a form of Calot or Galot of Normandy. *See* CALLOW.

Calow. *See* CALLOW.

Calowe. *See* CALLOW.

Calver, an abbreviation of CALVERT.

Calvert, from Calbert or Caubert, near Abbeville, the *b* being changed into *v*, as usual. David de Calvert, 1203, held lands by knight service, Notts and Derby (Rot. Canc.). In 1318-24 Henry Calverd was M.P. for York. Hence the Baronets Calvert-Verney, and the Lords Baltimore.

Cambray, from the lordship of Cambrai, Normandy, near Falaise. According to Des Bois this was a branch of the Barons de la Ferté. The Sire de Cambrai was at the battle of Hastings (Wace, ii. 267); Godefridus de Chambrai held lands in capite, Leicestershire, 1086; Henry de C. one fee in Derby, 1165 (Lib. Nig.); Ralph de C. paid scutage in Sussex and Hants, 1199 and 1203. The name was corrupted to Chambreys or Chambreis.

Camel, from Campelles or Campell in Normandy. Geoffry, Robert, and Hubert de Campelles occur (12th cent.) in Normandy (MRS).

Cameron. Although the majority of those who bear this name are Scoto-Celtic, there was an English family whose name is now written thus. The name was derived from

Champrond, near Coutances (De Gerville, Anc. Chat. de la Manche). In 1157 Ansger de Cambrun is mentioned in Essex (Rot. Pip.). Robert Cambron and John de Cambron occur in Scotland before 1200 and in 1234.

Camfield, or Camfyld, a corruption of Camville or Camvyle, a Norman baronial family, from Camville, near Coutances. *See* MILTON. Dugdale has treated of this family in his Baronage.

Camidge, for GAMMAGE.

Cammage, for GAMMAGE.

Cammegh, for GAMMAGE.

Camp, derived from Campe or Campes, Normandy. Walter, Ingulf, Rodolph, Gaufrid de Campe occur in the Duchy, 12th cent. (MRS); John and Matthew de Campes in England, 1199 (RCR).

Campe, for CAMP.

Campin, for CAMPION (Lower).

Campion. William Campion was living in Normandy, 1184 (Mag. Rot. Scac.); Geoffry Campion in England, 1194; and Gregory C., 1199 (Palgr. Rot. Cur. Regis).

Candelet, apparently foreign.

Candelin, from Gandelin or Gandelain, Normandy.

Candy, from Candé, near Blois. Nicholas Candie occurs in Normandy, 1195 (MRS).

Cane, for Caen. *See* CAIN.

Cane, or Cany. Richard Cane of Normandy, 1180; Warin, Odo, William, Thurstan Cani, 1180-95 (MRS); Hugh, Robert, Walter Cane of England, c. 1272 (RH).

Canfill, for Camville.

Cann, from Can, Normandy. Geoffry de Can of N., 1195 (MRS); Richard de Canne of England, c. 1272 (RH).

Cannel, from Chenel, now Cheneau, near Lille. William de Ganele of Hants, c. 1272 (RH). The name also occurs as Chenel and Cheynel (Robson).

Cannell, for CANNEL.

Cannon. Galfridus and Radulfus Canonicus or Le Chanoin of Normandy, 1180-95 (MRS); Gilbert and Robert Canonicus occur in England, 1189 (Rot. Pip.).

Cant, for GANT.

Cantis, for Candish or Cavendish (Norman baronial family).

Cantor. Gaufridus Cantor of Normandy, 1180-95 (MRS); Christian le Chaunter of England, c. 1272 (RH). The name was translated as 'Singer.'

Cantrell. William and Roger Cantarel, of Normandy, 1198 (MRS); Alberic Chanterhill, of England, 1199 (RCR); Richard Chaunterel, c. 1272 (RH).

Cantrill. *See* CANTRELL.

Cantwell, a corruption of De Cantelo or Chanteloup. *See* CODRINGTON.

Canty, for CANDY.

Canute, or Canu. Artur, Robert, Richard Canutus, Safrid, Bertin, Roger Canu, of Normandy, 1180-98 (MRS); John Canutus, England, 1180 (Rot. Pip.).

Cany. *See* CANE.

Cape, or Capes, from Chappes. *See* COPE.

Capel, a Breton family, from la Chapelle, Nantes (Morice, Hist. Bret. Pr. i. xiii.). Roald de Capella was living 1030, and in 1060, with Rainald, his son, made grants to St. Florent, Saumur. In 1096 his eldest son occurs in Bretagne, where the family long flourished. Rainald, the son, held lands in Essex from Alberic de Ver, 1086 (Domesd.). He

was succeeded by Alberic de C., whose son, Walter de C., was living 1199, when the pedigree was stated in a suit in the Curia Regis. The last-mentioned witnessed charters of Matilda, Countess of Essex, and Geoffry de Say (Mon. i. 461, 462). Robert C., 13th cent., held lands from Valoines in Essex (Testa); and William de C. was on an Inquisition in Suffolk (Mon. i. 289). From the latter descended the Lords Capel, Earls of Essex.

Capel, from La Chapelle, near Alençon. Gaufridus, Robert, and William de Capella, of Normandy, 1180-95 (MRS). This family became seated in the West of England.

Capell, for CAPEL.

Capern, for Capron. Gormond, Richard, Ranulph, Radulph Capron, of Normandy, 1180-95 (MRS); Roger C. of England, 1189 (Rot. Pip.), Robert C., 1194 (RCR).

Capes. Osbert, Hugh, Geoffry Cape or Capes, of Normandy, 1180-95 (MRS); William de Capes, of England, 1199 (RCR).

Caple, for CAPEL.

Caplin, Capelen, or Chaplain. Alvered, Robert, Rodolf, William Capellanus, of Normandy 1180-95 (MRS). Alan, Milo, Gervase, Richard C., of England, 1199 (RCR). In 1086 the name occurs in Kent, Northants, Devon (Domesd.). Fabian C. was of Essex, 1156 (Rot. Pip.). In 1202 Gilbert C. was of York, and Wymar of Norfolk (Rot. Canc.). In 1443 John Chaplyn, of Sleford, in Lincoln, is mentioned.

Capp, for Cape, or CAPES.

Cappel, for CAPEL.

Capps, for CAPES.

Capron. *See* CAPERN.

Carabine, for Corbin. Robert

Corbin, of Normandy, 1180–95 (MRS); Geoffry C., of England, 1194 (RCR); Walter C., of England, c. 1272 (RH).

Carbine. *See* CARABINE.

Carbonell. Pagan, William, Robert, Huismel, Richard de Carbonell, Normandy, 1180–95 (MRS); Carbonel held lands in Hereford, 1086; Hugh Carbonel in Normandy, 1165; Durand C. in Oxford, 1130. Thomas C. held of the Honour of Wallingford 13th cent. (Testa). Temp. Henry II., the family was seated in Devon, and long flourished in Hereford, Bucks, and Oxford.

Carden, in some cases an English local name, also a form of Cardon. Ralph, Richard, Robert, Paganus Cardon, or Cardun, were of Normandy, 1180–95 (MRS). William Cardun held lands in Essex in 1086. In 1165 the family was seated in Hants, Norfolk, Beds, and Lincoln (Lib. Nig.); temp. John in Bucks; and 1325, Adam Cardun was M.P. for Notts. Hence the Baronets Carden.

Cardwell, for Cardeville or Cardunville, from C., near Caen. Ernald de Cardunville held a fief from the See of Lincoln, 1165, and Peter de C. from the barony of Estoteville, York (Lib. Nig.). Paganus de C. had a grant in Hereford 1156 (Rot. Pip.) Walter de C. was witness, 1170, to a charter in Lincoln (Mon. ii.). Richard de Cardeville was witness (13th cent.) to a charter of the Bp. of Winchester (Mon. ii. 004). He held lands in Hants by serjeantry (Testa).

Careless. *See* CARLESS.

Cares, from Chars, in Normandy. In 1189 Geoffry de la Carice held estates in Hants (Rot. Pip.).

Carew, a branch of FITZGERALD.

Carey. *See* CAREW and CARY.

Carle, for Carel, or CARRELL.

Carles. *See* CARLESS.

Carless, or Charles, from St. Karles de Parcy, in the Cotentin. This family, then named Charles, was seated in many parts of England in the 13th century.

Carlish, for CARLESS.

Carloss, for CARLESS.

Carne. Robert and Geoffry le Caron, Normandy, 1180–95 (MRS). Wischard de Charun, Engl. c. 1272 (RH).

Carnell, from Carnelles, near Evreux. Geoffry and Odo de Carneilles were of Normandy, 1180 (MRS). Gilbert de C., about 1170, witnessed the charter of Hinkley Abbey, Leicester (Mon. i. 604). Ralph de C. was a benefactor of Studley Priory, Warwick (Mon. ii.). This family is armorially identified with that of CHARNELL. It was usually styled Charnel, or Charnels, in England.

Carpenter. Robert, Gaufrid, Ansketel, Richard, William, Bernard Carpentarius, of Normandy, 1180–95 (MRS). In 1189 Reiner, Adam, Roger, William C., of England (Rot. Pip.). Durand C. was a tenant in capite, Norfolk, 1086, and Rabel and Roger C. at the same time. The latter gave lands to Stoke-Clare Priory, 1090 (Mon. i. 1008). Simon C., 1165, held a knight's fee, Suffolk. William Carpentarius was father of Henry and Manasser Biset, Barons t. Henry II. (Mon. ii. 93, 95).

Carr, or Kerr. *See* KERR.

Carrall, for CARRELL.

Carrey, for CAREY.

Carrington, for Carentan, from

C. in the Cotentin. Robert de Carentan granted the mill of Stratton, Wilts, to Farley Abbey, c. 1125 (Mon. i. 621).

Carritt, or Caret, for GARET.

Carroll, in the case of English families, was a form of CARRELL. In Ireland it is Celtic.

Carson, probably from Corson, Normandy. William and Jordan de Kersun were witnesses, 1169, to a charter of Lanercost Priory, Cumberland (Mon. ii. 121). William de Carçun (13th cent.) held lands, Norfolk and Suffolk, by serjeantry (Testa).

Carter. William Cartier, of Normandy, 1195 (MRS); Ralph Caretarius, of Winchester, 1148 (Wint. Domesd.); Henry C., of Lincoln, 1203 (Rot. Canc.); Alured of Gloucester, and William of Warwick (Ib.). In 13th cent. Ralph C. held a fief from the See of Worcester (Testa).

Carterfield, or Quaterville. Aeliza de Quarteville held from Philip-Augustus, in Normandy, 1205 (Mém. Soc. Ant. Norm. v. 173).

Carrell, or Caril, from Caril, near Lisieux. Richard, son of Anchetil de Carel, or Quadrella, m. a dau. of Tancred de Hautville, and obtained the Principality of Capua from Robert Guiscard (Ord. Vit.). Richard C., his son, was unjustly deprived of his principality by Roger, King of Sicily, his uncle. Robert Carrel held the Castle of St. Ceneri for William Rufus, 1088 (Ord. Vit.). Temp. Henry II., William and Simon de Caril witnessed the charter of Keynsham Abbey (Mon. ii.). A descendant was created Baron Caryl by James II. after his loss of the throne.

Cartwright, armorially identified with Cateryke, or Catherick (Robson). Catherick was part of the demesne of the Earls of Richmond, and the surname therefore probably arose from tenure of the office of Seneschal by a branch of a neighbouring family. The arms (a fesse) are those of the adjoining family of De Smythton or Eschalers, with three cinquefoils for difference, which were afterwards corrupted into 'roses,' 'Catherine wheels,' and 'fire-balls with rays.' Of this family Ilbert de Catherege, or Catherage (a form of Catheric), occurs in Normandy, 1180-98 (MRS); which shows the Norman origin of the family. A branch long remained at Stanwick, in Richmondshire, close to Catterick. Another branch was seated in Notts, and one in Cambridge; and the name there changed from Cateryke to Cartwright. Of the former branch was Major Cartwright, the celebrated reformer, and of the latter, Thomas Cartwright, the great Puritan leader, temp. Elizabeth.

Carvell. Ranulph de Carville, 1180; Robert Carvel, 1195, in Normandy (MRS); Richard de Carville, of England, 1199 (RCR). Carvell is armorially identified with Carville.

Cary, or Pipart. William, Gilbert, Robert, Ranulf Pipart, of Normandy, 1180-95 (MRS). Waldin Pipart held Kari, Longdon, &c., 1086 (Domesd.). Longdon was held by William P., t. Henry II. (Pole), and in 13th cent. William Pipart held Kari; whence the name of De Kari or Cary. From this family descended the Lords Hunsdon, the Earls of Monmouth, and Viscounts Falkland.

Case, for Chace, which is armorially related to Chancy or Canci. *See* CHACE.

Casey, or CASSY, when it is an English family, is a branch of Canci, with which it bears armorial relations. The name is also Hiberno-Celtic.

Cash, for CASS.

Cashel, for CASSELL.

Cass, a form of CASE or CHACE.

Cassell, from C., Flanders. Maurice de Cassel witnessed a charter of Stoke-Clare, Suffolk (Mon. i. 1008). Hugo de C., of London and Middlesex, is mentioned 1130 (Rot. Pip.). *See* CECIL.

Cassells. *See* CASSELL.

Cassels, for CASSELLS.

Casson. *See* GASSON.

Castang, for CASTEYN.

Castell. Joceline and William Castel of Normandy, 1198 (MRS), Ranulph, Bartholomew, &c. 1189-95 (Ib.). Alexander de Castro (Castel) of England 1199 (RCR); John de Castro, c. 1272 (RH).

Castile, for CASTELL.

Castle, for CASTELL.

Castro. *See* CASTELL.

Cate or Catt. William and Roger Catus, of Normandy, 1180. Roger C. 1198 (MRS); Radulphus Cattus, of Lincoln, 1189 (Rot. Pip.). Alexander le Kat and others in England, c. 1272 (RH). The family long flourished in Norfolk.

Cates. *See* CATE.

Catherick. *See* CARTWRIGHT.

Catlin, Catline, or Castelline, from Castellan, bearing three castles in allusion to the arms. N. de Castellan occurs in Normandy, 1180-98 (MRS); Sire Reginald de Castellan in England, c. 1272 (RH). An

eminent chief justice of England bore the name of Catline.

Catling, for CATLIN.

Catlyn, for CATLIN.

Cato, from Catot or Escatot, in Normandy. Robert Catot, 1165, held one fee in Normandy (Feod. Norm. Duchesne). Hugh de Estcatot was of Salop, 1189 (Rot. Pip.), Hamond and Hugh de Asketot occur 1199 (RCR).

Caton. Herebert Katune, of Normandy, 1198 (MRS). This may mean the English family of De Catton, which it shows to have been Norman.

Catt. *See* CATE.

Cattel or Châtel, from some foreign family bearing the name of Du Chastel or De Castello.

Catton. *See* CATON.

Cattermole, from Quatremeulles or De Quatuor Molis, the locality of which I have not ascertained.

Cattermoul, for CATTERMOLE.

Cattermull. *See* CATTERMOLE.

Cattle, for CATTEL.

Cattlin, for CATLIN.

Caudel. *See* CAUDLE.

Caudle or Caudel. Roger Caldel or Caudel was of Normandy, 1180 (MRS); Anistina and William Caudel of Cambridgeshire, c. 1272 (RH).

Caulcott. *See* CALCOTT.

Caulfield, Calvel, Calfhill, or Caville. *See* CAVELL. The family was seated in Normandy, 1180-98 (MRS). In England Gilbert de Calvel was of Northumberland, and Richard C. of Kent, 1202 (Rot. Canc.). Malger de Cavel in 1261 paid a fine in Oxfordshire (Roberts, Excerpt.). James Calfhil or Calvel, otherwise Calfield, c. 1506, was Bishop of Worcester t. Eliz. and from his younger son, Sir Toby Caulfield, a renowned commander in Ireland, descended collaterally the Earls of Charlemont.

Cave. Adelina de Cava, and John Cave of Normandy, 1180-95 (MRS). Wyomar had a grant of Cave, Yorkshire, c. 1090, from Alan, Earl of Richmond; c. 1140 Margaret de C. and Richard de C. held from the Church of York (Mon. ii.). 1307-26 Sire Alexander de C., a commissioner of array and justiciary. The occurrence of the name in Normandy shows the origin of the family, though its name was derived from England.

Cavel, a form of CAVILLE.

Cavell. *See* CAVILLE.

Cavendish, Gernon, or de Montfichet. The descent of the Cavendish family from Gernon has been disputed, but (as I intend to show) without reason. The Gernons were a branch of the Barons of Montfichet, Montfiquet, or Montfiket in Normandy, so named after their Scandinavian ancestor. The castle of Montfichet long remained, as well as the Church of St. Catherine in the castle, a foundation of this family.

About 1050 Robert, surnamed Guernon (moustache), Baron of Montfichet, witnessed a charter of Duke William (Gall. Christ. xi. Instr. 229). He had issue, 1, William de Montfichet, who d. s. p., when the barony devolved on William, the son of his brother; 2, Robert Guernon or Gernon, who held a great barony in Essex, &c., 1086. From his elder son William de Montfichet descended the Barons of that name, whose seats were at Stanstead Montfichet, Essex, and Montfichet Tower, London, of which city the Montfichets were hereditary standard-bearers or military chiefs in time of war.

The younger branches retained the name of Gernon. Alured Gernon, brother of William de Montfichet, had estates in Essex and Middlesex 1130 (Rot. Pip.). Matthew, his son, 1135 witnessed a charter of William Montfichet (Mon. i. 803). Ralph, his son, 1165, held a fief from Montfichet in Essex, and was granted Bakewell, Derbyshire, by Richard I. (Testa). He had Ralph G., founder of Lees Priory, Essex, father of William G., who had two sons: 1, Ralph, ancestor of a line of Gernon frequently mentioned in Essex, Suffolk, and Derby, and which long continued; 2, Geoffry.

Geoffry, surnamed de Cavendish from his residence at Cavendish, Suffolk, appears in 1302 as bailsman with Walter de C., his son, for certain citizens of London who had been charged with the unlawful possession of some crown jewels (Palgr. Anc. Calendars, i. 205). Roger de C., another son of Geoffry, m. a dau. of Potton of Cavendish, by whom he acquired an estate there, and was father of Sir John Cavendish, chief justice t. Rich. II., and Roger Cavendish. The former, in 1359, purchased the Manor of Cavendish Overhall from De Odingselles, from which it has been too readily inferred that the statement that Cavendish had been acquired in the preceding generation by the heiress of Potton was unfounded (Archæologia, xi. 53). But the objector was not aware that at Cavendish there were five or six

191

manors, as the records clearly show, belonging to the families of De Grey, Hastings, De Clare, to the Abbot of Dereham, and De Odingselles, so that the Cavendishes may well have possessed property there before they purchased Cavendish Overhall.

The identity of the family of Cavendish with that of Gernon in the eastern counties appears in all the old heralds' visitations, where the two names bear indiscriminately the same arms; and the account of the descent of this family by Collins, which has been disputed on the above grounds, appears to be perfectly authentic. The Dukes of Newcastle, Devonshire, and other great families of the name of Cavendish, descended from the Gernons and Montfichets.

Caville or Cavill, identified by its arms (a calf) with Calvel or Cauvel. Hais, Peter, Robert Cauvel of Normandy, 1198 (MRS); William, Ranulph, and Gohier Caval, 1180–95 (Ib.). William Cavell, of Oxfordshire, c. 1272 (RH).

Cavit. Henricus Cauvet of Normandy, 1195 (MRS); Walter and Geoffry Cauvet, 1198 (Ib.).

Cawdery or Coudray, a branch of the Beaumonts, Viscounts of Maine (*See* Anselme, art. Beaumont). Benedict de Coudray was witness to a charter of Roger de Menilwarin to Deulacresse Abbey (Mon. ii.). Fulco de C. held one fee from Abingdon Abbey (Testa), and Matthew de C. one fee from Ralph de St. Amand (Ib.).

Cawdrey. *See* CAWDERY.

Cawley, for CALLEY (Lower).

Cawse, Calz or Caux, from C. near Abbeville. Ilbert de Chaz was a benefactor to Farley, Wilts,

c. 1125 (Mon. i. 620); Robert de Calz was of Wilts, 1158 (Rot. Pip.). Henry de C. witnessed a charter of Henry I. to Ramsey Abbey (Mon. i. 238). In 1130 Robert de C. and Walter, his son, were of Notts and Derby, William de C. of Beds. and Bucks (Rot. Pip.).

Cayley, from Cailly, near Rouen. Osbert and Samson de Calleio were of Normandy, 1180–95 (MRS). In 1086 William de Cailgi held lands in Berks in capite (Domesd.). In 1165 Jordan de Cailli held one fee from Marmion in Warwick, and one from Bigod in Norfolk; and Ralph Cailli held two fees in Yorkshire (Lib. Nig.). The Baronets Cayley are of this house.

Cecil, Cicelle, or Seyssel, from Kessel or Cassel, east of Bruges, Flanders. This is probably a branch of the Counts of Gand, whose arms (barry) it bears, with escutcheons charged with the lion rampant of Flanders. The arms are still borne in Flanders by a family of the same name. In 1180 Henry, Count of Cessele, witnessed a charter of the Emperor Frederick Barbarossa (Gall. Christ. iii. 138 Instr.), and 1203 Henry, Count of Kessele, witnessed a charter of the Duke of Brabant (Alb. Miræi Oper. Diplomat. i. 401). The Counts of Kessele probably bore that title as a younger branch of the Carlovingian Counts of Gand (*See* CONSTABLE). Maurice de Cassel of this family occurs in England t. William I. (Mon. i. 1008); and had issue Hugh de Alost, ancestor of the Counts of Kessel; and Robert de Kessel or Ciselle, one of the knights who, with Robert Fitz-Hamon, conquered Glamorgan, 1093. From his descendant Walter de Alterena, living

1165 (Lib. Nig.), descended the noble house of Cecil.

Of this family was William Cecil, Lord Burleigh, the greatest, perhaps, of all the statesmen of England.

Ceeley or Seily, from Silly, Normandy. Robert de Silleio, of Normandy, 1198 (MRS). Nigel de Cileio witnessed a charter of Henry I. for Colne Priory, Essex (Mon. i. 437).

Chabot or Cabot. Odo Cabot of Normandy, 1184 (MRS), and Robert Kabot, 1198 (Ib.). Roger Cabot of England, c. 1272 (RH).

Chace, Chase, or Chansey, armorially identified; also armorially identified with Channcy, or De Canci. Robert de Canceio, of Normandy, 1180 (MRS); Geoffry de Chansy of England, 1194 (RCR). The name appears in all parts of England as Chancey, Chancy, &c.

Chad, for CADD. Hence the Baronets Chadd.

Chaff, from Chauve. *See* CAFE.

Chaffer. *See* CHAFFERS.

Chaffers, from Chevrières, near Beauvais. Robert de Cheveriis of Normandy, 1195 (MRS); William de Caveres of Salop, c. 1272 (RH).

Chaffey, or Chaffy, a form of CHAFE or Chaff.

Chaffin, for CAFFIN (Lower).

Chaldecott. *See* CALDECOTT (Lower).

Chalie, for CAYLEY.

Challands, for Chalons. *See* CHALLEN.

Challen, a branch of the Counts of Chalons. Warin, Count of Chalons, was living 830 (Moreri); Manasses, 920; Lambert, t. Hugh Capet, whose grandson, Hugh II., was living 1072. Harduin de Chalons of this house, t. Henry II., m. Lady Florentia, heiress of Leigh,

Devon, from whom descended the house of Chalons of Leigh-Chalons, which flourished till the time of Henry VIII.

Challenger, or Challenge, from Chalonge or Chalinge, Normandy (MRS). The family of Challenge was seated in Gloucester.

Challice, for Callis or Calais. *See* CALLASS.

Challis. *See* CALLASS.

Chaloner, for CHALLONER.

Chaloner, probably foreign (Lower); perhaps from Chalons.

Chamberlain. Bricius, Robert, Gaufrid, Herbert, William, Henry, Serlo Camerarius, or Le Chamberlain, Normandy, 1180–98 (MRS). In England, 1194–1200, Henry, Hugh, Ralph, Robert, Thomas, Walter, Richard Turbert Camerarius (RCR). The principal family of these was descended from the Barons of Tancarville, Chamberlains of Normandy. *See* GRAHAM.

Chamberlaine. *See* CHAMBERLAIN.

Chamberlin, for CHAMBERLAIN.

Chamberlayne. *See* CHAMBERLAIN.

Chambers, or De Camera, armorially identified with Chamber. Stephen, Walter, Warin, William de Camera in England, 1189 (Rot. Pip.); Matilda de C. in Oxford, 1130 (Ibid.); Simon de C. in Essex, 1140 (Mon. i. 460); Elias de C. in Sussex, t. Rich. I. (Mon. Angl.). The family appears early in York, Wilts, and Norfolk. Chambre or Camera was in Brabant, whence the family seems to have come at the Conquest.

Chamen, for Chamon or Chamond (Robson). The latter was also written Chaumond or Chaumont, in Latin De Calvomonte (Lower). Childebrand, second son of Pepin the Elder, had issue Nebelon, Count of Vexin, whose descendant, Nebelon III., m. Ledgarda of Flanders, and had Waleran II., father of Geoffry de Vexin, Lord of Caumont and Mantes, whose son, Eudes de Caumont, is mentioned by Ordericus Vitalis. His son Otmund was a benefactor of St. Stephen's, Caen, t. William I. William de C., his son, occurs in Durham 1130, and Ralph de C. in 1165 held two fees of the Honour of Wallingford.

Champ. *See* CAMP.

Champion. *See* CAMPION.

Champness, for Champneys. *See* CHAMPNEY.

Champney, or Champneys, from De Champigné or Champagné, Normandy. In 1165 Geoffry de Champigné held one fee in the bailifry of Pont-Audemer. Nigel, Richard, Osbert, Ralph, Josceline de Campania of Normandy, 1180–95 (MRS); Robert de Campain of England, 1199 (RCR). · In the 13th century the name became Champney and Caumpeny.

Champneys. *See* CHAMPNEY.

Champniss, for CHAMPNEYS.

Chance, for Cance, which is armorially identified with Chansey or Cancy (Robson). *See* CHACE (Lower).

Chancellor. *See* CANCELLOR.

Chancillor, a Norman name. Ranulf, Richard, and Radulf Cancellarius occur in the Duchy, 1180 (Mag. Rot. Scac.); Geoffry and William C. in England, 1189 (Rot. Pip.); Richard C. in 1272 (Roberts, Excerpta).

Chaney, for CHEYNEY.

Channell, armorially identified

with Charnell. An eminent judge bears this name.

Channon. *See* CANNON.

Chant. *See* CANT.

'**Chanter.** *See* CANTOR.

Chantry, from Chaintré, near Mâcon.

Chaplin. *See* CAPLIN.

Chappel. *See* CAPEL.

Chappell. *See* CAPEL.

Chappuis. Hamon Cabus was of Normandy, 1195 (MRS). In 1165 William Cabus held a knight's fee, Bucks (Lib. Nig.). Hamon C. party to a suit, Wilts, 1199 (RCR). Reginald Cabus, 13th cent., held lands in Middlesex by serjeantry (Testa). In 1311 Richard Cabous was M.P. for Blechingley.

Chapple. *See* CAPEL.

Chapron, for CAPRON.

Chapuys, for CHAPPUIS.

Charge, for Gardge, Gordge, Gorges, or Gaurges, from G. in the Cotentin. Ralph de Gorges m. the heiress of Morville, and acquired her estates in Dorset (Lower). The Barons de Gorges who m. the heiress of the house were Russels (*see* Banks, Dorm. and Ext. Peerage).

Charles. *See* CARLESS.

Charlish, for CHARLES.

Charnell. *See* CARNELL.

Charter, for Chartres (Lower).

Charteris, the Scottish form of Chartres. *See* CHARTERS.

Charters, for CHARTRES.

Chartres. Reginald, Vidame de Chartres, was living 1020 (La Roque, Mais. Harc., 1568–9). Of this house Ralph Carnotensis (De Chartres) held estates in Leicester, 1086, and Ebrard de Carnot, 1148, held lands at Winchester (Wint. Domesd.). In 1165 Robert de Chartres held one fee from the Earl of Warwick

(Lib. Nig.). In the 14th cent. Robert and Roger de Chartres had writs of military summons.

Chase. *See* CHACE.

Chattell. *See* CATTELL.

Chattle, for CATTLE.

Chatty, for Cate, or CATT.

Chatwin, for CHETWIND.

Chaucer. Though this name does not occur in the London Directory, it cannot be passed over. Geoffry Chaucer, the poet, m. a dau. of Sir Paine Roet, sister of John of Gaunt's wife, and was valectus or esquire to Edward III. The family of Chaucer, Chaucier, Chaucers, or Chasur had been seated in the Eastern Counties, and some members were in trade in London. Richard le Chaucer was of London, 1328; John C. in 1349 (Riley, Liber Albus, 438; Nicholas, Life of C., 94). The poet was probably kinsman of Bartholomew Chaucer, who possessed estates in Cambridge, Hunts, Herts, and Essex, 1312 (Parl. Rot. i. 449, cited by Nicholas). In 1295 Gerard le Chaucer was of Colchester, Essex, and 1274 Alice de Chasar occurs as a tenant of the See of Ely in Cambridgeshire (Rot. Hundr.). In 1225 Ralph le Chauser is mentioned (Nicholas).

This family bore the arms of Malesoures (viz., per pale argent and gules), a Breton race (*see* WALDE-GRAVE) which had possessed estates in Essex, Rutland, and Northants from the Conquest. There are two other forms of these ancient arms of the Chaucers (Robson). The name Le Chaucier (Calcearius), may have arisen from some serjeantry connected with the tenure of land. It would seem probable that this was a branch of the family of Male-

soures: it was at least, from its name, of foreign origin.

Chayter, from Chatres in Maine, near Laval.

Cheek. William Cecus occurs in Normandy 1198 (MRS), and in Gloucester 1189 (Rot. Pip.); Walter Chike of England, c. 1272 (RH).

Cheese. John Formage of Normandy, 1195 (MRS); Peter Formage of England, c. 1272 (RH); afterwards translated.

Cheffins, for Chaffin or CAFFIN.

Chegney, for Cigony. Engelard de Cigony or Cigoine (now Chigné), one of the principal nobles of King John. This lordship was in Maine.

Cheiley, or Ceiley, a form of Cilly. *See* CEELY.

Chellingworth. *See* CHILLING-WORTH.

Chenery, probably from St. Ceneri, Normandy, the lordship of the Barons Geroie or De St. Ceneri. Hugo de S. Cinerino possessed lands in Hants, 1158 (Rot. Pip.).

Cheney. *See* CHEYNEY.

Chennell, a form of CHANNELL.

Chepmell, a form of Chemell. Roger Chemel held a knight's fee, c. 1205, from Philip Augustus in Normandy. John Kemel was of Oxfordshire, c. 1272 (Rot. Hund.).

Chequer. The name is territorial, and apparently foreign, perhaps from Sequerre, Picardy. Sire Roger de la Checker was of Cambridgeshire, c. 1270 (Rot. Hund.).

Cherry. 1. from De Cersaso, otherwise De Cerasio, or Cericio, Normandy (Lower). The early form was De Cerisy. John de C. and William de C. had a suit for land, Suffolk, c. 1200 (Palgr. Rot. Cur. Regis). In 13th cent. the heir of the latter held lands in capite (Testa) in Notts. 2. Also from Cheeri. William Cheeri of Normandy, 1180–95 (MRS).

Cherubin, a corruption of Carabin or Carbine. *See* CARABINE.

Chesney, from Quesnay, near Coutances, from which came De Chesneto or Kaineto in England (De Gerville, Anc. Chat. de la Manche). *See* CHEYNEY.

Chesterman, perhaps a corruption of Quatreman or Quatermaine, written or pronounced Catterman, or Chetterman.

Chetwynd, or De Verlai, from V., Normandy. In 1086 Turold de Verlai held thirteen lordships in Salop from Earl Roger, of which Chetwynd appears to have been the chief (Eyton, Salop). Robert his son was a baron t. Henry I., and before 1121 witnessed a charter in favour of Salop Abbey (Ib.). He was living 1141, and was father of Robert de Verlai, who, with his father, gave Verlai Church, Normandy, to Essay Abbey, which grant was confirmed by Henry II. (not Henry I. as erroneously stated in Gallia Christiana, xi. 234, Instr.). The next in descent was Adam de Chetwynd, 1180–1203; and 'in his time the barony, consisting of two knights' fees, was placed by the Crown under the feudal suzerainty of the Fitz-Alans (Eyton, viii.). The ancient arms of Chetwynd were two chevrons, probably the arms of Verlai. From John de C., son of Adam, descended the Chetwynds of Salop and Stafford, Viscounts Chetwynd, and the Baronets of the same name.

Chevalier, i.e. Miles. Gaufridus, Richard, Ralph, Walter, Robert

194

Miles, in Normandy, 1180–95 (Mag. Rot. Scac.); Richard Miles, Staffordshire, 1189 (Rot. Pip.); Hugh, Osmond, Reginald Miles in England, c. 1272 (Rot. Hund.); also Jordan and Walter le Chevaler.

Chevallier. *See* CHEVALIER.

Chew. William de Cayou, in Normandy, 1180–1195, and as De Kaen, 1198 (Mag. Rot. Scac.); John, Nicholas, and Walter le Keu or De Keu, in England, c. 1270 (Rot. Hund.).

Cheyne, a form of CHEYNEY.

Cheyney, from Quesnay, near Coutances. Ralph de Kaineto came to England at the Conquest. Ralph, his son, founded Tarrant Abbey, Dorset. Robert de Chesneto was Bishop of Lincoln, 1147. John de C. held lands in Oxford 13th cent., and William de C. in Cambridge. The Lords Cheyney were of this family.

Chick, or Chike, a form of CHEEK (Robson).

Child, the English form of Enfant. Roger, William, Walkelin Infans or l'Enfant, Norm. 1180–95 (MRS); William and John le Enfant, William and John Child, Engl., c. 1272 (RH).

Childers, a corruption of Chellers or Challers. *See* SMITHSON.

Chillingworth, or Rabaz. *See* RABAZ. William C., the celebrated writer, was son of John C., Mayor of Oxford in 1642. The name is very rare, and is derived by corruption from Killingworth, Kynelingworth, Kenilworth, or Kivelingworth, now Kilworth, Leicestershire. This lordship, now divided into North and South Kilworth, was granted, t. William I., by Robert, Earl of Mellent, to Ralph (Rabaz), a Norman.

Robert Rabaz, with Heloisa his wife, and Richard his son, granted the church of Kilworth to St. Mary de Pratis, Leicester, and the gift was confirmed by Henry II. (Nicholls, Leic. iv. 197). Stephen, son of Robert Rabaz, of Kilworth, gave lands to Sulby Abbey, Northants, in which county this family had large estates (Mon. ii. 630). About the time of King John this family divided into two branches, one retaining the name of Rabaz, the other that of Killingworth. Of the former was Stephen Rabaz, Viscount of Leicester, 1290, and M.P. for Northants, 1298. Robert Rabaz, of this line, was M.P. for Rutland 1313.

Roger de Killingworth was patron of the church of Kilworth, 1220; Robert, his son, lived t. Henry III., and Roger de K. was a benefactor to Sulby Abbey, t. E. I. In 1316 William de Killingworth received pardon as an adherent of the Earl of Lancaster. A branch seems to have settled not far from Oxford, for John K., late Proctor of the University, was buried at Merton College, 1444. His tomb bears three cinquefoils, evidently derived from those of the Earls of Mellent, the suzerains of Killingworth. In 1506 John K. was Archdeacon of St. Alban's (Coll. Top. et Geneal.), and t. Eliz., John K., Esq., possessed estates in Cambridge and the Eastern Counties.

Chilly, a form of Silly. See CEALY.

Chinn, a corruption of CHEYNE.

Chinery. See CHENERY.

Chinnery. See CHENERY. Hence the baronets of the name.

Chipperfield, a corruption of Chevreville, a lordship in the Cotentin. Robert de Chiefreville, 1165,

held two knights' fees from the Barony of Wormgaye, Norfolk (Liber Niger).

Chitty, in 1272, was Cette, when Roger Cette was of Suffolk (Rot. Hundr.). That name appears to have been a form of Catt or Cate, by alteration of a vowel. See CATE and CHATTY.

Chivell, a form of Chavell or Chaville. See CAVILLE.

Chivers, or Cheevers, from La Chievre or Capra, in Normandy. William Capra held forty-seven lordships in barony, 1086, in Devonshire (Domesd.). His name occurs in Normandy, 1070 (Gall. Christ. xi., Instr. 64). William Capre and Gosfred C. witnessed a charter of Montacute, Somerset, c. 1100 (Mon. ii. 910). William C. was one of the chief Barons of Rufus, and a justiciary (Mon. i. 997). The seat of the barony was at Bradninch, Devon; it was lost temp. Henry I., but the family remained. In Ireland they became Viscounts Mount-Leinster.

Choice, a form of CHOICY.

Choicy, a form of Chausy. See CHACE.

Chollett, a form of COLLETT.

Cholmeley. See CHOLMONDELEY.

Cholmondeley, a branch of De Toesni, of Normandy. William de Belwar, or Belvar, otherwise Belvoir, son of Berenger de Todeni, son of Robert de Todeni or Toesni, Baron of Belver, 1086, m. Mabilia, dau. and coheir of Robert Fitz-Hugh, Baron of Malpas, Cheshire; the other dau. having m. Richard Patrick, or Patry, of the great baronial house of that name, Patry de la Lande. From William de Belwar descended the houses of Cholmondeley and Egerton. The family of De Toesni was royal, descended from an uncle of Rollo.

Choules. *See* COWLES, a form of Cauls or Caulx.

Chrees, a form of Crease or CREASY.

Christen. *See* CHRISTIAN.

Christian. N. Christianus and Roger C., his son, Thomas, William C., of Normandy, 1180–1195 (Mag. Rot. Scac.). Walter Christianus, of Notts, 1199 (Palgr. Rot. Cur. Regis), Robert Crestien, Bricius, Ranulph, Robert Cristian or Cristin, and others in England, c. 1272 (Rot. Hund.).

Christien. *See* CHRISTIAN.

Christmas, a translation of the Norman-French Noel. Roger, Eynard, Stephen Noel of Normandy, 1180–1195 (Mag. Rot. Scac.), Thomas Noel of Staffordsh. 1189 (Rot. Pip.); Hugh, John, Richard Christmasse, &c., c. 1272, in England (Rot. Hund.).

Christofer. *See* CHRISTOPHER.

Christopher, from St. Christopher. Richard de St. Christopher occurs in Normandy, c. 1180 (Mag. Rot. Scac.). He appears to have been of the family of Harenc, and the estate was granted to new owners by Philip-Augustus, 1204.

Chuck, a form of Chokes or Chioches. *See* CHUCKS.

Chucks, a form of Chokes or Chioches, from Choques, in Flanders. Gunfrid de Cioches, a great Flemish noble, held a barony in Bucks, Leicester, and Northants, 1086. This passed, by marriage, to the Bethunes, Advocates or Protectors of Arras; but the male line continued as Cheokes and Chokes.

Church. *See* SEARCH.

Churchill, or De Corcelle. The

Churchills of Dorset, ancestors of the great Duke of Marlborough, are traceable, by the ordinary heralds' pedigrees, to the reign of Henry VII., bearing a lion ramp., debruised by a bendlet. Prior to this, they were of Devon and Somerset, still bearing the same arms (Pole, Devon). The C.s of Devon descended from Elias de Chirchille, t. Edw. I., who m. the heiress of Widworthy. In the same reign Richard de Churchulle occurs at Bruton and at Bath (Rot. Hundr. ii. 124; Anderson, Royal Geneal.). At the same time John de Corcelle, or Curcelle (the original form of Churchulle), occurs at Bruton (Rot. Hundr. ii. 124). Prior to this, Wandragesil de Curcelle is mentioned in Somerset, &c. (RCR), c. 1198. His father, Hugh de Curcelle, held five-and-a-half fees from the barony of Totness, 1165 (Pole, 12); and in a preceding generation lived Roger de C., who was granted Frome, Somerset, by Henry I. (Rot. Hundr. ii. 136). The latter was descended from Hugo Pincerna, who witnessed charters in favour of St. Amand, Normandy, before the Conquest (Mon. i. 996). His son, William de Corcelle (Gall. Christ. xi. 64), was father of Roger de Corcelle, who, in 1086, held a great barony in Somerset, &c., but lost it on taking part with other barons against Henry I. on his accession. He had brothers, Richard Pincerna or De Corcelle, Robert Pincerna, and Rainald, seated in Salop and Chester. His son, Roger de Corcelle, received a grant of the Hundred of Frome, Somerset, from Henry I., held by the service of one knight, where his descendants continued. Hugh de Corcelle, his son, above-mentioned, was living 1165 (Lib. Niger). The family of Walensis, or Wallace, in Scotland, was a branch of the Corcelles. *See* WALLACE. From this house descended the victorious Duke of Marlborough.

Churton, in some cases probably a corruption of Curton or CURETON.

Clabben. *See* CLABONE.

Clabone, for Calbone, or Calbony. William de Chalbeneys was summoned, 1251, to serve in Gascogne (Parl. Writs). The name was also written Chalviny or Chauveny, and was derived from a fief near Pontoise, Normandy. William de Calvigny occurs in the Duchy, 1180 (Mag. Rot. Scac.). Geoffry de Chalvennio witnessed a charter for Belver, Notts, t. Henry I. (Mon. i. 330). From Chalbeny, Chalbone, or Calbone, came Clabone.

Clapham, or De St. Ouen, from St. Andoen, near Arques, Normandy, which was held by William de St. Andoen from the Baron of Tancarville, c. 1050 (D'Anisy et St. Marie, Sur le Domesday). Bernard de St. A. in 1086 (Domesd.) held fiefs in Suffolk and Kent from William, Viscount of Arques and Rouen, and had several sons, of whom Atso or Azo, of Kent, occurs 1130 (Rot. Pip.); Gormund in Essex, t. Henry I. (Lib. Niger); and Gilbert in Sussex, who witnessed a charter of Philip de Braiose, 1103 (Mon. ii. 978). Roger de St. A. occurs 1153 (Mon. ii. 599). In 13th cent. Ralph de St. A. held two fees in Clopham (Clapham), Sussex, from the honour of Braiose (Testa). Hence the younger branches bore the name of Clapham, the seat of this family from nearly the Conquest. Another

family in Yorkshire, bearing the same name, is of unknown origin.

Clare. This probably includes different families : 1, Collateral descendants of the house of De Clare or Brionne, Earls of Hertford and Gloucester, descended from the Dukes of Normandy; 2, descendants of the Norman house of De Clere, whose fief lay in the Duchy. *See* CLEARE.

Claret. Walter Clarte occurs in Normandy, 1180-95 (Mag. Rot. Scac.); John Clarrot in Hunts, c. 1272 (Rot. Hundr.).

Clarges. Muriel de la Clergesse, Normandy, 1198 (MRS).

Claringbold. Geoffry Clerenbolt was of Normandy, 1180 (Mag. Rot. Scac.); N. Clarenbaut, in Sussex, 1199 (Palgr. Rot. Cur. Reg.); Roger Clerenbaud, in Salop, c. 1272 (Rot. Hund.).

Clark. This name includes persons of many different families. Some of these are Norman; at least the name frequently appears in the Duchy. Robert, Odo, Huard, Osbert, Philip, Richard, Branda Clericus, or Le Clerc, occur 1180-1195 (Mag. Rot. Scac.). Twenty of the name occur 1198 (Ib.); of these, nine also occur in England 1199; and the families of the name generally seem to have had members in both countries.

Clarke. *See* CLARK.

Clarmount, from Clermont, near Beauvais, the seat of the powerful baronial family of the name. William de Clermund (Clermont) granted lands to the Abbey of Shrewsbury, c. 1230 (Rot. Hundr.).

Clary. Lucas de Clarai occurs in Normandy 1198 (Mag. Rot. Scac.). The arms of the English family of

Clary occur in Robson; and are those of De Clare, with a label.

Class, or Claus. Odo de Clauso, of Normandy, 1180–95 (Mag. Rot. Scac.); Ralph de Clauso 1265 (Mém. Soc. Ant. Norm. v. 206). The arms of the English family of Claus appear in Robson. The French pronunciation makes it 'Close.'

Clavel, or Claville, a baronial family from C. near Rouen. Walter de C. in 1086 held 37 lordships in barony, Devon (Domesd.). In 1165 Walter de C. held 10 fees of the Honour of Gloucester (Lib. Nig.). Lomen-Claville according to Pole was the seat of the barony in Devon. Ralph de C. of this family held a fief in Dorset from Alured de Lincoln 13th cent. Various branches of this family continued for ages in Dorset. That of Smedmore in that county continued to 1774 (Hutchins, Dorset).

Clavering, a branch of the house of De Vesci or De Burgh. *See* VESEY.

Clay, from Claye, near Meaux. Peter de Claie occurs 1194, and Stephen de Claie 1199 in England (Palgr. Rot. Cur. Regis). Robert de Cladio held two fees in Oxford 1165 (Lib. Nig.). Henry de C. of York t. Henry II. (Mon. ii. 554). 1324 Thomas de C. (PPW). The name is borne by the baronets Clay.

Claye. *See* CLAY.

Clayfield, or Claville.

Clear. *See* CLEARE.

Cleare, or Clere, from the barony of Clere in the Vexin, Normandy. Reginald de C. was father of Matthew I., who m. Lucy de Hangest, and had Matthew II., who m. a sister of William de Longchamp, Bishop of Ely 1189. Roger de

Clere founded Little Mareis Priory, Yorkshire, t. Henry II. (Mon. i. 496), and Ralph and Roger Fitz-Ralph de C. were benefactors. In 1165 Roger de C. held two fees from Bigot in Norfolk, and Ralph de Clere from Fitz-Walter and de Clare (Lib. Nig.). The family was long seated at Ormsby, Norfolk.

Clears, a form of CLEAR.

Cleasby. Enisand Musard, brother of Hasculf M., Baron of Staveley, and son of Roald, Viscount of Nantes 1050 (Lobineau, Hist. Bret. ii. 117), was created Constable of Richmond by Earl Alan c. 1070. From him descended the family of De Richmond, Constables of R. His younger son obtained from him Cleasby, near Richmond, with Witcliffe, Torp, and Gerlington (Domesd.; Burton, Mon. Ebor. 273). Hasculph de Cleseby occurs t. Henry I. (Mon. Angl. i. 838), and his nephew Hasculf t. Stephen (Ib.). Hasculf, son of Hasculf t. John, possessed lands near Richmond which were granted to Roald, Constable of Richmond, on the death of Hasculf in Bretagne, (Gale, Hon. Rich. Add. 272, 3). T. Henry III. Hasculf de Cleseby held Wycliffe, Thorpe, and Gerlington (Ib. 29). In the next reign the family assumed the name of Wycliffe, Robert de W. holding the above estates (Ib. 50), and witnessing a charter of the Earl of Richmond 1278 (Mon. Angl. ii. 197). From a younger son descended the family of Cleasby. John Wycliffe, the Reformer, was brother of William, son of Roger W., son of Alan de Moresby, son of Robert de Wycliffe. One of the judges bears the name.

Cleere. *See* CLEAR.

Clemams. *See* CLEMENCE.

Clemence, from St. Clement, Normandy. Alured de St. Clement occurs there 1180–95 (Mag. Rot. Scac.); Robert Clement in 1198 (Ib.). William Clement and Matilda de St. Clement in England 1199 (Palgr. Rot. Cur. Regis).

Clemens. *See* CLEMENCE.

Clement. *See* CLEMENCE.

Clements. *See* CLEMENCE.

There is also a family of Cambro-Celtic origin of this name, from which descend the Earls of Leitrim.

Clemmans, a form of CLEMENCE.

Clemments. *See* CLEMENTS.

Clerc. *See* CLARK.

Clerihew, probably a corruption of Cleriveus or Clairvaux. The family of Clerowe is armorially identified with Clarvaux of Yorkshire (Robson). Clairvaux was near Rhodez, Aquitaine. Ranulph and John de Clervaus or Clerwaus occur in England c. 1272 (Rot. Pip.). The name long flourished at Croft, Yorkshire.

Clerke. *See* CLARK.

Clewett, from Cloet. Roger Cloet was of Normandy 1180–95 (Mag. Rot. Scac.). Peter and Philip Clouet are mentioned there at a later date.

Cliff, a Norman family, though bearing an English name. Lucas de Clive 1180 paid a fine in the bailifry of Rouen for disseisin (Mag. Rot. Scac.).

The family of Cliff or Clive was that of De Corneville, of which Robert de Corneville held 13th cent. a fief in Cliva of the Earl of the Isle (Testa).

Cliffe. *See* CLIFF.

Clifford, or De Pons. About 920 Manno and Pontius, Barons or Princes of Pons in Saintonge, nobles of Gothic race, were benefactors to Savigny Abbey (Bouquet, Hist. Franç. xi. 200), and in 1079 Pontius or Ponce, Prince of Pons, granted a church to the abbey of Cormery, in presence of his sons Anselm, Garnier, and Philip-Milo (Gall. Christ. xii. 14). From the first descended the Lords of Pons in Aquitaine, one of the most powerful families in France, who are frequently mentioned in history. Ponce had also other sons who went to England, of whom Drogo Fitz-Ponce and Walter Fitz-Ponce held important baronies in 1086 (Domesd.). Their younger brothers were: 1. Richard Fitz-Ponce. 2. Osbert Fitz-Ponce, ancestor of the VESEYS and BURGHS. The names of these sons are mentioned by Henry I. in his charter confirming their gifts to Malvern Priory (Mon. Angl. i. 366); and from the Monasticon (i. 365, ii. 876) it appears that they also bore the name of 'Pontium,' or des Pons, from which it appears that they were sons of Ponce 'of Pons.'

Richard Fitz-Ponce witnessed, with Bernard de Neumarché, a charter of Brecknock Priory c. 1120 (Jones, Hist. Brecon. ii. 75), and was ancestor of the De Cliffords, Earls of Cumberland, as is generally known; and from a remote junior branch of this family descended Thomas Clifford, who became a Roman Catholic; was a leading member of the Cabal, t. Charles II., and was created Baron Clifford.

Clift. *See* CLIFF (Lower).

Clifton. Families of various origin. The Cliftons of Notts bore also the Norman names of De Reborso or Ribercy. Arnulf de Reburso or Rebors occurs in the Duchy

1180-95 (Mag. Rot. Scac.). Richard and Humfry Rebors 1198 (Ib.). The lordship of Reborcy or Ribercil belonged to the family of Wac, and Hugh Wac granted the church there to Longues Abbey 1168 (Gall. Christ. xi. Instr. 83, 84). His son Geoffry Wac then mentioned appears to be the Geoffry de Ribercy or de Clifton who was ancestor of this family. *See* COLLINS.

Clinton. In 1086 Geoffry held Glinton, Northants, from Geoffry de Mowbray, Bishop of Coutances (Domesd.). Geoffry de Glinton or Clinton, his son, chamberlain to Henry I., gave the Church of Glinton, Northants, with others, to Kenilworth Priory 1120 (Mon. Angl. ii. 114). In t. Henry I., he, as Gaufrid de Dofera, was on an inquisition in Normandy (Mem. Soc. Ant. Norm.); and t. Henry II., before 1154, Gaufrid de Clinton, his son, acknowledged that he had pledged the estate of Dopra to the Bishop of Bayeux for 30l. Anjou (Mem. Soc. Ant. Norm.). In 1165 this baron returned his fees in England as 17 (Lib. Nig.). This was a branch of the family of De Douvres or De Dover, which was of great baronial consequence. *See* DOVER. The Dukes of Newcastle descend from this Norman house of Clinton.

Clisby. *See* CLEASBY.

Clissold. The old forms appear to have been Clisald and Clissolas (Robson). Probably derived from Clissolles or Glisolles, near Evreux.

Clixxard, probably a form of Clissald. *See* CLISSOLD.

Clode, for Claude (Lower); perhaps from St. Claude, near Blois. The arms appear in Robson as vairé or and az., and barry wavy of 6 or

202

and az. The name does not appear in Normandy.

Cloid, for Claude. *See* CLODE.

Close, the French pronunciation of CLAUS. *See* CLASS.

Closs, a form of Claus. *See* CLASS and CLOSE.

Cloud, a form of CLOUT.

Clout, a form of Cloet. *See* CLEWETT.

Clowes, a form of CLOSE.

Cluard, a form of Clouet or Cloet. *See* CLEWETT.

Cluett. *See* CLEWETT.

Clybeun, a form of CLABON.

Coad, a form of COAT.

Coat. Robert de Coete or Coiete was of Normandy 1180-95 (Mag. Rot. Scac.); David Cote of England 1199 (Palgr. Rot. Cur. Regis). The name was sometimes derived from places named Cote in England.

Coates. *See* COAT.

Coath. *See* COAT.

Coats. *See* COAT.

Cobb. N. Gobb, of Normandy 1180-95 (MRS). Walter, Robert, William Cobbe of England c. 1272 (RH).

Cobbett, or Cobet, from Coubet. Hugo Coubite was of Normandy 1180-1195 (Mag. Rot. Scac.). Robert Cobét was of Suffolk 1340 (Non. Inq. 89). Hence the famous political writer William Cobbett.

Cobbold, or Gobaud. Baldwin Wac granted to Robert Fitz-Gubold t. Henry I. one fee, held of the Barony of Brunne, Lincoln (Lib. Nig.), from whom descended John Gubaud 13th cent., who held of the same barony (Testa). Robert Goebald occurs in 1158 (Rot. Pip.), and Henry Gobaud in Devon (Testa).

Cobell, a form of Cabell. *See* CABBELL.

Cobham. Hamo, son of Serlo de Marci, was of Essex 1130 (Rot. Pip.). In 1198 William de Marci of Essex had a suit against the Prior of Bermondsey relating to the Church of Cobham, Kent (Palgr. Rot. Cur. Regis). Henry de Cobham, who was the first known to Dugdale (Baronage, ii. 65), was probably a cousin of William de Marcy. He was living 1199 (Palgr. Rot. Cur. Regis). *See* MARCY. Three branches of this family were barons by writ.

Cook, or Coke, from le Coq or Cocus. William, Gerold, Josceline, Radulphus Coqus or Cocus in Normandy 1180-95 (Mag. Rot. Scac.). Of these, William and Ralph occur in England 1189 (Rot. Pip.), also Bernard, Roger, Wascius Cocus, evidently foreigners. Others occur 1199 (Palgr. Rot. Cur. Regis).

Cooks, Cocus, or le Coq, from the feudal office of Coquus. Wymund le Coq, Hugh, Roger, Ralph of Normandy 1180-95 (MRS). Rodbertus Cocus held lands at Estraites, Kent, from Hugh Sire de Montfort 1086 (Domesd.). Hugo C., his grandson, witnessed a charter of Folkestone Priory 1137 (Mon. i. 560). Adam Cocus was dead before 1202, when the Hospitallers had a grant of his land in farm (Rot. Canc. 214). William Coc of Ospringe granted lands to Davington Priory, Kent, 13th cent. (Mon. i. 50). John le Cock of Ospringe was father of Walter le C., who d. 1328 seized of Ospringe (Inq. p. Mort.). Richard Cocks d. seized of O. in 1498; soon after which the family settled in Gloucester and Worcester; and from it descend the Earls Somers.

Cockerell, from Coquerel, near Evreux, Normandy. In 1165 Illyas de Kokerel held fiefs in Gloucester from Bohun and Neumarché, and William K. from Giffard E. of Bucks (Lib. Nig.). Fulco Cokerel held in Gloucester 18th cent. (Testa). In 1324 Sir William Cockerell was returned from Essex to attend a great council at Westminster, PPW. The baronets Cockerell (now Rushout) are of this race.

Codnor may perhaps be younger branches of Grey of Codnor. *See* GREY.

Codrington, or De Cantilupe, from Gotherington, Gloucester. Roger de Cantilupe, living 1201, had possessions in Wapley and Gotherington; and with his son Roger made grants there to St. Augustine's Abbey, Bristol (Fosbroke, Glouc. ii. 20; Mon. Angl.). The abbey made further purchases there from Richard, son of the above Roger (Ibid.). It appears that this family remained at Gotherington or Codrington, which name they bore. Geoffry de Cotherington was living here t. Edward III. (Atkins, Glouc., 391, 397). He was probably grandson of Richard de Cantilupe of this place. The Codringtons bore argent, a fesse gules, differenced by lions. Some branches of Cantilupe also bore argent, a fesse gules, differenced by lions' heads or fleur de lys (Robson); which shows that these were branches of the same race. The lords Cantilupe (barons by writ 1299) were from Chanteloup, near Coutances. William de C. occurs in Normandy 1124 (Gall. Christ. xi. 160). Walter de C. in Lincoln 1130 (Rot. Pip.). In 1165 Walter, Roger, Ralph, and Simon de C. held fiefs in England (Lib. Nig.). Roger de C., ancestor of the Codringtons, was brother of William de C., first baron of Brecknock.

Coffin or Cophin, perhaps from Couvain, near Coutances. The family came to England at the Conquest, soon after which Richard Cophin held fiefs in Devon (Pole), from the Earl of Mortaine (Testa); and Paganus Cofin, t. Henry I., held from Paganus de Beauchamp in Bedford (Mon. i. 245). Richard C. in 1263 had a writ of military summons (PPW).

Coffen. *See* COFFIN.

Coish, a form of Goish, or Goyes, which appears from Robson to be another form of Gorges; Goyes of Wilts being of Wraxall and Langford, Wilts, which belonged to Gorges, and bearing their arms, a gurges, or whirlpool. *See* CHARGE.

Coke, or Cocus. Godefridus Cocus, with other great men, witnessed a Norman charter 1066 (Gall. Christ. xi. 60). In 1086 Walter, perhaps son of Godfrey, held a barony in Essex (Domesd. Ess. 95). Ranulph Cocus, his son, occurs in Norfolk c. 1118 (Blomefield, iv. 430). William Coke, 1206, was father of Thomas C., who held a knight's fee and half in Didlington, from Earl Warrenne, 1239. His grandson Robert C. was Lord of D. 1280. His descendant Sir John C., banneret, was seneschal of Gascoigne t. Edw. III. (Blomefield, ix. 235), from whom descended the celebrated Sir Edward Coke, Lord Chief Justice, ancestor of the Earls of Leicester.

Coker, or De Mandeville, from the castle and barony of Manneville or Magneville, in the Cotentin. This family is said to have been a branch of the Bertrams, Barons of Briquebec (Wiffen, Mem. Russell, i. 6). *See* MITFORD. Geoffry de Manneville came 1066 to England, and

204

received a great barony in Essex. He had—1. William, ancestor of the De Mandevilles, Earls of Essex; 2. Stephen, father of Roger de M., Castellan of Exeter, ancestor of the M.s of Devon and Normandy; 3. Geoffry de Mandeville, who had grants in Barony from Henry I., of which Mersewood, Dorset, was the head (Pole, Devon, 233; Testa, 183). His barony consisted of 15 knights' fees, but t. Stephen the greater part was confiscated and given to De Tilly; and Geoffry de M., who returned his barony 1165 as only one fee, proceeded by law for the recovery of the remainder. William de M. of Dorset and Somerset, c. 1200, was engaged in the same suit (Hardy, Obl. et Fin. 44). In 1203 William Mandeville of Coker, Somerset, paid scutage for that lordship (Rot. Canc.). He obtained the barony of Mersewood. In 1205 Robert de M., probably brother of William, claimed Coker against him (Hardy, Obl. et Fin. 302), and obtained possession (Collinson, Somerset, ii. 341). Sir John de Mandeville was Lord of Coker 1275 (Ib.), and had Robert de M., whose sister and heir sold Coker to the Courtenays. Robert de Coker, brother of Sir John (Mon. ii. 10), witnessed a charter of Robert de M. regarding Coker. His descendants long held Coker. The arms varied slightly from those of Mandeville (three lions in pale, a bend), being a bend, charged with three lions' or leopards' heads.

Colbeck or Caldebeck, from Caudebec or Caldebec, Normandy. William de Caudebec occurs in the Duchy 1180–95 (Mag. Rot. Scac.); Jumel de C. 1198 (Ib.). Robson preserves the arms of the English line.

Colcote. *See* CALCUTT.

Coldrey. Robert, Roger, Reginald de Coldreio occur in Normandy, 1180–95 (Mag. Rot. Scac.). The fief of Coldrey was in Normandy (Ib.). William de Coldreto also occurs 1180; William de Coudray or Coldray in England, c. 1272.

Colebeck. *See* COLBECK.

Coleridge. In 1086 Colerige, Devon, was held in barony by the Bishop of Coutances, whose subtenant Drogo de Montacute had sub-enfeoffed Ingebald, probably a Norman follower of his (Domesd. 102 b), by whose descendants this place (whence they took their name) was held. Hence the poet Coleridge.

Colette. *See* COLLETT.

Coley, the French pronunciation of Colet. *See* COLLETT.

Collacott. *See* CALCUTT.

Collar. *See* COLLARD.

Collard. Hamon, William, and Geoffry Coillart of Normandy, 1180–95 (Mag. Rot. Scac.).

Collens. *See* COLLINS.

Coller. *See* COLLAR.

Collet. *See* COLLETT.

Collett. William Colet was resident in Normandy 1180–95 (Mag. Rot. Scac.); Humphry and William Colet in 1198 (Ib.); Alexander Culet in England 1199 (Palgr. Rot. Cur. Regis), Dyonisia and Walter Colet c. 1272 (Rot. Hundr.).

Colley, from Cuilly or Quilly, near Falaise, Normandy. Ralph de Cuillio, Nicholas de C., in Normandy, 1180–95 (Mag. Rot. Scac.).

Colley-Wellesley, from Cuilly. Robert Bordet, with his son Robert, witnessed a charter of the Count of Anjou, c. 1050. He had issue, 1. Robert; 2. Hugh, who, in 1086, held considerable estates in Leicester from the Countess Judith, and was ancestor of the Burdetts baronets, and of Baroness Burdett-Coutts.

Robert Bordet, the elder son, Lord of Cuilly, was dead before 1086, when his widow held from Hugh de Grentmenil, in Leicester (Domesd. i. 232 b.). He had been living in 1077 (Mon. i. 562), and his son Hugh de Cuilli in 1128 witnessed a charter of Richard de Beauvais (Mon. ii. 143). Hugh had issue, 1. Robert de Cuilli; 2. Walter de C.

The elder son Robert Bordet, Sire de Cuilli, m. Sibylla, d. of William de Chievre, a baron of Devon, and on undertaking to rebuild the city of Tarragona in Spain, and to defend it against the Saracens, obtained the suzerainty, with the rank of Prince of Tarragona. He in 1133, at the head of his Norman chivalry, rescued Alfonso, King of Arragon, and his army from destruction by the Saracens, at the battle of Fraga. William, Sire de Aguillon, his son, one of the barons of Normandy, 1165 (Feod. Norm.), lost the principality of T. in consequence of the accidental death of the archbishop, which was attributed to him. He appears to have been succeeded by Manasser de Aguillon, his brother, ancestor of the Barons Aguillon. Simon, a younger brother, was ancestor of the De Cuillys of Normandy.

Walter de Cuilly, brother of the first Prince of Tarragona, witnessed the foundation charter of Canwell, Stafford, 1142 (Mon. i. 440). In 1247 Hugh de C. paid a fine in Warwick (Roberts, Excerpt. ii.). William de Quilly (13th cent.) held

205

lands in Stafford from Marmion (Inq. p. Mort.), and also held Ratcliffe-Culey or Cuilly, Leicester, from the same (Nicholls, Leicester, iv. ii. 939). Hugh de Culey was Lord of Ratcliffe 1296, 1299. Hugh de Cuilly, 1309, was Constable of Kenilworth; and being taken prisoner with the Earl of Lancaster at the battle of Boroughbridge, died of his wounds in Pontefract Castle. He had issue John Culey, who had issue two sons, viz., Thomas, whose dau. and heir m. Sir John Stanhope, of Rampton (ancestor of the Earls of Chesterfield); 2. Richard, living 1361 (Rot. Origin., ii. 351), who was father of John Culley of Lubbenham, Leicester, who m. a dau. of Sir John Harrington (Harl. MS. 1558, fol. 35), and had issue John of Lubbenham, father of William Colley, of Glaston, Rutland, whose son John had issue, 1. Anthony, ancestor of the Colleys, Lords of Glaston, extinct; 2. Walter; 3. Robert. The two youngest sons went to Ireland t. Henry VIII., and from Walter descended the Lords of Castle-Carbery, the lineal male ancestors of Arthur Wellesley, Duke of Wellington, the greatest and most victorious general ever produced by England.

Collie. *See* COLLEY.

Collins. William de Colince or Colunce held lands at Chadlington, Oxford, c. 1272 (Rot. Hundr.). Hugh de Culunce had custody of Pont Orson t. John, c. 1200 (Mem. Soc. Ant. Norm., v. 119). Coulonces was near Alençon. Ernis de C. m. a dau. of William de Warrenne, Earl of Surrey, t. Henry I. Hugh de Colonches, 1165, held a barony of four fees, and Thomas de C. one

206

of equal dimensions. Adam de C. paid a fine to the King in Oxfordshire 1203, and Hugh de C. confirmed lands to Mottisfont Priory (Mon. ii.).

Colombine, a corruption of COLOMBELL.

Colombo. Roger Colombie or Colunbie, of Normandy, 1180-95 (Mag. Rot. Scac.).

Columba. *See* COLOMBO.

Columbell, from Colombelles in the Cotentin. William, Alexander, Eudo, Guido de Colombellis of Normandy 1180-95 (Mag. Rot. Scac.); Geoffry de Colombelles, Lincoln, 1199 (Palgr. Rot. Cur. Regis).

Colt, an abbreviation of COLET. Hence the baronets of the name.

Columbine. *See* COLOMBINE.

Colville, from Colleville, near Bayeux. Gilbert de Colavilla was of Suffolk, 1086 (Domesd.), and William de C. of York (Ib.). Temp. Henry I. William de C. held Colleville from Ranulph, Viscount of Bayeux (Mem. Soc. Ant. Norm. viii. 430). Temp. Stephen, Philip de C. resisted King Stephen in York, and was obliged to take refuge in Scotland, where, c. 1165, he witnessed a charter of Patrick, Earl of Dunbar (Chart. Mailros.). From him descend the Lords Colville of Scotland.

The English barons Colville descended from Gilbert C. of Suffolk, 1086. William de C. 1165, held four knights' fees of the Honour of Eye, also two in Lincoln from Wac and Deincourt. Roger de C. at the same time held one in Norfolk, and Richard de C. one in Devon (Lib. Nig.). The Colvilles of Lullington, Derby, descend from this family.

Colwell, a corruption of COLVILLE (Lower).

Colwill. *See* COLWELL.

Coman, a corruption of COMYN.

Combes. Theobald Comes of Normandy 1180-95 (Mag. Rot. Scac.). Gislebert, Nigel, Richard, Robert C. 1198 (Ib.). Ordulph Comes, Devon, c. 1272 (Rot. Hundr.); also Sire Richard, Nicholas, and Roger C. in Salop and Oxford (Ib.).

Combes. See COMBS.

Comins. See COMYN.

Commin. See COMYN.

Comper, from Camper or Champer, the arms of which are preserved (Robson). Perhaps from Champier, near Grenoble.

Comyn, from Comines in Flanders. Rodbert de Cuminis was created Earl of Durham 1068 (Ord. Vit.). The family continued after his death. Hugh Cumin witnessed the charter of Rievaux Abbey, York, t. Henry I. (Mon. Angl. i. 729). Odard C. witnessed a charter t. Stephen (Ib. i. 476). William C. occurs 1130, 1158 (Rot. Pip.). William C. became Chancellor of Scotland 1133 (Douglas, Peerage). His descendant William C. became Earl of Buchan 1210. Various branches existed in England.

Conde. See CONDY.

Condy, from Condé, near Bayeux. Amfrid Camerarius witnessed a charter in Normandy 1066 (Gall. Christ. xi. Instr. 60). In 1086 he held 26 lordships in Barony in England (Domesd.). Robert, his son, gave his estate of Condy to Holy Trinity, Caen, 1082 (G.C. 70). He is named Robert de Condy in England 1103 (Mon. Angl. i. 574). His brother Audin de C. was Bishop of Bayeux 1112, and Turstin de C. was Archbishop of York 1119. Another brother, Richard de C., accompanied Duke Robert to Pales-

tine 1096 (Des Bois). The family long remained of great consequence in England.

Coney, from Cony or Coigny in the Cotentin. Sire Hubert and Sire William de Coni held lands from Philip Augustus c. 1204. Robert Coignee occurs in Gloucester 1230 (Roberts, Excerpt.).

Conner, usually from the Celtic name O'Conor; but Connour was also an old English name, derived from Coneres, a form of Coisnieres or CONYERS.

Connett. Probably foreign. Sarah Conet occurs c. 1272 (Rot. Hundr.), perhaps a form of Cornet, several of which family occur in Normandy 1180-95 (Mag. Rot. Scac.).

Connew, i.e. Cannew or Canu, a form of CANUTE.

Conscience, a form of CONSTANCE.

Consedine, a corruption of CONSTANTINE.

Conquest, from Conquet, Bretagne. Geoffry de Conquest held Houghton, Bedf., from the Honour of Hunts, 13th cent. (Testa).

Constable, or De Gand. Witikind, the renowned opponent of Charlemagne, after many years of resistance was compelled to submit c. 780, when he was invested with the Dukedom of Angria (L'Art de Vérif. les Dates, xvi. 145). Ludolphus, one of his descendants, was Duke of Saxony, and d. 864, leaving by his wife, dau. of Eberhard, Duke of Friuli, Bruno, Duke of Saxony. He m. a dau. of the Emperor Arnold, and declined the Imperial throne. Bruno had two sons: 1. Henry the Fowler, Emperor in 919, father of the Emperor Otho, who succeeded 936; 2. Wickman. Wickman was created Count of

Gand 940 by the Emperor Otho, his nephew; and had two sons: 1. Theodoric, Count of Gand, ancestor of the Counts of Gand and Guines; 2. Adalbert, father of Ralph, father of Baldwin de Gand, Count of Gand or Alost, ancestor of the Counts of Alost, whose younger brother Gilbert de Gand became baron of Folkingham in England. The latter had, 1. Walter; 2. Hugh, ancestor of the house of Montfort; 3. Robert; 4. Thomas. Robert, the Constable (of Folkingham barony), granted to his brother Thomas de Alost, son of Gilbert de Alost (or De Gand), lands at Frestingthorpe, York (Burton, Mon. Ebor.). In 1130 the wardship of William (Constable) de Alost was granted to Walter de Gand, baron of Folkingham (Rot. Pip.), and William Constable's son Robert confirmed the grants of Thomas de Alost, his father's brother (Burton). Hence sprang the great house of Constable of Flamborough, who bore nearly the same arms as the De Gands and Alosts.

Constance, from Constans or Coutances, Normandy. Robert de Constans or Constance occurs in the Duchy 1180 (Mag. Rot. Scac.); Walter de Constantin in England 1190 (Palgr. Rot. Cur. Regis).

Constantine. Nigel was Viscount of C. or Coutances 1047, when he revolted against Duke William and lost his vast estates. Of his descendants, Ralph de Constantine was seated in Salop 1086 (Domesd.). Hugh de C., his son, granted lands to Salop Abbey before 1121. Umfrid de C. witnessed its foundation charter 1093, and Richard de C. that of Haghmond Abbey 1099. The family long flourished in Salop, and

208

t. Henry II. sent a branch to Ireland, of which Geoffry de C. witnessed the charter of St. Thomas, Dublin, 1177, and founded Tristernagh Abbey.

Conyers, from Coignieres, Isle of France. Roger de Conneris lived t. Stephen (Wiffen, Mem. of Russell, i. 16). In 1165 Roger de Coneres held three fees from the See of Durham, and Ralph de C. lands in Norfolk from De Albini. The elder line assumed the name of Norton from its 'caput baroniæ,' and from it descended the Lords Grantley, representatives of the eminent judge Sir Fletcher Norton. *See* NORTON.

Conyngham (Burton). *See* BURTON.

Cooch, a form of GOOCH.

Coode, a form of GOODE.

Cooley, from Culey or Cuilly. *See* COLLEY-WELLESLEY.

Cook, a form of Coq or COCK.

Cooke. *See* COOK.

Cookes. *See* COOK. Of this name was the founder of Worcester College, Oxford.

Coombes. *See* COMBES.

Coombs. *See* COMBS.

Coomes. *See* COMBES.

Coope. Turstin Coupe was of Normandy, 1180-95 (Mag. Rot. Scac.); Hugh Coupe, 1198 (Ib.); Robert and Walter Cope, c. 1272 (Rot. Hundr.). Coope, Cope, and Coup are armorially identified (Robson).

Cooper, or COWPER. 1. From Cuperius or Le Cuper, a trade. Salide le Cupere occurs in Norfolk, 1189 (Rot. Pip.). Norman, Jordan, Roger le Cupere and many others, 1272 (RH). Norman families are included. 2. From Cupparius, or Cup-bearer (Du Cange). Two families of importance bore this name. *See* ASHLEY-COOPER, and COWPER.

Coot, armorially identified with Chook or Choke (Robson). This is a branch of the Flemish family of De Choques or Cioches. *See* CHUCKS.

Coote. *See* COOT. The arms changed from three cinquefoils borne by Choke to a chevron between three cinquefoils borne by Coot, then to a chevron between three cootes borne by Coote. From this family descended the Earls of Bellamont, Lords Castle-Coote, and the Baronets Coote of the name.

Cootes, or Coutts, armorially identified with Coote (Robson).

Cope, or De Chappes, originally bore a fesse, which identifies it with the family of Chappes or Capes (Robson), the name being a translation of Chappe. Chappes was in Champagne. Osbern de Capes is mentioned, 1079, by Ord. Vitalis (p. 605). William de Capis, t. Henry I., with Albin his brother, witnessed a charter of Hugh Bussell for Evesham Abbey (Mon. i. 360). In 1200 Peter and Ralph de C. had a suit at Leicester with William de C. (RCR). Nicholas de C., t. John, m. the heiress of Robert le Prevost of Northampton, where the family long remained, and gave its name to Preston - Capes. The family of Chappes, Capes, or Cope appears in Northampton soon after. From it descend the Baronets Cope.

Copley, or De Moels, Baronets, from Meulles, Normandy. Descended in the male line from Moyle of Cornwall, of whom Reginald de Moyl, alias Moel, was dead before 1304, when Wm. M. was found to be his next heir (Roberts, Cal. Geneal. 676). The Lords Moels, of which this was a branch, descended from Roger de Molis, who

in 1086 held from Baldwin de Brionne in Devon.

Coppard, or Copart, from Coopertus or Covert. *See* COURT.

Coppen. *See* COPPIN.

Copper. *See* COOPER.

Coppin, probably foreign. Warin Copin was of Cornwall, 1189; Hervey and Ivo Copin of England, c. 1272. The name does not appear in Normandy, but it may be found elsewhere. The arms were or, a chief vair.

Copping. *See* COPPIN.

Coppins, for COPPIN.

Copus, for Capus or Cabus. *See* CHAPPUIS.

Coram, for Goram or GORHAM.

Corbell. Geoffry, Radulf, and William Corbel of Normandy, 1198 (Mag. Rot. Scac.); Richard Corbeil of England, 1189; William Corboil was Archbishop of Canterbury, t. Henry I.

Corben. *See* CORBYN.

Corbet, a Norman family too well known to need any detail. Hence the Barons Corbet of Caux, and the Baronets Corbet. *See* Eyton, Salop; Dugdale, Baronage, &c. The name also existed in Normandy. Ilbert, Reinold, and Richard C. occur there, 1180–95 (MRS).

Corbey, the Norman-French pronunciation of Corbet or CORBETT.

Corbitt. *See* CORBETT.

Corbould. Robert Corbaldus was of Normandy, 1180–95 (Mag. Rot. Scac.); John Carbul appears in England, c. 1272 (Rot. Hund.).

Corbyn. *See* CARABINE. Osbert Corbyn of Holne, Devon (Mon. i. 792). The name occurs in Notts, Derby, Devon, Wilts, in the records.

Cordeaux. The French form of Cordels or Cordeux. *See* CORDELL.

Cordelier, for Cordonier, or Corduaner. Fere Cordoanier, 1198; Robert Cordon, 1195, Normandy, (MRS); Stephen, Hugh, Randulph le Corduaner, England, c. 1272 (RH).

Cordell, or Cordall. Robert de Cordelles was of Normandy, 1180-95 (Mag. Rot. Scac.); Hugh Cordel of London, 1180 (Rot. Pip.).

Corden, a corruption of Carden. *See* CARDEN.

Corderoy, a corruption of Cordray. *See* CORDEROY.

Corderoy, or Cordray, from Corday or Corderay in the Cotentin. William de Cordai occurs in Normandy, 1195-98 (Mag. Rot. Scac.); Peter de Codrai in England (13th cent.). The family is frequently mentioned.

Cordery, a form of CORDEROY.

Cordeux. *See* CORDEAUX.

Cording. *See* CORDEN.

Cordroy. *See* CORDEROY.

Cordwell, for CARDWELL.

Corfe, probably a form of CORPE.

Core, or Cure. Robert Cur occurs in Normandy, t. Philip-Augustus, c. 1204 (Mem. Soc. Ant. Norm., v. 182); William Curre occurs in England, 1189; John Cure, c. 1272 (Rot. Hundr.).

Corker. Arnulf de Corcres occurs in Normandy, 1180-95 (Mag. Rot. Scac.); Geoffry Chorger or Churger in England, c. 1272 (Rot. Hundr.).

Corkhill, probably a form of Corcelle. *See* CHURCHILL.

Cormie, probably a corruption of Cormeilles, near Lisieux. Gozelin de Cormeliis was a baron in Hants, 1086, and Ansfrid de C. in Gloucester and Hereford (*see* Dugd. Bar.; Mon. i. 115, 553). Sire John de Cormayles,

210

1316, possessed estates in Dorset and Hants (Palgr. Parl. Writs).

Corn, from Corn, near Cahors. John, Richard, and William de Corne seated in England, c. 1272 (Rot. Hundr.).

Cornhill, or Corniole, a baronial family, of whom William Corniole held a barony in Kent, 1086 (Domesd.); Reginald de Cornhull in 1165 (Lib. Nig.); and Gervase de C. a fief from the Earl of Essex (Ib.). The latter was Viscount of Kent, 1168-73, and the family frequently held that office afterwards (Hasted, Kent). Robert Cornel occurs in Normandy, 1180-95 (Mag. Rot. Scac.).

Cornell. *See* CORNHILL.

Corner, from Cornerd or Cornart. Hugh and Sampson Cornard or Cornart were of Normandy, 1180-95 (Mag. Rot. Scac.); Robert, Alexander, and John de Cornherd or Corner of England, 1199 (Palgr. Rot. Cur. Regis).

Corney. The French pronunciation of Cornet. Richard, Reinold, Lucas, Ralph, Matthew Cornet of Normandy, 1180-95 (Mag. Rot. Scac.).

Cornew. *See* CORNU or Cornutus. Robert Cornu or Cornut, William and Richard in Normandy, 1180-95 (Mag. Rot. Scac.).

Corns. *See* CORN.

Cornu. Robert Cornu or Cornutus occurs in Normandy, 1180; William C. 1180-95. The family of Le Cornu in Normandy descended from them. Roger Cornutus held three fees of Tavistock Abbey, Devon, 1165 (Lib. Nig.).

Cornwell, or De Corneville, from C., near Pont-Audemer. Robert de Wenesley or De C. gave lands at

Corneville to Jumièges, t. Henry I. (Mon. ii.); Robert de C. held lands in Wilts, 13th cent. (Testa).

Corp. *See* CORPE.

Corpe, from the fief of Corp, in Normandy, held from Philip-Augustus by the Dean o Anjou, c. 1204 (Mem. Soc. Ant. Norm. v. 174).

Corry. *See* CORY.

Corsar, for Corvesar. William Corvesarius occurs in Normandy, 1180-90 (Mag. Rot. Scac.); Christina and Henry Corveser in England, c. 1272 (Rot. Hundr.).

Cort, from Court. *See* A'COURT.

Cortis. *See* CURTIS.

Corum. *See* CORAM.

Cory. Gilbert, Odo, William Coreie of Normandy, 1180 - 95 (MRS).

Cosen. John Cosen, Bishop of Durham, was descended from an ancient Norfolk family. In 1386 Edmond le Cosyn was bailiff of Norwich; in 1327 John C. Before this Roger C. held several manors in Norfolk by marriage (Blomefield, i. 485, ii. 491, 537), and Ralph C. possessed Choseley in the same county (Ib. x. 349); and 1217 Gilbert C., probably of this family, was bailiff of the Honour of Lancaster in Lincoln. The name of Le Cusin implies relationship to a distinguished family in Norfolk. The arms are those of De Limesi (with a change of tincture), which Norman family had a branch seated in Norfolk at an early date. The Cosins were probably descended from this branch.

Cosens, Cosin, Cousins (a French name) includes families of Norman and other descents. Herebert and Robert Cusin occur in England,

1189 (Rot. Pip.); Gilbert, John, Roger, and William C., 1199 (Palgr. Rot. Cur. Regis).

Cosham, a branch of the Bassets, Barons of Normanville in Normandy. *See* PALMER.

Cossart, apparently foreign. The arms are preserved by Robson.

Cosser, a form of COSSART.

Cost. Roger Costé was of Normandy, 1180-95 (Mag. Rot. Scac.); Ralph Coste in 1198 (Ib.).

Costen, or Costeyn, a known form of CONSTANTINE.

Coster, a form of Costard. Walter Costart was of Normandy, 1180 (Mag. Rot. Scac.); Anfrid and Roger C. in 1198 (Ib.); Oliver Costard was of England, 1194 (Palgr. Rot. Cur. Regis).

Costin, or Costeyn, a known form of CONSTANTINE.

Cotching, an English corruption of Cochon. William and Durand Cochon were of Normandy, 1180-95 (Mag. Rot. Scac.); Hugh Cochun of England, c. 1272 (Rot. Hundr.).

Cotell. William Cotel was of Normandy, 1180-95 (Mag. Rot. Scac.); Richard Cotel of England, 1189 (Palgr. Rot. Cur. Regis); Elias, Hugh, Robert, Roger, Thomas, Walter C., c. 1272 (Rot. Hundr.); Berengarius Cotel held lands in Wilts, in capite, 1083 (Exon. Domesd.).

Cotterell. Probably foreign. Walter Coteral was of Herefordshire, 1158 (Rot. Pip.). In 1130 William C. occurs in Middlesex (Ib.). He granted lands to the Knights Hospitallers (Mon. Angl. ii.). William C. was M.P. for Wilton, 1313-25.

Cotterill. *See* COTTERELL.

Cottle. *See* COTTELL.

Cottrell. *See* COTTERELL.

Cottrill. *See* COTTERELL.

Couch, or Couche. *See* CUST.

Couchy, from Coucy near Laon. Alberic de Coucy had issue Drogo, Sire de Coucy and Boves, living 1059. Eguerrand, Robert, and Anselm were his sons; also Alberic de Coucy or Cocy, who held lands in York and Bucks 1086 (Domesd.). He had Ingenulf, whose son, Geoffry de Cocy, occurs in Gloucester 1130 (Rot. Pip.). Richard Cose or Cocy occurs 12th cent. (Mon. Angl. i. 496). Of the French line was Eguerrand de Coucy, Earl of Bedford.

Coudray. *See* CAUDERY.

Coughtrey, altered from CAW-DERY.

Coulon, from ACOULON.

Coulter, or De Culture, from Culture, near Mende, Languedoc. In 1165 Henry de C. held a barony in Somerset (Lib. Niger). Henry II. confirmed his gifts to Plympton Priory (Mon. ii.). Henry de C. paid scutage in Dorset 1202; and Henry de C. held in chief in Somerset 13th cent. (Testa).

Counsel. William and Warin Consel were of Normandy 1180 (Mag. Rot. Scac.); John Cunsail of England, c. 1272 (Rot. Hundr.).

Count, an English form of Comes, or le Counte. *See* COMBES.

Courcy, a well-known Norman baronial family, from which sprang the barons De Courcy, the Earls of Ulster, and the Barons Kingsale.

Courtenay. In 941 Fromund was constituted Count of Sens (L'Art de Vérif. les Dates), and was father of Reginald or Rayner I., who built the Castle of Chateau-Raynard. From his elder son Fromund II. descended the Counts of Sens, extinct 1055. Reginald, the

younger son, possessed Chateau-Raynard, Courtenay, and Montargis, the hereditary estates of this line (Anselme, i. 473). Hatto, his son, built the Castle of Courtenay, and was thence surnamed (Bouquet, x. 222). This baron, according to authorities cited by Cleveland (Hist. House of Courtenay), had, 1. Milo; 2. Josceline, Count of Edessa; 3. Geoffry, slain in battle with the Saracens. Milo m. a dau. of the Count of Nevers, and had, 1. Reginald, whose dau. m. Peter, grandson of Louis VII. of France (Anselme), and was ancestor of the Counts of Nevers, Emperors of Constantinople; 2. Josceline. Josceline, the younger son, had two sons, Reginald and William, of whom Reginald m. Hawisa, dau. and heir of Maud de Abrincis or Avrances, widow of Robert de A., Viscount of Devon, and Baron of Oakhampton; and William de C. mar. Matilda, dau. of the same Maude by her second husband, Robert Fitz-Roy, who held Oakhampton in right of his wife 1165 (Lib. Niger). He appears to have left no issue.

Hugh de Courtenay, son of Reginald, in 1203 was possessed of the greater part of the barony, but Hawisa, his mother, still held eighteen knights' fees, Devon (Rot. Canc.). In 1205 Robert de C. succeeded his brother, and from this date the history of the Courtenays, Earls of Devon, Marquises of Exeter, and their various branches, is well known.

Courteney. *See* COURTENAY.

Counter, a form of Gounter or GUNTER.

County, from COUNT.

Couper. *See* COOPER and COW-PER.

Court. *See* A'COURT.

Courtice. *See* CURTIS.

Courtney. *See* COURTENAY.

Cousens. *See* COSENS.

Cousins. *See* COSENS.

Coureton, or Cureton, from Courtonne near Caen. William de Curtone was of Surrey 1130, Ernald de C. of Essex 1189 (Rot. Pip.). This family held three knights' fees in Normandy 1165 (Duchesne, Feod. Norm.). Gilbert and Geoffry de Cortone occur there 1180–95 (Mag. Rot. Scac.).

Courtauld, probably from Courtelles or Corteilles, near Evreux. Hugh de Cortilz and Gillebert de Corteles occur in Normandy 1180–95 (Mag. Rot. Scac.). John and Roger de Curteles in England, c. 1272 (Rot. Hundr.).

Coutts. *See* COOTE.

Coutts. *See* COOTE, COLLEY-WELLESLEY.

Couzens. *See* COSENS.

Covell, the Norman-French pronunciation of Cauvel. *See* CAVELL.

Cover, or Covert. *See* A'COURT.

Covey, or Covet, a form of Covert. *See* A'COURT.

Covil. *See* COVELL.

Cowan. 1. A Scottish local name. 2. A form of GOWEN.

Coward, from La Couarde, near Rochelle. Radulphus de Coarda occurs in Normandy 1198 (Mag. Rot. Scac.); Roger de Cowert in England c. 1272 (Rot. Hundr.).

Cowart. *See* COWARD.

Cow, from COWIE, or COWEY, armorially identified.

Cowdell. *See* CAUDELL.

Cowderoy. *See* CORDEROY.

Cowdery. *See* COWDEROY.

Cowe. *See* COW.

Cowell, a form of COVELL.

Cowen. *See* COWAN.

Cowens. *See* COWEN.

Cowie, from the fief of Cohy or Cuy in Normandy. Robert de Cui occurs 1180 (Mag. Rot. Scac.), Walkelin de Coweye in England c. 1272 (Rot. Hundr.).

Cowley. 1. An English local name, comprising families of various origin. 2. A form of De Cuilly. *See* COLLEY-WELLESLEY.

Cowney, a form of Cony or CONEY.

Cowvan. *See* COWAN.

Cowper, or De Columbers. The early history of the family has been noticed under ASHLEY-COOPER. In 1340 there were two branches in Sussex, as appears by the Non. Inquisitiones. From one sprang the Coopers of Harting, from the other the Cowpers of Strood, who bore the arms of the Norman line of De Columbers, viz. gules, a chief argent (Des Bois), merely exchanging the tinctures, and adding other marks of cadency. The Norman line were barons of La Haye du Puy. From the Cowpers of Strood in Sussex descended the C.s of Cheshire, ancestors of the Earls Cowper. Of this family were an eminent Lord Chancellor of England, and the poet Cowper.

Cox, Cocks, or Cocus. *See* COCK (Lower).

Coxe. *See* COX.

Coysh. *See* COISH.

Cozens. *See* COSENS.

Craft, or De Turville, from T. near Pont-Audemer, derived from Torf de Torfville (La Roque, Mais. Harc. ii. 1927), from whom descended Geoffry de Turville 1124 (Ord. Vitalis, 880 ; Mon. i. 519, ii. 309), who had grants from the

Earl of Leicester and Mellent in England. Ralph De Turville gave the church of Craft to De la Pré Priory, Leicester (Mon. ii. 312), to which Geoffry and Robert de Craft also contributed (Ib.). Roger de Craft and Simon de Turville Craft also held fiefs of the Honour of Leicester (Testa, 254, 255), being evidently of the same family.

Crakanthorpe, or Malcael, a branch of the LOWTHERS of Westmoreland, and of Breton origin. Of this family was the eminent divine Richard Crakanthorpe, t. Charles I.

Cramp, perhaps from Cremps near Cahors.

Cranwell (or Crenswell, as written in the Battle Abbey Roll), a corruption of Cramanville. This family of De Cramaville was seated in Essex from the Conquest (Testa), and in Kent held its lands by three knights' service (Ib.). In 1189 Ralph de Cramaville paid a fine for his estates in Northumberland (Rot. Pip.).

Crane, from Crannes in Maine. Andreas, John, Oliver, William de Crane in England, c. 1272 (Rot. Hundr.).

Craney. Ernald de Crenie occurs in Normandy 1180 (Mag. Rot. Scac.), and Odo de Crenea later (Ib.).

Crann. *See* CRANE.

Crannis. *See* CRANES.

Cranston, a local name in Scotland. The Barons Cranstoun seem to have been descended from a branch of the house of BERTRAM.

Crapnell, for Grapinel.

Crase, a form of Grace, Grasse, or GRAS.

Crast, for CREST. Winifred Crest occurs in Normandy 1180-95 (Mag.

214

Rot. Scac.). The English name of Cresett is probably a form of this.

Craven, or De Daiville, from D., Normandy. In 1056 Walter Barbatus, Lord of Daiville, witnessed the charter of Treport, Eu (Neustr. Pia, 589). Walter de D., his son, accompanied the Conqueror, and had grants from Roger de Mowbray in York, with the feudal dignity of Seneschal. He witnessed a charter of Pontefract Priory (Mon. i. 655). Richard de D. was living 1130 (Rot. Pip.). Robert, his son, was hereditary Seneschal, and held five fees from Mowbray in York, and one in Notts (Lib. Niger). He had a dispute with Byland Abbey (Mon. i. 1081), and had two sons: 1. Robert de Daiville, who m. a dau. of Agnes Percy by Josceline of Louvaine, and was ancestor of the Dayvilles, Daivilles, or Deyvilles of York; 2. Thomas. Thomas de D., whose brother was m. to a Percy, obtained the lordship of Roudon or Rawdon, in Craven (originally part of the Percy estates); and his descendants, who bore the fesse of Daiville with marks of difference, were indifferently styled Rawdon and Craven, the latter probably arising from the office of Seneschal of Craven, which belonged to the Earls of Albemarle, a family which possessed lands in Rawdon (Mon. ii. 103). Raginald de Rawdon, son of Thomas, occurs 1202 (Rot. Canc.). He had two sons: 1. Henry, whose descendants bore the name of Rawdon; of whom Simon de R., 'son of Henry,' did homage for his lands t. Henry III. (Rob. Excerpt. ii. 352), and was father of Isabel, a benefactress to Fountains (Burton, Mon. Ebor. 106), while Thomas, his brother

(Michael's son), was ancestor of the Rawdons, Earls of Moira, Marquises of Hastings; 2. Thomas de Craven, who with his descendants bore that surname. This Thomas de Craven held lands in Norfolk (Testa) as well as part of Rawdon. In 1316 William de Craven and Michael de Rawdon were joint Lords of Rawdon (PPW). The former granted to Fountains Abbey lands given to his father by William de Daiville (Burton, 149). From William de Craven descended the Cravens of Leveninge and Appletrewick in Craven, ancestors of the gallant Lord Craven renowned in the wars of Gustavus Adolphus, and of the Earls Craven.

Craweeur, a form of Cracure or Cravicure, which is armorially identified with Crevequer or Crevecœur (Robson). Crevecœur was a strong castle in the valley of the Auge, which still remains (MSAN, xxiv. 90, &c.). Its lord, according to Wace, was at Hastings. Hugh de C. occurs in Normandy t. Henry I., and held five fees from the Bishop of Bayeux (Ib. viii. 426, 427). Robert de C., probably his brother, founded Leeds Priory, Kent. A branch was seated in Lincoln.

Craze. See CRACE.

Crease, for CRACE.

Creasey, a form of CRESSY.

Creasy, a form of CRESSY.

Creese. See CRACE.

Crellin, from Crallan, which is derived from Crollon in the Cotentin, Normandy (Lower).

Crespin, from the family of Beccrespin, Normandy. See JOCKLYN.

Cressall. See CRESSELL.

Cressell. Turstan and Robert de Croissiles were of Normandy 1180 (Mag. Rot. Scac.); Richard de Creis-

selles 1195 (Ib.); Henry de Crissale of England c. 1272 (Rot. Hund.).

Cressey. See CRESSY.

Cressy. 1. From the Lordship so named, near Dieppe and Rouen. Hugh de Cressy, and Simon, occur in Normandy 1180–95 (Mag. Rot. Scac.). Anselm and Gilbert de Cressy c. 1119 held lands from the Earls De Warrenne in England. 2. Hugh de Cresseio was of Hunts, 1130 (Rot. Pip.). He was the son of Guy le Roux, Lord of Creci in La Brie, Seneschal of France (Ord. Vitalis).

Creswick. William de Cresek is mentioned in Normandy c. 1200, where estates were granted to him with Henry de Bailliolet (Mem. Soc. Ant. Norm. v. 110).

Crewe, a branch of DE LA MARE or Montalt, whose arms it bore, with a slight difference (Ormerod, Cheshire, iii. 165). Crewe was in the barony of Malbanc, and was possessed c. 1150 by Henry de Criwa, who attested a charter of Hugh Malbanc. Sire Thomas de Crue was living after 1241. Hence the Lords Crewe of Stene, maternally represented by the Lords Crewe.

Crews or **Crewys.** Hugh de Creus and Richard de Creos were of Normandy 1198 (Mag. Rot. Scac.). Creus-Anisy was in Normandy (Ib.). Richard de Crues also occurs in Devon 1199; and the family has remained there ever since.

Crickett. See CRITCHETT.

Criper. See GRIPER.

Crippen, for Grippon. Lescelina de Gripon occurs in Normandy 1195–8 (Mag. Rot. Scac.). Walter de Grippinge in England 1199 (Palgr. Rot. Cur. Regis).

Cripps, armorially identified with CRISP (Robson).

Crisp, an abbreviation of Crispin, a Norman name (Lower).

Crispin. Joceline, William, and Robert Crespin of Normandy 1180-95 (Mag. Rot. Scac.). *See* JOCELYN.

Critchett, from Crichet or Cruchet. Radulphus and Rainald Crochet of Normandy 1180 (Mag. Rot. Scac.). The name of Criquet and Crickett frequently occurs in England 12th and 13th cent. In 1313 William Cryket was bailsman for an M.P. for Bridport (PPW).

Critchfield, from Cricheville or Cristequeville, Normandy.

Croaker, or le Crochere, from Crocea, a cross (Ducange), crocearius, a cross-bearer. Simon le Crockere and William Crockare mentioned in England c. 1272 (Rot. Hundr.). Norman families may be included. John le Crochere held lands from De Pomeray, Devon, t. Henry I.

Crocker. *See* CROAKER.

Crocket. *See* CROCKETT.

Crockett. Radulphus and Rainald Crochett in Normandy 1180 (Mag. Rot. Scac.).

Crockitt. *See* CROCKETT.

Crofton, or De La Mare, from La Mare, Normandy. John de la Mare had a grant of Crofton from Roger de Poitou, t. William I. (Testa, 411). John de la Mara was lord, t. Richard I., and was a benefactor to Burscough Priory (Mon. ii. 305). Alicia was widow of Thomas de C. 1272; John de C., M.P. for Carlisle 1311 (PPW). The family then bore the name of De Crofton. From this branch of the De la Mares descend the baronets Crofton.

Crofton, or Lowther, Lords Crofton. *See* LOWTHER.

Croger. Perhaps a form of CROAKER.

216

Crokat. A form of CROCKETT.

Croke, a branch of le Blund. *See* BLOUNT.

Croker. *See* CROAKER.

Croll, for Crull or Cruel, appears to be a corruption of Criol. *See* KERRELL.

Crolls. *See* CROLL.

Crome, Croume, or Croune, a form of Crun or Craon. *See* CROWNE.

Croney, from Cronet in Normandy.

Crook, or Croc, a Norman baronial family. Hugh, William, and John de Croc occur in Normandy 12th cent. (Mag. Rot. Scac.). In 1086 Rainaldus Fitz-Croch, hereditary huntsman of the King, held fiefs in Hants, as did his father Croch (Domesd.). Osmond C. occurs 1130 (Rot. Pip.). In 1156 Matthew C. had charge of the forests in Hants, and 1165 Hugh Croc and William C. held fiefs in barony in Normandy (Feod. Norm.), as did John C. from William de Mohun, Ruald C. from the Earl of Gloucester, and William C. from the See of Bath (Liber Niger).

Crooke. *See* CROOK.

Crookes. *See* CROOK.

Croom. *See* CROME.

Croome. *See* CROME.

Croose. *See* CREWES.

Croot, for Groot or Grote. William, Thomas, and Robert Grut, in England, c. 1272 (Rot. Hundr.). Crot was in Normandy. Euric and Matthew de Crotis occur 1198 (Mag. Rot. Scac.).

Crop, or Croopes, from Cropus, near Dieppe, and Bellencombre. Walter de Cropus accompanied Bernard de Newmarch to the conquest of Brecknock 1087. He is mentioned by Ordericus Vitalis. Robert de Cropis had Norman estates 1165 (Duchesne, Feod. Norm.). The family remained in Brecknock.

Cropper. Simon de Croper, or Croperi, occurs in England 1199 (Palgr. Rot. Cur. Regis). This name seems foreign. Simon in 1194 claimed a knight's fee of the Honour of Mortaine, Northants.

Crosier, from Croiseur (Lower), probably of the same origin as le Crochere. *See* CROAKER.

Cross, from St. Croix, or Croix, in Normandy. Ralph de S. Cruce, and Adam, occur in the Duchy 1180 (Mag. Rot. Scac.). Reginald, Geoffry, Peter, Richard de Cruce in England 1199 (Palgr. Rot. Cur. Regis); Warin, Henry, Richard de Cruce in Normandy 1198 (MRS).

Crosse. *See* CROSS.

Crosson. *See* CRASSON.

Crotch, for Crouch, or CROSS.

Crouch, a form of CROSS (Lower).

Croucher, a form of CROSIER (Lower).

Crout. *See* CROOT.

Crowne or De Craon, armorially identified (Robson) ; descended from Hunrok, said by some to be a son of Desiderius, last king of the Lombards, and who was created Duke of Friuli by Charlemagne 795 (Art de Vér. les Dates). Everard, his grandson, was Duke of Friuli 846. Berenger, his son, was elected King of Italy 888. He was grandson of the Emperor Louis le Débonnaire, and was chosen Emperor 916. His dau. m. Adelbert, Marquis of Ivrea (son of Anscar, son of Wida, son of Everard, Duke of Friuli). His grandson Adalbert was King of Italy 950 (Ibid.). He was deprived by the Emperor Otho, but his son Otho William was adopted by the Duke of Burgundy, and became Count of Burgundy and Nevers c. 1000. His son Reginald of Bur-gundy had issue Robert, to whom the Barony of Craon in Anjou was granted by Geoffry Martel 1052. From his elder son descended the Barons of Craon (Du Paz, Mais. Bretagne, 735). His younger son Guy de Craon accompanied the Conqueror, and held 61 lordships in capite 1086, and was ancestor of the family in England.

Crozier. *See* CROSIER.

Cruft. *See* CRAFT.

Cruise. *See* CREWES.

Cruse. *See* CREWES.

Crussell. *See* CRESSELL.

Crutcher. *See* CROUCHER.

Crute. *See* CROAT.

Crux. *See* Crocks or CROOKES.

Cryer. Osmond le Crieor, Normandy, 1180–95 (MRS).

Cubison, for Corbizon. William de Corbucon occurs in Normandy, 1180–95 (Mag. Rot. Scac.). William Fitz-Corbezun was Baron of Studley, Warwick, 1086 (Domesd.). The family continued there till 1354 (Dugd. Warw.). Corbuzon the ancestor is mentioned in a charter of Duke Robert of Normandy (Gall. Christ. xi. 10). Robert Fitz-Corbezun also held a barony in the Eastern Counties, 1086 (Domesd.). The family long continued there.

Cubit. *See* COBETT.

Cubitt. *See* COBETT.

Cuel, or Cruel. *See* Crull or CROLL.

Cuell. *See* CUEL.

Culley, or CULEY. *See* COLLEY-WELLESLEY.

Cully. *See* CULLEY.

Cumin. *See* COMYN.

Cumings. *See* COMYN.

Cummin. *See* COMYN.

Cumming. *See* COMYN.

Cummings. *See* COMYN.

Cummins. *See* COMYN.

Cunditt, for Chenduit.

Cundy, for CONDY.

Cunnew, for CONNEW.

Cupison. *See* CUBISON.

Cupit, and CUPID. *See* CUBIT.

Curban, for Corbin. *See* CARABINE.

Curchin, probably a corruption of Curson or CURZON.

Curd, for Curt or COURT.

Cure, or De la Cour. Hunfrid, Alvered, Raginald, Radulf, Roger, William de Curia of Normandy, 1198 (Mag. Rot. Scac.); William Curre of England, 1189 (Rot. Pip.); John Cure, c. 1272 (Rot. Hundr.).

Curel, or Kerel. *See* KERRELL.

Cureton, from Curton, Normandy. William de Curtona of Surrey, 1130 (Rot. Pip.). In 1165 Robert de Corton held Esinanville, Normandy, as three knights' fees (Feod. Norm.). Richard I. in 1189 confirmed the gifts of Ernald de Curtune to Colchester Abbey (Mon. ii.).

Curle. *See* KERRELL.

Curley. Thomas de Curleio was of Normandy, 1198 (Mag. Rot. Scac.); John de Curli of England, 1199 (Palgr. Rot. Cur. Regis).

Curme, for CORAM.

Curr, for CURR.

Currall. *See* CURLE.

Currie. *See* CORY.

Currier. Richard Coriarius of Normandy, 1180 (Mag. Rot. Scac.).

Curson. *See* CURZON.

Cursons. *See* CURZON.

Curteis. *See* CURTIS.

Curtice. *See* CURTIS.

Curtis. William de Curtis was of Normandy, 1180 (Mag. Rot. Scac.); Robert Curteis gave lands to Gloucester Abbey, t. Rufus (Mon. i. 111); William le Curteis,

t. Henry II., was a benefactor to West Dereham Abbey, Norfolk (Mon. ii.).

Curtiss. *See* CURTIS.

Curzon, from Courçon near Caen, and Vire, Normandy. Robert de C. had estates, Norfolk, 1086 (Domesd.). He left descendants in Norfolk. Richard and Hubert de C., his sons, were seated in Derby, t. Henry I. From them descended two lines of Curzon in Derby, from one of which derive the Lords Scarsdale and De la Zouche, and Earls Howe.

Curt. *See* COURT.

Cusdin, for Custeyn, or Costin, a form of CONSTANTINE.

Cushen, for CUSHION (Lower).

Cushion, for CUSHON.

Cushing, for CUSHION (Lower).

Cushon. William le Cuchon, Normandy, 1180-95 (MRS).

Cuss, a form of CUST.

Cussens, from De Cusances, a foreign name. Cousances is near Bar-le-Duc.

Cust, or De Gouis or Gouvis, from Gouvis, near Falaise. William, Sire de Gouviz (incorrectly 'Souis' in Wace), was at the battle of Hastings, and 1082 witnessed a charter of King William (Gall. Christ. xi.; Instr. 74), in which he is styled a baron. Alured, his son, held from the honour of Senlis in Cambridge, 1086 (Domesd.); Richard de Guiz, 1130, was granted lands in York by Hugh de Laval. In 1165 Robert de Guiz or Guz held lands in Cambridge (Lib. Nig.), and witnessed a charter for Bernewall Priory in that county (Mon. ii.). He was seized of Gouviz, Normandy, where he made grants to St. Barbe en Auge (Feod.

Norm., i.; MSAN, vii. 97). Ralph, his son, had Andrew de Guiz of Cambridge, 1199 (RCR). As one of the confederate barons his estates were confiscated, 1216, but restored to his brother, Robert de G., who had also grants in Normandy (Hardy, Rot. Norm. 93). The family acquired great estates in Dorset by marriage, but a branch remained in Cambridge, of which William Cousche, Cushe, or Cust occurs,

13th cent. (Testa, 354). This family bore the arms since borne by the Custs. They acquired estates in Lincoln (probably by marriage), where they were seated 14th cent. From this line descend the Earls Brownlow.

Custance, a form of CONSTANCE, or DE COUTANCES.

Cutchey, for COCHY.

Cutt. See CUTTS.

Cutts. See COUTTS.

D

Dabbs or D'Abbes. See ABBISS.

Dace, Daisey, or D'Acy, from the fief of Acy, Normandy. Avere de Dayce occurs in England c. 1272 (RH). See Lower.

Dacre, or Fitz-Aculf, named from Dacre, Cumberland, descended from Aculf, a companion of the Conqueror. Theobald de Dacre or Aculf granted lands t. Henry I. to Carlisle Abbey (Mon. ii. 74). Gilbert Aculf, his son, made further grants (Ib.). Adam Aculf, son of Gilbert, confirmed the grants of Theobald de Dacre (Ib.). Adam Aculf was grandfather of William de D., with whom the Peerage accounts commence.

Dadd. William Dade occurs in Normandy 1180 (MRS); William Dad in England c. 1272 (RH).

Dadds. See DADD.

Dade. See DADD.

Daden, or D'Aden, from Hadon. William Hadon occurs in Normandy 1180 (MRS); Robert de Hadden in England c. 1270 (RH). See HADDEN.

Dadge, D'Agg, or De Angy. See DAGG.

Dady, a form of DADD.

Daer. William Dair of Normandy 1195 (MRS). Gilbert Dare in England c. 1272 (RH).

Daeth, from Belgium. Walter de Aath is mentioned by Bouquet, xii. 267, and seems to have lived c. 1000.

Daffen, for D'Avens. See AVENS.

Dagg, from D'Agg or De Augo. See AGG.

Dagnall, or De Agnellis. See AGNEW.

Dailey, from Ailly, Normandy. See ALLEY.

Daily. See DAILEY.

Dain, or D'Ain, from Asne, Normandy. See ANNE.

Daines, or D'Aines. See ANNE.

Daines. See AINS.

Dakin, Dakeyne, or De Acquigny, from A., near Louviers, Normandy. Herveius de Acquigny occurs 1058 (Morice, Hist. Bret. Preuves, i. 430). Roger de Akeny, 13th cent., held fiefs from the honour of Peveril of London (Testa). This family was numerous, and of great importance in England, as the records show.

Dakins, from DAKIN.

Dakers. See DACRE.

Dakyns, from DAKIN.

Dalby. See ALBY.

Dalley, or D'Alley, from Ally or Ailly, Normandy. See ALLEY.

Dallett, or D'Alet, from Alet or St. Malo.

Dallimore, a corruption of De la Mare. See DELLAMORE.

Dallman, or D'Aleman. See ALLMAN.

Dallow, or D'Alost, from Alost, Flanders. See CONSTABLE.

Dally or D'Ally. See ALLEY.

Dalmaine. See ALLMAN.

Dalman. See ALLMAN.

Dallow, or D'Alost, from Alost, Flanders. See CONSTABLE.

Dally or D'Ally. See ALLEY.

Dalmaine. See ALLMAN.

Dalman. See ALLMAN.

Dalston, or De Vaux, named from Dalston, Cumberland. Ranulph Meschin, t. William the Conqueror, granted the barony of Dalston, Cumberland, to Robert, brother of Hubert and Ranulph de Vaux (Nicholson and Burns, Cumberland, 316). All his descendants bore the name of Dalston, and for arms three daws or daws' heads. De Vaux came from Normandy. See VAUX.

Daltrey, D'Autrey, or De Alta Ripa, from Hauterive, Normandy. Philip and William de Alta Ripa were possessed of estates in Sussex and Lincoln 1189. The family founded Heringham Priory, Sussex, t. Henry II. (Lower).

Damer, or D'Amory. See DOR-MER.

Damarel, D'Aumerle, or De Albemarle, descended from William de Albemarle, Baron of Fougeres, Bretagne, who obtained grants at the Conquest (Morice, Hist. Bret. i. 76). See FOULGER. He is mentioned in Wace as at Hastings, and had Robert de A., a great Baron in Devon 1086, whose descendants long continued in Devon (Pole), and of whom William D'Aumarle had a writ of summons 1367 to Parliament with other barons and prelates. The name became Damarel.

Dames, or D'Ames. See AMES.

Damm, for Dame, or D'Ames. See AMES.

Damry, for Damory. See DAMER.

Dance, for DANCY.

Dancer, or D'Ancere. In 1130 Godwin Dancere occurs in England (Rot. Pip.); in 1198 Robert, Laurence, and William Ansere were of Normandy (MRS). William Ansera had a suit for lands in England 1198 (RCR). From this family descend the baronets Dancer. The fief of Anceres (de Ancariis) is mentioned t. Henry II. (Mem. Soc. Ant. Norm. viii. 438).

Dancy, or D'Anisy, from Anisy, near Caen. About 1042 Turstin de A. granted to St. Vigor, Cerisy, certain lands, with consent of Eudo, Ralph, and Ranulph, his sons (Mon. ii. 961). The Sire D'Anisy came to England at the Conquest (Wace, ii. verse 1355). William de A. occurs c. 1110 in the Winton Domesd. (536). William de A. of Wilts 1130 (Rot. Pip.). Richard de A. Hants 1165 (Lib. Nig.). Richard de Anesy was 13th cent. of Hereford (from whom the family of

Dansey). The family long continued in Normandy (La Roque, i. 996, 997).

Dancey. *See* DANCY.

Dando, from D'Anlo (Lower). Andelut or Andelot was near Mantes, Normandy. Robert de Andellou occurs in the Duchy 1198 (MRS). Sire Alexander D'Ando and others in England c. 1272 (RH).

Dane, for D'Ane. *See* ANNE.

Danes. *See* DANE.

Dansie. *See* DANCY.

Dangar, for D'Angers. *See* ANGER.

Dangerfield or D'Angerville, from Angerville, in the Cotentin. Benedict, Robert, William D'Angervillé and others in Normandy, 12th cent. (MRS). Walter de Angerville of England 1130 (Rot. Pip.).

Daniel. N. Daniel occurs in Normandy 1180-95 (MRS). Roger Daniel was possessed of estates Sussex 1086 (Domesd.). Petre and Ralph D. occur in the Duchy 1198 (MRS); Hugh, Ralph D., and others in England, c. 1272 (RH).

Danks, probably from Henges, or Hangest, near Amiens. The name De Henges occurs c. 1272 in England (RH). Hanks is also probably a corruption of it.

Dann, or D'Anne. *See* ANNE.

Dannell. *See* DANIEL.

Danvers, from Anvers, or Antwerp. Richard de A. witnessed a charter of Roger de Mowbray (Mon. ii. 395). Ralph de A. held two fees of the Honour of Wallingford 13th cent. (Testa). In 1316 Simon D. of Oxford, and William of Bucks, and 1324 Henry of Leicester, are mentioned (PPW). Hence descended the Earls of Danby, Lords Danvers.

Darben, an abbreviation of Darbenay or Dalbenay (Robson). *See* DAUBENY.

Darch, or De Arch. *See* DARK.

D'Arcy, a baronial family, from Arcy or Areci, Normandy, Barons D'Arcy, and Earls of Holdernesse. *See* Dugdale, Banks.

Dardenne, from Ardenne in Normandy. *See* ARDEN.

Dards. *See* ARDES.

Dare. *See* DARR.

Darell. *See* DARRELL.

Darens, for De Arenes. Adeliza de Arenis occurs in Normandy 1180, William de A. 1195 (MRS). Milo de Areines in England 1130 (Rot. Pip.).

Dargevel, or De Argeville (Robson). Mariscus de Orguil occurs in Normandy 1198 (MRS). In 1221 the lands of Geoffry de Orguevalle were granted to another by Philip-Augustus, probably as an adherent of King John.

Dark, or D'Arques. *See* ARCH, and SAVILLE.

Darke. *See* DARK.

Darker, or D'Orgeres, from Orgeres in Normandy. Ralph, Richard, and Gilbert de Orgeres occur 1180 (MRS).

Darkes. *See* DARK.

Darrell. The Castle of Airel, near St. Lo, was the seat of this family, which at the Conquest settled in Bucks and York. Marmaduc de Arel witnessed a Charter of William, son of Alan de Percy (Mon. ii. 395). Thomas de A. occurs in York 1158 (Rot. Pip.). In 1165 Ralph de Airel held in capite from the Honour of Wallingford (Lib. Niger). The name is frequent in all the records. Hence the baronets Darrell.

Darroch, for Darragh, or De Arras. *See* DOUGLAS.

Darvall, or D'Orival, from Orival, Normandy. Robert de Aurea Valle was of Devon 1130 (Rot. Pip.). Walter Dorival of England c. 1272 (RH).

Darvell. *See* DARVALL.

Darvill. *See* DARVALL.

Darville. *See* DARVALL.

Dasent. *See* DECENT.

Dash or Dast, from Dest. Emelot Dest occurs in Normandy 12th century (MRS). *See* EAST.

Date, for Teate or TATE.

Daubeny, or De Albini. A branch of De Toesni, baron of Belvoir, William I. The barons of Toesni and Conches, one of the greatest houses in Normandy, descended from Malahulcius, uncle of Duke Rollo. *See* Lord Lindsay's Lives of the Lindsays; Banks, Dorm. and Extinct Baronage; Dugdale, &c. The Lords Daubeney, Earls of Bridgewater, were of this line.

D'Aubeny. *See* DAUBENY.

Daubray. *See* AUBREY.

Daughtry. *See* DALTREY.

Dauney. *See* DAUNAY.

Daunton. Geoffry Dantan of Normandy, 1180–95 (MRS). Jordan de Donton, England, c. 1272 (RH).

Davall, or Daville. *See* CRAVEN.

Davenes. *See* AVENS.

Davey. William and John Davi or Davy, Normandy, 1180–95 (MRS); John and Martin Davi, 1198 (Ib.); Robert and William David, England, 1199 (RCR). Hence Sir Humphry Davy, so celebrated as a man of science.

David. *See* DAVEY.

Davidge, or Davids. *See* DAVEY.

Davie. *See* DAVEY.

222

Davison, or D'Avison. *See* IVESON.

Davy. *See* DAVEY.

Daw, from D'Awe, D'Owe, or De Eu. The family of De Eu or De Augo was extensively settled in England. *See* AEE. For Eu, *see* Dugdale and Banks.

Dauborn. *See* DAWBARN.

Dawbarn, a corruption of DARBEN.

Dawe. *See* DAW.

Dawes. *See* DAW.

Dawkins. *See* DAKIN.

Dawn, abbreviated from DAUNEY.

Daunay, or De Alneto, a branch of the baronial house of BASSETT, deriving from Fulco or Fulcelin de Alneto, brother of Osmond Bassett, Baron of Normanville, who witnessed a charter with him in Normandy, 1050. He had issue Ingelram (sometimes called Paganus) D'Alnai, who is mentioned at the battle of Hastings (Wace) as 'Sire d'Alnai.' He granted the Church of A. to St. Stephen's, Caen, 1082 (Gall. Christ. xi. 73). In 1115 Berenger de A. (son of Ingelram) witnessed a charter of Stephen, Count of Albemarle (Mon. ii. 999), and Gonthier his brother had custody of Bayeux, 1106 (Ord. Vitalis). William de Alneto, son or grandson of Berenger, held fiefs in Devon, 1165 (Lib. Nig.). William D'Aunay accompanied Richard I. to Palestine; and Fulco and Hugh de A. occur in Devon, &c., 13th cent. (Testa). John de A. was father of Nicholas, summoned by writ as a Baron, 1326. His son Thomas m. an heiress in York, where the family settled, and from them descend the Viscounts Downe.

Daws. *See* DAW.

Dawson, altered from DALSTON. The families of this name in York and Lancaster bear the three daws or martlets of Dalston. From them descend the Earls of Portarlington and Dartrey.

Day, from St. John de Day, near St. Lo, in the Cotentin. Henry and Ralph de Dai, 1165, held a fief from De Lacy in York (Lib. Nig.). Hugh, Richard, and William Day occur in England, c. 1272 (RH).

Dayes. See DAY.

Daykin. See DAKIN.

Dayman, changed from Deymont, or Dinant. See DINHAM.

Dayment, from Deynant or Dinant. See DINHAM.

Dayral, or De Airel. See DARRELL.

Deacon, armorially identified with Dakeny, or De Arquigny. See DAKIN.

Deakin. See DEACON.

Dean. William and Godfrey Decanus of Normandy, 1180–95 (MRS); Bartholomew, Ralph, and William Decanus of England, 1189 (Rot. Pip.); Thomas and Hugh D., 1199 (RCR).

Dear. See DARR.

Deards. See DARDS.

Deare. See DARR.

Dearen. See DARENS.

Dearing. See DERING.

Dearth, a form of DEATH.

Death, a form of DARTH.

Dearkeen, from Dakin or Dakeyne. See DAKIN.

Decent, from Disaunt, a foreign name, formed like Mordaunt, Poignaunt, and others. John Disaunt was of Bedfordshire, c. 1272 (RH).

Deeble, Dibble, or Diable (Robson). Ranulph Diabolus occurs in Normandy, 1180 (MRS); Gilbert

Devele in England, c. 1272 (HR). This family may possibly be descended from Robert Diabolus, Lord of Moulineaux, Normandy, before the Conquest.

Deed, a form of Dade. See DADD.

Deedes. See DEED.

Deedy, a form of Dade. See DADD.

Deemer, a form of DAMER.

Deer. See DARR.

Deere. See DARR.

Deering. See DERING.

De Fraine, or De Freane, De Fraxineto, a well-known Norman family.

Deeker, a form of DACRE (Lower).

De Lacy. See LACY.

De la Cour. See COURT.

Delahaye. See HAY.

De la Mare, from La Mare, near Pont-Audemer, a castle built on piles in a lake. Norman de la Mara lived c. 1030. Hugo de L. M. 1070 occurs in a Breton charter (Morice, Hist. Bret. Preuves, i. 434). He became seated in Cheshire, and is mentioned by Wace as a companion of the Conqueror (ii. 235). He had two brothers, William and Ranulph.

From Hugh descended the Barons of Montalt and Hawarden, seneschals of Chester, who bore the name of Montalt or Mohaut from the castle so named, and of whom Roger de M. was summoned by writ as a baron, 1299. From this line descend the Maudes Viscounts Hawarden, Barons Montalt, and also the Gerards, Earls of Macclesfield, and the Baronets Gerard, also the Crewes, Lords of Crewe, Barons of Stene.

William de la Mare, brother of Hugh, m. a dau. of Hugh Lupus, and from him descended the La Mares or Lechmeres of Worcester, and the Aldworths, Barons Braybrooke, Viscounts Doneraile.

From Ranulph de L. M., Dapifer of Chester, descended the Leighs of East Hall Leigh, and the Lords Leigh.

De la Mere. *See* DE LA MARE.

De Lane, or De L'Asne. *See* ANNE.

De Lisle. *See* ANDERSON-PELHAM.

Delivett, or De Livet. *See* LEVETT.

Dellamore. *See* DE LA MARE.

Dellow, from DALLOW.

Delly, from DALLY.

Delmar, an abbreviation of DE LA MARE.

Demant, for Dinant. *See* DINHAM.

Denman, or Plochet, a foreign name still to be met in France. Hugh Pluchet, Ploquet, or Pluket, t. Henry II., witnessed a charter for the Priory of Holy Trinity, London (Mon. ii. 80). He was granted Dunham, Notts, by Matthew, Count of Boulogne, and 1217 Ralph P. his son was restored on returning to his allegiance (Hardy, Lit. Claus. 323, 325, 356). In the wars of Henry III. the estates of Geoffry de Dunham, Notts, were confiscated. William de Denum occurs, t. Edward III. About 1430 Robert Denham was of Notts, and was grandfather of Sir John D. of Kirklington (Surtees Society, vol. xli.). The name of Denham changed to Denman, the arms of both names being the same. From this family descended the Denmans of Notts, ancestors of the great Lord Denman, Chief Justice.

224

Duncan. *See* DENEKAN.

Dunkin. *See* DENEKAN.

Dench, for Danish (Lower). *See* DENNIS.

Denchfield, or De Englishville, from Englesqueville in the Cotentin. Ralph and Robert De Engleskeville were of Normandy, 1180–95 (MRS); Sire Theobald de Englescheville and others occur in England, c. 1272 (RH).

Deneken. William Donekan or Donican was of Normandy, 1180–95 (MRS). In 1198 Richard Donecan or Donecamp (Ib.).

Denis. *See* DENNIS.

Dennes. *See* DENNIS.

Dennett, from D'Anet, or De Alneto. *See* DAWNAY.

Dennis, from St. Denis le Gaste in the Cotentin. Hugh de St. Dionisio, Roger, and Hugh of England, 1199 (RCR); Robert de St. Dionisio, 1194 (Ib.). *See* MURDOCH.

Dennis, Deneys, or Danois. Richard, Fulco, Geoffry, Roger, Hugh, Matthew, Robert Daneis of Normandy, 1180–98 (MRS); Hugh Daneis or Daniscus of England, 1189 (Rot. Pip.). In t. Henry I. John Danois held his estate from the See of Bayeux (Mem. Soc. Ant. Norm. viii. 431). Hugh Daniscus was of Devon, 1130 (Rot. Pip.). Robert Dacus or Le Daneys held from the Abbot of Tavistock, 1105 (Lib. Nig.); Osbert and Ralph Dacus held in Dorset (Ib.). Hence the Barons Tracton.

Denniss. *See* DENNIS.

Denney, the Norman-French pronunciation of DENNIS.

Denny, for DENNIS. Denny was Earl of Norwich.

Dennys. *See* DENNIS.

Denoon, or De Noyon. *See* NOON.

Denton, a branch of the Barons of Tatershall, descended from Eudo, a companion of the Conqueror (Banks, Dorm. and Ext. Peerage, Art. Tatteshall).

Denvall, or Devoll. *See* DIBBLE.

Denyer, or Daniers, otherwise Daniel, of Cheshire, from Asnieres, Normandy. Hugo de Asneriis occurs there, 1198 (MRS).

Dering. According to Philpot's Villare Cantianum, the ancestor of this family was Norman de Morinis (St. Omer in Flanders). His son was Deringus de Morinis, who lived in the reign of Henry I. Norman, son of Deringus, was Viscount of Kent, t. Stephen (Hasted), and is said to have married the daughter of William de Ypres of Flanders, Earl of Kent, t. Stephen. This family is therefore Flemish.

Derry, for D'Arry, or D'Airy. *See* AIRY.

Desson. William de Esson was of Normandy, 1183–4 (MRS).

De Vere. *See* VERE.

Dever, or De Vere. *See* VERE.

De Vear. *See* VERE.

Devereux, a branch of the sovereign house of Normandy, deriving from Robert Count of Evreux, Archbishop of Rouen, son of Richard I. of Normandy. This Count, by his wife Herleva (*see* Anselme, i. 477, &c.), had, 1. Richard, Count of E., father of William, Count of E., living 1086, whose sister, wife of Amaury de Montfort, was his heiress; 2. Ralph d'Evreux, Sire De Gacé, whose son Robert left his estates to the Count of Evreux, and d. a.p.; 3. William d'Evreux. He m., according to William of Jumi-

eges, the widow of Robert de Grentmesnil, and his dau. m. Roger, Count of Sicily. By a second marriage he had a son of his own name who came to England 1066 with Roger D'Evreux, his brother (who was of Norfolk 1086), and m. the sister of Walter de Lacy of Hereford. Helewysa, his widow, gave lands. to Gloucester Abbey (Mon. i. 115). Her son Robert de Evrois was a benefactor to Brecknock t. Henry I. (Mon. i. 320). In 1165 there were two branches of this family in Hereford. The Viscounts Hereford are of this house, as was also the unfortunate Earl of Essex, so celebrated temp. Elizabeth.

Devesey, from De Vesci. *See* VESEY.

Devey, from Devet, or Divet. *See* DEVITT.

Devine. William le Devin, Normandy 1180–95 (MRS). •

Devitt. Osulf de Diveta of Normandy 1180–95 (MRS); William le Desvet witness (12th cent.) to a charter of Henry de Tracy of Barnstaple (Mon. i. 685).

Devonald, a corruption of Davenant. Godefrid and Richard Avenant were of Normandy 1198 (MRS).

Devoy, or D'Ivoy. *See* IVY.

Dew, or D'Eu, from Eu, Normandy. The family of De Augo or D'Eu was widely spread in England.

Dewe. *See* DEW.

Dewrance, a form of AVERENCES, or D'Averances.

Dewy. *See* DEWEY.

Dey. *See* DAY.

Deykin. *See* DAKIN.

Diable. *See* DIBBLE.

Diamond, or Diamont, armorially identified with DINHAM or Dinaunt.

Diaper, from De Ipres, of Ipres in Flanders. William de Ipres was Earl of Kent, t. Stephen; William de Ypre of Oxfordshire, c. 1272 (RH).

Diball, for Dibell, DIBBLE.

Dibben, for DE BENE.

Dibbins. *See* DIBBEN.

Dible. *See* DEEBLE.

Dibble. *See* DEEBLE.

Dibley. *See* DIBBLE.

Dicey, from the fief of Dissey or Dessay, Normandy. Ralph de Diceto was an English historian temp. Edward I.

Dick, or Dike. N. Dica occurs in Normandy 1195 (MRS); Hamo and John Dike of England, c. 1272 (RH).

Dickens, appears from the name, and the arms (a cross patonce), to be of the family of DAKIN or Dakeyne, which also bore a cross (Robson). Hence DICKENS, the great novelist.

Digby. This family descends from Gacelin or Wazelin, probably a noble of Anjou, who held lands from Geoffry de Wirce in Lincoln 1086. His son, Thomas de Digby, t. Henry I., held his lands from Hanselyn (or De Beaugency of the Orleanois), and had William, whose son William de Digby, or Gacelin (Wazelin), witnessed, t. Henry II., the Charter of Cattley Priory, Linc. (Mon. ii. 814), and was dead before 1165, when William and Walter de Digby, his sons, minors, held a fee from the honour of Hanselyn, Notts. Soon after one branch bore the name of Gascelin, of whom John Wascelin was of Lincoln 1189, and Reginald held from Crevequer (Testa). *See* GHISLIN. William de Digby, above-mentioned, in

226

1165 had William and Thomas, from the former of whom descended the Digbys of Lincoln. Walter de D. was father of Robert, who acquired Tilton, Leicester, by marriage, and was ancestor of the Digbys, Earls of Bristol and Digby.

Diggles, or D'Eagles. The latter name bore a fesse between three eagles displayed (Robson). De Aquilis, three eagles displ. on a chief; and De Aquila, or an eagle close gu. It would seem that this is some branch of the De L'Aigles, Barons of L'Aigle, Normandy, of whom Richer de Aquila accompanied the Conqueror, and obtained the barony of Pevensey, Sussex.

Dike. N. Dica was of Normandy 1195 (MRS); Hamo and John Dike of England, c. 1272 (RH).

Dillamore, for Delamere, or DE LA MARE.

Dilley, from TILLEY.

Dillimore. *See* DILLAMORE.

Dillon, or De Gamaches. The Lords of Gamaches, in the French Vexin, were said to be descended from Protadius, Mayor of the Palace to Theodoric, King of Orleans, 604 (Des Bois). A branch became seated in England, and Godfrey de Gamaches, who held two fees from Hugh de Lacy, of Hereford 1165, was granted the barony of Dylon or Dilion, in the same county, by Henry II. 1158. His grandson, Matthew de Gamaches, was Baron of Dylon, and on his forfeiture as a Norman, William de G., his brother, had a grant of the barony 1217. He had Adam and Henry, the latter of whom passed into Ireland, and was ancestor of the Earls of Roscommon,

Viscounts Dillon, and Lords Clonbrock.

Dillwyn. *See* DILLON.

Dilly, for TILLY.

Dimes, for Deynes, D'Exmes, or De Hiesmes. *See* AMES.

Dimmett, for DIMENT.

Dimond, for Dimont, or DIMENT.

Diment, for Diamont, or Dinant. *See* DINHAM.

Dines. *See* DYNE.

Dingell, for D'Angle. *See* ANGELL.

Dingle. *See* DINGELL.

Dinham, a Devonshire family, Barons Dinham, and De Dinant, descended from the Viscounts Dinant of Bretagne. *See* STUART.

This name was variously written Dinant, Dinan, Dinam, Dimont, Diamond, Dinham, &c. *See* Banks, Dorm. and Ext. Baronage; Burke, Land. Gentry, art. 'Dayman.'

Dinn, for DINE, or Dines.

Dinsey. *See* DANSEY.

Diprose, for De Preaux (Lower). Preaux, Pratellæ was in Normandy. In 1180-95 we find John, Peter, Rostoldus, William, Osbert, Enguerran de Pratellis in Normandy (MRS); Ralph de P. and others in England.

Disney, from Isigny, Normandy, a well-known Norman family.

Dissard. Philip and William de Deserte of Normandy 1198 (MRS).

Distin, for D'Eston, or D'Astin. *See* ASTIN.

Dive, from Dives, Normandy, a baronial family which became seated in England at the Conquest, and occurs continually in the records. Bocelin de Dive accompanied the Conqueror, and became seated in Cambridge.

Diver. *See* DIVERS.

Divers, or Diverse (Robson).

Robert Divorce was of Normandy 1198 (MRS); Alan Diveres, of England c. 1272 (RH).

Dives. *See* DIVE.

Divett, or D'Ivetot. Geoffry de Iveto, Oxfordshire, 1156; Robert de Ivetot 1165 held in Normandy from the Honour of Montfort (Rot. Pip.; Duchesne, Feod. Norm.).

Dix, or Dicks. *See* DICK.

Dixie. 1. Armorially identified with Dicey. 2. The name also appears as Disa, Disce, or Disse, being taken from Diss, Norfolk, which belonged to Richard de Lucy, Governor of Falaise t. Stephen. One of his daughters and heirs m. Richard de Ripariis or Rivers (*see* RIVERS), and had part of Diss. Robert de Diss, mentioned (Rot. Canc.) 1203, was probably their son, and ancestor of this family, for they bear the arms of Rivers, Azure, a lion rampant or, with a chief for difference; and we find the names of Disse, Disce, or Dixy from the year 1200 in Norfolk. Hence the Baronets Dixie.

Doane. *See* DON. Hence the learned and pious Bishop Doane, of New Jersey.

Dobell, from Dolabella (Lower). Hugh Dolebel of Normandy 1180, Baldwin D. 1195 (MRS). This was probably the same as Doublel. Warin, Ralph, and Vitalis Doublel were of Normandy 1198 (Ibid.).

Doble. *See* DOBELL.

Dobree, from D'Aubri, Normandy (Lower). *See* AUBREY.

Doe, for DOUAY.

Doe. Raherius D'O, Normandy 1198 (MRS); Robert D'O, and the castle and manor of O (Mem. Soc. Ant. Norm. v. 226, 236); John Doe and William his father, Engl. c. 1272 (RH).

Doel, for Dowell, or Dol. *See* STUART.

Doggett, or Doget, from Doket, or Duket. Radulphus Doucet of Normandy 1180; Nicholas Douchet 1195 (MRS). Doget and Duket were frequent in England c. 1272 (RH).

Doggrell, probably from Dorgeril, a place in Normandy, mentioned 1180–95 (MRS).

Dold, or Dolt, for Dote. Roger Dote was of Normandy 1198 (MRS); Geoffry, Henry, and Hugh Dote, of England, c. 1272 (RH); Peter Dolte at the same time (Ibid.).

Dole, for Dol. *See* STUART.

Doley, or Dolley, for D'OYLEY; armorially identified (Robson).

Dollamore, from De la More, or DE LA MARE.

Doll, for Dol. *See* STUART.

Dollemore. *See* DOLLAMORE.

Dolmore. *See* DOLLAMORE.

Dommett, from Domet, near Orleans. Nicholas de Dommette was of Wilts 1264 (RH).

Domville, from Dumville, Normandy. Hugh, Roger, Alexander De Dumovilla of Normandy 1180–95 (MRS). Adam de Dunville 1182 witnessed a charter in Chester (Ormerod, ii. 295). Matthew de D., t. Henry III., was ancestor of the Domvilles of that county, and of the Baronets of the name.

Don. Richereld la Don, Normandy 1180–95 (MRS). Hence the Baronets Don.

Don, from Dune, Normandy. Ralph and Hervey de Duna, of N. 1180 (MRS). Richard de Duna, William, and Robert 1165 held several Knights' fees in Devon, Cornwall, and Derby (Lib. Nig.). Henry de Dona occurs Essex (Mon. ii. 954). William occurs in Normandy (MRS).

228

Done. *See* DON.

Donges, for Dongers, or D'Angers. *See* ANGER.

Donkin. *See* DENEKAN.

Donne. *See* DON.

Donnet, or Dannet, for De Anet, or D'Alneto. *See* DAWNAY.

Donnett. *See* Dannett, DENNETT.

Donville. *See* DOMVILLE.

Dorkes, for Darkes. *See* DARK.

Dormar. *See* DORMER.

Dormer, from Amars or Amory, near Caen. Gilbert D'Amory had grants from Robert D'Oylley in Oxford, and was a benefactor to Eynsham Abbey (Mon. i. 265). In 1129 Roger and Robert de Amar witnessed the Charter of Oseney (Mon. ii. 137). About 1180 Ralph was Lord of Hamars, Normandy (Wiffen, Mem. House of Russell, i. 75), and 1198 Alice Daumari and Geoffry her son were of Bucks (Lipscombe). In 13th cent. Roger de A. held part of the honour of D'Oylly in Bucks from the Earl of Warwick (Testa), and the Abbot of Oseney held from him 1 fee of the honour of Doylly (Ibid.). The name frequently occurs later in Oxford and Bucks; and 1326 Sir Richard Damory of Bucks, Oxford, and Somerset, was summoned by writ as a baron. From a younger branch derived William De Aumers of Bucks 1311, 1319, and Geoffry Dormer (Daumer) of West-Wycombe, Bucks, 14th cent.; ancestor of the Earls of Carnarvon, and the Lords Dormer. From a branch in Somerset descended the Damers or Damorys Earls of Dorchester.

Dorrell, for DARRELL, armorially identified (Robson).

Dorset, from DOSSETT.

Dorset. Thomas de Durset of Normandy 1180–95, MRS; Richard de Durset 1198, Ib.; Thomas de Dorset of England, c. 1272, RH.

Dorsett. *See* DORSET.

Dorvell, for De Orival, or De Aurea Valle, of Normandy. Geoffry, William, Ralph, Walter de Aurevalle of Normandy 1180 (MRS). This baronial family was seated in England 12th century.

Dossett. *See* DORSETT.

Dossett, from Doucet. *See* DOGGETT.

Dosson, from DAWSON.

Doubble. *See* DOBLE (Lower).

Doubell. *See* DOBELL.

Double. *See* DOBELL.

Douce, from Dulcia. *See* SWEET.

Doughty. William de Oughtia, Normandy 1180, 1198 (MRS); Geoffry, Henry de Dote, Engl. c. 1272 (RH). *See also* DOLD.

Douglas. This family descends from Theobald le Fleming (Flandrensis), who received, after 1147, lands at Douglas, Lanark, from Arnold, abbot of Kelso (Chalmers, Caledonia, i. 418, &c.) He was probably brother of Baldwin le Fleming (Flamingus), who about the same time had a grant of Biggar from David I., and was Viscount of Lanark. The latter, as Baldwin Flandrensis, in 1130 was excused payment of a fine in England at the instance of William, Castellan of St. Omer (Rot. Pip.). William Fitz-Baldwin, his son, held lands in Devon 1165, with Erchembald or Archembald le Fleming, his cousin (Lib. Niger). The latter was son of Stephen, and grandson of Archembald le Fleming or Flandrensis of Devon; the latter of whom held estates there 1086 (Domesd.). From the Devonshire line descended the Le Flemings, barons of Slane, in Ire-

land. Baldwin of Biggar was ancestor of the Le Flemyngs, who were invested with the earldom of Wigton 14th cent. Theobald le Fleming, of Douglas, had issue William, whose son Erchembald was ancestor of the Barons and Earls of Douglas, the Earls of Angus, now Dukes of Hamilton, Earls of Morton, of Selkirk, and many other families.

The connexion of William de St. Omer with this family has been noticed. The arms of the Earls of Wigton (a chevron) are those of the family of Bethune or De Arras, of which William de St. O. was a member. It is probable that Baldwin le Fleming, of Biggar (1130), was a nephew of William, his grandfather, Archembald le Fleming (1086), being of a branch of the house of Bethune. (*See* BEATON.) This joint connexion of the Le Flemyngs of Biggar, and the Douglases, with the Devonshire house, appears from the Liber Niger.

Douglass. *See* DOUGLAS.

Doust, from DOUCE.

Douste, for DOUST.

Dove. Simon D'Ove, Norm. 1150-95 (MRS); William Dovie, Eng. c. 1272 (RH).

Dove, or Dowe, from Eu or Owe, Normandy. *See* EU.

Dover, from Douvres or Dovera, Normandy, a baronial family, of considerable eminence, which derived its name from a Scandinavian Dover, at the Conquest of Normandy, 912. Fulbert de Dover, t. William I. and Henry I., had a barony in Kent, which his descendants, the De Dovers, held till the reign of King John (Dugdale, Banks). This baronial family has been supposed to have derived its name from Dover, in Kent; but it held no office in connexion with that Castle, nor were its possessions (though held therefrom) equal to those of others holding from the same Castle. It was the elder branch of the house of De CLINTON.

Dovey, a form of DOVE.

Dovey, from Auffai, Normandy (Lower).

Dow, or D'Eu. *See* EU.

Dowell, for Doel. Hugh Doel was of Normandy, 1180 (MRS).

Dowie. *See* DOVEY.

Dowle, or Doel. *See* DOWELL.

Down, or De Duna. *See* DON. Also a Devonshire family, of Breton origin, from which descended Bishop Jewell. *See* JEWELL.

Dowson, from DAWSON.

Dows, from DOUCE.

Dowse, from DOUCE.

Dowsett, from Doucet. *See* DOGGETT.

Dowsing, from DOWSON.

D'Oyley, a baronial family, from Pont Doylly or Duilly, Normandy; a branch of the BASSETTS. Robert of Pont D'oylly, brother of Osmond Bassett, Baron of Normanville, had issue Robert, Nigel, and other sons, who came to England 1066, from whom descended the barons and baronets DOYLEY.

Drabel, from D'Arables. Richard and Hugo De Arabilis occur in Normandy 12th century (MRS); Robert des Erables, t. John; Geoffry, Hervey, and Matthew Drabel, or Drabbel, in England, c. 1272 (RII).

Drake, Sir Francis, or De Montacute, the renowned Admiral, b. near Tavistock, 1545 (the son of Edmond D.), considered himself to be of the same ancestry as Sir Bernard Drake, of Ash; but the relationship being

230

remote, the latter disclaimed it. There is, however, no reason to doubt that the D.s of Devon were all originally of the same race. Drake or Draco, Fitz-Draco, was a form of Drogo, or Fitz-Drogo. Drogo de Montacute, 1086, held Chenolle, Somerset, in capite; Shepton, in the same county, from the Earl of Mortaine; and numerous lordships in Devon from the Bishop of Coutances. Among the last was Thornberie (Domesd., 103). Richard Fitz-Drogo granted this latter place to Montacute Priory (Mon. i. 670). Before 1146, Robert Draco (i.e. Fitz-Droco or Drogo) witnessed the foundation charter of Exeter Priory (Mon. i. 643). In 13th cent. Richard Fitz-Drogo held from Montacute Priory Thornberie, above-mentioned (Testa, 184). The Drakes of Devon bore a dragon (Draco), showing that their name had been Draco or Fitz-Draco.

Drage, or DRAKE, Draco (Lower).

Drain, for Traine. Petrus Traine was of Normandy, 1180; William Traine, 1198 (MRS); Simon Trane, of England, c. 1272 (RH).

Drane, for DRAIN.

Draper, or le Drapier, being a foreign name, probably included many Norman merchants.

Drapper. *See* DRAPER.

Dray, or Dreye (RH). (Lower.) Radulfus Droie, of Normandy, 1180–95 (MRS); Hugo and Stephen Dreye, c. 1272 (RH); Stephen Drois (Ib.).

Draysey, for TRACEY.

Dreaper. *See* DRAPER.

Dridge, for DRAGE.

Dressell or Drussell, for Trussell, a Norman family, formerly seated in Warwickshire.

Drew, or De Dreux, from Dreux, Normandy. Wado de Dreux was living 1050 (Ord. Vitalis). Amalric de Drewes, 1086, held lands in Wilts (Domesd.), also Herman de D. Hugh de Drocis (Dreux) occurs in Dorset, 1203 (Rot. Canc.). Walter Drew (13th cent.) held Littleton, Wilts. In 1316 Walter D. was Lord of Littleton. Their ancestor, William de Drocis, had held 2 fees, 1165, from Richard de Candos (Lib. Nig.). A branch became seated at a later period in Devon.

Drewell, or Drull, from the Norman Druel. Richard Druel occurs in the Duchy 1180–95 (MRS); John Druel in England, c. 1272 (RH).

Drewery. *See* DRURY.

Drewett, Druitt, or Drouet, a foreign name. Ralph Drueth, of England, c. 1272 (RH). N. Droart was of Normandy, 1180–95 (MRS).

Drewry. *See* DRURY.

Driver, from De Rivers, a name very frequent in Normandy (12th cent.), (MRS), when Serlo, Richard, Baldwin, William, John, Walter, Robert, Osbert, Paganus de Riperia, de Riveria, and De Riveriis, occur. It was also frequent in England.

Droop, or Drope, from De Rupe, or De la Roche. Oliver de Rupe occurs in Normandy c. 1200 (Mem. Soc. Ant. Norm. v. 99); Richard de Rupe in England 1189 (Rot. Pip.).

Druce, for Dreux. *See* DREW.

Druitt. *See* DREWETT.

Drury, or De Roueray, from Rouvray, near Rouen. Milo de Rouvray occurs 1180–95, Osbert de Rouvray 1198 (MRS); John de Rouverai in London and Middlesex 1189 (Rot. Pip.). In the 13th cen-

tury the name had been abbreviated to Drury. Adam D. of York, and William D. occur, and Sire Niel Drury was an Alderman of London 1312 (Palgr. Parl. Writs).

Dry, or Dreye. *See* DRAY.

Du Bois. *See* BOIS.

Ducat, or Ducket, from Douchet. *See* DOGGETT.

Duce, or DUCIE, from Ussey, in Normandy. Robert de Usseio occurs in the Duchy 1180 (MRS).

Duck, or Le Duc. Willelmus Dux was of Normandy, 1198 (MRS); Ralph Dux of Buckinghamshire, 1198 (RCR). *See* DUKE.

Duke. Osmond le Duc, Alexander and Robert le Duc, Norm., 1180–98 (MRS); Radulphus Dux of Bucks, 1199 (RCR). Hence the Baronets Duke. Robert D. and his father are mentioned in England (Testa, 120).

Duckett. *See* DUCAT. Ranulph Duchet was of Hants, 1130 (Rot. Pip.).

Duckitt. *See* DUCAT.

Duckworth, or De Abernon, from Abernon, near Orbec, descended from Roger D'Abernon, who held from Richard de Clare estates in Surrey, 1086 (*see* ADDINGTON). Jordan de Abernon held Duckworth, Cambridge, from the Honour of Mareschal, 13th cent. (Testa), whence the family and name of Duckworth. His ancestor, Hugo de Duckworth, occurs 1216 (Hardy, Obl. et fin., 587); and his descendant, Sire John D., was summoned to a great council, Westminster, 1324 (PPW).

Dudfield, from Dudeville, Normandy. In 1165 William de Dudeville held a fee of ancient enfeoffment in Oxford (Lib. Nig.). Baldwin de D. in the 13th century held lands in Essex and Herts (Testa).

Dudgeon, from Donjon. Petrus Donjon held lands in Normandy from Philip Augustus, c. 1204.

Dudley. In some cases descended from the Paganels or Paynels and Suttons, Barons of Dudley. The former were certainly Norman.

Duell, for Druel. *See* DREWELL.

Duer, for De Eure, a branch of DE BURGH and DE VESCI.

Duerre. *See* DUER.

Duggett, for DOGGETT.

Dukes. *See* DUKE.

Dumbrell, from Dumerle, connected armorially with Damarell of Devon, descended from Robert de Aumerle or Albemarle, a baron in Devon, 1086.

Dunman. *See* DENMAN.

Dummett. *See* DOMMETT.

Dumville. *See* DOMVILLE.

Dun. *See* DON.

Dunball, for Danabel. *See* ANNABLE.

Duncombe, or D'Engaine, from Engen or Ingen, near Boulogne. Richard and William de Ingen accompanied the Conqueror. The former in 1086 held a barony in Bucks, &c. (Domesd.). Vitalis D'Ingen, his son, t. Henry I., had Richard, who m. a dau. of Alberic de Ver, Earl of Oxford, and was Baron of Blatherwick, Northants. His son, Richard D'Engaine, 1165, held in Bucks from Paganel of Dudley (Lib. Nig.); and had, 1, Vitalis, ancestor of the Barons D'Engaine by writ, 1296; 2, Ralph D'Engaine (written Dungun or Dungeom in the Testa de Neville), who held Holcombe, Oxford, and in 1253 as Ralph D'Ungun was Lord of Tingewick, Bucks (Testa; Rot.

Hundr.). From him descended the Dengaines, Dunguns, or Dungeoms, gradually written Duncombe, Lords of Brickhill, Bucks, 16th cent.; and in the female line the Earls of Feversham and the Baronets Duncombe.

Duncombe. *See* PAUNCEFORT-DUNCOMBE.

Duncum. *See* DUNCOMBE.

Dunell, from Donell, or Doinell. William Doisnell occurs in Normandy, 1180–95 (MRS); Hugh and Robert Dunell in England, 1198 (RCR).

Dunger, from Donger or DANGER.

Dunham. *See* DENMAN.

Dunhill. *See* DUNELL.

Dunkin. *See* DONKIN.

Dunn. *See* DUN. In many cases, however, it is an Hiberno-Celtic name.

Dunscombe, a corruption of DUNCOMBE.

Dunsterville, or Dunstanville. *See* ADDERLEY.

Dunville, a form of DOMVILLE.

Durand, Durant, or Duredent. Geoffry, Roger, Henry Durant, &c., of Normandy, 1180–95, Aceline, Ralph, Richard, Robert D., 1198 (MRS); Everard D. of England, 1189 (Rot. Pip.); Roger, Robert D. in England, 1198 (RCR).

Durden, from Duredent (Lower). *See* DURAND.

Durrell, from DURELL.

Durell, armorially identified with DORRELL or DARRELL.

Durant. *See* DURAND.

Durrant, from DURAND. Hence the Baronets so named.

Durrans, from DURRAN.

Durran, from DURRANT.

Durroch. *See* Darroch, or DARRUGH.

Duvey, from Douay (Lower). In 1072 Walter, son of Urso de Douay, witnessed the charter of Wattignies Abbey, Flanders (Bouquet, xi. 106). In 1065 Walter, Castellan of Douay, witnessed a charter of Philip I. (Ib. xi. 111). He and Hugh his brother occur 1066 (Ib. 345). Walter de D. held a great barony in England, 1086 (Domesd.). From him descended the Barons of Bampton, Devon (*see* Pole, Devon, 22). The name was sometimes spelt Do, Dou, and Doe, and was widely spread.

Dwelley, from Dolley or D'OYLEY.

Dwight, from Doit. William de Doito, Ralph, Walter, Rainald, Richard, 1185-95, in Normandy (MRS); William del Doyt in England, 1272 (RH).

Deville, armorially identified with Deyville (Robson). *See* CRAVEN.

Dyason, for DYSON.

Dybell, for DIBBLE.

Dyble, for DIBBLE.

Dyce. Richard de Iz occurs in Normandy, 1180, and William de Iz, c. 1200 (MRS, and Mem. Soc. Ant. Norm. v. 202); Robert and Adam Dis and Disce in England, c. 1272 (RH).

Dye, for Deye, DAY.

Dyer. Radulphus Diore of Normandy, 1180, William and Robert Diere, 1195 (MRS); Nigel and Radulphus Tinctor of England, 1189 (Rot. Pip.). Hence the baronets of the name.

Dyke. *See* DIKE.

Dykes. *See* DYKE.

Dymes, for D'Hiesmes. *See* AMES.

Dymond. *See* DIMOND.

Dyne, a form of DIVE.

Dynes. *See* DYNE.

Dyson, a form of Tyson or Tesson. *See* PERCY.

Dyte, from Doit. *See* DWIGHT.

E

Eaddy. *See* EADY.

Eade. *See* EADY.

Eaden. *See* EDEN.

Eades. *See* EADE.

Eadie. *See* EADY.

Eady. *See* ADY.

Eagle, or De Aquila. *See* DIGGLES.

Eagles, or De Aquila. *See* DIGGLES.

Eagling, for Agyllon or Agulon. *See* ACOULON.

Eales, armorially identified with Eyles and Iles (Robson), probably the same as LISLE (Lower).

Eames. *See* AMES.

Earee. *See* AIREY.

Earl. 1, sometimes an English local name. 2, Theobaldus Comes of Normandy, 1180; Geoffry Comes, 1195; Gislebert, Maurice, Nigel, Richard, Robert Comes, 1198 (MRS). Richard, Nicholas, Roger Comes in England, c. 1272; also in England Agnes, Robert, Roger le Erl (RH). *See* EARLES.

Earle. Osmond and Roger le Cont or Counte, Norm. 1180-95 (MRS). *See* EARL.

Earles. *See* EARLE.

Earls. *See* EARL.

East. Amelot Dest, or D'Est, was of Normandy, 1195 (MRS). Est occurs in England frequently, c. 1272 (RH). Temp. Henry III. the lands of Richard de Este, Essex, are mentioned (Hunter, Rot. Select. 255); Walter Est, 31 E. 1., witnessed a charter of Wroxton Abbey, Oxford (Mon. ii. 327). Hence the Baronets East.

Easter, from L'Estre, near Valognes, Normandy (De Gerville, Anc. Chat. de la Manche). Richard de l'Estre held lands in Dorset from the time of the Conquest (Testa). In 1165 Richard de l'E. held a barony of four knights' fees in Somerset (Lib. Nig.). In 1272 Robert de l'E. was Viscount of Dorset.

Easterling, descended from some native of the Hanse Towns (Lower). The name occurs in England soon after the Conquest. *See* STRADLING.

Eastes. *See* EAST.

Eayres. *See* AYRES.

Ebbets, for ABBOTTS.

Ebbs, for ABBS.

Ebeling. *See* EVELYN.

Ebers, for EVERS.

Eddie. *See* ADDY.

Eddis. *See* ADDIS.

Eddowes. *See* EDDIS.

Eddy. *See* ADDY.

Ede. *See* EADE.

Eden, or De Torp. William de Torp or Torpes and his fief in Normandy are mentioned 1180 (MRS). He granted part of his lordship of Eden, Durham, to the Church of Durham before 1180 (Surtees, Durham, Append., vol. i. p. 281). His descendant, Eustace de Eden, granted part of Eden to the same church 1318 (Ib. vol. i. p. 40). Eustace

234

and Utred de Edene were witnesses to the charter of William de Torp of Eden, being probably his younger brothers. The family appears to have always remained seated in Durham. *See* LAMBTON.

Edenser, a branch of SHIRLEY.

Edes. *See* EADES.

Edgecumbe. In 1086 Milton with Lideton, Devon, belonged to Tavistock Abbey. Goisfrid then held them, from whom descended Reginald de Lideton, who 1165 held two fees from Tavistock (Lib. Nig.). Eggecumbe, a dependency of Lideton, was probably held by a younger branch of the De Lidetons or Liftons, as the arms are of the same origin. It appears that the Lidetons and Chanceaux, who were lords of Lideton, were the same. John de Eggecumbe (the first probably who bore the name) lived t. Henry III. Chanceaux was in Touraine; and of the English branch are mentioned Geoffry, Giles, and John de Cancellis, or Chanceaux, of whom the last named surrendered Lifton to Edward I. (Pole, Devon).

Edie. *See* ADDY.

Edington. *See* ADDINGTON.

Edis. *See* ADDIS.

Edlin, for Adlin, or Fitz-Adeline. Adeline frequently occurs c. 1272 (RH). William Fitz-Aldelm was frequently styled Fitz-Adeline. *See* DE BURGH, of which this may have been a branch.

Edmonds. 1. A patronymic. 2. A Norman name. Peter de St. Edmundo occurs in Normandy 1195 (MRS); Drogo de St. Edmundo in England 1199, and Richard (RCR), Lucas de St. Edmund, and others, c. 1272 (RH).

Edmunds. *See* EDMONDS.

Edward, from St. Edward. William de St. Edwardo and Jordan his son, t. Henry I., paid a fine for the lands of Roger, uncle of Jordan (Rot. Pip.). This was evidently a foreign family. Hugh de St. Edwardo occurs in Hereford and Bedford 1199 (RCR).

Edy. *See* EADY.

Edye. *See* EADY.

Eeede. *See* EDE.

Eedes. *See* EADES.

Eeles. *See* EALES.

Egerton, a branch of De Toeani and CHOLMONDELEY. Hence the Dukes of Bridgewater.

Eggens, for Aikens, or AIKEN.

Eggett. *See* HAGGETT.

Eglese. *See* EAGLES.

Eglon, for Aglon, or Agullon. *See* AGOULON.

Ewes. *See* IVES.

Eckert, Echard, or Acard. *See* ACHARD.

Ekins. *See* AIKIN.

Ekyns. *See* EKINS.

Elden. *See* ALDON.

Element, for Almont or ALMOND.

Elen, for ALAN.

Eley, or Elly, for ELY.

Eliot. N. Eliot occurs in Normandy 1195, and as the son of Anschar Elyot in 1198 (MRS); Eliot Fitz-William occurs in England 1198 (RCR); Reginald, Robert, William Eliot of England, c. 1272 (RH). From this Norman family descended the Eliots Earls of St. German's, the Elliotts Earls of Minto, Scotland, and the renowned Lord Heathfield, the defender of Gibraltar.

Eliott. *See* ELIOT.

Ell, for Elles, or Helles. *See* HILLS.

Ellard, for ALLARD.

Ellen, for ALLEN.

Ellerd, for ALLARD.

Ellers. Radulphus de Illeriis Normandy 1198 (MRS).

Elles, for ELLIS.

Ellett, for ALLETT.

Ellice, for ELLIS or ALIS.

Elliot. *See* ELLIOTT.

Elliott. *See* ELIOT.

Ellis, or Alis, from Alis near Pont de l'Arche. In 978 Hugh d'Ales witnessed a deed of the Abbey of Chartres, and was a favourite of Fulco Niger, Count of Anjou (Des Bois). William Alis is mentioned as a Baron in Normandy by Ord. Vitalis (344). He held lands in barony in England 1086 (Domesd.). He was a feudal tenant of William de Breteuil in Normandy. Philip Alis 1165 held a fief in Hereford (Lib. Niger). The dau. of Sir Roger Alys or Halys m. Thomas Earl of Norfolk, son of Edward I. From this family descend the Lords Howard de Walden, Seaford, and Dover.

Ellison. *See* ALLISON.

Elliss. *See* ELLIS.

Ellisson. *See* ELLISON.

Ells. *See* ELLES.

Elvery. *See* ALVAREY.

Elvey. *See* ALVEY.

Ely, or Fitz-Ely. Adam, Ralph, and William Fitz-Elie of Normandy 1180-95 (MRS); William, Alan, Geoffry, &c., Fitz-Elie of England 1198-9 (RCR): Sire William Fitz-Elie, Thomas, Peter, Richard, and others in England 1272 (RH).

Etty. *See* ATTY.

Elwes, or Helwish. Galterus Helouis, Normandy 1198 (MRS).

Emary, for AMORY.

Embelin, for Hambelin, or Hamelyn. *See* HAMLYN.

Emblem. *See* EMBLIN.

Emblen. *See* EMBELIN.

Emblin. *See* EMBELIN.

Emes. *See* AMES.

Emett. 1. A local name. 2. From Amiot. N. Amiota of Normandy 1195; Robert and Roger Amiot 1198 (MRS); William Amiot of England c. 1272 (RH).

Emler, for AMBLER.

Emm, for EMES.

Emmett. *See* EMETT.

Emmott. *See* EMMETT.

Emms. *See* AMES.

Emory. *See* AMORY.

Emperor. Gilbert, Roger, William Imperator, Normandy 1180–95 (MRS).

Enefer. John Enfer was of Normandy 1195 and 1198 (MRS).

Enes. *See* AINS.

Eness. *See* ENES.

Enever. *See* ENEFER.

Engall. *See* ANGELL.

England, or of England, equivalent to ENGLISH.

Engle. *See* ENGALL.

English, borne by numerous Norman families. Adam, Alexander, Alvered, Asceline, Bernard, Henry, Elias, Gaufrid, and twenty more, bore, 1180–95, the name of Anglicus in Normandy (MRS). Twenty-four of the name of Anglicus are mentioned in 1198 (Ib.). The families of English or Inglis are all Norman. 'England' is another form of Anglicus.

Ennals, from Annel in Normandy. Henry de Enhal and Alicia de Henhil occur in England c. 1272 (RH).

Ennever. *See* ENEFER.

Ensor, for EDENSOR.

Envill, for Anneville. Alexander

236

de Anneville occurs in Normandy 1195. *See* ANVILLE.

Enzor, for ENSOR.

Erle. *See* EARL.

Ernes, for Arnes, or ARNE.

Errol. *See* ERLE.

Esquilant. Roger Escollant was of Normandy 1195 (MRS). Geoffry Escolland 1130 witnessed a charter of Durham Abbey (Surtees, iv. 149), and held the see of Durham in farm 1130 (Rot. Pip.). Geoffry E. occurs in England 1198 (RCR).

Esson, from Esson, Normandy. William de Esson occurs in the Duchy, c. 1200 (Mem. Soc. Ant. Norm. v.).

Estell, for ASTELL.

Estelle. *See* ESTELL.

Eustace. William Eustachius occurs in Normandy 1198 (MRS); Eustace and Robert Eustachius in England 1198–9 (RCR); Geoffry, John, Roger, Ralph Eustace in England, c. 1272 (RH). Of this name were the Viscounts Baltinglas in Ireland.

Evanson, for IVISON.

Evatt, or Ivaz. *See* IVES.

Eve, Eves, or Ives. Radulphus, Maingot, and Osbert Ivas of Normandy 1180, 1195 (MRS). The name of Ive and Eve frequent in England c. 1272 (RH).

Eveling. *See* AVELING.

Evelyn. Roger Ivelin, Normandy 1198 (MRS).

Evelyn, Avelin, armorially identified. Avelin armorially connected with Abelin or Abelyn, and the latter similarly identified with Abilon. *See* ABELON. The notion of Burke, who derives the name from Evelyn near Shifnal, Salop, appears to be incorrect. The name of that place was formerly Evelyth, which has never been that of the family of Evelyn.

Eveness, for Evens, or AVENS.

Everard. N. Everard of Normandy 1180–95 (MRS); William Evrard 1198 (Ib.) ; Richard Everard of England, 1199 (RCR); Richard and William E., c. 1272, in England (RH).

Everet, for EVERARD, armorially identified (Robson).

Everett. See EVERET.

Evers. See HAVERS.

Every, a Norman name. Ranulph Ivrou occurs in the Duchy, 1180; Tustin Evrie, 1198 (MRS); Prinet Evrie of Normandy had a safe conduct from Henry V. (Mem. Soc. Ant. Norm. v. 216); Ralph, Nicholas, Walter Avery of England, c. 1272 (RH). Of this name are the Baronets Every.

Eves. See EVE.

Evetts. See DIVETT.

Evil, Eville, or Deyville (Lower). See CRAVEN.

Evitt. See DIVETT.

Evry. See EVERY.

Ewart. William de Huart, Normandy, 1180–95 (MRS).

Ewer, for EURE, a branch of De Vesci, and De BURGH, formerly Lords Eure.

Eyles. See ELES.

Eyre. 1. A local English name. 2. From Le Heir, Heres. William and Wymarc Heres occur in Normandy 1198 (MRS). Adam, Geoffry, John, Nicholas le Eyr, and others in England, c. 1272 (RH). Hence the Earls of Newburgh and Lords Eyre.

Eyrl. See EARL.

Eyton, a branch of Pantulf, Baron of Wem 1086, from whom Warin, his relative, held Eton or Eyton (Domesd.). Robert de E. was living c. 1170. This family bore the arms of Pantulf quarterly (Eyton, Salop, viii. 27–35).

F

Faber. Richard, Hugo, John, Robert, Roger Faber, were both of Normandy and England 1180–98 (MRS and RCR). Thirty-two persons bore the name in Normandy, and fourteen in England, at that time. Sixty-one occur in England c. 1272 (RH). The name was afterwards usually translated as 'Smith.'

Facer, for Fasart, the arms of which are preserved (Robson). Roger Fessart, Ralph, William, and John of Normandy 1180–95 (MRS).

Facey. Geoffry Fasse was of Normandy 1195. In 1198 Geoffry

Farsi and Roger F. also occur (MRS). Hugh Faci was of England, c. 1272 (RH).

Fache, for FACEY.

Facy. See FACEY.

Fage or Fagg. John, Robert, and Simon de Fago of Normandy 1198, William de Fago 1180 (MRS); Walter Fegge of Norfolk 1199 (RCR). William le Fag paid a fine in Sussex 1265 (Roberts, Excerpta). Of this line were the Fagges of Sussex, Baronets.

Fagg. See FAGE.

Fail, for Faiel. See FELL.

Faint, for Fant, or FAUNT.

Fair. Radulphus Fere of Normandy 1180, 1195 (MRS). Reginald Fer of England 1199 (RCR). Walter Fere of England, c. 1272 (RH).

Fairbridge, a form of FAIRBRASS.

Fairer, for FARRER.

Fairfield, or Fierville. Lovel, Ralph, and Roger de Fiervilla of Normandy, 1180-95 (MRS).

Fairhead, Fairet, or Freret. Richard Freret, of Normandy, 1195 (MRS). Oinus, Richard, Robert F. 1198 (Ib.). Thomas Ferrator, of England, c. 1199 (RCR). Robert Ferot, c. 1272 (RH).

Fairman. Walter Farman was of Normandy, 1180-95 (MRS). N. Fereman occurs in Devon 1189 (Rot. Pip.).

Fairs, from FAIR.

Fairbrass or Firebrass. Radulphus Fierebrache of Normandy, 1198 (MRS). Henry Ferebraz occurs in England c. 1272 (RH). The Baronets Firebrace were of this family.

Fairy, for FERRY.

Faith, from St. Faith, or De S. Fide. Geoffry de Sancta Fide was of Normandy 1198 (MRS); William de S. F. of England, 1194; and Gilbert de S. F. 1109 (RCR).

Falconer. This name includes families of various origin, especially Norman. Henricus Falconarius occurs in Normandy 1198 (MRS); and also frequently in England (RCR). Henry de Wada, Geoffry, Walter de Maner, and Hugh de Hanville of Normandy 1180-1200, are mentioned as Falconarii Regis (MRS).

Falkner. See FALCONER.

Faley, the Norman pronunciation of Falet. William Falet of Nor-

mandy 1180-95 (MRS); Robert Fellei of England, c. 1272 (RH).

Fallace, for FALAISE, a great baronial family. Geoffry de Falaise, son of Ameline, witnessed 1075 a charter of William de Braiose in Sussex (Mon. i. 581). William de Falaise in 1086 held the barony of Dartington, Devon, and 29 lordships (Domesd.). The family was spread in all parts of England in the 12th cent., and long remained eminent.

Fallowfield, armorially identified with Fauville or FAVELL.

Fallows, from FELLOWES.

Fallwell, for Falvel or FAVELL.

Fancourt, from Vandelicourt, near Beauvais. Helias de Fanacort held a fee of ancient enfeoffment from Deincourt in Lincoln 1165 (Lib. Nig.). Gerard de Phanucort was a benefactor to Thurgarton Priory (Mon. ii. 94). Sire Bertin de Fanecort was pardoned as an adherent of the Earl of Lancaster 1318, and was summoned from York to a great council 1324 (Palgr. Parl. Writs).

Fanner, for FENNER.

Fannin. See FANNING.

Fanning, from Fainent or Faineant. John and William Faitneant, or Fainent, of Normandy 1198 (MRS).

Fannon, from FANNING.

Faraday, or Fereday, from Ferté or La Ferté, Normandy. The family of De la Ferté had branches in England from the Conquest. See BROWNE.

Farden, for Vardon, or VERDON.

Farey, for FERRY.

Farish, for FARISS.

Fariss, for FERRIS.

Farley. See VARLEY.

Farman. See FAIRMAN.

Farment, for FARMAN.

Farmer, no doubt includes families of Norman and other origins. The earliest mention of the surname seems to be in Normandy 1195, when John Fermor occurs (MRS). The name was unfrequent in England c. 1272 (RH). Of this name were the Fermors Earls of Pomfret, and the Baronets Farmer.

Farnes. *See* FARREN.

Farr, for FAIR.

Farra, for FARRER.

Farrah. *See* FARRA.

Farran, for FARREN.

Farrance, for FRANCE.

Farrant, for Ferrant or Ferrand. William Ferrand held one fee of the Honour of Montford, Normandy, c. 1165 (Feod. Norm. Duchesne). In 1203 Roger Ferrand, man at arms of the Earl of Leicester, was appointed to a serjeantry at Caen (Hardy, Rot. Norm. 83). In 1203 the estate of William F. was granted to others by King John (Ib. 76, 99). In 1305 Hugh was found son and heir of Henry Ferrant, and petitioned for the custody of Skipton Castle, York, as hereditary in his family (Roberts, Cal. Geneal. 708, 795).

Farre, for Fere, or FAIR.

Farren. Robert and Guarin Farin were of Normandy 1180 (MRS); Geoffry and Roger Ferun of England c. 1272 (RH).

Farrer, armorially identified with Ferrers of Bere-Ferrers. *See* FERRERS.

Farrier, for FERRIER.

Farries, for Farris, or FERRIS.

Farrin. *See* FARREN.

Farris, for FERRIS.

Farrow, for Farra, or FARRER, armorially identified.

Farthing, for FARDEN.

Fase. Geoffry Fasse occurs in Normandy 1195 (MRS); Simon Fesse in England c. 1272 (RH).

Fast, for FASSETT.

Fassett. William Facetus of Normandy 1198 (MRS); Radulph le Facet in England c. 1272 (RH).

Fathers, or Fethers, from Le Feutrier. Reinfrid and Osmund le Feutrier of Normandy 1195 (MRS). Walter le Feuteror c. 1272 in England (RH), and Isabella le Fetor.

Faulconer, for FALCONER.

Faulkner, for FALCONER.

Faulks, for Faukes, or VAUX.

Faulls, for Vaulx, or VAUX.

Faultless, for FALLACE.

Faunt, for Font, or De Fonte. Norman, Peter, William, Hugh, Robert, Umfrid, Richard, Ralph, Ranulph de Fonte of Normandy 1180-95 (MRS). Reginald and Emma de Fonte of England 1198-9 (RCR). Many of the name occur here c. 1272 (RH). The family of De Fonte flourished in Norfolk (*See* Blomefield) and other counties.

Faupel, for Fauvel. *See* FAVELL.

Faussett, armorially connected with FOSSETT, or Fossart.

Fauntleroy, or Enfauntleroy, appears to be of foreign origin, but its date is uncertain.

Favell, or Fauvel. *See* FOWELL. The name frequently occurs in Normandy 1180-98 (MRS). William Fauvel or Falvel held from Oliver de Tracy, Devon, in 1165. The family occurs 13th cent. in York, Northants, Rutland; and Sir William Fauvel was M.P. for Derby 1314.

Faviell, for FAVELL.

Fawell. *See* FOWELL.

Fawkes, a form of VAUX.

Fawn, from Vannes, or Vane. Galfridus de Fane witnessed the foundation charter of Tywardereth Priory, Cornwall (Mon. i. 587). Reginald Fane, c. 1300 manucaptor of an M.P. for Pershore. Gueroch or Werok was Count of Vennes or Vannes c. 630 (Albert le Grand, Vie des Saints: Vie de St. Gildas).

Fawsitt. *See* FAUSSETT.

Fay, from Fay, Normandy. Reginald du Fai, Geoffry and Ralph de la Faia of Normandy 1180-98 (MRS). Ralph de Faia possessed estates Surrey 1156 (Rot. Pip.), and 1223 the king received the homage of John, son of Ralph de Fai, for a knight's fee in Surrey, held in capite (Roberts, Excerpta, i. 102). His sisters m. Roger de Clere, and Richard Longespée.

Fayle. *See* FAIL.

Fayors, for Fairs. *See* FAIR.

Fayrer, for FARRER.

Fearis. *See* FERRIS.

Fear, or Fere. *See* FAIR.

Feare, or Fere. *See* FAIR.

Fearman. *See* FAIRMAN.

Fearn, for FEARON.

Feasey, for Veasey, or Vesci. *See* VESEY.

Feast, for Fast, or FASSETT.

Fearon. N. Feron of Normandy 1180, Geoffry, John, Odo, Richard, Robert, Roger, Sulpice, and William Feron 1198 (MRS). Geoffry and Roger Ferun of England c. 1272 (RH).

Fee. *See* FAY.

Feesey, for VESEY.

Felix. Radulphus Fellex of Normandy 1195, Nicholas Feliz 1198 (MRS). Gilbert, Hugh, John Felice of England c. 1272 (RH).

Fell, from FAIEL. William Faiel of Normandy 1180, Gilbert Faiel 1198 (MRS). Petronilla and Reginald Fale, and William de Fall of England c. 1272 (RH).

240

Fellowes, for Felice, or FELIX.

Fellows, for Felice, or Fellex. *See* FELIX.

Fells. *See* FELL.

Felton, a branch of the Lords Bertram of Mitford, Northumberland (Banks, Dorm. Peerage, Art. Bertram). *See* MITFORD.

Fenn, armorially identified with Vene or Venn (Robson). Rualan de Vein of Normandy 1195, John de Vein 1198 (MRS); Thomas and Ralph de Vein in England 1199 (RCR); Roger, Henry de Fen and others c. 1272 (RH).

Fenner. Odo Fenarius of Normandy 1180-95; Walter Fannere of England c. 1272 (RH).

Fenning. *See* FANNING.

Fennings, for FENNING.

Fereday. *See* FARADAY.

Fermor. *See* FARMER.

Ferne, for Feron. *See* FEARON.

Fernee, for Verney. *See* FERNEY.

Ferney, for Verney or Vernai, from St. Paul de Vernai, near Bayeux. Gereline de Vernaco, c. 1080, was a benefactor to Conches, Normandy (Gall. Christ. xi. 132); and soon after Ralph de V. In 1158 Walter de Vernai was of Cambridgeshire (Rot. Pip.). In 1223 Ralph de V. paid a fine for having m. Agnes Wac without royal licence (Roberts, Excerpt.); Simon de Verney, 1268, had a suit with Berenger le Moyne relating to his lands, Northants. From this family descended the Lords Willoughby de Broke.

Fernie, for FERNEY.

Feron. *See* FEARON.

Ferrand. *See* FARRANT.

Ferrar. *See* FERRERS.

Ferrer. *See* FERRERS.

Ferrers, a baronial family, from Ferrières St. Hilary, near Bernai, Normandy. Walchelino de F., c. 1031, had a war with Hugh Barbatus, Baron of Montfort (Ord. Vitalis); Henry de F. held a barony in England, 1086. In 1096 William de F. was a chief leader in the Crusade (Ord. Vit.). The history of this family, Earls of Derby, and of its various branches in England, is too well known to need detail.

Ferrey, the Norman pronunciation of Feret. Richard Feret, Robert, and Oinus F. of Normandy, 1180–98 (MRS); Robert Ferot of England, c. 1272 (RH).

Ferry. *See* FERREY.

Ferrie. *See* FERREY.

Ferrier, for FERRERS.

Ferries. *See* FERRIS.

Ferriman, for Ferman, or FAIRMAN.

Ferry, for VERRY.

Ferris, or Ferres, a form of FERRERS (Lower).

Ferns. *See* FERNE.

Fethers. *See* FATHERS.

Fetherston. Ralph de F. granted lands to Nostel Priory, York, t. Henry I. The Church of Fetherston was at the same time granted by Hugh de Laval (Mon. ii. 34), from which it seems probable that the Lords of Fetherston were of the family of Laval. The latter came from Laval, Maine. Gui, Sire de Laval, lived c. 1000 (Des Bois); John de Laval witnessed a charter in Normandy, c. 1065. His descendants possessed a barony in Northumberland.

Fever, or Le Fevre, the usual Norman-French form of FABER.

Few, for Viel, the terminal letter softened to u. Agnes, Milo, Robert,

John Viel or Vyel of England, c. 1272 (RH); Richard and William V., 1180 (Rot. Pip.); Rad. Vitulus or Vetulus, 1158 (RP); Robert Viel occurs in Normandy, 1198 (MRS).

Fewtrell, from the French Vautrel, a hunter (*see* 'Vautrarius,' apud Ducange). William Falterellus held lands by knight service from the See of Chichester, 1165 (Lib. Nig.); Ralph Futerel occurs in a suit, Herts, 1198 (RCR). The name also remains as Fottrell.

Fey, for FAY.

Finch, for FINCH.

Fitch. *See* FITCH.

Ffrench, for FRENCH.

Fiander, for Viander. N. Viandier occurs in Normandy, 1198 (MRS).

Fichett. Osbert Fichett of Normandy, 1198 (MRS); Ralph, Hugh, Robert F. held, 1165, in Sussex and Somerset (Lib. Nig.); Thomas F. of Norfolk, in 1199 (RCR, &c.). In 1198 the name occurs several times as Fiket.

Fick. Joanna de Vicques occurs in Normandy, t. Henry V., Grimald Vic. t. John; Robert de Vico in England, c. 1272 (RH). The fief of Vec or Vic is mentioned in Normandy.

Ficken, from Vicinus. Goumond and Empire Veisin of Normandy, 1198 (MRS); Henry and William le Veysin or Vicinus of England, c. 1272 (RH).

Fickling. Richard de Wyclyne occurs in Rutland, c. 1272 (RH). This lordship I have not found in England.

Fiddes, from St. Fides. Geoffry de Sancta Fide occurs in Normandy, 1198 (MRS); Gilbert and Walter de S. Fide in England (RCR).

Fiddey, from St. Fides. *See* FID-
DES.

Fiddy. *See* FIDDEY.

Fiddymont, for Vaudemont,
from V. near Nancy; the only place
of the name in France.

Fidge, for FITCH.

Fidgen, for FICKEN or VICINUS.

Fidler, armorially identified with
Fidelow, which is armorially identified with Vis-de-lou, from Vis de
lou in Normandy. William Vis de
lou occurs there, 1198 (MRS). Humfrid Vis de lou held a barony, Berks,
1086 (Domesd.), and Ralph V. was
seated in Norfolk. In both counties
the family flourished for many ages.
Walkelin Vis de lou held a barony
in Berks, 1165.

Field, or De la Felda, embraces
both English and Norman families.
Richard de la Felda is mentioned in
Normandy, t. John (Mem. Soc. Ant.
Norm. v. 126).

Fielden, for FIELDING.

Fielder, from Feltrier, or Feutrier.
Reinfrid Feutrier occurs in Nor-
mandy, 1180-95 (MRS) ; Walter le
Feuterer in England, c. 1272 (RH).

Figes, or Figeys, from Figg or
Vic. *See* FICK.

Figgess. *See* FIGES.

Figg, a form of FIC or FICK.

Figgins, for FICKEN or Vicinus.

Fielding. This family ought
not perhaps to be introduced, being
not earlier in England than the
thirteenth century. Its history as
a branch of the Counts of Habs-
bourg is well known.

Filer. Robert Vidulator or Le
Vielur, and Reginald of England,
c. 1272 (RH); Turstan le Violur
in 1199 (RCR); Geoffry Vielator
of Devon, 1130 (Rot. Pip.). Evidently a foreign family.

242

Filder. *See* FIELDER.

Fillary, or Villary, for Valery or
St. Valery. Reginald de St. Valery
held a barony in Lincolnshire, 1086
(Domesd.). Reginald and William
Fitz-Herbert de St. V. occur in
England 1130 (Rot. Pip.); Wido
and Thomas de St. V. in 1199
(RCR). Reginald, son of Wido
de St. V., was granted the Barony
of Yvery in Oxfordshire by Henry II.
Bernard, his son, died at the siege
of Acre, Palestine, leaving Thomas,
who left a dau. and heir, m. to
Robert de Dreux.

Filler, for Le Vielur. *See* FILER.

Fillpot, or Philpot. N. Philipot
of Normandy, 1180-95 (MRS). *See*
PHILPOTT.

Finch. An English sobriquet
converted into a surname. It no
doubt included families of various
origin, Norman and otherwise.

Finch, or De Vendôme. Acfred,
Baron of Preuilly, founder of Preuilly
Abbey, Anjou, m. Beatrice of Issodun (Anselme, viii. 723, &c.; Gall.
Christ. xiv. 55, 302). His son,
grandson, and greatgrandson were
all named Geoffry. The latter
became, 1085, Count of Vendôme.
From his elder son descended the
Counts of V. Geoffry, the second,
accompanied Geoffry Count of Anjou
in his invasion of Normandy, 1136,
and had issue Herbert de Vendôme,
who came to England with Henry II.,
and is mentioned in a charter of
Count Burchard of V. as his relative (Gall. Christ. xiv. 324). He
had two sons, William de V., one
of the nuncii of Henry III. (Hardy,
Lit. Claus.), and Herbert de Vendôme or Veneum, who in 1203 paid
a fine (Rot. Canc.). John Fitz-
Herbert his son held lands in Kent

in capite (Testa), and had issue Herbert Fitz-Herbert, surnamed Le Finch, living 1299 and 1301, who held in capite in Kent. Herbert Fitz-H. his son was father of Vincent Herbert or Finch, ancestor of the Earls of Winchilsea, and Lord Finch of Fordwich.

Fines, a baronial family, from Fiennes in the county of Guines. Eustace, Baron of Fiennes, c. 1020, m. Adela, Lady of Ardres, dau. of Everard de Furnes, and had Conon de Fiennes, who founded Beaulieu Abbey, Boulogne, and had issue Conon, father of Eustace, ancestor of the Barons of F. (Des Bois). This family was seated in Kent at an early date, and held the office of hereditary castellans of Dover.

Fingerhut, or Vingraut, apparently from Vingrau, near Perpignan.

Finnes, armorially identified with Fiennes or FINES.

Finney. William Fenie of Normandy, 1198 (MRS); John Venie of England, c. 1272 (RH).

Finnis, or Fenys. *See* FINNES.

Finter, for VINTER, or Venator.

Firmin. N. Firmin of Normandy, 1180-95 (MRS), and William Forman, 1198 (Ib.).

Firminger, from the Norman-French Fromageur (Lower), probably a family of foreign origin.

Firrell. *See* FURRELL.

Fish. The English form of Piscis. Osmond de Piscis or Pisce, William and John, occur in Normandy, 1180-95 (MRS); William de Piscis in England, c. 1272 (RH). The name was afterwards translated.

Fishe. *See* FISH.

Fisher, or Piscator. Ernis Piscator and Galterus of Normandy,

1180-98 (MRS); Robert and Godwin P. of England, 1189, and Geoffry Fitz-Ralph Piscator, 1199 (Rot. Pip.; RCR). The name common c. 1272 (RH). It no doubt includes families of different origins.

Fisk, or Fyske, armorially identified with Fyshe or FISH.

Fison, for Veisin or Vicin. *See* FICKEN.

Fitch, for Fitz (Lower). Fitz or Le Fils, evidently foreign, occurs in England c. 1272, when Gilbert, Walter, and William Fitz are mentioned (RH).

Fitchew, for FITCHETT.

Fitter, for Fetter or Feutrier. *See* FIELDER.

Fitzgerald, or De Mortaine. About A.D. 660 Aother or Other, a great noble of Aquitaine and probably of Gothic descent, was deprived of estates in Aquitaine by Clotaire III. (Bouquet, x. 342). Sacerge, one of these estates, was afterwards in possession of the family, and was granted by another Other, c. 987, to the Abbey of Fleury near Orleans (Ibid.). Other or Autier, his son (whose name was Latinised Austerius), was Lord of the Castle of Mortaine, Aquitaine, c. 1030, and had issue Gilbert, Lord of Mortaine (Gallia Christ. ii. 48, Instr.), and Walter Fitz-Other, who accompanied the Conqueror to England, and received from him a barony and the office of Castellan of Windsor, whence his descendants bore the name of De Windsor. From a younger son descended the house of Fitzgerald. The Earls of Kildare, Dukes of Leinster, the Earls of Desmond, the Marquises of Lansdowne, the Barons and Viscounts Windsor, Barons of Decies,

Earls of Totness, Barons Carew, and other great families, descended from the same house. The name of Fitzgerald, being a clan name in Ireland, was adopted there by numbers of persons of Hiberno-Celtic descent in no way related to this house.

Fitzgibbon, a branch of FITZ-GERALD, and formerly Earls of Clare.

Fitzmaurice, a branch of Fitzgerald, Marquises of Lansdowne and Earls of Orkney.

Fitzwater, a branch of the Counts of Brionne, descended from Richard I. Duke of Normandy. Its ancestor was Robert de Tonbridge, fifth son of Richard Fitz-Gilbert, son of Gilbert, Count of Brionne, in Normandy. His son Walter Fitz-Robert was the progenitor of the great house of Fitz-Walter, Barons Fitz-Walter, who possessed the great barony of the Baynards in Essex. The name was frequently written Fitzwater.

Fitzwilliam. This family has been supposed, but erroneously, to be of Anglo-Saxon origin. It was of Flemish origin, and derived its original name of De Clerfai from Clerfai, Clarefay, or Clarfait, near Avesnes. Of this family was Henry de Clarofageto, Abbot of Tournay, 1227 (Gall. Christ. iii. 299). Godric de Clarefai was living t. Henry I. His son William Fitz-Godric or De Clarefai was of note in the reign of Stephen. He is mentioned, 1142, by John Prior of Hagulstad as having escaped from Randolf, Earl of Chester, to Tickhill Castle (Hunter, South Yorkshire, i. 333). Some time before 1156 he as William de Clarafai with Alicia de

244

Tanai his wife and Albreda de Lisures founded Hampole Priory, York (Mon. i. 831). He married 2ndly Albreda de Lisures, by whom he acquired Sprotboro and Plumptre, and had issue William Fitzwilliam, Lord of Sprotboro, who confirmed the gifts of his predecessors, especially of his mother Albreda de Lisures to Hampole (Hunter, Ibid.). The chief seat of this family was Plumptre, Notts, and from it descended the Fitzwilliams of Sprotboro, the Earls of Southampton, Viscounts Fitzwilliam, and Earls Fitzwilliam.

Flamank. Elye, Geoffry, and John Flamenc of Normandy, 1198; Clement, Serlo, Petre, Elye, Alard Flamenc or Flameng, 1180 - 95 (MRS); William, Robert, Ranulph Flameng in England, 1199 (RCR).

Flanders, or Flaunders. The English version of Flandrensis, a common name in England from the Conquest, and which speaks for itself. *See* FLEMING.

Flather, or Flatter, for Falter, Felter, or Felterer, derived from Feltrier or Feutrier. *See* FIELDER.

Flavell, for Falvel or Fauvel, from Fauvel, or Fauville, near Evreux. John, Robert, Hugh de Fauvel of Normandy, 1180 - 95 (MRS). William Fauvel held half a fee in Devon, 1165 (Lib. Nig.). Sire William Fauvel was of Northants and Rutland, c. 1300, other branches seated in Derby and York. In Worcester the name by transposition of letters became Flavell.

Flavelle, for FLAVEL.

Flawith, for Flawit, Floete, or Flote, from La Flotte, near Rochelle. John de la Flode occurs in England, c. 1272 (RH). The arms of Flowde, Flote, or Floelte are preserved by Robson.

Flawn, for Filaun or Villan. Ranulph Villanus, Richard, Haward, Gilbert, Simon, Ivo, of Normandy 1180–98 (MRS). Hugh, John, Richard le Vilein or Vileyn of England, c. 1272 (RH).

Flaws, for FELLOWES.

Fleet, for Floete or Flotte. *See* FLAWITH.

Fleming, or Flandrensis, borne by many Flemish families who accompanied the Conqueror. Walter Flandrensis was a Baron in Herts, Bucks, Bedf., &c., 1080. *See* WENTWORTH. The family of Flandrensis, of Devon, was probably a branch of Bethune or De Arras. *See* FLEMYING. The mention of the name is frequent from the Conquest. Of this name are the Baronets Le Fleming; and the Earls of Wigton and the Barons of Slane bore the same name.

Flemming, for FLEMING.

Flemwell, a corruption of Flamville, from Flamanville near Yvetot, Normandy. Roger de Flamville witnessed a charter of Walter Espec for Rivaux, York, t. Henry I., being one of his tenants (Mon. i. 729). He is mentioned 1130, also Hugh de F. in York, and in 1165, Roger de F., York, who held eight and a half fees from Mowbray (Lib. Nig.). The family long flourished in great eminence in England. William and Lohout de Flamonville occur in Normandy 1195 (MRS).

Fletcher, or Le Flechier. Robert Flechier occurs in Normandy 1198 (MRS); Adam le Flecher in England, c. 1272 (RH); Denis Flecharius of Lincoln occurs 1203 (Rot. Canc.). Robert le Flecher and Denis

held by serjeantry in Lincoln (Testa, 347, 371), 13th cent. Of this name are the Baronets Fletcher.

Fleury, from Flory, Normandy, held from Philip Augustus by Walter de Flori. Serlo, Walter, Robert de Flori of Normandy, 1180 (MRS). Hugh de Fluri held three fees in Hants, 1165 (Lib. Nig.). He granted lands to Taunton Abbey, Somerset, before 1162 (Mon. ii. 83). A branch of the family long flourished at Combe-Flory, Somerset.

Flewitt, for Floete or Flotte. *See* FLAWITH.

Fley, for FLY.

Flick, for FLECK.

Fliess, or Flyes, for FLY.

Flight, armorially identified with FLY or De Flagio.

Float, for Flotte. *See* FLAWITH.

Flood, or Flode, from Flote. *See* FLAWITH. The Baronets Flood descended from this family.

Florence, probably from St. Florent or St. Florence, near Orleans. The arms preserved by Robson, az., a cross floretty, are of early date.

Flower, or de Flore, otherwise de Janville, seated in Rutland 14th cent., and previously at Flore, Northants. The estate of William Tilli and Robert de Leicester (i.e. Flore) was restored to them in 1222 (Roberts, Excerpta). Flore of Northants bore fleur-de-lys, as did De Leicester. The families are therefore armorially identified. *See* LEICESTER. The Viscounts Ashbrook are of this family.

Flowerday, or Flowerdue, from Foladoube. Robert Foladoube in 1180 paid a fine in the Viscounty of Bayeux, Normandy (MRS). Lower derives the name from Fleur-Dieu, given as a sobriquet.

245

Flowers, for FLOWER.

Flude. *See* FLOOD.

Fludger. *See* FLUDYER.

Fludyer, or Fludger, a transposition of Fullager, which is a corrupt form of Fulger or FOULGER. Of this name were the Baronets Fludyer.

Fluker, for FULCHER. N. Fulchere of Normandy, 1195 (MRS). The arms of Fulcher of Derby are preserved by Robson.

Flurry, for Flory, or FLEURY.

Flutter, for Flatter or FLATHER.

Flux, for Flex or Fellex. Radulphus Fellex of Normandy, 1195 (MRS); Richard Flisk and Gilbert Felice of England, c. 1272 (RH).

Fly, from Fly or Flagium, Normandy (Lower). Robert, William, Henry de Flagie, Normandy, 1180-95 (MRS); Richard de F., 1198 (Ib.); Oda, Ralph, Roger Flie of England, c. 1272 (RH).

Foakes. *See* FOWKES.

Foale, for Foel or FOWELL.

Foget, for Faget. Radulphus Faget of Normandy, 1195 (MRS); Richard Faggot of England, 1199 (RCR).

Fogg, for FAGG.

Folder, for Felder or FIELDER.

Foley, from La Folie or Folia, near Bayeux. Robert Folie occurs in Normandy 1195 (MRS). John de Folia was a benefactor to St. Frideswide's, Oxford (Mon. Ang. i. 175), and the gift was confirmed by Pope Adrian (Ib.). Richard de la Folie in 1165 held one fee of ancient enfeoffment in Wilts (Lib. Nig.). Roger de la F. held Stratton, Wilts, as one fee in 13th century (Testa). At this time Robert de la F. held lands from the See of Worcester (Ib.). In 1304 Adam, son of Guido de la F., occurs in Worcester (Ro-

berts, Cal. Geneal.). Temp. Eliz., Richard Folly had a suit at law in the same county; and Edward Foley of the same county was ancestor of the Lords Foley. Of this family was the celebrated Richard Foley, the founder of an important branch of the iron manufacture, whose adventurous and successful career has been described by Mr. Smiles in 'Self-Help.'

In the reign of Henry II. Theobald De Moulines confirmed to Barbarie Abbey, Normandy, the grants made by Walter, Robert, and William de la Folie, brothers (Mem. Soc. Ant. Norm. vii. 141).

Foljambe, Fulgeam, or Fowlchampe, from Fulgent, originally Fulmechon, near Alençon. William and Josceline de Fulmechon of Normandy, 1180; Aubry, Gilbert, and others of the name, 1198 (MRS); Thomas, Robert Folejambe of England, c. 1272 (RH).

Folk, or Fitz-Fulco. *See* FOWKES.

Folkard, or Fokard. Radulfus Fochart of Normandy 1198 (MRS); William Fouquart. do. t. Henry V.; John Folkard of England, c. 1272 (RH).

Folks. *See* FOWKES.

Folkes. *See* FOWKES.

Follenfaunt. Hubert Folenfant in 1066 held Gouberville, Dainonville, and Oouverville, Normandy, from Adelais, dau. of Turstan Halduc (Wiffen, Mem. Russell, i. 17). Ralph Folefant held by knight service in Bedford from Simon de Beauchamp, 1165 (Lib. Niger). Hugh Folenfaunt was of England, 1272 (RH).

Follett. Gilbert, Mainard, and Robert Folet of Normandy, 1195-8 (RCR). William Folet held lands in Kent, 1086 (Domesd.); William F. in Gloucester and Worcester, 1165 (Lib. Nig.). Milo, Robert, and William F. of England, 1180 (Rot. Pip.); Reginald F. in 1199 (RCR).

Folley. Roger Folli of Normandy, 1195 (MRS); Horold Folie of England, c. 1272 (RH).

Folliott, a baronial family. Before the Conquest, Lord Roger Foliot in 1050 granted Omonville, Normandy, to Lessay Abbey (Gall. Christ. xi. 237). William Folet of Kent, 1086 (Domesd.), was father of Otbert and Adelulph, predecessors of Roger Foliott, who in 1165 held a barony of fifteen knights' fees in Northants (Lib. Niger; Bridges, Northants, i. 234). Several branches of this family existed in England t. Henry II., from one of which descended the family of De Ryther. *See* RYDER.

Follit, for FOLLETT.

Folser, for FULCHER.

Fooks. *See* FOWKES.

Footitt. Andolt Fotet was of Normandy, 1198 (MRS).

Force. Gerelm de Forz in 1165 was one of the Barons of the French Vexin (Feod. Norm. Duchesne); William de Forz was Earl of Albemarle in England. William and Isabella de Forz occur, c. 1272 (RH). Gerelm and Helie de Forz and Supplicius de Forz are mentioned in Normandy 1180-08 (MRS). Robson mentions the name as Forts or De Fortibus.

Foreman, or Forman, for FAIRMAN or Ferman.

Fores, for Force.

Forge. William de Forgis occurs in Normandy, 1180 (MRS); William de Furcis in England, 1199 (RCR); William de Furches, c. 1272 (RH).

Forgan, for Forican, which is armorially identified with Foricall or Ficault. The latter appears to be identical with Foucault. Ranulph, Richard, Adam Foucholt or Foukolt of Normandy, 1198 (MRS).

Forman. *See* FOREMAN.

Formon, for FORMAN.

Forrest, from Forez, Normandy. Guerard and Nicholas de Foresta of Normandy, 1198 (MRS). William Forist held lands in Hants 1086 (Domesd.). Hugh de Forester witnessed a charter of Hugh de Cahanes for Luffield Priory, Northants (Mon. i. 522), and a charter of William Earl of Albemarle for Gerondon, Leicester (Mon. i. 773). The Baronets Forrest are of this race.

Forrester. Vitalis, Rualen, Geoffry, Hugo, Radulphus Forestarius, and four others, of Normandy, 1180-95; and Geoffry, Gilbert, Hugh, Lambert, Vivian Forestarius, 1198 (MRS). Several of these appear in England (RCR). Fifteen or twenty of the name occur here, c. 1272, bearing Norman Christian names (RH). Of this name were the Lords Forrester of Scotland.

Forrestt, for FORREST.

Forrow, for Farrow, armorially identified with FARRER.

Forsey. *See* FURSBY.

Forster. *See* FORRESTER. Of this name are the Baronets Forster.

Fort. Robert and William de Fort of Normandy, 1198 (MRS); Sampson Forte and Adam F. of England, c. 1272 (RH).

Fortescue, a Norman family, from near Valognes, which continued till the 15th century (La Roque, Mais. Harc., i. 1023, 1247, 1443;

ii. Preuves, 766). Rainald was Lord of Winestane, Devon, 1086 (Domesd.). John Fortescue, his descendant, had a confirmation of W. in 1208 (Pole, 310). Robert F., his son, held a knight's fee in capite, as of the honour of Mortaine (Testa). From this family descend the Earls Fortescue, and other noble houses.

Fortey, for Forte, armorially identified with Fortibus or Forz (Robson). *See* FORCE.

Fortens, or Forten. Osbert, Radulphus, William Fortin, and their fiefs in Normandy, 1180-95, Berenger F. in 1198 (MRS); Richard de Forten of England 1199 (RCR). *See* FORTUNE.

Geronymus and Baldwin Fortinus witnessed a charter in Normandy 1077 (Mem. Soc. Ant. Norm. v. 197).

Fortt. *See* FORT.

Fortune, or Forten. *See* FORTENS.

Forty. *See* FORTBY.

Fory, the French pronunciation of Forêt or De Foresta. *See* FORREST.

Foss. Geoffry, Hubert, Ralph, Richard, Stephen de Fossa, or De la Fosse of Normandy, 1198 (MRS); Roger de Fossa, Richard de la Fosse of England, c. 1272 (RH).

Fossett. Geoffry, Gilbert, Robert, William de Fossato, Normandy, 1198 (MRS); Richard de Fossato of England, 1199 (RCR).

Fossey. John de Fosseio of Normandy 1198 (MRS); Richard Fossey of England, c. 1272 (RH).

Fossick. *See* FOSSETT.

Foster. *See* FORSTER. The Baronets Foster, also the Viscounts Ferrard, bear this name.

Fottrel. *See* FUTTRILL.

248

Foucard. *See* FOLKARD.

Foulds, for Fowles or FOWLE.

Foulger, or De Fougeres, a baronial family descended from Alan, Baron of Fougeres or Fulgiers in Bretagne, c. 900, father of Maino, whose grandson Maino was living 1050. From his brother Frangualo descended the Lords Bohun of Midhurst (Herald and Genealogist, vi. 481, &c.). The Barons of Fulgiers or Filgiers had many branches in England. Ralph de Filgeres, 1083, held lands in Devon in capite (Domesd.).

Henry de Filgeres occurs in 1130 (Rot. Pip.); Ralph de F. in 1180 (Ib.). William de Fulgeres held a barony in York 1165 (Lib. Nig.). Wace (ii. 231) mentions Ralph de Fulgeres as present at the battle of Hastings.

Foulkes. *See* FOLKES.

Fountaine, or De Fonte. Norman, Peter, William De Fonte, and seven others, of Normandy, 1180-95, eight others of the name, 1198 (MRS). Twenty-six of the name occur in England c. 1272 (RH); after which the name was translated into 'Fountain' and Spring.

Fountain. *See* FOUNTAINE. These names comprise the descendants not only of the family of De Fonte, but of that of De Fontibus of Normandy, of whom Gonduin, Gervase, and others were living 1180 (MRS); when Roger and Reginald de Fontibus were of England (RCR).

Fourneaux, or Fornels, from Fourneaux near St. Lo, and Coutances. Odo de Furnell held in capite in Somerset, 1083 (Ex. Domesd.). Geoffry de F. was Viscount of Devon 1130, and Robert de F. occurs in Yorks. Adam de F., 1165, held one and a half fee, Devon, as mesne lord; and Alan F. one fee. He was one of the Justiciaries (Mon. i. 999). Ralph de Fornellis occurs in Normandy, 1070 (Ord. Vit. 575); Richard and Philip de F. 1180–95 (MRS).

Fouracres. Ranulph de Quatuor Acris of Normandy, 1180–95 (MRS).

Fowell, Fauel, or Fauvel. John, Robert, Hugh, Geoffry de Fauvel of Normandy, 1180–95 (MRS). William Fauvel held from Oliver de Tracy, Devon, 1165 (Lib. Niger). The name changed to Fauel, Fouel, Voghill, Vowell, and Fowell; the family was seated at Bolterscombe, Devon, and from it descended the Baronets Fowell and the Vowells, ancestors of 'Judicious Hooker.'

Foweraker. See FOURACRE.

Fowkes, or Folkes, otherwise Fitz-Fulco. William, Richard, Henry, Guido Fitz-Fulco of Normandy, 1180–95 (MRS); Robert, Geoffry, Theobald, William F. Fulco of England, 1199 (RCR). Robert Fulco, one of the Justiciaries, 1267 (Roberts, Excerpt., ii. 460, &c.). The Baronets Folkes and Fowke are of this race.

Fowl, for FOWLE.

Fowle, armorially identified with FOWELL.

Fowler. Rainerus Auceps or Fowler of Normandy 1198 (MRS). Gamel Auceps paid a fine in York 1158 (Rot. Pip.). Stephen and Thomas Aucuparius of England, c. 1272, also Juliana, Adam, Walter Foulare (RH).

Fowles. See FOWLE.

Fowls. See FOWLE.

Fox. Robert Reinard (Fox) of Normandy, 1198 (MRS); Turstain Renouard t. Henry VI.; also Aeliz and Ranulph Renouard 1198 (Ib.). Gilbert le Fox and others of the name in England, c. 1272 (RH), the name being translated. Before this time the name was Rainer, Renard, &c. William Vulpis or Renard in 1148 held lands from the Bishop of Winchester (Wint. Domesd.). The family long continued there as Le Fox, and from it descended the Earls of Ilchester and Lords Holland. Other families, both native and foreign, bear the name.

Foy, for St. Foy or St. Fides. See FAITH.

Foyel, for Fayel. See FAIL.

Foyle. See FOYELL.

Fosard, for Fossart, a baronial family descended from Nigel Fossart, Baron of Doncaster, t. William I. The family does not seem to have been Norman, but Frank, perhaps from Fossard, near Fontainebleau. William Fossard held in 1165, 33½ knights' fees in barony. At the same time Geoffry, William, and Geoffry F. held knights' fees from Fossard, the Bishop of Durham, and De Stuteville.

Fraiser. See FRASER.

Frame. William Fitz-Fram of Normandy 1180–95 (MRS). William Frampe of England, c. 1272 (RH).

France. Radulphus France of Normandy 1198 (MRS); Alexander Fraunc of England, c. 1272 (RH), and William Frense (Ib.).

Frances. See FRANCIS.

French, for FRENCH.

Franchet, for Freschet. Bertrand Freschet of Normandy, 1180–95 (MRS).

Francis, Francus, or Le Franceys.

William le Franceys or Francus 1180-98 in Normandy (MRS); Richard, Azo, Robert, Umfrey, Walter, William le F. of England 1189 (Rot. Pip.). The name is thenceforth frequent in England, and speaks for itself as to origin. William le Franceys and several others of the name held knights'-fees in England 1165 (Lib. Nig.). The Lords De Freyne and Barons French bear forms of this name. *See* FRENCH.

Franck, or Frank. *See* FRANCIS.

Francklyn. *See* FRANKLIN.

Franks. *See* FRANK.

Franey, from Fresnay, Normandy. Roger de Fresnay living 1180 (MRS). Robert and Roger de Fraisnio 1198 (Ib.).

Frank, for Francus. *See* FRANCIS.

Frankish, for FRANCIS, an English form of Le Francois or Le Franceys.

Frankland, a form of FRANKLIN. Of this name are the Baronets Frankland.

Franklen. *See* FRANKLIN.

Franklin, Franchilanus, or Le Fraunclein, meant a free tenant, holding by military service (Du Cange). It included both native and foreign families, but probably the latter bore chiefly the name Fraunclein, the former the English form Freeman. The name was not used in Normandy.

Frankling, for FRANKLIN.

Fraser or Fresel. This name does not appear in Normandy; it was of Touraine, where René Frezel, c. 1030, was a benefactor to Notre Dame de Noyers. He had issue—1. René, living 1084, who was ancestor of the house of Freseau, Marquises of La Frezeliere; 2. Simon (Des

Bois). The latter came to England at the Conquest. His descendants bearing the name of Fresel or Frassel long continued in England, and t. David I. Simon Fresel settled in Scotland and c. 1150 granted the church of Keith to Kelso (Chart. Kelso). From him descend the Lords Saltoun and Lovat of Scotland, and their branches. The Celtic followers of these barons assumed the same name.

Fray, for Viré, in Aquitaine. Gilbert and Hugh de Viridi, and John Viry, c. 1272, in England (RH). Other forms of the name are Frey, Fry, and Frie.

Fraye. *See* FRAY.

Frazer. *See* FRASER. Many persons who bear this name are Celts, it being a clan name.

Frazier, for FRASER.

Frean. *See* FRAYNE.

Free. *See* FRAY.

Freebody, a corruption of FREEBOUT or Frebois.

Freebout, for Friebois. Robert de Friebois occurs in Normandy t. Phil. Augustus. The family is frequently mentioned in Yorkshire (Burton, Mon. Ebor.).

Freed, for FREE.

Freeland. Richard Frolant or Froland of Normandy 1180 (MRS); Hugh Frelond or Frilond, and Matilda Frelond, c. 1272, in England (RH).

Freeling, for FREELAND. The Baronets Freeling are of this family.

Freeman, corresponds to Franklin, and meant a free tenant. It is sometimes used for FORMAN (Robson). Some families bear fleur de lys, and their name is a form of De Fremond, Fremont, or De Frigido-monte, of whom Radulfus de Frigido Monte occurs in Normandy 1180 (MRS); Matthew and Simon de Friemont 1198 (Ib.). The arms of Fremond in England are preserved by Robson. The name doubtless is borne by Saxon, Danish, and Norman families. In Yorkshire, 1259, Nicholas Freeman, son of Margery, daughter of Walter de Belun of Winkesley, made a grant to Fountains Abbey; and Nicholas De Bellun was a benefactor (Burton, Mon. Ebor. 165). Alicia, widow of Gilbert F. of York, occurs 1267. Thomas F. of Walton, York, 1259 (Roberts, Excerpt.). The name of De Bellon occurs in Normandy t. Philip-Augustus. The fusils in fesse borne by various branches appear to have originated in Yorkshire.

Freemantle, from Fromanteau, Isle of France. William Freismantel occurs in England 1198 (RCR). The name of Freemantle is armorially identified with Fromantrill (Robson). Nigel de Fremantel occurs Northants 1216 (Hardy, Lit. Claus.). Richard and Thomas F. appear in Surrey and Dorset 1315, 1316. Richard F. one of the gentry of Oxford 1433. The Baronets Fremantle are of this family.

Frees, from FREE.

Freezer, for FRAZER.

Frere. Ansgot Frater of Normandy, 1198 (MRS). Walter le Frere (13th cent.) paid scutage in Essex (Testa de Neville, 364). Thomas F. of Framlingham, 1326, man at arms, attended the array at Loose, Suffolk (PPW). The fief of this family was held from the De Mandevilles, Earls of Essex.

Freshfield, armorially identified with Freacheville of Derby. In-

gelram de Frissonville witnessed a charter of Henry, Count of Eu, to Robertsbridge, and one of Ralph de Issodun (Mon. ii. 920, 921). Ralph de Fressonville in 1225 had seizin of the estates and barony of Hubert Fitz-Ralph in Notts and Derby, as his heir (Roberts, Excerpta). The chief seat of the barony was at Boney, Notts. The family of the Barons Freacheville long continued.

Frei. See FRAY.

Freeman, for FREEMAN.

French, the English translation of le Franceys. See FRANCIS.

Frend, or Amicus. Willielmus Amicus of Normandy 1180, Robert Ami 1198 (MRS); Gilbert and Hugh le Frend, and others in England c. 1272 (RH).

Fretwell, identified by Camden with Freacheville (Lower). See FRESHFIELD.

Frewer, for Frere, or FRIER.

Frey, or Fry. See FRAY.

Friend. See FREND.

Frier, armorially identified with Frere (Robson).

Frigent. Richard Frigant or Frigaut of Normandy 1195 (MRS).

Fripp. Alanus Freeb of Normandy 1180–95 (MRS).

Friswell, or Fritzville, armorially identified with Freacheville. See FRESHFIELD.

Frith, by transposition for Firth, a form of Fireth (See Robson). The latter a form of Feret, or Feirot. Oinus, Richard, Robert Feret of Normandy 1180–95 (MRS). John le Frith of England c. 1272 (RH).

Frizell. See FRASER.

Froud, or Parsons. Christopher and John Parsons alias Frowde were of Wilts t. Elizabeth (Proc. Chanc.

t. Eliz.). Froude bears three lions rampant in a bordure, and Person or Parsons three lions rampant on a fesse. The family subsequently appears in Devon. *See* PARSONS. The name of Froud occurs 1261, when Ivo Fitz-Alan de Frode, with Adam, John, and Richard his brothers, paid a fine in Kent (Roberts, Excerpta).

Froude. *See* FROUD.

Frow, for FROWD.

Frowd. *See* FROUD.

Frowde. *See* FROUD.

Fry. *See* FRAY.

Fryatt, for Friart. Gislebert Freiart of Normandy 1180 (MRS).

Fryer. *See* FRIER.

Fryett. *See* FRYATT.

Fudge, for Fuge, or Fugers, a form of Fulgers. *See* FOULGER.

Fuge. *See* FUDGE.

Fuggle, for Voghil, or Vowell, a form of FOWELL.

Fuggles, for FUGGLE.

Fulcher. N. Fulchere of Normandy 1180-95 (MRS); Aeliz Garin, Radulf Fouchier, Ricard Folkere 1198 (Ib.). The family of Fulcher was seated in Derby.

Fulker, for FOLKER.

Fulkes, for FOWKES.

Fullager, for Folger, or Fulger. *See* FOULGER.

Fulljames, for Foljambe (Lower).

Fullalove, a corruption of Valdeloge. Lucas, and William de Valle de Logis, occur in Normandy 1198 (MRS).

Fullard, from Filard. Ralph Filard of Normandy 1180-95 (MRS).

Fullcher, for FULCHER.

Fuller, being the name of an employment, comprises, doubtless, families of Norman as well as other origins.

Fulllove. *See* FULLALOVE.

Fulling, or Fullin, from Folin. Wascius Folin of Normandy 1198 (MRS), also Arnulf and Walter Folon.

Fulloon. *See* FULLING.

Fundell, like Funnell, is probably a corruption of Fontanelle, from F. in Normandy (Lower). Droco de Fontenel occurs there t. Philip-Augustus.

Funnell. *See* FUNDELL.

Furber, or Furbisher. N. Forbeor or Forboer of Normandy 1180, Ralph 1195 (MRS); Alexander, Roger, William le Furbur of England c. 1272 (RH). Hence the famous Sir Martin Frobisher.

Furbin, probably from Forbin, apparently a foreign name, but not Norman.

Furlong. N. Forlon of Normandy 1195 (MRS).

Furlonger, from Valancre. Warin de Valle-Ancre was of Normandy 1195 (MRS). The name appears in England c. 1272 as Varencher, then Wallenger, then as Fullanger, or Furlonger.

Furmage, for FROMAGE.

Furnell, from Fourneaux, near Coutances. Ralph de Fornellis is mentioned c. 1070 (Ord. Vitalis, 575). Anquetil de F. witnessed, t. William I., the foundation charter of Swavesey Abbey, Cambridge (Mon. i. 572). Robert de Fornell occurs in York 1130 (Rot. Pip.). Philip de F. (13th cent.) held Fen Ottery, Devon, by grant of Henry I. to his ancestor. Alan de Fornell was a justiciary.

Furner, or Forner. Durand Fornier of Normandy 1195, Hugo Furnarius 1180 (MRS), William le Furner and Juliana his wife of England c. 1272 (RH).

Furness. *See* Furnes.

Furness, from Fournes, near Lille, Picardy. Everard de Furnes is mentioned before 1000, whose daughter m. Eustace, baron of Fiennes. In 1165 Gerelm de Furnis held lands in the county of Breteuil, Normandy. Robert de Furnes was baron of Ulverston, Lancashire, before 1100 (Baines, Lanc. i. 115); and William de Furnes had a writ of military summons 1257.

Furney, or Forney, the Norman French pronunciation of Fornet. Sylvester Fornet of Normandy 1195, Nicholas and Sylvester de Fornet 1198 (MRS). Fornet was in the Cotentin.

Furnice. *See* Furness.

Furnival, from Fournival, near Beauvais. Gerard de Fournival was in the service of Richard I., and is mentioned in Normandy 1195 and 1198 (MRS), and 1202 had grants in Essex (Rot. Canc.). Long before

1279 Christiana de F. had held the Barony of Wardon, Northants, with fifteen fees. The Lords Furnival were of this family. Their barony was in Yorkshire.

Furrell, or Forel. Robert Forel of Normandy 1198 (MRS); John and William Forel of England c. 1272 (RH).

Furse, or Fursey. Geoffry and Roger Farsi of Normandy 1198 (MRS). The name also occurs as Forcy and Falsy (Mem. Soc. Ant. Norm. v.). Geoffry Farsi is mentioned at the siege of Dol 1173.

Fussell, or Fuisel. Ralph Fuisel of Normandy 1198 (MRS); Geoffry Fussel of England c. 1272 (RH).

Fussey. *See* Fossey.

Furze. *See* Furse.

Futcher, for Fudger, or Fulger. *See* Foulger.

Fuzzard. *See* Fozzard.

Fysh. *See* Fish.

Fyson. *See* Fison.

G

Gabb, or Gapp. William Gaipi of Normandy, 1198 (MRS); Robert Gappe of England, c. 1272 (RH).

Gabel. *See* Cabbell.

Gabell. *See* Gabel.

Gabbett, for Chabot.

Gable. *See* Gabel.

Gabriel. William Gabriel of Normandy, 1195 (MRS). In 1327 John Gabriel was M.P. for Winchester. Of this name are the Baronets Gabriel.

Galey, for Caley, or Caylby.

Gadd, for Cadd. *See* Cade.

Gade, for Cade.

Gadban, for Cadban, from Chabanne in Aquitaine. *See* Cabban.

Gael. William Cael of Normandy, 1198 (MRS); William Gayl of England, c. 1272 (RH).

Gaffin. *See* Caffin.

Gaffney, for Cafney, or Chaveny, from Chavigny, near Evreux. Henry de Chavignie occurs in Normandy, 1180–95 (MRS).

Gagan, from Gacon. William Gacon or Gachon of Normandy 1180 (MRS); Thomas Gagun of England, c. 1272 (RH).

Gage, from Gaugy, Normandy.

Ralph de Gaugy occurs there, 1180 (MRS). Gauchi, Gaugi, or Gaacy was near L'Aigle, Normandy. Warin de Gaacy or Wacy occurs in Bedford, 1140 (Mon. i. 326). In 1165 Ralph de Gauchi or Gaugi held a fief in Northumberland, which he had acquired by marriage. Robert de Gaugi was Baron of Slesmouth, Northumberland, 1165 (Lib. Niger), and had a brother, Roger de Gauchi, to whom King John, 1208, committed the custody of Argentan Castle and Forest (Hardy, Rot. Norm.). William de Gaugi, his son, of Northampton, was father of John de Gaugi, who in 1260, with Petronilla, his wife, paid a fine in Essex (Roberts, Excerpt.), and in 1269 he occurs in Suffolk (Hunter, Rot. Select. 221). Roger Gaugi, 1324, was returned from Suffolk to a great Council at Westminster (PPW). John Gage, of this family, settled in Gloucestershire, from whom descended the Viscounts and Barouets Gage.

Gagen. *See* GAGAN.

Gaggis, for Gagges, or Gaggo, a form of GAGE. Henry Gagge and Robert Gagse occur in England, c. 1272 (RH).

Gailey, for CAYLEY.

Gaimes. *See* GAMES.

Gain. *See* CAIN.

Gaine. *See* GAIN.

Gaines, for GAIN.

Gairdner, for GARDINER.

Gait. Hugo de Gaiet occurs in Normandy, 1176 (Mem. Soc. Ant. Norm. v. 198). Robert Gait, Miles, founder of Thame Abbey, Oxford, 1138 (Mon. i. 802). Henry II. confirmed the gift of Reginald de Geyt to Thame.

Gaites. *See* GAIT.

Gaitskell. *See* GASKELL.

Gaitz. *See* GAIT.

Gale. *See* GAEL.

Galer. *See* GALLIERS.

Gales, for Cales, or Calais. *See* CHALLICE.

Galey, for Caley, or CAYLEY.

Gall. Roger, Walter, Radulphus Gal, Durand, Gislebert, Radulphus de Gal of Normandy, 1180–98 (MRS). Hugh, Sibilla, Thomas Gall of England, c. 1272 (RH).

Galland, for GARLAND.

Gallant, for GARLANT.

Gallard, for CALLARD.

Gallavin, for CALVIN. *See* CAFFIN.

Galley, the Norman-French pronunciation of Galet. Gilbert Galet of Normandy, 1180–98 (MRS). From the same origin is probably derived the name Galt, by abbreviation.

Galliers, from Challiers, or Challers. *See* SCALES.

Gally. *See* GALLEY.

Gallyon. Udonus Galien of Normandy, 1198 (MRS); Fulco, Symon, William Galyon of England, c. 1272 (RH).

Gamage, from Gamaches, in the Vexin, Normandy. Peter, Roger de Gamaches occur in Normandy 1180–98 (MRS). *See* DILLON.

Gamain. *See* GAMMON.

Gaman. *See* GAMMON.

Gamble. Auberil Le Gemble, Norm. 1198 (MRS).

Gamble, from the patronymic Gamel, a Danish and Norman name (Lower). This may include other families besides Norman.

Gambier. William Gambier of Normandy, 1180 (MRS). Hence the brave Admiral, Lord Gambier.

Game. *See* GAMES.

Games, for Cames, or Cambes. Richard and Geoffry de Cambes of

Normandy, 1180–95 (MRS); William Caim of England, c. 1272 (RH), and Robert del Cam.

Gamester, from Cambitor, or le Changeur. Gaufridus, Sylvester, Helibec, Herbert Cambitor of Normandy, 1180–95; Geoffry, and four others of the name, 1198 (MRS). Petrus Cambestre or Cambitor of England c. 1272.

Gamlen, from Fitz-Gamelin, a Norman patronymic. Reginald, Roger, and Radulf Gamelyn of England c. 1272 (RH).

Gamlin. *See* GAMLEN.

Gammage. *See* GAMAGE.

Gamman, for GAMMON.

Gammell. *See* GAMBLE.

Gammon, for Camin. Gillebert Camin of Normandy 1180–95 (MRS); William Gamen, Adam Camin, Geoffry Gamon of England c. 1272 (RH). Hence the Baronets Gamon-Grace.

Gancell. Rainer, Richard, and Geoffry Gansel of Normandy 1180–95 (MRS).

Gandell, for CANDEL.

Gander, or le Ganter (RH), the designation of some Norman-French maker of gloves.

Gandy, for Candy. Nicholaus de Candie of Normandy 1180–95 (MRS).

Gane. *See* GAIN.

Ganeval, or Ganfield, for Jeneville or Janville. *See* LEYCESTER, LEICESTER.

Gange. Muardus de Ganges held lands in Normandy t. Phil. Augustus (Mem. Soc. Ant. Norm. v. 181); Thomas and William de Gangia in England c. 1272 (RH).

Gann. *See* CANN.

Gannaway, for Canoway, or Canevet. *See* KNIVETT.

Gannell, for CANNELL.

Ganney, or Canney, from Canet or Canut. Nicholas and Robert Ganet, and Philip Canet of England c. 1272 (RH). *See* CANUTE.

Gant, or De Gand. *See* CONSTABLE.

Ganter. *See* GANDER.

Gantlett, or Gantelo, from Cantelo or Cantelupe. *See* CODRINGTON.

Gapp. *See* GABB.

Garbett, from Gerböde (Lower). Hamo and William Gerbode of England 1199 (RCR). The name Gerbode is Flemish, derived probably from an ancestor who accompanied the Conqueror from Flanders.

Garbutt. *See* GARBETT.

Gard, or Garde. *See* WARD.

Garden. William, Osmond, Gervase, Richard, Umfrey De Gardino, &c., of Normandy 1180–95 (MRS); Walter de Gardan of England 1199 (RCR); Henry and Nicholas de Gardin c. 1272 (RH); Sire Thomas de Gardyn of Cambridge c. 1300 (Palgr. Parl. Writs).

Gardener, or Le Gardener, le Jardinier, probably Norman, from the office of gardener to the King or to great nobles. In 1202 William le Gardeiner possessed estates in Rutland (Rot. Canc.). The name occurs 13th cent. in Derby and York; 14th cent. in Wilts and Somerset.

Gardiner. *See* GARDENER.

Gardiner. *See* GAIRDNER.

Gardner. *See* GARDENER.

Gardom, for GARDEN.

Gardyne, for Gardin. *See* GARDEN.

Gare, from Gare, or Gere, Normandy. William Gere and Robert de Gera mentioned there 1198 (MRS); Robert Gere of England c. 1272 (RH).

Garey, for GEARY.

Gargon, for Carchon. Robert de Carchon of Normandy 1180–95 (MRS).

Garland. John de Garlande and William de G. mentioned in Normandy .1180–98 '(MRS). William de Garlande, Seneschal of France, Lord of G. and Liury, t. William I., was father of Ansel de G., Seneschal of France, whose son Gilbert was Butler of France (La Roque, Mais. Harc. ii. 1815). William de G. in 1165 held Neuchatel in the Norman Vexin, and a barony in Normandy (Feod. Norm. Duchesne). Roger, William, and Richard Garlande held a fief in Devon 13th century, from Henry de la Pomeraye (Testa). This great family is extinct in France.

Garlant, for GARLAND.

Garlick, for Garlec or Garlayk. John Garlayk of Bretagne, and John Garlec, occur t. Henry V. (Mem. Soc. Ant. Norm. v. 216, 246). Probably a corruption of Gerloch, a Breton name.

Garman, for GERMAN.

Garment, for GARMAN.

Garner, or GUARNIER. Robert, Richard, Hubert, Thomas Garnerus or Guarnier of Normandy 1198 (MRS); Henry, John, Matilda Warner or Garner of England c. 1272 (RH).

Garms, for Garm, Gorm, or GORHAM.

Garnet, or Gernet. William Gernet of Normandy 1180–95 (MRS). William de Chernet was of Hants 1086 (Domesd.). William G. was of Bedford, Alexander and Geoffry of Essex 1165 (Lib. Nig.). Alexander had estates in Lancashire, and was dead before 1202, when Mat-

256

thew Gernet obtained seizin of his lands (Rot. Canc.). The family long flourished in Lancashire. Henry Gernet was Viscount of Essex and Herts, 1341.

Garnier. *See* GARNER.

Garot, for GARRETT.

Garrad, for GARRETT.

Garrard, for Gerard. Ralph, Walter, Gilbert, William Gerard, and others of Normandy 1180–95 (MRS). Twenty-six of the name mentioned in England c. 1272 (RH).

Garratt, for GARRETT.

Garrett. Roger and William Garet of Normandy 1180, Arnulph and William Garet 1198 (MRS). Henry and Richard Caret c. 1272 (RH).

Garritt. *See* GARRETT.

Garrod, for GARRETT.

Garrood, for GARROD.

Garrould, or Gerould. Roger Gerald or Geroud was of Normandy 1180–95 (MRS); Mabilia and Richard Gerold of England c. 1272 (RH).

Garrud, for Garrett.

Gascoine. *See* GASCOYNE.

Gascoyen. *See* GASCOYNE.

Gascoyne, or De Gascoigne. The name speaks for itself. Wiliiam de Gasconia and Geoffry de G. are mentioned in England 1209, 1210 (Hardy, Rot. de Libertate). In 1266 Ismenia, widow of Philip le Gascoyn, paid a fine in Salop (Roberts, Excerpt.), and Philip le G. had a suit in the same county 1254 (RH). An ancient family of this name was seated near Coutances, Normandy (Des Bois). Of this family Girard de Gasconia occurs in Normandy 1180 (MRS).

Gashion. William Gachou of

Normandy 1180 (MRS). The name of Gayson is a form.

Gaskell, or Gaskill, from Gascuil, Vascœuil, or Wascuil, near Andelys, Normandy. Gilbert de Wascuil occurs there 1180–95 (MRS). Ingelram de Wascuil obtained a pardon in Warwick 1130 (Rot. Pip.). William de Wascuill occurs in England 1199 (RCR).

Gaskin, for GASCOYNE.

Gasking, for GASKIN.

Gass, for Cass, or CASE.

Gasson. See GASHION.

Gastrell, probably a form of Gastnell, or Gastinel. Richard and Wido Wastinel of Normandy 1180–95, Richard and William W. 1198 (MRS). William Gastinel is mentioned in 1070, Gerard Gastinel 1080 (Ord. Vitalis, 575, 576). The family is said to have been originally of Anjou (Des Bois). Richard Wastinell occurs in England 1199 (RCR).

Gate. See GAIT.

Gater, for CATER.

Gates, for Gate, or GAIT. Sir John Gates was beheaded t. Philip and Mary.

Gattey, for GAIT, or Gate.

Gattle, for Gate, or GAIT.

Gaubert. Richard Gaubert of Normandy 1195–8 (MRS).

Gaudin. Richard Gaudion of Normandy 1195–8 (MRS). Roger Gaudin of England c. 1272 (RH). Hence Gauden Bishop of Exeter.

Gaul. See GALL.

Gaunt, or De Gand. See CONSTABLE.

Gauntlett. See GANTLETT.

Gaved, for Gavet, or Cauvet. Henry Cauvet of Normandy 1180–95 (MRS).

Gavey, the French pronunciation of Gavet. See GAVED.

Gaviller. Petrus Gablarius of Normandy 1180–95 (MRS).

Gavin. See GAWEN (Lower).

Gawdery. See CAWDERY.

Gawen, or Goin. William Goin of Normandy 1180 (MRS). Andrew Goiun of England c. 1272 (RH). The family of Gawen was seated in Wilts, and that of Goin or Going settled in Ireland.

Gawler. See GAYLER.

Gautrey, for Caudrey. See CAUDERY.

Gay. Ralph Gai and Geoffry de Gaio of Normandy 1180 (MRS). Philip Gai 1138 was a kinsman of the Earl of Gloucester (Flor. Wigorn. ii. 109). Robert de Gay was a benefactor to Osney, Oxford (Mon. ij. 142). Adam de Gay held lands in Oxford and Wilts (Testa).

Gaye. See GAY.

Gayer. See GARE.

Gayler, or GAWLER, for Goler. Roger Golier of Normandy 1198 (MRS). The name Gallard, Gayeler, occurs in England c. 1272 (RH).

Gaylor. See GAYLER.

Gaynar. Hamelin Gener occurs in Normandy 1198 (MRS).

Gaynor. See GAYNAR.

Gaxe. See GASS.

Geal, for GALE.

Gear, for GARE.

Geard, for GARD.

Gearing, for Gerin, or Garin. Hugh, Richard, Robert Garin of Normandy 1180 (MRS). Hubert Gerin of England c. 1272 (RH).

Gearl, for Carle, or CARRELL.

Geary, Gere, or Gerry, armorially identified. William de Gueri 1165 held lands in capite in Passy, Normandy (Feod. Norm. Duchesne). He or his son occurs in Normandy as William Gere 1195–8 (MRS). In

1194 Radulph Gari was of North-ants (RCR). In 1235 Roger le May had a suit at Bedford against Walter Gerey (Roberts, Excerpt.). Of this name are the baronets Geary.

Geater. *See* GATOR.

Geare, for GARE.

Geddes, Gaddes, or Gaddez. Arnulph Cades of Normandy 1180–95 (MRS); Margaret, Ralph Cade, &c., c. 1272 (RH).

Gedge, for Gadge, or GAGE.

Gedye, or Gaddy, armorially identified with Gaddes, or GEDDES.

Gee, the French pronunciation of Gui, Guy, or Wido. Robert Guide of Normandy 1180, William Guido 1198 (MRS); Magister Guido, and Robert Gy of England, c. 1272 (RH).

Geen, for GAINE.

Geer, for GEARY.

Geeres, for Geers, or GEER.

Geering, for GEARING.

Geers, from G., a fief of the honour of Mandeville or Magneville, Normandy (MSAN, v. 190). Robert de Guerres and Geoffry de G. held a fief from Philip-Augustus, and Ralph de Guerris paid a fine in Normandy 1198 (MRS). Manasser and William de Guerres 1165 held fiefs from the honour of Mandeville in Essex (Lib. Niger). The latter m. the sister of Hugh de Bayeux of Lincoln (Ib.). Ralph de Gueres witnessed a charter of Roger de Mortimer and Isabella his wife to Kington Priory, Hereford (Mon. ii. 887). Hence the family of Geers in Hereford, now represented by Geers-Cotterell, baronet.

Geers, for GEER.

Geeves, Geffe, or Geffy: the latter a form of Gafet, as pronounced

258

in Norman-French. William Gafet occurs in Normandy 1180–95 (MRS).

Geere, for GEARY.

Geils, for GILES.

Gell. *See* GALL.

Gellett, for Galet, or Galot. Gilbert, Ralph, Peter Galet, or Galot, of Normandy 1180–95 (MRS). Hence the names Jellett and Gillett.

Gelley. *See* GALLEY.

Gellion. *See* GALLYON.

Gemmill, for GAMBLE, or Gamel.

Gender, for GANDER.

Genet, for GENT.

Genge, for GANGE.

Genner, from Gener. *See* GAYNAR.

Gennery, for Chenery, or Chinnery, from St. Cineri, or St. Serenicus, Normandy. Augustus de S. Serenico, and Robert, of Normandy 1180–95 (MRS). A branch of the Geroies barons of St. Ceneri.

Gennys. *See* JANES.

Gent, for GANT.

Gentil, a foreign family, by the evidence of the name, Le Gentil.

Gentle, for GENTIL.

Gentry. *See* CHANTRY.

George, from St. George. Richard and William de St. Georgio of Normandy 1198, Ivo, Robert, William, Ralph de S. G. 1180–95 (MRS). Alan de St. Georgio of England 1189 (Rot. Pip.). Several families of the name appear by the arms to be of the house of Gorges.

Gepp. *See* GABB.

Gerald. Peter, Gerold Ralph, Gerold of Normandy 1180 (MRS). Henry and Walter Gerald of England c. 1272 (RH).

Gerard. Ralph, Walter, Gerard, Gilbert, William Gerard, or Gerart of Normandy 1180–95 (MRS).

Many of the name in England c. 1272 (RH).

Gerard, baronets. The origin of the family of Gerard, which had been derived from the Fitzgeralds, is traced by Ormerod (Cheshire, ii. 61) to William G., who was summoned from Lancaster to a great Council at Westminster 1324 (PPW); descended from William Fitz-Gerard of Hawarden, Flint, who m. the heiress of Kingsley, Cheshire. He is presumed to have been of the house of Montalt, barons of Hawarden, as his descendants bore the arms of Montalt with a bend for difference. *See* DE LA MARE.

Germain. Matthew, Ralph, Richard de St. Germano of Normandy 1198 (MRS); William de St. German of England 1199 (RCR); Henry, John Simon Germeyn of England c. 1272 (RH). The lands of Osbert de St. German were granted to Troarn Abbey by Roger Montgomery. Roger de St. G. possessed lands in Suffolk 1086 (Domesd.). There are numerous notices of this family in England, and it long flourished in Normandy (Des Bois).

German. *See* GERMAIN.

Germyn, or Germain. Of this family were Lords Jermyn, and Dover.

Gerner. *See* GARNER.

Gerrish, for GERRES.

Gerrard. *See* GERARD.

Gerrett, for GARRETT.

Gerson, for Garson or CARSON.

Gervis. N. and Richard Gervasius of Normandy, 1180–95; Fulco G. in 1198 (MRS); Robert Gerveis of England 1199 (RCR); Alicia and Stephen Gerveys, c. 1272 (RH).

Gery. *See* GEARY.

Gesell. Tustin Gisle of Normandy, 1180 (MRS).

Gess, for GASS.

Geylin, for GALLYON.

Ghewy, or Goey. Robert Goie of Normandy, 1180–95 (MRS). Bartelot Govi and others of England, c. 1272 (RH).

Ghent, for GAUNT.

Ghislin, for Gascelin, from Anjou. Geoffry Gascelyn was summoned to Parliament by writ, 1259. Roger and Robert Wacelin are mentioned 13th century (Testa).

Ghosley, from Gouseley, which is armorially identified with Goushill, a branch of De Ver. *See* THOROLD, WARHAM.

Ghurney, for GURNEY.

Giar, for GEER.

Gibb, or Wibb. Ralph and Richard Wibue, Richard and William de Wibo, Normandy, 1189–98 (MRS). The forms of this name include Jebb and Webb. Adam de Wybe occurs in England, c. 1272 (RH).

Gibbard, for Gilbard or GILBART.

Gibbens, for GIBBONS.

Gibberd, for GILBART.

Gibbes, for GIBBS. Hence the Baronets Gibbes.

Gibbin, for GIBBON.

Gibbings, for GIBBON.

Gibbins, for GIBBON.

Gibbon. Balduin Gibon of Normandy, 1180 (MRS); Philip Gibun of England, 1194 (RCR). Some families of Gibbons who bear paly, are branches of Gobion. *See* GUBBINS. Hence the historian Gibbon.

Gibbons. *See* GIBBON.

Gibbs, for GIBB.

Giblett. Deva Gibelot of England, c. 1272 (RH). The name evidently foreign.

Giblin, for Gablin or Caplin. *See* CHAPLIN.

Gibling. *See* GIBLIN.

Gibson, a corruption of some earlier name. Perhaps CUBISON, from Curbizon of Normandy.

Gibus, armorially identified with Gibbons (Robson).

Gidden, Gideon, or Gidion (Lower), from Guiton. Ralph Guiton of Normandy, 1180–95, William Guido, 1198 (MRS); William Gydon of England, c. 1272 (RH).

Giddens. *See* GIDDEN.

Giddings, for GIDDENS.

Giddy. *See* GEDYE.

Gideon. *See* GIDDEN. Hence the Lords Eardley.

Gieve, or Gives (Robson). Perhaps from Guifosse in the Cotentin. Robert de Gauiz of England, 1199 (RCR); Richard Geves, c. 1272 (RH).

Giffard, from Giffard, Barons of Bolbec, Counts of Longueville and Buckingham, a Norman family too well known to need further detail. *See* Dugdale, Banks, &c. The Lords Gifford are of a Devonshire line, descended from Berenger, brother of Walter Giffard, first Earl of Bucks, who held lands in barony, Wilts and Dorset, 1086 (Domesd.). His son Osberne occurs in Devon 1130 (Rot. Pip.); Osberne G. held fiefs there 1165, Baldwin 1203, from whom the Giffords, Lords of Buckton, Devon, who terminated in an heiress 1372; but the G.s of Brightley, a collateral branch, continued long afterwards. From this family descend the Lords Gifford.

Giffen. *See* GAVIN.

Giffin. *See* GAVIN.

Gifford, for GIFFARD.

Gigg. Walter le Gig, Norfolk,

c. 1272 (RH); William Gigan, same county, 1198 (RCR); Robert and William Gigan or Gigon, Normandy, 1198 (MRS).

Giggs, for GIGG.

Gigney. *See* CHEGNAY.

Gilbart. N. and Richard Gilbert, 1180–95, Walter, Richard, Vacar G. 1198, Normandy (MRS). The name frequent in England, c. 1272 (RH).

Gilbert. *See* GILBART.

Giles, from La Gile or Gueilles, Normandy. Robert de Gueilles of Normandy 1198 (MRS); Godfrey Gile of England, 1189 (Rot. Pip.); John, Thomas, and Matilda G., c. 1272 (RH).

Gill, or Gille, armorially identified in some cases with Giles or Gills. *See* GILES, of which it is a form.

Gillard. *See* GAYLARD.

Gillatt. *See* GILLETT.

Gilles. *See* GILL, GILES.

Gilliatt, for GILLATT.

Gillies, for GILLES.

Gilliver, for Gulliver, or Gulafre. Roger Gulafre claimed property from St. Evroult, Normandy, 1061 (Ord. Vit. 483). He was Lord of Mesnil Bernard (Ib. 466). William Gulafre, t. William I., gave tithes to Eye Abbey (Mon. i. 356). He had great estates in Suffolk, 1086 (Domesd.). Roger G. was of Suffolk 1130 (Rot. Pip.). Philip G. held four fees in barony Suffolk, 1165 (Lib. Nig.). The name occurs afterwards in Oxford and other parts of England. In Normandy, William, Roger, Hugh, John Golafre occur 1180–95 (MRS).

Gillman. *See* GILMAN.

Gilloch, for GILLOW.

Gillon, or Gaillion. Udon Galien

of Normandy, 1198 (MRS). Robert and William Gilion of England, c. 1272 (RH).

Gillow, for Galot. *See* GALEY.

Gilly. *See* GUYLEE.

Gilman. Walter Gilmin of England, c. 1272 (RH). Walter Galman or Galmon, and the estate of Galman, Normandy, 1198 (MRS).

Gilpin, armorially identified with Galpine, a form of Galopin. Bernardus Galopin of Normandy, 1198 (MRS); Nicholas Galopin of England, c. 1272 (RH); also N. Gelopin. Hence the excellent and devoted Bernard Gilpin.

Gingell, for Gansell. Ralph and Ranulph Gansell of Normandy, 1198 (MRS); Robert Gaunsil of England, c. 1272 (RH).

Ginger, for Gingan. Ralph Gingan of Normandy, 1198 (MRS).

Ginn. N. and William Guenes, William Guenes or Guines of Normandy, 1180–98 (MRS); Osborne, Henry, William de Gene, England, c. 1272 (RH).

Ginner. *See* GENNER.

Gipps. *See* GEPPS.

Girard. *See* GERARD.

Gire. *See* GEER.

Girtanner, from Courtomer near Alençon. William de Cortemer occurs in Normandy t. John.

Gladding, for GLADWIN.

Glading, for GLADDING.

Gladwin, or Gladisfen, a branch of the Montfichets of Normandy. *See* CAVENDISH.

Glanville, from Glanville, near Caen, Normandy. *See* BUTLER.

Glanfield, for GLANVILLE.

Glave, for Gleave or Gleue. *See* GLEW.

Gleaves. *See* GLAVE.

Glen. William Glin 1180, and

as Glene, 1198 (MRS); Hugh Glenie, England, c. 1272 (RH).

Glenie. *See* GLEN.

Glenn. *See* GLEN.

Glennie. *See* GLEN.

Glenny. *See* GLEN.

Glenton, for Glinton, or CLINTON.

Glew, or Gleue, from Glos or Gloz with the French pronunciation. Emma, Nicholas de Gloz, Normandy, 1180–98 (MRS). Geoffry Glosus, England, 1189 (Rot. Pip.). Roger Gleiue, England, 1199 (RCR).

Glidden, for GLADWIN.

Glindon, or Glinton, for CLINTON.

Glover, the English translation of Gantier, probably includes families of Norman extraction.

Glydon, for GLIDDON.

Glyn, in some cases for GLEN.

Goater, or Gotard, for GODDARD.

Gobbett, for COBBETT.

Gobby, for Gobet, with the French pronunciation. *See* COBBETT.

Gobey. *See* GOBBY.

Goble, for Gobel or Gabbel. *See* CABBELL.

Godart. *See* GODDARD.

Goddard. Reinald, Reginald, Roger Godard or Godart, Normandy, 1180–98 (MRS). Several of the name in England, c. 1272 (RH).

Godefroy. Robert Godefroy, Gonduin, Robert, Symon, William Godefridus of Normandy, 1180–98 (MRS). Many of the name Godefroy, &c., in England, c. 1272 (RH).

Godfree. *See* GODEFROY.

Godfrey. *See* GODEFROY. Hence the Baronets Godfrey.

Godier. Hubert Fitz-Goduere of Normandy, 1180–95 (MRS).

Godsell, or Godschall, apparently

from Godescalus, a mesne lord in Wilts 1086, of foreign origin, for his name is not amongst the landowners of Anglo-Saxon times.

Godward, for GODDARD.

Godwin. Geoffry and Roger Godvinne, Normandy, 1198 (MRS); Walter Godvein, England, 1199 (RCR); Roger, Thomas, William, &c., Godwine, c. 1272 (RH).

Goggin, or Gogun. Durand Cocon, Normandy, 1195 (MRS); Isabel Cogun, Malin Gogun, Nicholas Gogging, England, c. 1272 (RH).

Gogging. See GOGGIN.

Goher. See GOWER.

Gold, or Gould. Alexander and John Golde (Goude) of Normandy, 1195; John and Odo Goude, 1198 (MRS); Elias, Gilbert, Isolda, &c., Golde, England, c. 1272 (RH).

Goldie, probably a form of Gold, from the arms.

Goldring, probably for Goldoury or Goldourg (Robson), apparently foreign.

Golds, for GOLD.

Goldsmith. Geoffry, Roger, William, Nicholas, Gerard Aurifaber (Goldsmith) of Normandy 1180-95, three more in 1198 (MRS); John, Robert, Hamo, Hugh, Jordan, William A. of England, 1194-9 (RCR).

Gollop. William le Golu, Normandy, 1198 (MRS).

Goman, for Comen, or Comin. See COMYN.

Gondie, for CONDY.

Gooch. Odo de la Coce, Normandy, 1180 (MRS).

Gooch, or De Gouiz. See CUST. William le Cousche held lands, Cambridge, 13th cent. In 1205 Richard Goche of Suffolk was party

to a suit there (Hardy, Obl. et fin.). William Gouche and John le Gose were present at an array in that county (PPW). Hence descend the Baronets Gooch.

Good. In some cases for Gooch or Goodge (Robson), in others from Godes. Alvered and Ralph Godes of Normandy, 1198 (MRS); Henry, William, Hugh Godde, England, c. 1272 (RH).

Goodair. See GODIER.

Goodall. See GOODALE.

Goodale. Roger Godel of Normandy, 1198 and 1180 (MRS); Ralph Godhale of England, 1199 (RCR); Alicia Godebil, c. 1272 (RH).

Goodban, for Gadban, or CABAN.

Goodchild, the English translation of the Norman name Bonenfant. See BULLIVANT.

Goodday. See GOODEY.

Goode. See GOOD.

Goodes. See GOOD.

Goodey, from GOODES. See GOOD.

Goodfellow, a translation of the Norman Bonenfant. See BULLIVANT.

Goodger. See GODIER.

Goodhart. See GODDART.

Goodheart. See GODDART.

Goodhew. Richard Gaudiou of Normandy, 1198 (MRS). He was of Quillebœuf, Normandy, t. John (Mem. Soc. Ant. Norm. v. 115). William Godio of England, c. 1272 (RH).

Goodhugh. See GOODHEW.

Gooding. See GOODWIN.

Goodinge. See GOODWIN.

Goodman. Ranulph Godeman of Normandy, 1198 (MRS). N. Godeman in 1086 owned large estates Suffolk and Essex (Domesd.);

Ralph and Henry Godman of England, c. 1272 (RH).

Goodred, by transposition for Godderd or GODDARD.

Goodwill, for GOODWIN.

Goodwin. *See* GODWIN.

Goody, for GOODDEY.

Goodyear, for GODIER.

Googe, for GOOCH.

Gook, for COOK.

Goold. *See* GOLD. Hence the Baronets Gould.

Goosey, or Gossey. The French pronunciation of Goucet. *See* GOSSETT.

Goozee. *See* GOOSEY.

Goram, for GORHAM.

Gorard, for GARRARD.

Gordon. 1. From Gordon, Berwick, granted c. 1130 to a family of Anglo - Norman origin (Douglas). 2. A branch of the Norman family of Say, deriving from Picot de Say living 1030, whose son, Robert Fitz-Picot, Lord of Aunay, was co-founder of St. Martin, Seez, 1060. He had issue, who came to England at the Conquest, 1, Picot, Baron of Clun and Stoke-Say, Salop; 2, Robert Fitz-Picot; 3, William de Say, ancestor of the Lords Say in England. Robert Fitz-Picot, Baron of Brunne, Cambridge, 1086, had issue, 1, Robert Fitz-Picot, the Viscount, who forfeited the Barony of Brune, t. Henry I.; 2, Saher de Say, who is stated to have taken refuge in Scotland, and obtained grants from Alexander I., named after him Sayton. Alexander, his son, was a baron of Sayton and Wynton (Chalmers, Cal. i. 517; Douglas, Peerage). From him descended the Lords Seyton or Seton, Earls of Wintoun and Dunfermline, Viscounts Kingston, and (under the name of Gordon) Marquises of Huntley and Dukes of Gordon. Gordon is a clan name, and is of course chiefly borne by persons of Celtic race.

Gordge, for Gorges. *See* CARDGE.

Gore, or Goher. *See* GOWER. The name Gore is armorially identified with 'Goare,' and 'Goare' with 'Gower.' One branch of the latter family bore a fesse, which seems to be the original form of the Gore arms. The Gowers of Warwick and Worcester bore the same arms as the Earls of Arran, merely doubling the number of crosslets (Robson). It is clear, therefore, that the Gores are Gowers of the Warwickshire line, of which Hugh de Goher held a knight's fee from the Earl of Warwick in 1165 (Lib. Nig.). From this line derived the Gores, Earls of Arran and Ross, and the Baronets Gore.

Gorham, a well-known family from Bretagne.

Goring, or Bygod. Hugh Bygod was Lord of Garringes or Goring, Sussex, 13th cent. (Testa). He was executor of the will of the Countess of Norfolk, 1248 (Roberts, Excerpt. ii. 33). John de Garringes, his son, had a dau. and heir, who m. Henry Tregoz, M.P. for Sussex 1309 (PPW). The bailsman of Henry T. was John Goring, probably nephew of John de Goring or Garringes (Ib.). From the latter descended the family of De Goring, afterwards Lords Goring, Earls of Norwich, so distinguished in the Civil Wars 17th cent., and the Baronets Goring. This family appears to be a younger branch of the Bygods Earls of Norfolk.

Gornall. William Gornel of Normandy, 1195; Robert Guernuel, 1198 (MRS).

Gornell, for GORNALL.

Gorringe, for GORING.

Gorrud, for GARRET.

Gorrum, for GORHAM.

Gorst, or Jors, from Jort near Falaise. The Sire de Jort was at the battle of Hastings (Wace, ii. 245). Anchetil de Jorz occurs in England, 1110 (Wint. Domesd.); John de Jorra in Normandy, 1138 (Ord. Vit. 916); Robert de Jorz held a fief in Hunts 1165 (Lib. Nig.); Ralph, Ranulph, and Robert de Gorz, 13th cent., were seated in Warw. and Leicester, Geoffry de G. in Notts and Derby (Testa); Robert de J. was commissioner of array and M.P. for Notts, 1300–1306 (PPW).

Gorvin, for Corbin. *See* CARABINE.

Goslin. *See* GOSLING.

Gosling, or Goslin. Peter, Anchitel, Ralph, Robert Goscelin, Normandy, 1180–95; Richard G., 1198 (MRS); Ralph G. of England, 1199 (RCR); Roger and Walter Gosselin and Gosselyne, c. 1272 (RH).

Gosney, or Cusney. Bernard de Cusneio of Normandy, 1180 (MRS).

Goss. *See* GASS.

Gosse. William Gosce, Normandy, 1198 (MRS); Amauri de Gosse of Normandy, t. Henry V. (Mem. Soc. Ant. Norm. v.); John and Walter Gosce, England, c. 1272 (RH).

Gosset, for GOSSETT.

Gossett. Richard and William Gocet of Normandy, 1180 - 95 (MRS); Gerard and John Gosset occur in Normandy, t. Henry V.

Gostling, for GOSLING (Lower).

Gothard, for GODDARD.

Goude. *See* GOOD.

264

Goudge. *See* GOOCH.

Goulard, or Gollard, a form of COLLARD.

Goulborn, a branch of De Toeni, being descended from William de Belwar or Belvoir. *See* CHOLMONDELEY.

Gould. *See* GOLD. Hence the Lords Tredegar.

Gouldsmith. *See* GOLDSMITH.

Goullee. William Gollay of England, c. 1272 (RH). Golletum, Golley, or Golet was a parish in Normandy.

Goullet. *See* GOULLEE.

Goult, for GALT.

Goundry. Robert de Gundrea, Normandy, 1198 (MRS).

Goupil. Roger Goupil of Normandy, 1198 (MRS); Peter Gupil of England, c. 1272 (RH).

Gourlay, for GOURLEY.

Gourley, for Courley. Thomas de Curleio of Normandy, 1198 (MRS); John de Curli of England, 1199 (RCR).

Gouyn, for Goin. *See* GAWEN.

Gove, for Chauve. *See* CALF.

Gover, or Le Cuver, probably a foreign name (RH).

Govers, for GOVER.

Govett, for Gobet. *See* COBBETT.

Govett. Geoffry Guvit of Normandy, 1195 (MRS).

Govey, for GOVETT—the French pronunciation.

Govier, for GOVER.

Gowar, for GOWARD.

Goward, for COWARD.

Gowen, for GAWEN.

Gowens, for GOWEN.

Gower, or Goer, a Norman family from Goher, Normandy, which name was transferred from Scandinavia. Thomas Goher paid talliage at Caen, 1195, as did Ralph G. Ralph paid a fine at Bayeux; Thomas in 1198 paid a fine at Coutances; and Osmond Gohier at Caen, where he also made a loan of 15l. to the king (MRS). In England the name appears in 1130, when Walter de Guher paid scutage for his lands at Carmarthen (Rot. Pip.). He had probably been one of the Norman knights who accompanied Arnulph de Montgomery. Adelard de Guer witnessed a charter of Geoffry de Mandeville, Earl of Essex, 1136 (Mon. i. 460), from which family Roger de Guer held a fief in 1165 (Lib. Nig.), when also Hugh de Goher held a fee from the Earl of Warwick (Ibid.). William 'Guhier' obtained a pardon in Oxford, 1158 (Rot. Pip.), being also of Essex, for after 1152 the Abbey of Tilteney, Essex, acquired lands of the fief of William 'Goer' (Mon. i. 889).

This William Goer or Guhier was Lord of Stittenham, Yorkshire, and was dead A.D. 1200 (RCR). He confirmed the grant of Godfrey Fitz-Richard of Stitnam to Rivaux Abbey (Burton, Mon. Ebor. 363). Walter Goher, his son or grandson (Mon. ii. 822), had issue William, 'son of Walter Goher,' who in 1270 paid a fine to the Crown (Roberts, Excerpt. ii. 513). This William G. had a park in Dorset, t. Henry III. (Placit. Abbrev. 281). His son John was summoned in 1300 for miltary service in Scotland; and in the same year Robert Gouer (probably his brother) was commissioner of array in Yorkshire (PPW). From this family descend the Dukes of Sutherland, Earls of Granville, Ellesmere, and Cromartie.

Gower, John. The Poet's origin has been treated by Sir Harris Nicolas (Retrospective Review, Series ii. vol. 2, and in the Kentish Archæologia, vol. vi.). It appears from these authorities that G. was born c. 1330; acquired the Lordship of Aldington, Kent, in 1365; that of Kentwell, Suffolk, and another in Essex by purchase from the dau. of Sir Robert Gower, Knt.; also Multon, Suffolk, and Feltwell, Norfolk, in 1382; and a lease of Southwell, Notts, which with Multon he left to his widow on his decease, 1408.

The poet was probably nephew and heir-male of the above Sir Robert Gower. The latter resided in Kent. In 1359 King Edw. III. took up his abode at Stonar, Isle of Thanet, in a house formerly belonging to 'Robert Goviere' (Hasted, Kent, iv. 385). In the preceding generation 'Richard Gouiere' was bailsman for an M.P. for Sussex, 1313, and was not of that county, but probably of Kent; and from the continual interchange of families between Kent and Essex was doubtless of the Essex family of Goher or Guhier, as the name is not an early Kentish one. The family of Guhier or Goer in Essex was Norman and of great antiquity (see GOWER, Duke of Sutherland).

The arms of Gower of Essex were a chevron between three wolves' heads erased. The poet and the Kentish family bore the chevron charged with three heads, whether of lions, leopards, or wolves, it were hard to say. Archdeacon Todd was not so much in error as Nicolas and others have supposed, in making the poet of the same family as the Gowers of Stittenham.

Gowers, for GOWER.

Gowing, for Goin. *See* GAWEN.

Gowrley. *See* GOURLEY.

Goy, from Goi, Normandy. Robert Goie of N. 1195 (MRS); Robert de Gois of England, 1199 (RCR).

Gozar, for GOZZARD.

Gozzard. *See* COSSART.

*Grace, for Le Gras, Le Gros, or Crassus. Roger, Richard, Osbert, Arnulph, William, Nicholas C. of Normandy, 1180–95 (MRS); Richard Crassus or Grassus of England, 1199 (RH); Roger le Gras, c. 1272 (RH); William and Richard le Cras. The English forms are Grace, Grose, Gross, &c. The Irish family of Grace appears to be a branch of the FITZGERALDS. For the Baronets Grace, *see* GAMMON.

Gracey, or Grancey, from Grancey in Burgundy. The arms are preserved by Robson.

Gracie. *See* GRACEY.

Graefe, for GRAFF.

Graff, for Craff or CRAFT.

Graham, or De Tancarville. Graham in all the early records of England means Grantham in Lincoln; and William de Graham, who settled in Scotland t. David I., c. 1128, and obtained Abercorne and Dalkeith (Douglas), came from Grantham. He must have been of an important family there, and the only family of that kind was that of De Tancarville, which held the Barony of Grantham in farm from the Crown after the Conquest for above a century. The English branches of the De T.s were generally named Chamberlain, and the Chamberlains of Lincoln, probably a branch of the T.s, bore three escallops, which three escallops appear in the arms of the De Gra-
266

hams or Granthams, originally from Lincoln also. It may therefore be inferred that William de Grantham was a younger son of the Baron of Tancarville, who had held the office of Seneschal of Grantham under his father.

The family of Tankarville probably derived from Tancred, c. 912, whose fief on the settlement of Normandy was named Tancardivilla. Rabel, his son, left his name to Rabel's Isle, and Rabelsfoss, mentioned in early records. Gerold, Baron of Tancarville, towards the end of the 10th cent. (D'Anisy et St. Marie, Sur Domesday), was father of Rabel II., t. Duke Robert, who had two sons: 1. Ralph; 2. Almeric D'Abetot, ancestor of the Viscounts of Worcester.

Ralph was guardian to Duke William, hereditary Chamberlain of Normandy, and founder of Bocherville Abbey. William, his son, had 1. Rabel, ancestor of the Chamberlains of Normandy; 2. William de Graham. From this family descended the famous Marquis of Montrose, and the brave Viscount Dundee; also Sir James Graham of Netherby, the eminent statesman.

Grain. Richard de Grana, Normandy 1180–95 (MRS); William de Grana of England c. 1272 (RH).

Grainger, or le Grangier (RH). Probably of foreign origin.

Grammer. William Grammaticus, a juror at Evreux t. Philip-Augustus (Mem. Soc. Ant. Norm. v. 162). John and William Grammaticus of Middleton, Yorkshire, 1189 (Rot. Pip.).

Grand. Robert, Richard, Serlo, Roger, Nicholas Grand, Normandy 1180–95 (MRS); Simon, William,

Robert Grant or Le Grant (Grand) 1199 (RCR).

Grane. See GRAIN.

Grange. William de Grandeis of Normandy 1198 (MRS); Adam de Granges, England, c. 1272 (RH).

Grange. See GRAINGE.

Granger. See GRAINGER.

Grant. For English families of the name, see GRAND; Scottish families of the name are Celtic.

Granvell, for GRANVILLE.

Granville. The Grenvilles or Greenfields of Neath and Bideford adopted, instead of the paternal coat (a cross), the three rests of the Earls of Gloucester, their feudal suzerains. The name, however, was still written Grenville, Greenfield, and Grenfell, though the Earls of Bath adopted the form of Granville. A fabulous pedigree was concocted for this family in the 17th cent., making them descend from Fitz-Hamon; but this descent is absolutely without proof. See GRENVILLE. Hence the Earls of Bath and Lords Granville.

Gras, or Le Gras. See GRACE.

Grassett, for Gresset or Crest. Umfrid Crest of Normandy 1180–95 (MRS). John and Roger Cruste of England c. 1272 (RH).

Grassie. See GRACIE.

Gravell. Guido, Adam, Robert de Gravelle or Graville, Normandy, 1180–95 (MRS). William de Gravale, England, 1199 (RCR). See GREVILLE.

Graves. Walter de Grava (De la Grave) occurs in Normandy 1198 (MRS), and in Bucks t. John (Hunter, Fines, i. 194). Osbert de Grava or De la Grave, in Gloucester 1203 (Rot. Canc. Hardy, Obl. et fin. 462). Richard de la Grave 1267

(Hunter, Rot. Select. 137). Thomas de la G. occurs 1295; and 1316 Sibilla de la G. of Gloucester (PPW). Hence the Graveses of Mickleton, Gloucester, ancestors of the gallant admiral Lord Graves, and the Baronets Graves-Saule.

Gravett, originally Crefeyt or Creflet, probably foreign, but I have not been able to identify it.

Gray. See GREY.

Greasley or De Toesni. See GRESLEY.

Greathead. Richard Groceteste of England c. 1272 (RH). Robert Grosteste, bishop of Lincoln. Probably a foreign family from the name. Name translated.

Greatorex, or Greatorick, from Gayteric, the old form of Catterick, York, in which county the name remains common. See CARTWRIGHT.

Great-Rex, for GREATOREX.

Greatrex. See GREATOREX.

Greaves. See GRAVES.

Gredley, or Grelly, from Gresillé, Anjou. Albert Grealet, Baron of Manchester under Roger de Poitou, occurs in Domesd. (270) in 1086. Robert Grealet had a suit in York 1130, with Eustace Fitz-John (Rot. Pip.), and paid a fine in Lincoln (Ib.). Robert de Greley m. Hawise de Burgh, of the family of Burgh, Earl of Kent, and his son Sir Thomas de Grelly was summoned by writ as a baron 1307. The name was often written Gredley, Gridley, and Grealey; but the family is altogether different from that of GRESLEY.

Greely, for Grelley. See GREDLEY.

Greener. Berenger Granarius of Normandy 1180 (MRS).

Greenfield, armorially identified with GRANVILLE.

Greenlees, or Greenly, from Grin-
ley, Notts. Roger Gringelai was of
Normandy 1180-95 (MRS). The
family seated in Notts c. 1272 (RH),
where the lordship of Gringele is
mentioned.

Greenner, for GREENER.

Greer, for Gregor (Lower). *See*
GREGO.

Greest, for Crist or Crest. Umfrid Crest, Normandy 1180 (MRS).

Greeves. *See* GRAVES.

Greey, for GREY.

Grefield, for Grenfield, Greenfield, or GRANVILLE.

Greg. *See* GREIG.

Gregg. *See* GREIG.

Grego, for Gregor. William Gregor of Normandy 1180-95 (MRS);
William Fitz-Gregory, England
1199 (RCR); Adam Gilbert, Elias,
Robert, &c., Gregori, England, c.
1272 (RH).

Gregora, for GREGORY.

Gregory. *See* GREGO. In Scotland some of the name may be Celtic.

Greig. Radulfus Groig, Richard
Grege, Normandy 1180 (MRS);
Robert Grege, Serlo Grigge, Eng-
land, c. 1272 (RH).

Grenfell, armorially identified
with GRANVILLE.

Grenville, De Greinville, De
Grainville, Granville, &c., derives its
name from Greinville, in the Cotentin, a fief of the Barons of St. Denis
le Gaste, of which noble family this,
with the families of Bigod, Trailly,
Beauchamp, Montague, St. Denis,
and Meurdrac, are supposed to have
been branches, and the supposition
is confirmed by the arms. The first
Lord of Greinville was probably
brother of Wigod de St. Denis,
Baron of St. Denis and Meurdra-
268

quière, who, in 1050, subscribed a
charter of Duke William before all
the Barons of Normandy. William de
Grenville, the next in descent, with
Robert his son, witnessed a charter of
Walter Giffard for Bolbec Abbey in
1061 (Neustria Pia, 402). The
latter accompanied the Conqueror,
and received from the same Walter
Giffard three knights' fees in Bucks,
which passed to his descendants.
He had, 1. Gerard; 2. Richard,
ancestor of the Grenvilles or Gran-
villes of Neath and Bideford, the
Earls of Bath, and the Earls of
Warwick. Gerard de Grenville was
living 1130 (Rot. Pip.), and Gerard
II. de Greville was living 1158 (Rot.
Pip.), who, 1165, held three fees
from Giffard, Earl of Bucks (Lib.
Nig.). William, his son, was living
1207 (Hardy, Obl. et Fin.). In
1230 Eustace, his son, did homage
as a baron on m. the dau. and coheir
of Robert Arsic, Baron of Coges
(Roberts, Excerpt. i. 193). In 1293
Sir Eustace de Greinville held two
fees at Wooton, Bucks, of the
Honour of Giffard, and Robert de
G. one fee (Testa). The Norman
estates appear to have belonged to
a branch of this line. In 1200
Eustace de Grenville was indebted
to William de Martigny in Normandy (Hardy, Rot. Norm. 44),
and 1298 Richard de Grenville was
son and heir of Eustace de G. of
Normandy (Roberts, Cal. Geneal.
578).

From this family sprang the brave
Sir Beville Granville, the hero of
Lansdown, and the Grenvilles so
renowned as English statesmen.

Gresham or Branche. The Norman family of Branche, whose estates lay in the Caux, accompanied

William de Warrenne to England 1066, where Ralph Branche received a grant of two knights' fees, of which Gresham was the chief seat. Barsham was also held from the De Wancis, tenants of Warrenne. Ralph and his son Richard occur in the charters of Walsingham Abbey. The latter had Walter, who in 1165 held the Norman estate of half a knight's fee in capite in the bailifry of Caux. William B. of Gresham, his brother, had issue Richard, who t. Henry II. confirmed to Castle Acre Priory the tithes of his lordship of Gresham, which had been granted by his ancestors. This Sir Richard Branche was one of four knights summoned in 1200 to select 12 knights for the grand assize, Norfolk (RCR, ii.). Sir Peter, his grandson, held Gresham and Aylmorton by the service of two fees from Earl Warrenne, and 1241 had a writ of summons to pass into France, and had a grant of market, fair, and free warren. He had two sons, Nicholas and Roger, the former of whom with his descendants bore the name of Branche, the latter that of De Gresham. Both continued to bear the same arms (a chevron between three mullets), merely varying the tinctures. In the 16th cent. the Greshams added a chief variously charged to their arms.

Roger Branche or Gresham was a benefactor (with his wife) to Marrig Priory, York. Roger de G., his son, was living 1313 (Blomfield, Norf. ix. 368). Edward de G. had lands in Bodham, Norfolk, 1363. Another Edward, living c. 1400, was father of John Gresham, who resided at Holt, Norfolk, and was the direct ancestor of the celebrated Sir Thomas Gresham. (*See* Blomefield's Norfolk.)

Gresley, Baronets. A well-known branch of the house of De Toesni, Barons of Toesni and Conches, Normandy.

Gressley, for GRESLEY.

Greville or Grenville. The names are used interchangeably in the early records, and the arms of Greville are those of Grenville with a bordure to mark a younger branch. The Grevilles, Earls of Brooke and Warwick, Lords Brook, Greville, &c., probably descend from a branch of the house of Grenville or Greville, of Wotton, Bucks. *See* GRENVILLE.

The arms are those of a younger branch of this house. This branch was possessed of Drayton, Oxfordshire (the adjoining county to Bucks), and was descended from John Greville (or Grenville), who appears to be the same who is mentioned by Collins as of Wotton 1308, and whose father John, son of John de Greinville, was living 1305. There can be little doubt that the present branch sprang from the Grenvilles at about this date, both from the arms and the recurrence of the same contemporary Christian names.

Grey, or De Grai, from Gray, Normandy, near Caen. Arnulph was Lord of Gray, c. 970, and his son Nigel de Gray witnessed a charter c. 1020 (Lobineau, Hist. Bret. ii. 171). Turstin succeeded as Baron of Gray and Dounville, near Caen. In 1082 Gisla, his daughter, granted, with consent of her nephew Turstin de Gray (son of Turgis), lands to Holy Trinity, Caen (Gall. Christ. xi., Instr. 71), and Turstin, 'son of Turgis,' executed a charter 1096 (D'Anisy et St. Marie, Sur Domesd.).

Anchetil de Gray, son of Turgis, and brother of Turstin de Gray, came to England with the Conqueror, and 1086 held lands in Oxford, viz. Redrefield (Rotherfield), and five other lordships, from William Fitz-Osborne (Domesd.). Columbanus de Grae, son of Anchetil, witnessed a charter of Ralph de Limesi, t. Henry I. (Mon. i. 331). He had issue: 1. Robert; 2. Roger, a tenant of the See of London, 1165, father of Henry de Gray, first Baron of Codnor, ancestor of the Lords Grey of Ruthin, Wilton, Codnor, and Walsingham, the Earls of Kent and Stamford, Marquises of Dorset, and Dukes of Suffolk.

Robert de Gray of Rotherfield, Oxford, in 1165 held lands from the barony of Windsor, Bucks (Lib. Niger). The Bolbecs, a branch of the Giffards, were barons in Bucks and Northumberland, and t. Henry II., Robert de Gray and his son Robert witnessed a charter of Walter de Bolbec of Northumberland (Hodgson, North. i. i. 167). Robert de G., the younger, of Rotherfield, had, 1. Walter; 2. Robert, who in 1200 had a suit in Bucks (RCR); and in 1226 was of Schotton, Northumberland, and became baron of Rotherfield in 1245, on his brother's resignation (Dugdale).

Walter, the elder son, was Chancellor 1205, Archbishop of York 1216, and in 1245 resigned his barony of Rotherfield to his brother Robert, who had issue, 1. Walter, ancestor of the Lords Grey of Rotherfield, Barons by writ 1296; 2. Richard; 3. William, of Langley, Northumberland, 1240 (Testa, 388);

270

4. Hugh, ancestor of the Barons Gray of Scotland.

Richard de Gray and William his brother paid a fine in Northumberland 1233 (Roberts, Excerpt. i. 250). He was Viscount of Northumberland 1236; and from him descended the Greys Earls of Tankerville, and the Earls Grey.

Gribble, or Grebell, from Grabol. Richard Grabol, Normandy, 1180-95 (MRS).

Gribbon. Liescelina Gripon, Normandy, 1198; the Lady of Gripon, 1195 (MRS).

Grice. Richard de Grisy, Normandy, 1180; Richard de Grise, or Grisey, 1198 (MRS). Eustachius Gris, England, 1189 (Rot. Pip.).

Gridley. See GREDLEY.

Grieve. See GREAVES.

Grieves. See GREAVES.

Grigg. See GREGG.

Griggs, for GRIGG.

Grigs, for GRICE.

Grindale, or Percy. Edmond G., Archbishop of Canterbury, was son of William G., who settled, on the dissolution of the Monasteries, near St. Bees. There were others of the name in London, Hunts, and especially in York, where Grindale or Grendale, afterwards Handale, was situated. This place belonged to a branch of the Percys. Richard de Percy was younger son of William I. de Percy (Mon. Angl. i. 74), and brother of Alan de P. He obtained from his father Dunsley, Lofthouse (in which Grendale was situated) and other estates. He had, 1. Ralph de Grendale, 2. William de Percy, 3. Walter Fitz-Richard. The second gave lands at Dunsley to Whitby Abbey (Mon. i. 74). Ralph de Grendal was father of Ralph, both living at the foundation of Bridlington Priory. Walter, their younger brother, succeeded, and, 1165, with his uncle William de Percy, held a knight's fee from William, son of Alan de Percy (Lib. Niger). From Walter de Grendale descended the G.s of the North, of whom Walter de Grendale was returned in 1300 as possessing an estate above 40*l.* per ann. in York, &c., and was summoned by writ for military service in Scotland, and in 1312 was summoned by writ to the Parliament of York as a baron of the realm.

The arms of Grendale were, a cross moline, flory, or pattée, which was also the coat of a branch of the Percys (Robson).

Grint. Henry Grente, N. de Grento, Richard, Simon Grento, Normandy, 1180–98 (MRS); Eustace, Geoffry Grinde, England, c. 1272 (RH).

Grinyer. *See* Graner.

Gripper. Ralph de Griperia, Normandy, 1180 (MRS).

Grist. *See* Greest.

Groco. *See* Grogan.

Grogan. John Grogon, mentioned in England c. 1272 (RH). The name probably foreign, from its formation.

Grokes, for Croke.

Gros. *See* Grose.

Grose. Josce, Matthew le Gros, Normandy, 1198 (MRS). Crassus, or Le Gros, was a name of the Geroies, Barons of Eschaufour.

Grose, for Gross.

Gross. Ralph, Matthew, Roger, Robert de Grosso, Normandy, 1180–95 (MRS). Henry Gros, Thomas de Gruce, and others, England, c. 1272 (RH).

Grosse. *See* Gross.

Grote. The lands of William Grout at Goudere, Normandy, were confiscated by Philip Augustus (Mem. Soc. Ant. Norm. v. 159). William Grote, England, c. 1272 (RH).

Grouse, for Grosse.

Grosvenor, so named from the office of Venur, or Venator (huntsman) of the Dukes of Normandy, borne by this family. Walter de Venur was eminently distinguished 960 at the battle of the Fords, between Lothaire, King of France, and the Normans, where he was rescued by Duke Richard I., and remounted by him on his best horse (Palgrave, Hist. Normandy, ii. 738). The name occurs about the same time in the Charters of the Gallia Christiana. The ancient seat of the Le Venours appears to have been Venables, near Evreux, and they bore or, or argent, a bend azure (La Roque, Hist. Harcourt, ii. 1181), which was also borne by several of their English descendants, especially by the family under consideration. Three brothers of this family came to England with Hugh Lupus: 1. Gislebert Venator, or De Venables, ancestor of the barons of Kinderton, of whom Gislebert Venables of Cheshire is mentioned in Normandy 1180 as 'Gislebert Venator' (MRS). The French line of Le Venur, descended from him, bore argent, a bend azure, fretty or, for difference (Anselme, viii. 256). From another brother probably derived the Butlers of Chester, Barons of Warrington, who also bore or, a bend azure, differenced by the wheat sheaves of Chester. 3. Radulph, or Ranulph.

Ranulph Venator, a baron of Chester, held in capite from Hugh Lupus in 1086 (Domesd.). He witnessed the foundation charter of Chester Abbey, and was a benefactor to it (Mon. i. 201). His descendants all bore or, a bend azure, till the 14th cent. Robert le Venur, his son, received from Earl Hugh, t. Rufus, Over Lostock, Cheshire (Ormerod, iii. 82). His son Robert had, c. 1153, a grant of Budworth, with the office of forester or grand-huntsman of Delamere Forest (Ormerod, ii. 115), from Earl Hugh Kevelioc. Robert Grosvenor 1178 witnessed a charter of John, Constable of Chester, for Stanlaw Abbey (Mon. i. 897). Ralph, his son, t. John (Ormerod, iii. 87), was ancestor of the Grosvenors of Cheshire. In the reign of Richard II., Lord Scrope objected to their use of their paternal arms, as his own ancestors had used the same, at which time it was proved that the G.s had borne their arms from the remotest ages; but the influence of Scrope obtained a decision depriving this family of their original arms. The Marquises of Westminster, Earls of Wilton, and Lords Ebury descend from this house.

Grout. *See* GROTE.

Gruchy, or Grochy, the French pronunciation of Grochet. Clarus de Grochet, Normandy, 1180 (MRS); Richard Grucet, England, c. 1272 (RH).

Grumell. Peter and Robert de Grumuell held lands at Nogent, Normandy, from Philip-Augustus (Mem. Soc. Ant. Norm. v. 182).

Gubbins, or De Gobion, from Bretagne. Guido Gobio witnessed a charter of Geoffry de Dinan, c. 1070, as one of his knights (Morice,

272

Hist. Bret. Preuves, i. 439), and William Gobio occurs in a charter of the same date (Ibid.). Hugh Gubiun was of Northants 1130 (Rot. Pip.), and 1165 Richard Gubiun, or Gobio, held fiefs in Bedford and Derby from Beauchamp, and Ferrars Earl of Derby (Lib. Niger). The name was corrupted to Gubbins. Sir Hugh Gobyun of York occurs c. 1300 (PPW).

Gubby. N. Gob, Guislanus Gobe, Normandy, 1180-98 (MRS); Geoffry, Walter, &c., Cobbe, England, c. 1272 (RH).

Gude, for GOOD.

Gudge. *See* GOODGE.

Gudgen. *See* GUDGEON.

Gudgeon, for Cucon. *See* GOGGIN.

Guest. Guest was near Caen, Normandy. This family settled in Salop at the Conquest, and held Lega from the De Dunstanvilles. In 1150 Alan de D. granted the lands of Alric de Lega to Wembridge Priory (Eyton, Salop, ii. 273). Thomas de Lega, his son, occurs 1180 (314); Walter and Leonard, his sons, 1194–1230; Henry, son of Leonard, 1240 (315). Roger de Lega, or Guest, brother of the latter, had Thomas, who gave lands to Wembridge Priory (Eyton, Salop, ii. 313). In 1295 Adam Gest was assessor of parliamentary aids in Salop (PPW). From this Norman race descended Bishop Guest, one of the Reformers, and the eminent manufacturer, Sir John Guest.

Guise, or Gouiz. *See* CUST. In 1165 Richard de Guiz held five knights' fees in Gloucester from the Earl of Gloucester (Lib. Niger). In 1203 Robert de Gouvis also held five fees of the honour of Gloucester, for which fees the service was performed in Normandy (Rot. Canc. 57). This Robert de G. is frequently mentioned t. John, in Bedford, Cambridge, &c. (RCR); Hardy (Rot. Claus. &c.); and a manor was styled Apsley Guiz or Guise after the family. About 1300 Sir John de Gyse, Bucks, bore gules, six mascles vair, a quarter or, being nearly those borne by the baronets Guise of Gloucestershire. The original arms of Gouiz were vair.

Gull. Petrus Goles, Normandy 1198, Gervasius Gouel 1195 (MRS); Laurence, Richard, Matilda Gule, England c. 1272 (RH). Hence the baronets Gull.

Gulley. *See* GOULLEE.

Gulliver, or Golafre. *See* GIL-LIVER.

Gully. *See* GOULLEE.

Gun. William de Gons, Normandy 1180–95, Gilbert de Gons, Richard Goon 1198 (MRS); Elias Goun, William Gun, England c. 1272 (RH).

Gundry. *See* GOUNDRY.

Gunn. *See* GUN.

Gunnell, for Gunwell, Gonville or Conteville, descended from Herluin, Lord of Conteville, Normandy, by his first marriage, the issue of which, Ralph de Conteville, is stated by Orderic Vitalis to have had grants from the Conqueror in England. Accordingly in 1083 he appears holding lands in Somerset, but as mesne lord (Exon. Domesd.), his barony being in Gloucester, and being held 1086 by his son Roger Fitz-Ralph (Domesday). This barony in 1165 was held by his grandson Roger Fitz-Ralph, whose brothers Hugo, Hamelin, Philip, and Robert de Gundeville all held fiefs in the same county (Lib. Niger).

Hugo de G. also held two fees in Somerset, and Robert de G. two (Lib. Niger). Adam de Conteville, or Gundeville, one of the family, acquired Dodington, Somerset, t. Henry II.; from whom descended the family of Dodington, which continued in the male line to 1720. The Gunvilles or Gonvilles of Dorset were of this family, also the founder of Gonville and Caius College, Cambridge.

Gunner, for CONNER.

Gunning. William Ginon, Normandy 1180 (MRS); Rufus de Genun, England t. John (Hardy, Rot. de Libert. 100); Geoffry Gannon c. 1272 (RH). Hence the baronets of the name.

Gunter. N. Gontier, Normandy 1180 (MRS); Sir Peter Gontier or Gunter accompanied Bernard de Neumarché in the conquest of Brecknock 1088, and obtained a fief there (Jones, Brecknock, i. 92).

Gunther. *See* GUNTER.

Guppy, for Gopil. Ursel and Aufrid Gopil, Normandy 1180–95 (MRS); John and Richard Gopil, England c. 1272 (RH).

Gurdon, from Gourdon or Gorden near Cahors, a Gothic race. Adam de G. of Hants 1207 (Hardy, Obl. et fin.). Aimeric de G. 13th cent. was a benefactor to the church, and had grants from King John in England (Testa); and William de G. founded Gourdon Abbey 1240 (Gall. Christ. xi. 133, 174, 187). In 1231 Henry III. granted to Ralph Mareschal part of the estate of Sir Adam de Gourdon (Roberts, Excerpta). In 1257 Adam G. was bailiff in fee of Wolmer Forest (Ib.). In 1251 William, son of Roger G., paid a fine in Lincoln (Ib.). The family still remains of consequence.

Gurney, for De Gournay, one of the greatest and most ancient baronial families of Normandy, which was also seated in England, but which is too well known to need details.

Gurr, for GORR.

Gush, or Goshe. *See* GOOCH.

Guy. *See* GEE.

Gustard. *See* COSTART.

Gutch. *See* GOOCH.

Guyatt. *See* WYATT (Lower).

Guye, for GUY.

Guylee. William de Guilie, Normandy 1195 (MRS); William Gilly, England c. 1272.

Gyde. Robert Guide of Normandy 1180–95 (MRS).

Gye, for GUY.

Gyles, for GILES.

Gynne, for GYNN.

Gyan, or Gynney. Richard de Gisnei, Normandy 1180–95 (MRS); Roger de Gisneto, England 1199 (RCR).

H

Haberfield, Alberville, or Auberville, from A. near Caen. William de Aubervilla, Normandy, 1180 (MRS); Hugh de Albertivilla, Kent, 1130 (Rot. Pip.); William de A., Norfolk, 1194 (RCR); Richard de Haubervyle, c. 1272 (RH).

Hablin, for ABELINE, or ABELON.

Hackett, or ACHET. Robert Haket, Normandy, 1180–95; Alvered, Robert, H., 1198 (MRS); Walter Haket, England, 1194 (RCR). Walter Achet, 1086, held from Walter Giffard in Bucks. Bertram Haget witnessed a charter of Robert Mowbray (Mon. i. 754), and 1200 Bertram H. founded Helaugh Abbey, York. The family of Achet, Hachett, Hatchett, Hacket, or Haget, spread into all parts of England and Ireland.

Haddan. William Hadon, Normandy, 1180 (MRS); De Haddon, England, c. 1272 (RH).

Hadden. *See* HADDAN.

Haddon. *See* HADDAN.

Haden. *See* HADDAN.

Hadow, for Hoto, or Hotôt. Emma, Roger, Nicholas de Hotot,

Normandy, 1180–95 (MRS); William de Hotot, England, 1130 (Rot. Pip.). The name occurs continually afterwards. *See* OTTO.

Hace, for HASE.

Haggett, armorially identified with Hackett. Rolland Haget, of England, 1158 (Rot. Pip.); Geoffry Haget, 1189 (Ib.).

Haggis. *See* AGGIS.

Haight. *See* HAIT.

Haile. Denis, Ralph, Fulco, Haisle, Normandy, 1180 (MRS).

Hailes. *See* HALES.

Hailie, for Hailly, or D'Ally. Walter Allie, Normandy, 1180 (MRS). *See* ALLEY.

Hain, for Asnes. Durandus Asnes, Normandy, 1195 (MRS). *See* ANNE.

Haines, from Haisne near Arras. Hugh de Haynes witnessed a charter of Payen de Beauchamp, founding Chicksand Priory, 12th cent. (Mon. ii. 793); also Walter de Haynes. William Hayne, 1325, bailsman for the M.P. for Ilchester (PPW).

Haines, for HAIN.

Hains, for HAIN.

274

Haire, for HARE.

Hait. Gervase Haitie, Normandy, 1180-95 (MRS). Henry Hat, Thomas del Hat, England, c. 1272 (RH).

Haldane. Robert Alden, Normandy, 1180-95 (MRS). *See* HAWTIN.

Halden. *See* HALDANE.

Hale, for HALL. *See* also HAILE.

Hales, for HALYS or ALIS. *See* ELLIS—sometimes also a local name.

Haley. *See* HAILEY. Irish families of the name are Celtic.

Haliday, from Halyday, Normandy (Mém. Soc. Ant. Norm. v. 159). Philip and Reginald de Halyday of England, 1194 (RCR).

Halkett, armorially identified with HACKETT. Hence the gallant General Sir Colin Halkett.

Hall. Serlo de Haula, of Normandy 1198 (MRS); also Robert de Hala. In 1165 Thomas de Hal and Richard de la Hale held in Lincoln from De Senlis. The family was of importance in the west of England. *See* HAWLEY. The name includes families of various origin, some perhaps not Norman.

Hall, or De Clarefai. The learned Joseph Hall, Bishop of Norwich, was son of Hall, seneschal to the Earl of Huntingdon, President of the North, and by his arms is identified as one of the Lincolnshire family of Halls of Grantham, the ancestor of which, on marriage with an heiress of the Halls, assumed the name and arms. William Fitzwilliam, son of Thomas, and brother of John Fitzwilliam, 14th cent., was the person alluded to who took the name of Hall, as appears from the Lincoln Visitation, 1592. *See* FITZWILLIAM.

Hallatt, for ALLOTT.

Hallett, for HALLATT.

Halley, for ALLEY.

Halliday. *See* HALIDAY.

Hallowes. *See* HALLOWS.

Hallows, or HALLOW, for Halot. Roger Halot, Normandy, 1180-95 (MRS).

Halls, for HALL.

Hally, for HALLEY.

Hallybone, for ALLIBONE.

Halse, for HALSEY.

Halsey. William de Halasa, Normandy, 1180 (MRS); Britia de Alisy and Silvester, 1180-95 (Ib.); Robert de Alsey, England, c. 1272 (RH).

Haly. *See* HALEY.

Ham, from the Castle of Ham, Normandy. William du Ham, Normandy, 1180-98 (MRS); William and Alexander de Ham, England, c. 1272 (RH).

Hambelton. *See* HAMILTON.

Hambleton. *See* HAMILTON.

Hamby. Gaufridus Hambee, Normandy, 1198 (MRS); Roger de Hambeia, and others, 1180-95 (Ib.).

Hamel. Robert Hamel, Ranulph, Turstan, Savaric, and eleven more, Normandy, 1180-95 (MRS); Alexander de Hamel, England, c. 1272 (RH).

Hames. *See* AMES.

Hamilton. Gislebert, Lord of Blosseville (now Blouville), Normandy, in 1086 held Newton and Brayfield, Bucks, and Harold and Falmersham, Beds, from the Countess Judith (Domesd.). William de Blosseville was of Beds 1130 (Rot. Pip.). Robert de B., his son, c. 1150 granted lands at Harold, Turvey, and Lavendon to Harold Abbey. Jordan de Blosseville, brother of Robert, possessed the estates of Newton-Blosseville, &c., in Bucks, and was in 1157 Viscount of Lincoln.

He probably held the office of seneschal of the great Crown demesne of Hameldon, Bucks, and thence was named 'De Hameldon,' and under that name he held lands, 1165, from the see of Durham (Lib. Nig.), and in 1156 he had a Crown grant of lands in Surrey (Rot. Pip.). He had two sons: 1. Gilbert de B., who occurs in Normandy c. 1180 (MRS). 2. Thomas.

Thomas de Hameldon occurs in Northumberland (where the family had estates), 1170 (Hodgson, iii. iii. 16, 18). He had issue—1. Robert; 2. Roger de Hameldon, who occurs in Northumberland c. 1200 as security for the Abbot of Kelso (Ib. ii. ii. 250), and in Normandy as Roger de Blosseville (MRS).

Robert de Hameldon, the elder son, occurs as a knight of Northumberland 1207 (Ib. ii. ii. 148, 258). He was also Lord of Newton-Blosseville 1203-9 (Lipscombe, Bucks, iv. 257), and occurs in a suit in that county 1199 (RCR). His son, Gilbert de Blosseville, or de Hameldon, was Lord of Newton-Blosseville 1254, when he sold it to another branch of the family (Lipscombe). He also possessed the estates in Surrey (Testa); and holding his lands from the Honour of Huntingdon, and therefore from the kings of Scotland, he received a settlement in Scotland 13th cent., and in his latter years became an ecclesiastic (Chart. Paisley). His elder son, Walter Fitz-Gilbert de Hameldon, was one of the barons of Scotland, and obtained the barony of Cadzow, afterwards Hamilton. From this line descend the Dukes of Abercorn, the first Dukes of Hamilton, and many other noble families of the name.

276

Hamis, for AMISS.

Hamley. John, Reginald, Richard de Amblia, Normandy, 1198 (MRS); Geoffry de Amblie, England, 1199 (RCR).

Hamlin. Ralph, Robert, Roger, William Hamelin, Normandy, 1198 (MRS); William Hamelyn, England, c. 1272 (RH).

Hamling. See HAMLIN.

Hamlyn. See HAMLIN.

Hamman, for HAMMOND.

Hampnant, for HAMMOND (Lower).

Hammat, from Amatus, or Amée. Ralph Amée, Normandy, 1180-95 (MRS).

Hammett. See HAMMATT.

Hammie, for HAMBY.

Hammon. See HAMMOND.

Hammond, or HAMON. Geoffry, Ranulph, Waleran, Richard, Stephen Hamon, or Hammon, Normandy, 1180-98 (MRS); John Hamon, England, c. 1272 (RH). Hence the baronets Hammond.

Hampden. See HAMPTON.

Hampton. William de Hantona, Normandy, 1198 (MRS). William, Aelis, Gervase, Osbert, Walter de Hantona, Normandy, 1180-98 (MRS); Alexander, Reiner, Roger, Simon de Hamton, England, 1198 (RCR). The family of Hampden, Bucks, from which descended the patriot John Hampden, derived from Alexander de Hamptona.

Hams, for HAM.

Hance, for HANNS, or ANNS.

Hancock, or De Sprenchaux, from S. in Burgundy. Agilric de Sprenchaux, Lord of Longnor and Westley, Salop, lived t. Stephen (Eyton, Salop, vi. 26). William his son was bailiff at Hencot for the Abbey of Lilleshall, and Lord of H. by gift of the same Abbey (Ib. 368).

In 1208 Roger Fitzwilliam, his son, was of Encot, and 1274 Thomas Hancoc, or Hencot, sub-escheator of the king, Salop, set forth the lands held by Sir Robert Springhouse (Sprenchaux, his ancestor, Ib. 29). The name gradually changed to Hancock, and hence derived the Viscounts and Barons Castlemaine.

Handley, or D'ANDELY (Lower), from Andelys near Rouen. Richer De Andeli occurs in England, 1083, as a baron (Exon. Domesd.). The name occurs in the Winchester Domesday (560), and in 1165 (Lib. Niger), when this family had estates in Hants and North Hants, and in Normandy. In England the name remained 14th cent. (Mon. Angl. i. 106, 1026; PPW; D'Anisy et St. Marie sur Domesday.) It bore the forms of Dandeleigh, Daundely, and Handley.

Hanes, for HAINES.

Hankers, or HANKER, from Ancore, Normandy, mentioned 1198 (MRS).

Hankey, from Anché in Poitou. Robert de Anké accompanied Boamund to the Crusade 1096 (Roger Wend. ii. 76). Thomas de Hanchet of Cambridgeshire, 1316 (Palgr. Parl. Writs).

Hanley, for HANDLEY.

Hann, for ANNE.

Hanne, for ANNE.

Hannes, for HANNS.

Hannuell, or HANWELL, for HANDVILLE, or ANDEVILLE, from Andeville, a castle near Valognes, where the name occurs before 1030. The family as Andeville and Anneville had possessions in many English counties, and frequent writs of military summons. (See De Gerville, Anc. Chateaux; Mon. Angl. i. 592, ii. 905;

Lib. Niger; Testa; PPW; Rot. Canc.; Des Bois, Dict. de la Noblesse.) The name remained in Kent 17th cent. as HANVILLE or HANDVILLE.

Hansell, for ANCELL.

Hansor. See ENSOR.

Hanton. See HAMPTON.

Hanwell. See HANNUELL.

Harbar, for HARBERT. See HARBERD.

Harben. See HARBIN.

Harberd, or Harbert, for Herbert. Peter, Hugh, Serlo, William, Herbert, &c., Normandy, 1180-95 (MRS); Herbert Herbert, England, 1199 (RCR); Geoffry, Gilbert H., and others, England, c. 1272 (RH).

Harbin. Aeliza de Harpin, Normandy, 1180-95; Ralph H., 1198 (MRS). Hence the name of Orpen.

Harbord, Morden, or De Bercy, from Bercy, Normandy. Serlo de Burcy was a baron in Somerset and Dorset 1086 (Domesd.). Robert Fitz-Serlo, his son, had grants in Cheshire from Hugh Lupus (Mon. i. 201). These appear to have descended to Nigel de B., who confirmed lands to Chester (Mon.), and 1165 held lands in Wilts as Nigel de Morden (Lib. Niger). His son or grandson 13th cent. held Morden, Wilts (Testa), and his brother Nicholas de M. held lands in capite in Essex, which passed to John his son, on whose decease, 1258, Nicholas de M., his cousin, paid homage for them (Roberts, Excerpt.). His brother Guido de Bercy de Morden occurs in 1249 as indebted to Isaac the Jew, of Norwich. William de M., his descendant, d. 1362, seized of lands in Middlesex. Robert M. occurs in Essex t. Elizabeth, from whom descended the Mordens of Suffield (now Harbord), Lords Suffield.

Harbord, for HARBORD-MORDEN.

Harbour, for HARBORD.

Harbutt, for HARBOLD. Thomas Herbolt, Normandy, 1180 (MRS).

Harcourt, a well-known Norman family, ancestors of the Earls of Harcourt (*See* Collins), and descended from Bernard the Dane, Regent of Normandy c. 940.

Harden, for Hardern or Ardern. *See* BRACEBRIDGE.

Hards, for ARDES.

Hardy. Roger, Hunfrid, Robert, Nicholas Hardi, Normandy, 1180-95 (MRS); John, Thomas, Henry, William Hardi, England, c. 1272 (RH).

Hare, or Leigh, baronets, probably from the family of Leigh, a branch of DE LA MARE.

Hare. Wymarc Heres, and William of Normandy, 1198 (MRS); Robert Hare, Norfolk, 1199 (RCR); Henry, Hugh le Hare, and others, England, c. 1272 (RH); also Geoffry le Heyr, and others. In 13th cent. Roger le Hare occurs in Norfolk (Blomef. ii. 449). In 1319 William le Eyr occurs in N. (v. 311). In 1264 Roger le Hayre occurs in N. (v. 310). Hence the Hares of Stow Bardolph, and the Earls of Listowell. *See* EYRE.

Harefield. Fulco and William de Herouville, Normandy, 1180-95 (MRS).

Harenc. Ralph Harenc occurs in Normandy 1118 (Ord. Vit. 848). In 1203 Ralph H. was father of Roger H., Lord of Gauville. Walkelin, 1165, held lands in Wilts, Terric H. in Warwick (Lib. Nig.). The name was changed frequently to Harenge or Herring. Of this latter name was Thomas H., Archbishop of Canterbury.

278

Harker, for HARCOURT (Lower).

Harle, for HARRELL.

Harlot, for HALOT, from Halot, Normandy. Roger Halot, Normandy, 1198 (MRS); Hugh and Robert Harlot, England, c. 1272 (RH).

Harman, or Herman. Ralph, William, Richard, Hugh Herman, Normandy, 1180-98 (MRS); Ralph, Nicholas Herman, England, c. 1272 (RH). Hence the Earls of Rosse.

Harmer. John, Ralph, William Hermer, Normandy, 1180 - 98 (MRS).

Harmony, from Aumenil, Normandy. Richard and Ralph Aumesnil, 1198 (MRS).

Harms. *See* ARMES.

Harnell, for Arnell or ARNOLD (Lower).

Harold. Radulphus Herolt, Normandy, 1180-98 (MRS); Robert Harald, England, 1199 (RCR); Reginald, Roger Harald or Haralt, c. 1272 (RH).

Harrah, for ARRAS. *See* BEATON.

Harrall, for HARRELL.

Harrell. Peter, Roger, Osbert, &c., Harel, Normandy, 1180-95 (MRS); Agnes, Robert Erl, England, c. 1272 (RH).

Harrild, for HAROLD.

Harrill. *See* HARRELL.

Harris, for Heriz. Ralph Heriz, Normandy, 1180-95 (MRS); Ivo de Heriz, England, 1130; Ivo de H., 1199; Hugh de H. and Roger Herice, c. 1272 (Rot. Pip.; RCR; RH). Harris and Heriz are armorially identified, each bearing three herissons (hedgehogs) in allusion to the name. Landric de Baugency of B. in the Orleanois had issue John and Hericius, or Herice, who in 1022 were prohibited by King Robert of France from making inroads on the estates of a neighbouring abbey (Bouquet, x. 607). Landric witnessed a charter of King Robert, 1028 (Gall. Christ. viii. 297, instr.), and was ancestor of the powerful Barons of Baugency. Hericius was father of Ancelin de Beaumont (styled Alselin in Domesd.), who, 1086, held a great Barony in Notts, &c. Ivo Fitz-Herice or De Heriz, his son, was Viscount of Notts before 1130. He had issue, 1, Ralph Hanseline, who held the Barony in Notts in 1165; 2, Robert Fitz-Herice mentioned in a charter of Barberie Abbey, executed by Henry II.; 3, Josceline, mentioned in Hunts, 1156 (Rot. Pip.); 4, William, who held, 1165, two fees in Notts and four in Lincoln; 5, Humphry.

Humphry Hairez was of Berks, 1158 (Rot. Pip.). William Herez, 18th cent., possessed estates, Wilts. From him descended William Harrys, one of the principal inhabitants of Salisbury, 1469 (Hoare), ancestor of the Earls of Malmsbury, who bear the three herissons, the arms of Heriz. Lord Harris bears the same.

Harris. Wymund Harace, Normandy, 1198 (MRS).

Harrison. Gilbert and Philip Heriçon, Normandy, 1180 – 98 (MRS); Henry Harsent, Engl., c. 1272 (RH). The name no doubt includes other families as a patronymic. *See* HARSANT.

Harriss. *See* HARRIS.

Harrold. *See* HAROLD.

Harrop. Geoffry de la Herupe held lands, Normandy, t. Philip-Augustus (Mém. Soc. Ant. Norm. v. 165); Andrew, Nicholas Harpe, England, c. 1272 (RH).

Harrow. William Herou, Normandy, 1180–95 (MRS); Richard Hero, England, c. 1272 (RH).

Harry. Ralph Harry, Normandy, 1180–95 (MRS); John Harre, England, c. 1272 (RH).

Harryman, for HARMAN.

Harsant. Richard and Ranulph Fitz-Hersent, Richard and Roger Hersent, Normandy, 1180 – 98 (MRS); Henry Harsent, England, c. 1272 (RH).

Hart, or Le Cerf. William, Richard, Walter, Ralph Cerfus, Normandy, 1180–98 (MRS); in England translated into Hert before 1272 (RH). Hence the Baronets Hart-Dyke.

Harte. *See* HART.

Harter, or Hartery, perhaps from Artres, near Valenciennes. William Artur, England, c. 1272 (RH).

Hartland. Alan de Hertalanda, Norm. 1198 (MRS). The house of Dinan were Barons of Hartland, Devon. *See* DINHAM.

Hartree. *See* HARTRY.

Hartry. *See* HARTER.

Hartt. *See* HART.

Harvest. Richard Hervest of Oxfordshire, c. 1272 (RH). This seems to be a Norman patronymic, derived from Erfast, a Norman name.

Harvey. William Herveus, Normandy, 1198 (MRS), and England, 1199, Surrey and Suffolk (RCR). Probably several families of different origin bore the name. *See* HERVEY.

Harvie, for HARVEY.

Hase. Bartholomew de la Hase held a knight's fee, Hereford, 1165 (Lib. Nig.). The name probably from Hayes near Blois.

Haseler, for Hoseler. *See* OSLER.

Hasell or Hasle. *See* HAILE.

Maskey, for Askey, or ASKEW.

Masler. See HASELER.

Massard. William Hasart and Richard, Normandy, 1180 – 98 (MRS); Hugh Hasard, England, 1189 (Rot. Pip.).

Massell. See HASELL.

Massett, or Haste. Hugh Heste, Normandy, and Henry H., 1180–98 (MRS); John Hest, Geoffry Hassot, England, c. 1272 (RH).

Mastie, for Haste. See HAST.

Mastin, for ASTIN.

Mastings, or De Venoix. The Barons of Venoix, near Caen, held their fief as hereditary Marshals of the Stable (Masters of the Horse), whence they bore the name of 'Le Mareschal,' or 'Mareschal of Venoix' (MSAN, xii. 15). Milo le Mareschal, b. probably c. 980, and Lescelina his wife, were living 1050, when the Duchess Matilda purchased lands at Vaucelles from them for Holy Trinity, Caen (Ibid.). He had issue Ralph le Mareschal and other sons, who came to England 1066. R. was living 1086, and had issue, 1, Robert; 2, Roger le Mareschal, who, 1086, held lands in Essex; 3, Gerold, owner of estates Suffolk, 1086; 4, Goiafrid, owner of estates in Hants and Wilts, 1086, father of Gilbert, ancestor of the Mareschals, Earls of Pembroke.

Robert, the elder son, is sometimes styled Fitz-Ralph, elsewhere 'De Hastings,' and 'Le Marischal' (Domesd. 17, 73, 74 b, 160 b; Essex, 107 b). He was Lord of Venoix, and was the king's viscount or seneschal at Hastings, where and at Rye his descendants long held the revenues in farm from the Crown. He had William de Hastings, who, c. 1100, m. Juliana, granddau. and

280

heir of Waleran, a great baron of Essex, and was living 1130 (Rot. Pip.). He, with Robert de Venoix his brother, instituted a suit against his cousin Gilbert Mareschal and his son to recover the office of hereditary marshal, which G. or perhaps Goiafrid, his father, had obtained to the prejudice of the elder line (Dugdale). The suit failed, but in compensation William de H. was created Dapifer. His son, Hugh de H., in 1130 held estates in Leicester and Bucks by m. with the heir of De Flamville, by whom also he acquired estates in Norfolk (Blomefield, i. 168, 339). He had issue, 1, Ralph, ancestor of Hastings, Barons of Bergavenny and Earls of Pembroke; 2, Thomas, ancestor of Hastings, Lord Hastings, Earls of Huntingdon. There were numerous branches of these families. From the latter descended in the female line the Marquises of Hastings.

Matchard. See ACHARD.

Matcher, for HATCHARD.

Matchett. See HACKETT.

Matherill, or Hauterill, armorially identified with Hautevill (Robson). This family, which also appears under the form of Hovell and Hauvell, is one of the most historically interesting in Europe, being a branch of the Norman kings of Naples and Sicily. Hialtt, a Northman viking, c. 920, was its probable founder, whence the fief of Haultville or Hautville, Latinised Altavilla. Third in descent was Tancred, b. c. 980–990, Sire de Hautville, who was in the court of Richard II., whose favour he gained in the hunting field by an exploit narrated by Galfrid de Malaterra. He was leader of ten knights in the

Duke's service (Bouquet, xi.). He m. and had Drogo, Umfrid, Galfrid, Serlo, Robert, Malger, Alvered, William, Humbert, Tancred, and Roger, who were the most renowned warriors of their age. Serlo was taken into the Duke's household in reward for a remarkable feat of chivalry, and Geoffry, according to Orderic Vitalis, obtained the paternal fief, when his father went to spend his last days in Italy.

The other sons joined the Norman chivalry in Apulia, where William, surnamed 'Bras de Fer,' became leader of the Normans and Lord of Ascoli, Drogo Lord of Venosa, and the other Norman chiefs great barons. In 1043 William was elected by the chiefs their general and Count of Apulia. He was succeeded 1046 by his brother Drogo de Hautville, Count of Venosa, who was succeeded by Humphry his brother, who dying 1057 was succeeded by his brother Robert de Hauteville, surnamed Guiscard (the Adroit), Duke of Calabria, Apulia, and Sicily. Roger his brother became Count of Sicily, and from him descended the De Hautevilles, kings of Naples and Sicily. Bohemund, Prince of Antioch and Tarento, so renowned in the First Crusade, was son of Robert Guiscard, and from him descended the Kings of Cyprus and Jerusalem.

A branch of this royal house became seated in England. Geoffry de Hautville, who remained in Normandy, was father of Ralph de Hautville or Altaville, who in 1086 held a Barony in Wilts (Domesd.). His descendants were a renowned race of warriors. Sir John de Hautville accompanied Edward I. to Palestine. In 1316 John de Hautville was Lord of Norton-Hawtfield or Hautville, Somerset, and 1316-24 Sir Geoffry de H. was M.P. for Somerset, Bucks, and Wilts. He bore sable crusilly argent, a lion rampant argent, being nearly the same as those borne by the Kings of Italy as descendants of the Kings of Cyprus. Hautville's quoits, two great rocks, which he is said to have used as quoits, are still shown in Somerset, where popular tradition describes him as a giant (Collins, Somerset).

The Hautvilles or Hauvilles were seated in Northants and Rutland, t. John; and in Norfolk by grant of Henry II., where they held the dignity of hereditary falconer to the king. The name changed in that county to Auville, Haville, Hovell, and Dunton. The name in Normandy in 1198 had changed to Haville, when Hugh, Hubert, and Walkelin de H. occur (MRS).

Hatherell. *See* HATHERILL.

Hatt. *See* HAITE.

Hattrell. *See* HATHERILL.

Haughton. *See* HOGHTON.

Haven. *See* AVENS.

Havers, for Alvers or Auver. Richard de Auvere of Normandy, 1198 (MRS).

Haviland. Robert de Haverland, Normandy, 1180 (MRS).

Haweis, for HOWIS.

Hawes, in some cases armorially identified with HASE.

Hawker, the English form of Le Fauconer or Accipitrarius. *See* FALCONER.

Hawkins, from the manor of Hawkinge, Kent, held by Walter Hawkin, 1326 (PPW). The family had previously borne the name of

Flegg, for William de Flegg, 18th
cent., held a fief in Hawking (Testa).
The family had been seated at
Flegg, Norfolk, and t. Henry II.
Ralph Curzon of Flegg occurs
(Blomefield, v. 414). Arthur, Roger,
and William de Flegg occur 1121–
1145 (Ib. xi. 194); and the latter
may be William de Curzon, mentioned 1165 (Lib. Nig.). Hence the
Baronets Hawkins.

Hawkins. 1. A local name as
above; 2, for DAWKINS, DAKEYN,
DEACON, or De Akeny, armorially
identified.

Hawley, from La Haulle, Nor-
mandy. Warin de Haulla occurs
in Somerset, 1156, and 1165 he held
a barony of eight fees in Devon
(Lib. Nig.). Roger de Aula of
Somerset and Dorset, 13th cent.
From this family descended the
Lords Hawley and the Baronets H.

Haws, for HAWES.

Hawten. See HAWTIN.

Hawtin. In 1086 Godwin Hal-
dein, Norfolk (Domesd.). May have
been Danish as Blomefield contends
(x. 390, 425), but the name appears
also in Normandy. See HALDANE.
The family in England bore the
name Hauteyn, then Houghton.

Hawtrey, or De Hauterive, Al-
taripa, from Hauterive, Normandy.
A barony possessed by a branch of
the Paganels, with whom this family
is armorially identified, bearing three
lions passant instead of two, as
borne by P. of Bahantune. The
name occurs in England from the
Conquest.

Hay, or De la Haye. Richard,
surnamed Turstin Halduc, the first
known ancestor of this family, was
probably a younger son of Turstin
de Bastembourg, ancestor of the
282

Bertrams (see MITFORD), as might
be inferred from several reasons.
He in 1056 with Eudo his son
founded Essay Abbey, Normandy,
endowing it with vast and princely
possessions (Gall. Christ. xi. 224
instr.). Eudo accompanied the
Conqueror. He is mentioned by
Wace as the 'Sire de la Haie,'
and in 1086 was a great baron in
England (Domesd.). His d. and
heir m. Geoffry de Mandeville, Earl
of Essex, Seneschal of Normandy
in her right (Dugd. Bar. 110).
Eudo had a brother Ralph, Dapifer
or Seneschal to Robert Earl of
Mortaine. In 1086 Ralph Dapifer
held in capite in Lincoln, and from
the Earl of Mortaine and Earl Alan
in Northants (Domesd.). He accompanied Duke Robert to Palestine,
1096 (Des Bois). In 1105 Robert
de Haia his son as heir confirmed
the charter of Turstin Halduc and
Eudo (Gall. Christ. xi. 227, Instr.);
and 1105 as Robert de Haia, 'son
of Ralph the Seneschal of the E.
of Mortaine' and nephew of Hudo
(Eudo) Dapifer, granted Boxgrove
to Essay Abbey (Ib. 233). The
confirmation charter of Henry I.,
1126, recites the gifts of Turstin,
Eudo, and the confirmation by
Robert de Haia and his sons Richard
and Ralph (Ib. 234), also the grants
of Richard de Haia in Britville,
Normandy (Ib. 235). Robert had
issue, 1, Richard de la Haye, whose
barony in Lincoln was of twenty
fees, 1165, and who left coheiresses;
2, Ralph, who held a Norman barony
1165; 3, William. The latter held
fiefs in Hereford, Devon, and Worcester, 1165, and held the office of
Pincerna or Butler of Scotland
(Douglas). From his eldest son

descended the Earls of Errol, and from his younger the Marquises of Tweeddale. Many other branches of De la Hay existed in England and Scotland.

Hayden. *See* HADDEN.

Haydon, for HADDON.

Hayer, for HARE.

Hayes, from Hayes near Blois. In 1165 Bartholomew de la Hase held a fief in Hereford (Lib. Nig.). William de Hayes of Northants, 13th cent., was a follower of John Giffard, and his house was plundered after the Battle of Evesham (Hunter, Rot. Sel. 185). Hence the Baronets Hayes.

Hayles, for HALES.

Hayley, for HALLEY.

Hayman, for HAMON. *See* HAMMOND.

Haymen, for HAYMAN.

Hayne, for HAINES.

Haynes. *See* HAINES.

Hayr, for HARE.

Hays, for HAYES.

Hayser, for HASSARD.

Hazard, for HASSARD.

Hazell, for HASSELL.

Hazill, for HASSELL.

Hazle, for HASSELL.

Head, or Teste. Robert Teste (Tête), Normandy, 1180-95 (MRS); Nicholas Tate, Robert Hedde, England, c. 1272 (RH). Hence the Baronets Head.

Headen, for HADDON.

Heales, for Eles, or EYLES.

Healey: for English families *see* HALEY.

Healy. *See* HEALEY.

Heaman, for HAYMAN.

Heard, for Harde, or HARDY.

Hearn, for Heron, from Heron, near Rouen. William Heron held a fief, Normandy, t. Philip-Augustus

(Mem. Soc. Ant. Norm. v. 175). Odonil Heron, t. Will. Rufus, witnessed a charter in Durham (Raine, N. Durh. Ap. 3). Alban de Hairun held a barony Hertf. 1165 (Lib. Nig.).

Hearne. *See* HEARN.

Hearon. *See* HEARN.

Hearsey, from Hericy, Normandy. Hugh de Hersy, Galter Hericie, Normandy, 1180-95 (MRS); Hugh de H. England, t. John (Hardy, Rot. de Libertate).

Heavens. *See* HEAVEN.

Heaven, for HAVEN.

Heaver, for HAVERS.

Hebard. Geoffry Hebart, Normandy, 1180-95 (MRS); Henry, Reginald, Nicholas Hebart or Hebard, England, c. 1272 (RH).

Hebbard. *See* HEBARD.

Hebbert. *See* HEBARD.

Hebert. *See* HEBARD.

Hector, from Le Acatour. *See* CATOR.

Hedge, or Hegge (RH). *See* AGG.

Hedges. *See* AGGES.

Heed, for HEAD.

Heelas, for HEELIS.

Heelis, for Eales, or EYLES.

Heely, for Ely. Walter, Peter de Ely, Normandy, 1180-98 (MRS).

Helas, for HEELIS.

Helbert, for ALBERT.

Heley, for HEELY.

Heller, for HELLIER.

Hellier, for Illiers, or Hellier, fro St. Hellier, near Rouen. Ralph Illeriis, Normandy, 1198 (MRS).

Helie, for HEELY.

Hellis, for ELLIS.

Hellond, for HELLIER.

Hellyer. *See* HELLIER.

Helmes. *See* HELM.

Helm. Emma de Haume (Halme) Normandy, 1198 (MRS); Andrew de Helum, Engl. c. 1262 (RH).

Helps. Hugo de Helpe, Normandy, 1180–95 (MRS); Henry Helbe, England, c. 1272 (RH). *See* ALPE.

Hely. Walter de Hely, Normandy, 1198 (MRS). *See* HEELY.

Hemans, for Emmens, or EMMETT (Lower).

Hember, for AMBER.

Hemblin, for HAMLIN.

Hemens, for HEMANS.

Hemmens, for HEMANS.

Hemment, for Hamant or AMAND.

Hemory, for AMORY.

Hems, for Hams, or HAM.

Hence, for HANCE.

Hender. *See* HENDRE.

Hendra, for ANDREW.

Hendre, for André or ANDREW.

Hendrey, for André. *See* ANDREW.

Hendrie, for HENDREY.

Hendry, for HENDREY.

Henery, for HENRY.

Herbert. 1. *See* HARBERD. 2. A well-known English family, Earls of Pembroke, probably, from the ancient arms (3 chevrons, with a chief vair), of the family of St. Quintin of Normandy. *See* ST. QUINTIN.

Herd, for Hert, or HART.

Hereman, for HERMAN.

Hering. *See* HARENC.

Heriot, or Harriet, from De Ariète. *See* RAM.

Hern, for HEARN.

Heron. Tihel de Herion was of Essex 1066. In 1165 Alban de Hairun held in Hertford, Richard in Essex, Dru in York, and Jordan in York and Northumberland. In the latter county the Herons were of great note, and William Heron was summoned as a baron 1369. *See* HEARN.

Herron, for HERON.

Herries, or Heriz. *See* HARRIS.

284

Herring. *See* HARENC.

Herriott. *See* HERIOT.

Herrman. *See* HARMAN.

Hermon, for HERMAN.

Hersant. Richard, Roger, Ranulph Hersent, Normandy, 1180–98 (MRS); Henry Harsent, Engl., c. 1272 (RH).

Hersee. *See* HEARSEY.

Hersey. *See* HERSEE.

Hervey, or De Bourges. Geoffry Papabos was made Viscount of Bourges 920 (Anselme, iii. 216). Geoffry III., his grandson, rebuilt the Abbey of St. Ambrose, Bourges, 1012, and 1037 was at war with the Lord of Chateau-Raoul. He had issue: 1. Geoffry N., whose son Stephen, Viscount of Bourges, left Matilda de Sully his niece and heir; 2. Maldalbert, father of Hervey.

Hervey de Bourges (Bituricensis), cousin of Stephen the viscount, accompanied the Conqueror, and 1086 held a great barony in Suffolk (Domesday). Henry Fitz-Hervey, his son, witnessed a charter of Roger de Clare (Mon. i. 731). The barony passed from the family t. Stephen. Hervey, brother of Henry, held fiefs of Peché in Suffolk, and his son paid a fine 1130 (Rot. Pip.). Osbert Fitz-Hervey, 1165, held a fief from Peché, being then styled ' De Haffield,' from one of his lordships (Lib. Niger). He was, t. Richard I. and John, one of the king's justiciaries (Mon. i. 854; Rot. Canc.; RCR). Henry Fitz-Hervey, his son, was, 1203, in charge of the royal forests beyond Trent (Rot. Canc.). Adam Fitz-H., his son (Blomefield, Norf. xi. 231), had issue John Fitz-Hervey, who m. Joan, dau. of John Hammon, Lord of Thurley, Bedford, and d. 1292, and from him lineally descend the Marquises of Bristol and the Baronets Bathurst.

Hervey. *See* HARVEY.

Hesse, or Hese, for HASE. There are foreign families also of the name.

Hessey, for Hese, or HASE.

Hester, for Ester. William, Robert, Andrew, Estor or Estur, Norm. 1180-98 (MRS). *See* ASTOR.

Hett, for Hatt or HAITE.

Heugh, for HUGH.

Hewat, for HEWETT (Lower).

Hewell, a corruption of Hoel or Huel. *See* HOILE.

Hewer, for Eure, a branch of De Vesci. *See* VESEY.

Hewett, from Huest or Huet, near Evreux. The Norman family of Huet long continued (Des Bois). William de Huet paid a fine, apparently in Lincoln, 1204 (Hardy, Obl. et fin.). Peter Hughet occurs in Sussex 1278, and in 1311 Robert H. (PPW). Sir Walter Hewet was a distinguished warrior in France t. Edw. III., and from him descended the Hewets, created baronets 1621 and 1660, and Viscounts Hewet 1689, also the eminent lawyer James H., Lord Chancellor of Ireland, and first Viscount Lifford.

Hewetson, for HEWSON.

Hewitt, for HEWETT.

Hews, for HEWES.

Hewson. Fulco de Hueçon, Norm. 1198 (MRS); William and Guido de H. 1180-95 (Ib.).

Hey, or De la Hey. *See* HAY, armorially identified.

Heyer, or Le Heyr. *See* HARE.

Hibbard, for HEBARD.

Hibbart, for HEBERT.

Hibberd, for HEBARD.

Hibbert. *See* HEBARD.

Hibbitt, from HIBBERT.

Hickey. Alvered Hequet, Norm.,

1180-95 (MRS); John and Basilia Hicchi, Engl., c. 1272 (RH).

Hickie, for HICKEY.

Hickling. William and Hugh de Ikelon, Norm. 1180-95 (MRS), probably of Hickling, Notts.

Hicks, Hick, or Hycke, or Hecke, from Hitchin, Herts (anciently Hich). Henry de Hic witnessed the charter of Bernard de Bailliol t. Henry l. (Mon. Angl. ii. 98). Henry was probably Seneschal of Hitchin under his father Bernard de Balliol, who was lord. Temp. Henry II. lived William de Heck, whose son Herman occurs 1204 (Hunter, Fines). In 1298 Payne de Hyche was bailsman for the M.P. for Hertford; Robert de H. was soon after M.P. for the same. Hence the Viscounts Campden.

Higg. *See* HEDGE.

Higgin. Richard Hegent, Norm. 1180-95; John and David Hicun, England, c. 1272 (RH).

Higgins. *See* HIGGIN. Irish families of the name are probably Celtic.

Higgs. *See* HEDGES.

Hight, for HAITE.

Hilbert. Gaufred de Heldebert, Restoldus H., Normandy, 1180-95 (MRS); Robert Ilberd, Engl. c. 1272 (RH).

Hildebrand. N. Heldebrant occurs in Norm. 1180 (MRS); the name occurs in Engl. c. 1272 (RH).

Hilder, for Elder (Lower). Ranulph Heldeier, Normandy, 1180 (MRS); Cristina le Heldere, Julian Hildegar of England, c. 1270 (RH).

Hildyard, armorially identified with Hilliar, Helliar, and HELLIER.

Hill. 1. Local English in many instances. 2. The English form of De Monte. *See* MOUNT. 3. For Helle, or De Heille, from H. near

Beauvais. Gozelin de Heilles 1059 witnessed a charter of Henry I., King of France (Bouquet, xi. 579). A branch settled in England 1066, and bore a bend azure on a field sable, afterwards changed to a fesse, the tinctures remaining the same. The French line bore a bend fusilly. Theobald de Helles was living t. Stephen. His son Thomas Fitz-Theobald gave, temp. Henry II., a tenement at Canterbury to the Hospitallers (Mon. ii. 411, 412). In 13th cent. Bertram de Helles was Constable of Dover Castle. Thomas de H. possessed Helles Court in Ash, t. Edward I. Henry de H. was M.P. for Kent, t. Edward III., Gilbert Viscount of K., 1355, and his arms remain, sa. a bend argent (Hasted). In the church of Ash the arms are, argent, a chev. sable, between three leopards' faces or, being the foundation of the modern arms. The family was spread throughout Kent and Surrey, and from it probably derived Sir Moyses Hill, ancestor of the Marquises of Downshire, whose origin has been ascribed to the Devonshire family of Hill, but the arms of the latter are wholly different, and there is no assignable evidence of connexion.

Millard, for Hilliard. *See* HIL-DYARD.

Millary, from St. Hilary, Normandy. Jane, Hubert, Peter, Ralph de St. Hilary, 1180–98 (MRS). The Baronets Hillary are of this family.

Milleard, for HILLIARD.

Milleary, for HILLARY.

Millen, for Hellen, Hallen, or ALLEN.

Miller, for HILLIER.

Milliar. *See* HILDYARD.

286

Miller, for St. Hellier. *See* HILDYARD.

Mills, for Heilles. *See* HILL.

Millyard, for HILLIAR.

Millyer, for HELLYER.

Milson, for Helson, Elson, or ALISON.

Mimes, for Hiemes. *See* AMES.

Minge, or Hinges, for Henges or Hangest, from H. near Amiens.

Minks, in some cases from Hinges. *See* HINGE.

Minvest, perhaps a corruption of Hangest. *See* HINGE.

Mierns, for HIRONS.

Miron. *See* IRONS.

Mirons, for IRONS.

Mitt. Richard de Iz, Normandy 1180 (MRS); John Hitti, Engl. c. 1272 (RH). William de Iz, Norm. c. 1200 (MRS).

Moale, for HOLE.

Moar. *See* HOARE.

Moard. *See* HOARE.

Moare, the Norman-French pronunciation of Aure, with an aspirate. The name Aure, Alre, or Auré was Breton, derived from Auray, in Bretagne, of which this family were hereditary Castellans. The family is mentioned in that province in the 12th cent. (D'Anisy et St. Marie, Sur le Domesday). William de Aure or Alre held lands in Devon 1083 (Ex. Domesd.). William de Aure witnessed a charter of Robert Malerbe, granting his estate of Cheddok to his son. He was Viscount of Salop 1199. Hubert D'Aure witnessed the charter of Emma D'Auvers to Thame Abbey, Oxford. John de Aur was summoned 1263 to march against the Welsh. In the 13th cent. this John, son of Adam Aure, held lands in Dorset and Somerset (Testa, 168), and in Wilts held half a fee from Peter de Chaurcis, and another fee in capite (Ib. 144, 160). In the next century the name appears in Wilts as Hore or Le Hore (PPW). Hence the Baronets Hoare of England and Ireland.

Hobart. 1. Roger, Ralph Hubert, Norm. 1198 (MRS); John and Geoffry H., England, c. 1272 (RH); 2. Hobart or De Criquetot, from C. near Dieppe, Normandy; a baronial family in England. Ansgar de C., who accompanied the Conqueror, held lands in Suffolk from Mandeville in 1086. Hugo Fitz-Ansgar occurs 1130 (Rot. Pip.). In 1165 Hubert de Criketot, his son, held two fees from Mandeville (Lib. Nig.). He had, 1. Humfrid de Criketot, ancestor of the Barons C.; 2. Hubert Fitz-Hubert; 3. Richard Fitz-Hubert, who were parties in a suit in Essex 1194 (RCR). From Hubert Fitz-H. descended the Fitz-Huberts or Huberts of Tye and Hubert's Hall in Harlow, Essex, which places were within the Honour of Mandeville. Geoffry H. of this line, t. Henry III., had Simon; and t. Edward III., Robert Hubard or Hubert was of Harlowe, Essex (Morant, ii. 484). In 1389 John H. was Lord of Tye. Collins gives an account of the family from this time till c. 1450, when it passed into Norfolk, and his account is confirmed by Blomefield, Norfolk (v. 395). In the reign of Henry VII. Sir James Hubert or Hobart became Attorney-General. His great grandson was Lord Chief Justice, and from him descend the Earls of Buckinghamshire.

Hoblyn. Ranulph Hupelin, Normandy, 1198 (MRS).

Hodding. Richard de Hodenc, William Hodin, Norm. 1180–95 (MRS).

Hody, for Hodac. Robert and Walter de Hudac, Normandy 1180–95 (MRS). Hoger Hodi, Engl. c. 1272 (RH). The family was long seated in Dorset.

Hody. *See* ODY.

Hogard. *See* HOGGARTH.

Hogarth. *See* HOGGARTH. Hence the famous painter.

Hogg, or De Hoga, from La Hogue, in the Cotentin. In 1040 Hubert de Hoga granted lands to Cerisy Abbey (Mon. ii. 960). Henry and Adam de H. in 1250 occur in the Kelso Chartulary. Godfrey de la Hoge was a benefactor to Gisborne Priory, York (Mon. ii. 150). Hence the Baronets Hogg, and the poet Hogg.

Hoggarth, or Hogarth. Radulphus Hogart, Norm. 1180–98 (MRS); John Hochard, Engl. c. 1272 (RH).

Hoggett. Petrus Hugot, Normandy 1198 (MRS).

Hoghton. This family, according to the Testa de Neville, and Baines (Lancaster), descends from Hamo Pincerna, who, in the reign of William Rufus (or Henry I.), obtained Hocton in marriage with the dau. of Warin Bussel. This Hamo cannot have been of the house of Butler, Earls of Ormond (as the Peerages suppose), because the name Pincerna was not borne by the latter till much later. He was probably a son of Richard Pincerna, (and it may be observed that his own son bore the name of Richard). The latter was ancestor of the Pincernas or Butlers, Lords Boteler of Warrington (1295), Butlers of Chester. Richard Pincerna made grants in Cheshire to Chester Abbey c. 1090 (Mon. i. 201). He is mentioned 1086 as holding great estates in Salop and Cheshire (Domesd.). About 1134 Robert Pincerna founded Pulton Priory, Cheshire (Mon. i. 890). It appears from the early arms of these barons that they were a branch of the house of Venables or Le Venur. *See* GROSVENOR.

Holle. Ingulfus Hoiel, Bartholomew Hoel, Norm. 1180–98 (MRS); N. Hoel, Engl. c. 1272 (RH).

Hoinville, for Henville, from Henouville, Normandy, which fief often occurs (MRS). Robson preserves the arms of the English branch.

Holbech, for HOLBECK.

Holbeck. Hugh Faber de Holbec, Nicholas de H. Norm. 1198 (MRS).

Holburd, for Alberd or ALBERT.

Holden, for ALDEN.

Holding, for HOLDEN (Lower).

Hole. Walter Hole or Holes, and Richard H. Norm. 1180–95 (MRS). Richard de la Hole, Engl. c. 1272 (RH).

Holiday. *See* HALLIDAY.

Holl, for Hole.

Holland, or Du Grelly. *See* JUXON.

Holland. 1. Anschetil de Hoilant. Robert de H., Rochier de H. Normandy 1180–98 (MRS). Robert de H. of England c. 1198 (RCR). 2. names from other places in England.

Hollands, for HOLLAND.

Hollebone, for ALLEBONE.

Holleley, corruption of HOLLIDAY.

Holles, for HOLLIS.

Hollings. Eguerrand de Holene, Norm. 1180–95 (MRS); A. Holing, Engl. c. 1272 (RH).

Hollis. Robert de Holia, Norm. 1198 (MRS). William Houles, Engl. c. 1272 (RH). Hence Holles, Earls of Clare, Dukes of Newcastle.

Holliss, for HOLLIS.

Hollond, for HOLLAND.

Hollot, for HALLATT.

Holly. *See* OLLEY.

Hollyer, or Hollier. Osmund Huielor or Hoielor, Norm. 1198 (MRS).

Hollyman, for ALLEMAN, or Allemagne.

Holm. *See* HOLMES.

Holman, for ALLMAN.

Holmes. William du Holme, Norm. 1180–95; William de Homes 1198 (MRS). In England it included probably Norman and other families.

Holms. *See* HOLMES.

Holsey, for HALSEY.

Holyday. *See* HALLYDAY.

Homer, or St. Omer, a branch of the house of Bethune of Picardy, with which it is armorially identified. William, Castellan of St. Omer, was a distinguished historical character t. Henry I. The family was extensively settled in England. William de St. Omer was a justice itinerant t. Edward I. (Mon. ii. 809), and had a writ of military summons 1263. Sir Thomas de St. O. was Lord of several Manors, Norfolk and Wilts 1316 (PPW). Hugh, Richard, and William de St. O. occur in Norfolk, London, &c., 1130 (Rot. Pip.).

Homere, for HOMER.

Homes. *See* HOLMES.

Homfray. Joslin Onfrey or Onfroy, Norm. 1180–95 (MRS); Roger, Walter, Thomas Humfrey, &c., of England, c. 1272 (RH).

Hone, probably a form of Huan of Normandy. *See* HUGHAN.

Honeyball. *See* ANNABLE.

Honeybell. *See* HONEYBALL.

Honeywell, probably from Anville or Handeville. *See* HANWELL.

Honiball. *See* ANNABLE.

Honniball. *See* ANNABLE.

Honywill. *See* HANWELL.

Hooker. Barnabé Hucherer 1180-98, Guarner Huchier 1198 Norm. (MRS). John Hochard, Engl. c. 1272 (RH).

Hooker. Richard Hooker, 'the Judicious,' was nephew of John Vowell or Hooker, of Exeter (MP), a writer of note. The original name was Vowell or Fowell, and the family had been seated at Fowelscombe t. Henry IV. or earlier; and a younger son marrying an heiress assumed the name of Hooker.

The family of Fowell, Fauvel, Falvel, or Fouel, was Norman, and in 1165 William F. held a fief (of ancient tenure) from De Tracy in Devon (Lib. Nig.). Prior to this in 1151, Thomas Fauvel witnessed a charter of Odeliza de Rumelli in Yorkshire (Mon. Angl. ii. 101). Geoffry Fauvel occurs in Normandy 1203 (Hardy, Rot. Norm. i. 83). The name long continued in Normandy and Picardy.

Hoole. Walter de la Huel, Normandy 1180 (MRS).

Hoole, for HOLE.

Hooley, for HOWLEY.

Hooper. John Hooper, Bishop of Gloucester and martyr, was born in Somerset. The name was old there, for in 1325 it occurs in that county, and 1274 William le Hopere possessed lands in the adjacent county of Dorset. The name 'Hopere' was the Norman-French term for a cloth merchant, and it may be presumed that the family which bore this French name was foreign.

Horder, for Order or Ardre. Richard Ardre, Normandy 1180-95 (MRS). Richard de Ardres, Engl., c. 1272 (RH).

Hore. *See* HOARE.

Horey, for Harey, or Harry. Ralph Harri, Normandy 1180-95 (MRS); John Harré, Engl. c. 1272 (RH).

Horner. Gaufridus Le Cornier Norm. 1180-95. Roger le Corneor, 1198 (MRS). John le Corner, Matilda le Hornere, Engl. c. 1272 (RH).

Horrell or HURRELL. Gislebert, Philip, Richard, Robert Hurel, Norm. 1180-95 (MRS); John, Richard Hurel, Engl. c. 1272 (RH). Ralph H. Engl. c. 1198 (RCR).

Horry. *See* HORBY.

Horsell, from Ussel near Cahors. Ralph and Reginald Ursel held in Berks 13th cent. (Testa).

Horsfall. Orsval or De Arseville, from Arseville, Normandy, now Ossonville near Estampes. Richard de Arseville, c. 1125, witnessed a charter of Humphry de Bohun in favour of Farley Priory, Wilts (Mon. i. 621). The change of ville into fall in this name is similar to that of Waterville into Waterfall.

Hort, or De L'Orty, a baronial family, from Ortiac, in Aquitaine, which bore a cross, as the Baronets Hort still do. In the 13th cent. Henry de Urtiaco paid scutage for two fees, Somerset (Testa). In 1209 Richard de U. occurs (Roberts, Excerpta); and 1293 Henry L'Orti, or De Urtiaco, was summoned to parliament as a baron. The family long continued as Lorty, Lort, and at last Hort.

Hort, or De Lort. Robert, Peter, Richard Orte, De Ortis, or De Ortie, Norm. 1180–1200 (MRS).

Hosack, apparently foreign, but not yet verified.

Hose, or Hoese. Osbert, John, Walter, Martin, &c., De Hosa or De la Hose, Norm. 1180–95. The Lords Hussey of Sleaford descended from this family, and the Earl of Beaulieu; also the Husseys of Harting, Sussex.

Hoste, for Haste. Roger Haste, Normandy 1198 (MRS); Geoffry Hassot, Engl. c. 1272 (RH). The baronet's family, however, came from Flanders more recently.

Hotten. Henry de Hostona or Hotona, Normandy 1180–95 (MRS); John, Robert, William de H. England, c. 1272 (RH).

Houchin. William, Guido de Huechon, Norm. 1180–95 (MRS); Fulco, Ib. 1198.

Houl, for HOULE.

Houle. See HEWELL, HOOLE.

Houlden, for HOLDEN.

House, for Hoese or Hussey. See HOSE. It is armorially identified with Hussey.

Houseman. See HOUSMAN.

Housman. Guido de Houcemaine and Roger de H. Norm. 1198 (MRS).

Horsenail, formerly Horsenel, foreign, but not identified, original form probably Ursenel, a dim. of Urso.

Hovell, armorially identified with HAVILLE.

Howchin. See HOUCHIN.

Howden. Morel de Hodene, Norm. 1198 (MRS); Stephen de Hovetone, Engl. c. 1272 (RH).

Howel. 1. Bartholomew Hoel, Normandy 1189–95 (MRS); 2. a Cambro-Celtic name. See also HOLE.

Howes, for HOUSE.

290

Howeth, for HOWETT.

Howett, for HEWETT (Lower).

Howis, for HOWES.

Howitt, for HEWETT (Lower).

Howley. Gislebert de Houlei, Norm. 1198 (MRS). John Houle, Engl. c. 1272 (RH). Hence William Howley, Archbishop of Canterbury.

Hows. See HOUSE.

Howse. See HOUSE.

Howson. Roger Housin, Norm. 1198 (MRS).

Hoyland. See HOLLAND.

Hoyle, for Hoel. See HOILE.

Hoyle. See HOILE.

Hoyte, for Huet. See HEWETT.

Huband, for Hubald or Huband, armorially identified. Radulphus Hubout or Hubolt, Norm. 1198 (MRS); Adam and Robert Hubald, Engl. c. 1199 (RCR).

Hubbard or HUBERT. Roger, Ralph Hubert, Normandy, 1180, &c. (MRS). Henry, John, Nicholas H. Engl. c. 1272 (RH).

Hubberd. See HUBBARD.

Hubbert. See HUBBARD.

Hubble, for HUBEL.

Hubel, a foreign name, not identified. The arms of Hoble remain in Robson.

Huber, for HUBERT.

Hubert. See HUBBARD.

Hucker, for HOOKER.

Huckle, for Hogel. Radulfus Hogel, Normandy 1180–95 (MRS); Richard Hockele, Engl. c. 1272 (RH).

Huckvale or Huckville. William and Simon de Hugerville, Roger de Huglevilla, Norm. 1180–98 (MRS). The family was seated in Devon.

Huddard. Richard Hetart, Normandy, 1198 (MRS).

Huddert. Roger Odard, Norm. 1189–95 (MRS).

Huddy. *See* HODY.

Hudson. Nicholas Heudesent, Norm. 1198 (MRS). Of this family are the Baronets Hudson, now Palmer.

Huelin. *See* WHELLING.

Huffell, or Heuville. Geoffry de Heuville, Norm. 1198 (MRS).

Huggard, for HOGGARD.

Huggett. Petrus Hugot, Norm. 1198 (MRS).

Hughan. Robert Huan, Norm. 1180-95; John Huene, Engl. c. 1272 (RH); Roger, William Huan, Norm. 1198 (MRS).

Hughes, generally Cambro-Celtic; but occasionally for Huse, a form of Hoese or HUSSEY.

Hughesman, for HOUSEMAN.

Hugo. Petrus Hugot, Norm. 1198 (MRS); Henry, Robert, John H., Eng. c. 1272 (RH).

Hugoe, for HUGO.

Huitson, for HEWSON.

Hulbert. *See* ILBERT.

Hulburd, for HULBURT.

Hulme. Robert and William de Hulmo, Simon de H., Normandy 1180-98 (MRS); Malger, Richard, William de Hulmo, Eng. 1189 (Rot. Pip.).

Hulse, for Huse, Howse, or HUSSEY. It bears the arms of Howes, which is armorially identified with Hussey. Geoffry de Hosa was of Berks 1194 (RCR), and 1201 (Hardy, Obl. et fin.). In 13th cent. Bartholomew de la Huse was of the same county (Testa); and in 1322 Peter de la Huse or Hoese was returned from Berks for Knight Service (PPW). The family of Hulse is a branch, as appears by its arms. Hence the baronets of the name.

Hulse, or Houssay. Godfrey, Richard, Robert, Osbert de Houseio, or Holseio, Norm. 1198 (MRS); armorially identified with HOWES.

Humbert. *See* IMBERT.

Humfrey. *See* HOMFRAY.

Humphery. *See* HOMFRAY.

Humphrey. *See* HOMFRAY.

Hunt. Robert Le Huant, Normandy 1198 (MRS). Hence the Baronets De Vere (Hunt).

Hunter, the English form of Venator or le Veneur. Arnulph, Gilbert, Geoffry, Hugh, Richard, &c., Venator, Normandy 1180-95 (MRS). Families of this name are considered to be generally Norman (Lower).

Huntley, or Fitz-Baderon. William Fitz-Baderon held the barony of Monmouth, including 22 lordships, 1086 (Domesd.), and had, 1. Wyenoc, father of Gilbert, whose son Balderon held the barony 1165, from whom descended John de Monmouth, t. Henry III. 2. Balderon, ancestor of the Huntleys. He, with his son John Trone, witnessed a charter of Wyenoc of Monmouth (Mon. Angl. i. 600). Balderon is mentioned as brother of Wyenoc (Ib.). In the next generation Richard de Huntilande or Huntley held, 1165, with Balderon of Monmouth, a knight's fee from the See of Hereford (Lib. Niger). In the time of King John, Walter de Huntley held Hope Maloysel from John, Baron of Monmouth, and it was held of him by the Abbey of Gloucester (Testa, 63). Thomas de H., t. Henry III., witnessed a charter of the same Baron (Mon. Angl. i. 601).

The ancestor of this house, William Fitz-Baderon or Baldran, appears to have been a scion of the lords or princes of Jarnac, in Angoumois and Saintonge, probably of Gothic race. In 973 Hugh, a son of this house, was Bishop of Angoulême (Bouquet, x. 248). Wardrade Loriches, Prince of Jarnac, with his wife Rixindis, founded the Abbey of Bassac, Saintonge, 1014 (Vigier de la Pile, Hist. Angoumois, ii. 19). He was succeeded by his nephew Baudran or Baldran, Prince of Jarnac, who had issue, 1. Peter (Gall. Christ. xiv. 151 instr.), ancestor of a powerful line of princes or lords of Jarnac, which became extinct; 2. William Fitz-Baldran, Baron of Monmouth 1086.

Huntsman. *See* HUNTER.

Hurle, for HURRELL.

Hurlin, from Hurlon-Sarqueri, Normandy (Mém. Soc. Ant. Norm. v. 189).

Hurn. *See* HEARN.

Hurndall, for ARUNDELL.

Hurran, for HURN.

Hurrell. *See* HORRELL.

Hurren. *See* HURN.

Hurry. *See* HORRY.

Hurt, for HART or Hert.

Husbands. *See* HUBAND.

Husey. *See* HUSSEY.

Huson, for HEWSON.

Hussey. *See* HOSE.

Husson, for HUSON.

Hutcheon. *See* HUTCHINGS.

Hutchens. *See* HUTCHINGS.

Hutchence. *See* HUTCHINGS.

Hutchings. *See* HOUCHIN.

Hutchins. *See* HUTCHINGS.

Hutson, for HUDSON.

Hutt, for HETT. Hence the Baronets HUTT.

Hutton. Alan Bussel, of Hoton, York, witness to a charter 1153 (Mon. i. 916, 917). Robert de Hoton witnessed a charter of William Fitz-Fulco to Hoton Priory, York, and Humphry de H. witnessed a charter of Ernald de Percy to the same (Mon. i. 84). The name changed to Hutton.

Hyatt. *See* HOYTE.

Hyett. *See* HYATT.

Hyland, for Hoyland, or HOLLAND.

Hymns, for Hesmes, or AMES.

I

Ibbetson, for Abison. *See* IVISON.

Ibbett, for IVETT.

Ibbs, for EBBS.

Ibbotson. *See* IBBETSON. Of this family are the Baronets SELWYN-IBBOTSON.

Ibison, for Abison. *See* IVISON.

Ibotson, for Abison. *See* IVISON.

Ife. *See* IVE.

Ikin, for Eykin, AIKIN.

Ilbert, or Helbert. Geoffry, Heldebert, and Restoldus H., Norm. 1180 (MRS). *See* ALBERT.

Iles, or Isle, armorially identified with several branches of LISLE.

Ilett, for AYLETT.

Ilott, for AYLOTT.

Imbert, probably foreign, but not identified.

Imeson. *See* EMPSON.

Imray, for EMERY.

Imrie, or Imbrie, for EMERY, from the arms.

Ims, for AMES.

Ingall, for Angall, or ANGELL.

Ingamells, for Angerville. Benedict, Robert, William, &c., De Angervilla, Normandy 1180–95 (MRS).

Ingarfield, from Ingarville, Normandy. Geoffry Ingarville, and Richard I. 1180–95 (MRS).

Ingle, for ANGLE.

Ingleheart. William Engeart, Normandy 1180–95 (MRS). Isabel Ingelard, Eng. c. 1272 (RH).

Inglish, for INGLIS.

Inglis, or Anglicus. *See* ENGLISH. This family was early seated in Scotland; Ralph Anglicus being witness, 1110, to the foundation charter of Kelso (Chart. Kelso, Ed. Bannatyne). The Baronets Inglis were of this family.

Ingpen, or De Sauquemont, from Saumont, near Gournay. Peter de Sukemond granted his lands at Ingpenn to Tichfield Abbey — grant witnessed by Nicolas Fitz-Gervas de Ingpenn (Mon. Angl. ii. 663). This name frequently occurs in the Rolls of Parliament, t. Edward I.

Ingram. Robert Engerranus, Gervasius E., Brumes, William E., Normandy 1180–98 (MRS). William Ingelram, 1103, witnessed a charter of Philip de Braiose (Mon. ii. 973). John I. was of Yorkshire 1130 (Rot. Pip.). Walter Engelram was witness to the foundation charter of Hoton P., York (Mon. i. 840). The Viscounts Irvine were of this family.

Innocent, for HINSON, or Enson.

Innes. This family derives from Beroaldus Flandrensis, who had a grant from Malcolm IV. of Scotland (12th cent.), of the barony of Innes and Easter Urchard in Elgin (Douglas). The name Beroald appears to have been peculiar to the Counts of Egmond, Flanders, descendants probably of Theodoric, Count of Friesland in 923, who had a grant of Egmond. Beroaldus de Egmond d. 1093, Beroald his son in 1114, and Beroald his son was living 1143 (Art de Vérif. les Dates, xv. 112, xiv. 417). The latter had issue,

1. Dodo, ancestor of the Counts of Egmont, Dukes of Gueldres; 2. probably, Beroald de Innes. From this family descend the Dukes of Roxburgh, and the Baronets Innes.

Inns, for INNES.

Ionn, for ION.

Ion. William, Alexander De Aion, Normandy, 1180–95 (MRS). Richard Ion, Engl. c. 1272 (RH).

Irby, or De Amondeville, from A. near Caen. In 1066 two brothers came to England: 1. Nigel de A., ancestor of the barons of Folkstone; 2. Roger de A., seneschal to Remigius, bishop of Lincoln. John, his son, occurs 1130. Walter de A. was Viscount of Lincoln, 1156; and 1165 his son William de Amundeville held Irby from the barony of Craon, and three other fees from De Senlis (Lib. Niger). Temp. John, William de Ireby m. the dau. and heir of Fitz-Odard of Cumberland (Testa). Their descendants bore the arms of Amondeville, azure fretty or, merely altering the tinctures. Hence the Irbys, Lords Boston.

Ireland. Ralph de Hibernia, Normandy, 1180 (MRS); Richard Hiberniensis, brother of Thomas Fitz-Adam; occur t. John (Hardy, Rot. de Libert. 232). Adam de Hibernia was witness to a charter of Whalley Abbey, Lancaster, 1316 (Mon. i. 305), and 1324 was summoned to a great Council at Westminster (Palgr. Parl. Writs).

Irish, or Ireys, for HERIZ.

Iron. *See* IRONS.

Irons, from Airan, Normandy (Lower). Gervasius de Airan, Norm. 1180–95 (MRS).

Irton, or Ireton, a branch of ENSOR and SHIRLEY.

Isbel. N. Isabella, Normandy,

1180-95 (MRS); Richard and William Fitz-Isabell, Engl. c. 1272 (RH).

Isbister, perhaps for Ilbister or ALABASTER.

Isier, for OISELEUR. *See* OSLER.

Isles, or LISLE.

Ismay, for Esmay or Esme, a form of Esmes or Hieames. *See* AMES.

Ison. William de Aison, Normandy, 1180 (MRS); John de Eisenne, Engl. c. 1272 (RH).

Ivall, for Eyville. *See* CRAVEN.

Ivatt, or IVAS. *See* IVES.

Ivatts, for IVATT.

Ivers. *See* IVOR.

Ive. Radulphus, Mangot, Osbert Ivas, or Ivata, Normandy, 1180-95 (MRS); Reginald Ivaus, Geoffry, Ralph Ive, &c., Engl. c. 1272 (RH).

Ives. *See* IVE.

Ivey. *See* IVY.

Ivey, the English pronunciation of Ivet or Ivetta. *See* IVE.

Ivimey, a corruption of Evermue. Joscelin de Evermou, Normandy, 1180 (MRS); Rainer de Evermou, Engl. 1130 (Rot. Pip.); Alicia de E., Engl. c. 1272 (RH). Evermue was Yarmouth, but the family was Norman.

Ivimy. *See* IVIMEY.

Ivison, for Avison, or Abison, from Abison, Aquitaine. King John, 1213, gave direction to the Viscount of Abison regarding certain affairs at Limoges (Hardy, Rot. Claus.); Peter de Abiscon was of Salop, c. 1272 (RH).

Ivor. William Iver, Normandy, 1180-95 (MRS).

Ivory. *See* EVORY.

Ivy, from Ivoi, near Namur. Geoffry de Ivoi had a pardon in Oxfordshire 1156, and Geoffry de Ivei occurs 1157 (Rot. Pip.).

Izant, for Esson, from E. Normandy (MRS). William de Esson, 1198.

Izard, from Essarts, Normandy. Radulphus de Essartia, and Mauger, Normandy, 1180-98 (MRS).

Izod, for IZARD.

Izzant. *See* IZARD.

J

Jack, for Jacques or Jacobus (Lower). Adam Jacob, Normandy, 1180-95; Jacobus J., 1198 (MRS); Geoffry, Henry, Jordan Jacob; William Jak, Engl., c. 1272 (RH).

Jackes. *See* JACK.

Jacks. *See* JACK.

Jackson, a name of the family of LASCELLES, but includes many other families.

Jacob. *See* JACK.

Jacques. *See* JACK.

Jaeger, for JAGER.

Jaffray, or Goffroi. *See* GODFREY.

Jager. *See* JAGGARD.

Jaggard, or Jacquard, foreign, but not identified.

Jagger, for JAGGARD.

Jaggers, for JAGGER.

Jagget, for JAGGARD.

Jaggs, for JAQUES.

Jago, for JACOB.

Jakins, or Jaquin. N. Jaquinus, of Normandy, t. Phil. August. (Mém. Soc. Ant. Norm. v. 181).

James. 1. From St. James, Normandy. Richard de St. Jacobo, 1180-95 (MRS); Hasculph, son of

Hasculph de St. Jacobo, Engl. 1180 (Rot. Pip.). 2. A patronymic, chiefly Cambro-Celtic.

Jandrell, for JAUDRELL.

Jane, for JANES.

Janes, for Genes, or GENNYS. Philip and Roger de Geneiz, Normandy, 1180-95; Philip de Genez, 1198 (MRS).

Jaques. See JACQUES.

Jardine, for GARDEN. Hence the baronets of the name.

Jarmaine. See GERMAINE.

Jarman. See GERMAINE.

Jarratt. See JARRETT.

Jarred, for JARRETT.

Jarrett. See GARETT.

Jarritt, for JARRETT.

Jarrold, for GEROLD.

Jarvie, for GERVIS.

Jarvis. Richard Gervasius, Norm. and N. Gervasius, 1180-95; Fulco G., 1198 (MRS); Robert Gerveis, Engl., c. 1199 (RCR).

Jary, for Gary. See GEARY.

Jason, for CASSON.

Jauncey, for CHAUNCEY.

Javal. Roger Javala, Normandy, 1198 (MRS).

Javal, for Jarville, or Jarpenville, from Jarpenville, near Yvetot. Geoffry de J. held lands in Essex, 1165 (Lib. Nig.). In 1322 Henry de J. was summoned from Bucks for the war, Scotland. 1325 Roger de J. summoned to serve in Guienne under Earl of Warrenne (Palgr. P. Writs).

Javan, for Chabannes. See CABAN.

Javens, for Chabannes. See CABAN.

Jay, for GAY.

Jaye, for GAYE.

Jayes, for JAYE.

Jeakes, for JACQUES.

Jeakins, for JAKINS.

Jeal, or JALE, for GALE.

Jean, for JANE.

Jeanes, for JANES.

Jeanne, for JANE.

Jeanneret, apparently foreign.

Jeanes, for JANES.

Jeans, for JANES.

Jeapes, for Chapes. See COPE.

Jearred, for JARRED.

Jearum, for Geron. Robert Geron, Normandy, 1180-95 (MRS); Ralph Gerun, Engl., c. 1272 (RH).

Jeavons, for Jevone or Joven. See YOUNG.

Jebb, for Guebb, or GIBB. Hence the eminent and learned Bishop Jebb.

Jeckell. See JEKYLL.

Jecks, for JAQUES.

Jeckyll. See JEKYLL.

Jee, for JAY.

Jeems, for JAMES.

Jeeves, or Jeffs. Peter de Cheef, Normandy, 1180-95 (MRS).

Jefferay. See GODFREY.

Jefferey. See GODFREY.

Jeffries. See JEFFEREY.

Jefferies. See JEFFEREY.

Jefferis, for JEFFEREY.

Jeffery, for JEFFEREY.

Jefferys, for JEFFEREY.

Jeffree, for JEFFEREY.

Jeffrey, for JEFFEREY.

Jeffs. See JEEVES.

Jehu, or Jew. William de Juis, Henry, and Robert, Norm., 1180-95; Mauger, Osbert, Juas, 1198 (MRS); Thomas Jeu, England, c. 1272 (RH). This family gave name to Market Jew, Cornwall.

Jekyl, or Jackel. William Jackel, Normandy, 1180-95; and the fief of Jacle (MRS); John Jocel, 1198 (Ib.); William and Richard de Jakele, Engl. c. 1272 (RH).

Jelen, for CHALLEN.

Jelf, for Jellif. *See* JOLLIFFE (Lower).

Jell, for Gell, or GALL.

Jelley, for Joli, or JOLLIFFE (Lower).

Jemmett. Robin, John, William, Jamet of Normandy, mentioned t. Henry V. (Mém. Soc. Ant. Norm. v. 216, 279).

Jenet. Durand Chenet, Normandy, 1180 (MRS); Walter, William Gent, England, c. 1272 (RH).

Jenn, for JANE.

Jennens, for JENNINGS.

Jenner, from Gener. *See* GAYNAR. Of this family are the baronets Jenner.

Jennett, armorially identified with Genet. Durand Chenet, of Normandy, 1180 (MRS).

Jennette, for JENNETT.

Jenning, from Genon, or Canon. Petrus de Canon or Kanon, Normandy, 1198 (MRS); Richard Chanum, Engl. c. 1199 (RCR); Henry, Walter, Canoun, c. 1272 (RH). The name became Chanon, and Chenoun, thence Jenun, or Jenning.

Jennings, for JENNING.

Jenour. *See* JENNER.

Jentle, for GENTLE.

Jepp. *See* JEPPS.

Jepps, for Gapp. *See* GAPE.

Jerdein, for JARDINE.

Jeremiah, for JEREMY.

Jeremy, for JERMY.

Jermey, for JERMY.

Jermy, armorially identified with Jermyn or GERMAINE.

Jerningham, or Jernegan, descends from the Lords of Pontchateau, Bretagne, of whom Daniel le Rich was living, c. 1020, and Jarnegan Fitz-Daniel, who also witnessed a charter in 1060 (Lobineau, Hist. Bret. ii. 171). The latter had,

1, Daniel Fitz-Jarnegan, Lord of Pontchateau, 1080, ancestor of that noble family (Des Bois); 2, Ludovicus Fitz-Jarnegan, who witnessed a charter, 1065 (Morice, H. B. preuves, i. 426); 3, Jarnegan. The latter occurs in Bretagne, 1083, as 'Jarnegan forestarius' (Morice, 457), and in 1086 held lands as Jarnacot, Suffolk. Hugo his son had Hubert de Jarnegan, 1165 (Lib. Nig.), of Suffolk, whence the Jerninghams, Lords Stafford.

Jerome. *See* JEARUM.

Jerram. *See* JEROME.

Jerrard. *See* GERRARD.

Jervis. *See* GERVIS. Hence the brave admiral, the Earl of St. Vincent.

Jerwood. *See* JARROD.

Jesmei, probably for Chesmy, or CHESNEY.

Jessamy, perhaps for Chesmey, or CHESNEY. *See* JESSMEI.

Jesse, for CHASE, or CASS.

Jessett, for Gessett, or GUEST.

Jessey. *See* JESSE.

Jesson, for JASON.

Jeune, or Le Jovene. William, Robert Juven or Juvenis, Norm. 1180-95 (MRS); Adam, Henry, &c., Le Juvene, Engl. c. 1272 (RH). The name includes different families. *See* YOUNG.

Jeves. *See* JEEVES.

Jewell, John, Bishop of Salisbury, the famous divine, was born at Bowdon, Devon, where the family of Juel or Fitz-Joel had been long resident. A Juell occurs c. 1450 (Pole, Devon, 375), and in 1242 Warin Fitz-Juel held a knight's fee, which had been granted by the Earl of Mortaine at the Conquest (Testa de Neville, 184). Thomas Fitz-Juel at the same time held lands from the Barony of Totness (Ib. 176). The Jewells descended from a younger son of this line.

This family derived probably from Juel or Judael de Mayenne, Baron of Totness and Barnstaple, t. William I. (*see* MAYNE, MAINE), a Breton noble. · He held lands from the Earl of Mortaine, besides his own barony; and a portion of the former, as well as a fief created in the Barony of Totness, seems to have passed to the younger branch named Fitz-Juel. The name of Juel long continued in the descendants of Judael de Mayenne.

Jewell. Helias and Robert Juels, Normandy, 1180–95 (MRS); William Joel, &c., Engl. c. 1272 (RH).

Jewett, or Guet. Geoffry Guuit, Normandy, 1180–95 (MRS); Matilda Joute, Richard Joyet, William Juet, Engl. c. 1272 (RH).

Jewiss, for Jewes or Jew. *See* JEHU.

Jewitt. *See* JEWETT. ·

Jewson, for JESSON.

Jex, for JEEKS.

Jeyes, for JOY.

Jibb, for JEBB.

Jiggens, probably Chigon, or Cigony.

Joblings, from Jublains, Mayenne (Lower).

Jocelyn, a branch of the Barons of Briquebec: *see* MITFORD. The first Baron of B. had two sons: Oslac, ancestor of the Barons of B.; 2, Amfrid the Dane. The latter had two sons, Turstan Goz, ancestor of the house of Avranches, Earls of Chester, and William. The latter was Baron of Bec and ancestor of the Barons of Bec-Crespin. His son or grandson, Gilbert Crespin, Baron of B. and Castellan of Tilli-

eres, aided 1034 in founding the Abbey of Bec. He had, 1, William, 2, Gilbert de Tillieres. William II. of Bec supported Duke William against the French in 1054 (Wace, ii. 73), and came to England 1066. He had, 1, William; 2, Gislebert, Abbot of Westminster; 3, Milo, a great baron 1086, who d. s. p. William III. of Bec had Jocelyn Crispin, Baron of Bec, who combated Henry I. at the Battle of Nogent, but was pardoned. In 1158 he paid fines for his lands in Essex and Hertford (Rot. Pip.). In 1165 he still possessed Bec, but is not mentioned in England, having transferred his estates to his younger sons, William and Robert. Of these, William Fitz-Jocelyn, 1165, held two fees in Essex, and Robert Fitz-Jocelyn one in Hertford (Lib. Nig.). The former had issue Richard Fitz-William, who occurs in Essex and Herts, 1203 (Rot. Canc.). Jocelyn Fitz-Richard, his son, occurs in Hertford (RCR); and William Fitz-Richard held the estates in Essex, 1236 (Testa), which, however, appear to have passed to the descendants of Jocelyn.

Thomas Jocelyn of Herts, 1248, acquired Hyde in that county by marriage (Morant, i. 466). Ralph, his son and heir, in 1315 was assessor of aids in Herts (PPW). His descendants always held estates in Essex and Herts (Morant), and from them descended Robert Jocelyn of Hyde, Lord Chancellor of Ireland, ancestor of the Earls of Roden. Genealogists have furnished a fabulous pedigree for this family.

Joel. *See* JEWELL.

John. 1, Hugh and Ralph Joannes, Norm. 1198 (MRS); Thomas, John, Alicia Joannes, Engl. c. 1272 (RH); 2, for St. John.

Johns. See John.

Jollands, or Jollans, for Challens. See Challen.

Jolley. See Jolliffe.

Jolliff. See Jolliffe.

Jolliffe. N. Giolif of Normandy, 1195 (MRS); Robert Jolif, 1198 (Ib.). In 1295 William Jolyf was bailsman for the M.P. for Thirsk, and 1305 Robert Jolyf for the M.P. for Arundel (PPW). Hence the Lords Hylton.

Joly. See Jolly.

Jordain, for Jordan.

Jordan. Richard, Robert, William Jordanus, Norm. 1198 (MRS); Martin, Ralph, Robert Jordan, &c., Engl. c. 1272 (RH).

Jordon, for Jordan.

Jory, for Jury.

Joselin, for Jocelyn.

Josland, for Joselin.

Joslin, for Jocelyn.

Josolyne, for Jocelyn.

Jost, or Just, for Gost. See Gossett.

Josselin, for Jocelyn.

Josslyn, for Jocelyn.

Joule, for Jull.

Jourdain, for Jordain.

Jourdan, for Jordan.

Jowers, for Jorz, near Falaise, Normandy. The Sire de Jort was at Hastings (Wace, Pluquet, ii. 245); Galfridus de Jorz, Engl. c. 1272 (RH). See Gorst.

Jowett. See Jewett.

Jowitt. See Jewett.

Joy. Ralph le Goie or Goix, and Geoffry, Norm. 1180–95 (MRS). Reginald and William le Goix 1198 (Ib.).

Joy, from Goi or Gouy, near Evreux. Hugh de Goi 1148, held

lands at Winchester (Wint. Domesd.). John de Joe 1165, held lands in the Viscounties of Pont-Audemer and Beaumont, and Helto de Jay one fee from Geoffry de Ver, Salop (Lib. Nig.).

Joyce, a form of Jorz or Gorst. The family of Joyce or de Jorse t. Edward I., obtained extensive possessions in West Connaught by m. with the O'Flahertys, where their descendants remain in Joyce's country.

Joyce or Joce. William Fitz-Joce Normandy 1080–98, England 1199 (MRS; RCR). He was of co. of Northampton.

Joynes, for Gines, or Gennys.

Joynes, or Geynes. See Gennys.

Judd, for Jude.

Jude, for Jew. See Jehu.

Juden, for Jurdan, or Jordan.

Judge, for Goodge or Gooch.

Jukes or Jokes, for Chokes, or de Chokes. See Chucks.

Julian. 1. St. Julian, from St. J. Normandy (MRS); 2. a patronymic.

Julien, for Julian.

Juller or Jeweller. Ranulph and Alan Joculator, Norm. 1180–95 (MRS).

Jull, for Jule, or Jewell.

Julyan, for Julian.

Junior. Walter and Bernard Junior, Norm. 1198 (MRS).

Juniper, for Chenefar, probably foreign. William de Chenefara occurs in Leicester and Warwick 1130 (Rot. Pip.).

Junner, for Jenner.

Jupp, for Jepp, or Gapp.

Jury, for Ivry. See Every.

Just, for Jost.

Justice. Probably from La Justice, Normandy (MRS); but not identified.

Juxon, Euxton, or De Grelly.
William Juxon, Archbishop of
Canterbury, son of Richard Juxton
(d. 1583), whose father John Juxton of London probably came from
Lancashire. The name of Juxton
or Euxton occurs there as late as
1641 (Ducat. Lancastr. i. 105).
The Manor of Euxton was acquired
t. Edw. I. by a branch of the Hollands by m. with an heiress of the
Buscels. In 1323 it was held by
William Holland de Eukestone.

The name was adopted by a younger
branch of the Hollands, for they bore
orig. a cross between four Moors'
heads for difference—the Hollands
bearing a cross. The Hollands were
a branch of the De Grellys or Greslets, Barons of Manchester, who came
with Robert de Poitou t. William I.,
and who also bore a cross. The
name Holland was derived from H.
near Wigan (Robson; Baines, Hist.
Lanc. ii. 187).

K

Kail, or Kayle, or Cayle, armorially identified with CAYLEY.

Kain, for Kaines, or De Keyneto.
Herbert de Cahaignes, William Cahaines, Normandy 1180-95 (MRS);
William Cahaignis, England 1189;
WilliamFitz-RicharddeC.(Rot.Pip.).

Kamman, for GAMMAN.

Karet, for GARET.

Karpen, for Carpen, Carben, or
CARBINE.

Karr, for CARR.

Karslake, for Carslacke, or Carsacke (armorially identified), from
Carsac in Perigord, Aquitaine.

Kates. See CATTS.

Kay, armorially identified with
Cay and GAY.

Kaye. See KAY.

Kays, for KAY.

Keable, for KEBBEL.

Keast, for Gest, or GUEST.

Keat, for Cate, or CATT.

Keatch, for KEATES.

Keates, for KEATE.

Keats, for KEATE. Hence Keats,
the poet.

Keays, for KAYS.

Kebbel, for CABBEL.

Kebbell, for KEBBEL.

Kebble, for KEBBEL.

Keble. See KEBBEL. Hence the
Christian poet Keble.

Keeble. See KEBBEL.

Keel, for KAIL, armorially identified.

Keele, for KEEL.

Keep, for Cape, or CAPES.

Keeson, for Cason, or CASSON.

Keeton, for CATON.

Keeys, for KEAYS.

Kefford, for GIFFORD.

Keil, for KAIL.

Keirie. See KYRLE.

Kell. See CAIL (Lower).

Kellaway. William de Callouey
witness to a charter of Robert de
Gouiz, Normandy 1190 (Mém. Soc.
Ant. Norm. v. 199).

Kellow. Ralph and Peter Galot,
Norm. 1180-95 (MRS). Walter
Gelay, Engl. c. 1199 (RCR).

Kett, for Cate or CATT.

Kemball. See KNATCHBULL.

Kembell. *See* KNATCHBULL.

Kemble. *See* KNATCHBULL.

Kerly, for Kerle, or KYRLE.

Kerley, for Kerle, or KYRLE.

Kemmish, for Camoys or Kames, a branch of the De Umfravilles, descended from Martin Sire de Tours, Normandy, one of that house.

Kemp. Walter de Campe, Campis, or Des Camps, Ingulf, Radulphus, Gaufridus, Gervasius, Helta, Richard, Wymarc, of Normandy 1180-98 (MRS). John and Matthew de Campes Engl. c. 1199 (RCR). John de C. was of Essex, and 1324 Roger Kempe was of Suffolk (PPW). Hence the baronets Kempe.

Kempe, for KEMP.

Kempster, for Cambistor. *See* GAMBSTER.

Kempt, for KEMP.

Kennell, for Chenel, or CHANNELL.

Kentain, for Kintan, Quentin, or QUINTIN.

Kentfield, for Centeville or Sequainville. In 1324 John de Centeville returned from Somerset to attend a great council at Westminster (PPW). Sir Richard de Ceintval of Oxford c. 1300 (Ib.). William de Cestvill 13th cent. held lands in Kent (Testa).

Kenny. Autoel de Kaigny, and Hugo de K. 1180-95; Brusli and Guerold de Kani 1198, Normandy (MRS).

Ker. *See* KERR.

Kerdel. *See* CORDELL.

Kerr. The origin of this family has not hitherto been traced; it appears to be a branch of the Norman house of Espec. Ranulph Espec held lands at Aunou and Astelle, Normandy, from the barony of Albini c. 1080. In 1056 they

300

were granted, with consent of his sons, to Essay Abbey (Gall. Christ. xi. 236 Instr.).

Of these sons, William Espec was a great Baron in England 1086, and his brothers Walter and Richard occur.

Walter Espec, his son, t. Henry I. possessed estates in York and Northumberland, and on the death of his son he founded Kirkham Abbey, to which he gave the Church of Carr on Tweed (Burton, Mon. Ebor.). The lordship, however, appears to have been granted to Walter Espec, brother of William, whose sons Robert and William de Carum (Carr or Kerr) held it t. Henry I.; for the former 1165 returned his barony as one fee held by him and his brother t. Henry I. (Lib. Nig.). Walter de Carum, his son, was deceased before 1207 (Hardy, Obl. et Fin.). Thomas de Carro, his son, was father of William, whose son Richard Fitz-William, with Michael Ker and John Ker (his kinsmen), paid scutage together in Northumberland. This Richard Fitz-William Carr or Ker was seated in Scotland before 1249, as appears by the Chartulary of Melrose (i. 232). His son was father of, 1. Ralph, living 1330; 2. John Kerr of Selkirk Forest, living 1357, ancestor of the Kerrs of Cessford, Earls and Dukes of Roxburgh. Ralph held lands from the Earl of Douglas, named after him Kersheugh. From him (who d. c. 1350) descended the Kers of Fernihurst, Earls and Marquises of Lothian.

Kerrell, for Kerell, or KYRLE.

Kerrey, for CAREY.

Kerslake. *See* KARSLAKE.

Kerry, for Carri or CARY.

Kerry. Radulphus de] Kirie, Normandy 1180–95 (MRS).

Kerrison, or Kerdeston, from K. in Norfolk, the estate of Geoffry Baynard or De Beaumont, t. William I. (*See* BEAUMONT.) He granted his tithes at Kerdeston to Castle-Acre Priory (Mon. i. 646). Roger de Kerdeston (son of Geoffry), and William, his son, frequently occur in the records. From them lineally descended (the evidences being full throughout) William, son of Sir Roger de Kerdeston, who m. Margaret, sister and heir of Gilbert de Gand, Baron of Folkingham, and 1281 had a writ of military summons (PPW). Roger de K. was summoned to Parliament by writ 1331, from whom descended the Lords Kerdeston. Various branches continued in Norfolk, whose names gradually became changed to Kerrison. Hence the Baronets Kerrison.

Kettle. Anscher and William Ketel, Normandy, 1198 (MRS); Geoffry Fitz-Ketel, Engl. 1199 (RCR); Geoffry, Henry, Roger Ketel, Ib. c. 1272 (RH).

Kew, for Cayou or Le Ku.

Kewell, from Keuel, Kevell, or CAVILLE.

Kewer, for CURE.

Key, for KAY.

Keybead, the corruption of some foreign name, perhaps Cabot.

Keyes, for KEY.

Keys, for KEY.

Keysell, for Kessel, or CECIL.

Keyte, for KEAT.

Kibbels, for KEBLE.

Kibble, for KEBLE.

Kidd, written Kede, c. 1272, in England (RH); probably a form of CADE.

Kiddell. Muriel and Odelina de Kidel, Normandy, 1180–95 (MRS).

Kiddle. *See* KIDDELL.

Kidds, for KIDD.

Kiell, for KEEL.

Kifford, for GIFFORD.

Kight. *See* KITE.

Kilberd, for GILBERT.

Kilbey, for Killebue, or Quilleboeuf, from Quilleboeuf, Normandy. Robert de Kilebeuf, 1180 (MRS).

Kilby. *See* KILBEY.

Killby. *See* KILBY.

Killett, for GILLETT.

Killinger, for CHALLENGER.

Killingsworth. *See* CHILLINGWORTH.

Killon, for GILLON.

Kilpin, for GILPIN.

Kilsby, for KILBY.

Kilvert. *See* CALVERT.

Kimbel, for KEMBLE.

Kimbell, for KEMBLE.

Kimble. *See* KEMBLE.

Kimmins, for CUMMINS.

Kimmis, for Cameys, or KEMMISH.

Kindell, for Candel, or Candela. *See* ANSTRUTHER.

King. Roger le Roi, William le Rei, Roger, Odo, Robert, Norm. 1180–95 (MRS).

King. William, Gislebert, Roger, Gerald, Walter, Geoffry, Herbert Rex or le Roy, Normandy, 1180–95 (MRS); also Durand, Hugo, Peter, Ralph, Richard, Robert, Roger, Theobald, Walter, William Rex, 1198 (MRS). Of these, Roger King occurs in Middlesex 1199 (RCR); Adam and John Rex, Engl. c. 1272 (RH). The great number of this name in Normandy explains the number in England. Hence the Earls of Kingston and Lovelace, and the Baronets King.

Kinepple, for Kenebel. *See* **Knatchbull.**

Kinnell, for Chenell. *See* CHAN-NELL.

Kinninmont. William Quiene-ment, Norm. 1180 (MRS). The arms of a Scottish branch as well as an English occur in Robson.

Kinns, for KEYNES.

Kinsey, or Kensey, from Cansey, Canci. *See* CHAUNCY.

Kinze, from KINSEY.

Kipling, for Kapling, or Capelin. *See* CHAPLIN.

Kipps, for CAPPS.

Kirk, or Quirk. Geoffry, Oliver, Golnir de Quercu, Norm. 1180–95; Geoff., Oliver, Ranulph, 1198 (MRS); Nicolas, and William de Quercu, Engl. 1189 (Rot. Pip.).

Kirke. *See* KIRK.

Kiss, for KEYS.

Kissell, for Kessel, or CECIL.

Kite, for KEYTE, armorially iden-tified. *See* KEATE.

Kittle. *See* KETTLE.

Kitto, for CATO.

Kittoe. *See* KITTO.

Kiver, for COVER, or COVERT.

Knapp, for Knapwell, or Kenap-peville. Emma, John, Robert, Wil-liam de K., Normandy, 1180–98 (MRS); John Knappe, John and William de Knappewell, Engl., c. 1272 (RH).

Kenyon, or Banastre. Warin B. was baron of Newton, Lancashire, t. William I. Lawton within that barony was held, t. Henry II., by Adam de Lawton, whose descend-ants bore a modification of the Banastre arms (probably as a younger branch). William de L., his son, had, besides other issue, Jordan, who took the name of Kenyon from that manor in Lancashire, and whose descendants bore the same arms with slight difference. Hence

302

the eminent Lord Chief Justice Ken-yon and the Lords Kenyon.

Knatchbull, or De Molbec, from M. in the Cotentin. Hugh de Mol-bec held Chenebella, Bucks, from Walter Giffard, 1086 (Domesd.). His descendants were named De Kenebel, Kenebol, Kenetbole, Ken-echbole, and Knatchbull. In 1165 Matilda de [Mol]bec held a fee from Earl Walter Giffard, Humphry de Kenebelle (her son), in Gloucester, and William Fitz-Matilda, another son, four fees in Bucks, from Earl Walter (Liber Niger). In 1205 Adam de Kent paid a fine to have custody of the land and heirs of Hugh de Kenebel in Kent and Bucks (Hardy, Obl. et Fin.). The Viscounts of Kent and Bucks were informed 1217 that John de Kenebell had returned to his allegiance (Hardy, Rot. Claus. 327). Temp. Richard II. Kenebel, Bucks, was styled 'Gentbole' (Hunter, Fines, 172), and in Kent the name had become Kenechbole t. Henry VIII., as ap-pears in the records. The name of Kemble is the modern form of Kenebel, and the arms of Kemble bear resemblance to those of Knatch-bull.

Knebel, for Kenebel. *See* KNATCH-BULL.

Knell, for Canell. *See* CHAN-NELL.

Knevitt, or Canivet. William and Richard de Kenivet, Norm. 1180–95 (MRS). From St. Pierre de Canivet. John Knyvet 1316 was possessed of estates in Cambridge (PPW). The Lords Knyvett and Baronets Knyvett were of this family.

Knight. Between 1180–98, twenty-two persons named Miles or

Knight occur in Normandy (MRS). The name probably came thence, and in 13th cent. was in England Miles and Knight (RH). English families may have been included.

Knights, for KNIGHT.

Knill, for Canell, or CHANNELL.

Knobel, for Kenobel. *See* KNATCH-BULL.

Knott, for Canot, or CANUTE.

Knotts, for KNOTT.

Knowlin, for Canolin.

Knyvett. *See* KNEVITT.

Kydd, for KIDD.

Kyle, for Keyle, or CAYLEY.

Kyrle, Kirle, or Kirell, armorially identified with Kyriell and De Criol. *See* ASHBURNHAM.

L

Laby, for L'Abbé. *See* ABBOT.

Lacelles. William and Ralph de Lacella, or Lacele, and the estate of Lacella, Normandy, 1180–95 (MRS). The De Lacelles, Barons of Messie, derived their name from Lacella, near Falaise, which with its church belonged 1154 to the Abbey of St. Sauveur, Evreux (Gall. Christ. xi.). Temp. Henry I. this family, which had been seated in Yorkshire at the Conquest, was divided into two powerful branches, viz., 1. the Lacelles of Kirby, of whom are mentioned Roger 1130, Picot 1139–1165, Roger 1165, Robert Fitz-Picot, and Roger summoned to parliament as a baron 1294. 2. Lascelles of Herlsey.

Of the latter house Radulphus de L., 1086, held lordships in York of Ilbert de Lacy (Domesd.). Horlsey, Bingley, and Buskerby, were soon after granted to this family by the crown. Radulphus was a benefactor to Nostel Priory (Mon. ii. 35), and had issue Jordan and Turgis of Yorkshire 1130 (Rot. Pip.). The former was a benefactor to Nostel, and 1154 Henry II. confirmed his grants (Mon. ii. 37). About 1146 Gerard and Alan, his sons, were benefactors to Byland Abbey (Mon. i. 1032). The former had issue Ralph, whose nephew William was plaintiff in a suit against him for Lacelle and the barony of Messie in Normandy, which Ralph yielded to him as his inheritance (MSAN. xv. 92). Alan de L., brother of Gerard, was father of 1. Simon; and 2. William, who 1165 held two fees, Yorkshire. Simon at that time held three fees from Lacy (Lib. Niger), and had John de L., from whom descend lineally the Earls of Harewood. The particulars are too long for insertion here.

Lacer. William Laceore, Normandy, 1180–95; also A. de Lacoire, Raginald and Rich. Lachoire, and William Lacoere, 1198 (MRS); Derekin de Lacre, Engl. 1189 (Rot. Pip.).

Lacey. *See* LACY.

Lacon. John de Lakon was summoned 1324 to attend a great Council at Westminster. Of this name are the Baronets Lacon. Roger and William de Laccon, Serlo and William de Lachon or Lacon, and the fief of Lacon occur in Normandy 1180-95; Petrus de Lacon 1198 (MRS).

Lacy, a baronial name, from Lassy, Normandy, formerly borne by the Barons of Pontefract, York, and of Evias, Hereford. The branches of this house were so numerous that Robson mentions above 40 coats of arms of different houses. Lacy or Lassy was between Vire and Aulnay. Walter de Lacy is mentioned by Wace at the Battle of Hastings, and witnessed a charter of William Fitz-Osborne, and from him descended the Barons of Evias, Earls of Ulster and Lincoln, Barons of Pontefract, and Palatines of Meath.

Ladell. *See* LEDELL.

Laidet. N. Laidet, Guiscard Laidet, Normandy 1180-95 (MRS), a baronial family in England.

Laight. *See* LYTE.

Lait. *See* LYTE.

Lake, from St. Martin du Lac, Burgundy. Derkin de Lake before 1198 granted lands to Wudeham Abbey, Essex (Mon. Angl. i. 889). John de Lacu held by serjeantry in Gloucester 13th cent. (Testa de Neville).

Laker. *See* LACER.

Lakin, for LACON.

Lamb. Robert Agnus, and Ralph, Normandy 1180-98 (MRS). This and the name De Agnis, then frequent in Normandy (MRS), may have been sometimes translated to Lamb in England. The latter name was not frequent here c. 1272 (RH). It may include English families. Hence Lamb, Viscounts Melbourne, and Barons Beauvale.

Lambard. *See* LAMBERT.

Lambe. *See* LAMB.

Lambell. Petrus de Lambale, Normandy 1180-95 (MRS).

Lambert, descended from Haco, a Norman chief, who 1066 held Witham, Lincoln, from Ralph Paganel (Domesd.). He appears 1091 as Haco de Multon (Mon. ii. 100, new ed.). Thomas de Multon, his son, a benefactor to Spalding, had Lambert de M., living t. Stephen (Lib. Niger). From his elder son descended the Lords Multon of Egremont. His younger son, Henry Fitz-Lambert, was a benefactor to the Church in Lincoln, and had Richard Fitz-Lambert, living 1235 (Roberts, Excerpt.). In 1325 William Lambarde was security for an M.P. Yorkshire, and the family continued to be of importance in York and Lincoln till t. Elizabeth. A branch became seated in Surrey, of which was the distinguished General, Sir Oliver Lambert, t. Elizabeth, ancestor of the Lords Lambart, Earls of Cavan.

Lambert. William Fitz-Lambert, William Lambert, Peter, Flodus L., Normandy 1180-98 (MRS); Robert, Walter, William Lambert, Eng. c. 1272 (RH).

Lamberth, for LAMBERT.

Lambeth, for LAMBERTH.

Lamble, for LAMBELL.

Lambole. *See* LAMBELL.

Lamboll, for LAMBELL.

Lamborth. *See* LAMBERT.

Lamburd, for LAMBERT.

Lambton. The origin of this Durham family, like that of Eden in the same county, appears to have been from the Barons of Torp in Normandy. *See* EDEN, THORP. Ernulph de Torp, of this family, appears to have held Lambton from the see of Durham, t. Henry I. In 1165

Geoffry Fitz-Ernulph de Torp held half a knight's fee from the see of Durham (Lambton), as appears by the Liber Niger. John de Torp, son of Geoffry, executed a charter in Durham, c. 1200, which was witnessed by his son John de Lamtun (Surtees, Durham, ii. p. 170, &c.). In 1260 another John de Lamton witnessed at Newcastle a charter of Alexander, King of Scotland. The lordship of L. was held as half a knight's fee from the see of Durham, and the arms of De Torp and De Lambton appear to have been originally the same—viz. a fesse—to which the former added three fleur de lys or lions, and the latter three lambs, in allusion to the name. The Earls of Durham descend from this family.

Lambard, for LAMBERT.

Lamborne. Alvered de Lamborne, Normandy 1180–95 (MRS). Gilbert Fitz-Maurice de Lamborne, Robert and William de L., England 1194–1200 (RCR).

Lamert. William La Mort, Normandy 1180 (MRS). Robert Mort, England 1194–1200 (RCR).

Lamey, for AMY.

Lamotte. See MOTE.

Lampard, for LAMBARD.

Lamport, for LAMBERT.

Lancaster, or Taillebois. See PRESTON.

Lance. Galterus Lance, Normandy 1198 (MRS); Mabilia and Joanna Lance, Eng. c. 1272 (RH).

Lancefield, probably foreign.

Lancelay. Aeliza and Ralph de Lancelevee, Normandy, and their fief 1180–98 (MRS). Roger Lancelevee, Dorset 1203 (Rot. Canc.).

Lanceley. See LANCELAY.

Land. Jordan, William, Warin,

Nicholas, Thomas, John de Landa, and the fief of Landa, Normandy 1180–95 (MRS); Richard de Landa, Eng. 1189, Reginald 1203, &c. (Rot. Pip.; Rot. Canc.). See PATRICK. William de la Lande 13th cent. held from Roger de Mowbray, York.

Landale. William and John de Landell, William Bacon de Landells, Normandy 1180–98 (MRS).

Landau, for LANDEAU.

Landel. See LANDELL.

Landeau, the French form of Landell. See LANDALE.

Landell. See LANDALE.

Lander, from Landres, Burgundy. Almaric de Landres held lands Bedford and Bucks (Testa de Neville), in the 13th century. Hence Landor, the poet.

Lander, for LANDOR.

Landfield, probably foreign.

Landon. Geoffry Landon, Normandy 1180 (MRS). Amicia de Laundon Eng. c. 1272 (RH).

Lands, for LAND.

Lane, probably from English localities in some cases. See ANNE.

Lang. See LONG.

Langmead. The fief of Longum Pratum was in Normandy (Mem. Soc. Ant. Norm. v. 174). The English branch in Devon translated their name (see Lower).

Lankester, for LANCASTER.

Lanning. William Lanone, Normandy 1180–95 (MRS); Roger and Thomas de Lanun, Engl. c. 1272 (RH).

Lansley. See LANCELEY.

Lara. Nicholas de Larre, Normandy 1198 (MRS); William Larie, Engl. c. 1272 (RH); Oliver de Lare, Normandy 1180 (MRS).

Larcher. Radulphus and Roger Larchier or Larker, Normandy 1198

(MRS); Richard Larcher, Eng. c. 1199 (RCR).

Lardant. Tuff and Tustin Lardant, Normandy 1180–95; Fulco Lardant, 1198 (MRS).

Larder, equivalent to LARDINER. Oilard Lardarius, Hunts 1086 (Domesd.); Bernard and Durand Lardarius, Wilts and Surrey 1130 (Rot. Pip.). The names are foreign.

Lardiner. Peter de Larderario, Normandy, 1180 (MRS); Robert Lardenier (Ib.), 1198.

Lardner, for LARDINER.

Large. Radulphus Large, Normandy 1198 (MRS); Wymar de Largo, and William de Largo, Normandy 1180–95 (MRS); Matilda, and Philip Large, Engl. c. 1272 (RH).

Lark. *See* LARKE.

Larke, for LARGE.

Larken. *See* LARKIN.

Larkin, for Largen, or Largan. Eudo Largant, Normandy 1180–95; Eudo and Ion Largan, 1198 (MRS). It was also written Larcamp.

Larking. *See* LARKIN.

Larkins. *See* LARKIN.

Larnder, for LARDNER.

Larner, for LARDNER.

Larrad, for LARRETT.

Larrance, for LAWRENCE.

Larratt, for LARRETT.

Larrett, for LART.

Larritt, for LARRETT.

Lart, for LORT.

Lascelles. *See* LACELLES.

Lash, for LOSH.

Laskey, for LASCY, or LACY.

Last, for LAS, or LOS. Philip Augustus granted lands, Normandy, to Robert de Los (Mem. Soc. Ant. Norm. v. 158). Probably of the same family as Walter and William Luz, 1198 (MRS).

Latimer. Hugh, Bishop of Wor-

cester, and Martyr, was the son of a farmer in Leicestershire, a distant branch of the Latimers, Barons of Braybroke, who possessed five manors in Leicester 1300–1400 (Nicholls, Leic. iii. 1062). Several churches retain their arms. Hugh L. was probably fifth or sixth in descent from a younger son of Thomas L., who was summoned as a baron 1297, 1299. The latter was descended from the Latimers of York, where William le Latimer held a knight's fee from Vesci 1165 (Lib. Niger). He was descended from Radulphus le Latimer, or Latiner (Latinarius), Secretary to the Conqueror, who held lands in Essex as a baron 1086, and who from his surname and the French name borne by his posterity was doubtless Norman or foreign.

The Barons Latimer of the North were of the same race.

Lattimer, for LATIMER.

Lattimer, for LATIMER.

Laud, or De St. Laudo. The immediate ancestry of Archbishop Laud has not been as yet ascertained. His father, William Laud, a cloth manufacturer at Reading, who d. 1594, was in ample circumstances. He was born at Wokingham, Berks, to which place the Archbishop was a benefactor (Lysons, Berks). The family of Laud was also seated at this time at Tiverton, Devon, the great seat of the cloth manufacture, where John Laud occurs t. Eliz. (Chanc. Proceedings, t. Eliz.). The name is evidently an abbreviation of St. Laud, or St. Lo, and the arms of Laud (a chevron between three mullets) bear relation to those of St. Lo; a chevron between three spear heads; or perpale; three cinquefoils; or two bars, in chief three mullets. The family was probably a remote and early branch of St. Laud.

St. Laud, or St. Lo, was near Coutances, Normandy; and was a barony. Simon de St. Laud, who had grants at the Conquest, witnessed a charter of William, Earl of Mortaine, in favour of Keynsham Abbey (Mon. ii. 299). The widow of Geoffry de St. Laud held from the Bishop at Winchester 1148 (Winton Domesday). Adam de St. Laud was Viscount of Lincoln 1278, and Ralph de St. L. 1329. Thomas de St. Laud, 1297–1300, was returned as holding estates in Notts and Lincoln. The principal branch was seated at Newton St. Laud, or St. Lo, Somerset, where it flourished till c. 1400, when the heiress m. Lord Botreaux. The male line continued in Sir John St. Lo, Constable of Bristol Castle, t. Henry VI.; and in the St. Los of Dorset. Younger branches also continued to possess considerable estates in Somerset (Collinson, Somerset, iii. 342, &c.). Leland, t. Henry VIII., mentions a Sir John St. Lo then living (Itin. vii. 97). The St. Los of Dorset came from Somerset (Hutchings's Dorset, iii. 354). See Lowe.

Lauer, for LAVER.

Laugher, for LAVER.

Launder, or Loundres. See LONDON.

Launders. See LAUNDER.

Laurel. Hugo Lorel, Normandy 1198 (MRS). Robert Lorle, Normandy 1180–95; Hugh Lorel 1198 (MRS).

Laurance, for LAURENCE.

Laurence. William Lorenz, Normandy 1180–95 (MRS); John, Richard, William Laurenz or Lau-

rence Engl. c. 1272 (RH). Also for St. LAURENCE.

Lavars. See LAVER.

Laver. Osmond Lavarde, Normandy 1180 (MRS); John le Laverd, Theobald Laver, Engl. c. 1272 (RH).

Lavers, for LAVER.

Law. 1. a local name; 2. for LOWE or St. LOWE.

Lawes. See LAW.

Lawn, for Lawnde, or LAND.

Lawrance, for LAURENCE.

Lawrell. See LAUREL.

Lawrence. See LAURENCE.

Laws. See LAW.

Lawson. Walter Loison, Normandy 1180–95 (MRS).

Laysel. Hugh Loisel, Normandy 1180 (MRS). From L'Oisel or L'Oiseau comes the English name Bird.

Layt. See LYTE.

Lazard. See IZARD.

Leach or Medicus. Robert, William, Odard, Hugh, Nicholas, Matthew, Durand, Arnulph, Robert, William Medicus, Normandy 1180–98 (MRS). William, Robert, Julian, Alexander M. England 1194–1200 (RCR).

Leahair, for LEAR.

Leal. See LEALE.

Leale, for Lille or LISLE.

Lear, for Lyre, from L. Normandy. Oliver de Lyre Norm. 13th cent. (MSAN. plate 14). William de Leyre held in Warwick and Leicester 13th cent. (Testa).

Leason. See LEESON.

Leatt. See LYTE.

Leaver. See LEVER.

Leavers, for LEAVER.

Lebeau. See BELL.

Leche, for LEECH.

Lechmere, for De la Mare. As

is elsewhere stated, in 1165 Robert de la Mare held 10 fees of the honour of Gloucester. From him sprang several branches in Gloucester, Worcester, and Hereford. In 13th cent. Thomas de Hanley or De la Mare held Hanley-Thorn of William de la M., who held of H. of Gloucester (Testa). Doddesham was also held from William de la M. by William le Manus (Mara), as was Redmarley (Testa), and Thomas de Hanley held in Dodesham from William de la Mare (Ib.). Gilbert de Hanley held from Sir Reginald de Hanley or De la Mare. The Lords of Hanley, where the La Mares were afterwards seated, were evidently a branch of De la Mare. It was usual to write the name 'Lamare,' as appears in the records, and it afterwards became 'Lachmare' by the same mode in which Lile became Lidle, and Kenebel Knatchbull. Hence the Lords and Baronets Lechmere. *See* DELAMARE.

Leddell, for LIDDELL.

Ledgar, for LEDGER.

Ledgard, for LEDGAR.

Ledger. William de St. Leodgario, and the fief of St. Leger, Normandy 1180-95 (MRS). Gilbert, Gisbert, and Robert de St. L. 1198 (Ib.). Hence the Lords Doneraile.

Lee, for LEIGH, also local English of unknown origin.

Leech. *See* LEACH.

Leechmore, for LECHMERE.

Leeman, for LEMON.

Leemans, for LEEMAN.

Leeming, for LEEMAN.

Leer, for LEAR.

Leers, for LEER.

Leeson. *See* LISSON.

Leetch. *See* LEACH.

Leete. *See* LYTE.

308

Lefever. *See* FABER.

Lefevre. *See* FABER.

Legard. Galterus Legara, Normandy 1198 (MRS). Hence the baronets Legard.

Leggatt. Herveius Legatus (from his name of foreign origin) held in capite in Bucks 1086. In 1290 and 1301 John and William Legat were bailsmen for the M.P. for Hertford (PPW). Helming Legat was Viscount of Hertford 1401.

Leggett, for LEGGATT.

Leggitt, for LEGGATT.

Leggott, for LEGGATT.

Legh. *See* LEIGH.

Leicester or De Ganville. Thomas de Joannisvilla and his fief mentioned in Normandy 1180-95, Ralph de Jehanville 1198 (MRS). Of this family Roger de Geneville gave the Church of Pictariville c. 1000 to St. Taurin Abbey, Evreux, Normandy (Gall. Christ. xi. 139 Instr.). His descendants came to England 1066, and t. Henry I. Hugh [de Janville], Viscount of Leicester, witnessed the charter of Lenton Priory 1100-1108 (Mon. i. 646). He was Viscount of Leicester 1130, and Seneschal to Matilda de Senlis (Rot. Pip.; Mon. i. 672). Ivo de Leicester, his son, was living 1130 (Rot. Pip.). The family then became widely spread. In the same century Odo de L. and Ralph de Leicester gave lands in Normandy to Plessis Priory (MSAN, viii. 156, 157). William de Ganville, M.P. for Leicestershire 1322, occurs as 'William de Leicester' (PPW). Roger de Leicester of this family possessed estates Leicestershire, t. Richard I. (he was son of Robert de L., witness to a charter of Salop Abbey, c. 1170, son of Ivo de L.). He witnessed 1190 the charter of

Cokersand, Lancashire (Mon. ii. 631) and was of that county c. 1200 (RCR), and in 1208 paid a fine in Leicester (Hardy, Obl. et Fin.). From this line descended the Lysters of Rowton, Salop. He had two grandsons: 1. Sir Nicholas, of Lancashire, who acquired Tabley, Cheshire, and was ancestor of the Leicesters of Tabley; 2. Thomas, father of, 1. Geoffry de L., M.P. for Derby 1311; 2. John of Derby, who, in 1321, obtained pardon as an adherent of Roger Mortimer, of Wigmore, and to whom in 1311 the Abbot of Salop was commanded by the king to make a payment of 20*l.* (PPW). He m. 1312 Isabel, dau. and heir of John de Bolton of Bolland, Lancashire, and had Richard Leicester, whose son John inherited estates in Craven from the De Boltcns, and was ancestor of William Lister, Lord of Midhope Craven, ancestor of the Listers, Barons Ribblesdale.

Leicester or Lester. Robert de Lestre, Normandy 1180 (MRS); Geoffry and Richard de L. Engl. 1203 (Rot. Canc.). Robert de Lestre, c. 1272 (RH).

Leigh, a branch of the Norman house of DE LA MARE; also borne by other families.

Leighton. Eyton remarks that in the early history of this family 'invention has supplied the place of fact' (Salop, vii. 326). It descends from Tihel, who t. Henry I. held from the Fitz-Alans (Ib.). The name Tihel is Breton, as were the Fitz-Alans. Richard Fitz-Tihel held a fief from Fitz-Alan 1165 (Lib. Nig.). His son Richard de Lecton, Knight, was living 1203 (Rot.Canc.). Hence the Leightons, Baronets.

Leitch, for LEECH (Lower).

Leite. *See* LYTE.

Lely. Simon Lele, Normandy 1180–95 (MRS). William de Leelay, Engl. 1189 (Rot. Pip.). Robert de Lelay 1194–1200 (RCR).

Leman, for LEMON.

Lemann. *See* LEMON.

Lemere. *See* LECHMERE.

Lemmon, for LEMON.

Lemmons. Roger Leminz, Normandy 1180–95 (MRS).

Lemon. Godefridus Lemon, Normandy 1180–95 (MRS). John Leman, England 1194–1200 (RCR). Hence the Baronets Lemon.

Lenard, for LENNARD.

Lendon. *See* LANDON.

Le Neve. *See* NEAVE.

Leney. *See* LENNEY.

Lenney, from Lannai, Normandy. Walter, Joscelin, Hugo de Launay, Normandy 1198 (MRS). Henry de Laune, William Leny, Engl. c. 1272 (RH).

Lennard, for LEONARD.

Lennox, Dukes of Richmond. *See* STUART.

Lenny, for LENNEY.

Leonard, or St. Leonard, from St. Leonard, near Fécamp, Normandy. William Leonard, Engl. c. 1272 (RH). Robert de St. Leonard held that fief from Philip Augustus (Mem. Soc. Ant. Norm. v. 187). Hence the Lennards, Earls of Sussex.

Leonards, for LEONARD.

Leopard, for LEPARD.

Lepard, for Le Pere, or LEPER.

Leper. Robert le Per, Normandy 1180–95 (MRS). William, Geoffry, Nicholas, &c., Le Pere, or Le Pare, Engl. c. 1272 (RH).

Leppard. *See* LEPARD.

Lerche, for L'Arche, perhaps

Pont de L'Arche, an ancient Norman name. William, son of Walter Pontelarche, was Viscount of Berks 1130 (Rot. Pip.). Osbert de Pont-delarche is mentioned in Normandy (Ib.). Robert and Ralph P. held fiefs Berks and Hants 1165 (Lib. Nig.).

Lerner, for LARNER.

Lesiter or Lestre. *See* LEICESTER.

Lessey, for LACY.

Lester, or Lestre. *See* LEICESTER.

Lestock. Ranulphus de Lestac, Normandy 1180 (MRS).

Lestrange. This family descends from Ruald Lestrange, who witnessed a charter of Alan Fitz-Flaald in Norfolk 1112 (Mon. i. 627). The descent of the Lords Lestrange of Knockyn has been treated by Eyton (Salop, x. 259, &c.). Ruald was of Breton origin, and was probably son of Payne or Judicael de Peregrino, whose father Ruald or Rodaldus de Peregrino (or extraneus, le Strange) granted part of the island of Noirmoutier to the Abbey of St. Saviour, Bretagne 1060 (Lobineau, Hist. Bret. ii. 176). Hence the Barons Strange of Knockin and of Blackmere.

Leteh, for LEECH.

Lett, for LETT.

Letts, for LETT.

Lever. Petrus Lievre, Normandy 1180-95 (MRS). Also from an English locality.

Leversha, for Levesey, or LIVESEY.

Levesque. Ralph Leveske and John, Normandy, 1180-98 (MRS). Henry Eveske, England, c. 1272 (RH).

Levet, from Livet, Normandy.

310

Ralph, William, Roger, Gilbert, Hugh Livet, Normandy, 1180-95 (MRS). From John de Livet, banneret c. 1200, descended the Marquises of Barville (Des Bois). Roger de Livet granted lands in Stafford to Tetbury Abbey, t. William I. (Mon. i. 355). Robert de Livet held two fees Warwick, t. Henry I. (Lib. Niger). Thomas and Ralph L. held lands in Normandy 1165 (Feod. Norm.). William Livet of Yorkshire, c. 1200 (RCR); Eustace Livet, York, 13th cent. (Testa); John L. York, 1316 (PPW).

Levett, for LEVET.

Levette, for LEVETT.

Levick, for LEVESQUE.

Levison, from Levasson, Normandy. Robert de la Veneison, 1180-95 (MRS); Adam, Richard, Robert de Leveson, Engl. c. 1272 (RH).

Levitt. *See* LEVETT.

Lewer. *See* LOWER.

Lewers, for LEWER.

Lewis. 1. A patronymic, chiefly Cambro-Celtic. 2. William de Lues, Walter Luiz, Normandy, 1180-95 (MRS); John, Robert Lews, or Lewis, Engl. c. 1272 (RH). Osbert de Leus of Worcestershire, 1199 (RCR); Adam de Lewes, Gloucester, 1203 (Rot. Canc.). Hence Sir G. Cornewall Lewis, the eminent scholar and statesman.

Lewsey, for Lucy (Lower). Richard de Luceio, Alexander, Roger, William, Nicholas, Herbert, Normandy 1180-1200 (MRS. and Mem. Soc. Ant. Norm. v.) *See* LUCY.

Leycester, or De Janville. *See* LEICESTER.

Leyland. *See* LELAND.

Lezard. Roger Lisiart, Normandy, 1180-95 (MRS).

Lezard. Hugo Lesiardus, Normandy, 1198 (MRS).

Libby, for L'Abbé. *See* ABBOT.

Liberty. Roger Livardé, Normandy, 1198 (MRS); Ralph Levarde, Alan Leyberd, Engl. c. 1272 (RH).

Liddall, for LIDDELL.

Liddell, probably descended from Turgis Brundoz (Rot. Pip. 31 Hen. I.), a Norman, to whom Liddel or Lydale, on the borders of Scotland, was granted by Ranulph Meschin, t. Henry I. It remained with his descendants till t. John, when it passed away by an heiress to the house of De Stuteville, and then to that of Wake. The younger branch of the De Liddels settled in Scotland, where John de Lidel in 1292 held the revenues of Dundee in farm (Rot. Scot. i. 17), while about the same time William de Lydel was seneschal of the Bishop of Glasgow, and led the forces of the see to the support of Robert Bruce (Palgrave, Documents illustr. Hist. Scotland, i. 345). In 1383 William Lidell had licence to enter England for mercantile purposes with his train (Rot. Scot. ii. 54). In 1406 Sir William de Lydale witnessed a charter of Robert Duke of Albany (Registr. Mag. Sigill. Scot. 225). Robert L. of Balnure was Dapifer to the king 1453, Sir James of Halkerstoun ambassador to England 1474, and 1477 George de L. had licence to purchase bows in England for the Duke of Albany (Rot. Scot. ii. 454), and appears to have settled in England. His son Thomas Liddel m. Margaret, dau. of John de Leybourne, and had issue, of whom Thomas L. was Sheriff of Newcastle, and William alderman of Morpeth. From the former descended the Liddels Lords Ravensworth.

Liddle, for LIDDELL or LISLE.

Liddon, for Ledun, from Lidon near Saintes, Aquitaine. Henry Ledun held in Wilts part of a fee from Simon Ledun 13th cent. (Testa, 153). Hence Liddon, the noble Christian apologist.

Lidgett, for LEGHTT.

Lidle, for LISLE.

Liell, for LISLE.

Liggett, for LEGGATT.

Light, for LYTE.

Lile, for LISLE.

Liles, for LISLE.

Liley, for LELY.

Lill, for LISLE.

Lilley, for LELY.

Lillie, for LELY.

Lilly, for LELY.

Limebear, for LIMEBEER.

Limbert, for LAMBERT.

Limebeer, for LIMBIRD.

Limbird, for LAMBERD.

Lincoln. Alured de Lincoln came from Normandy with the Conqueror. He witnessed a charter in Normandy 1080 (Gall. Christ. xi. 23), and 1086 held a great barony in Lincoln and Bedford. In 1130 Robert de L. occurs (Rot. Pip.), and 1165 Alured de L. held a barony of thirty fees. There were various collateral branches, from one of which probably descended Abraham Lincoln, President of the United States.

Lind, from Lynde, near Lille and Hazebrook, Flanders. The family of De la Lynde was seated in Dorset at an early date.

Linder, for LANDOR.

Linde. *See* LIND.

Lindesay, for LINDSAY.

Lindley. The name is derived from Lindley, Yorkshire, which was

311

held (13th cent.) from Roger de
Mowbray by knight service, by Wil-
liam de Rodeville or Rudeville, of
Normandy (Testa de Neville, 92-96).
Rudeville, now Rouville, is near
Gisors. The family of R. probably
took the name of its manor, Lindley.

Lindon, a branch of LASCELLES.

Lindsay, or De Limesi, a branch
of the baronial Norman house of De
Toesni, of Toesni and Conches. This
was one of the sovereign families
which formerly ruled in Norway
from immemorial ages, but were dispossessed by Harold Harfager c. 860.
Malahulcius, who accompanied Rollo,
his nephew, had issue, Hugo, Lord
of Cavalcamp in Neustria, whose
sons were, Ralph or Ranulph, and
Hugo, Archbishop of Rouen 942-
980, the latter of whom gave Toesni
to his brother Ralph. The grandson of Ralph, also named Ralph,
was c. 1011 appointed Castellan of
Tillieres, jointly with Nigel Viscount
of Coutances. He had issue, Roger
de Toesni, surnamed D'Espagne, on
account of his prowess against the
Saracens in Spain, progenitor of the
De Toesnis, hereditary standard-
bearers of Normandy, barons of
Toesni and Conches, Normandy, and
of Stafford and Belvoir in England,
ancestors of the English houses of
Cholmondeley, Egerton, Gresley, and
others. Roger D'Espagne's brother,
Hugh de Toesni, was surnamed De
Limesay from his Norman seigneurie,
and was living 1060. He had several
sons, who accompanied the Conqueror, viz.: 1. Ralph de Limesay,
baron of Wolverley, Warwick, 1086,
whose barony ultimately passed in
part to the Scottish line of Limesay;
2. Baldric de L., who held lands
from the Earl of Chester 1086; and

313

was father of Walter de Limesay or
Lindesay, who obtained grants in
Scotland, and witnessed the inquisition made in 1116 into the possessions of the see of Glasgow. From
this baron descended the great house
of Lindsay, Limesy, or Limesay in
Scotland, Earls of Crawford and
Balcarres, Dukes of Montrose (*see*
Lord Lindsay's Lives of the Lindsays); while various branches in
England continued to bear the same
name under various forms, and with
armorial identifications evidencing
their common origin.

Lindsey, for LINDSAY.

Linnell. Robert Lunel, Normandy, 1198 (MRS).

Linney, for LENNY.

Linom, for Limon or LEMON.

Liney, for LINNEY.

Linsey, for LINDSAY.

Lintott. John de Lintot and the
fief of L. Normandy, 1180 (MRS).
This fief was near Dieppe. Richard
de L. and William, his brother, were
benefactors to Belvoir Priory, Rutland, t. William I. (Mon. i. 328).
Richard de Lintot held a fief in
Normandy 1165 (Feod. Norm.). The
name often occurs in England.

Lion. *See* LYON.

Lisle. *See* ANDERSON-PELHAM.

Lisson, from Lison, Normandy
(Mem. Soc. Ant. Norm. v. 185).
William Lesson, Engl. c. 1272 (RH).
Hence Leeson, Earl of Milltown.

Lister. *See* LEICESTER.

Littell. Ralph, William, Bernard, Herbert Parvus or Le Petit,
1180-95, Normandy (MRS). Fourteen of the name occur in Normandy
1198 (Ib.); many in England, c.
1198 (RCR).

Little. *See* LITTELL.

Littleton. *See* LYTTELTON.

Livesey. Warner Levezied, and Ralph, Normandy, 1180 (MRS); Hunfrid Leuveyse, Engl. c. 1272 (RH).

Livett, for LEVETT.

Loach. See LOCH.

Loader. William Lodres, Normandy, 1180–95 (MRS); Agnes, Emma la Lodere, Engl. c. 1272 (RH).

Lobb. William Lobes, Normandy, 1180–95 (MRS). Mabilia and Henry de la Lobe, Normandy, 1180–95 (MRS).

Lobs. See LOBB.

Loch. Thomas de Loches, Normandy, 1180–95 (MRS); Laurent de Lochea, Engl. c. 1272 (RH).

Locker. Roger Locheor, Normandy, 1180–95 (MRS); John, Jordan Lokar, Engl. c. 1272 (RH); Richard Lokere, Normandy, c. 1185 (MRS).

Locket, for LOCKHART.

Lockhart, or Locard, probably foreign. Stephen Locard witnessed a charter of Richard de Morville before 1153 (Douglas, Baronage, i. 323). Jordan Locard 1165 witnessed a charter of Walter Fitz-Alan, Dapifer (Kelso Chart.).

Lockett, for Lockard or LOCKHART.

Lockitt, for LOCKHART.

Lockyer. See LOCKER.

Locock, perhaps for Lovecot, or Lovetot, from L. Normandy, of which Durand was lord, c. 1030. William de Lovetot founded Worksop Priory, Notts, t. Henry I. His barony passed to the Furnivals. Nigel, his younger son, had descendants, who are mentioned t. Edward I. Richard de L. held fees in Notts from Paganel 1165. The name of Lovecote or Lovecock is afterwards found in various parts of England, Bucks, Leicester, Devon, Wilts, &c. The name of Locock appears to be an abbreviation of it.

Lodder. See LOADER.

Loddidge, for LODER.

Loder. See LOADER.

Lodge, or Lodges. Richard, William, Ralph, Robert de Loges, Normandy, 1180–95 (MRS); Geroius de Logis occurs in Normandy 1050. From him descended Bigod de Loges, Baron of Aldford, Chester, and Odard de Loges, Baron of Wigton, Cumberland, t. William I. The family also appears in Berks and Devon.

Loe. William de Loe, Normandy 1180–95 (MRS); Ralph de la Lowe, Engl. c. 1272 (RH).

Lomer. Durand Loemer, Normandy 1198 (MRS); Margery Lumber, Engl. c. 1272 (RH).

Lond. Richard, Robert, &c. De Londa, Normandy 1180–95 (MRS). Anschetil de Lunda witnessed a charter (12th cent.) in York (Mon. i. 656); Stephen de Lund of Yorkshire 1250 (Roberts, Excerpta).

London. William, Robert London, Norm. 1180–95 (MRS). Of this family was William de Londres, one of the conquerors of Glamorgan, 1090, ancestor of the Lords Loundres of Naas, and Thomas de L., who settled in Scotland before 1163 (Chart. Mailros.).

Lone, for LOND.

Long. 1. Petrus de Longa, Normandy, t. Phil. Augustus (Mem. Soc. Ant. Norm. v. 177); Emma de Longues, Normandy 1198 (MRS); Agnes Longa, Engl. c. 1272 (RH); 2. from Le Long.

Longe. See LONG.

Longes. See LONE.

Longfeld, for LONGVILLE.

Longville. A branch of the house of Giffard, barons of Langueville and Bolbec near Dieppe, Normandy. Osberne de Longueville or Bolbec, with William de Bolbec, Robert Malet, and Gilbert de Menill c. 990, gave the church of Pictariville, Normandy, to religious uses. In 1165 Henry de Longavilla held from Nigel de Luvetot in Hunts (Lib. Nig.). Richard de Logvil occurs in Bucks 1199, William in Herts 1198, and Roger de Longavilla in Hunts c. 1200 (RCR). John de L. had a writ of military summons 1259. Hence Longueville, Lord Grey de Ruthyn, and probably the Longfields, Viscounts Longueville.

Looker. See LOCKER.

Loomes. Hugo Lomme, Normandy 1180-95 (MRS); Henry Home, Philip, Ralph Lomb, Engl. c. 1272 (RH).

Loos. See LOOSE.

Loose, from Los, Normandy. Robert de Los, 1219 (Mem. Soc. Ant. Norm. v.). Hugh de Luxa, Engl. c. 1272 (RH).

Loraine. John, Robert, Simon, Henry Laurane or Laurone, and the fief of Lauraine, Normandy, 1180-95 (MRS). Albert de Loraine (Lothariensis) was a baron in Hereford and Bedford 1086. Roger Loering was of Bedford 1165. In 13th cent. William Loharing was a benefactor of Gisborne Priory, York (Mon. ii. 151). In 1333 Eustace de Lorreyne was a Commissioner, Berwick-on-Tweed (Rot. Scotiæ, i. 260). The descent is traced by records to the family of Lorraine, Baronet.

Lorek. Rufus de Lorec, Normandy, 1180-95 (MRS).

Lord. Osmond de Lavarde, Nor-

314

mandy 1180 (MRS); John le Lavord, Engl. c. 1272 (RH).

Lordan. Elye Loradin, Normandy 1198 (MRS); Jane le Lordi[n]g, Engl. c. 1272 (RH).

Lorenz. William Lorenz, Normandy 1180-95 (MRS); William Lorenz, Engl. c. 1272 (RH).

Lorie. Robert Lorre, the fief of Lurre, Fortin de Luri, Roger de Lury, Normandy 1180-95 (MRS); Richard Lure, Engl. c. 1272 (RH).

Lorimer. Robert and John Lauremarius, Normandy 1180-95 (MRS); Geoffry, Lambert, Maurice, William Loremer, 1198 (Ib.), Adam, Ralph L., Eng. c. 1272 (RH).

Lorimer. Richard, Walter, Peter, John, William Loremarius, Normandy 1180-95 (MRS); Nicholas Lorimar, &c. Engl. c. 1272 (RH).

Lorimier. See LORIMER.

Loring. Henricus Loherene, Normandy 1180, and Asketil (MRS). See LORAINE.

Lorkin, for LARKIN.

Lorking, for LARKING.

Lormier, for LORIMER.

Lort. William Lortie, Robert, and William de Lortie, Normandy 1180-98 (MRS). See HORT.

Lorymer, for LORIMER.

Losh. Gaufridus Loske, Normandy 1180-95 (MRS); Michael, Nicholas Losse, Engl. c. 1272 (RH).

Lottimer, for LATIMER.

Louch, from Loches, Touraine. Laurence de Luches mentioned in Oxford 1270 (Roberts, Excerpta, ii.). Warin de Luches and others charged with entry on the Manors of the De Spencers, Bucks (PPW). Thomas de Luches summoned from Berks to a great Council 1324 (PPW).

Louisson. Walter Loison, Normandy 1180–95 (MRS); Ralph Lussing, Engl. c. 1272 (RH).

Lound, for LOND.

Loup. Herbert, Joscelin, William Lupus or Le Loup, Normandy 1198 (MRS); John, Rich., Robert, William Lupus, Engl. c. 1272 (RH).

Lovatt, for LOVETT.

Louis. *See* LEWIS. Hence the baronets of the name.

Love, a form of Le Lou, or Lupus (Lower). *See* LOUP.

Loveday, from Loveday, or Loudet, Toulouse. William Loveday was a benefactor to the Knights Templars (Mon. i. 545). Richard L. 13th cent. witnessed a charter of Almaric Peché (Mon. ii. 84). In 1297 William L., of Oxford, a writ of military summons (PPW).

Lovell. Roger, William, Nicholas, Adam Loyel, or Louvel, Normandy 1180 (MRS). The Lovells, Barons of Cary, were a branch of the house of Ivry. *See* PERCEVAL.

Lover, from Louviers, Normandy. John de Loviers 1180–95 (MRS).

Levering. *See* LORING.

Lovesy, for LIVESEY.

Lovett. Richard, Peter, Ralph Louvet, or Lovet, Normandy 1180–95 (MRS); William L. 1086 held lands Berks, Bedford, Northampton, Leicester, in capite. Robert L. 1165 held lands Normandy. Hence the baronets Lovett.

Lovis, for LEWIS.

Lovitt, for LOVETT.

Low. *See* LOWE.

Lowe. 1. for St. Lo, or St. Laud, bearing a bend. William de St. Laudo, 1180, the canons, forest, ville, castle, and fief of, in Normandy (MRS). *See* LAUD. 2. for Le Loup, or Lu, bearing wolves. *See* LOUP. 3. from La Loe, or La Lupe,

Normandy. Thomas, and Hugh de la Loe, Norm. 1180 (MRS). *See* LOE.

Lowen. William de Loven, Normandy 1180–95 (MRS). Robert de Lovent, Eng. c. 1272 (RH).

Lower. Hugo de Luera, Normandy 1195 (MRS); the heirs of Lower, England c. 1272 (RH).

Lowery. *See* LOWER.

Lowes. Richard Lowes, Normandy 1180–95 (MRS); Robert Loys, Engl. c. 1272 (RH).

Lowndes, for LOND.

Lownds, for LOND.

Lowson. *See* LAWSON.

Lowther, or Malcael. Hervey, Ralph Malcael, Normandy 1180 (MRS). One of these paid a fine in the Bailifry of Coutances 1198 (Ib.). Also Tieric Malus Catulus 1198 (Ib.). Helto Malus Catulus or Malcael, t. William I. had a grant of Crakanthorpe and other estates Westmoreland. He granted lands to Holm Cultram Abbey, and had, 1, Ralph of Crakanthorpe, father of William Mauchael, t. Stephen, whose son William Malus Catulus granted to Geoffry M. lands in Crakanthorpe 1179, and was ancestor of the Malcaels Lords of Crakanthorpe, and the family of Crakanthorpe; 2, Humphry Malcael, Lord of Lowther, who granted part of that Church to Holm Cultram (Mon. ii. 74). His son Geoffry Malcanelle, t. Henry II. granted lands at Crakanthorpe to Alexander de Crakanthorpe, and had issue William and Thomas de Lowther, who, 12th cent., witnessed a charter to Holm Cultram Abbey (Ib. 428). Roger Malus Catulus, a third brother, was Vice-Chancellor to Richard Cœur de Lion (Madox, Exch. i. 77). These particulars have been chiefly gathered from Nicholson and Burns (344, 345). From this family descend the Earls of Lonsdale, the Lords Crofton, and the Baronets Lowther.

Luard. *See* LUER.

Lubin, or St. Lubin. The fief of St. Lubin, Normandy (Mem. Soc. Ant. Norm. v. 179).

Lucas. 1, from De Lukes, or Luches. *See* LOUCH. Lady Eliza de Lucas, 1275, was the widow of Raymond de Lukes (Roberts, Calend. Geneal.). 2, a patronymic. 3. *see* LUKE.

Lucey. *See* LUCY.

Luck, for LUKE.

Luckett, for LOCKETT.

Lucy, a baronial family (*see* LEWSEY), from Lucy, near Rouen. Richard de Lucy occurs in Normandy t. Hen. I. (MSAN, viii. 428). In 1165 Richard de Lucy's barony in Passy consisted of 19 fees. He also held 19 in Devon, besides others in Kent, Norfolk, Suffolk (Lib. Niger), and in 1156 in Northumberland. Geoffry de Lucy 1165 held one fee Devon. In 13th cent. William de Lucy held Charlcote, Warwick (Testa), and 1312–24 William Lucy was MP. for that county (PPW). This branch was sometimes named de Charlcote. Sir Thomas Lucy and others of Kent c. 1300 (PPW).

Lucock. *See* LOCOCK.

Luer. *See* LOWER.

Lugg, for LUKE.

Luke. William de Leuca, Normandy 1198 (MRS).

Luke, from St. Luc, near Evreux, Normandy. Simon de St. Luc, England c. 1272 (RH).

Lukes. *See* LUCAS.

Luks, for LUKES.

316

Lumb, for LOMB.

Lund, for Lound, or LOND.

Lunel. Robert Lunel, Normandy 1198 (MRS). This family was seated in Warwickshire.

Lunt, for LUND.

Lush. *See* LOSH. Simon de Lusco, and Godefrid, Normandy 1180–95 (MRS).

Lusher, for Lusers or Lisores. This family, like Lusers and Lisores, bears a chief. William de Lusoris, Normandy 1180–95 (MRS). The Barons of Lisores, Normandy, were a branch of the BASSETTS. Hugh de Lisures granted lands to Thorney Abbey, t. Henry I. (Mon. i. 247), and 1128 witnessed a charter of Jocelyn Crespin in Normandy (La Roque, ii. 1816). In 1165 Warner de Lisures held a barony in Wilts, Robert in Hunts, and R. was forester in fee, Northants (Lib. Niger). Nigel 13th cent. held in Notts (Testa).

Lusk, for LUSH.

Luton. Robert and William Luiton, Normandy 1198 (MRS). Petrus Luittin, Normandy 1180–95 (MRS). Gilbert and Roger de Luiton, Engl. c. 1199 (RCR).

Luttrell, a baronial family. Ralph and Robert Lottrel, Normandy 1180, Ramald and Martin Lottrel 1195, Osbert Lottrel 1198 (MRS). Robert Lotrel and Hugh his son were benefactors to the Abbey of Barberie, Normandy, at its foundation (Gall. Christ. xi. 85 Instr.). Symon Lutro mentioned in England 1130 (Rot. Pip.), Geoffry Luterel in Lincoln t. Richard I. (Dugdale), from whom descended the Barons Luttrel, and the Earls of Carhampton.

Lyall, for LISLE.

Lycett. Hubert, Sylvester Lesot,

Normandy 1198 (MRS). E. Lesote, Engl. c. 1272 (RH).

Lydall. *See* LIDDELL.

Lyddall. *See* LIDDELL.

Lyddon, for LIDDON.

Lyell, for LISLE. Hence the celebrated geologist, Sir C. Lyell.

Lyle, for LISLE.

Lyel, for LISLE.

Lynd. *See* LIND.

Lynde. *See* LIND.

Lyon, from Lions, Normandy. Ingelram de Lions came to England 1066 (Mon. Angl. ii. 604), and held Corsham and Culington from the King. He had Ranulph, whose brother William de L. had a grant in Norfolk from Earl Walter Giffard, and left descendants there. Ranulph had Ingelram de Lions, named Parcar, as being forester of Croxton, Leicester, by exchange with the King (Mon. Angl.). William Parcarius de Lions was a benefactor to Croxton Abbey, t. Henry II., and was brother of Hugh de Lyons, who was deprived of his estates 1203 (Nicholls, Leicester). From him descended the family of Parcar, or Parker, and the Earls of Macclesfield. Roger de Lyonn, of the same family, held Begbroke, Oxford, 13th cent., from Walter de Lucy (Testa, 112). Sir Richard de Lyons held lands in Oxford and Bucks 1275, and was father or grandfather of John de Lyons, who 1334 was summoned from Oxfordshire to attend the King with horses and arms at Roxburgh (Rot. Scot. i. 306). He in 1343 had charters for lands in Perth and Aberdeen, and from David II. obtained the reversion of the thanedom of Glamis. His son Sir John Lyon, of Glamis, was Great Chamberlain of Scotland, and from him descended the Lords Glamis, Earls of Strathmore and Kinghorn.

Lyons. Roger de Leona, and the Castle and Forest of L, Normandy 1180–95 (MRS). The name is derived from Lions, Normandy (*see* LYON), descending from William de L., t. Henry I., of Norfolk, where the family continued in 1346, after which they extended to Essex, Middlesex, and Ireland. Hence the Lords Lyons.

Lys. Richard Liesce, Normandy 1198 (MRS); William de la Lesse, Engl. c. 1272 (RH).

Lysley, for LISLE (Lower).

Lysons, for LESSON.

Lyte. Radulphus Lichait, Normandy 1198 (MRS). Geoffry, Walter, Roger, Lete, Engl. c. 1272 (RH). The family was of note in the West of England.

Lyttelton, or Westcote, appears to be a branch of De Vautort or Valletort, from Vautort, Maine, of which family Reginald, Hugh, and Goisfrid de Valletort came to England 1066. Reginald held thirty-three lordships from the Earl of Cornwall, 1086. From him descended Hugh de Valletort, who in 1165 held one fee in Devon and fifty-nine in Cornwall (*see* Dugdale for the later history). Joel de Valletort, a younger brother, was living 1165, and held estates in North Tawton, Derth, and Alfeton, Devon, of the Earls of Devon (Lib. Nig.; Testa). From him descended the Valletorts of North Tawton, who bore argent, three bends gules, within a bordure bezantée. The same arms, with slight difference of tincture, were borne by the family of Westcote in Marwood, near North Tawton, whence it may be inferred that they were a younger branch. Of this line Eustace de Marwood occurs, 13th cent. (Testa). Henry de Westcote, his son or grandson, possessed W. 1279 (Collins), and in 1314 John de Westcote occurs. Robert W. is mentioned in Devon, 1424, and his brother, Thomas Westcote of Westcote in Marwood, m. the heiress of Lyttelton of Worcester, and was father of the famous Lyttelton, Lord Chief Justice, author of the treatise on Tenures, and ancestor of Lord Lyttelton the historian. Hence the existing Lords Lyttelton.

Lytton-Bulwer. This family, the original name of which was Wiggott, Wigott, or Bygod, is a branch of the Bigods, Earls of Norfolk; and its ancient arms as 'Wygott' are those of the Bigods, with appropriate differences (viz. a cross quarterly pierced or, between four escallops arg., a fifth in the centre point). The Bigots or Wigots appear, from various circumstances too long to be detailed, to be descendants of Wigot de St. Denis, one of the greatest nobles of Normandy, who made grants to Cerisy Abbey in 1042, and in 1050 subscribed a charter of Duke William at the head of the Norman barons. He was married to a sister of Turstin Goz, father of Richard D'Avranches (father of Hugh Lupus), and had a younger son, Robert Wigot, Fitz-Wigot, or Bigot, who was introduced by Richard D'Avranches to the favour of Duke William. He had, 1, Roger, ancestor of the Wigots or Bigots, Earls of Norfolk; 2, William.

William Bigot, the second son, went into Apulia, but returned with Geoffry Ridel, t. William I. (Domesd.), and had a grant of Dunmow and Finchingfield, Essex, where he made gifts to Thetford Abbey (Mon. i.). He had Ilger, who in 1096 was chief commander in Palestine under Tancred, who left him in command of 200 knights to defend Jerusalem (Ord. Vitalis, 755). He had two sons, Humphry and William Bigot, who witnessed a charter of William, son of Roger B., for Thetford (Mon.). Raymond B., son of Humphry, held one fee in Suffolk, 1165 (Lib. Nig.). William his grandson (Blomefield, ii. 258) was father of Bartholomew, who was despoiled of his goods at Dunmow and Alfreton, t. Henry III. His grandson, Sir Ralph Bigot of Dunmow, M.P. for Essex, had issue 1, Walter, whose line terminated in coheiresses, t. Henry IV.; 2, John, of Marham, Norfolk, 1315, whose son Roger, of Norfolk, 1324 (PPW), left descendants, of whom Robert Wygod, a clergyman, occurs 1350, John Wygott in 1480, William Bigot in 1555, and John Wygot in 1580, when the last was possessed of the lordship of Geist, Norfolk. From him descended the family of Wiggott of Geist, which assumed the names of Lytton, Earle, Bulwer, and from which sprang Edward Lytton Bulwer, Lord Lytton, the celebrated writer, and his brother, Henry Lytton Bulwer, Lord Dalling, the eminent diplomatist. Another branch of this family assumed the name of Chute, whence the Chutes of the Vine, Hants.

M

Maas, for MACE.

Mabbert. Hugh and Roger Mabire, Normandy, 1180–95 (MRS); John de Mapert, Engl. c. 1272 (RH).

Mabbett, for MABBERT.

Mabbitt, for MABBERT.

Mabey, for MALBY.

Mabin, for MAPPIN.

Maby, for MALBY.

Mace. William de Mes, Normandy, 1180–95; Rener Mape, Ib. 1198 (MRS); Adam, John, Richard Mace, Engl. c. 1272 (RH).

Macey, or MASSY, from Macy, Normandy, a lordship and parish. See MASSY.

Machell, or Malcael. See LOWTHER.

Machin, from Le Machun or Le Meechin, a Norman sobriquet (Lower).

Mackney. See MAGNAY.

Mackrell. Ralph and Robert Makerel, Normandy, 1198 (MRS). Charlton Mackrell, Somerset, preserves the name.

Mackrill, for MACKARELL.

Mackrill. See MACKRELL.

Macer, for MARE.

Macers, for MARES.

Mager, for MAJOR.

Maggot. Richard Margot, Normandy, 1180 (MRS); Robert Maggote, Engl. c. 1272 (RH).

Maggs. Hugo Mages, Normandy, 1180 – 95 (MRS); John Magge, Engl. c. 1272 (RH).

Magnay. Gillebert Magné, Richard and Jordan de Maigniai, Normandy, 1180–95 (MRS), also Robert and Nigel de Magny (Ib.). Of this

family was Oliver de Mangny or Manny, so famous in the reign of Edward III., and a peer of England.

Magner. Ralph le Maigner Normandy, 1180–95 (MRS).

Magnus. Gilbert, Warin, Ralph, Robert, Tustin, William Magnus, or Le Grand, Normandy, 1198 (MRS); William and Simon Magnus, Engl. c. 1198 (RCR).

Maile. Gislebert de Maisle, Normandy, 1180–95 (MRS); Geoffry, William Mal, William Mayle, Engl. c. 1272 (RH).

Maillard. Gerold, Vivan Maillard, Normandy, 1180–95 (MRS). The arms of the Mallards are preserved by Robson.

Main. See MAINE.

Maine, or De Mayenne. See MAYNE.

Mainwaring, or Mesnil-Garin, a well-known Norman family. Robert de Mesnil Garin, Normandy, 1180 (MRS); William de Menil Garin, and the churches of St. John and St. Mary, Menil Garin, Normandy, 1198 (MRS). Ranulph de Mesnilgarin was Lord of M. near Coutances, and in 1086 held twelve lordships in barony from Hugh Lupus (Domesd. Chesh. 267). Richard and Roger de Menilgarin, his sons, were benefactors to Chester Abbey in 1093, and before 1119. Roger de Menilwarin (son of William de M.), t. Henry II., gave one-third of Tabley to Chester Abbey. From this baron descended the Mesnilgarins or Mainwarings of Peover, Baronets. A branch was seated in Norfolk, t. Henry II., of which was Ralph Meyngaryn, Miles, founder of Waybourn Abbey, Norfolk, whose descendants long continued (Mon. i. 490).

Mair, for MARE.

Maire, for MARE.

Maisey. Geoffry Mazue, Normandy, 1198 (MRS); Roger de Maisie (Ib.).

Maitland, or Maltalent. Robert Maltalent, Normandy, 1198 (MRS). Maltalent was near Nantes. Ralph Maltalent, c. 1135, witnessed a charter in York (Mon. ii. 192), as did Gilbert Mantalent, t. Henry II. (i. 733). The family was seated in York in 1165, when Richard Maltalent held half a knight's fee from Vescy of Alnwick, of which he had been enfeoffed by Eustace Fitz-John (Lib. Nig.), and also half a fee from Percy. He witnessed a charter of Eustace F. John (Mon. ii. 592) to the priory of Alnwick. Richard M. paid a fine to the Crown in Northumberland, 1231 (Hodgson, iii., iii. 163). Thomas de Matulant, a younger brother, settled in Scotland, t. William the Lion (Chart. Mailros.), and d. 1228. His son, William de Matulent, witnessed charters of Alexander II. and d. c. 1250. From him descended the Dukes and Earls of Lauderdale.

Major. Warin, Ralph, Robert Major, Normandy, 1198 (MRS); William Mair, Engl. c. 1272; William Maior, Normandy, 1180–95 (MRS); William le Magere, Engl. c. 1272 (RH).

Majors, for MAJOR.

Makin, for MACHIN.

Makings, for MACHIN.

Makins, for MACHIN.

Malby, for Malbisse. Hugh
320

Malbisse, Normandy, 1180 - 95 (MRS); Hugh Malbisse, Engl. c. 1272 (RH).

Male. *See* MAILE.

Malet, a well-known Norman baronial family, Barons of Gerardivilla or Graville, near Havre, Normandy. The ancestor was probably Gerard, a Scandinavian prince, one of the companions of Rollo, who gave his name to his fief. Maleth, his son or grandson, was father of Robert Malet, who c. 990 united with Osberne de Longueville, William de Breteuil, Gilbert de Menill, and others in giving the Church of Pictariville to religious uses. The gift was confirmed by his family (Gall. Christ. xi.; Instr. 139). William Maleth, whose name is conspicuous in the history of the Conquest, witnessed a charter before the Conquest (Gall. Christ. xi. 328). Robert M. his son, 1086, held the vast barony of Eye, Suffolk, and was one of the greatest proprietors in England. From him descended the Malets of Normandy. Several brothers of the family settled in England, of whom Durand M. occurs 1086 in Leicester, Notts, and Lincoln; Gilbert and William in Suffolk. From a branch possessed of the Lordship of Corry Malet, Somerset, 1165 (Lib. Nig.), descended the Malets of Somerset and the baronets of the name.

Malin, for MALINS.

Maling, for MALIN.

Malings, for MALIN.

Malins, or De Malines, from M., Flanders. The Lords of Malines descended from Bertold, living c. 800, and were established as Advocates or Protectors of Malines by the Bishops of Liege. They became extinct soon after 1300. In England Godeschal de Maghelenis had custody of the barony of Montgomery, t. Henry III. In 1312 Henry de Malines paid a fine for delaying to take the order of knighthood; and 1322 William Malyn was Bailiff of Ipswich. Hence the eminent Vice-Chancellor of the name.

Mallalue, for MELLADEW.

Mallan, for MALIN.

Mallett, for MALLET.

Mallock. Henry, William de Mailloc, Normandy, 1180–95 ; Henry de Maloc, 1198 (MRS).

Malmains. Roger, Frederick, Gilbert, Fatric le Malesmains, or Malis Manibus, Normandy, 1180–95 (MRS). In England this family was seated in Kent. The original name seems to have been Berville. *See* BARWELL.

Malpas, or De Malpassu, a branch of the ancient Barons of Malpas. *See* EGERTON.

Malyon, formerly Malaon, the arms of which, arg. a lion ramp. gu. crowned az., are preserved by Robson, and correspond with those of the Viscounts de Mauleon of Poitou, a branch of the Carlovingian Viscounts of Thouars.

Man. *See* LOMB.

Mancel. Alvered, Ralph, Gislebert, John Mancel or Mansel, Normandy, 1180–95 ; Warin, Ranulph, William M. 1198 (MRS); John M. was of Rutland, Worcester, and Leicester ; Ranulph of Oxford ; William of Cambridge and Gloucester (RCR). Hence the Mansells Baronets and the Lords Mansell.

Mander, for MANDERS.

Manders, from Mandres, near Evreux.

Mandeville, or Manneville, from Manneville in the Cotentin, Normandy, a well-known baronial house, Barons of Mersewood, Earls of Essex. This family probably derives from Manno, a Northman viking, who gave his name to the fief, c. 930. It appears that the family of De Sottevast was a branch (Wiffen, Hist. Russell, i. 6, 7). That of De Vere also appears from the arms (which are those of Magneville, with a mullet for difference) to have been a branch. Geoffry de Magnavilla was one of the greatest grantees, t. William I.; and his descendants were numerous and powerful both in England and Ireland.

Mandrell, Maundrel, or Munderel, identified armorially with Mundevill or Amundeville. *See* MONCKTON.

Mandrey, from Mandray in Lorraine. The arms are preserved by Robson.

Mandry. *See* MANDREY.

Mandy, for MONDAY.

Maney, or Mayney. *See* MAGNAY.

Mangin. Radulphus Mangeant, or Maniant, and William, Normandy, 1180–95 (MRS); Alexander Mangant, Engl. c. 1198 (RCR).

Manins, for MONYNS.

Mann. *See* MAN.

Mannell. *See* MANVELL.

Mannering, for MAINWARING.

Manners, or De Maneriis, from Mesnieres near Rouen, granted probably t. Rollo to Mainer, a Viking ancestor. It was held as half a knight's fee t. Philip Augustus by the Abbey of Lyre. The family of Mesnieres long continued in Normandy, Ralph and Roger de Mesnieres being mentioned 1198 (MRS), and William de M. 1232, whose descendants continued to be of consequence till c. 1400, when the male line ceased. Richard de Manieres came to England 1066, and in 1086 held from Odo of Bayeux, Borne, Kent, and Benested, Surrey (Domesd.). He was father of Tirel de Manieres, who, with Helias de St. Saen, a neighbouring noble, devoted himself to the cause of William Clito, the dispossessed heir of Robert of Normandy, and the legitimate heir to the throne. These faithful adherents of Clito lost their estates, and had to endure extreme sufferings on his behalf. On his death-bed he recommended them to his uncle, King Henry I., who accepted their submission. Tirel de Manieres, who was surnamed 'Peregrinus,' or 'the Wanderer,' from his adventures with William Clito, granted the church of Benested, Surrey, to St. Mary Overy t. Henry I. (Mon. ii. 85), and gave the manor of Benested in free marriage with his dau. to William Earl of Salisbury. Hugh de Maniere, his son, was also surnamed 'Peregrinus,' and with his son Richard 'Peregrinus,' or de Manieres, made grants in Hants to Waverley Abbey (Manning and Bray, ii. 146). He had another son, Robert, who is mentioned in the charters, and whose gift, as well as that of his brothers, was confirmed by Eugenius III. in 1147 (Mon. Angl. ii.). Robert, a son of Hugh Manieres above-named, held part of a fee Northumberland, 1165. His sons, Walter and Thomas de Maners, witnessed a charter of William de Vesci, 1178 (Mon. ii. 502). Their elder brother, Henry, had issue Reginald de Manieres, who witnessed a charter of Hugh, Count of Eu, temp. John (Mon. ii. 921), and as

322

'De Maisneriis' is also mentioned in Normandy 1198 (MRS), at which time Ralph and Roger M. are also mentioned in Normandy (Ibid.). From Reginald descended the house of Manners of Ethal, Northumberland; and thence the Lords Ros of Belvoir, Earls and Dukes of Rutland, Barons Manners, and Viscounts Canterbury. From another branch descended Baldwin de Maners, a baron by writ, 1309.

Mannett. Richard Mennet, Normandy, 1180-95; Osbert Minete, 1198 (MRS); William Monet, Engl. c. 1272 (RH).

Mannevy. John and Robert de Manorbia, Normandy, 1180-95 (MRS). The arms of Minifie, England, are preserved by Robson.

Manning. Lambert Maignon, 1180; William, Ansketel le Maignen, Normandy, 1180-95 (MRS); Richard, Henry Maning, Engl. c. 1272 (RH).

Mannion, for MANNING.

Mannix, for Mannis or Manse. Durand Manse, Normandy, 1180-95 (MRS); Cristiana Manus, Engl. c. 1272 (RH).

Manns, for MANN.

Mansell, for MANCELL.

Manser. Richard Manesier, Normandy 1198 (MRS).

Mantell. William de Montellis, Normandy, 1198 (MRS). The name as Mantel dates from the Conquest in England.

Mantle, for MANTELL.

Manse, or Manse. *See* MANNIX.

Mantor. John, and Walter Fitz-Richard Minutor, Normandy, 1180-95 (MRS); Henry le Munetor, Engl. c. 1272 (RH).

Manvell. Roscelin, and Nicholas de Manneval, and the fief of M.

Normandy, 1180-95 (MRS); Robert de Manevil, Engl. c. 1272 (RH).

Manwaring. *See* MAINWARING.

Manwell. *See* MANVELL.

Mapp, for Mapes or MALPAS.

Mappin. Roger Magnepeine, Normandy, 1180-95 (MRS); John, Richard Manipenyn, c. 1270 (RH), Engl.

Mapson. William Maubeysin, Engl. c. 1272 (RH); Michael Maubuisson, Normandy, t. Henry V. (Mem. Soc. Ant. Norm. v. 244).

Marborough. *See* MARLBOROUGH.

Marbury. *See* MERBURY. Nicholas Merbury, Butler of the King, Normandy, 1180-95 (MRS).

March, from Marché, Normandy, as Newmarch from Neumarché. Nicholas, William, Stephen, Roger de Mercato, Normandy, 1180-95 (MRS); Bartholomew, William de Marche, Engl. c. 1198 (ROR).

March, or de la Marche. Fermer, and Robert de Marchia, Normandy, 1198 (MRS).

Marchant. Rainald, William, Stephen, Ranulph, Robert Mercator, Normandy, 1180-95 (MRS). Everard, Gilbert, Herbert, Richard, 1198 (Ib.). Of these, Robert, Richard, William, appear in England, 1189-99.

Marcot. William, Richard, Marcote, Normandy, 1180-95 (MRS).

Marcy, from Marcy, Laon. In 1086 Ralph de Marcy held in Essex and Suffolk. The family long continued in Essex, Herts, and Gloucester. It appears that the Cobhams of Kent, Lords Cobham, were a branch.

Mares. William des Mares, Normandy, 1180-95; Angevin, Asa, William de Maria, Normandy, 1198

(MRS); John, Richard, Robert de Mareya, Engl. c. 1272 (RH).

Maret. Richard Mareta, Normandy, 1180-95 (MRS); Alexander Mirthe, Engl. c. 1272 (RH).

Marett, for MARET.

Margrie. William de St. Margareta, Normandy, 1180-95; William Margarita, 1198 (MRS); John Margerie, Engl. c. 1272 (RH).

Margries, for MARGRIE.

Marin, for de Marinis, a Norman name.

Maris. Ivo, Drogo, Gilbert, Robert de Maris, and the lordship of Maris, Normandy, 1180-95 (MRS); William de Mareis, Engl. c. 1272 (RH).

Mark, or De Marc, from M., Normandy. Geoffry de Marco and his sons are mentioned by Ordericus Vitalis (591). In 1148 Robert de Marc had lands at Winchester (Wint. Domesd.). The name occurs t. Stephen (Mon. ii. 109).

Marke, for MARK.

Markes. *See* MARKS.

Marks. 1. For MARK. 2. A Hebrew name.

Marlborough. Alured de Merleberge, 1086, was a great baron, Wilts. William de Merleberge gave lands for a chaplain at Isle Bruers, Somerset (Inq. p. mort.). This was probably a Norman family.

Marler. N. Marruglarius, Normandy, 1180 (MRS); Alice le Marler, Engl. c. 1272 (RH).

Marley, or Merley. William and Ralph de Merlai, and the fief of M. Normandy, 1180-95 (MRS). Roger de Merlai, Engl. 1189 (Rot. Pip.). The Merlais were barons of Morpeth.

Marling. *See* MERLIN.

Marmion. Robert, William, Geoffry, Marmion, Normandy, 1180-

95 (MRS). A well-known baronial family, Lords and Viscounts of Fontenay le Tesson, Normandy. They appear to have been a branch of the Tessons.

Ralph Tesson, who brought 120 knights of his dependence to the aid of Duke William at the battle of Val des Dunes 1047, founded c. 1055 the Abbey of Fontenay near Caen (Gall. Christ. xi. 413). A charter of Ralph Tesson was witnessed by William Marmion or Marmilon, probably his brother, c. 1070 (Ibid.), who with his family possessed part of Fontenay. Robert Marmion, his son, Viscount of Fontenay, passed into England with the Conqueror, and had extensive grants, his descendants a century later holding seventeen fees in England and five in Normandy (Lib. Niger; Feoda Norm. Duchesne; also the paper of M. Vaultier, Mem. Soc. Ant. Norm. x. 94). The Tessons of Normandy bore gules, a fesse ermine; the Marmions vair, a fesse gules; and the Percys, another branch, azure, a fesse indented or. *See* PERCY.

Marney. Rohais de Marreiny and the fief of Marigny, Normandy, 1180-95 (MRS). The Lords Marney of England were of this house.

Marr, for Mare, or De la Mare. *See* MARE.

Marrable, from Mirabel, Normandy. Lucia Mirable, Engl. c. 1272 (RH).

Marratt, for MARET.

Marriage, for MARCH.

Marrian, for MARRIN.

Marrin, from Marines, Normandy. The name Marines often occurs in the early records.

Marrin. Richard, Robert, Morein, Normandy, 1180-95 (MRS);

Geoffry, John, Ralph, Morin, Engl. c. 1272 (RH).

Marris. *See* MARIS.

Marritt, for MARRETT.

Mars, for MARES.

Marsh. 1. A local English name. 2. Robert, Simon, William, de Mariscis; Roger, Robert, Gervase de Marisco, Normandy, 1180-95; Alpais, Gervase, Robert de M., 1198 (MRS). William was of Kent, Robert of Gloucester, Richard of Hants, and York, and Lancaster.

Marshal, for MARSHALL.

Marshall. This being a name of office (the Marshal being a feudal officer of eminence appointed by each great baron) includes a number of different families. Robson has preserved sixty-two coats of arms of this name. It may be presumed that those who held this office were generally Norman; and numerous families of the name were possessed of estates. The principal was that of the Marshalls Earls of Pembroke, and the Lords Marshall of Hingham, Norfolk.

Marshall, or le Marischal, Earl of Pembroke. *See* HASTINGS.

Marsham, or Baynard (*See* Beaumont), descended from Geoffry Baynard or de Beaumont, whose son William Baynard had issue Roscelin Lord of Stratton and Marsham, who had issue William Fitz-Rosceline, and Robert Fitz-R., whose sons William de Stratton, and Bartholomew de Marsham, living t. Henry II., were ancestors of the Strattons and Marshams of Norfolk; from the latter of whom descend the Earls of Romney. *See* ROSLING.

Mart, for MORT.

Martel. John, Roger, Geoffry, Martel, Normandy, 1180 (MRS).

The name occurs in all the English records.

Martell, for MARTEL.

Marten, for MARTIN.

Martin. Diel, Guido, John, Ralph, Roger, Tustin, William Martin, Normandy, 1198 (MRS); Nigel, William M. Engl. c. 1198 (RCR); Robert, William, Richard, Ansketil, Peter, Roger, Ralph Martin, Normandy, 1180–95; 2. from St. Martin, Normandy. Alured, Roger, Hervey de St. M., Normandy, 1180–95 (MRS). 3. A patronymic from Martin de Umfraville, Sire de Tours, Normandy, conqueror of Cameys, Wales, t. William Rufus, whose descendants bore the name of Fitz-Martin or Martin, and were barons by writ.

Martins, for MARTIN.

Martyn, for MARTIN.

Martyr. Ranulph and William Le Martre, Normandy 1198 (MRS); Wymarc La Martre 1198 (Ib.).

Marvel. Richard de Marvil or Maruil, Normandy 1198 (MRS); Sire John de Marville of Normandy occurs c. 1270 (Mem. Soc. Ant. Norm. v. 151); Warin Merveyl, England c. 1272 (RH). Of this family was Andrew Marvell, the patriot.

Maryon, Mervyn or Mering. Radulphus Mervain, Normandy 1198 (MRS); Matilda Marwyn, Engl. c. 1272 (RH).

Mascall, for MARSHALL (Lower).

Masey, for MASSY.

Mash, for MARSH (Lower).

Masi, for MASEY.

Maskall, for MASKELL.

Maskell, for MASCALL.

Maskelyne. Eustachius de Masseline, Normandy 1180–95 (MRS). Roger Fitz-Mazeline 1180; John Mazelyn, Engl. c. 1272 (RH).

Maskens, for Meschins. *See* MAKINS.

Maslen, for MASLIN.

Maslin, or MASKELYNE.

Mason. Godfrey, Richard, William le Mazon, Normandy 1198 (MRS); Hugh le Mazun, Engl. c. 1198 (RCR). This name doubtless includes families of various origin.

Massey. *See* MASSY.

Massie, for MASSY.

Massinger, or Messenger, the English form of LEGGATT, or Legatus.

Masson, or Le Masson. *See* MASON.

Massy, a well-known Norman family. Macey, whence the name is derived, was near Coutances and Avranches, Normandy. In 1086 Hugo de Maci held lands in Hunts (Domesday), and Hamo or Hamund de Macy held nine lordships in barony from Hugh Lupus in Cheshire, and 1193 subscribed the foundation charter of Chester Abbey, and granted lands to it (Mon. i. 985). Robert de Macy witnessed a charter of Ranulph Meschines E. of Chester 12th cent. (Mon. i. 986). From this line sprang many houses of eminence, bearing the name of Massy, Massey, or Massie, and the Barons Massey, and Clarina.

Mast, for Most or MOSSE.

Master. John le Meteier, Normandy 1198, Osbert and William, Ib. (MRS); Alan and John le Mayster, Engl. c. 1272 (RH).

Masters. *See* MASTER.

Mathams. Robert, William, Samson de Matom, Normandy 1180–95 (MRS); Richard and Thomas de Matham, Engl. c. 1272 (RH).

Matland, for MAITLAND.

Maton. Robert, William, Samson de Maton, Normandy 1180–95

(MRS); Beatrix Motun, Engl. c. 1272 (RH).

Matterface, for MARTINVAST (Lower).

Maud. *See* MAUDE.

Maude, de Mouhaut or De la Mare. *See* DE LA MARE. This branch of De la Mare descends from Ranulph, Dapifer of Chester 1093, whose sons Robert de Montalt and William de la Mare occur in York-shire 1130 (Rot. Pip.). Roger de Mara, son of the former, was a bene-factor to Roche Abbey, York (Mon. i. 839), and from him descended Roger de Montalt, summoned as a baron 1299. William, above men-tioned, had issue Simon de Muhaut, witness to a charter of Cecilia de Rumelli (Mon. ii. 101) for Bolton Abbey, York; and to another char-ter with Simon Mohaut, his son (i. 655). The latter held lands of the honour of Skipton, York, 1165 (Lib. Nig.). John de Montalt of Ma-therley, York, gave lands to Drax (Burton, Mon. Ebor.), and in 1300 Adam de Mohaut or Maude was re-turned as liable for military service in person against the Scots (PPW). Hence the Maudes of Holling, Woodhouse, Alverthorpe, and Rid-dlesden, York, from the latter of whom sprang the Maudes, Barons Montalt, Viscounts Hawarden.

Mauditt, or Mauduit, from M., near Mantes, Normandy. Geoffry Maudit held in Wilts in capite 1086. William, his brother, held a barony, Hants 1086. Hence the Barons Mauduit, Earls of Warwick.

Maudslay, or Banastre.. *See* NELSON. Of this family was Maudslay, the eminent engineer and inventor of machinery of various descriptions.

326

Maudsley. *See* MAUDSLAY.

Mauger. John, Erenger Mauger, Normandy, 1180-95; eight of the name, 1198, Norm. (MRS); Robert and Walter Mauger, Engl. c. 1272 (RH).

Maul. *See* MAULE.

Maule, from Maule in the French Vexin, the history of which family has been preserved by Du-chesne from the time of Guarin, who lived c. 980, father of Ansold, father of Peter Lord of Maule. The family is frequently mentioned by Ordericus Vitalis, and a branch be-came seated in Scotland, and hence sprang the Earls of Panmure (Douglas).

Mauleverer, from M. near Rouen, Normandy. Helto M. 1086 held in Kent, and 1120 Helto, his son, witnessed the charter of Bolton, York (Mon. ii. 101). From this time the notices of the name in Notts and York are continual.

Mauley. *See* MAWLEY.

Maull, for MAUL.

Maunder, for MANDER.

Maunders, for MANDERS.

Maunsell, for MANCEL.

Maurice, from St. Maurice, Nor-mandy. N. de St. Maurice 1180-95 (MRS); Isabella, John, Margerie Morice, Engl. c. 1272 (RH). N. de St. Maurice and the fief of St. M. Normandy 1180-95 (MRS).

Mawby, for MALBY.

Mawditt. *See* MAUDIT.

Mawley, from Mauley, Poitou. Peter de Malo Lacu acquired the barony of Mulgrave and Doncaster by marriage. Hence the Lords de Mauley summoned by writ 1260.

May. Robert, Ralph de Mai, Robert Mai, Normandy 1180-98

(MRS). Henry de May, Hugh Mey, Engl. c. 1272 (RH).

Mayall. *See* MIALL.

Maybank, or Malbanc. Henry, Hugh, Alberic Malebenc, Normandy 1180–95 (MRS); Roger and William 1198 (Ib.). This family was possessed of the barony of Wich-Malbanc, Cheshire.

Maybin, for MAYBANK.

Maybury. Hugh, and Roger de Mabire, Normandy 1180–95 (MRS).

Maychell. *See* MACHELL, or Lowther.

Mayell. *See* MAILLE.

Mayer, in some cases for MARE or De la Mare.

Mayers, for MAYER.

Mayes, for MACE.

Mayhew, for MAYO.

Mayho, for MAYO.

Maylard, for MALLARD.

Mayle, for MAILLE.

Mayles, for MAYLE.

Maylin, for MALIN.

Maynard. N. Mainart or Mainard, Ralph, John, and the estate of the Mainards, Normandy 1180–95 (MRS); Richard Mainard, Engl. c. 1198 (RCR). From this family descended the Viscounts Maynard.

Mayne, or Mayenne, from Mayenne in Maine, a powerful baronial house, of which Walter de M. occurs in 976 (La Roque, i. 159, 160). Judael de Mayenne had a vast barony in Devon 1086, and his family long continued there. In 1165 Walter Fitz-Juel de Mayenne (de Meduana) held a barony of twenty-one knights' fees in Kent (Lib. Niger). Many branches of these houses remained; the name changing gradually to Main and Mayne. Hence the Lords New-haven.

Mayo. Roger de Maio, Normandy 1180–95 (MRS); Acon de Maeio, and Robert 1198 (Ib.). Ralph Mayot, Engl. c. 1272 (RH).

Mayor. William Maior, Normandy 1180 (MRS); William Mair, Engl. c. 1272 (RH).

Mays, for MACE.

Mayou. *See* MAYO.

Mays. *See* MACE.

Mayse, for MACE.

Meachin, or Meschin. *See* MACHIN.

Mead, the English form of De Prato. William, Robert, Matilda, Reginald de Prato, Normandy 1180–95 (MRS); Richard and Robert de P. 1198 (Ib.). Stephen, Peter de P., Engl. c. 1272 (RH).

Meade. *See* MEAD.

Meadow. *See* MEAD.

Meadows, the English form of De Pratis. Simon, Gilbert, Hugh, Fulco de Pratis, Normandy 1180–95 (MRS); Henry and Richard de P. 1198 (Ib.); William de Pratis, Engl. 1189 (Rot. Pip.).

Meads, for MEAD.

Meadus, for MEADOWS.

Meager, for MAUGER.

Meakin, for MAKIN.

Meakins, for MEAKIN.

Meal, for MALE.

Mealin, for MALINS.

Mealing, for Maling or MALIN.

Meall, for MALE.

Mean, for MAINE.

Means. *See* MEAN.

Meares, for MARES.

Mears, for MARES.

Mease, for MACE.

Measer. Gilbert and William Masuer, Normandy 1180 (MRS); William de Masura 1198 (Ibid.). Geoffry le Massor, Engl. c. 1272 (RH).

Measures. *See* MEASOR.

Meates, or De Meautis, from that place, Normandy. The arms are preserved by Robson.

Meatyard. Ralph le Meiteier, Normandy 1180-95 (MRS).

Meayers. *See* MARES.

Mee. Robert de Mieie, Normandy 1180-95 (MRS); Robert Miee, 1198 (Ib.); Hugh, Richard Mey, Engl. c. 1272 (RH).

Meech. Hugh de Meche, Normandy 1180-95 (MRS); Henry Mache, Engl. c. 1272 (RH).

Meed, for MEAD.

Meek, for MEECH.

Meeke, for MEEK.

Meeking, for Mechin or MACHIN.

Meekins, for MEEKINGS.

Meers, for MEARS.

Meeres, for MEARS.

Mees, for MEE.

Meeson, for Mauvesin or Malvoisin (Lower). Berenger, Geoffry, Manasser, Peter, Ralph, Ranulph, Robert, Roger Malveisin, Normandy 1198 (MRS). This family is considered to have been a branch of the ancient Counts of the Vexin (Wiffen, Mem. Russell, i. 49). In 1070 Ralph Malvoisin, Sire de Rosny (who occurs as 'Malusvicinus' in Suffolk 1086), gave lands to the Abbey of St. Evroult, Normandy (Ord. Vitalis, 604). Hugo Malusvicinus, founder of Blitheley Abbey (Mon. i. 468), appears in Stafford 1130 (Rot. Pip.); Henry Malveisiu in Salop and Stafford 1165 (Lib. Niger). Gilbert M. was of Normandy at this time (Mem. Soc. Ant. Norm. viii. 266). Ridware Mauvesyn, Leicester, still bears the name of this family.

Meggs. *See* MAGGS.

Mehary, for Mary. Richard and

William de St. Marie, Normandy 1180-95 (MRS); William de St. Maria, Engl. c. 1198 (RCR); Adam de St. M. c. 1272 (RH).

Melborne. Henry, Hugh, Roger Malberne, Normandy 1180-95 (MRS).

Melby, for MALBY.

Melen, for MALINS.

Melhuish, for MELLERSH.

Melladew, for Malduit. *See* MALDITT.

Meller. Eguerran and William Mellers, Normandy 1180 (MRS). Simon le Meillur, Engl. c. 1272 (RH).

Mellersh, or Mellers. William de Mesleriis, Eguerrand, Fromund, Simon, Walter de Meuleriis, Normandy 1198 (MRS). The arms of Mellers are preserved by Robson.

Melles, for MILLS.

Mellett. Petrus de Melleto, Normandy c. 1200 (Mem. Soc. Ant. Norm. v. 118, 121); William Melite, Normandy 1198 (MRS); Geoffry, and William Melt, Engl. c. 1272 (RH).

Mellifont. Thomas Malenfant, Normandy 1180-95 (MRS).

Mellin, for MALIN.

Mellish. *See* MELLERSH.

Mellodew. *See* MELLADUE.

Mellon. Radulphus Meloan, Normandy 1180-95, and the fief of Mellon, Normandy (MRS); Robert Millun, Engl. c. 1272 (RH).

Mellor. *See* MILLER.

Mellhuish. *See* MELLERSH.

Melon, for MELLON.

Melvil, for MELVILLE.

Melvill. *See* MELVILLE.

Melville, from Esmaleville or Maleville, a barony in the Pays de Caux, Normandy. William de Smalavilla held lands in Suffolk 1086

(Domesd.); Robert de Malavilla t. Henry I. witnessed a charter in Yorkshire (Mon. Angl. i. 660), and one of Roger of Poitou (Ibid.). Roger de Malavilla held a fief 1165 from William de Ros; and other branches were seated in Bucks and Scotland, where Geoffry M. was Grand Justiciary t. David I. Hence the Earls of Melville.

Mence. Durand Manse, Normandy 1180-95 (MRS); Thomas Minch, Engl. c. 1272 (RH).

Menday, for MONDAY.

Mendes, for MENDS.

Mendis, for MENDS.

Mends, for MENCE.

Mennell, for MEYNEL.

Mennie, for Manny or MAGNAY.

Menzies, or De Maners, an early branch of the house of Manners in Scotland, which still bears the ancient arms of the family. Hence the baronets Menzies.

Mercer. Bertin and Buno le Mercier, Normandy 1180-95; Guinard, Ralph, &c. 1198 (MRS).

Mercer. Hubert, Hugh, Richard, Odo Mercer or Mercier, Normandy 1180-95. Nineteen of the name as Mercator and Mercennarius in 1198 (MRS). In England, no doubt, the name included Norman and other families.

Merchant. See MARCHANT.

Mercier. See MERCER.

Merck. See MARK.

Mercy, for MARCY.

Merfield. Gislebert Mirfaut or Mirfalt, Normandy 1198 (MRS); Geoffry de Merrifeud, Engl. c. 1272 (RH).

Merges, for Marges or Mages. See MAGES.

Merifield. See MERFIELD.

Merivale, from Merrival or Mer-val, Normandy, which was held by Simon de Bello Sacco t. Philip August. (Mem. Soc. Ant. Norm. v. 189). William de la Marival held a knight's fee from the Abbot of Jumieges c. 1200 (Ib. 173). Geoffry de Mariavalle, Normandy 1180-95 (MRS).

Merle. Simon Merel, Normandy 1180-95 (MRS); Adam de Meriel Engl. c. 1272 (RH).

Merlin. Robert Merlin 1180, Ralph 1180-95, Norm. (MRS); Roger de Merlene, Engl. c. 1272 (RH).

Merrall. See MERLE.

Merralls. See MERRALL.

Merrell. See MERLE.

Merrett, for MARETT.

Merrick. William de Meric or Meri, Normandy 1180-95 (MRS); John de Merc, Engl. c. 1272 (RH).

Merridew, for MELLADEW.

Merrill, for MERLE.

Merriman, a corruption of MARMION (Lower).

Merrin, for MARRIN.

Merritt, for MARETT.

Merry. Walter de Mereio or Mery, Normandy 1180-95 (MRS); Robert de Mery 1198 (Ib.); Alicia, John Marie, Engl. c. 1272 (RH).

Merryman. See MERRIMAN.

Merser, for MERCER.

Messenger, or Massenger. Osberne Legatus Regis, a diplomatic agent of the Conqueror, held estates Lincoln 1086. From him descended the family of Legat or L'Enveyse of York and other counties. The name was translated 13th cent. Hence the dramatic poet Massinger.

Messent. Gervasius de Maisent, Normandy 1180-95 (MRS).

Messent, probably for Mucedent.

Alexander, Hugh, Robert Mucedent, Normandy 1180-95 (MRS).

Messer. Jacobus Mesoart, Normandy 1180-98 (MRS); Adam, Aubry, &c., Messer, Engl. c. 1272 (RH).

Messiter, for MASTER.

Metherell, or Meterell, for MEVERELL.

Meuse, from Mues, Moes, or Muisa, in Normandy. Gilbert de Moes held from Philip Augustus c. 1200. Roger Miaz 1180-95 (MRS). Mieuce was in the Vexin. Ketel de Melsa 1066 came to England, and gave his estate in Holderness the same name. He was father or grandfather of John de Melsa, with whom the Earl of Albemarle 1138 exchanged lands for Melsa, and founded there Melsa or Meaux Abbey. The family of Melsa or Meaux of Yorkshire descended from John, and branches of it settled in the South. Hence the baronets Meux.

Meux, for MEUSE.

Mew, for MEUSE.

Mewes, for MEUSE.

Mews, for MEUSE.

Meyers, or Moirs. Robert de Moire, Normandy 1180-95 (MRS); Haimeric, Robert, William de M. 1198 (Ib.); Robert Moyere, Engl. c. 1272 (RH); also a modern foreign name.

Meymot, or Maymot, for Mamignot. Hugo Maminot, Normandy 1198 (MRS). Robert Maminot, Sire de Curbespine, near Bernai, was father of Gilbert M., Bishop of Lisieux, and Ralph de Curbespine of Kent, t. William I. The family became seated in England, and 1165 Walter M.'s barony in Kent was of twenty-eight fees. Walchelin M. was of Salop, and nephew of Ralph

Peverel (Ord. Vitalis, ed. Forester, iii. 287). The Norman fief of M. consisted of five knights' fees (MSAN. viii. 427).

Meyrick. See MERRICK.

Meynell, a baronial family, from Mesnil, Normandy. Stephen, Sire de Mesnil t. William I., obtained great estates in York and Notts. His son Robert and grandson Stephen joined with him in the foundation of Scarth Abbey, York (Burton, Mon. Ebor. 357). Hence the Lords Meynil of York. Gilbert, second son of Stephen I., was of Notts 1130, and was ancestor of the M.s of Meynil-Langley, barons of Parliament 1326. The family of Mesnil, Normandy, is mentioned c. 980, when Gilbert de Menill joined with Osberne de Longueville and Robert Malet in granting the church of Pictariville for religious uses. In 1027 Duke Richard confirmed the grant of Odo, son of Gilbert de Menill (surnamed Episcopus), viz. Menil St. Melan, with its Church, and also the Church of Bulville, to religious uses (Neustria Pia, 217).

Meysey. Roger de Maisie, Normandy 1198 (MRS).

Miall. Ricardus Mihial, Normandy 1180 (MRS); William Mayle, Engl. c. 1272 (RH).

Miatt. Roger Miaz or Miata, Normandy 1180-95 (MRS); Walter Mite, Engl. c. 1272 (RH).

Michael. Radulphus Michael, Normandy 1180-95, Geoffry and Selle Michael 1198 (MRS); Geoffry and William de St. Michael, Engl. 1198 (RCR).

Michel. See MICHAEL.

Michell, for MICHAEL.

Michels, for MICHAEL.

Michells, for MICHAEL.

Middleton, of Middleton-Morel, Northumberland, probably a branch of Morel (Testa de Neville, 382).

Mieling, for MALING.

Miell. See MIALL.

Mihell, for MIALL.

Mier. See MEYERS.

Miers. See MEYERS.

Milbank, armorially connected with Malbanke of Lancashire. The family of Malbanc or Malbeding came to England with Hugh Lupus, Earl of Chester, and held the barony of Wich-Malbank, Cheshire, t. William I. Henry, Hugh, Alberee Malbenc occur in Normandy 1180-95 (MRS). Richard Malbanc gave the Church of Bency to Troarn Abbey, Normandy, t. Henry I., and Alured M. gave his lands to the same abbey t. William I. (MSAN. xv. 174, 175). He was contemporary with William M., Baron of Wich, Cheshire. Branches of the family in later times occur in Dorset and Lancashire, from the latter of which descend the Malbankes, now Milbankes, baronets.

Milborn. Henry, Hugh, and Roger Malberne, Normandy 1180 (MRS); Hugo de Meleburn, Engl. c. 1272 (RH).

Milbourn. See MILBORN.

Milbourne. See MILBORN.

Milburn. See MILBOURN.

Mile, for Miall. Sometimes for MOYLE or Moels.

Miles. Geoffry, Richard, Ralph, Walter, Robert, William, Miles, Normandy 1180-95 (MRS); Richard Miles, Engl. 1189 (Rot. Pip.). Of this name are the baronets Miles.

Miley, for Milly. Roger de Milleio, and the fief of Milly, Normandy 1180-95 (MRS).

Mill. William and Geoffry Mil, Normandy 1180-95 (MRS); Oliver Mile 1198 (Ib.). Hence the baronets Mill.

Millar, for MILLER.

Millard. William Milart, Normandy 1189-95 (MRS).

Millbank, for MILBANK.

Millbourn, for MILBOURN.

Millen, for Melan. Roger de St. Melan, William de St. M., Normandy 1180-95 (MRS).

Miller, or Milner, Molendinarius, le Mouner. Walter, Hugh, Joscelin, Ralph, Raginald, Richard, Robert, William Molendinarius, Normandy 1198 (MRS). The same name occurs frequently in England 13th cent., and was afterwards translated. It includes Norman and other families.

Millett. See MELLETT.

Millhouse. William Milhous, Normandy 1180-95 (MRS); Margery Milys, Engl. c. 1272 (RH).

Milliard, for MILLARD.

Millicent. Petrus Millesent, Normandy 1198 (MRS); Petrus Milesant, Engl. c. 1272 (RH).

Millie. See MILEY.

Millin. See MELLON.

Million, for MILLIN.

Millisent. See MILLICENT.

Millish. See MELLISH.

Mills. 1. from MILES. 2. for De Molis. Oger, Ralph, Richard de Molis, Normandy 1198 (MRS); Hugh, Roger de Moles, Engl. c. 1272 (RH). 3. from an English locality, Norfolk.

Miln, for MILNE.

Milne, or Milon. Robert Milon, Normandy 1180-95 (MRS); Geoffry Milne, Engl. c. 1272 (RH).

Milner. Roger, Alvered, Bertram, Geoffry, Henry, Ralph, Richard Le Mounier, Normandy 1180-

98 (MRS); Roger, Martin Molendinarius, Engl. c. 1199 (RCR).

Milner. *See* MILLER.

Milnes, or Mills, otherwise de Moels. Roger de Molis held in Devon 1083, 1086. The name was derived from Meulles, Normandy. Geoffry de Molis was of Notts and Derby 1130 (Rot. Pip.), and 1165 William de Moles held fiefs of Mowbray, Yorkshire. In 1243 Geoffry de Molendino, or Moles, temporarily forfeited his lands in the North (Roberts, Excerpt.). John del Milne 1315 was bailsman for an M.P. for Lancashire (PPW). Hence the Baronets Milnes, and the Lords Houghton.

Milns, for MILNES.

Milo, for Milon. *See* MILNE.

Milton, from several English localities. Sometimes a contraction of Middleton, as in the case of the poet Milton. Professor Masson, in his Life of John Milton the poet, shows that John Milton his father, a scrivener in London 1603, was son of Richard M., of Stanton St. John, Oxfordshire, living 1577, son of Henry M., of the same place, who d. 1558. He also remarks that it has been found impossible to connect the name with any place called Milton in Oxford or Berks; and cites the statement of the poet, that he was born of 'an honest and honourable stock,' i.e. of a good family. The name of Milton was however only an abbreviation (of which we have many examples, such as Milton Abbas, Dorset, formerly Middleton); and Middleton, Oxfordshire (the original of Milton), was the baronial estate of the Norman family of De Camville, whose arms, a double-headed spread eagle, were

332

borne by the poet as his paternal coat, confirmed by Segar the herald, t. Charles I. He was therefore, on the evidence of name and arms, one of the De Camvilles.

Camville or Campville was in the Cotentin, and t. William I. William de C. was a benefactor of the Church of Jumieges (Mon. Angl. ii. 978). Richard de C. his son, surnamed Puignant, had a grant of Middeltune and Godendune, Oxford, in barony. William de C., his brother, whose son occurs as Hugh Fitz-William, held Godintune from him 1086 (Domesd.). The Camvilles of Milton appear continually in the subsequent records. Gerard de C., baron of Milton, had three sons: 1. Richard, whose d. and heir carried the barony to William Longespee, c. 1230. 2. Thomas, d. s. p. 3. Gerard, living 1205 (Hardy, Obl. et fin. 241). The latter was probably ancestor of the Miltons, of whom Roger de Milton was security for an M.P. for the adjacent county of Bedford 1318, while in 1322 Ralph de Milton occurs in Oxfordshire (PPW). In 1340 John de Middleton or Milton was a juror in Oxfordshire (Nonar. Inq.). In 1428 John de Milton held Burnham, Bucks, and 1433 Roger de M. was returned as one of the gentry of Oxfordshire, and in 1437 was an assessor and collector of Parliamentary aids in that county. The family is said to have suffered during the Wars of the Roses. In 1526 Henry Middleton (Milton) was rector of Marden, Bucks, and 1534 John Middleton was sub-prior of Bicester, Oxfordshire. These ecclesiastics were probably uncles of Henry Milton of Stanton St. John, the poet's great grandfather, and this connection accords with the family tradition that the poet's ancestors had been strong supporters of Popery, and that his father had been disinherited in consequence of his change of religious opinions.

Minn, for Men, or MANN.

Minet. *See* MINNETT.

Minnett. Ricardus Mennet, Normandy 1180–95 (MRS); Osbert Minete 1198 (Ib.); Petrus Minnot, Engl. 1202 (Rot. Canc.).

Minnitt, for MINNETT.

Minns, for MENCE.

Minors. Gislebert and Henry de Mineriis, Normandy 1198 (MRS). They also occur in England 1198 (RCR). William, Eguerran, Ivo, de M., t. John appear in Normandy.

Minter, for Munter, or Muntator, equivalent to a knight or man-at-arms—including chiefly Norman or foreign families.

Miott, probably foreign.

Miskin, for MACHIN, or Meschin.

Misson, for MESSON.

Misson, for MESSON.

Mister, for Mestre, or MASTER.

Mitchell, for MICHELL.

Minchin, or Manchin. Robert, Geoffry, Lucas Manchon, Normandy 1180–95 (MRS). Warin, Gervase, Ranulph M. 1198 (Ib.); Philip Mincan, Engl. c. 1272 (RH).

Mineards, for MINORS.

Minier, for MINERS.

Mitchell. *See* MICHAEL.

Mitford, or Bertram. This family was founded probably by Brico, a Norwegian Viking, who gave his name to the barony of Briquebec, its inheritance. Oslac or Auslec, his son, filled a great part in Norman history. His brother Amfrid the Dane was ancestor of the earls of Chester, and the barons of Bec-

Crespin. Oslac had: 1. Torstin. 2. Hugh Barbatus, ancestor of the barons of Montfort. Torstin, t. Richard I., witnessed his charter in favour of St. Denis 968 (Bouquet, ix. 731), and was a benefactor 960 to Fontenelle (Wiffen, Mem. Russell, i. 60). William, surnamed Bertram, son of Torstin, living 1012, was father of Robert Bertram, Baron of Briquebec, living 1066 (Gall. Christ. xi. 60, 229 Instr.). From Robert, his elder son, descended the barons of Briquebec, whose barony consisted of 40 knights' fees. His younger son, William, became Baron of Mitford and Bothal, Northumberland, probably after the forfeiture of Robert Mowbray. He m. the dau. of Wido de Bailliol (and not of an imaginary Sir John de Mitford, as alleged by some). He had four sons, of whom two left issue, viz. Richard B., ancestor of the barons of Bothal, and an elder son, Roger Bertram, Baron of Mitford. The latter had issue, William, living t. Stephen, father of Roger II. t. Henry II., who in 1165 held five knights' fees in barony. He had issue three sons, viz.: 1. William B., whose son Roger III. was summoned as a baron by writ 1260 as 'Roger Bertram de Mitford,' and had Roger IV., who d. s. p. 1311. 2. Richard. 3. John de Midford, who t. Richard I. subscribed a charter of Eustace de Bailliol. He had Matthew de M., whose sons, Nicholas and Peter de Mitford, lived t. Henry III., and held lands near Mitford. (Matthew and Nicholas are transferred to the time of the Conquest by modern writers.)

Richard de Midford or Mitford, above mentioned, witnessed the charter of Eustace de Baillioi, before referred to. The surname De Midford or Mitford was borne as that of the paternal barony. Eustace de M., 1254, had a grant from Roger III. of part of the demesne of Mitford (Hodgson, ii. ii. 49). His son Hugh de M. lived t. Edward I., and from him the descent is clear to the present family of Mitford, Barons of Mitford, and Lords Redesdale.

The manor of Molesden was purchased by this branch 1369, and, in allusion to it, they adopted three moles in their arms, the descent from the Bertrams being probably then forgotten, through lapse of time; and so entirely has this been the case, that this, the legitimate male representative of one of the most illustrious Norman families, is now traced to imaginary Anglo-Saxon ancestors.

Mizen, for le Mazun. *See* MASON.

Mizon. *See* MIZEN.

Moakes, from Moches or Muches, Normandy. (Mem. Soc. Ant. Norm. v. 118.)

Moase. Philip and Beatrix Moaz or Moiaz, Normandy 1180-95 (MRS); William Mose, Engl. c. 1272 (RH).

Mote, or De la Mote. Oger, and Robert de Mota, and the fief of Mote-Ebrard, Normandy 1180 (MRS). Simon le Mot, Engl. 1189 (Rot. Pip.). Richard Mote, c. 1272 (RH).

Moates, for MOATE.

Mobbs, for MABBS.

Mockler. Walter Mauclerc, Normandy 1180-95; Hubert Malcler, 1198 (Ib.).

Mode. Hugh Mode, Normandy 1180 (MRS); Reginald Mody, Engl. c. 1272 (RH).

Mogg, for MAGGS.

334

Mogge, for MOGG.

Moginie, for MAGNAY.

Mohan, for MOHUN, Mohon, or Moion, from Moion, near St. Lo, Normandy. This lordship in 1026 was part of the Ducal demesne, and was granted by Richard III. to his consort in that year. It was subsequently granted to the ancestors of this family, of whom William de Moion or Mohun accompanied the Conqueror 1066, and obtained a great barony in Somerset (Domesd.). From him descended de Mohun, Earl of Dorset, t. Stephen, and the Lords M., of Dunster and of Oakhampton (*see* De Gerville, Anc. Chateaux de la Manche; Wiffen, Mem. Russell, i. 85; Dugdale, Banks, &c.). The barony of Dunster was held by the service of 40 knights (Testa, 162). In 1165 William de M.'s barony in Normandy consisted of 16 fees (Feod. Norm. Duchesne).

Moir. HAIMERIC, Robert, William de Moire, Normandy 1198 (MRS); Robert Moyere, Engl. c. 1272 (RH).

Moist, for Miast, or Miats. *See* MIATT.

Moister, for Mosters, or MUSTERS.

Mokler. *See* MOCKLER.

Mole, for Moela, a well-known Norman family.

Moles. *See* MOLE.

Molesworth, or De Limesy. This branch of the Norman house of Limesy is mentioned in Lord Lindsay's 'Lives of the Lindsays,' but without notice of the later descent. Sir Walter de M., with whom the peerages commence, bore the same arms as Sir Gilbert Lindesey, Hunts (PPW), and of Walter de Lindsay, c. 1250, the latter being Lord of Lamberton, Scotland, a branch of the house of

Lindesay or Linsay. William de Lindesey held Molesworth 13th cent. (Testa). Hence the Viscounts and Baronets Molesworth.

Moline, from the Castle of Molines, Normandy. William de Molines 1198 (MRS). The baronial family of Molines in England was of this house.

Molineux, for MOLYNEUX.

Molyneux, from the Castle and ville of Molinelles or Molineus, Normandy. Robert, surnamed le Diable, built the castle in 11th century. Gervase de Molinelles 1180-95 (MRS). The family appear to have been castellans of this fortress. Richard de Molinelles, t. William I., witnessed a charter of William de Braiose in favour of the abbey of B. (MSAN. xxii. 120). He acquired from Roger de Poitou land in Lancashire, where Adam de Molinaus held a fee temp. Stephen, which descended to his grandson Richard de M. 1203 (Rot. Canc.). Hence the Earls of Sefton and the Baronets Molyneaux.

Moll, for MOLE. There was a Castle of Mol, Normandy (Mem. Soc. Ant. Norm. v. 18).

Moll, for Mole or MOLES.

Mollendinia, for Molendinar. Walter, Hugh, Joscelin &c. Molendinarius, Normandy 1198 (MRS); Achard de Molendinar, Engl. c. 1272 (RH).

Mollett. *See* MULLETT.

Mollineux. *See* MOLYNEUX.

Moloney. In some cases this is an Irish Celtic name; in others for Malauney (Lower), or De Malo Alneto, a Norman name.

Molyns, or Molines, descended from Walter, Lord of Falaise, Normandy, c. 1030, who m. the heir of Guitmond, baron of Molines. Wil-

liam de Molines, his son, who d. 1100, was baron of Dartington, Devon, in 1086, which he held as William ' de Falaise.' The family of Molines and Falaise occurs thenceforth in many parts of England. The barons Ventry bear the name.

Monck, or Le Moin. William, Walter, Robert, Ralph, Peter Monachus, Normandy 1180-95 (MRS). Of these the first three also appear in England c. 1198 (RCR); Robert in Engl. 1189 (Rot. Pip.). From this name came the Dukes of Albemarle and Earls of Rathdown.

Monckton, or De Amundeville, from A. Normandy. Ranulph de Munneville had possessions in Warwick 1130 (Rot. Pip.), and in York as Ranulph de Monkton, whose son Robert de M. confirmed his gifts to Fountains (Burton, Mon. Ebor. 202), and as Robert de Mundeville held five fees in York of the see of Durham 1165 (Lib. Niger). He had a brother Ralph de Amundeville, who 1165 held a fief Yorkshire, and was father of Ralph de A., who 1200 had a suit for a fief in Monkton (RCR). The family of Monkton continues to appear 13th, 14th, and 15th cents. Hence the Viscounts Galway.

Money, from Monnay, Normandy (Lower). William de Monay, a benefactor to Bliburgh, Suffolk, before t. Henry II. (Mon. ii. 593). Robert de Monei held a fief from Bigot, Earl of Norfolk 1165 (Lib. Niger).

Monday, believed to be foreign, but the reference has been mislaid.

Moneypenny. Roger Magnepeine, Normandy 1180-95 (MRS); Hubertus Manipeni, John Manipenyn, England c. 1272 (RH). Hence the Lords Monypeny or Manypeny of Scotland.

Monk. *See* MONCK.

Monks, for MONK.

Monkton. *See* MONCKTON.

Monnery, for Malnuri. Simon, Walter, William, Malnorri or Malnuri, Normandy 1180 (MRS).

Monsell. Warner, Roger de Moncello, Normandy 1198 (MRS); Roger du Moncel 1180 (Ib.); Robert de Muncel, Engl. c. 1272 (RH).

Monson, for Monceaux, descended from the ancient lords of Maers and Monceaux, Counts of Nevers. Landric IV. became Count of Nevers c. 900, by marriage, and had a younger son Landric of Nevers, baron of Monceaux, grandfather of William de M., who is mentioned by Wace 1066. He appears as William de Moncellis in the Exeter Domesday, and as William de Nevers in Norfolk 1086. His descendants occur in Sussex, but chiefly in Yorkshire and Lincoln. Thomas de Monceaux d. 1345, seized amongst others of the manors of Killingholm, Keleby, &c., Lincoln (Inq. p. Mort.). His son, Sir John de Monceaux (or Monson), d. 1363, seized of Burton and Keleby, Lincoln, which continued in this family t. Elizabeth. John Monceaux or Monson was of Lincoln 1378; sixth in descent from whom was Sir John Monson, who was possessed of Burton and Keleby at his death 1593. From him descended the Lords Monson, Viscounts Castlemaine, and Lords Sondes. (*See* Anselme, iii. 105; Rot. Pip. 31 Henry I.; Mon. i. 410, 922, 923, ii. 152, 911; Hardy, Lit. Claus. 376; Testa; Burton, Mon. Ebor. 245.)

Montagu, from Montaigu, or Montacute, Normandy, near St. Lo in the Cotentin. It was held from the barons of St. Denis le Gaste, who were probably descendants of Meurdrac, a Scandinavian Viking, who was seated there c. 930, and it is believed that the families of Meurdrac, Trailly, Grenville, Beauchamp, and Montagu, whose arms were closely related, and whose fiefs were parts of the barony of St. Denis, were of the same origin. Drogo, who succeeded to Montacute, was living 1067, when he commanded the forces of King William in the West of England. He had three sons: 1. William de Montacute, living 1086, ancestor of the barons de Montacute, Earls of Salisbury, and the Dukes of Manchester and Earls of Sandwich; 2. Drogo de M., living 1086, ancestor of the DRAKES; 3. Anschar de M. of Somerset, living 1086. For the history of this family *see* Dugdale, Baronage; Banks, Dorm. and Extinct Baronage.

Montague, for MONTAGU.

Monte. *See* MOUNT.

Montford, from M. sur Rille, Normandy, a great baronial family descended from Auslec or Oslac, Baron of Briquebec, c. 940 (*See* MITFORD). Hugh Barbatus, Baron of Montfort, was slain in battle with Walchelin de Ferrars, c. 1035. The M.s, Barons of Beaudesert, descended from the house of De Gand paternally. The name spread to all parts of England. *See* Dugdale and Banks.

Montgomery. Arnulph, Hugh, Roger de Monte Goumeril, Normandy 1198 (MRS); Ralph, Robert, Bartholomew, Arnulph, Roger, Hugh de Montgommeri, 1180-95 (Ib.). These were branches of the house of Montgomeri near Alençon, Earls of Arundel and Salop, of which several branches remained in England and Scotland. Hence the Earls of Eglinton.

Montgomrai, for MONTGOMERY.

Montgomerie, for MONTGOMERY.

Montis, for Mountis or MUNZ.

Monyns. Nicholas Manens, Normandy 1198 (MRS). The name was of distinction in Kent.

Moodie. *See* MOODY.

Moody, for MODY or MODE.

Moon, or De Mohun. *See* MOHUN. Various branches continued till a late date. The name as Moone occurs in Dorset t. Elizabeth.

Moone, for MOON.

Moor. Vitalis Maurus, Normandy 1198 (MRS); Alan le Mor, Engl. c. 1272 (RH).

Moore, or More, a local name including families of Norman and other origin. The Moores of Kent derive from Ralph Fitz-Richard, t. William I., who held Rochinge, Kent, from Hugh, Baron de Montfort in 1086 (Domesd.). This Ralph appears to have been son of Richard, Sire de Beaufort in Anjou, whose dau. m. Hugh, Baron de Montfort (Des Bois, Dict. de la Noblesse), ancestor of the Montforts of Beaudesert. Ralph Fitz-Richard held Alington, Kent, from the see of Canterbury 1086, and his descendants, who bore the names of De Roking and De More, or atte More, continued in the vicinity till the time of Elizabeth, when Sir Thomas and Sir Edward Moore settled in Ireland, and became ancestors of the Earls of Tullamoore and the Marquises of Drogheda.

Moores. *See* MOORS.

Mooring, or Moring. William, Herbert, Robert, Richard Morin, Normandy 1180 (MRS); Gilbert,

Ralph, William M. Engl. 1180 (Rot. Pip.).

Moors. Hugo Mores, Normandy 1180–95 (MRS); Geoffry de Mores, Engl. c. 1272 (RH).

Moorton, for MORETON.

Moos. John and William de Musca, Normandy 1180 (MRS); Isabel Mus, Engl. c. 1272 (RH). *See* MOSSE.

Mopsey, perhaps for Mumpesson or Montpinçon, from M. near Evreux, a baronial family. Ralph de Montpinson was Dapifer to William the Conqueror (Ord. Vit.). He witnessed a charter in Normandy 1074 (Gall. Christ. xi. 66), and granted lands to St. Evroult Abbey. His son Hugh, who m. a dau. of Hugh de Grantmesnil, and his grandson Ralph, are mentioned by Ordericus. Philip de M. witnessed 1132 the foundation Charter of Fountains Abbey, York (Mon. v. 306, 307, New Ed.). The family appears afterwards in Lincoln, Essex, Hertford, Norfolk, Wilts, and in 1165 the barony of Montpinsun, Normandy, consisted of fifteen knights' fees (Feod. Norm. Duchesne).

Moran. 1. A Celtic name. 2. For Morin. *See* MOORING.

Morand, for MORANT.

Morant. Oliver, Ralph, William Morant, Normandy 1180–95 (MRS). The arms of the English branch are preserved by Robson.

Morath. William de Moreto, Normandy, 1180–95 (MRS); Robert Moret 1198 (Ib.); Robert Mort, Engl. 1198 (RCR).

Mordan, for MORDANT.

Mordant. *See* MORDAUNT.

Mordaunt. William Mordent, Normandy 1180. The Mordents or Mordants were probably Lords of St.

Gilles, near Coutances and St. Lo. The first mentioned in the records is Ralph M., who witnessed a charter in Normandy, 1126 (MSAN, v. 197). Baldwin M. occurs in Bedford t. Stephen (Mon. Angl. ii. 202). In 1148 William M. held lands at Winchester from the bishop (Wint. Domesd.). In 13th cent. Richard de Ardres and Eustace Mordent held a fief at Turvey, Bedford (Testa). Hence the Baronets Mordaunt, and the Earls of Peterborough and Monmouth.

Morden. See HARBORD.

More, for MOORE.

Morel. See MORRELL.

Morell. See MORRELL.

Moreton. 1. An English local name. 2. for de Mauretania. See FITZGERALD. The name occurs early in England.

Morey, the French pronunciation of Moret. See MORATH.

Morfee, for Maufee (Lower), or Malfey. John Malfe, Ralph Malfei, Normandy, 1180–95 (MRS); Geoffry, Simon Malfey, Engl. c. 1272 (RH).

Morile, for MORRELL.

Morice. See MAURICE.

Morin. See MOORING.

Moring. See MOORING.

Morisse. See MAURICE.

Morling. Ralph, Albareda Morillon, Normandy 1180–98 (MRS); Hugh Morlyng, Engl. c. 1272 (RH).

Morrall, for MORRELL.

Morrell. Ralph, Tustin, William, Ansketil, Richard, Robert, Walter Morel, Normandy 1180–95 (MRS). John Morel was seated in Norfolk 1086 (Domesd.). John M. held a fief in Northumberland 1165 (Lib. Niger). The family extended throughout England.

338

Morrill. See MORRELL.

Morrin, for MORIN. See MOORING.

Morse. See MOORS.

Morss, for MORSE.

Mort. William (de) la Mort, Normandy 1180–95 (MRS); Simon Mort, England, c. 1272 (RH).

Mortain. Petrus, Robert de Mauretainia, Normandy 1180 (MRS). Laurence de Moretaine 1198 (Ib.). Ralph de Morteine, Engl. c. 1198 (RCR).

Morten. See MORTAIN.

Morter, for MARTYR.

Mortimer, a well-known Norman baronial family. This family descends from Walter, Lord of St. Martin, Normandy, who, about 980, m. a niece of the Duchess Gunnora. William de St. Martin, his son, was father of Roger, Lord of Mortimer, and of Ralph, Sire de Garenne, and of the Sire de St. Martin, from whom the family of St. Martin in England and Normandy (Mon. ii. 950).

Roger, Sire de Mortemer, was a leader of the army of Duke William, and defeated the French in 1054 (Ord. Vit. 639). Roger de Mortimer, who was a leader at Hastings, was his son, and was father of Ralph de M., who in 1086 held a great barony in Hants, Berks, Wilts, Somerset, &c. (Domesd.). From him descended the Lords Mortimer of Wigmore, Earls of March. William de Mortimer, who held t. William I. estates in Norfolk from his kinsman William de Warrenne, was father of Robert de M. t. Henry I., and of Ralph de M. or de St. Victor, and from this line descended the Lords Mortimer of Attilburgh (by writ 1296), and the Lords Mortimer of Richard's Castle.

Mortimore, for MORTIMER.

Morton. 1. An English local name. 2. For Mauretaine. *See* MORTAN.

Mose, for MOSSE.

Mortyn, for MARTYN.

Moser. Henry de Museriis, or Museres, Normandy 1180 (MRS).

Mosey. Raherius de Musie, Normandy, 1180–98 (MRS); Ralph and William de Mose, Engl. c. 1272 (RH).

Moslin. *See* MASLIN.

Moss, for MOSSE.

Mosse. Godefridus de la Mosce, Normandy, held a fief from Philip Augustus of the honour of Malherbe (Mem. Soc. Ant. Norm. v. 176).

Mote. *See* MOUAT.

Moth, for MOTE.

Motion, for Moton. Geoffry, Hugh, Mouton, Normandy 1198 (MRS); Nicholas de Muton, Engl. c. 1198 (RCR). Motons was in the Cotentin. Walter Moton 1311, M.P. for Guildford; William M. Knight 1324–1327, M.P. for Leicestershire (PPW).

Mott. *See* MOUAT.

Motte, for MOUAT.

Mouat. Philip Moaz or Moats, Normandy 1180–95 (MRS). The fief of Mouet at Apreville mentioned t. Philip Augustus.

Moudy, for MOODY.

Moul, for MOLE.

Moulder. Robert de Moudre, Normandy, 1180 (MRS).

Moule, for MOLE.

Moules, for MOLE.

Moull, for MOLE.

Moullin, for MOLINE.

Mounsey. *See* MUNCEY.

Mound, for MOUNT.

Mount. Robert, Richard, Ralph, John Ranulph de Monte, Normandy 1180 (MRS); William de Monte, Engl. 1189 (Rot. Pip.).

Mountague, for MONTAGU.

Mountain, or De Monte. *See* MOUNT. Was derived from the French form de la Montagne.

Mounteney, from Montigni near Falaise, Normandy. Roger de Montigny gave lands to St. Vigor's, Cerisy, t. William I. (Mon. i. 961.) William de M. m. a dau. and coheir of Jordan Briset, a great baron of Essex t. Henry I. (Mon. ii. 505.)

Mountford, for MONTFORD.

Mountfort. *See* MONTFORD.

Mountjoy, from the Isle of France. Paganus de Monte Gaii occurs in Normandy 1097 (Ord. Vit. 766). William de Montegai witnessed a charter of Pontefract (Mon. i. 657). The family was seated in Notts and Derby.

Moussell. *See* MUSSELL.

Mouttell. *See* MOWTELL.

Mouzon. John de Mouçon, Normandy, 1180–95 (MRS); Geoffry Mussun, Engl. 1198 (RCR).

Mowat, for MOUAT.

Mowatt, for MOUAT.

Mowbray. A well-known Norman baronial family, from the Castle of Molbrai or Moubrai, near St. Lo in the Cotentin. (*See* De Gerville, Anc. Chateaux de la Manche.) This name probably includes in its first syllable the name of the Scandinavian grantee c. 930, which is also preserved by Molbec, another place in the Cotentin. Robert de Molbray witnessed a charter in Normandy c. 1056 (Gall. Christ. xi. 227). Geoffry de Moubray, his son, bishop of Coutances, accompanied the Conqueror with a great force, and was at the battle of Hastings (Wace, ii. 185). He had vast grants in England. Roger de Molbray, brother of Geoffry, witnessed a charter in Normandy in 1066 (Gall. Christ. xi. 60), and was father of Robert de M., Earl of Northumberland, who witnessed a charter in Normandy 1082 (Gall. Christ. xi. 86). He lost his English earldom and estates, and the next heir was Nigel de Albini, who assumed the name of Moubray, and from whom the English barons Mowbray, Earls of Nottingham and Dukes of Norfolk, descended. *See* Dugdale and Banks.

Mowells, for MOULES.

Mowl, for MOULE.

Mowser, for MOSER.

Mowtell. Francis Mustel, Normandy, 1180–95 (MRS); Hugh Mosteil 1198 (Ib.) ; Constance, Geoffry Mustel, Engl. c. 1272 (RH). *See* MUSTELL.

Moy. Robert, Roger, Bartholomew de Moeio, Normandy, 1180–95 (MRS); Hugh, Richard Mey, Engl. c. 1272 (RH).

Moyce, for MOYES.

Moye, for MOY. ·

Moyer. *See* MOIR.

Moyes, for MOYE.

Moyle, for MOLE or Moel.

Moyns, for Moin. *See* MONCK.

Moyse, for MOYES.

Moysey. Alan Moisi, Normandy, 1198 (MRS); Hasting, Richard, Walter Moyse, Engl. c. 1272 (RH).

Mudd, for MODE.

Mudge, for Mugg or Mogg.

Mudie, for MOODY.

Muffey, for MORFEE.

Mules, for MOLES or Moels, a well-known Norman baronial family.

Mull, for MOLL.

Mullen, for MOLINE.

Mullens, for Molines. *See* MOLYNS.

Mullett. Ansketil Mulet, Nor-

mandy 1180 (MRS); John Mulet, Engl. c. 1272 (RH).

Mulley. William de Moleio, Normandy 1180 (MRS).

Mulley, the French pronunciation of Mulet. *See* MULT.

Mully, for MULLEY.

Mulliner, for Molonar. *See* MILLER.

Mullineux, for MOLYNEUX.

Mullings, for MULLENS.

Mullins, for MULLENS.

Mullis, for MOLIS.

Mullord, for MALLARD.

Mumford, for MONTFORD.

Mummery, probably for Montmorice, the English form of Montmorency, the history of which family from the fifth century has been written by Duchesne. This line descended from Geoffry, son of Burchard II. of Montmorency (Anselme, iii. 660), who had: 1. Hervey de M. 2. Theobald, named Paganus, Castellan of Gisors in the Vexin. He was ancestor of the family of Gisors seated in England. Hervey de Montmorency, the elder son, came to England 1066, and was father of Geoffry Fitz-Hervey (Duchesne, 67). He held several manors in Essex, of which his descendant Hervey de Montmorency, Constable of Ireland, was possessor a century later. He m. Adelaide de Clermont, whose name appears with his in charters (Parkin, Hist. King's Lynn, 171). He had Burchard de M., who was a benefactor of Thetford (Mon. i. 667), and Robert Fitz-Geoffry, who was a baron 1165. He is mentioned in Lincoln 1165 as Robert Maurenciacus (Lib. Niger). He had Hervey, Constable of Ireland, whose nephew Geoffry was Deputy of Ireland t. Henry III., and from whom descended the Barons de Marisco, Ireland, and the Viscounts Mountmorres and Frankfort. The spelling of this name varied greatly, as Montemorentii, Montemarisco, Montemoraci, Montemorentino, &c.

Muncey, from Monchy, near Arras. Drogo de Moncy came to England 1066, and was in Palestine 1096 (Ord. Vitalis, 723). Drogo de M., his son, had a pardon in Sussex 1130 (Rot. Pip.). In 1299 Walter de M. was summoned to Parliament as a baron.

Munday, for MONDAY.

Mundey, for MONDAY.

Mundy, for MONDAY.

Munfort, for MONTFORT.

Munk, for MONCK.

Munn, for MUNNS. See MUNTZ.

Munnings, for MONYNS.

Munns. See MUNTZ.

Munsey. See MUNCEY.

Munson. See MONSON.

Munster. See MINISTER.

Munt, for Mont. See MOUNT.

Munting, for MOUNTAINE.

Munton, for MOUNTAINE.

Muntz. Geofíry and Ralph de Montibus, Waleran, Herbert, Matilda, Robert, Roger de Montibus, Normandy, 1180–1200 (MRS). Eight of the name occur in 1198.

Murch, for MARCH.

Murden, for MORDEN.

Murdoch, or De St. Denis, a branch of the great Norman house of Meurdrac, barons of St. Denis and Meurdraquiere, Normandy. Finche, Robert, Stephen Murdac occur in Normandy, 1198 (MRS). The name is continually found in the English records from the beginning.

Murdock, for MURDOCH.

Murduck, for MURDOCH.

Murfin, for MERVIN.

Murley, for MERLEY, or MARLEY.

Murralls, for MORRALL.

Murrell, for MORRELL.

Murrells, for MURRELL.

Murrill. See MURRELL.

Murton, for MORTON.

Muschamp, from Moschaus, Normandy. Richard de M., Normandy 1180–95 (MRS); Thomas, William de Muschamp, Engl. 1189 (Rot. Pip.). See WILLOUGHBY.

Musgrove or Mucegros. Matthew, John, and Robert Mucegros, Normandy 1180 (MRS). M. is near Ecouis, Normandy. Robert de Mucelgros occurs 1080 (Ord. Vitalis, 576). Roger de M. 1086 held lands in Hereford in capite (Domesd.). In 13th cent. the family held estates in Somerset, Dorset, Gloucester, and Hereford. Charlton-Musgrove, Somerset, is named from it. The baronets Musgrove are hence derived.

Mushet, for Montfichet. See CAVENDISH. See also MUSKETT.

Musk, or De Musca. See MOSSE.

Muskett. Richard Mosket occurs in Normandy c. 1200 (Mem. Soc. Ant. Norm. v. 174); Robert and William Musket in Engl. c. 1274 (RH).

Mussard, for Musard. See WYCLIFFE.

Mussell. See MOWTELL.

Musson. See MOUZON.

Mustard, for MUSTERS.

Musters. Garin de Moster, Normandy, 1198 (MRS). Robert de Mosters, a tenant of Earl Alan in Notts 1086 (Domesd. 282 b). The family is frequently mentioned thenceforward in the English records.

Mustell. See MOWTELL.

Mustill. See MOWTELL.

Mutimer, for MORTIMER.

Myall, for MIALL.

Myatt. *See* MIATT.

Myers, in some cases a Hebrew name ; generally, however, for Moirs or MOIR.

Myhill, for MIALL.

Myles, for MILES.

Mylne, for MILL—the Northern form.

N

Nages. Aubert de Nages, Normandy 1180–95 (MRS).

Nagle, for NANGLE.

Nail, for NEAL.

Naish, for NASH.

Naldrett, for MALDRETT. Ranulph de Maldreit, Normandy 1198 (MRS).

Nance, from the fief of Nans or Les Nans, Normandy (Mem. Soc. Ant. Norm. v. 174).

Nangle, or De Angulo. *See* ANGELL.

Napier, Nappator, or Napparius. William Nappator, Engl. 1198 (RCR) ; William le Naper 1189 (Rot. Pip.) ; Robert le Napier, Engl. 1202 (Rot. Canc.).

Napper, for NAPIER.

Nares. Hugo de Neirs, Normandy 1198 (MRS) ; Walter le Neyr, Engl. c. 1272 (RH).

Nash, for NAS. *See* NESS. Also an English local name.

Natt. *See* NOTT.

Nave, for NEVE.

Navin. Gervasius Navine, Normandy 1198 (MRS).

Nayer. *See* NARES.

Neagle, for NAGLE.

Neal. Elias de Neel, 1180 ; Ranulph and John de N. 1195 ; Warin de Neel, c. 1200 ; Walter, George, Richard, Ralph, Robert Neel, Normandy 1198 (MRS) ; Simon, Thomas, Adam, Geoffry,

&c. Neel or Nel, Engl. c. 1272 (RH).

Neale, for NEAL.

Neall, for NEAL.

Neape, or Nape, for NAPPS or Nepos. *See* NEVE.

Neat, or Net. Reginald de Niz or Nita, Normandy 1180–95 (MRS) ; John and Avicia Net, Engl. c. 1272 (RH) ; Gilbert and John de Nes (Ib.). *See* NEATS.

Neate. *See* NEAT.

Neats, for NITS or NEAT.

Neave. *See* NEVE. Of this family are the Baronets Neave.

Neaves. *See* NEAVE.

Nebel. Roger de Nebula, Normandy 1180–95 (MRS).

Need, for NEAT.

Needes. *See* NEED.

Needham. Frodo, brother of the Abbot of St. Edmund's, Suffolk, a favourite physician of the Conqueror and a Norman, held in Suffolk and Essex 1086. He had a younger son, to whom he gave Mendham with Needham, from whom descended the families of M. and N. in Norfolk (Blomefield). The Earls of Kilmorey are a branch.

Needs, for NIZ or NITS. *See* NEAT.

Neeld, a form of NEAL. Hence the Baronets Neeld.

Neeve, for NEVE.

Neeves, for NEVE.

Negus, for Nages. *See* NAGGS.

Neil, for NEAL, when the name is English.

Neill, for NEIL.

Nell. *See* NEAL.

Nelson. *See* BOLTON-NELSON.

Nelson. The Norman family of Banastre (*see* BANNISTER) were barons of Newton, Lancashire, t. Henry I. In 1287 John Banastre held in Maudsley, Lancash., two bovates from the heirs of Ferrars. Adam, Thomas, and the heirs of Robert B. held adjacent estates (Baines, Lanc. iii. 392; Testa, 398, 399). The Banastres of Maudsley adopted the name of Maudesley, and bore the cross sable of Banastre. In 1377 Richard Nelson (Fitz-Nigel) of Maudsley (a branch of the Maudsleys), whose descendants bore the arms of M. (with a bend), granted lands at M. with remainder to George, son of Robert Nelson. In 1405 Robert Nelson of Maudsley conveyed lands to Peter Banastre and Edward Maudesley, and sealed with the above arms. Richard N. was of M. 1508, t. Henry VIII. Richard Banastre had a suit with Thomas Nelson (Ducat. Lanc.), and Ellen B. claimed rent from him. A younger son of the Nelson family, t. Henry VII., accompanied Dr. Stanley, Bishop of Ely, and settled in Norfolk. He was the direct ancestor of Admiral Lord Nelson (*see* Burke, Peerage; Hoare, South Wilts, Hundr. Downton). *See* MAUDSLAY.

Ness, from the fief of Nas, Normandy. Durand de Naso 1198 (MRS); John and Thomas de Nes, Engl. c. 1272 (RH).

Nettelfeld, for NETTERVILLE.

Netterville, from Netreville, Normandy. Hence the Viscounts N.

Nettlefold, for NETTLEFIELD.

Neve. Robert, Roger, William Nepos, Normandy 1180–95; Godfrey, John, Richard, Robert N. 1198 (MRS); Hugo Nepos Huberti was of Essex 1086 (Domesd.); Adam le Neve of Norfolk, t. Edw. I., ancestor of the Le Neves or Neaves baronets.

Nevell, for NEVILLE.

Nevett. William Nevvet, Normandy 1180–95; Ralph Nivet 1198 (MRS).

Nevil, for NEVILLE.

Nevill, for NEVILLE.

Neville. Peter, John, Hugo (Forestarius), Robert de Neville, or De Nova Villa, Normandy 1180–95 (MRS). The Earls of Westmoreland of this name were descended in the female line, also the Earls of Abergavenny. This family descended from Baldric Teutonicus, who with his brother Wiger came to Normandy c. 990 to offer his service to the Duke (Ord. Vit. 479). From him descended the families of Neville, Courcy, Beaugency, Baskerville, and D'Aunou. The Nevilles were widely spread in England, but were most numerous in Lincoln.

Nevin. *See* NAVIN.

Nevins. *See* NIVIN.

New, or Neveu (Lower). *See* NEVE. It seems also to be the English form of Le Novel. *See* NOVELL.

Newe, for NEW.

Newey, for NEWE. *See* NEVE.

Newitt, for NEVETT.

Newmarch, a baronial family, from the Castle of Neumarché, Normandy. Turketil de Newmarch

(Novus Mercatus) was slain in the civil wars of Normandy c. 1035 (Ord. Vit. 567). The Castle of Newmarch was seized c. 1060 by Duke William to the prejudice of its inheritor Geoffry de N. (Ord. Vit.). Hugh de Moriomonte, brother of the latter, was slain c. 1053 (Ibid.). Bernard de N., conqueror of Brecknock c. 1088, was son of Geoffry. Collateral branches are found in various parts of England. William de Newmarch of North-umberland was dead before 1130 (Rot. Pip.). Henry de N. held in 1165 a barony in Worcester and Gloucester (Lib. Nig.), consisting of nineteen knights' fees. Adam de N. of Lincoln 1243 had writ of military summons, and was sum-moned to parliament as a baron 1260, 1264. Branches occur in Dorset and Wilts.

Newmark, for NEWMARCH.

Newmarsh, for NEWMARCH.

Newns, for NUNNS.

Newton. It appears from Sir David Brewster's Life of the great philosopher, that according to a statement verified by the latter, he was the son of Isaac Newton of Woolsthorpe, Lincoln, Esq., and was fifth in descent from John N. of Westby in Basingthorpe, Lin-coln, who, judging from the dates, was probably born c. 1470.

The earlier history has been dis-puted ; but none of the origins assigned to the family have any evidence in their favour, except that from the N.s of Barr's Court, Gloucester, whose representative en-tailed his estates and baronetcy on the Newtons of Gonnerby, Lincoln (who were certainly of the same family as Sir Isaac Newton). Lord

344

Monson, however, has shown that the similarity of name to that of the family of Barr's Court was merely accidental, and that there was no relationship (Notes and Queries, i. 190, 3d Series). The arrangement arose from a mortgage.

The family of Newton was of far older standing in Lincoln ; it had formerly been of considerable im-portance, but its estates had in a great measure passed away.

Newton was between Folkingham and Sleaford, a few miles from Westby, Gonnerby, and Wools-thorpe, the later seats of the family, the direct ancestor of which was William Pesson, or Peisson, a Nor-man, whose estates lay in the Caux, and who in 1086 held Neuton from Odo Arbalister. Of this estate Ouvesby, Uvesby, or Osbornby, and Trikingham (which are adjacent), appear to have been members. He also possessed Bottingdon, Lincoln, where he made grants to the Knights Templars (Mon. Ang. ii. 535). Ingelram Peisson, his son, t. Henry I. (Mon. Angl. i. 773) appears to have acquired other lands at Neuton, Trikingham, and in Lincoln by grant from De Craon, and De la Haye.

Reginald de Neuton or Niweton and Alan Pescams (Pesson) his brother, held in 1165 a knight's fee by ancient tenure from De la Haye (Lib. Nig.), and granted lands to Barlings Abbey, Lincoln (Mon. ii. 644). At this time Osmond Piscis or Pesson (probably his brother) held the Norman estate in the Caux.

Sir Richard N. t. Henry II. was Constable of Nichola de la Haye (Mon. ii. 1015), and had William de Niuton, who was also Constable of De la Haye, and with Peter de N. is mentioned in Normandy 1198 (MRS). To omit other names, Sir Robert N., t. Edward I., claimed free warren at Neuton by immemorial right (Rot. Hundr. i. 256), and t. Edward III., John Willoughby, Knt. enfeoffed John de Neuton and others in lands, parcel of the manor of Haconby in the Hundred of Aveland near Neuton (Inq. p. mort.). A century later we find the ancestors of Sir Isaac Newton resident in the same vicinity in the Hundred of Aveland. The principal estates probably passed away by heiresses.

Niblett. *See* NOBLETT.

Nicholas. Richard Nicholas, Normandy 1198 (MRS); Nicholas Nicolaus, Engl. 1198 (RCR); John, Philip, Stephen Nichole, Engl. c. 1272 (RH). The name in England included families of different origins.

Nicholes, for NICHOLAS.

Nicholl. *See* NICOLAS.

Nicholls, for NICHOLL.

Nichols, for NICHOLLS.

Nickells, for NICHOLLS.

Nickless, for NICHOLAS.

Nicol. *See* NICHOLAS.

Nicolas. *See* NICHOLAS.

Nield, for Niel or NEAL.

Nightingale. P. Rossinoil (Rossignol) Normandy 1195 (MRS); Andreas Nightyngale, M.P. Cricklade 1307; Thomas Nightegale, Gloucester 1286; Ralph Niktegale, Norfolk 1273 &c. Hence the baronets of the name. William Nuitummel, Normandy 1198 (MRS).

Nish, for NAISH.

Nives, for NEAVES.

Noad. Roger Node, Normandy 1180 (MRS); Geoffry, John, Note, Engl. c. 1272 (RH).

Noah. William de Noa, Normandy 1180–95 (MRS). The arms of Now are preserved by Robson.

Noall, for NOEL.

Noble. Walter and Gillebert le Noble, Normandy 1180 – 95 (MRS); Robert and Roger Nobilis, Eng. 1194–1200 (RCR).

Nobles. *See* NOBLE.

Noblett. Alexander Noblet, Normandy 1180–95 (MRS); Reginald, William Noblet, Engl. 1198 (RCR).

Nodes, for NOAD.

Noel. Roger and Einard Noel 1180; Stephen N. 1195; Geoffry, Hugh, Ralph, Robert, Stephen N. 1198 Normandy (MRS); Hugh, Thomas, William, England 1198 (RCR). Thomas was of Sussex and Salop; William of Kent; Hugh of Hertford.

Robert Fitz - Noel and Robert Noel and others of the family, t. Henry I., founded Ranton Priory, Stafford (Mon. i. 53). Hence the Noels of England, Earls of Gainsborough.

Nohill, for NOEL.

Noldaritt, for NALDRETT.

Noon, or De Noion. Paganus de Noion, Normandy 1198 (MRS). In 1064 Hugo, Castellan of Noyon, witnessed a charter of Hugh, Bishop of N. (Gall. Christ. x. 367, Instr.). Richard de Nugun occurs 1203 in Norfolk (Rot. Canc.). In 1322, 1324, Sir John Noiun was M.P. for Norfolk. The name long remained there as Noon, and has been corrupted to Nunn.

Noone, for NOON.

Norie. William Norri, Normandy 1198 (MRS); John Nore, Engl. c. 1272 (RH).

Norman. Robert, Ralph, Gillo

345

Normannus, Normandy 1180–95; Osmund, Richard Normandus (Ib.), 1198 (MRS); Geoffry, Henry, &c. Norman, Eng. c. 1272 (RH).

Normand. *See* NORMAN.

Normansell, for NORMANVILLE.

Normanville, a branch of BASSETT of Normandy, descended from Hugh Fitz-Osmund, who held in capite Hants 1086. From him descended the barons of Normanville, a younger branch of whom (the Bassets) held the barony till c. 1500 (La Roque, Mais. Harc.). Gerold de N. had possessions in Sussex t. Henry I. (Mon. i. 318). Gerold de N. witnessed a charter of Humet t. Henry II., and Norman de N. was a baron in Sussex 1165 (Lib. Niger). Sir Ralph de N. lost his Norman barony t. John, and had grants in Lincoln, and from him descended the great family of N. in York and Lincoln.

Norreys, for NORRIS.

Norris. Andomar and William Norensis, Normandy 1180–95 (MRS); Petrus Norreis N. 1198. Thomas Norensis, Engl. c. 1198 (RCR); Osbert, Roger (Ib.), also William, Richard, Henry, Ralph, Roger N. (Ibid.). *See* NORTH.

Norrish. *See* NORRIS.

Norriss, for NORRIS.

North, Norreys, or Norensis. The Lords North, Earls of Guilford, descend from the family of Norreye of Notts (ancestors of the N.s of Speke, Lancashire). Henry le N. was seized of estates in Notts, which on his death King John granted to Alan le N., his brother. They were probably sons of Robert Norensis, who held three fees in Hants 1165, whose ancestor, Richard de North, occurs 1103 (Mon. ii. 973). *See* NORRIS.

Northcoate. *See* NORTHCOTE.

Northcote, or De Colville. *See* COLVILLE. Northcote (with Affeton), Devon, was 1086 the property of the Bishop of Coutances in demesne. It appears to have been granted to Tavistock Abbey, which enfeoffed them to Richard de Colville, who held 1165 one fee from the abbey (Liber Niger). He was a benefactor in Lincoln to the Hospitallers (Mon. ii. 536). He seems to have had a brother, Edil de Northcote, 1165 (Lib. Niger), and two sons or nephews, William de Northcote, and Robert de Affeton (in Northcote), who occur in the Northcote Charters (Harl. MS. 1080). In 13th cent. Geoffry de Northcote held a fief in N. from Tavistock Abbey (Testa). In 1295 a charter was granted by Andrew de N. to Robert de N. (Harl. MS. 1080). Hence the baronets Northcote, who bear the cross crosslet or cross moline of the Colvilles, with distinctions.

Northcott. *See* NORTHCOTE.

Northeast. Joanna Nordest, Normandy 1180–95 (MRS).

Northway. *See* NORWAY.

Norton, or Conyers. The elder branch of the family of Conyers, from Coignieres, Normandy, named from the barony of Norton, York, the chief English seat of the family. Robert de C. came to England 1066, and held from the see of Durham, 1086, Norton, Yorkshire (Domesd. 304 b). Roger, his son, had grants in Yorkshire from the see of Durham before 1126 (Surtees, iii. 244). He had also lands in Durham. Sir Robert Conyers of Norton was summoned by writ as a baron 1312. The representative of the younger line in Durham was created Lord Conyers

1509. From the Yorkshire line descended Sir Fletcher N., Speaker of the House of Commons, Lord Grantley.

Norvall, for NORVILL.

Norvell, for NORVILL.

Norvill, for NORMANVILLE.

Norway, for Norey. See NORIE.

Nott, for Note, or NOAD.

Novell. Gaufrid, Osbert, Richard Novel, Normandy 1198 (MRS); John le Novel, Engl. c. 1272 (RH).

Nowell. See NOEL.

Nowill, for NOWELL.

Nowme, for NOON.

Noyce. See NOYES.

Noyer. Richard, Gerald, Gervase de Noiers, Normandy 1180–95 (MRS). This family of De Noers was of importance in England. Gilbert de Noyers witnessed a charter of Duke Richard to Fontanelles 1024 (Neustria Pia, 166). See Banks, Baronia Angl. Concentrata.

Noyes. Richard Nois 1180–95. Osbert and William de Nois, Normandy 1198 (MRS).

Nudd, for NOAD.

Nugent, a branch of the Counts of Perche, as correctly detailed in Burke's Peerage. Hence the Earls of Westmeath, Baronets Nugent, Earls Nugent, &c.

Nunes, for NOON.

Nunn, for NOON.

Nunns, for NUNN.

Nurse, or Nutrix. The lands of the Nutrices, at Cremie, in Normandy, are mentioned 1180 – 95 (MRS). Gilbert Nutricius held from Geoffry de Clinton in Warwick, t. Henry I. (Mon. ii. 115).

Nurton, for NORTON.

Nutt, for NOTT.

Nye, for Noye. See NOYES.

O

Oake, the English form of De Quercu. Geoffry, Oliver De Quercu, Normandy 1180–95 (MRS); Nicholas and William de Q., Engl. 1189 (Rot. Pip.). Walter and Philip de Oke, Engl. c. 1272 (RH). Hence the baronets Oakes.

Oakes. See OAKE.

Oastler. See OSLER.

Obbard, for HOBART.

Obeney, for Aubeny. See DAUBENY.

Obré, for AUBREY.

Odell, or Woodhall, a baronial family. See Dugdale, and Banks, Dorm. and Ext. Peerage. The family was Flemish, and derived from the Castellans of Cambray, of whom Walter is mentioned by Baldric of Noyon, in his Chronicle, as Lord of the Castle of Lens, c. 950. Walter II., his son, was constituted hereditary Castellan of Cambray soon after, who had issue: 1. Walter. 2. Sicher, Bishop of Cambray. 3. Ada de Cambray, who m. the Baron of Oissy, and had issue Walter III., Castellan of Cambray 1049. Hugh I., son of Walter, had issue Hugh II., Viscount of Meaux, living 1096, and Fastre D'Oissy, Advocate of Tournay 1098, ancestor of the great house of Avesne (Des Bois, Dict. de la Noblesse). Walter Flandrensis or De

847

Cambray, a younger brother, came to England 1066, and 1086 held a great barony in Bedford, Bucks, &c., of which Woodhall or Wahul was the chief seat, and from him descended the barons Wahull, by writ, 1295 (*see* Dugdale, Banks). This family bore three crescents for their arms, the house of Cambray bearing one crescent. From a branch, seated in York, derives the family of WENTWORTH.

Oddie. *See* ODY.

Oddy. *See* ODY.

Odlin. Ralph Fitz-Odeline, Normandy, 1180-95 (MRS); Richard Fitz-Odeline, Engl. c. 1272 (RH).

Odling. *See* ODLIN.

Ody. Simon Audé, Normandy 1180-95 (MRS); Henry, John Ode, Engl. c. 1272 (RH).

Offer. *See* OFFOR.

Offor, for OFFORD.

Offord, or Ufford, a baronial family, Lords Ufford, Earls of Suffolk, a branch, according to Camden, of the Peytons, who were of the Norman house of Malet. *See* MALLETT.

Ogg, for AGG.

Ogg, for HOGG.

Oglander. Roger, Alan de Orglandes, and the barony of O., Normandy 1180-95 (MRS). This well-known Norman family is represented in England by the Baronets Oglander.

Olley, for DOYLEY.

Oke, for OAKE.

Olding, for Olden, or HOLDEN.

Oldrey, for Aldrey, or AUDREY.

Oliphant, for Olifant, or OLIVER. Oliver held in Devon 1086, Jordan Oliver in Wilts 1165 (Lib. Niger). Hugo and William Olifard occur 1130, 1165 in Hants and Northants (Rot. Pip.; Lib. Niger). William O. witnessed a charter of Sautre

Abbey 1147 (Mon. i. 851). David O., t. Stephen, settled in Scotland, and was ancestor of the Lords Oliphant.

Olivant. *See* OLIPHANT.

Oliver. Harvey, Nicholas Oliver, Normandy 1180-95 (MRS). Ranulph, Robert, William O. 1198 (Ib.). William O., Engl. c. 1198 (RCR). Twenty-three persons of the name, c. 1272 (RH). *See* OLIPHANT.

Olley. William Olie, Normandy 1180-95 (MRS), and the fief of Olly. *See* HOLLEY.

Ollivant, for OLIVANT.

Ollivier, for OLIVER.

Olver, for OLIVER.

Ombler, for AMBLER.

Omer, or St. Omer, armorially identified with Homer and St. Omer. *See* HOMER.

Onslow, or Arundel. De ARUNDEL, descended from Wido, son of Roger de Arundel, who held Pourton, Dorset, from him 1086 (Domesd.). He was probably brought by the Montgomerys to Salop, where the Arundels held Habberley and Ondeslawe from the Barons Corbet (Eyton, iv. 351). The names of Arundel and Ondeslawe were borne indifferently by this family, as appears throughout from the pages of Eyton; and they also bore the six hirondelles of the Arundels, with a fesse for difference. Hence the Earls and Baronets Onslow.

Orange. William, Walter, Ralph, John Orenge, Normandy 1180-95 (MRS); William de Orenge, of Bucks 1086 (Domesd.). William de O. held in Bedford 1165 (Lib. Niger).

Ore. *See* HOARE.

Orfeur, for Aurifaber, or Orfrere.

Grimbald Aurifaber 1086 held lands in Wilts, and Otto or Odo in Essex by barony (Domesd.). The latter was Goldsmith to the Conqueror, and constructed his tomb of gold, silver, and precious stones (Ord. Vit.). William A., his son, occurs 1130 (Rot. Pip.), and 1165 William Fitz-Odo A. held a fief from the honour of Gloucester (Lib. Nig.). The name occurs 13th and 14th cent. in Southampton and Surrey (Testa), also in Hunts, Stafford, Oxford, Sussex, Kent, and changed to Orfevre, and Goldsmith.

Orgar. Ralph, Richard, and Gilbert Orgeriz, Normandy 1180 (MRS); Bernard, Robert, William Orgar, Engl. c. 1272 (RH). Osberne de Orgers was slain in N. Wales, c. 1080 (Ord. Vitalis, 609, 670).

Orger. *See* ORGAR.

Orgill. Mariscus de Orguil, Normandy 1198 (MRS). The fief of Orguil or Orgoil (Mem. Soc. Ant. Norm. v. 188, 189). The name was also translated into Pride in England.

Orgles. *See* ARGLES.

Oriel. William Orielt, Normandy 1180–95. Robert, William Orient 1198 (MRS). The arms of Orell are preserved by Robson.

Ormsby, of Lincoln, a branch of the house of De Bayeux, of Normandy. Roger de Bayhus, or Bayeux de Ormsby made grants at Ormsby to Osney Abbey, Oxford (Mon. ii. 151), as did Reginald Bayhus (Ib.).

Orpin, for HARBIN.

Orson. William Orsin, Normandy 1198 (MRS).

Orth, for Ort. *See* HORT.

Ory, for De Oyry, from Oiray, near Chartres, a family formerly of importance in Lincoln.

Osborn, for OSBORNE.

Osborne. This family descends from a Kentish branch of the family of Fitz-Osberne, seated in that county early in the reign of Henry VI., when Thomas Osberne appeared to a writ of Quo warranto for the Abbey of Dartford. The family had come from Essex and Suffolk, where the name is traced to Thomas Fitz-Osborne 1227–40, who granted lands to Holy Trinity, Caen (MSAN. viii. 224, 229, 230, 231). His grandfather, Richard Fitz-Osberne, or Fitz-Osbert, held a fief from Earl Bigot 1165, and was ancestor of the Lords Fitz-Osbert, summoned by writ 1312. Richard's father, Stephen Fitz-Osbert, living 1152 (Mon. Angl. i. 640), was son of William Fitz-O., son of Osberne Fitz-Letard, who came to England 1066, and who held lands from Odo of Bayeux, 1086. Letard is mentioned in Normandy before the Conquest. Hence the Dukes of Leeds.

Osbourne, for OSBORNE.

Osler. Geoffry and William le Oiselor, or Loiseleor, Normandy 1198 (MRS); Henry and Roger le Oyselur, Engl. c. 1272 (RH):

Osman, for OSMOND.

Osmont, for OSMOND.

Osmint, for OSMENT.

Osmon, for OSMOND.

Osmond. William Osmond, Normandy 1180–95 (MRS); Hugh, Robert, Simon, &c., Osmond, Engl. c. 1272 (RH).

Ostler. *See* OSLER.

Ott, for Hott, or HUTT.

Ough, for Owe, or EU.

Ovens, probably for AVENS.

Overall, for AVERELL.

Overell, for AVERELL.

Overs. Robert Ovriz, Normandy

1180–95 (MRS); Richard de Overe, Engl. c. 1272 (RH).

Overy, for Auvery, or ALFREY.

Owen, Baronet. *See* LORD.

Owen, in some cases from De St. Ouen, or Audoen, from St. Ouen, near Caen, Normandy. Bernard de St. Audoen held in Kent 1086 (Domesd.). Gilbert St. A. 1103 witnessed a charter of Philip de Braiose (Mon. ii. 973). The name thenceforth occurs in all parts of England. The Claphams of Sussex were a branch of St. Ouen. The name is also borne by Cambro-Celtic families.

Oxenford. Stephen de Ocsene-fert, Normandy 1198 (MRS); Vitalis de Oxineford, Eng. 1189 (Rot. Pip.).

Oxford. *See* OXENFORD.

Oyler. William Hueliet, and Roger, Normandy 1180–95 (MRS).

P

Pace, for PASS.

Pacey, from the fief and Castle of Pacey, Normandy. Paganus de Paceio 1198 (MRS); Roger de Pasci, Engl. 1198 (RCR); Hugh Pacy c. 1272 (RH).

Packard, for PICARD (Lower).

Packer, for PACKARD.

Pacy, for PACEY.

Padgett. *See* PAGET.

Paget. William Pachet, Normandy 1180 (MRS). Robert Paget occurs in Norfolk t. Henry I. (Mon. i. 633) soon after 1113. Robert Pachot occurs 1195 (RCR). About 1272 Gilbert Pachet in Suffolk (Rot. Hundr.), and 1302 John Pachet of Westminster (Palgrave, Anc. Calendars, i. 283). From him descended the first Lord Paget (whose name is spelt Pachet in the State Papers t. Henry VIII.), and the Earls of Uxbridge, represented in the female line by the Marquises of Anglesey.

Pagitt, for PAGET.

Paiba, probably for Pabœuf. Hugo de Pede Bovis, Normandy 1180–95 (MRS); Fulco Pie de Bœuf 1198 (Ib.).

Paice, for PACE.

Pailes, for Pale or PEILE.

Pain. Robert Payen or Paganus, Normandy 1180, 1198 (MRS); Gilbert, John, &c. Pain, Engl. c. 1272 (RH). Hence the baronets Payne.

Paine. *See* PAIN.

Painell, or Paganel. Fulco, Robert, Gervase, Peter Paynel, Paenel, Paienell, Paignel or Paganellus, Normandy 1180–95 (MRS). A great baronial family in Normandy and England. *See* Dugdale, Banks.

Pairpoint, for PIERPOINT.

Paisey, for PACEY.

Paish, for PASS.

Pakenham, or De Pirou, from the Castle of Pirou, Coutances, Normandy. The Baron of Pirou came to England 1066, and is mentioned at Hastings by Wace (ii. 236). William de P., his son, was Dapifer to Henry I., and was lost with Prince William 1120. His son William held the office of Dapifer

(Mon. ii. 7). He or his son W. held a barony of eleven fees in Normandy 1165. William Pirou also held five fees from Earl Bigot in Norfolk, and one from Montfichet, and William Fitz-Humphry (of the same family) held a fee of the honour of Eye (Lib. Nig.). In 1198 William, son of William (Pirou), complained that the Earl Bigot had seized his lands as feudal superior (RCR); and the Earl was obliged to restore his fief, which was Pakeham or Pakenham. This name now was adopted as the family surname, and William de P. and Simon de P. occur 1199 (RCR). The arms of this family, quarterly or and gules, are those of Pirou with a change of gules for azure, and the addition of an eagle as a sign of cadency. Hence the Pakenhams of Suffolk, and the Earls of Longford.

Pakington, Baronet, derived paternally from Russel, a branch of the RUSSELLS, Dukes of Bedford.

Palce, for PALEY.

Pales. *See* PEILE.

Paley, for Peley, the French pronunciation of Pelet. *See* PELLETT.

Palfrey. Richard, Roger Palfrei or Palefridus, Normandy 1180-95. It occurs in the early records of England.

Palin. William Palain, Normandy 1198 (MRS); Richard Palling, Engl. c. 1272 (RH).

Pallet, for PALLETT.

Pallett, for Pollett, Polet, or PAULETT.

Palmar, or Palmarius. *See* PALMER.

Palmer. Hugh le Paumier, Normandy 1180-95. Ennore, Peter, Robert le Paumer 1198, Ranulph, Robert, Warin, William, John Pal-

mer or Palmarius 1180-95, also Richard and William Paumier. Arthur, Fulco, Peter, William Palmer, Paumer 1198 (MRS). Reginald, Robert, Roger, William, Engl. 1189 (Rot. Pip.). Hugh and William 1203 (Rot. Canc.). Geoffry, Richard, Robert, William, Engl. 1194-1200 (RCR). Palmarius or Le Paumer in the 11th and 12th centuries meant a Crusader in Palestine, and included families of different origin. In England four families of the name are traceable to a Norman origin, viz. 1. The Palmers of Lincoln, of whom Roger P. held from William de Roumar, Earl of Lincoln (Mon. i. 823), and William P. was living 1203 (Rot. Canc.). He also occurs in Normandy 1203 (MRS). 2. The P.s of York, of whom Robert le Paumier gave lands to Fountains (Burton, Mon. Ebor. 166), and is mentioned in Normandy 1189 (MRS). From the Yorkshire line are stated to be descended the P.s of Warwick, ancestors of Lord Selborne. 3. The P.s of Northampton, of whom Hugh paid scutage 1203, and appears in Normandy at the same time (MRS); from whom the P.s of Carlton, baronets. 4. The Palmers of Hants and Sussex.

This family is a branch of the BASSETTS, deriving from Anchetil Fitz-Osmund or Basset, Lord of Cosham, Hants 1086, who went to Palestine 1096, and appears 1110 as Anchetil Palmarius at Winchester (Wint. Domesday). His son Geoffry Fitz-Anchetil or Basset, living 1103, was father of Herbert Fitz-Geoffry or Palmarius 1148 (Ib.), father of Herbert Fitz-Herbert of Hants 1165 (Lib. Niger), who had, 1.

Peter de Cosham, mentioned in Normandy as 'de Pont-Doylly;' 2. William le Paumer or de Cosham (Testa) t. John. The latter had issue, Sir William Basset of Sussex, Knight (where the family had long held estates called Basset's Fee in Billinghurst from the Abbey of Fescamp, Normandy), whose daughter Lucy was admitted a nun at Easeborne by letter of Archbishop Peckham (Mon. Angl.). His sons Ralph and Adam Basset occur in Sussex c. 1281 (Dallaway, West Sussex). They were subsequently resident at Steyning, bearing the name of Palmer, 1305, 1308 (PPW.; Dallaway).

From Ralph descended the P.s of Angmering, who bore the Bassett arms, barry of 6 or and gules, or two bars and a bend, from whom the baronets Palmer and Earl of Castlemaine.

Palmes, from Palmes in Languedoc. Manfred de Palmes in England t. Stephen.

Pammer, for PALMER.

Pamphilon, for PAPILLON (Lower).

Pamplin, for PAMPHILON.

Pane, for PAIN.

Panks, for BANKS.

Pannell, for PAINEL.

Pannett. William Painet had a grant in Normandy from K. John (Mem. Soc. Ant. Norm. v. 122), and held from Philip Augustus. William Pant of Engl. c. 1272 (RH).

Panniers. Ascius, Adam Panier, Normandy 1180–95 (MRS); Editha Panier, Engl. c. 1272 (RH).

Pantin. See PANTON.

Panting. See PANTIN.

Panton. N. Panetarius of Normandy t. Philip Augustus (Mem. Soc. Ant. Norm. v. 166). Sire

352

Simon de Panton, Engl. c. 1272 (RH).

Papillon, from Pavillon, Nantes, Normandy. Torald de Papilion present in a great Council, London 1082 (Mon. Angl. i. 44). The name occurs thenceforth frequently.

Papillon. Joscelin, William Papeilon, Normandy 1180 (MRS); Walter and William de Papeillon 1198 (Ib.).

Papprill. See PEPPERILL.

Paramore. Richard and William Paramor, Normandy 1198 (MRS). The arms of the English branch are preserved by Robson.

Parches, for PURCHASE.

Pardew, from PARDY.

Pardy. Radulphus de Pardé, Normandy 1180–95 (MRS); William de P. 1198 (Ib.).

Parfett. Roger Perfectus or Parfait, Normandy 1180–95 (MRS); Eudo, Ralph Parfey, Engl. c. 1272 (RH).

Parfit. See PARFETT.

Parfitt. See PARFETT.

Parfrey, for PALFREY.

Paris. William, Roger, Walter, Odelina Paris, Normandy 1180–95 (MRS); Alan, Eguerran, Garin, Gislebert de Parisiis (Ib.) 1198. Hugo, Peter de Paris, Engl. c. 1198 (RCR).

Parish, for PARIS.

Pariss. See PARIS.

Park. Richard, William, Sylvester, John, Robert, Philip de Parco, Normandy 1180–95 (MRS); Richard, William, Thomas de P., Engl. c. 1198 (RCR). Parc was near Valognes. Hence descended Baron Park.

Parke. See PARK.

Parker. See LYON for the early history. William le Parker or De

Lions gave the park at Croxton for the foundation of an abbey (Mon.), and Hugh, his brother, accompanied King Richard I. to Palestine. The family appears after this in Essex, Norfolk, Bucks, and Stafford, whence a branch removed to Notts, t. Richard II., and were Lords of Norton Lees, Derby, where, and in Stafford, they resided till Thomas Parker became Lord Chancellor, and Earl of Macclesfield.

Parker. Matthew, Archbishop of Canterbury, was lineally descended from a Norfolk family, one of whom, Nicholas P., in 1450, became principal registrar of the Archbishop of Canterbury (Strype's Parker; Blomefield, Norfolk, iii. 306). In 1396 Roger P. had been bailiff of Norwich. About 1218 Hugo le Parker held the hundred of South Erpingham from Hubert de Burgh, Earl of Kent, and it was also held 1274 by Hugo le Parker, his son (Blomefield). The family had come from Leicester; for c. 1200 Hubert de Burgh, E. of Kent, had a grant of Croxton in Leicester, where the family of le Parker or de Lions had been long seated. Hugo le Parker was hereditary Parker or Forester of the royal park at Croxton, and accompanied Hubert de Burgh to Normandy, and was his tenant (Mon. Angl. ii. 604). Through Hubert de B. this branch became seated in Norfolk. *See* PARKER, or De Lions.

Parker, descended from Norman le Parcar or Forester, who held from Queen Matilda in 1083 (Exon. Domesd.). He appears to be the same as Norman Venator of Salop 1086 (Eyton, ix. 361, 362; Mon. i. 375), brother probably of Hugh

Fitz-Norman De la Mare. *See* DE LA MARE. From him descended Hugh Parcarius of Devon, 13th cent. (Testa); Roger le Parker 1313 (PPW), and the Parkers Earls of Morley.

Pashley, for Passelu. *See* PARSLOW.

Parkes, or De Perques, from les Perques near Valognes, a castle belonging to a branch of the Bertrams of Briquebec. *See* Gerville, Anciens Chateaux, and MITFORD.

Parkin. *See* PARKINS.

Parkins, or Perkins, perhaps a corruption of Perkes, Perkys, or Perques. *See* PARKES.

Parks, for PARKES.

Parkyn. *See* PARKINS.

Perles, or PARLES.

Parlour. Warin le Parlier, Normandy 1180 (MRS).

Parmenter. John, Ranulph, Parmentarius, Normandy, 1180–95 (MRS); Geoffry P. 1198 (Ib.); William, Godwin, John P. Engl. c. 1198 (ROR).

Parminter. *See* PARMENTER.

Parmiter. *See* PARMENTER.

Parnell. Richard, Robert, William, Parnelor Pernel, Engl. c. 1272 (RH) of Cambridge. Pernelle was near Valognes, Normandy. Hence the Lords Congleton.

Parnwell, for BARNWELL.

Parratt, for PERROTT.

Parren. William Parent, Normandy 1180–95 (MRS).

Parrett, for PERROTT.

Parris, for PARIS.

Parrish, for PARRIS.

Parriss, for PARIS.

Parritt, for PARRETT.

Parron, for PERRIN.

Parrott, for PERROTT.

Parsell, for Porcell or PURCELL.

Parsey, for PERCY.

Parsley, for PARSLOW, or Passelewe.

Parslow, or Paslow, for Passelewe. From Pasloup, Etampes, Isle of France. Ralph Passelewe was of Norfolk 1165; and William P. of Bucks (Lib. Niger).

Parson. *See* PARSONS.

Parsons. In t. Eliz. Christopher and John P., alias Frowde, occur in Wilts, also Richard Parsons (Proceedings in Chanc.). In 1318 John Parsons had been bailsman for an M.P. for Wilton, Wilts (PPW); Matilda Persona paid talliage, Norfolk, t. Richard I. (Rot. Canc.), and the name seems to have come from Normandy, for t. Philip Augustus Odo Persona held lands in Normandy (MSAN, v. 181), and the family of De La Personne long continued there. Hence the Parsons, Earls of Rosse.

Parsonage. Hugo Pasnage, Normandy 1198 (MRS).

Part. N. Pert 1180, William P. 1198 Normandy (MRS).

Partrick, for PATRICK, armorially identified.

Partridge, for PATRICK.

Partrige, for PARTRIDGE.

Pascall, probably foreign.

Pash, for PASS.

Pashley, for Passelewe. *See* PARSLOW.

Paskell. *See* PASCALL.

Pasley, for Passelewe (Lower). *See* PARSLOW.

Pass. Odo Paste, Normandy, 1198 (MRS); Avicia Paste, Robert Passe, Engl. c. 1272 (RH).

Passenger. Hugh de (le) Passeor, Normandy 1198 (MRS); Richard, Henry le Passur, Engl. c. 1272 (RH). Petrus Passator 1189 (Rot. Pip.).

Passey, for PACEY.

Passmore, or PASSMERE. N. Passemere, Normandy 1180 (MRS); Ralph Passemer, Engl. c. 1198 (RCR).

Patch, for PASS; also from Peche (Lower). *See* PEACH.

Pate. Richard and Tustin Peet, Normandy 1198 (MRS); Richard Pet, Engl. c. 1272 (RH).

Pater, for PETER.

Paternoster. Roger Paternostre, Normandy, 1180–95, 1198 (MRS); Robert Paternoster, Engl. 1202 (Rot. Canc.)

Pates, for PATE.

Patey, for PETTY.

Patie, for PATEY.

Patient, for Pashent, or Passavant. Matilda and Adam Passavant, Engl. c. 1272 (RH).

Paton. Geoffry Patin, Normandy 1198 (MRS); Alice Patun, Engl. c. 1272 (RH).

Patrick. This great Norman house, Patry, or Patrick de la Lande, was from La L. near Caen. William Patrick de la Lande is mentioned by Wace as the entertainer of Harold during his visit to Normandy, and as challenging him to combat at Hastings for breach of his oath (Wiffen, Mem. Russell, i. 73). In England he held from King William a barony of fifteen fees in Norfolk and Suffolk. William, his son, witnessed a charter of William I. to Savigny Abbey, and had Ralph, whose son William joined Ralph de Fulgeres and the sons of Henry II. in their revolts. Eguerrand, his son, lost his barony, which was given to William de Say.

Branches were seated in the north of England. Paganus de la Lande held three fees in 1165 from the see of York. Robert Patric of this line acquired half the barony of Malpas, Cheshire, by marriage 12th cent. Richard Patric was of Lincoln t. Henry III. Richard Launde in 1433, Thomas Patrick t. Henry VIII. Simon t. Elizabeth are mentioned.

The latter, who possessed a considerable estate near Caistor, Lincoln, was grandfather of the learned Simon Patrick, bishop of Ely. The Patrics bore vairé arg. and sa., a chief sa. The bishop's line added three pales.

Patridge, armorially identified with Partrick and PATRICK.

Patry, for PATRICK.

Patten. *See* PATON.

Pattle, for PETTY.

Pattle, for Battle or BATTAIL. *See* BABINGTON.

Patton, for PATON.

Pattrick, for PATRICK.

Pattyn. *See* PATON.

Paul, or St. Paul, branches of the Counts of St. Paul, descended paternally from the Counts of Ponthieu, who acquired St. P. c. 991 (Moreri). These Counts had considerable estates in England, and numerous branches were seated there. The estates of the E. of St. P. in Essex are mentioned 1198 (RCR). Robert de St. Paul of Lincoln 1158, Roger de St. P. Stafford 1157 (Rot. Pip.). Hence the baronets Paul, and St. Paul.

Paulet, or POWLET. This family has been derived from Hercules de Tournon; but he appears to be a mythic personage. It is really descended from the Norman house of D'Aunou. Baldric Teutonicus, living c. 990, was ancestor of the Courcys, Nevilles, and D'Aunous. Fulco, Sire D'Aunou, his son, was father of Fulco, Sire D'Aunou, mentioned by Wace as present at Hastings (ii.

237). He occurs t. Will. I. (Gall. Christ. xi. 61, 330 Instr.) In 1082 Fulco de Alno, perhaps his son, occurs (Ib. 70); and 1124 Fulco de Alnou is mentioned in a charter of Henry I. to Dive, Normandy (Ib. 159). These barons, and Fulco De Alnou 1165, were amongst the magnates of Normandy; their barony consisting of thirty-eight fees. (Duchesne, Feoda.)

In the reign of Henry I. Fulco de A. had a grant from the Crown of Grandon in Somerset, a member of North Petherton, and Poolet another member. The latter was held as half a knight's fee (Testa, 162). Another part of Poolet belonged to a different owner, and descended to the family of De Gaunt. In 1165 Alexander De Alno, a younger son of Fulco, held a knight's fee in Somerset (Lib. Niger). As Alexander 'de Puilleta' (Poolet) he paid monies in Normandy (MSAN, viii. 365). He had two sons: 1. Walter de Poeleth, who 1203 paid a fine in Somerset (Rot. Canc.). 2. Robert de Polet, mentioned in Bucks 1198 (RCR), and again in 1200 (Ib.). William Pauleth, 1220 (son of Walter) held the Lordship of Leigh, Devon (Testa). His descendant, William de Paulet, was returned as Lord of Paulet, Stretchill, and Walpole, Somerset, in 1316 (PPW). The family remained in possession of Paulet till the time of Elizabeth. From it descended the Marquises of Winchester and Earls Poulett, and the Dukes of Bolton.

Pauley. Gerold Pauli, Normandy 1180–95 (MRS); Geoffry and William Pauly, Engl. c. 1272 (RH).

Paulin. John and Ivo Polain,

Normandy 1180–95 (MRS); Roger Paulyn, Engl. c. 1272 (RH).

Pauline. *See* PAULIN.

Paull, for PAUL.

Paulyn. *See* PAULIN.

Pauncefote. *See* PAUNCEFORT.

Pauncefort. In 1083 Bernard Pancevolt, a foreigner, held lands in capite Somerset (Exon. Domesd.), also in Hants (Domesd.). Humphrey Pancevolt witnessed the foundation of Shireburn Abbey, Hants (Mon. i. 578). In 1165 Humphrey P. held fiefs in Gloucester from Newmarch (Lib. Niger). The name long continued in Gloucester and elsewhere. Hence the baronets Pauncefort-Duncombe.

Pausey, armorially identified with Passey or Passy. *See* PACEY.

Pavely, or De Pavilly, a baronial family. Rainald and William de Pavilli and the fief of P., Norm. 1180–95 (MRS). (*See* Banks, Baronia Angl. concentrata.)

Pavely, or Pavilly, from Pavilly near Rouen, Normandy. A monastery was founded here by Amalbert Lord of Pavilly 664, which was restored by Thomas de Pavilly c. 1090 (Neustria Pia, 328). Reginald de P. died in the first Crusade at Acre (Des Bois). Ralph de P. witnessed a charter of William Earl of Surrey t. Henry I. (Mon. i. 625). The family afterwards appears seated in Northants, Notts, and Derby; also in Wilts. Of the latter line was Reginald de P., who was summoned 1260 as a baron to attend the King in Council. Walter de P., also 1295 had a writ to attend Parliament at Newcastle-upon-Tyne. Sir Walter de P. was famous in the wars of Edward III., and a knight of the Garter.

Paver, for Pevre or Pauper. Roger Pauper, Norm. 1180 (MRS); Robert and William P. 1198 (Ib.); Hubert Pauper, Engl. c. 1198 (RCR); Gilbert P. 1202 (Rot. Canc.)

Pavey. *See* PAVY.

Pavia. *See* PAVY.

Pavier. *See* PAVER.

Pavy. Roger Pavé or de Pavia, Normandy 1180-95 (MRS); N. Pawei, Engl. c. 1272 (RH).

Pavyer. *See* PAVER.

Pawle. *See* PAUL.

Pawley. *See* PAULY.

Pawsey. *See* PAUSEY.

Pawson. Girard Paisant, Normandy 1180-95 (MRS).

Pay. John and Fulco Pie de Buef 1180-95, Normandy (MRS); John, Roger, Simon Pie, Engl. c. 1272 (RH).

Paybody. *See* PEABODY.

Payn, for PAIN.

Payne, for PAINE.

Payne-Galway, Baronet. *See* PAYNE.

Pays, for PACE.

Payton, for PEYTON.

Pea, for Pie. *See* PAY.

Peabody, or Papady. Pabode held a fief from the see of Durham, t. William I. He was probably of Flemish origin. Henry Pappede held this fief 1165 (Lib. Nig.), and from him descended the family of Pappady, Pabody, or Peabody, from which the celebrated philanthropist of the name.

Peace, for PACE.

Peacey, for PEACHEY or PACEY.

Peachey, or Peché. *See* PEACH.

Peachy, or Peché. *See* PEACH.

Peach, or Peché, a branch of De Clare and Fitz-Walter.

Peacock. Robert Pavo, Normandy 1180 (MRS); Adam and

Geoffry Pocok, Engl. c. 1272 (RH). Hence the Baronets Peacock and Pocock.

Pead, for Pied or Pie. *See* PAY.

Peak, armorially identified with PECK.

Peake. *See* PEAK.

Peal. *See* PEEL.

Peall, for PEEL.

Peaple. *See* PEOPLE.

Pear, for St. Pierre or St. Peter. *See* BUNBURY.

Pearce, for PEARS.

Pearcey, for PERCY.

Pearcy, for PERCY.

Peard. Ralph and William de Parde, Normandy 1180-95 (MRS).

Pearkes, for PARKS.

Pearks, for PARKS.

Pearl. John and Tustin Peril or Perol, Normandy 1198 (MRS); Egidius and Richard Perles, Engl. c. 1272 (RH).

Pearless, for Pearles. *See* PEARL.

Pearpoint, for PIERPOINT.

Pears. Richard, Odo, Thomas de Piris, Normandy 1180 - 95 (MRS); eight of the name 1198 (Ib.); Richard, William Peris, John Pers, Engl. c. 1272 (RH).

Pearsall, said to be of Norman origin.

Pearse. *See* PEARCE.

Pearson, for Person or PARSONS, sometimes a patronymic, including various families.

Peart. *See* PEARD.

Peartree, for Partry or Patry. *See* PATRICK; also perhaps local in some cases.

Pease, for Peace, or PACE.

Peasley, for PASLEY.

Peat. Richard and Tustin Peet, Normandy 1198 (MRS); Richard Pet, John Pitte, Engl. c. 1272 (RH).

Peate. *See* PEAT.

Peavey, for PAVEY.

Peay, for Pied. *See* PAY.

Peberdy, for PEABODY.

Pebody, for PEABODY.

Pech, for PEACH.

Peck, for Peché (Lower). It is armorially identified with the latter. *See* PEACH.

Peckett, for BECKETT.

Peckitt, for BECKETT.

Peed, for Pied. *See* PAY.

Peek, for BEEK or Bec.

Peek, for PEAK.

Peeke, for PEAKE.

Peel. Radulphus Pele occurs in Normandy 1180; Robertus Piel 1180 - 95; William Pele 1198 (MRS). Of these, Robert, son of Robert le Pele (c. t. Henry II.), gave lands in Monk Bretton, York, to the abbey there (Burton, Mon. Ebor. 93). Hugh le Pele occurs 1242 (Roberts, Excerpta, i. 377). Richard and William Pelle were bailsmen for the M.P.s for Preston, Lancashire (PPW). From this northern family descended the Peels of Yorkshire and Lancashire, ancestors of the celebrated minister of England, Sir Robert Peel.

Peele. *See* PEEL.

Peeling, for PALIN.

Peell, for PEEL.

Peen. William Peigne, Normandy 1198 (MRS); Richard Peine, Engl. 1194 (RCR).

Peerless, for PEARLESS.

Peers. Roger de la Perre, Normandy 1180 (MRS). *See* PIERS.

Peers. *See* PEARS.

Pees, for PEASE.

Peet. *See* PEAT.

Peete. *See* PEAT.

Peever. *See* PAVER.

Peevor, for PEEVER.

Pegg, or Pigg. *See* PORCAS.

Peggs, for PEGG.

Peil. *See* PEEL.

Peile. *See* PEEL.

Peill. *See* PEEL.

Peine. *See* PEEN.

Pierce. *See* PEARS.

Piercey, for PERCY.

Pelham, or De Bec, from Bec-Crespin, Normandy (*see* JOCELYN). This family descended from a brother of Auslec or Oslac, Baron of Briquebec, Amfrid the Dane, c. 940 (*see* MITFORD). Gilbert surnamed Crespin, Baron of Bec and Castellan of Tillieres, had issue William de Bec, who had, 1, Goisfrid de Bec, a great baron in Herts 1086; 2, Gilbert, Abbot of Westminster; 3, Ralph.

Ralph de Bec held Pelham and Eldeberie, Herts, from the see of London 1086, other estates Herts from his brother Goisfrid, and in Cambridge estates from Picot de Cambridge (Domesd.). The barony of the latter (Picot) passed to the Peverells, and from them to the De Dovres and Peché.

Ralph had issue, 1, Robert de Bec or Bech, who witnessed a charter of William Peverel (Mon. i. 247); 2, Alan de Bec, Dapifer to the same baron. Robert was father of Gilbert (Mon. i. 355), who held lands from Hugh de Dovres in Cambridge, which 1165 belonged to his son Alan, then a minor (Lib. Nig.). Everard de Bec, his brother, held part of the estate from Hamon Peché and Hugh de Dovres (Ibid.).

Ralph de Pelham or De Bec, brother of Gilbert above mentioned, was a tenant of the see of London 1165 (Ibid.), and appears to have been the first of his family to bear

358

the name Pelham. He had, 1, Helias de P.; 2, Walter de P.; 3, Peter de Bec or De P. About 1172 Helias and Walter claimed lands in Cambridge, but resigned them, as appears by a deed of Everard de Bec, then Viscount of Cambridge (RCR). Peter de Bec or Pelham 1194 was party in a suit for lands, Cambridge (Ibid.). He is mentioned in Cambridge 1218 as Peter de Pelham (Hardy, Lit. Claus. 376). The early arms of the Pelhams were a fesse between two chevrons, those of their feudal suzerains, the Pechés of Cambridge. The principal residence of the family was in that county. About 1273 Robert de Pelham and Geoffry de P. occur in Cambridge (Rot. Hundr.); but the chief of the family was Walter de Pelham, who held from Walter de Bec le Chamberlain, a tenant of Peché, descended from Alan de Bec, Dapifer (Rot. Hundr.). The last-mentioned Walter P. d. 1292. Walter his son acquired lands in Sussex, and from Sir John P., of Sussex, one of the heroes of Poitiers 1356, descended the Pelhams, Lords Pelham, Dukes of Newcastle, and Earls of Chichester.

Pell, armorially identified with some families of PEEL.

Pellatt. *See* PELLETT.

Pelle. *See* PELL.

Pellett. Hugo, Ranol, Gislebert, Odo Pelet, Normandy, 1180–95 (MRS). The family was of Sussex, 13th cent. (Lower).

Pellew, or Peleve, from P. Normandy, held from the Church of Bayeux (Liber Rubeus, apud Ducarel). Gerbode Peleve, t. William I., held from Ilbert de Lacy Yorks. Ranulph P. held in York

1165 (Lib. Nig.). About 1240 William Peleve held a fief in Devon and Cornwall from Reginald de Valletort (Testa). From him descended the Peleves or Pellews of Devon, of whom sprang the brave admiral Sir Edward Pellew, first Viscount Exmouth.

Pelling, for PALIN.

Pells, for PELL.

Pelly, or Pelley. The French pronunciation of Pelet. See PELLETT.

Pelu. Walter Pelutus, Normandy 1180-95 (MRS).

Penhey, for PENNY.

Pennell. William Pinel, Normandy 1180-95 (MRS); Ranulph, Robert, William P. 1198 (Ib.); Henry, &c. Pinel, Engl. c. 1272 (RH).

Pennell, armorially identified with PANNELL.

Penhall. See PENNELL.

Penhey, for PENNY.

Penney. See PENNY.

Penny. Serlo Penné, Normandy 1180-95 (MRS); John le Penny was of Bayeux, t. Henry V. (Mem. Soc. Ant. Norm. v. 258); John Pinne, Engl. c. 1198 (RCR); Alexander, Elyas Peny, c. 1272 (RH).

Peny. See PENNEY.

Penton. Ralph de Pentonne, Normandy 1198 (MRS); Helena de Pentyn, Engl. c. 1272 (RH). See PANTON.

Pepall. See PEOPLE.

People. Robert Populus of Normandy held lands at Anet and Saucey from Philip Augustus, Normandy, c. 1200 (Mem. Soc. Ant. Norm. v. 180).

Pepperell. See PEPPERILL.

Pepperill, or Piperellus, a form of PEVERELL of Normandy.

Pepin. Osbert, William, Nicholas, Osbert Pepin, Normandy 1180-95 (MRS); Richard, William P. Engl. c. 1272 (RH).

Pepper, for Peppard or Pipard. William, Gilbert, Robert, Walter, Ranulph Pipart, Normandy 1180-95 (MRS); Gilbert Pipard, England 1189 (Rot. Pip.). See CARY.

Pepperall, for PEPPERILL.

Peppin. See PEPIN.

Perceval, or D'Ivry. Judicael, Count of Rennes, grandson of Erispoe, King of Bretagne, was slain 890. From him descended the Counts of Bretagne (See Anselme, iii. 44; L'Art de Vérifier les Dates, xiii.). Eudo, Count of B. 1040, had eight sons, of whom Robert, Lord of Ivry, Normandy, received from the Conqueror Kari, Quantock, Harptre, Somerset, and d. 1082, leaving Ascelin Gonel de Percheval, surnamed Lupus, whose exploits in Normandy are recorded by Ord. Vitalis. He had, 1. William; 2. John, ancestor of the Barons of Harptre. The former had, 1. William, ancestor of the Barons of Ivry; 2. Ralph, surnamed Lupellus or Lovel, ancestor of the Lovels, Barons of Cary, Viscounts Lovel; 3. Richard, ancestor of the Percevals of Somerset. From the latter descended Richard, who went to Ireland t. Elizabeth, and founded the House of Perceval, Earls of Egmont.

Percival, for PERCEVAL.

Percivall, for PERCIVAL.

Percy. It has been noticed elsewhere (Chapter III.) that the early Percy pedigree is not authentic. The real origin may now be considered. Percy after 1026 became the property of a branch of the

Tessons, the greatest baronial house in Normandy, and so continued in the reign of Richard I. (Stapleton, Mag. Rot. Scac. Norm. 1. lxxxiii., 2. xiii.) Ralph Tesson was of Anjou in the tenth century. Ralph Taxo, his son, witnessed with Fulco, Count of Anjou, a charter of King Robert 1028 (Gall. Christ. viii. 297 Instr.). He, or his father, acquired a barony in Normandy, perhaps by marriage, and founded the abbey of Fontenay (Gall. Christ. xi. 413); and in 1047 Ralph Tesson of Cinquelais led 120 knights of his dependence to aid Duke William at the battle of Val des Dunes (De Gerville, Anc. Chateaux). The Tesson barony 1165 consisted of 60 knights' fees (Feod. Norm., Duchesne).

From this House descended the MARMIONS, of whom William Marmilon of Fontenay (a Tesson estate) witnessed a charter of Ralph Tesson, probably his brother, in 1070 (Gall. Christ. xi. 413). The BYRONS seem to have been another branch. The Percys probably derive from Ernegis or Erneis Tesson, brother of Ralph and co-founder of Fontenay 1050 (Gall. Christ. xi. 413). He had William, Serlo, and Ralph de Percy, who came to England 1066, and from whom the English Percys descended. The arms of these families show their common origin. The Tessons bore a fesse, the Marmions the same, the Percys a fesse indented, the Percys of the South fessy or barry, and the Byrons bendy for fessy. The distinction is chiefly made by tinctures.

Percy-Louvain. This House, which inherited by marriage from the Norman House of Percy, and was the source of the great historical

Earls of Northumberland, is too well known to require detail.

Percy-Smithson. See SMITHSON.

Percy. John, Ralph, Normandy 1180–95; Hugh, Ralph 1198 (MRS); Hugh Percehaie 1180 (MRS). These were collaterals of the great House.

Perfect. See PARFAIT.

Perfet, for PARFAIT.

Perken, for PARKINS.

Perks, for PARKS.

Perkes. See PARKES.

Perkin. See PARKINS.

Perkins. See PARKINS.

Perou. A baronial family. Fulco Piro, William de Pirou, Normandy 1180–95 (MRS); Hugo, Rener, Robert, Serlo, William de Pirou, Norm. 1198 (Ib.). See PAKENHAM.

Perratt, for PERROTT.

Perreau, for PEROU.

Perren. Osbert and Walter Perrin or Perron, Normandy 1180–95 (MRS); John and William Perin, Engl. c. 1272 (RH).

Perrett, for PERROTT.

Perrie, for PERRY.

Perrier. Odo, Robert, Hugh, Ralph, &c. de Periers, Normandy, 1180–95 (MRS); Robert de Pereres, Engl. c. 1198 (RCR).

Perrin. See PERREN.

Perring. Albarede de la Perine, Normandy 1180–95 (MRS). See PERREN.

Perrings, for PERRING.

Perrins. See PERRING.

Perrot. See PERROTT.

Perrott. A baronial family, descended from Pirot, probably a foreigner, who held in 1086 from Eudo Dapifer, in the eastern counties (Domesd.).

Perry, identified by its arms with Pereres. The family of Perry was seated in Devon (See Pole) in 1370.

That of Perier was of P. in Bretagne (Des Bois), and descended from Budic, Count of Cornouailles c. 900, whose younger son Periou gave name to Perieres, Bretagne. A branch came to England 1066, and Matilda de Perer was mother of Hugo Parcarius, who lived t. Henry I. The name continually occurs in all parts of England: hence the Perys, Earls of Limerick. There was also a Norman family of Perers (*See* PERRIER, SHAKSPEARE), which bore different arms.

Perse, for PEARCE.

Persey, for PERCY.

Pescott. *See* PESKETT.

Peskett. Walter Pesket, Normandy 1180-95 (MRS).

Pestell. N. Pestoil, Normandy 1180-95 (MRS); Alexander, Richard, Gilbert, Pestel, Engl. c. 1272 (RH).

Pester. Roger de Pistres, Normandy 1180-95 (MRS), also from Pistor. *See* BAKER.

Pestle, for PESTELL.

Petch, for Pech, or PEACH.

Petchy, for Peché, or PEACHEY.

Peter. 1. Henry de Petra, Normandy 1180-95; Warin de P. 1198 (MRS); Hugh de Petra, Engl. c. 1272 (RH). 2. From Fitz-Peter. Thomas, Robert, Rainald, Ausfrid, Fitz-Peter, Norm. 1180-95 (MRS).

Peters. *See* PETER.

Petery, for PETRIE.

Pether, for PETER.

Petit. Ralph, William, Bernard, Herbert Parvus or le Petit, Normandy 1180-95 (MRS). Eleven of the name 1198. Gilbert, John, Ralph, Robert, William P., Engl. c. 1198 (ROR).

Petitt, for PETIT.

Peto, Peytou, or Peitou, from Poitou. The Chevalier de Peitou is mentioned by Wace as a companion of the Conqueror. Robert Pictaviensis was a benefactor to St. Peter's and Noëtell, York (Mon. ii. 34, 393). The name occurs afterwards as Peytevin, and De Peitou or Peyto: hence the Baronets Peto.

Peto. William and Ralph Pitot, Normandy 1180-95 (MRS). Gislebert, Thomas, William Pitot, 1198 (Ib.). Petrus de Pitou, Engl. 1189 (Rot. Pip.).

Petre. *See* PETER.

Petrie, for PETRE.

Pett. *See* PEAT.

Petter, for PETER.

Petters, for PETTER.

Pettet, for PETIT.

Pettey, the French pronunciation of PETIT.

Pettie. *See* PETTEY.

Pettis, or Petts, for PETT.

Pettit, for PETIT.

Pettitt, for PETIT.

Petts. *See* PETT.

Petty. *See* PETTEY.

Peverall, for PEVERELL.

Peverell, a baronial family. Nicholas and Robert Pevrel, Norm. 1180-95; Godfrey, John, William P., 1198 (MRS). *See* WALLOP.

Pevier, for PAVER.

Peyton, a branch of Malet of Normandy. *See* OFFORD.

Phair, for FAIR.

Pharaoh, for FARROW.

Phare, for FAIR.

Pharoah, for FARROW.

Phear, for PHAIR.

Pheasant. Radulphus le Paisant, Normandy 1180-95 (MRS); Walter Peysun, Engl. c. 1272 (RH).

Phelp, for PHILIP.

Phelps, for PHILIP.

Pheysey, for VESEY.

Philip. Richard, Roger Phylippus, Normandy 1198 (MRS). Generally in England from Fitz-Philip, a patronymic, which included families of various origin.

Phillimore. See FILMER. Armorially identified.

Phillipp. See PHILIP.

Philip. See PHILIP.

Philpot. N. Philipot, Normandy 1180–95 (MRS).

Philpott. See PHILPOT. Hence the celebrated Henry Philpott, Bishop of Exeter.

Philpotts. See PHILPOT.

Philpp, for PHILIP.

Phipos, for PHILPOTTS.

Phipponel, or Pipponel. See PEPPERILL.

Phippen, perhaps for Vippan, or Weapont. See VIPAN.

Phippos. See FEYPOE.

Phipps. Descended, according to the Peerages, from Col. William P. t. Charles I. Sir John Phippes possessed estates in Lincoln t. Elizabeth (Blomefield, Norfolk, ii. 457). This, and the family of P., Wilts, bearing the same arms (sable, semy of mullets argent), came from London, where those arms were borne by a family, probably descended collaterally from Sir Matthew Philip, Lord Mayor 1463, who bore sable semy of fleur de lys. His arms are those of the Mortimers of Attleburgh, Norfolk, reversing the tinctures; and it appears that John Philip, of Middlesex, 1403, was connected with Norfolk (Blomefield, xi. 195). The name of Philip or Fitz-Philip is traced in successive generations in Norfolk (See Blomefield, ii. 194, xi. 28, vi. 415) to Philip de Mortimer, third son of Robert de M. of Norfolk t. Henry I., son of William de

362

M., who held lands from De Warrenne in Norfolk, 1086 (ancestor of the Lords Mortimer of Attilburgh, 1296). See MORTIMER.

Phoenix, for Feynis, or FIENNES.

Physick, for FISK.

Picard. Ralph, Engeram, Richard, Peter, Geoffry, Walter Picard, Normandy 1180–95 (MRS); Robert Pichard, Engl. c. 1198 (RCR); John Pikart, c. 1272 (RH).

Pick, for PECK.

Pickard, for PICARD.

Picken. Radulphus Picon, Normandy 1180–95 (MRS); Richard Phycun, Engl., c. 1272 (RH).

Picker. Radulphus Pichere, N. Picore, Normandy 1180–95 (MRS); William le Pikkere, Engl. c. 1272 (RH).

Pickett. Herbert, Richard, Gilbert, William Picot, Normandy, 1180–95 (MRS); Robert Pikede, Engl. c. 1272 (RH).

Pickin, for PICKEN.

Picking, for PICKIN.

Pickles, or Pickel. Herbert Pigole, Normandy 1180–95 (MRS); Robert Pikel, Engl. c. 1272 (RH).

Pidgeon. John Pichon, Normandy 1180–95 (MRS); Richard, William Pigun, Engl. c. 1272 (RH).

Pie. See PAY.

Pierce. See PEARS.

Piercey, for PERCY.

Piercy, for PERCY.

Pierpoint, a Norman baronial family. See Dugdale, and Banks, Dorm. and Ext. Bar.

Pierpont. See PIERPOINT.

Piers, from Pierres near Vire, Normandy. Hugh de Piers had a grant in Salop 1156 (Rot. Pip.). Richard and James Peres possessed estates in Notts 1316 (PPW). Hence the baronets Piers.

Pierse. *See* PEARS.

Pierson, for PEARSON.

Pigeon, for PIDGEON.

Pigg. *See* PORCAS.

Pigge. *See* PORCAS.

Piggin, for PIGEON.

Piggott, or Picot. Bartholomew, Hubert, William, Lambert, Ralph, Reginald, Richard, Roger Picot, Normandy 1198 (MRS). *See also* PICKETT.

Pigot, or Avenel. *See* AVENEL. C. 1030 Osmeline Avenel, Lord of Say, made grants to St. Martin's, Sees, which were confirmed by Picot Avenel, his son, and Robert and Henry, his sons (Gall. Christ. xi. 152, 153). This Osmeline was probably a brother of Hervey A. Baron of Biars 1035. Picot de Say or A. had great grants in Salop. One of his younger sons, Picot Miles, obtained from him the barony of Clun. His younger son William Picot or De Say held one fee in Salop from De Ver 1165 (Lib. Niger), which Ralph P. also held before 1180. His son Robert was living 1200–1260. From this time the P.s have been seated in Salop, and from them descend the baronets Pigot in England and Ireland, and the Lords Pigot of Ireland.

Pigot. *See* PIGGOTT.

Pigott. *See* PIGGOTT.

Pike. Radulphus and Ibert Pikes, Normandy 1180–95 (MRS); Ralph P. 1198 (Ib.); Richard, Walter Pik, Engl. c. 1272 (RH).

Pilcher. Robert and William Pelegars, Normandy 1180–95 (MRS); Ralph Pilkere, Engl. c. 1272 (RH).

Pile. William Pile, Normandy 1180–95 (MRS); Henry, John, Peter Pille, Engl. c. 1272 (RH).

Pilgrim. Robert, John, Thomas,

Pelerin, Normandy 1180–95 (MRS); Henry, John, Symon Pelrim, Engl. c. 1272 (RH).

Pill, for PILE.

Pilley. Ansger Pilet, Normandy 1180–95 (MRS); Richard Pilet 1198 (Ib.); Michael and Walter Pilat, Engl. c. 1272 (RH).

Pillmer. Simon Pelinart, Normandy 1180–95 (MRS).

Pillivant. *See* BULLIVANT.

Pillow, from Pilot. William Pilot, Normandy 1198 (MRS). *See* PILLEY.

Pinchard. Walter and Durand Pinceart, Normandy 1180–95 (MRS); Albreda Pinchard, Engl. c. 1272 (RH).

Pinchin. William Pincon, Normandy 1180–95 (MRS); Ralph P. or Pinzon, Roger, Stephen, Simon 1198 (Ib.); Reginald Pinzun, Engl. c. 1272 (RH).

Pinching. *See* PINCHIN.

Pinckard. *See* PINCARD.

Pinckney, a baronial family. *See* Dugdale, and Banks (Dorm. and Ext. Peerage). This family descended from the Viscounts of Picquigny, one of the greatest houses in the North of France, and maternally descended from Charlemagne. (*See* Bouquet, Ord. Vitalis).

Pindar, le Pinder or le Bailli, probably descended from William, a Norman of distinction, Dapifer to Earl Warrenne t. William I., whose son Wymer Dapifer was living 1066 (Domesd.). From him descended the family of De Gressenhall, of whom William de G. t. Henry II. had several brothers, of whom John le Pinder (le Bailli) was father of Richard le P., living 1252 (Roberts, Excerpta, ii. 127), whose son, with Wymar his brother, gave lands to Castle-Acre (also benefited by Wymer Dapifer, and others of the family; Blomefield, ix. 168, vii. 519, vi. 35, &c.). In the next generation Thomas le P. was of Lincoln, where the family remained till recently, and from which sprang the Pinders, now Beauchamp, Earls Beauchamp.

Pinder. *See* PINDAR.

Pine. Durand, William de Pinu, Normandy 1180–95 (MRS); Henry, Peter, Robert de P. 1198 (Ib.). This family was long seated in Devon.

Pingeon, for Pinceon. *See* PINCHIN.

Pinkerton, for Punchardon or Pont Cardon (Lower). William and Robert de Ponte Cardun, Normandy 1180–95 (MRS). Pontcardon was near Neaufle, Normandy. Robert de Pontcardon 1083 held lands in Devon from Baldwin the Viscount (Exon. Domesd. 277, &c.) In 1165 William de P. held four fees in Devon, and two in Somerset, and Roger de P. held in Lincoln, and Matthew de P. in York or Northumberland (Lib. Niger). In 1216 the estates of Sir William Pontcardon at Aureville, Avesnes, and St. German, Roche, and Cetrentost, were granted to another by Philip Augustus, probably as an adherent of King John (MSAN. xv. 156).

Pinkett. N. Pincet, Normandy 1180–95 (MRS).

Pinkney. *See* PINCKNEY.

Pinn, for PINE.

Pinnell, for PANNEL or Painel.

Pinner. Geoffry Pinar, Normandy 1198 (MRS); William Pennard, Engl. c. 1272 (RH).

Pinney. *See* PENNY.

Pinnion. Robert Penon, Normandy 1180–95 (MRS).

Pinsent. *See* PINCHIN.

Pinyon. *See* PINNION.

Piper, or Pipard. *See* PEPPER.

364

Pipere. *See* PIPER.

Pirie. *See* PIRRIE.

Pirkis, for Perkys or PERKS.

Pirrie. *See* PERRY.

Pisey, perhaps for Paysey or PACEY.

Pitcher. Radulphus Pichere, Normandy 1180 (MRS); Paulinus Peckere, Engl. c. 1272 (RH).

Pitcher. *See* PICKER.

Pite, a form of PITT.

Pitfield. Ralph de Petiville, Normandy 1180 (MRS); Godfrey de Petitvilla 1198 (Ib.).

Pither, for PETER.

Pitman. Maingot Piteman, Normandy 1198 (MRS); John Piteman, Engl. c. 1272 (RH).

Pitt. This name occurs in Normandy, where Richard and Turstin Peet are mentioned 1198 (MRS); Richard Pet and John Pite occur in Engl. c. 1272 (RH). From the arms the well-known family of Pitt is the same as that of Pet or Pette of Kent and Sussex. Gervase P. occurs in Sussex 1199 (RCR). From this family derived the Pitts of Dorset, t. Henry VI., ancestors of the great Earl of Chatham; William Pitt, his still more famous son; the Earls of Londonderry, Barons of Camelford and Rivers. The name also was taken by other families from English localities.

Pittar. Richard Pitart, Normandy 1180–95 (MRS).

Pittard. *See* PITTAR.

Pittis, for PITT.

Pittman, for PITMAN.

Pitts, for PITT.

Pitz, for PITTS.

Piver, or Pever. *See* PAVER.

Place, armorially identified with Plais or De Plessetis, a Norman baronial family. Radulphus, Gardinus, Ascius de Plaissecio, Plaisuz, Pleiz, or Plessys, Normandy 1180–95 (MRS). Giles de Playz was summoned by writ as a baron 1293.

Plackett, for BLACKETT.

Plaice. *See* PLACE.

Plaister. *See* PLASTER.

Plank, or De la Planche, a baronial family. Richard and Henry de Planca and their fief, Normandy 1180–95 (MRS). Ralph de la Planche c. 1119 witnessed a charter of Leeds Abbey, Kent (Mon. ii. 113). Planche was near Alençon.

Planner. William Plenier, Normandy 1180–95 (MRS), also 1098 (Ib.).

Plant. Durand, Emeric de la Plante, Normandy 1180–95 (MRS). Robert, Roger, William Plante, Engl. c. 1272 (RH).

Plante. William Planet, Normandy 1180 (MRS). Ralph de Planez or Planets, Engl. 1189 (Rot. Pip.); Robert, Roger, William Plante, Engl. c. 1272 (RH).

Plaster. Andreas Placitor, Normandy 1180–95 (MRS).

Plater. Warin Peletier, Normandy 1180–95 (MRS); John Pellitar, Engl. c. 1272 (RH).

Platt. Gislebert de Platea, Normandy 1198 (MRS); Adam, Richard Plot, Engl. c. 1272 (RH).

Platts. Robert de Plateis, Normandy 1198 (MRS); Stephen de Platell, Engl. c. 1272 (RH).

Platts. *See* PLATT.

Plaw, for BLAAW.

Player. Andreas Placitor, Normandy 1180–95 (MRS).

Playle, perhaps for PLAYNE.

Playne. Robert, Henry de Playnes or Planis, Normandy 1180–95 (MRS), and the fief of Planes. Roger de Planes, Engl. c. 1198 (MRS).

Pleasant. *See* PLEASENCE.

Pleasants. *See* PLEASENCE.

Pleasence. N. Plaisence, Normandy 1198 (MRS); Hugh de Plesence, Engl. c. 1272 (RH).

Pleister. *See* PLESTER.

Plester. *See* PLASTER.

Plews. Ralph de Plus nigro, Normandy, 1180–95 (MRS); Ralph Plusneir 1198 (Ib.). Richard de Pleys, England, c. 1272 (RH).

Plimmer, for PLUMMER.

Plough, for PLOWES.

Plow, for PLOWES.

Plowes, for PLEWS.

Pluck. Ralph Peloc, Normandy 1180–95 (MRS); Henry Pilloc, Engl. c. 1272 (RH).

Plucknett, or De Plukenet. *See* PLUNKETT.

Plum. Robertus Plumme, Normandy 1180 (MRS); Rob. Plome 1198; John Plum, Engl. c. 1272 (RH).

Plumb, for PLUM.

Plumbe, for PLUM.

Plume, for PLUM.

Plumer. William Plemer, Normandy 1180–95 (MRS); Gilbert, Thomas le Plumer, Engl. c. 1272 (RH).

Plumm, for PLUM.

Plummer. *See* PLUMER.

Plumptre, or De Clarefai, a branch of the house of FITZ-WILLIAM, deriving from Paul Fitz-William de Plumtre, living 1285, son of William Fitz-Thomas, whose father, Thomas de Plumtre, or Fitz-William of Plumtre and Sprotboro, was son of William Fitz-William, son of Albreda de Lisures. (*See* FITZ-WILLIAM.) Thomas de Plumtre, or Fitz-William, 13th cent., held Plumtre, Normanton, Stanton, Keyworth, Rutingdon, Riseley, and Clipstone, Notts, by the service of half a knight's fee, from the Countess of

Eu (Testa de Neville, 7). From his grandson Paul descended the De Plumtres of Notts and of Kent. Of this branch was John Plumtre of Nottingham, who in 1392 had license from Richard II. to found an hospital with two chaplains at Nottingham, which he accordingly founded in 1400 (Mon. ii. 448).

Plunkett, or De Plugenet, from Plouquenat near Rennes, Bretagne. Alan de Plugenoi occurs in Oxford 1158 (Rot. Pip.). Hugh de Plugenet mar. Sibil, dau. of Joce de Dinant, and acquired Lamborne, Berks. His son Alan P. 1219 paid 100 marks for livery of Lamborne. Alan P. 1267 was Lord of Kilpeck, Hereford, and was a baron by writ 1295. John Plunket (probably his nephew) settled in Ireland, and was ancestor of the Earls of Fingall, Lords Louth and Dunsany, and the eminent Lord Plunket, Chancellor. The family bears the bend of the Lords Plugenet of England.

Poague, for BOAG.

Poate, for BOAT.

Pochet, for PACHET. *See* PAGET.

Pochin. Aitard Pocin 1157 witnessed a charter Normandy (Mem. Soc. Ant. Norm. v. 107).

Pochin. Gaudin, William Pocin, Normandy 1180–95 (MRS); Thomas, William Poucin 1198 (Ib.).

Pockett, for POCHET.

Pocock, or Pacock. *See* PEACOCK.

Pococke, for POCOCK.

Podger, for BODGER.

Poett. *See* POTE.

Poge, for BOGUE.

Poile. *See* PILE.

Poingdextre, Richard Poindestre, Normandy 1180 (MRS).

Pointer. William Pontier, Normandy, 1198 (MRS); John and

366

Richard Ponter, Engl. c. 1272 (RH).

Pointing. Richard Pontin, Normandy 1180–95 (MRS); Jordan Ponteyn, Engl. c. 1272 (RH).

Poland. John and Ivo Polain, Normandy 1180–95 (MRS). Nine of the name 1198 (Ib.). Richard Pulein, Eng. c. 1198 (RCR); John Polein, c. 1272 (RH).

Pole. Roger de Pola, Normandy 1180–95 (MRS). This Roger de Poles is mentioned in Devon 1189 (Rot. Pip.).

Poley. John de Poleio and his wife paid a fine 1221 for lands in Normandy (Mem. Soc. Ant. Norm. v. 141); Ralph de Poillie or De Poelai 1180–98 (MRS). Poley appears to be in Herts (Lower).

Polhill, armorially identified with POLLEY.

Pollard. Robert, Roger, Geoffry Polard, Normandy 1180–95 (MRS). Godfrey and Robert P. 1198 (Ib.); Bernard, Godard, Richard, Robert, Walter Pollard, Eng. c. 1198 (RCR).

Pollen, for Polein. *See* POLAND.

Pollett, for Polet or PAULETT.

Polley, armorially identified with POLEY.

Pollitt. *See* POLLETT.

Polly, for POLLEY.

Polyblank, probably for Peilblanche, but not identified.

Pomeroy, a baronial family, Castellans of La Pomerie, Normandy (De Gerville, Anc. Chat.). Ralph de la Pomeraye held 51 lordships in barony in Devon 1086. *See* Dugdale and Banks. Hence the Viscounts Harberton.

Pomroy, for POMEROY.

Pond, the English form of De Stagno. William de Stagno, Normandy 1180–95 (MRS), also 1198.

Gilbert de Stangno, Engl. c. 1198 (RCR); Hervey and Edmund de Stanho c. 1272, and Roger de Pond, Engl. (RH).

Ponder. Geoffry, Gilbert Ponhere, Normandy 1180–95 (MRS); William Pontier 1198 (Ib.); William and Simon le Pondere, Engl. c. 1272 (RH).

Ponders. *See* PONDER.

Ponsford, for PAUNCEFOOT.

Ponsonby. The name is derived from P., Cumberland, so named from Ponzo or Poncio, t. William I. This name was, as appears from Gall. Christ. vol. vi., and from Bouquet, equivalent to that of Pontius; and was peculiar to Aquitaine. John Fitz-Ponzo granted the church of P. to Coningshead Priory (Mon. ii. 424). From him descended Richard de P., t. Edward I., ancestor of the Earls of Bessborough and Viscounts Ponsonby.

Pont. Arnulph, Berenger, Raynald de Ponte, Normandy 1180–95 (MRS); John, Robert, Sylvester de P. Engl. c. 1198 (RCR).

Ponton. Richard Pontin held lands in Normandy from Philip Augustus (Mem. Soc. Ant. Norm. v. 183); Philip de Ponton, Eng. c. 1198 (RCR).

Ponting, for PONTIN.

Pontis, or Ponts. *See* PONT.

Ponton. *See* PONTIN.

Pool, for POLE.

Pooley, for POLEY.

Poore, the English form of Pauper or Le Poer. *See* PAVER.

Popert, for BOBART.

Popkin. *See* POPKISS.

Popkins. *See* POPKISS.

Popkiss, for Popkins. William Popekin, Normandy 1180–95 (MRS). The arms of Popkin are preserved by Robson.

Pople, or Populus. *See* PEOPLE.

Porcas. Hugh, Ranulph Porcus, Normandy 1198 (MRS).

Porcher. Eguerran, Osbert, Anfrid, William, Bernard Porcarius, Normandy 1180–95 (MRS); Hugh, William Porcarius, England c. 1198 (RCR); John le Porcher, c. 1272 (RH).

Porrett. Phylippus Poret, Normandy, 1198 (MRS).

Port. 1. A baronial family. Adam, Robert, Henry, Ralph, Engelram de Portu, Normandy 1180–95 (MRS). *See* Dugdale, Banks. The main line took the name of St. John. Hence the Earls and Viscounts Bolingbroke, and Lords St. John. 2. From Porta, Normandy. Roger de Porta, and many others 1180–98 (MRS). From this family probably descended the Ports of Derby.

Porter. Thomas, Engerran, Robert Portarius, Normandy 1180–95 (MRS); Hugh, Roger, Thomas, William P. 1198 (Ib.); Godfrey, Simon Portar, Engl. 1189 (Rot. Pip.).

Porters. *See* PORTER.

Posener. Harduin Pocenarius, Normandy 1180–95 (MRS).

Posenere. *See* POSENER.

Posner. *See* POSENER.

Post, for Past. *See* PASS.

Postans, for Postern. Geoffry de Posterna, Normandy 1180 (MRS).

Postill. Richard, Alexander, Ralph Postel, Normandy 1180–95 (MRS); Richard Potel, Eng. c. 1272 (RH).

Portwine, a corruption of Poitevin (Lower). *See* POTWINE.

Pote. Osbert Poeta, Normandy 1180–95 (MRS); Reginald Pot, Engl. c. 1272 (RH).

Potier. *See* POTTER.

Pott. *See* POTE.

Potter. John, Raimond Potier, Normandy 1180–95 (MRS); Cardois and Ralph P. 1198 (Ib.); Henry, John, Nicholas le Potere, Engl. c. 1272 (RH). The term meant an apothecary or druggist.

Pottier. *See* POTTER.

Pottinger, for POTTER, old English for an apothecary (Lower).

Pottle. *See* POSTILL.

Potts. *See* POTT.

Potwine. N. Petevin, Normandy 1180–95 (MRS). *See* PETO.

Poulter. Robert le Pautre (Paltre), Normandy, 1180–95 (MRS); Richard le Poleter, Engl. c. 1272 (RH).

Pouncy, armorially identified with Pounse. Wigot Ponce, Normandy 1198 (MRS).

Pound, for POND.

Poupard. Walter, Warner Poupart, Normandy 1198 (MRS).

Poupart. *See* POUPARD.

Power. Robert Poher, Normandy 1180–95 (MRS); Richard, Robert Pohier, or Poher, 1198 (Ib.).

Power, Poher, or Poncaer, descended from the Lords of Poncaer, Bretagne, of whom Rivallon was living 846 (Morice, Hist. Bret. Preuves, i. xi.). From him descended the Viscounts of Poncaer or Poher, of whom Tanegui occurs c. 1100, and Rivallon previously. A branch settled 1066 in Devon, with Alured de Mayenne; and in 1165 Ranulph Poher held three fees of his barony (Lib. Niger). Bartholomew P. at the same time was Lord of Blackborough, Devon, and was father of Robert Poher (Pole, 165). This Robert Poher or Poer settled in Ireland, and was ancestor of the Lords Poer, Barons of Dunnoyle, and of Curraghmore. This family bore a

368

chief indented, or per pale indented. The latter were the arms of Poher of Devon. Hence descended the Lords Poer, Earls of Tyrone (ancestors in the female line of the Marquises of Waterford, and Lords Decies), and the Baronets Power, and other families of importance. The name also remains in England.

Powers, for POWER.

Powle, for POWLES.

Powles. Unfrid Poles, Normandy 1198 (MRS). Hugh Poul, Eng. c. 1272 (RH).

Powley, for POLEY.

Powling, for Polin, or Polain. *See* POLAND.

Powney, the French pronunciation of Ponet or Poinet, a foreign name, locality unascertained.

Powning, for Poynings (Lower), a baronial family, considered to be a branch of PIERREPONT.

Powter, for PORTER (Lower).

Poynter. *See* POINTER.

Poyntz, or Ponz, a branch of Fitz-Ponce. *See* CLIFFORD, VESCI, BURGH.

Practor. *See* PRATER.

Praill. Ranulph de Praelliis, Norm. 1198 (MRS). The name also occurs as de Praeriis (Ib.). Robert de Praeriis, Engl. 1189 (Rot. Pip.). Henry de Prahors, c. 1198 (RCR), a baronial family in Normandy and England.

Prall, for PRAILL.

Prater. Richard de Pretot, Norm. 1198 (MRS).

Prato, for Peretot, Normandy. Ralph and Roger de Peretot 1198 (MRS).

Pratt, from Pratum, or Pré, near Lisieux, where Duke Richard, in 1024, gave lands to Fontanelles Abbey (Neustria Pia, 166). In

Normandy Richard and Robert de Prato occur 1198, Matilda, Reginald, Roger de Prato 1180–95 (MRS). The latter occurs in Essex 1199 (RCR), and Walter de P. in Hertford (Ibid.). Hervey de Prato 1200, in Normandy, was King John's 'faithful knight' (Hardy, Rot. Norm. i. 32), and the custody of Rouen Castle was given to his brother. Elyas de P. occurs in Suffolk in 1236 (Roberts, Excerpta), William de P. in 1259 (Hunter, Rot. Select.), from whom descended the Pratts of Riston, Norfolk, a branch of whom, settling in Devon, were ancestors of the Lord Chief Justice Pratt, and the Marquises Camden. The name was translated Mead, Meade, Mede, Meads.

Predavalle, for Perdeville, from Perdreauville, near Mantes, Normandy. Hugh de Perdeville witnessed a charter of Peter de Falconburgh to Pontefract Priory, York (Mon. i. 656).

Preeston, for PRESTON.

Preist. William, Durand, Symon, Peter, Ansketil, Thomas, Harvey Presbyter, Norm. 1180–95 (MRS). Hugh, John, Martin, &c., Prest, Engl. c. 1272 (RH).

Preede, for PREIST.

Pressey, for BRESSEY, or BRASSEY.

Prest. See PREIST.

Preston, or Tailleboia. Renfrid Taillebosc, of Normandy, c. 1050, had issue: 1. Ralph Taillebosc, Viscount of Bedford, whose widow was a tenant in capite Bedford, &c. 1086. 2. William Taillebosc, of Lincoln 1086. 3. Ivo Taillebosc, of Lincoln and Norfolk 1086. 4. Gilbert Fitz-Renfrid. The latter was provided for by his brother Ivo, who held Kendal, Westmoreland, t. William

I.; and inherited his barony. His son, William de Lancastre, had issue, Renfrid, who was father of, 1. William de Lancastre II.; 2. Roger, whose son Gilbert m. the heiress of William II. de L., and dying 1219 left William III., whose sisters were his heirs; 3. Warin de Lancastre, to whom Henry II. confirmed the estates at Preston formerly held by Gilbert Fitz-Renfrid (his great grandfather). In 1199 King John confirmed the rents of Preston to Henry Fitz-Warin de Lancastre (Baines, iv. 297, 298). Hence descended the important family of De Preston in Lancashire, who bore the arms of the De Lancastres, with a slight difference. A younger son, Philip de Preston, settled under the patronage of the Butlers (Barons of Amounderness, Lancashire, and Earls of Ormond), in Ireland, t. Edward I., and adopted the arms of Butler, with a slight variation, probably as a feudal tenant, or from intermarriage. From him descended the Prestons, Viscounts Gormanston, and Lords Tara.

Prett, for PRATT.

Pretty. See PRITTIE.

Previte. See PREVITT.

Previtt, or Prevot. Alan, Alvere, Bartholomew, &c. Prepositus, Norm. 1198 (MRS). Many of the name in England, c. 1272 (RH).

Prevost. See PREVITT.

Prevot. See PREVITT.

Prew, for Pirou. See PAKENHAM.

Pride. See ORGILL.

Prier, for Prayer, or Praers. See PRIOR.

Priest. See PREIST.

Pring, for PERRING.

Prior, armorially identified with Praers, or Praels. See PRAILL.

Pritt, for PRETT.

Prittie, or De Pratis, appears from the arms to have been originally of Norfolk; the crest of the N. family being the basis of the arms of P. in Ireland. Henry Prettie occurs in Norfolk 1681; William Praty, Suffolk, t. Elizabeth; William Praty, Norfolk, 1490 (Blomefield, vi. 277.), Stephen 1400, Thomas 1397, Simon de Pratis 1397, Lord of Dalling, Norfolk (Ibid. v. 145). William de Pratis, Suffolk, 1259; Jordan de Pratis, earlier (Ibid. vii. 73), Peter de Pratis, of Suffolk and Essex, 1207. Probably from Preaux, Normandy.

Pritty. See PRITTIE.

Privett, for PREVITI.

Proud. Radulphus Superbus, Norm. 1198 (MRS). Hugh, Walter le Proude, Eng. c. 1272 (RH).

Prouse. See PROWSE.

Prout, for PROUD.

Prouts. See PROUT.

Proviss, for PROVOST.

Provost. See PREVOST.

Prowett, for PROUT.

Prowse, or Preux. Drogon Prose, Norm. 1180–95 (MRS); Ralph, Richard Probus homo 1198 (Ib.); William Prous, Engl. c. 1272 (RH).

Proy. See PROYE.

Proye, for Broy, an ancient baronial family of Champagne (see Des Bois), settled in England 1066, and which held fiefs in 1165 (Lib. Niger).

Pruce. See PROUSE.

Prust, for PREST.

Pryor. See PRIOR.

Puckett, for POCKETT.

Puckle, for BUCKLE.

Pullar, or Pullard, for POLLARD.

Pull. Thomas, Warin, Tustin Pullus, Norm. 1180–95 (MRS); Hugh Poul, Engl. c. 1272 (RH).

370

Pullen, for Polein, or POLAND.

Puller, for Polard. See POLLARD.

Pulley, for Pooley, or POLEY.

Pulleyn. See POLAND.

Pullin. See PULLEN.

Pulling, for PULLEN.

Pullinger, for BULLENGER.

Pullins. See PULLEN.

Punch, for Punce, or Ponce. See POYNTZ.

Punchard, for Punchardon, or PONTCARDON. Robert de Pontcardon held lands in Devon 1083 (Exon. Domesday). Pontcardon was near Neauffle, Normandy. William de Punchardon in 1165 held six fees in Somerset and Devon; Roger de P. in Lincoln; and Matthew in Northumberland or York (Lib. Niger). William de Punchardon, of Heanton-Punchardon, Devon, was living 1242 (Pole), and in 1261 Oliver P. had a writ of military summons for the war in Wales.

Punchard. Walter, Durand Pinceart, Norm. 1180–95 (MRS); Grenti, Manaud, Roger Pinchart 1198 (Ib.); Albreda Pinchard, Engl. c. 1272 (RH).

Puncheon, armorially identified with Pincheon. See PINCHIN.

Puncher, for PUNCHARD.

Punshon. See PUNCHEON.

Punt, for PONT.

Punter, for Ponter. See POINTER.

Purcell. William Porcel, Norm. 1180 (MRS); Andrew Bertin P. 1198 (Ib.); Roger, Simon, Thomas P. Engl. c. 1272 (RH). Of this name were the Barons of Loughmoe, Ireland.

Purchase. See PORCAS.

Purches. See PORCAS.

Purchese. See PORCAS.

Purday, from PARDY.

Purdey. See PURDAY.

Purdie, from PARDY.

Purdon, for BURDON.

Purdue, for PARDÉ.

Purdy. *See* PURDIE.

Purkess. *See* PORCAS.

Purkins. *See* PERKINS.

Purkis. *See* PERKINS.

Purkiss. *See* PURKIS.

Purle, for PERLE.

Purnell, probably foreign, but not identified. The arms differ from Burnell. Robert, son of Haniser de Pruneto, or Purnelai, occurs Ord. Vit. 834, 843.

Purney, for BURNEY (Lower).

Purrier, for PERRIER.

Purrott, for PERROTT.

Pursell, for PURCELL.

Purser, for BURSER. *See* BOURCHIER.

Pursey, for PERCY.

Purslove. *See* PURSLOW.

Purslow, for PARSLOW, or Passeleu.

Purss. Radulphus Borse, Norm. 1198 (MRS); Gilbert, Henry, Richard Purs, Engl. c. 1272 (RH).

Purssell, for PURCELL.

Purssey, for PERCY.

Purt. William Pert, Normandy 1180-95 (MRS); Walter Purt, Engl. c. 1272 (RH).

Purves. *See* PURVIS.

Purvis, for Parvus. *See* PETIT.

Pury, for BURY.

Puryer, for PURRIER.

Putman, for PITMAN.

Putt. *See* POTT.

Putts. *See* POTTS.

Pusey, for Pudsey, or de Puisay, from PUISAZ, or Puisay, in the Orleanois. Everard de Pusac commanded a division at the Battle of Antioch 1098 (Rog. Wendover, ii. 120). William de Pusaz was Bishop of Durham 1189. Henry de Pusac, or de Puteaco, witnessed a charter of William, son of Rodbert de Percy, in favour of Bolton Priory, York (Mon. ii. 35), and subscribed the foundation charter of Ellerton Priory, York, t. John (Ib. 822). Henry III. confirmed to Wilberfosse Abbey, York, lands near those of Hugh de Pusac (Mon. i. 524). William de Putat (Pusac) had a writ of military summons 1233 to proceed to Bretagne. The English name of 'Pusey' or de Pesey was local, from a place in Berks.

Pyatt. *See* PIATT.

Pye, for Pie. *See* PAY.

Pyemont. Osbert Piman, Normandy 1180-95 (MRS); Osbert Piment 1198 (Ib.); John Pigeman, Engl. c. 1272 (RH).

Pyett, for PYATT.

Pyk, for PIKE.

Pyke, for PIKE.

Pyle, for PILE.

Pyne, for PINE.

Pyott, for PYATT.

Pyrke, for Perk, or PERKS.

Q

Quall. *See* QUAILE.

Quaile, for Cail. *See* CALL.

Quain, for KAIN or CAIN.

Quaintrell, for Canterel, or Quin-terel, foreign. Richard Queynterel, Engl. c. 1272 (RH); Walter Q., M.P. for Worcester, 1298 (PPW).

Quallet. Eustace Quillot, Norm.

1180 (MRS); Barth. and Eustace Quillot 1198 (Ib.).

Quantrell. See QUAINTRELL.

Quarell. Hugo de la Quarelle, Robert, and Reginald, Norm. 1180–95 (MRS). See CARELL.

Quaritch. Arnulf de Quarroges, and the Honour of Q., Norm. 1180 (MRS).

Quarrell. Roger, Turstin, Acard, Bertin, William Quarrel, Norm. 1180–95. See CARELL. William Q. held a fief in Somerset (Mon. i. 280).

Quarrier. Ansketel Quareter, Norm. 1180–95 (MRS); Hugh le Quarreur, Engl. c. 1272 (RH).

Quatermass. Robert de Quatuor Mare, Norm. 1198 (MRS), from Quatremars near Rouen. Lucas de Q. 1165 held from Ridel in Northampton (Lib. Nig.). Sir Adam de Q. witnessed a charter of Roesia de Verdun 1244 (Mon. i. 933). The family was of importance Lincoln and Leicester.

Quartermain, for Quatremaines, appears to have been the same as Quatremass. Hubert de Quatremaines of Lincoln 1165. Hubert Q. paid 1203 a fine in Oxford for one fee (Rot. Canc.). William Q. was summoned from Oxford 1263

to attend with horses and arm⁻. Thomas Q. summoned from Oxford to a council at Westminster, 1324 (PPW).

Quartermaine. See QUARTERMAIN.

Quarterman, for QUARTERMAIN.

Quay, for KAY.

Quebe, for Guibe or GIBB.

Queely, for DE QUILLY. See COLLEY-WELLESLEY.

Queintrell. See QUAINTRELL.

Quennell, for Chenell or CHANNELL.

Quentin, for St. Quentin, a baronial family. See ST. QUINTIN.

Quentery, for Cantery or CHANTRY.

Quilley, or De Ouilly. See COLLEY-WELLESLEY.

Quincey, a baronial family from Quincé, Maine. La Roque (Mais. de Harc. i. 213) traces the house of De Quincy to that of De Rohan, Bretagne, whose arms they bore. See BAILLIE, and for the Earls of Winchester Dugdale and Banks, Dorm. and Ext. Baronage.

Quinney, for CHEYNEY.

Quinnel, for Quesnel, or CHENNELL.

Quinton, for QUENTIN.

Quintrell, for QUAINTRELL.

R

Rabbage, for Rabaz. See RABBITS.

Rabbeth, for Rabaz. See RABBITS.

Rabbits. Hugh Rabace, Norm. 1180–95 (MRS); Gerard de Rabes 1198 (Ib.). Robert Rabaz gave Ke-

nilworth or Chillingworth Church, Northants, to De la Pré Abbey, which gift was confirmed by Henry II. (Mon. ii. 312). Stephen Fitz-Robert R. of N. Killingworth was a benefactor to Sulby Abbey (Ib. 630). John R. (13th cent.) held half a fee from John de Bayeux (Testa, 24). Stephen de R., M.P. for Northants 1298 ; Robert R., M.P. for Rutland 1313–1316, Lord of Preston, Ridlington, and Ayston, Rutland.

Raby, from the forest and castle of Raby or Rabeium, Normandy. John Raby had a safe conduct in Normandy t. Henry V. (Mem. Soc. Ant. Norm. v. 243).

Racine. Robert Racine, Normandy 1180–95 (MRS); Arnulph, William Racinne 1198 (Ib.); Richard Raison, Engl. c. 1272 (RH).

Rackett. Radulphus Racate or Rachate, Normandy 1180 – 95 (MRS) ; Peter, William Ragat, Engl. c. 1272 (RH).

Radcliff. *See* RADCLIFFE.

Radcliffe. An English local name borne by different families. The Radcliffes of Radcliffe, Notts, were originally named De Mendrei, being a foreign family. In 1165 R ·ginald de Radclive held lands of ancient enfeoffment from the barony of Hansel in Notts (Lib. Nig.). In the next cent. Reginald de Mendrei paid scutage for a fee in Radeclive, Notts (Testa, 20). Walter Fitz-Stephen de R. was a benefactor to Thurgarton Priory, Notts (Mon. ii. 95).

Radclyffe. *See* RADCLIFFE.

Rae, for RAY.

Ragg, for Rack or RAIKES.

Ragge. *See* RAGG.

Raggett. Symon Ragot or Ragotus, Normandy 1198 (MRS); Richard le Raggide, Engl. c. 1272 (RH).

Raikes. Andreas Rake, Normandy 1180–95 (MRS); Walter Rake, Engl. c. 1272 (RH). *See also* REEKS, REX.

Rain, for RAINE.

Rainbird. Radulphus Reinbert, Normandy 1180–95 (MRS); William Reinbert, Engl. c. 1198 (RCR).

Rainbow. Warin, John, Roger Rainbaut, Normandy, 1198 (MRS) ; Robert Reynbaut, Engl. c. 1272 (RH).

Raine. Warenger Reine, Normandy 1180 – 95 (MRS); Alicia Reine, Engl. c. 1272 (RH).

Raines, for RAINE.

Rainger. *See* RANGER.

Rains, for RAINES.

Rainy. *See* RENNIE.

Raiser. William Raser, Normandy 1180 – 95 (MRS) ; Ralph Rasur, Engl. c. 1272 (RH).

Raison. Arnulph, William Racinne, Normandy 1198 (MRS); William Raisoun, Engl. c. 1272 (RH).

Rake. *See* RAIKES.

Rallings. *See* RAWLINS.

Ralls, for ROLLS.

Ralph, or Fitz-Ralph, comprises Norman and other families.

Ram. Richard de Ariete (Ram), Normandy t. John (Mem. Soc. Ant. Norm. v. 103). Ram or Ramy is mentioned in Normandy (MRS).

Ramm, for RAM.

Ramsay, or De Beauchamp. Hugh de B. of Normandy, first Baron of Bedford t. William I., was father of Oliver, father of Paganus de Beauchamp of Eaton, Bedford, founder of Chicksand Priory c. 1150 (Banks, D. and Ex. Bar.). His son Hugh appears to have had a brother Simon.

Simon de Beauchamp being seneschal to the Abbey of Ramsey, was surnamed De Ramsey, and had grants in Scotland c. 1140. William de Ramsey, probably his grandson, witnessed a Scottish charter before 1198. Branches of the De Ramseys occur in Hunts, Bedford, and Essex 12th cent. (RCR). They appear to have held the office of seneschal of Ramsey. Roger 'the Seneschal' occurs c. 1199 as Roger 'de Ramsie.' He also appears as Roger 'Fitz-Simon' (RCR). This Simon with Hugh his brother appears 1165 as Simon 'de Bellocampo,' holding lands from the Abbot of Ramsey, no doubt as seneschal (Lib. Nig.). The English line of Ramsay bore 'argent a fesse gules,' merely varying in tincture from that of the De Beauchamps, who bore 'or, a fesse gules.' The Earls of Dalhousie are of this family.

Ramsey. *See* RAMSAY.
Randal, or RANDALL.
Randall. *See* RANDOLF.
Randell. *See* RANDALL.
Randells. *See* RANDALL.
Randle. *See* RANDALL.

Randolf, or Randulf. Randulf or Ranulf, brother of Ilger, held in 1086 a great barony in Essex, Suffolk, Norfolk, Herts, &c. (Domesd.). His name indicates a foreign origin. William Randolph or Fitz-Ranulf 12th cent. was a benefactor to the Hospitallers of Cressing, Essex (Mon. ii. 544). In 1165 William Fitz-Ranulph or Radulf held fiefs in Kent and Sussex (Lib. Nig.). Hugh Randolph in 1199 witnessed a charter of King John (Mon. i. 179). In 1300 Sir John Randolf was summoned for military services against the Scots, and in 1307 to the coronation of Edward II. (PPW). From this family descended Sir Thomas Randolf of

874

Kent, the ambassador to Scotland t. Eliz.; John R., Bishop of London and the family of R. in Kent, Wilts and Virginia, who bear the arms o Sir J. R. 1300, viz., a cross charged with five mullets.

Raney. *See* RENNIE.
Ranger. Robert Reignier, Normandy 1180–95 (MRS).
Ranken. *See* RANKIN.
Rankin. Ralph, William, Bernard Roncin, Normandy 1180–95 (MRS).
Ranking, for RANKIN.
Ransom, armorially identified with Ranson, from Ronson or Roncin. Bernard Roncin and others, Normandy 1180–95 (MRS).
Ransome, for RANSOM.
Ranson. *See* RANSOM.
Ranyard, for Rainard. Robert, John, Roger Rainard or Reinert, Normandy 1180–95 (MRS); William Rener, Engl. c. 1272 (RH).
Raper, for ROPER (Lower).
Rapier, for RAPER.
Rasell, for RASTELL.
Rastall. Baldwin Rastel, Normandy 1180–95 (MRS); Sire Ralph Rastel, Engl. c. 1272 (RH).
Rastrick. Andrew, Eudo, Galter, Oger, &c., Rusticus, Normandy 1198 (MRS).
Ravell. *See* REVELL.
Ravenhill, for Ravenel, from Ravenel, near Beauvais and Clermont, in the Beauvoisin. Jordan de Revenell and Thomas his son witnessed a charter of Richard de Luretot, confirming his father's grants to Worksop Abbey (Mon. Angl. ii. 57). This was in the reign of Stephen.

The name occurs in the Duchy. Ranulf Ravenel, Normandy 1180–95 (MRS) Mariota, Robert Ra venild occur in Engl. c. 1272 (RH).

Ravenshear. N. Ravenger, Normandy 1180–95 (MRS).

Ravey, for Raville. *See* REVELL.

Raw, for ROWE (Lower).

Rawding, for RAWDON.

Rawden. The early pedigree of this family from the Conquest stated in the Peerages is mythic, and unsupported by any evidence. The family was the same originally as that of CRAVEN, which see. From this house descended the Earls of Moira, Marquises of Hastings.

Rawe. *See* RAW.

Rawle, for ROLLE.

Rawlence, for RAWLINS.

Rawles, for ROLLE.

Rawlin. *See* RAWLINS.

Rawling, for RAWLIN.

Rawlings. *See* RAWLINS.

Rawlins. Robert Roillon, Normandy 1180; William Raillon 1198 (MRS).

Rawll. *See* RAWLE.

Ray. Turstin de Rea, or Ree. Robert and Turstin de Rea, Normandy 1180–98 (MRS). Ralph, Robert de Ree, Engl. c. 1272 (RH). William de Radio (Raye) in 1083 held lands Somerset (Exon. Domesd. 74).

Raybould, for Ribald. Ribald, Baron of Middleham t. William I., was of the house of Bretagne. Adam Ribald 1180 (Rot. Pip.). Ribald was a brother of Alan, Earl of Richmond and Penthièvre, of the house of Bretagne, and father of Ralph Ribald, Lord of Middleham, who m. Agatha, dau. of Robert de Brus of Skelton. From him descended Ralph Ribald, Baron of Middleham, who m. a dau. of Lord Percy, and d. 1269, leaving daugh-

ters his heirs. *See* Dugdale, Banks.

Raynbird. *See* RAINBIRD.

Rayne, for RAINE.

Rayner. Gaufridus Ranier, Normandy 1180 (MRS). William Rener, Engl. c. 1272 (RH).

Raynes, for RAINE.

Rayney. *See* RENNIE.

Raynor, for RAYNER.

Rea. *See* RAY.

Reaney. *See* RENNIE.

Reason. *See* RAISON.

Reavell. *See* REVELL.

Rebanks, for Rebeck. *See* REBBECK.

Rebbeck, a Flemish family. Balduinus de Rabeca of Flanders 12th cent. *See* Albert. Miræi, Opera Diplomatica, i. 396.

Reboul, for RIBALD. *See* RAYBOULD.

Reckitt, for RACKETT.

Record. Hugh Ricoart, Normandy 1180–95 (MRS). Robert, William Rikeward, Engl. c. 1272 (RH).

Reddall, for RIDDELL.

Reddalls. *See* REDDALL.

Reddel, for RIDDEL.

Redgate. Richard Retgate, Normandy 1198 (MRS). Sewall de Retcote, Engl. c. 1272 (RH).

Redley, for RIDLEY.

Ree. *See* REA.

Reecks. *See* REEKS.

Reek, for REEKS.

Reekes, for REEKS.

Reeks, for Rex. William, Gislebert, Roger, Gerald, Walter, Geoffry Rex, Normandy 1180–95 (MRS). Adam, John Rex, Engl. c. 1272 (RH). *See* REX. Hence the name of King.

Reeson, for RAISON.

Rein, for RAIN.

Relfe, for RELPH.

Relph, for RALPH.

Relphs. *See* RELPH.

Remy, for St. Remy. William and Robert de St. Remigio held lands in Normandy t. Philip Augustus. Richard de St. Remigio, Normandy 1198 (MRS). Lady Juliana de St. R. Engl. c. 1272 (RH).

Renard. *See* RANYARD.

Rendall, for RANDALL.

Rendel, for RANDALL.

Rendell. *See* RANDELL. A distinguished engineer bears the name.

Rendle. *See* RANDLE.

Rennell. *See* REYNELL.

Rennels, for REYNOLDS.

Renner, for RAYNER.

Rennie. Hugh de Ranny, Normandy t. John (Mem. Soc. Ant. Norm. v. 124). Eguerran de Reinni, Normandy 1198 (MRS). The celebrated engineer Rennie bore this name.

Rennies, for REYNOLDS.

Rennolls, for REYNOLDS.

Renny, for RENNIE.

Repington. Geoffry, William de Rapendon, or Repondon, Normandy 1180–95 (MRS). Geoffry de R. 1198 (Ib.). This family was seated in Warwick and Leicester.

Repuke, for REBBECK.

Rest. Nicholas Fitz-Reste, Normandy 1180–95 (MRS). Hugh Ress, Engl. c. 1272 (RH).

Restall. *See* RESTELL.

Restell. Baldwin Rastel, Normandy 1180–95. Arnulph R. 1198 (MRS). William Rastell, Engl. c. 1198 (ROR).

Revel. *See* REVELL.

Revell, a baronial name, from Reville or Raville, Normandy. Sansom and Roger de R. and the fief of R. are mentioned in N. 1180–95

(MRS). The ancestor came to England with the Conqueror. Paganus and Robert Revel had estates in Hertford and Northants 1130 (Rot. Pip.). Richard R. held two fees in barony in Somerset 1165, and two from William Fitz-William. Robert R. held lands in Norfolk, Essex, Northants (Lib. Niger). Henry Revel was one of the nobles taken at Alnwick Castle 1174 (Hov. i. 382); and in the 13th cent. Richard R. the younger held Langport and Cory, Somerset, by grant of Richard I.; by service of two knights. Hence 'Cory - Revel' (Testa, 160). The family long continued of consequence in various parts of England.

Revett. *See* RIVETT.

Revill, for REVELL.

Revnell, for RAVENELL.

Rew. John, Peter, Richard, Robert, Roger de Rua, Normandy 1180–95 (MRS). John and Matthew Rue, Engl. c. 1272 (RH).

Rex. The original form of REEKES and Raikes still existing.

Rey. *See* RYE.

Reynal. *See* REYNELL.

Reynell. *See* REYNOLD. Hence the Baronets Reynell.

Reynold. Godfrey, Robert, Torketil, William Renoldus, Normandy 1198 (MRS). Giffard, John, William Reynold, Engl. c. 1272 (RH).

Reynolds. *See* REYNOLD. Sir Joshua Reynolds, the great painter.

Rhodes. Gerard, Richard de Rodes, Engl. 1202 (Rot. Canc.). Gerard de Rodes held Clifton and Langar, Notts, of the Honour of Peverel (Testa, 6). This name and family were derived from Rhodez, Aquitaine, and its ancient Counts, who were dispossessed by the Counts of Toulouse 1147.

Ribbands, for RIBBANS.

Ribbans, or Rabayn. The family De Rabayne came from Saintonge, Aquitaine, where it possessed the marquisate of Piscay. The Castle of Rabaine still remains. The family was of eminence 1018 (Des Bois). Elias de Rabayn had writs of military summons for the war in Gascoigne 1251 ; and another El. de R. had writs of summons 1277, 1282 (PPW). In 1316 Matilda de Raban was Lady of Edmonsham, Dorset.

Rich. Riche was near Nancy, in Lorraine. In 1278 Richard de la Riche was manucaptor for John Marmion, M.P. for Sussex, and was distrained to oblige him to receive knighthood (PPW). John de Riches 13th cent. held lands in Fotherby, Lincoln, from Walter Bec (Testa de Neville, 318). The Earls of Warwick and Holland, and the Baronets Rich, bore this name.

Richer. See RIDGERS.

Riches, for RICH.

Richmond, a baronial name derived from the office of Constable of Richmond. See BURTON-CONYNGHAM.

Rickard. See RECORD.

Rickards. See RECORD.

Ricket, for RICKARD.

Rickets. See RICKET.

Rickett, for RICKARD.

Ricketts. See RICKARDS. Of this name are the Viscounts St. Vincent.

Ricks. See REEKS.

Riddall, for RIDDELL.

Riddell, a baronial name, derived from a Gothic race in Aquitaine. Gerard, Baron of Blaye, c. 1030, granted lands to the Abbey of Fons Dulcis near Bordeaux, which

grant was confirmed by his brother Gerald de Blavia, and his sons Geoffry Rudelli (Ridel) and William Frehelandus (Gall. Christ. ii. 484, Instr.). The last-named, who was living 1079–1099 (Gall. Christ. ii. 459, Instr.), m. a sister of William de Albini Brito of England, and had Warin, Oliver, and Geoffry. The latter (Geoffry Ridel) went to Scotland t. David I., from whom he had grants, and was ancestor of the Riddells, Baronets. Another Geoffry Ridel, of the preceding generation, came to England from Apulia t. William I. with William Bigod, and is mentioned in Domesday 1086. He was a Crown Commissioner with Ralph Basset 1106 (Mon. Angl. i. 172), and succeeded the latter as Justiciary 1120. A collateral branch in 1165 possessed estates in Normandy. There is a Scottish family of Riddell which takes its name from R., Scotland. Geoffry Ridel occurs in Normandy 1180, Roger R. 1195, Geoffry 1198 (MRS).

Riddett. Victor le Retit, Normandy 1180-95 (MRS). The name appears as Ridhut (RH).

Riddle. See RIDDELL.

Riddles, for RIDDLE.

Rideal. See RIDDELL.

Rider. See RYDER.

Ridet. See RIDOUTT.

Ridge. See RUDGE.

Ridgers, for Richers or Richer. Robert Richerus, Normandy 1198 ; Robert, Thomas, Walter Richer, Engl. c. 1272 (RH).

Ridley, or De Loges. Nicholas R., Bishop of London and martyr, was descended lineally through the Ridleys of Ridley and Willmotwick, Northumberland, from Nicholas de Redley or Ridley living 1306. His father, Odard de R., witnessed a charter in Northumberland c. 1280 (Hodgson, Northd., ii., ii.); and c. 1250 Nic. de R. (son of Thomas) executed a charter (Ib.). His grandfather, Nicholas de Wilmotswyk (a place close to Ridley), lived t. John, and was son of Odard de W., who witnessed a charter of Hexham Abbey t. Henry II. (Ibid.) He was probably brother of John Fitz-Odard, Baron of Emildon (living 1161–1182), and son of Odard, Viscount of Northumberland, mentioned as such 1130, and in 1110 when Governor of Bamburgh. He was son of Odard de Loges, Viscount of Cumberland. See Loges.

Ridoutt. See RIDDETT.

Ridout. See RIDETT.

Rillatt. William, Geoffry Roillied or Roilliet, Normandy 1180 (MRS).

Rimboult. John Raimbault or Reinbaud, Nicholas, and Roger, Normandy 1180–95 (MRS). See RUMBOLD.

Rimer, for ROMER.

Ringer, for RANGER, Reignier.

Rivers, or De la Rivière, a baronial family from Normandy, where they were Lords of St. Germain de Crioult, near Bayeux (Des Bois). In 1083 Goscelin de Riveria held lands in Wilts (Exon. Domesday 1), also Walter de R. (Ib. 2). In 1130 Walter de R. paid a fine Berks (Rot. Pip.). In 1194 Ralph De la Rivere had a suit in Oxford (RCR). Richard de Rivers 1241 had m. one of the daughters and heirs of John Biset, and Richard de la Rivere was of Wilts 1258 (Roberts, Excerpt. i. 358, ii. 291). William de Ripariis of Essex had issue John of Berks, whose son John was Baron of Angre, Essex; and was summoned by writ

378

as a baron 1299 (P.P. Writs). The name continually occurs afterwards, and the Baronets Rivers were of this family.

In Normandy we have Serlo, Richard, Baldwin, William de Riveriis 1180–95 (MRS).

Rivett, foreign, probably not from Normandy.

Rivington. Hugh and John de Raveton, Normandy 1198 (MRS). The name was derived from Rivington, Lancashire.

Rix. See REX.

Roach. See ROCHE.

Road. See ROADES.

Roades. See RHODES.

Roads. See RHODES.

Roak. See ROAKE.

Roake. Gervas, John, Jocelin de Roca, Normandy 1180–95 (MRS). Agnes de Roka of Cambr. and Hunts 1205 paid a fine not to be obliged to marry (Hardy, De Obl. et Fin. 309). Richard Rake with Richard Malbanc had estates in Hereford 13th cent. (Testa) which were held from Sir Robert Tregoz of Ewyas. Nicholas Roc was a benefactor to Tupholme, Lincoln, temp. Henry III. (Mon. ii. 597). Hugh Roc, c. 1272 (RH), &c.

Roalfe. See ROLFE.

Roan, or De Rouen, a baronial name derived from the Viscounts of Arques and Rouen. (See SAVILLE.) Anselm, Viscount of Rouen, was of Oxford and other counties 1130 (Rot. Pip.), also Laurence and Nicholas de R., and Ralph de R. (Ib.). In 1165 Ralph de Rouen was of Lincoln, and John de R. of Devon (Lib. Niger); and the family long continued.

Robarts. Gilbert Robart, Normandy 1180 (MRS); Richard, James Robertus, 1198 (Ib.); John, Richard

Roberd, Engl. c. 1272 (RH). Of this name were the Earls of Radnor.

Robb. *See* ROBB.

Robbins. *See* ROBINS.

Robe. Robert Robe, Normandy 1198 (MRS); Henry Fitz-Richard Robbe, Engl. 1189 (Rot. Pip.).

Robin. *See* ROBINS.

Robins. Radulphus Robin, Normandy 1198 (MRS). John, Roger Robin or Robins, Engl. c. 1272 (RH).

Roche, a baronial name from La Roche, Normandy. In 1097 Wido de Rupe surrendered his castles of Roche and Veteuil to William Rufus (Ord. Vit. 767). In 1165 Wido de R. held a fee at Passay in the French Vexin (Feod. Norm.); Oliver de R. was at the same time one of the barons seated between Normandy and Brittany, and Ralph Roche held lands in Devon; Sansom R. in Dorset (Lib. Nig.); and 1203 Ralph de Rupe held three fees of the honour of Mortaine and Cornwall (Rot. Canall. 94). Adam de Rupe, ancestor of an Irish branch, built Roche Castle and Pill Priory in Pembroke, and accompanied Henry II. to Ireland, where he was ancestor of the Viscounts Fermoy, and the Barons Fermoy. In 1180–95 Roger, Hugh, and John de la Roche are mentioned in Normandy (MRS).

Rochefort. *See* ROCHFORT.

Rochfort, from Rochfort in the Viscounty of Rouen. Wido de R. held three fees in Bucks from the Earl 1165 (Lib. Niger), and witnessed a charter of Walter Giffard E. of Bucks, t. Henry II. (Mon. ii. 154). Another Guido de R. was summoned for the war in Wales 1257, and in Gascony 1251. Of this family was Milo de Rupeforti,

witness to a charter of Henry II. confirming the foundation of Dunbrody Abbey, Ireland 1178 (Mon ii. 1028), from whom descended Maurice de Rochfort 1295, 1302, one of the fideles of Ireland; and the Earls of Belvidere. In Normandy occur Paganus, Guido de Rupefort, 1180–95 (MRS); Radulfus Rochefort, 1198 (Ib.).

Rock. *See* ROAKE.

Rockall, from Rochelle in the Cotentin, Normandy. In 1130 Humfrid de Rochella had lands in Dorset, in 1165 William de Rochelle in Essex (Rot. Pip.; Lib. Niger). The former witnessed the charter of William de Mandeville, Earl of Essex, founding Walden Abbey (Mon. i. 460). The family of De la Rochelle in Normandy 1396 bore 2 bends argent with 7 escallops. (Douet-Darcq, Armorial de la France, p. 28.) The family long continued of importance in England, where the name was written Rokele.

Rocke. *See* ROAKE.

Rockhill, or ROCHELLE. *See* ROCKALL.

Rockley. Robert de Rokela, Normandy 1198; Philip de la Rochella, and Robert de la R., 1180 (MRS).

Roden, for RAWDON.

Rodney, or De Reyney. This family has been traced (Collinson, Somerset, iii. 602–605) from Walter de Rodney, t. Stephen; but the name Rodney is apparently not found in the records prior to the 14th century. It is a corruption of Reiny or Rayney, afterwards Radenay. The family of Reyney bore 3 pairs of wings in lure, from which the present arms of Rodney (3 spread eagles) are derived. The family of De Reiney or Rigny came from Champagne. Hagebert de Rigneio 1101 witnessed a charter of the Bishop of Tulle (Gall. Christ. xiii. 480 Instr.), and may be the same who possessed lands in Essex 1086 (Domesday). Roger de Reigny witnessed a charter of Bishop Roger of Sarum, t. Henry I. (Mon. i. 424); and Robert de R. held five fees, Devon 1165 (Lib. Niger). John de R. of Devon, and William de R., occur 1200 (RCR). John de Reiney or Rayney was of Devon and Somerset, and d. 1247 (Roberts, Excerpta). Thomas de R. occurs in the same year, and 1303 Sir Richard de Reyney or Radeney, and Lucia his wife, occur (Roberts, Cal. Geneal.). This noble acquired Stoke, Somerset, by m. with the heiress; and from him descended the brave Lord RODNEY, and the barons of that name.

Gaufridus de Radeneio, Normandy 1180 (MRS), paid a fine in the bailifry of Argentom; from which it appears that the name of Rayney had early adopted the D. The case is similar to those of Kenetbol for Kenebal, Lachmere for Lamare, Lidle for Lisle.

Roe. See ROWE.

Roebuck, for Rabeck. Baldwin de Rabeca occurs in Flanders 12th cent. (Al. Miræi Opera Diplomatica, i. 396). The name is Flemish.

Rofe. Symon de Rof, Normandy 1180–95 (MRS); William Roffe, Engl. c. 1272 (RH).

Roff. See ROFE.

Roffey. Garin de Raffeio, Normandy 1198 (MRS); Reginald and Henry de Ruffi, t. Philip Augustus (Mem. Soc. Ant. Norm. v. 173, 181); Lucia Rufe, Engl. c. 1272 (RH).

Roffway, for ROFFEY.

Roger. N. Rogere, Normandy 1180; Robert R. 1195 (MRS); Alexander, Richard, Roger, Engl. c. 1272 (RH).

Rogers, for ROGER. This name is borne by the Baronets Rogers.

Rokeby, or De Spina, from Rokeby, Yorkshire. Henry de Spina of Rokeby was a benefactor to Fountains Abbey, and Reginald de Spina, son of Hugh de Rokeby, confirmed the gift of Stephen de R. to the same abbey (Burton, Mon. Ebor.). Sire Henry de R. witnessed a charter of the Earl of Richmond 1275 (Mon. ii. 197). This appears to be a branch of the Norman family of De la Spine or De Spina.

Roland. Odo, Nicholas, Gaufrid Rollant or Rolland, Normandy 1180–95 (MRS). Robert, William Rouland, Engl. c. 1272 (RH).

Roles. See ROLL.

Rolfe. See ROFE. Of this name was Lord Chancellor Cranworth.

Roll. Peter and William Roeles, Normandy 1198; William de Rodolio 1180 (MRS); Girald de Roel, t. Phil. Augustus; Robert Rolle, Matilda Rolles, Engl. c. 1272 (RH).

Rolle. See ROLL. Hence the Barons Rolle.

Rolles. See ROLL.

Rolleston. Henry de Rolleston, Normandy 1195 (MRS). This Norman family took its name from Rolleston, Notts. Malger de R. (Mon. i. 840). Thomas de R. 1165 held a fief from Deincourt (Liber Niger). Sir Benedict de R. t. Edward I. (Mon. ii. 605).

Rolland. See ROLAND.

Rollings. See RAWLINS.

Rollo, or De Rullos, from Rullos, now Ruelles, near Vernon, Normandy. Richard de Rullos or

Rollos was Chamberlain to William the Conqueror, and m. Isabella, dau. of Richard Baron de la Haie despuits (De Gerville, Anc. Chat. de la Manche); whence came the connection of this family with Lincoln. His son William de R. m. the dau. and heir of Hugh de Evermue and Turfrida, dau. and heir of the famous Hereward by his first marriage; and received the barony of Bourn and Deeping (Liber Niger). He had, 1. William de Rullos, ancestor of a Norman line. 2. Richard, whose dau. m. Baldwin Fitz-Gilbert (from which union sprang the house of Wake, Barons of Bourn or Brunne). Richard afterwards settled in Scotland, where he had received grants from David I. (Douglas, Peerage Scotl.); and from him lineally descended John de Rollo, who in the 14th century had a grant of Duncrub, and was ancestor of the Barons Rollo of Duncrub.

Rolls. *See* ROLL.

Rolph. *See* ROFE.

Rolt. Peter Roald, Normandy 1180–95 (MRS); John, Peter, Robert Ruaut or Roalt (Ib.) 1198; Robert Ruaut 1180-95 (Ib.).

Romans. William Romant, and the Ville of M., Normandy 1180–95 (MRS). The arms of Romanes of Scotland are preserved by Robson.

Rome. Orsellus Rohom, Normandy 1180 (MRS).

Rome. William Rom, Normandy 1180–95 (MRS); Robert Rome 1198 (Ib.); Robert Rome, Engl. c. 1272 (RH.).

Romer, or De Roumare, from Roumare near Rouen, Normandy. Geroldus the Dapifer granted 1067 his church of Roumare to St. Amand, Rouen. He had issue Robert Fitz-Gerold de Roumara (father of William de Roumare, Earl of Lincoln) and Edward of Salisbury, Viscount of Wilts, living 1119, whose grandson, Patrick of Salisbury, was created Earl of S. by Matilda. William I., Earl of Lincoln, had a son William II., whose son William III. returned the fees of his barony in Lincoln in 1165 as 58, and in 1194 was with Richard I. in Normandy (Bowles, History of Laycock Abbey; Banks, Dorm. and Ext. Bar.). Collaterals, viz. William, John, and Matthew de Romara, occur in Normandy 1180–95 (MRS); Erenborc de Romara 1195 (Ib.); and the forest and estate of Romare are also mentioned. The name in England derives from some collateral branch.

Roney. William Roenai, Normandy 1180–95 (MRS); Hugh de Roenai 1198 (Ib.). The arms of Roney in England are preserved by Robson.

Roof, for ROFE.

Rooff, for ROPE.

Rook. *See* ROAKE.

Rooke. *See* ROAKE. Of this Norman family was the gallant Admiral Sir George Rooke, the captor of Gibraltar.

Rooks. *See* ROOK.

Rooksby. *See* ROKEBY.

Room. *See* ROME.

Roome. *See* ROME.

Rooney. *See* RONEY.

Roop, for De Rupe, or ROCHE.

Rooper. Richard de Rupetra; Ralph de Ruperia, Normandy 1180–95 (MRS); Ralph and Richard de Rupetra 1198 (Ib.). *See* ROPER.

Roos. *See* ROSS.

Root. *See* ROOTS.

Roote. *See* ROOTS.

Roots. Ranulph de Rotis, Normandy 1180–95 (MRS); Hugo de R. 1198 (Ib.); Ralph, Robert, Simon, &c. Rote, Engl. c. 1272 (RH). Hugo de Rotis held a fee of Montfort in Normandy 1165 (Duchesne, Feod. Norm.).

Rope. *See* ROBE.

Roper, or De Rupierre. This family has been supposed to be descended from a member of the house of Musard, who is said to have assumed the name of 'Rospear or De Rubruspatha;' but there is no evidence for the statement.

The name is derived from Rupierre near Caen, Normandy, the lords of which were of great importance in the 11th and 12th centuries (Des Bois). William de Rupierre (who came to England with the Conqueror) is mentioned by Ordericus Vitalis; in 1090 he commanded the forces of Duke Robert. The Counts of Rupierre continued in Normandy till the last century (Ib.). In 1099 William de R. possessed Trenouville, Grenteville, and Fremont, and was a benefactor of Troarn (MSAN, xii. 53). The seal of Roger de R. (MSAN, plate xvii.) represents a shield divided into twelve squares, each containing a martlet, the original evidently from which the modern Roper arms are derived. In England Robert de Ruperia paid fines in Notts and Derby (Rot. Pip.); and the heiress of John Rooper of Turndish, Derby, m. De Fourneaux, who assumed her name (Mon. i. 503). Roger de Rupere, of the Norman line, held lands in Warwick or Leicester, t. John, where he granted the advowson to Tewksbury Abbey (Testa de Neville, 87). From this family

382

descend the Roopers and the Barons Teynham.

Ropes, for ROBBS.

Rose, for ROSS.

Roser. Peter Roceart, Normandy 1180–95 (MRS); Peter de Rochier 1198 (Ib.); Richard le Rockare, Engl. c. 1272 (RH).

Rosher, for ROSER.

Rosier. *See* ROSER.

Rosling, for ROSCELIN, a baronial family, a branch of the Carlovingian Viscounts of Maine and Beaumont. *See* BEAUMONT. Geoffry de Bellomont or Baynard, brother of Hubert Viscount of Maine, held fiefs 1086 from the barony of Baynard, and from Percy and Earl Alan in Yorkshire (Domesd.). He had amongst other sons Roscelin de Bellomont, who had a grant of Stratton and Marsham, Norfolk, t. Henry I., whose son, William Fitz-Rosceline, had issue William de Stratton (Blomefield, vi. 331). Robert Fitz-Rosceline, brother of William Fitz-Rosceline, was father of Bartholomew de Marsham, ancestor of the Earls of Romney. William de Stratton also appears as 'Fitz-Rosceline,' and Robert Fitz-Rosceline his son held a lease of Newton, Norfolk, from Henry II. (Blomefield, v. 65). This estate was held in 1235 by Peter de Rosceline, and in 1317 by Thomas, son of Sir Peter Fitz-Roscelin (Ibid.). Sir Peter was summoned by writ as a baron in 1294. *See* MARSHAM.

Ross, or De Ros, a baronial name derived from an English locality. The origin of this family not ascertained.

The Norman name of De Ros, also established in England, came from Ros, now Rots, near Caen

(D'Anisy et St. Marie, sur le Domes-day). Temp. William I. Anchetil de Ros held in Kent from Odo of Bayeux, and Ansgot, Goiafrid, and Serlo de Ros were mesne lords in England 1086 (Domesd.). In 1130 Geoffry de Ros was of Kent (Rot. Pip.); in 1165 Geoffry de R. held two fees Essex; Everard de R. one in Suffolk and seven in York (Lib. Nig.). The family long continued of note in Normandy, and in several parts of England.

Rossall. *See* RUSSELL.

Rosser. *See* ROSER.

Roswell, for Rosel or RUSSELL.

Rotch, for ROCHE.

Rothwell, or De Warneville. William de Warnaville gave lands in Rothwell, Northants, to De la Pré Abbey, Northamptonshire (Mon. i. 1018). The family afterwards bore the name of Rothwell.

Rouch, for ROCHE.

Rougemont. Richard de Rubeomonte, Normandy 1180 – 95 (MRS).

Rought, for ROOT.

Rougier. Peter de Rochier, Normandy 1180-95 (MRS).

Round. In 1130 Radulphus Rotundus occurs in Essex (Rot. Pip.); Wiard de Rotundo, Normandy 1180-95 (MRS).

Roundell. Lucas, Geoffry, John Roondel, Normandy 1180 – 95; Stephen Roundel, Geoffry, Hugh, Lucas Roondel 1198 (MRS).

Roupell, for Rochelle. Robert de Rupella and Philip de Rupella paid scutage for lands in Essex held from M. de Mandeville, Countess of Essex (Testa de Neville, 364). *See* ROOKALL.

Rous, or Le Roux. This family is Norman, and in 1165 held lands near Rouen from the County of Breteuil (Duchesne, Feod. Norm.). Ralph le Roux was sent 1119 by Henry I. to the aid of Ralph de Guader (Ord. Vit. 857), and 1120 was one of the nobles who perished with Prince Henry in the Blanche Nef. His nephew Simon le Roux was living 1137 (Ord. Vit. 197). The English line descends from Turchil Rufus or Le Rous, who came to England 1066 and held lands in Norfolk from Alan Fitz-Flaald, ancestor of the Fitz-Alans (Mon. Angl. i. 627). Fulcher Rufus of Norfolk lived 1130 (Rot. Pip.); Henry Rufus of Norfolk 1156 (Rot. Pip.); Alexander R. 1165 (Lib. Nig.); also Richard R., who held from De Albini in the Eastern Counties, and half a knight's fee at Booville, Normandy, from the County of Breteuil (Duchesne). Hugo Rufus was Viscount of Norfolk 1225, and in 1232 was deceased (Roberts, Excerpta, i. 227). Roger le Rus of Flixton, Suffolk, was dead before 1271; Richard of Norfolk d. 1277, and had Alan, who in 1316 was Lord of Dunham and E. Lexham, Norfolk, and had Peter le Rous of Dennington, ancestor of the R.s of that place, from whom descended the Rouses of Henham, Earls of Stradbroke.

Rouse. *See* ROUS.

Rout, for ROUTH.

Routh, or De Scruteville. Richard de Scruteville, from Escretville, Normandy, was Lord of Routh, Yorkshire, 1136 at the foundation of Meaux Abbey (Mon. i. 794). Hence was derived the family of De Routh or De Ruda, of which was Martin Routh, D.D., late President of Magdalen Coll. Oxford, the most learned divine of his age, who died in his 100th year in the full possession of all his faculties. *See* SCURFIELD.

Roux. *See* ROUS.

Row, for Roe, or ROWE.

Rowatt, or Roalt. *See* ROLT.

Rowan, in some cases for ROAN.

Rowbury. *See* RUBERY.

Rowden, for RAWDON.

Rowe, Roe, or Roo, for Le Roux. *See* ROUS.

Rowes. *See* ROWE.

Rowles, for ROLLES.

Rowley, from Roelly, Reuilly, or Roilly, near Evreux, Normandy. Ralph de Roileio came over with the Conqueror, and held Stockland, Devon 1083 (Exon. Domesd.) from Ralph Paganel. In 1165 Ralph de Ruelli held a fee in the Viscounty of Evreux, Robert de Roilli in Essex, and Roger de R. in Gloucester (Lib. Nig.). Galfridus de Roeli witnessed a charter of Gervase Paganel to Tikford Abbey 1187 (Mon. ii. 911). Ralph de Rolli gave tithes in Yorkshire to Holy Trinity, founded by Ralph Paganel of Drax (Mon. i. 564). In 1301 William Roilly was bailsman for an M.P. Wilts (PPW). The name became spread widely in England, and hence derived the Baronets Rowley and the Viscounts Langford.

Rowling. *See* RAWLINS.

Rowse. *See* ROUS.

Rowsell, or Rowsewell, for RUSSELL, armorially identified.

Roxby, for ROOKSBY.

Roy. *See* KING.

Royall. *See* ROYLE.

Royle. John Roiale, Normandy 1180-95 (MRS); Hugh Royl, Engl. c. 1272 (RH).

Rozier. *See* ROSIER.

Rubery. Radulphus Rebree, Normandy 1180-95; Gislebert, Peter de Riperia 1198 (MRS). The name occurs in England as Roubery amongst the Parliamentary writs.

Ruck, for Roke, or ROAKE.

Rucker, for ROOKER.

Rudall. *See* RUDDELL.

Ruddell. Petrus Rudellus, Normandy 1180-95 (MRS); John de Rodhall, Engl. c. 1272 (RH).

Ruddle, for RUDDELL.

Rudge. *See* RUGG.

Ruel. Martin, Guillan, Goislin de Ruella, Normandy 1180 - 95 (MRS); Peter and William de R. 1198 (Ib.). The arms of the family of Rule are preserved by Robson.

Ruf. *See* ROOF.

Ruff. *See* ROOF.

Ruffell, perhaps for Raville or REVEL.

Ruffie. *See* RUFFELL.

Ruffles, for RUFFLE.

Rufus. *See* ROUS.

Rugg. Radulphus Rogue, Normandy 1180-95 (MRS); William de Roges t. Philip Augustus; Henry, Hugh Robert Ruge, Engl. c. 1272 (RH).

Ruggles, from the ville and castle of Rugles, Normandy. *See* Lower (Patronym. Britann.).

Rule. *See* RUELL.

Rumball. *See* RUMBOLD.

Rumble. *See* RUMBALL.

Rumbel, for RUMBOLD.

Rumbold. A Norman family, styled Rimbaud or Rimboult, in the Duchy (*See* RIMBOULT), where it continued in the twelfth century. The Norman ancestor of the English and Norman lines was Rumbaldus, who held lands in Gloucester 1086 (Domesday, 107 bis). Richard I. confirmed to Wickham Abbey, Essex, lands granted by Robert Rumbold

(Mon. i. 889). The latter was party to a suit, Essex, 1194 (RCR), and in 1200 exchanged lands in Hertford (Ib.). Walter Rembald is mentioned c. 1272 (RH). From this family descend the Baronets Rumbold.

Rumboll. See RUMBOLD.

Rumens, for ROMANS.

Rumley, from Romilly, near Evreux. Robert de Romeliolo and Roger, Earl of Salop, granted lands to Horsley Abbey, Essex, t. William I. (Mon. i. 604). Aaliza de Romilly was foundress of Bolton t. Henry I. In 1165 Agnes de Romilli held lands in Normandy, and Philip de Rumelli a knight's fee in Somerset (Lib. Niger). In 1199 Alexander de R. was of Oxfordshire, as was Alan 13th cent. Baldwin de R. held from De Tony in Worcester (Testa, 41, 28, 100). Richard de Romilly, 1180–95 (MRS) was of Normandy.

Rummans. See ROMANS.

Rummer. See ROMER.

Rummens. See ROMANS.

Rundall, for ROUNDELL.

Rundell, for ROUNDELL.

Rundle, for RUNDELL.

Rupp. See ROOP.

Ruse, for ROUS.

Rush, for RUSE.

Rusher. Richardus Risher, Normandy 1195 (MRS). See also ROSIER.

Rushmere. Richard de Ruskemara, Normandy 1180–95 (MRS). The arms of Rosmer are preserved by Robson.

Rushout, or Rouault, a baronial family. This family is Breton, deriving from Roald or Rouault, a Breton noble living c. 1000, whose son Hasculph, Viscount of Nantes, c. 1050, had four sons, who accompanied the Conqueror, viz. 1. Ruald;

2. Hasculph; 3. Hugh; 4. Enisand. See CONYNGHAM.

Ruald, surnamed Adobé (i.e. dubbed knight), held three lordships in capite 1086 in Devon (Domesday, 114 b). His son Ruald was father of Alan Fitz-Ruald, who m. Lady Alis de Dodbroke, and acquired estates by her (Pole, Devon). Roald Fitz-Alan, his son, had John Fitz-Rohaut, father of Alan, whose grandson Sir Roger Fitz-Rohault had a dau. and heir (Pole).

Theobald Rouault, a younger son, became seated in France temp. Edward II., as Sire de Boismenard. From him descended Joachim Rouhault, Marshal of France, who d. 1478, and whose posterity settled in England t. Charles I., from whom descend the Barons Northwick.

Russ, for ROUS.

Russel. See RUSSELL.

Russell, or De Rosel, a baronial family. This name is derived from the Lordship of Rosel in the Cotentin, Normandy, of which the Russells were the ancient lords. They were a branch of the great baronial house of Bertram, Barons of Briquebec (see Wiffen, Mem. House of Russell), whose descent is stated under the name MITFORD.

William I., fourth Baron of Briquebec, living 1012, had—1. Robert, ancestor of the houses of Briquebec, Mitford, Bothal, and St. Pierre; 2. Hugh.

The latter received the castle and fief of Rosel, and in 1077, being then old, granted, as 'Hugh de Rosel,' with consent of his son Hugh the younger, lands in Normandy, given to him by the Conqueror, to St. Stephen's, Caen (Mon. Angl. ii. 937). Hugh II. of Rosel came to England with the Conqueror, and is mentioned in a charter of the time of Stephen as father of Robert Russel (Wiffen, i. 531). In Domesday he appears as holding lands in Dorset in capite by the serjeantry of being Marshal of the Butlery of England (Domesday, 84 b), a feudal dignity, which conferred rank, and was hereditary. Robert Russel I., his son, granted t. Stephen lands at Cannington, Somerset, with consent of William de Moune, Earl of Somerset, to the abbey there (Wiffen); and had issue Robert de Rosel II. This baron held the fief of Kingston, Dorset, in capite, and in 1165 one fee in that county from Alured de Lincoln, another from the Abbot of Cerne (Lib. Niger). The latter had apparently been acquired by authority of the Crown t. Stephen.

Odo, Eudo, or Hugh Russel, who succeeded, is mentioned in a charter of King John, granting an advowson of a church in Gloucester to his son John Russel, who in 1202 m. the sister and coheir of Dodo Bardolf, one of the greater barons, and was constable of Corfe, Dorset. From this house descend the Russels, Dukes of Bedford, Earls Russel, Lords De Clifford, &c. The name often occurs in Normandy, where Joscelin, William, Hugo, Bertin, Ansketil, Richard, Jordan, Osbert, Gauder de Rosel or Rossel occur 1180–95, also the fief of Rosel (MRS).

Russen. Michael de Rucino, Normandy, held a fief from Philip Augustus (Mem. Soc. Ant. Norm. v. 173). Bernard Roncin 1198 (MRS). Richard Resen, Engl. c. 1272 (RH).

Russom, for Russon.

Russon. See Russen.

386

Rust. See Raste.

Rutt, for Root.

Ruth, for Routh.

Rutter, for Rotar. Fulco des Rotors, Normandy 1180–95; Fulco de Rotor, 1198 (MRS); Richard and Thomas Rotor or Rotour, Engl. c. 1272 (RH).

Rutty. Hugh de Rotis, Normandy 1198 (MRS); Ralph de R. 1180 (Ib.); Alicia Rute, Engl. c. 1272 (RH).

Ryall. See Royle.

Ryalls. See Ryall.

Ryder, or Foliot, a baronial family. The English Ryders descend from the Foliots, Sires of Omonville, or Osmondville, Normandy, whose probable ancestor was Osmond, a companion of Rollo. In 1050 Roger Foliot granted the advowson of Omonville to Essay Abbey (Gall. Christ. xi. 237; De Gerville, Anc. Chateaux). Several of this family came to England at the Conquest, of whom William F. held lands 1086 from the See of Canterbury, and Otbert F. large estates in Northants, Herts, and elsewhere from Fitz-Ansculph. His son Adelulf had issue Roger Foliot, who in 1165 returned his barony in Northants as fifteen fees and a half (Lib. Niger).

From William (t. William I.) came his son Henry, who t. Henry I. m. Lucia, dau. and coheir of Jordan Briset, a great baron (founder of St. John's Priory, Clerkenwell). He had—1. William F., whose line was seated in Worcester (Mon. Angl. ii. 505); and 2. Jordan Foliot, who obtained estates in Yorkshire, and was the first to bear the name of 'De Rither.' He in 1165 held five fees of ancient enfeoffment from the barony of Pontefract (Lib. Niger).

Thomas de Ryther, his son, confirmed his father's gift to Fountains Abbey (Burton, Mon. Ebor., 154). William de R., a benefactor to Nun-Appleton, occurs as William 'Foliot' granting lands to Nostel Priory (Ib. 304, 306). From him descended the Rythers or Ryders, Lords of Harewood, Yorkshire, and the Earls of Harrowby.

Rye, a baronial family, from Rie, near Bayeux. Geoffry de Rie was living c. 980. His son Odo Fitz-Geoffry gave half the church of Rie to Fescamp Abbey, which was confirmed 1027 by Richard II. of Normandy (Neustria Pia, 218). In 1047 Hubert de Rie, after the battle of Val des Dunes, saved the life of Duke William, and sent his three sons to guard him to Falaise (Roman de Rou, Ed. Pluquet, ii. 23). Hubert was sent ambassador to Edward the Confessor, and after the Conquest, with his sons, was sent into Normandy to maintain the Duchy in quiet. Ralph de Rie, his elder son, was Castellan of Nottingham, Robert the second Castellan of Norwich, whose son Hubert de Rie held in Norfolk a barony of 40 knights' fees 1165 (Lib. Niger). The family long continued to be of great rank and power in various parts of England.

In Normandy we have Robert, Richard de Ria, Rie, or Rii, and the Ville of Rie 1180–95 (MRS).

Ryle. *See* ROYLE.

Rymer, for RIMER.

S

Sabey. Robertus Saba, Normandy 1180 (MRS); Robert, William Sabe, Engl. c. 1272 (RH).

Sach. *See* SACK.

Sacheverell, from Saultchevreuil in the Cotentin, Normandy. The family held a fief in Derby from the barony of Chaources. In 13th cent. Patricius de Saucheverel held one knight's fee at Sallow and Hopewell, Notts and Derby (Testa de Neville, 13). The descent is regularly traced from him. George S., of Sallow or Callow, c. 1710, left great estates to the celebrated Henry Sacheverell, D.D., his near relation.

Sack. Samuel, Peter, William, Richard, Thomas de Sac, Normandy, 1180–95 (MRS); Thomas Seck, Engl. c. 1272 (RH).

Sacker. *See* SECKER.

Sackett. Nicholas Saget, Normandy, 1180 (MRS).

Sackville. Joannes and Gilo de Sakenvilla, Normandy, 1180–95 (MRS). The history of the English family, Lords Buckhurst, Dukes of Dorset, is well known.

Saddler, the English form of LORIMER.

Sadleir, for SADLER.

Sadler. *See* SADDLER.

Safe. Ricardus Soef, Normandy, 1198 (MRS).

Saffell. Roger and Girart de Sevele, or Savale, Normandy, 1180–95 (MRS); Roger Sevale, Engl. c. 1272 (RH).

Saffery, for SAVORY.

Saffran. William Sabrin, Normandy, 1180–95 (MRS); Simon de Sabrin, Engl. c. 1272 (RH).

Saffrey, for SAVORY.

Sage. Richard Sapiens, Normandy, 1180 (MRS); John, Ranulph, Richard, William Sapiens or le Sage, 1198 (Ib.); John le Sage, Normandy, 1180–95 (MRS); Hugh, John, Ralph le Sage, Engl. c. 1272 (RH).

Sager. See SEAGUR.

Saggers. See SEAGER.

Saillard, or Sailer. Robert Selier, Normandy 1198 (MRS); Hugh and William le Saillur, England, c. 1272 (RH).

Saint. William Sent, Normandy, 1180–95 (MRS); Bernard Sain, Normandy 1180 (MRS); Thomas Seynt, England, c. 1272 (RH).

St. Amand. Richard de S. Amanda, Normandy, 1180–95 (MRS). St. A. was in the Cotentin. Hence the Lords St. Amand of England. See Dugdale, Banks. See AMAND.

St. Aubyn. Benedict, Galfridus, Herbert, Ranulph, Roger, Thomas de S. Albino, Normandy 1108 (MRS). St. A. was near Evreux. Astho de S. A., soon after 980, granted his tithes to St. Taurin, Evreux (Gall. Christ. xi. 139, Instr.). Fulco de S. A. was a benefactor to St. Evroult, t. William I. (Ord. Vitalis, 596). Malger de S. A. witnessed the foundation charter of Barnstaple Abbey, Devon, t. William I. Hence the baronets St. Aubyn.

St. Barbe, from St. Barbara, in Normandy. Jordan de St. Barbe, 1322–5, was an adherent of the Earl of Lancaster, and had a writ of military summons (PPW).

St. Clair, from St. Clair, near St. Lo, in the Cotentin, Normandy. Wace mentions the Sire de St. Clair at Hastings (ii. 239). This was

388

Richard de S. C. who held lands, Suffolk, 1086 (Domesd.). Britel de S. C., his brother, held in Somerset (Ibid.). He witnessed a charter of the Earl of Mortaine (Mon. ii. 910). Richard was succeeded by Hamo de S. C., living 1130 (Rot. Pip.) William de S. C., probably a son of Britel, held in Dorset, 1130 (Rot. Pip.), and had from David I. a grant of Rosslyn, Scotland; whence descended the great house of St. Clair, Earls of Orkney and Caithness, &c.

St. Denis. Geoffry de St. Dionysio, Normandy, 1180 (MRS).

St. George, from St. George, near St. Lo, Cotentin. The family came to England 1066. Temp. Henry I. Helyas de St. George occurs in Sussex (Mon. i. 593), and Baldwin de St. G. as witness to a charter of William Peverel of Dover (Mon. i. 382). The family was of importance in Cambridge 1300. Hence the Baronets St. George, and the Lords St. George.

St. John, a baronial name. William de S. Joanne, Normandy 1180; Geoffry, John, Robert, William de S. Joanne, 1198 (MRS). St. John was near Avranches (De Gerville, Anc. Chateaux). Roger and John de S. J. were in the service of Henry I., Normandy 1119 (Ord. Vit. 844). The former was of Hants, 1130, and was son of Roger de St. John (Rot. Pip.); and John was of Oxford, ancestor of the Barons de St. John. The history of this family appears in Dugdale, Banks, &c. The name was taken by the Barons de Port.

St. Laurence. Symon de St. Laurent held a fief from Philip Augustus in Normandy (Mem. Soc. Ant. Norm. v. 172). St. Laurent was in the Caux, near Yvetot, Normandy; and its owners are mentioned as 'an illustrious race of barons' by Ordericus Vitalis (853). Roger de S. L. came to England 1066, and witnessed a charter of William Giffard, Bishop of Winchester (Mon. i. 1026). His descendant, Adam, held from Walter Gi`ard, Earl of Bucks, 1165 (Lib. Niger). The family became widely spread in England. In 1165 Nicholas de St. L. held a knight's fee, Salop, from De Ver. The name does not afterwards appear in Salop, for Nicholas joined in the invasion of Ireland, and became baron of Howth. He d. c. 1190, and was succeeded by Almaric de S. L., to whom John, Earl of Mortaine, confirmed Howth, as held by his father (Lodge, Peer. Ireland, iii. 183), who had aided in the conquest of Ulster by John de Courcy. He had three sons—Adam, Robert, and Nicholas—who inherited successively. The latter had Robert, who lived t. Edward I. From this baron descend the Earls of Howth. There is much error in Lodge's account.

St. Lodger. *See* ST. LEGER.

St. Leger. Robert de S. Leodgario, or St. Leger, William, John, Gilbert, Normandy 1180–95 (MRS); Gislebert, Robert, Simon, William, 1198 (Ib.). St. Leger was near Avranches, Normandy. Robert St. L. was of Sussex, 1086, and appears to have been father of William de S. L., who, with his son Clarembald, granted lands to Battle Abbey, t. Henry I. (Mon. i. 318). Hence the St. Legers of Kent and Devon, and the Viscounts Doneraile.

St. Martin. Alvered de S. Martin, Normandy, 1180 (MRS); Bur-

nulf, Warin, Geoffry, Henry, Hugh, Nicholas, Ralph, Roger, William de S. M., 1198 (Ib.).

St. Ouen. Robert de S. Andoeno, Normandy 1180–95; Nicholas, William, 1198 (MRS). *See* CLAPHAM.

St. Paul, or St. Pol. *See* PAUL.

St. Quintin, a baronial name. Osbert de S. Quintino, Normandy 1198 (MRS). St. Q. was near Coutances, in the Cotentin, Normandy. Wido de St. Quentin, t. William I., granted lands to Cerisy on assuming the monastic habit (Mon. i. 960). Alured de St. Q., his son, t. Will. I., gave lands to the same abbey (Ib.). The latter was brother of Hugo, one of the Conqueror's companions, 1086, who held lands in Essex and Dorset in capite 1086; also in Hants. He had, 1. Robert, who joined in the conquest of Glamorgan 1090, and whose descendants sat in Parliament as barons; 2. William, mentioned in Normandy 1120 (MSAN, viii. 426); 3. Herbert. The latter held houses at Winchester 1110 (Winch. Domesd.), which he granted to Godstowe (Mon. i. 528). He held estates Lincoln and York 1149 (Mon. ii. 198). He had issue Walter and Alan (Mon. i. 474). Hence the St. Quentins, Baronets. It is probable that the family of Herbert was of this house. Herbert, the father of Herbert Fitz-Herbert, Chamberlain to Henry I., was perhaps a brother of Alured de St. Quentin; for the ancient arms of the Herberts and St. Quentins were nearly the same, viz., one or more chevrons and a chief vair.

Sait. Richard Saete, Normandy 1180–95 (MRS); Richard Saiete, 1198 (Ib.); Robert Seyot, Engl. c. 1272 (RH).

Saker. *See* SACKER.

Salaman, for SALMON.

Sale. Hubert and Odo de Sella, Normandy 1180–95 (MRS); John and Ralph de Salle, Engl. c. 1272 (RH). Hence the brave General Sale.

Salenger, or Sellenger, for ST. LEDGER.

Sales, for SALE.

Salinger, or Sellinger, for ST. LEDGER.

Sallmann, for SALMON.

Salman, for SALMON.

Salmon. William Salmon, Normandy 1180–95 (MRS); Ralph, Raginald, Richard Salomon, 1198 (Ib.); Richard Saloman, Engl. c. 1272 (RH).

Salomon. See SALMON. Some families are Hebrew.

Salter. William Salatre, Normandy, 1198 (MRS); Beatrice and William le Salter, Engl. c. 1272 (RH).

Salvage. Umfrid Salvage, Normandy 1180; Walter, 1195 (MRS); Ralph, Ranulph Salvage or Sauvage, 1198 (Ib.); Walter Salvage, Eng. c. 1272 (RH).

Salvin. Wido, Richard, William Silvain or Silvanus, Normandy 1180–95 (MRS); Hugh Silvanus, Engl. 1202 (Rot. Canc.).

Samler. Geoffry Somelier, Normandy 1198 (MRS).

Sammann. See SALMON.

Sammon. See SALMON.

Samons. See SALMON.

Samper, for ST. PER or ST. PIERRE.

Sampson, or De St. Sampson, from that lordship near Caen, Normandy. Ralph de St. Sansom accompanied the Conqueror, and 1086 held estates in several counties (Domesd. 16, 87 b, 247 b, bis). Wil-

liam Sampson, his descendant, was summoned to Parliament as a baron 1297–1304. The Sampsons of Playford, Suffolk, an ancient branch of this family (who bore the arms), were ancestors of Thomas S., Dean of Christ Church, so celebrated in the Puritan controversy, t. Elizabeth. Robert de S. Sansom, Normandy 1198 (MRS); Nicholas, William, Christian, Henry, Walter Sanso, or Sanson, 1180–95 (Ib.)

Samson. See SAMPSON.

Sancroft. William, or De Bosco, Archbishop of Canterbury, one of the seven bishops so renowned t. James II., was descended from the Norman family of De Bosco or Bois. William de Bois-Guillaume, of the bailifry of Caux, in 1086 possessed estates in Essex (Domesd. Ess. 81). Baldric de Bosco was of Suffolk 1130; William de B. of Essex 1165. The family of De Bois or Bosco held lands in South Elmham from the Conquest, as appeared by a suit at Ipswich 1285 (Davy, Coll. Suffolk, vol. xxxv.). Sandcroft or Sancroft was in South Elmham; and the family so named bore three crosses with a chevron (as the distinction of a younger branch), while the De Boscos of Elmham bore a cross. In 1198 Robert de Bosco had a suit against Robert de Sandcroft for lands in Elingham and Hennersfield, Suffolk (RCR). Robert de S. presented to the Church of Sancroft 1319 (Suckling, Suff. i. 208). The family soon after migrated to Fressingfield, a few miles south, where they continued seated 1463, 1534, 1555, and 1616, when William S. (the archbishop) was baptized there.

Sandfield. See SANDWELL.

Sandford. Ralph and Richard de

Sanfort, Normandy 1198 (MRS).
Richard is mentioned in Cambridge,
Hunts, and Lincoln, 1202 (Rot.
Canc.).

Sandifer, for SANDFORD.
Sandiford. *See* SANDFORD.
Sanford, for SANDFORD.
Sandwell. Geoffry de Sando-
ville, Normandy 1180 (MRS);
Robert de Sanderville, Engl. c. 1198
(RCR); Gilbert de Sannerville,
1189 (Rot. Pip.).

Sanger. *See* SINGER.
Sangster. *See* SINGER.
Sansom, for SAMPSON.
Sansum. *See* SANSOM.
Saint, for SAINT.
Santer. Osbert Saintier, Nor-
mandy, 1180 (MRS); Oliver le
Seyntour, Engl. c. 1272 (RH).

Santhan, for St. Anne, Normandy.
Geoffry de St. Agna, Normandy
1198 (MRS).

Sanville, or Sandeville, from San-
darville, near Chartres, France. In
1165 William de Sandville held four
fees of the honour of Skipton, York,
and Gervasius de S. one fee (Lib.
Niger). Manasses de Sanderville held
13th cent. lands in Hants (Testa).
William de S., t. Henry II., witnessed a charter of Boxgrove Priory,
Sussex (Mon. i. 593); and Thomas
de S. in 1301 was summoned from
Oxford and Berks for service against
the Scots (PPW).

Saphin, for Savin, or SALVIN.
Sard. *See* SART.
Sarel, for SORREL.
Sargant, for SERJEANT.
Sargeant, for SERJEANT.
Sargood. Odo de Sire-bone, Nor-
mandy, 1180-95 (MRS).
Sarjant. *See* SERJEANT.
Sarjeaunt, for SERJEANT.
Sarjent, for SERJEANT.

Sarl, for SARLE.
Sarle. *See* SORRELL.
Sarll, for SORRELL.
Sarson. William Sarazin, Nor-
mandy, 1180-95 (MRS); Robert,
Thomas, William Sarcenas, 1198
(Ib.); Petrus Saracenus, Engl. 1202
(Rot. de Libertate).

Sart, for Essart. Ralph de Essar-
tis, Normandy 1180-95; Mauger
and Ralph, 1198 (MRS); Richard
de Essart, Engl. c. 1198 (RCR).

Sarvent, for Serviens. *See* SER-
JEANT.

Sass. Rener, John, Roger, William de Sace or Saceio, Normandy
1198 (MRS); Simon, Evain, &c. de
Saceio, 1180-95 (Ib.); Robert de
Sauce, Engl. c. 1272 (RH).

Sasse. *See* SASS.
Satchell. *See* SATCHWELL.
Satchwell, or Sachville. Robert
de Sacheville, Normandy 1180
(MRS); Denis de Siccavilla, 1198
(Ib.). This family was seated in
Devon.

Saul. *See* SALE.
Saull, for SAUL.
Saulter. *See* SALTER.
Sausse. Walter, John, Ascelin,
William de Sauceio, Normandy 1180-
95 (MRS); Robert de la Sausei,
Robert de Salceton, Engl. c. 1198
(RCR).

Savage. Unfrid le Salvage, Normandy 1180-95 (MRS).

Savage. *See* SALVAGE.
Savell, for SAVILLE.
Savery, for SAVORY.
Savidge, for SAVAGE.
Savigny. Thomas de Savigny,
Normandy 1180 (MRS); Eureia
and Nicholas de Savigneio, and
Guido de Savinisco, 1198 (Ib.);
Ralph William Saveney, Engl. c.
1272 (RH).

Savile, for SAVILLE.

Savill, for SAVILLE.

Saville, or De Arches. *See* ARCH. This family is descended from the Viscounts of Arques and Rouen, a branch of the Giffards. Geoffry, Viscount of Arques or Arches, had, 1. William, Baron of Folkestone; 2. Osbern, a great baron in York 1086: he had issue, 1. William; 2. Thurstan. The former founded Nun-Monkton, York, t. Stephen; the latter was Pincerna of the Barony of Sandal, and obtained from his brother Kettlewell and other lands in York. His son Peter D'Arches, Pincerna, granted part of Kettlewell to Fountains Abbey (Burton, Mon. Ebor. 174). His son Hugo Pincerna was living 1216 (Hardy, Rot. Claus. 245), and had issue, 1. Richard de Sayville, who describes himself in a grant to Pontefract as son of Hugo Pincerna (Whittaker), and was summoned to the coronation of Rich. I. (Bromton, 1158); 2. Henry de Sayville, Lord of Golcar. From Richard derived Peter de S., 1285 (Inq. p. m.); Sir John, 1300 (PPW); Sir John, Viscount of York, 1379; and the Savilles of Copley, Methley, &c., Marquises of Halifax, Earls of Mexborough, &c.

Savory. Peter Savore, Normandy 1180 (MRS), also 1198 (Ib.); Richard Savaria, Engl. 1202 (Rot. Canc.); Laurence de Savore, Richard Saveri, Engl. c. 1272 (RH).

Saward, for SAWER.

Sawer. *See* SAWERS.

Sawers. Radulphus de Sahurs, and the Ville of Sahurs, Normandy 1198 (MRS); Nicholas Sawere, Engl. c. 1272 (RH).

Sawle. *See* SAUL.

Sawyer, for SAWER.

Saxby. *See* SHAKSPEARE.

Say, a baronial name. Geoffry de Saie, and the fief of Saie, Normandy, 1180–95 (MRS); Geoffry de Say, 1198 (Ib.). This was a branch of the house of Avenel. *See* PIGOT, AVENEL. The Barons de Say descended probably from Jordan de Say, t. William I., brother of Picot de S. or Avenel (MSAN, xv. 174). He founded Aunay Abbey; from whom descended Henry de S. of Warwick, 1130, William de S. of Norfolk, Hunts, and Middlesex, t. Henry II., and the Barons Say.

Sayer. *See* SAYERS.

Sayers. Ralph de Sahurs, and the Ville of S., Normandy 1198 (MRS); Richard Sare, Engl. c. 1272 (RH).

Sayle. *See* SALE.

Sayles, for SALE.

Saytch, possibly a form of SECH or SUCH.

Saywell, for Sayvell or SAVILLE.

Scales, a baronial name, derived from Harduin de Scalers or Scales, a great baron 1086, whose barony lay in Cambridge and Herts. Hence the Barons Scales, summoned by writ 1298. *See* SMITHSON-PERCY.

Scamel. *See* SCAMMELL.

Scammell, perhaps from Escameul-ville, Normandy (MRS).

Scannell. *See* SCARNELL.

Scardefield, for Scardeville, from Escardanville, Normandy (Lower). This family was seated in Sussex. Eskerdeville is mentioned (MRS).

Scarf, for Scarp, or SHARP.

Scarfe. *See* SCARF.

Scarff. *See* SCARF.

Scarffe. *See* SCARF.

Scarle, for SARLE.

Scarles. *See* SCARLE.

Scarlett, from Carlat or Escarlat, Aquitaine. Bernard was Viscount of

Carlat 932 (Anselme, ii. 695, &c.). From him descended Richard, Gilbert, and Raymond, joint Viscounts of C., who appear to have accompanied the Conqueror, 1066. From the first descended Hugh the Viscount, d. before 1150, who had Hugh de C., Count of Rhodez 1190. In 1195 the Hospitallers held lands in York, the gift of Hugh Scarlet or Carlat; and at the same time occur William S. in Somerset and Kent, Gilbert S. in Middlesex, Mon. ii. 540 (RCR). The family thenceforth appears in various parts of England. It bears the lion rampant of the Viscounts of Carlat. Hence the eminent Lord Chief Justice Scarlett, Lord Abinger.

Scarnell, perhaps from Scarville or Escarville, from E. Normandy. Alan de S. 13th cent., Warwick and Leicester (Testa).

Scarvell. *See* SCARDEFIELD.

Schofield. Richard and Nicholas Escoville, and the fief of E. Normandy, 1180-95 (MRS); Fulco and William de Escovilla, 1198 (Ib.); Humphry de Scoville, Engl. c. 1272 (RH).

Scholefield. *See* SCOFIELD.

Scholfield, for SCHOLEFIELD.

Scholey. Richard de Scoleio, Normandy 1198 (MRS).

Schooley, for SCHOLEY.

Scofield. *See* SCHOFIELD.

Scofield, for SCOFIELD.

Score, for SCURR. Simon, Ralph, Henry Scures or Escures, Normandy 1180-95 (MRS). *See* SHORE.

Scot. Hugh and Alan le Scot, Normandy 1180-95 (MRS).

Scovell. *See* SCHOFIELD.

Scrivener. Rainbald Scriba or Scriptor, Normandy 1180-95 (MRS).

Scudamore. Walter de Escude-more, Normandy 1195 (MRS). In 1165 Geoffry de Scudimore was a baron in Wilts (Lib. Niger), and had subenfeoffed Waleran de Scudimore and Walter Gifford. He also held four fees of ancient enfeoffment from Robert D'Evias of Hereford (Ib.). Hence the Viscounts Scudamore.

Scurfield, armorially identified with De Scruteville, from Escretville, Normandy. Richard de Scruteville of Yorkshire, t. William I. (Mon. i. 794). William Le Gros, Earl of Albemarle 1131, exchanged lands with Alan de Scruteville, Yorkshire (Mon. i. 795). *See* ROUTH.

Scurr, for ESCURES. *See* SCORE.

Seaborn. William Sabrin, Normandy 1180 (MRS); Simon de Sabrin, Engl. c. 1272 (RH).

Seaborne. *See* SEABORN.

Seabourne. *See* SEABORN.

Seagars. *See* SEAGER.

Seager, from Segre in Anjou.

Seaker. *See* SECKER.

Seal, for SALE.

Seale. *See* SALE.

Sealey. Robert de Silly or Silleio, Normandy 1198 (MRS). He held lands in Normandy from Philip Augustus. William de S. was living at the same time.

Seales, for SEALE.

Sealy. *See* SEALEY.

Seamarle, for Seamar, or SEA-MER.

Seamer, for SEYMOUR.

Sear. *See* SAYER.

Search. Thomas de Cherches, Normandy 1180-95 (MRS). *See* CHURCH.

Searcy, from Cerisy, Normandy. The arms of Cercy are preserved by Robson.

Seare, for SAYER.

Seares, for SAYERS.

Seargeant, for SERJEANT.
Searl. *See* SARLE.
Searle. *See* SARLE.
Searles. *See* SEARLE.
Searls. *See* SEARLE.
Sears, for SAYERS.
Searson, for SARSON.

Seaward, for Suhart. Philip, Roger, Ralph, William Suhart, and the fief of S. Normandy 1180–95 (MRS); Philip, Ralph, William Suart, 1198 (Ib.) Hence the eminent American Statesman.

Secker, armorially identified with Sacre, probably a foreign name, and perhaps meant for Segre. *See* SEAGER.

See, for SAY.
Seear, for SAYER.
Seeger. *See* SEAGER.
Seeley, for SEALEY.
Seelie, for SEALEY.
Seely. *See* SEALEY.
Seeney, perhaps for CHEYNEY.
Seers, for SAYERS.
Segar. *See* SEAGAR.
Self. *See* SELFE.

Selfe. Roger Saife, Normandy 1180 (MRS); Walter Selve, Engl. c. 1272 (RH).

Sell. *See* SALE.
Selle. *See* SALE.
Sellar. William Cellarius, Normandy 1180–95 (MR); Ralph, William de Celar, Engl. c. 1272 (RH).

Sellars. *See* SELLAR.
Seller. *See* SELLAR.
Sellers. *See* SELLARS.
Selley, for SEALEY.
Sellis, for SELLS.
Sells, for SELL.
Selmon, for SALMON.
Semon, for SALMON.

Sellon. Peter and Ralph de Sellant, Normandy 1180–95 (MRS).

Semer. Richard le Semer, Nor-

mandy 1180–95 (MRS); Robert, William, Simon Semer, Engl. c. 1272 (RH).

Semon, for SIMON.
Senger. *See* SINGER.

Senior. Ralph Seignor, Muriel his wife, Thomas and Roger S., Normandy 1180–95 (MRS); Hugh, Robert, Roger, Thomas, William Seignore, 1198 (Ib.); Henry Senior, Engl. c. 1272. (RH).

Sentance, perhaps for Septvans, from Sept Vents, Normandy, a family formerly of great importance in Kent.

Sennett. *See* SINNETT.
Sennitt. *See* SINNOTT.
Senyard, for SENIOR.

Seraphim, for Servain. Adam, Richard Servain, Normandy, t. Philip August. (Mem. Soc. Ant. Norm. v. 174, 201); John Serwynd, Engl. c. 1272 (RH).

Sergeant, for SERJEANT.
Sergent, for SERJEANT.

Serjeant. Malger and Gislebert Serviens, Normandy 1180–95; Gislebert, Horsel, Roger S., 1198 (MRS); Robert Serviens, William Sergent, Engl. c. 1198 (RCR); Henry, Herbert, Simon, Walter Serviens, 1202 (Rot. Canc.).

Serle. *See* SARLE.
Serrell. *See* SERLE.

Service. William, Richard, Walter Cervus, Normandy 1180–95 (MRS).

Severn. William Sabrin, Normandy 1180 (MRS); Geoffry, William Sebern, Engl. c. 1272 (RH).

Severne. *See* SEVERN.

Severs. Hubert Saveire, Normandy 1180–95 (MRS); John le Severe, Engl. c. 1272 (RH).

Seville, for SAVILLE.
Sevin. Gaufrid Savon, or Sa-

vonier, Normandy 1180–95 (MRS);
Nicholas and Roger le Sevon or
Sevoner, Engl. c. 1272 (RH).

Seward. *See* SEAWARD.

Sewell. Girart de Sevele, Normandy 1180 (MRS); Roger Sevale,
Engl. c. 1272 (RH).

Sewells. *See* SEWELL.

Seybold. William Sebolt or
Sebout, Normandy 1180 (MRS);
Robert Sebode, Engl. c. 1272.

Sexby. *See* SAXBY.

Seyer, for SAYER.

Seymer, for SEYMOUR.

Seymour, or St. Maur, a baronial name, from St. Maur, near
Avranches, Normandy. William de
S. Mauro, Normandy 1198 (MRS).
The early arms, two or more
chevrons, appear to imply that this
was a branch of the family of
Avranches, which also bore chevrons.
Wido de St. Maur came to England
1066, and was deceased before 1086,
when William Fitz-Wido, his son,
held a barony in Somerset, Wilts,
and Gloucester; and ten manors in
Somerset (of which Portishead was
one) from Geoffry, Bishop of Coutances. He made conquests in Wales
c. 1090, which his family afterwards
held. He had, 1. Peter de St. Maur,
who granted Portishead to the Hospitallers (Mon. ii. 530), and was ancestor of the Lords St. Maur, barons
by writ 1314, who bore arg. two
chevrons gules; 2. Richard Fitz-
William, who inherited the Welsh
barony, and t. Stephen granted four
churches in Wales to the abbey of
Kadwalli (Mon. i. 425). This mar-
cher barony was reconquered soon
after by the Welsh. His son Thomas
de St. Maur held three knights' fees
from Humphry de Bohun in Wilts
(Lib. Niger), and had issue Bar-

tholomew, who witnessed the charter
of Keynsham Abbey, c. 1170 (Mon.
ii. 298). His son, William de St. M.,
conquered Woundy and Penhow,
Monmouth, from the Welsh about
1235, and was ancestor of the Sey-
mours; from whom sprang Queen
Jane Seymour, the Protector Duke
of Somerset, and the Dukes of
Somerset, the Marquises of Hertford,
and other families.

Shaen, or Shane. Hugh de Sena,
Normandy 1180–95 (MRS). G. de
S. 13th cent. in Normandy (Mem.
Soc. Ant. Norm. v. 144); Simon
Scan, Engl. c. 1272 (RH).

Shafe, for Saife. *See* SELFE.

Shakspeare. The immediate ancestry of William Shakspeare, the
poet, has been carefully investigated
by Mr. Halliwell, in the Life of
Shakspeare prefixed to his works.
The family had been one of the
middle class. John S., the poet's
father, combined agricultural and
commercial employments at Stratford, where he settled c. 1550. Richard S., father of John, with
Henry, his brother, were occupants
of land at Snitterfield, two miles
north of Stratford. Prior to this,
the family had been resident eight
or ten miles further north, in the adjoining parishes of Rowington, Pack-
wood, and Wroxall. Amongst others
of the family, Isabella Shakspeare
occurs in 1501, as Prioress of Wroxall; Richard, of the same parish,
probably c. 1464; John, of Rowington, 1464; and Richard, of Wol-
diche, or Oldish, in Temple Balsall,
who had died before 1460 (Halliwell). From these facts we may
infer, that the family were seated in
that vicinity temp. Henry VI., and
probably for some time previously.

Of any earlier mention of the name of Shakespeare in Warwick or elsewhere in England, I have found no trace. There is a lacuna in the publications of the Record Commission after the time of Edward II., and I have failed to find early subsidy rolls referring to that vicinity in Warwick.

While, however, we lose sight of this family in England in the 15th century, a light is incidentally thrown on the subject by the records of Normandy three centuries before, where we should have little anticipated the existence of the name.

The name of 'Sacespee,' or 'Sakeespee,' which occurs several times in the Norman records 1180–1200, appears to have been a French form of the same name as 'Shakspeare.'

It appears from the Great Rolls of the Exchequer, Normandy, that

In 1195 Roger Sake espee paid a fine of 10s. in the bailifry of the Caux, near Lillebonne. In 1198 William Sake espee occurs in the same bailifry.

In 1195 William Sake espee owed two marks as security for Reginald le Blaier in the bailifry of Hiesmes.

In 1203 Roger Sac espee paid a fine in the bailifry of Coutances, and Godfrey Sac espee another fine at the same time and place (MRS).

The name of Sac espee or Sake spee, thus found in Normandy, is one which, although its termination is French, can scarcely be supposed to be of Norman origin. It is impossible to make sense out of this name, or to comprehend it as it stands. We may infer, therefore, that it is a corruption of another name, and an English name. That name appears

396

to have been 'Saxby,' derived from the manor of that name in Leicestershire, which, according to Nicholls, was written in ancient deeds 'Saxeby, Shakkesby, Sasby' (Hist. Leic. ii. 308). The name of 'Shakspeare' is an English corruption of the same name, and is nowhere to be found prior to the 15th century.

We have now to consider Saxeby in Leicester. In 1086 it was held in part by Hugh Musard, and another part appears to have passed soon after into possession of the Norman family of De Perers, who, in the person of Henry de Perers, were seated at Dalby and elsewhere in Leicester in 1086 (Domesd.) In 1174 Henry de Pirariis, or Perers, had a dispute regarding lands at Saxby with William de Pirariis (Nicholls, Leic. ii. 308); which implies that the family had been long seated there. This William de Perers of Saxby appears to be the same who is mentioned in Normandy as 'William Sakespee' in 1195, 1198; and in 1202 Nicholas de Saxeby paid money to the Crown in Warwick and Leicester in behalf of the same William de Saxeby, his brother (Rot. Canc.). In 1207 Gaufrid de Saxeby gave security for seven marks, which he owed to the King in Leicester (Hardy, Rot. de Fin. 303). This Gaufrid de Saxeby appears to be the same as 'Godfrey Sacespee' mentioned in Normandy 1203. The name also appears in Yorkshire 1280, when 'Henry Sakespeye,' who seems to have been a clergyman, quitclaimed land to Fountains Abbey (Burton, Mon. Ebor. 185). From what has been said, it appears that the family of Saxby, Shakkesby, Saxeby, Sakespee, Sakespeye, or Shakspeare, was a branch of that of De Perers; and this appears to be confirmed by the armorial. The arms of one branch of Perire or Perers were, argent, a bend sable (charged with three pears for difference); those of Shakspeare were, argent, a bend sable (charged with a spear for difference); and those of Saxby or Shakkesby, a bend engrailed sable (on a field barry for difference). The family of Perers came from Periers, near Evreux, Normandy, where it remained in the 15th century (La Roque, Mais. Harcourt, ii. 1360, 1361). Hugo de Periers possessed estates in Warwick 1156 (Rot. Pip.); Geoffry de P. held a fief in Stafford 1165; and Adam de P. in Cambridge (Lib. Niger). Hugh de Pererers 13th cent. held a fief at Sixtenby, Warwick, and Leicester from Roger Mowbray (Testa). Sir Richard de Perers was M.P. for Leicestershire 1311; for Herts 1316-24; and Viscount of Essex and Herts in 1325.

Shakespear, for SHAKSPEARE.

Shalders, perhaps for Shallers, Challers, or SCALES.

Shales, for SHALLIS.

Shalless, for SHALLIS.

Shallis, for CHALLIS.

Shannon, for CHANOIN. See CANNON.

Sharman. See SHERMAN.

Sharmon. William Sarmon, Normandy 1180-95 (MRS); Geoffry, John Sarpman, Eng. c. 1272 (RH).

Sharp. Roger Poinant, Normandy 1180 (MRS); Denis and Roger Poignant 1198 (Ib.); Richard Poinant, Hugo Scarp, Engl. c. 1272 (RH).

Sharpe, for SHARP.

Shayer, for SAYER.

Shayler, for Shaller, or Challers. See SCALES.

Sheaf, for Saife. See SELF.

Sheaff, for SHEAF.

Shean, for SHAEN.

Shear, for SHAYER.

Shearer. See SHERARD.

Shearman. See SHARMAN.

Shears, for SHAYERS.

Sheat. Richard Saete, Normandy 1180-95 (MRS); Robert Seyot, Engl. c. 1272 (RH).

Sheath. See SHEAT.

Sheen, for SHAEN.

Sheerman, for SHERMAN.

Sheers. See SHEARS.

Sheeres, for SHEERS.

Sheirs, for SHEARS.

Shellard, for Shaller. See SCALES.

Shelley. This family, according to tradition, came from Huntingdon originally (Collins). It appears that the old arms (argent a fesse engrailed between three escallops) were those of a branch of the family of Scales, which bore three escallops, and a fesse between three torteaux. John de Scales had writs of military summons for Scotland 1297, 1298 (PPW), and d. 1302, seized of the Manor of Chavele or Chevely, Cambridge (Inq. p. mort.). Hence the name of de Chavele, Schievely, and by abbreviation Shelley. John, his son, was father of John, who bore the Scales arms, three escallops. The latter was father of Sir William, the known ancestor of this family, who possessed 'Chelsey,' said to be in Sussex. There is, however, no Sussex place of this name, which is probably a form of Chelley, Cheveley, or Shelley. From this family descended the poet Shelley, the Baronets Shelley, and the Lords

De Lisle. Shelley, in York, furnishes a similar instance of change. In the records it appears as Skelfleg and Chelively (PPW).

Shelly, for SHELLEY.

Sherar, for SHERARD.

Sherard. Godefridus Sirart, Normandy 1180–95; Hugh Scherhare 1267, Rutland (Hunter, Rot. Select. 178), Adam Scirart, Dorset, 13th cent. (Testa). From the former descended the Lords Sherard, Earls of Harborough.

Sherer, for SHERARD.

Sheriff. See SHERRIFF.

Sherley, for SHIRLEY.

Sherman. Gaufridus Sire-horne, Normandy 1180–95 (MRS); John and William Sireman, Engl. c. 1272 (RH). Hence the distinguished American General. See SHARMAN.

Sherrard. See SHERARD.

Sherriff. Roger le Viscomte, Normandy 1180–95 (MRS); Denis, Robert, Ralph, Vicecomes 1198 (Ib.).

Sherry. Hugh de Siry, Normandy 1180 (MRS); Henry, Thomas Shiré, Engl. c. 1272 (RH).

Shervill, for SURVILLE.

Sherville, for SURVILLE.

Sherwell, for SHERVILL.

Sheward, for Suhart. See SEAWARD.

Shewill, for SEWELL.

Shide, for CHIDE.

Shield, for CHILD.

Shiells, for GILES.

Shier, for Sire. See KNIGHT.

Shiers, for SHIER.

Shiles, for GILES.

Shillito. The fief of Hugh de Siletot, Normandy, held from Philip Augustus (Mem. Soc. Ant. Norm. v. 191).

Shillitoe. See SHILLITO.

Shine. See SHINN.

398

Shinn. Robert and Geoffry de Siena, Normandy 1180 (MRS).

Shirley. This family descends from Sasualo, who held vast estates from Henry de Ferrars 1086. He has been supposed of Anglo-Saxon origin, but the name does not occur amongst the proprietors t. Edward Confessor (Domesd.); nor is it probable that such vast estates (nine knights' fees) would have been given to an Anglo-Saxon. The name is probably foreign. Sasualo or Saswalo was Castellan of Lisle, Flanders, c. 1000, and 1039 founded the Abbey of Palempin (Albert Miræus, Op. Diplom. i. 54). His son Robert, Castellan of Lisle, had 1. Roger, whose grandson went to the Crusade 1096, and from whose brother Hugh descended the powerful Castellans of Lisle. 2. Sasualo, or Sigewalo, who witnessed a charter of Baldwin, Bishop of Tournay 1087 (Ib. 60). He appears to be the ancestor of this family, who came to England 1066. From him descended the families of Edensor, Ireton, and Shirley, who bore respectively the arms of Ferrars and Ridel. Hence the Earls Ferrars.

Shirreff. See SHERRIFF.

Shirville. See SHERVILL.

Shone, for SONE.

Shonfield, for Johnville, or Jemville. See LEYCESTER.

Shoppee, for CHAPUIS (LOWER).

Shore, or D'Escures, a branch of the house of Falaise or De Molines (see MOLYNS). The estate of Escures belonged to Alan de Escures or Falaise t. Henry I. (MSAN, viii. 428, Rot. Pip. 31 Hen. I.). He was son of Alured de Falaise, of York t. William I. (Burton, Mon. Ebor. 340), and ancestor of William de

Scures, of York 1165 (Lib. Niger).
The name changed gradually to
Scurs, Schur, Schor, Scor, Skewers,
Scunes, Skiers, Skurer, Schures, &c.
A branch became seated in Derby,
of which was Robert Shore, one
of the gentlemen of that county
1433, ancestor of the eminent
Governor-General of India, Sir John
Shore, first Lord Teignmouth.

Shore. Gerold, Alan, German le
Sor, Norm. 1180–95 (MRS); Elena
le Sore, William le Sour, Engl. c.
1272 (RH).

Shores. *See* SHORE.

Sherman, for SHARMAN.

Short, for SART.

Shorter. William Sartor, Norm.
1180–95 (MRS).

Shortt. *See* SHORT.

Shout, for SHUTE, or CHUTE.

Shovel. *See* CHAUVEL. Hence
the brave Sir Cloudesley Shovell.

Shoveller, for Chevaler, or le
Chevalier. *See* KNIGHT.

Showard, for COWARD.

Showell, for SCOVELL.

Showler, for SHOVELLER.

Shrapnell, apparently of foreign
origin, but not identified.

Shreeve. *See* SHERIFF.

Shrivell, for Chervel, or CARVILL.

Shufil, for ESCOVILLE.

Shum, for SOME.

Shurley, for SHIRLEY.

Shurr. *See* SHORE.

Shynn, for SHINN.

Sibbald. *See* SEYBOLD.

Sich, for SUCH.

Sidnell, for SIDWELL.

Sidney. The celebrated Sir Henry,
and Sir Philip Sydney, and Algernon
Sydney were of the family of Sidney,
originally Sithney, of Sussex. This
family is stated to have come from
Aquitaine t. Henry II. The original

seat was probably what is now
called Sathonay, near Lyons. The
older form occurs in Normandy 1180
(MRS), when Robert de Setingneio
is mentioned.

Sidwell. Warin de Sidevilla,
Normandy 1180–95 and 1198 (MRS).
William de Siwell in Engl. 1210
(Hardy, Rot. de Libert.).

Sier. *See* SYER.

Siers. *See* SYERS.

Siggers, for SEAGER.

Sillar, for SELLAR.

Silley, or de SILLEIO. *See* SEA-
LEY.

Sillis. *See* SELLS.

Sillito. *See* SHILLITO.

Sills, for SELLS.

Silvester. Rainald, Robert, Ra-
nulph Silvester, Normandy 1180–95
(MRS); Warin, Humphry, Ralph,
William S. 1198 (Ib.); Roger and
William Fitz-Silvester, Engl. c.
1198 (RCR); John, Thomas S.,
Engl. c. 1272 (RH).

Sim. *See* SYME.

Simes. *See* SYME.

Simeon. Geoffry Simeon, Normandy 1180 (MRS). Henry Fitz-
Simeon, Engl. c. 1198 (RCR).
James and Richard Simeon, Engl.
c. 1272 (RH). Hence the baronets
of the name.

Simes. *See* SYMES.

Simond. *See* SIMMONDS.

Simon. *See* SIMMONDS.

Simms. *See* SYMES.

Simmonds, or Fitz-Simon, comprises Norman and other families.

Simmons. *See* SIMMONDS.

Simms. *See* SYME.

Simonds. *See* SIMMONDS.

Simons. *See* SIMMONDS.

Sims. *See* SYME.

Sinclair, for ST. CLAIR.

Singer. Gaufridus Cantor, Normandy 1180–95 (MRS). Christiania le Chaunter, Engl. c. 1272 (RH).

Singfield, probably from Centeville, or Sequanville, Isle of France.

Sinnott. Sinodus, a tenant (probably Norman) of Geoffry de Ros, Kent, paid a fine 1130 to obtain his inheritance (Rot. Pip.).

Sinton. William and Richard Santon, Normandy 1180–95 (MRS). David de Santon, Engl. c. 1198 (RCR).

Sirles, for SEARLE.

Sisson, for Cisenne, a foreign name.

Sitch, for SUCH.

Sitwell, for Sideville. *See* SIDWELL.

Sivell, for SEYVILLE or SAVILLE.

Sivil. *See* SIVELL.

Sivyer, for SAVIOUR. This appears to be a branch of the Sires de St. Sauveur, Viscounts of Constantine, of which other branches remain in England under the name of CONSTANTINE. In 920 Richard Sire de St. Sauveur le Viconte gave to Nigel his son the lordship of Nehou, the castle of which belonged for above a century to the barony of St. Sauveur (De Gerville, Anc. Chateaux). Nigel was made hereditary Viscount of the Cotentin 938. In 1047 Nigel de St. Saveur revolted, and was defeated at the battle of Val des Dunes, when he lost his estates. He afterwards recovered a part of them, but the Viscounty passed to the Tessons. In 1066 Nigel was at the battle of Hastings (Wace, ii. 231). In England we find Roger de S. Sauveur (Salvatore) witnessing the foundation charter of Binham Priory, Essex, by Geoffry de Valognes t. Henry I. (Mon. i. 344.)

400

Sixen, for Cisenne. *See* SISSON.

Skeats, for KEATS.

Skeere, for Sceres, or Scures. *See* SHORE.

Skeet. *See* KEAT.

Skerman, for SHERMAN.

Skidmore, for SCUDAMORE.

Skipwith, or De Estoteville, of Normandy, a well-known family, which need not be dwelt on. The arms confirm the descent, which, however, is not exactly in the line usually supposed. *See* STUTFIELD.

Slate. William Salate, Normandy 1180–95 (MRS). Robert, William Seled, Engl. c. 1272. Hence the name Sleath.

Slater, probably Sellator, or le LORIMER.

Slatter. *See* SLATER.

Slaytor. *See* SLATER.

Slee. *See* SLY.

Sleet. *See* SLATE.

Sleigh, for SLY.

Sleight. *See* SLATE.

Slemmon, for LEMON.

Slight. *See* SLEIGHT.

Sloan, for SELLON.

Sloane. *See* SLOAN.

Sloman. *See* SALAMON.

Slowman. *See* SLOMAN.

Sly, for SILLY. *See* SEALEY.

Smale. *See* SMALL.

Small, for MAULE, or Masculus.

Slyth, for Slit, or SLATE.

Smalley, for MAULEY.

Smallfield, for Malville. *See* MELVILLE.

Smallpiece, for MALPAS.

Smeaton, for Smithton. *See* SMITHSON-PERCY. Hence the celebrated engineer.

Smedley, for SMILY.

Smeley. *See* SMILY.

Smellee. *See* SMILY.

Smeeton. *See* SMEATON.

Smiles, for MILES.

Smily. William de Semilly, Similly, or Semellie, and the Castle of S., Normandy 1180–95 (MRS); also 1198, and the Park of Similly (Ib.).

Smith, originally Faber or Le Fevre. *See* FABER. This name, arising from an important industry, the iron manufacture of the Middle Ages (which was chiefly employed in the fabrication of arms), comprises families of Norman and other origins. The name S. does not appear till the 13th cent., being then a translation from Faber or Le Fevre. Alberic Faber witnessed in 1075 a charter of William de Braiose of Sussex (Mon. i. 581). Reginald Faber, t. William I., gave lands at Egremont to St. Mary's, York (i. 389). Godric Faber 1086 held lands at Walton, Suffolk, from Roger Bigod (Domesd. Suff. 339 b). The name occurs frequently among the early benefactors of Bridlington and Gisborne Priories, York (Burton, Mon. Ebor.). In Durham, Mildred, Simon, and Humphrey Faber are mentioned as landowners in Boldon Book 1183; in Norfolk Richard Faber 1199 (RCR); in Suffolk Henry Faber 1190 (RCR); in Lincoln Ulestan Fitz-Godwin Faber paid a fine 1130 (Rot. Pip.). In Middlesex Roger Faber possessed estates 1130 (Rot. Pip.); in Surrey Alured Faber occurs c. 1200 (RCR); Andrew F. in Berks, and Henry F. in Lincoln, at the same time (Ib.). William F. occurs in Leicester c. 1200 in a suit with Earl Ferrars (RCR).

Smithson-Percy. This is a branch of the baronial family of De Scalis or De Scallariis, deriving from Harduin de Scallers t. William I.

The origin of the name is apparently not Norman, as it is not found in the Duchy till the time of Philip Augustus. It was probably derived from Aquitaine, where the Viscounts of Scales had been of importance since the time of Charles Martel c. 730, at which epoch they had a grant of the ruined Abbey of Tulle and its estates. These were restored to the church by Aldemar, Viscount of Scales 930 (Gall. Christ. ii. 262). Gausbert, his brother, was ancestor of the family of Scales, which continued at Limoges 1201 (Ib. vi. 200 Instr.). Harduin de Scales, probably one of this family, had extensive grants in Herts and Cambridge 1066, and he and his posterity also held three knights' fees in Yorkshire by gift of Alan Earl of Richmond (Gale, Hon. Richmond, App. 26). Soon after 1086 Smydeton, or Smithton (now Smeaton), part of the demesne of Earl Alan near Richmond, York, was granted to Malger, son of Harduin de Scalers. Turgis Fitz-Malger t. Stephen gave lands to Fountains Abbey. William de Scalers, his son, confirmed his gifts (Burton, Mon. Ebor. 149, 201). Richard Fitz-Turgis, another son, named also De Smydeton and De Scalers, was living 1147–1164 (Burton, 319; Mon. Angl. i. 855, 51). The eldest son, Ranulph, had issue: 1. Geoffry; 2. Brian de Scales, who joined in the invasion of Ireland 1171. Ranulph had Geoffry Fitz-Ranulph, or De Scalers, who granted lands to Waltham Abbey (Mon. ii. 18); and at Smydeton to St. Mary's, York (Drake, Ebor. 504). The succession of the family is regularly traced (its name changing to Smithson) till it adopted that of Percy, and acquired the Dukedom of Northumberland.

Smyley, for SMILY.

Smythe. *See* SMITH.

Smythe. *See* SMITH. The Smythes, Viscounts Strangford, were descended from a family seated at Corsham, Wilts, t. Henry VIII., one of which, Henry Faber (Smith), was mentioned in a suit-at-law in Wilts 1198 (RCR), and in 1189 in a charter of Richard I. (Mon. i. 868.) In 1202 Richard Faber was appointed by the Crown to superintend the works at Salisbury Castle (Rot. Canc.). In 1272 Nicholas Faber, of Wilts, was complained of for withdrawing his tenants from the Hundred Court (Rot. Hundr. ii. 78). In 1307 William Faber was bailsman for the M.P. for Marlborough; and 1313 Edward le Smyth was M.P. for Chippenham (near to Corsham), and Henry le Smyth M.P. for Ludgershall, Wilts (PPW). The early arms of this family, six lions rampant, on a bordure (Harl. MS. 1443), appear to indicate descent from the family of de St. Martin of Wilts, a branch of Warrenne.

Smythson. *See* SMITHSON.

Snart. Fulco Senart held lands in Normandy from Philip Augustus (Mem. Soc. Ant. Norm. v. 170). Margery and Richard Sinard, Engl. c. 1272 (RH).

Sneezum, for Senesom, or SANSOM.

Snowball, for Senebol, or Chenebel, or KENEBEL. *See* KNATCHBULL.

Soame, for SOANE.

Soames, for SOANES.

Soane. Radulphus Sone, Normandy 1180–95 (MRS). R. Sone, or Sonne 1198 (Ib.). Roger Soun, Engl. c. 1272 (RH).

Soanes. *See* SOANE.

Soar, for le Sor. *See* SHORE.

Soares. *See* SOAR.

Soars. *See* SOAR.

Soddy. William de Sundaye, Normandy t. John c. 1200 (Mem. Soc. Ant. Norm. v. 105). John Sodde, Engl. c. 1272 (RH).

Soer, or le Sor. *See* SHORE.

Sole, for SOLEY.

Sole. The estate of Ranulph de Sola, Normandy, was granted 1209 by Philip Augustus to another (Mem. Soc. Ant. Norm. v. 158). Ranulph, William, Salemon de Sola, Normandy 1198 (MRS). William Sole, Engl. c. 1272 (RH).

Soley. William de Solio, or de Soliis, and Richard 1180–95, Normandy (MRS). Richard de Solies or Soliers (Ib.). Mabilia, William, Simon, Walter de Soliers or Solers, Engl. c. 1198 (RCR).

Solly. *See* SOLEY.

Somerfield, for SOMERVILLE.

Somers, for De Someri, a baronial family. Ralph de Summeri of Normandy t. John. From Sommeri, near Rouen. They were barons of Dudley in England by m. with the heiress of Paganel. The families of Somers and Summers are armorially identified with the family of De Sommeri. *See* Dugdale, Banks, Dorm. and Ext. Bar.

Somervail, for SOMERVILLE.

Somervell. *See* SOMERVILLE.

Somerville, from Sommerville, now Sommervieux, near Caen. The history of this family, Lords Somerville in Scotland, is well known. William de Sumerville witnessed a charter of Malcolm King of Scotland for Sautre Abbey, Hunts, c. 1150 (Mon. i. 851), and 1158 was indebted to the Crown twenty marks of silver

(Rot. Pip.); but was in Scotland (Ib.). In 1165 Walter de Summerville held a fief from the Earl of Derby, two fees from the barony of Stafford, and one in York from De Lacy (Lib. Niger).

Sommers. *See* SOMERS.

Somes, for SONES.

Sommerville, for SOMERVILLE.

Sommerwill, for SOMERVILLE.

Sone. *See* SOANE.

Sones, for SONE.

Soole. *See* SOLE.

Soper. *See* SEVIN.

Sorel. *See* SORRELL.

Sorge. Roger Sorice, Normandy 1180 (MRS).

Sorrell. Robert Sorel, Normandy 1180–95 (MRS). Hugh Sorel, Matilda Sarle, Engl. c. 1272 (RH).

Sorrill. *See* SORRELL.

Soul, for SOLE.

Sounes, for SONES.

Soutar. *See* SUTER.

Souter. *See* SUTER.

Southwell, descended from Bardulph, a brother of Bodinus (mentioned in Domesday), and of the family of the Earls of Richmond (Gale, Hon. Richm.). He had Akaras Fitz-Bardulph, and Hugh Bardulph, of Lincoln 1158, whose son, William B., was Viscount of Norfolk and Suffolk t. Henry II., and had issue: 1. Dodo, ancestor of the Barons Bardolf 1293; 2. Walter, who held in York from the Honour of Pontefract 1165 (Lib. Niger); 3. Ralph B., who was father of Robert, who as Robert 'de Southill' had a suit in Norfolk (ROR); 4. Hugh Bardolf, who t. John granted lands at Hoton-Bardolph to Kirkham Abbey, York (Burton, 375), and had issue, John 'de Sothul,' who was found to die seized of Suthill and West Hoton

(Hoton-Bardolph), York, and other estates in that shire (Inq. p. Mort.). Sir John de Sothull c. 1300 bore gules an eagle argent, the arms of Bardolph. These were exchanged at a later date for others, which, however, were also borne by the Lords Bardolph. Sir John was Seneschal of Gascoigne t. Edward I. His descendants continued to possess estates in Norfolk, and from them descended the Viscounts Southwell and Barons de Clifford.

Soutter, for SOUTER.

Soward, for SWORD.

Sowler, for Sollers. *See* SOLEY. The name was derived from Soliers, near Caen, Normandy, and the family came to England at the Conquest. Thurstan de Solariis settled in Hereford, and Humphry de Sollers his brother in Brecon, with Bernard de Newmarch 1088 (Jones, Brecon, i. 92). The family continued in the 17th century in Brecknock. Richard de Solariis in 1165 held three fees of ancient enfeoffment (Lib. Niger). Walter de Solar held Hope-Solar, Hereford, 13th cent. (Testa); and Henry and Richard S. occur 1297, 1307 (PPW).

Sowter, for SOUTER.

Spaight, for Spade, or SPEED.

Spain, or De l'Espagne, from Espagne, near Pont-Audemer, Normandy, a baronial name.

Walter de Hispania is mentioned 1080 (Ord. Vitalis, 576); and his sons Hervey and Alured de Ispania occur 1086 in England (Domesd.). The latter was a great baron. From the former descended the Spains of Essex, who long continued to flourish.

Spake, for SPEER.

Spark, for Esparc, or PARK.

Sparkes, for Esparks, or PARKS.

Sparks. *See* SPARKES.

Sparling. Ralph de Esparlon, Normandy 1180 (MRS). Jordan Esperling, Engl. c. 1198 (RCR).

Speak, for SPEKE.

Speck. Robert Espec, Normandy 1180–95 (MRS). The fief of William Espec at Kesnoi-Espec, Faugernon, and Tylia was in the hands of Philip Augustus. Robert and William E. mentioned 1198 (MRS). The Barons Espec were Norman in origin (*see* KERR); and the Kerrs of Scotland are a branch descended from Walter Espec t. William the Conqueror. His brother Richard Espec was of Devon, and a charter of his granted to Osbert Prous or Probus lands held by the service of two knights, which had belonged to his brother William P. before he left for Jerusalem, probably in 1096 (Pole, Devon, 235). His descendant William Espec of Devon in 1202 paid a fine to the Crown (Rot. Canc. 204); and in 13th cent. the heir of Richard de Espec held in Bramford, Devon, half a knight's fee from the honour of Barnstaple (Testa). The descent of this family is traced by Pole in Devon and Somerset, where it still continues, bearing now the name of Speke.

Speed. Ivo de Spada, Normandy 1180–95 (MRS); John and Roger Sped, Engl. c. 1272 (RH).

Speight, for SPEED.

Speke. *See* SPECK.

Spellar. Walter Espenlard, Normandy, held lands from Philip Augustus (Mem. Soc. Ant. Norm. v. 172).

Speller, for SPELLAR.

Spencer, includes various families who held the office of Dispensarius to the king or the great barons. The Spencers so famous in English

404

history appear to have derived from Odard, a Baron of Chester, who with Nigel, Baron of Halton and Constable of Chester, and other brothers, came with Earl Hugh Lupus, being probably of the house of Avranches. This may be inferred from the ancient arms, which were preserved by the Warburtons, descendants of Odard, who bore two chevrons, like the St. Maurs; the house of Avranches also bearing chevrons. The Spencers, however, and the Duttons adopted the arms borne by the Constables of Chester, the Claverings, Eures, Lacys, and other branches of the house of Vesci or Burgh.

Odard seems to have had two sons: 1. Hugh of Dutton, ancestor of the great house of D. of Cheshire, and of the Warburtons, baronets; 2. Thomas Fitz-Odard (Mon. Angl. ii. 799), who appears in Cheshire c. 1130 as Thomas 'Dispensarius,' having been created Dispencer or Steward in fee by Rufus or Henry I., to which office was attached the manor of Rollright, with other estates, Oxfordshire. He had issue— 1. Thomas, ancestor of the Earls of Winchester, father of Fulco of Cheshire 1178 (Mon. i. 897), and of Thomas, who gave Bollington, Cheshire, with his daughter to Hugh de Dutton (Ormerod, i. 479). Thomas had Hugh, father of Hugh the Justiciary, father of Hugh, Earl of Winchester; 2. Geoffry, who appears in Cheshire 1150 (Mon. i. 987), and who was Joint-Dispencer. Gerold his son occurs 1200 (Hunter, Fines). Geoffry his son held Stanton, Oxford, also estates in Worcester from De Stuteville, and elsewhere (Testa). John Despencer, his son, a minor 1251 (Roberts, Excerpta, ii. 108), died 1274, seized of lands held from Hugh the Justiciary, and of estates in Worcester. William Despencer, of Worcester, d. 1328 (Nash, i. 82), and had William, whose son William was living 1428 in Worcester (Ibid. ii. 106). In the next generation John D., who possessed estates in Worcester, with Henry his brother or kinsman, became seated in Northants. The latter bore the arms of the Spencers and Duttons; and from the former descended the Lords Spencer, Earls of Sunderland, Earls Spencer, Dukes of Marlborough, and Barons Churchill. Spenser the poet appears to have claimed descent from this family, but there were so many other families of the name, and the data in his case are so limited, that it is not possible for the writer to form an opinion on the matter.

Spikes, for Pike.

Spinney, or De Spiney. Anscher, Robert, Eustace, William, Ranulph, de Spineto, the honour of Spiny, Normandy 1180–95 (MRS). The family was seated in Devon, where it long continued at Samford-Spiney.

Spratt, for Pratt.

Spring, or De Fonte. Norman, Peter, William, Hugh de Fonte, Normandy 1180–95; Reginald and Emma de Fonte, Engl. c. 1198 (RCR).

Sprunt, for Esperon. Ranulph and Fulcher D'Esperon, Norm. 1180–95; Durand E. or de E. 1198 (MRS); Thomas Esperun, Engl. c. 1272 (RH).

Spryng, for Spring.

Spurrier, for Purrier.

Spurin, for Esperon. See Sprunt.

Spurling. See Sparling.

Spurr, the English form of Esperon. See Sprunt.

Squirrel, for Carrell.

Squirrell. See Squirrel.

Stable. N. de Stables, Normandy 1180 (MRS).

Stables. See Stable.

Stacey, for Tacy.

Stacy, for Tacy.

Staff. See Steff.

Stafford, or Bagot. The younger branch of the Bagots (see Bagot), who acquired the Barony of Stafford by m. with the heiress of Toesni, and became Earls of Stafford, Dukes of Buckingham. See Dugdale and Banks.

Stagg. See Tagg.

Staight. See Tate.

Staines. See Stanes.

Stains. See Stanes.

Staley. See Stella.

Stamp, or D'Estampes. Lucas de Estampes, Normandy 1180–95 (MRS). The Ville of Stampes, Norm. t. Phil. Augustus (Mem. Soc. Ant. Nor., v. 158). Ferric de Stampis is mentioned by Ord. Vitalis (908).

Standley, for Stanley.

Standly. See Stanley.

Stanes. William de l'Estan, Normandy 1180–95 (MRS); Robert Estan, Engl. c. 1272 (RH).

Stanhope, or de Colville, a baronial family. See Colville, Northcote.

William de Colleville, who came to England 1066, had issue: William, who t. Henry I. was Lord of Colleville, Normandy (MSAN, viii. 430). It was held from Ranulph the Viscount and from the Church of Bayeux. From Philip, his elder son, descended the Lords Colville of Scotland. Thomas de C., the younger son, obtained Eversley or Ifferley, York, where he granted lands to

Byland Abbey (Burton, Mon. Ebor., 72). He had issue—1. Philip, father of William de Colville or De Everley, who t. Rich. I. granted lands to Whitby Abbey, and was ancestor to the Everleys of Yorkshire; 2. Richard de Everley or De Stanhope. The last-mentioned occurs in Boldon Book 1183 as Richard 'De Stanhop,' otherwise 'De Ifferley or Yrealey.' He held lands at Stanhope from the See of Durham, with the office of Seneschal. His descendants, who bore the name of Stanhope, continued to bear the arms of Colville, viz. a cross, until the 15th century, when the present modification was adopted (Collins). Bernard, son of Richard 1199 (RCR), was ancestor of William de S. t. Edward I. (Rot. Orig. Cur. Scac. i. 86), whose son Richard had issue: Robert and Richard, who are mentioned at Berwick 1334, 1345. The latter had Sir John Stanhope, M.P. for Newcastle, who acquired Rampton, Notts., by m. with the heiress of Maulovel, and was ancestor of the Earls of Chesterfield, Harrington, and Stanhope.

Staniland. Herbertus de Stanelonda, Normandy 1180 (MRS).

Stanhow, for De Stagno. William de Stagno, Normandy 1180–95 (MRS), and in 1198; Gilbert de Stangno, England 1198 (RCR); Harvey and Edmond de Stanho, c. 1272 (RH).

Stanley, or De Valecherville, from V. in the Caux, named also Wallichville, Warlanville, probably from Valenger, a companion of Rollo. Fulco de V. was living 1063 (Ord. Vit. Ed. Forester, iii. 489). His son William de W. accompanied the Conqueror 1066, and had grants in Derby, but died before 1086, leaving: 1. Robert; 2. Ralph, to whom Henry I. granted lands in Notts., which were carried by his dau. and heir to Robert de Ohaus; 3. Walter, mentioned in Normandy 1124 (Ord. Vitalis). Robert, the elder son, in 1086 held Stanley, Derby (Domesd.), and several lordships in Notts. in barony, and was, as 'Robert de Stanley,' Viscount of Stafford 1124–1120 (Rot. Pip. 31 Hen. L.). He appears to have obtained a grant of Aldithley, Balterley, and Talk in Stafford, on the death of Gamel, the former owner (mentioned in Domesday), and also part of the adjacent forest, which when cultivated bore his name, Stanley. He had issue—1. Ralph, father of William Fitz-Ralph, Seneschal of Normandy, who was of great eminence t. Henry II., and who before his death granted Stanley in Derby to found an abbey, afterwards styled Stanley or Dale. His dau. and heir m. William de Salicosa Mara (Mon. ii. 612); 2. Liulph, who had Aldithley during his father's life, and Balterley and Stanley (Stafford) after his decease. In 1130 he as Liulph de Aldithley paid a fine in Stafford (Rot. Pip.). He had issue—Adam, from whom descended the Lords Aldithley or Audley; 3. Adam, who obtained the Lordship of Talk, which his son William t. Henry II. exchanged with his cousin Adam de Aldithley for Stanley and part of Balterley (Dugd. Bar. ii. 247; Ormerod, Cheshire). From him descended the Baronets Stanley, the Earls of Derby, so famous in English history, the Lords Monteagle, and Stanley of Alderley.

Stannah. *See* STANHOW.

Starbuck. *See* TARBUCK.

Stark. *See* STIRKE.

Starling, for Easterling. *See* STRADLING.

Starr. *See* STORR.

State, for TATE.

States, for STATE.

Staute, for STOUT.

Steabben, for STEPHEN.

Steains. *See* STANES.

Steal. *See* STEEL.

Stean. *See* STANE.

Steane. *See* STANE.

Steff. *See* STIFF.

Steel. *See* STELLA.

Steele. *See* STELLA: hence Steele, baronet.

Steete. *See* STATE.

Stella. Ingrie and Domingo de Stella, Normandy 1180–95 (MRS); John Stel and Isabel his mother, Engl. c. 1272 (RH).

Stemp. *See* STAMP.

Stephen. N. Stephanus, Normandy 1180–95 (MRS); John, Ralph, Stephen, Engl. c. 1272 (RH).

Stephens, for Fitz-Stephen; contains Norman families in all probability.

Stearn. *See* TARN.

Sterling, for Esterling. *See* STRADLING.

Stevens. *See* STEPHENS.

Steward. *See* STEWART.

Stewart, or le Seneschal. Hugo and Nicholas Senescallus, Normandy 1198 (MRS); Roger, Tebald, William, Alan, Bernard, Nicholas, Roger Senescallus, Engl. c. 1198 (RCR). Nicholas is mentioned in Hertford. The office of Seneschal or High Steward was a chief feudal dignity in each earldom and barony, and must have been generally held by Normans. Of course different families were included under the name in England. In Scotland it is equivalent to STUART.

Stickland, for STRICKLAND.

Stiff. Radulphus Rigidus, Normandy 1180–95 (MRS); John, Robert Stife, Engl. c. 1272 (RH).

Stiffe. *See* STIFF.

Stiffin, for STEPHEN.

Stimp, for STAMP.

Stirk. *See* STIRKE.

Stirke. Richard Lesterc, Normandy 1198 (MRS); Henry Sterck, Engl. c. 1272 (RH).

Still. *See* STEEL.

Stirling. *See* STERLING; also a Scottish local name.

Stoate. *See* STOTT.

Stocks. *See* STOKES.

Stokes. Petrus and John de Stokes, Normandy 1180–95 (MRS). Peter de S. is mentioned in Northants, Wilts, Bedford, and Bucks. Other families bore this local name.

Stolte. Herveus Stultus, Normandy 1180–95 (MRS); Joannes Stout or Stolt, t. Henry V.; John Stuhte, Engl. c. 1272 (RH).

Stoneley, for STANLEY.

Stones. *See* STANES.

Store, for STORR.

Storr. Stephen (de) La Stur, Normandy 1180–95 (MRS); Margaret Stur, Engl. c. 1272 (RH).

Storrs, for STORR.

Stott. *See* STOUT.

Stout. *See* STOLTE.

Stower, or Sture. William Fitz-Estur, Robert Estur, Normandy 1180–95 (MRS); Andrew Estor, 1198 (MRS); Margaret Stur, Engl. c. 1272 (RH).

Stowers. *See* STOWER.

Stradling, or le Esterling, came from Flanders t. William I., and joined in the Conquest of Glamorgan, where the family long re-mained of great eminence.

Strang, or Strong, the English form of Le Fort. Richard le Fort, Normandy 1198 (MRS); Adam, Samson le Fort, Simon Strong, Engl. c. 1272 (RH).

Strange, for L'Estrange, a baro-nial name. *See* LESTRANGE.

Stratten, for STRATTON.

Stratton, a branch of Baynard, or De Bellomont, of Norfolk. *See* MARSHAM.

Streatfield, for De Stratavilla or Estréeville. Robert de Estréeville occurs in Normandy t. Phil. Augustus (Mem. Soc. Ant. Norm. v. 161); Roger de Estrainvilla, 1198 (MRS).

Strick, for STIRK.

Strickett. *See* TRICKETT.

Strickland, or De Vaux. Hubert de Vaux, Baron of Gillesland t. William I., granted Castle Carrock, with Hayton, Cumberland, to Eus-tace de Vaux (his son), as appears from Nicholson and Burns (West-moreland, 511). Eustace gave parts of Castle Carrock and Hayton to Lanercost Priory. In the time of Henry II. these manors were owned by Robert de Castle Carrock, and from him passed to Robert his son, and Richard his grandson, who d. t. Edward I. Robert de C. C., t. Henry II., had a brother, Sir Walter de Stirkland, as appears by the grant of the latter of lands at Strike-land to St. Mary's, York, witnessed by Robert de C. C., 'brother of the said Walter' (Ib. 89). This seems conclusive. The family of Strickland descended from Sir Walter. Hence the baronets Strickland, and the emi-nent historian, Agnes Strickland.

Strong. *See* STRANG.

Stuart, or De Dinan. The Stew-

ards, afterwards kings of Scotland, as has been shown by Chalmers (Cale-donia), descended from Walter Fitz-Alan, created Steward of Scotland by David I. He was son of William Fitz-Alan (founder of Haughmon, Salop), son of Alan Fitz-Flaald, Baron of Oswaldestre, Salop, and Mileham, Norfolk, who came to England with the Conqueror, and whose origin has not yet been deter-mined. In 1098, however, Alan Fitz-Flaald (Flaud) granted the Church of Gugnan, Bretagne, to the Abbey of Combourne or Combourg, a place where a great castle of the Viscounts of Dinan existed from 1000 (Morice, Hist. Brit. Preuves. i. 492). In 1079 the name of Flaald, father of Alan, occurs in that vicinity, when, at the foundation of the Abbey of Mezuoit, near Dol (a cell of St. Flo-rent, Saumur, of which William de Dol or Dinan was then abbot), a grant was made by 'Alan the Seneschal' (of Dol), confirmed by his brother Fledaldus or Flaald, of the site of the abbey at Mezuoit; the gift being confirmed by Oliver, Viscount of Dinan, whose charter is witnessed by Alan the Seneschal (Lobineau, Hist. Bretagne, ii. 138). About the same time Geoffry, Viscount of Dinan, granted lands at Dinan to the same abbey, which were part of the estate of 'Alan the Seneschal, son of Guienoc,' which were given with consent of Rivallon, Alan's brother (Ib. 139).

Rivallon, in the preceding deed (p. 138), is mentioned as brother of Alan and Flaald, and is received as a monk into the abbey of Mezuoit. It appears, then, that Alan Fitz-Flaald was nephew of Alan Senes-chal of Dol, and grandson of Guienoc.

The latter was probably a son of Hamo I., Viscount of Dinan, representative of the ancient Counts of Dol and Dinan.

The identity of the families appears from their arms. The house of Dinan bore a fesse indented; that of Fitz-Alan and Fitz-Flaald bore fessy or barry; the Stuarts a fesse checquy. The historical importance of this family seems to demand some additional space. The principality of Dinan and Dol appears to have extended from Alet (St. Malo), by Dol, Dinan, and Combourg, to the central hills of Bretagne, over a tract of ninety miles by sixty. Its chiefs (on whom numerous barons were dependent) were rather sovereigns than magnates: their origin is lost in antiquity. In all probability they represented the patriarchal sovereigns of the Diaulites, the nation who held that part of Armorica in the time of Julius Cæsar. The alleged colonisation of Armorica from Britain in the third or fourth century is rejected by Niebuhr, and seems to rest upon no authentic data. The Bretons were indigenous, although there was a close intercourse between them and Great Britain. About A.D. 500 the Frisians invaded Armorica, at the instigation of Clovis; but in 513 Hoel, son of Budic, king of Armorica, returned from exile with the principal chiefs, and re-established the national independence (Morice, Hist. Bret. i. 15).

From this time the Counts of Dol begin to appear. Frogerius is mentioned as possessed of great power there in the time of Samson, Abbot of Dol, c. 570 (Alb. le Grand, Vies des SS. de Bretagne, 423). Count Loiescan, his successor, granted to the Abbey of Dol an estate in Jersey, part of which had been formerly given to Samson. 'Quidam comes, nomine Loiescan, valde divitiarum opibus obsitus.' (Acta SS. October x. 756; see also Vita Maglorii, apud Bouquet, iii. 435.) Rivallon, who is mentioned as a 'tyrannus' or dynast of great power, 'potentissimus vir,' c. 710, restored a monastery at request of Thurian, Bishop of Dol (Acta SS. Jul. 3, 5, 615). Early in the following century Salomon appears to have been Count of Dol. Rivallon, his son, with his brothers Alan and Guigan, witnessed a charter of Solomon, King of Bretagne, c. 868 (Lobineau, Hist. Bretagne, ii. 59, 62, 68). About 919, according to Ogee (Dict. Hist. et Geogr. de Bretagne, Art. Dinan), Alan, Count of Dol, gave his daughter in marriage to Ralph, Lord of Rieux in Bretagne. About 930 mention is made of Salomon as 'Advocate' or Protector of the Church of Dol (Bouquet, x. 188, 214), being evidently the dynast of the surrounding territory, and representative of the founders, Frogerius and Loiescan. He appears to have been succeeded by Ewarin, whose son Alan, 'son of Ewarin,' with Gotacelin de Dinan (his brother), witnessed, c. 980, a charter of Bertha, mother of Duke Conan (Lobineau, ii. 114). This Alan, 'son of Ewarin,' Count of Dol, was probably succeeded by his brother Hamo, Viscount of Dinan, who had six sons; viz., 1. Hamo, Viscount of Dinan, ancestor of the Viscounts of Dinan and the Barons De Dinant of England (by writ 1294); 2. Juahoen, or Junkeneus, Archbishop of Dol, c. 1000; 3. Rivallon, Seneschal of Dol, ancestor of the Counts of Dol;

4. Gosselin de Dinan; 5. Salomon, Lord of Guarplic, ancestor of the renowned Du Guesclin; 6. Guienoc, ancestor of the Stuarts, kings of Scotland.

Stuchfield, for STUTFIELD.

Stump, for Stemp, or STAMP.

Sturch, for Sturcke, or STIRK.

Sturcke. *See* STIRK.

Sturge, for STURCH.

Sturgeon. King John granted to N. Sturgon, of Normandy, Stoteville, the estate of Hugh de Gornai, 1203 (Mem. Soc. Ant. Norm. v. 122). He was Viscount of Fescamp (Ib.)

Sturges, for STURCE.

Sturgess, for STURGES.

Sturgis, for STURGES.

Stutfield, or Estoteville, a baronial name. William de Estoutville, Normandy 1180-95; Eustace and William de E., 1198 (MRS); William and Henry de Stotevilla (Ib.) Estoteville was near Yvetot, and this family was one of the greatest houses in Normandy. Robert de E. came to England 1066. He is mentioned in Normandy 1070 (Ord. Vit. 575). The family had great possessions in all parts of England, particularly in the North.

Such. *See* SUCHE.

Suche, Souche, or Zouche, a baronial name. *See* ZOUCHE.

Suchwell, for Suchville, or De Siccavilla. This family came from Sageville, Isle of France, and was seated in Devon. Richard de Sachevilla occurs in Essex 1086 (Domesd.); and in 13th cent. Robert de Saccaville held a fief in Devon, and John de Siccavilla one in Cornwall from Henry de la Pomeraie (Testa). Heanton-Sachville, Devon, retains the name.

Sugden, or De Rotors. Fulco de

410

Rotors, Normandy 1180-95 (MRS); Fulco de Rotor, 1198 (Ib.). Rotors was in the Cotentin, and was held from the barony of Litehaire (MSAN, xv. 81, 170). In England William de Rotor occurs 1130 (Rot. Pip.). His son Guiomar de Rotor in 1165 held a fief in Salop from Fitz-Alan, and had Guiomar II., De Rodington or De Sugden, so named from his estates in Salop (Eyton, vii. 373). Godfrey de Rotur, his brother, was Lord of Sugden (Ib. 380, 382), and from him descended the family of S., long of great importance in Salop, a branch of which, anciently settled in London, gave origin to Sir Edward Sugden, Lord St. Leonards, Lord Chancellor of England.

Sully. Walter de Sully, Suilli, or Suilleio, Normandy 1180-95 (MRS). Robert de S. Ibid. and 1198; Walter de Sully, Engl. c. 1198 (RCR).

Sulman. Radulphus Sorlemun, Normandy 1180-95 (MRS); John and Ralph Solyman, Engl. c. 1272 (RH).

Sumerfield, for SOMERVILLE.

Sumfield, for SUMMERFIELD.

Summervill, for SOMERVILLE.

Summerfield, for SOMERVILLE.

Summers, for SOMERS.

Sumption, for Sumpson, or SAMPSON.

Supple, for Chapel, or CAPEL.

Surman, for Sarmon. *See* SHARMAN.

Surmon. *See* SHARMAN.

Surr, for SIRR.

Surrell, for Sorel.

Surridge. Roger Sorice, Normandy 1180 (MRS); Seman le Sureys, Engl. c. 1272 (RH).

Surville. Roger de Survilla, and

the fief of S., Normandy 1180–95 (MRS). Robert de Surevilla 1198 (Ib.). *See* SHERVILLE.

Sutch, for SUCHE.

Suter. Geoffry, Roger, Gerald Sutor, Normandy 1180–95 (MRS). Seven of the name 1198 (Ib.). Many in Engl. c. 1272 (RH).

Suter, for SOUTER.

Suter, for SOUTER.

Sutterfield, from Soteville, Normandy. Robert de Sotevilla, and the fief of S., Norm. 1180–95 (MRS); Norman, Robert, Walter de S. 1198 (Ib.); Roger de Sotewille, Engl. c. 1272 (RH).

Sutton. Thomas, founder of the Charter House, was son of Richard Sutton (who d. 1558), Steward of the Courts in Lincoln, and a tenant of the See of Lincoln (Bancroft, Life of S.). The family is armorially identified with the Suttons of Washingborough, &c., who descended from Hamon Sutton, living c. 1430, and Viscount of Lincoln, who bore the same arms (Harl. MS. 1550).

These arms are entirely different from those of the Suttons of Holderness, and those of Dudley. We do not find the name of S. in Lincoln before 1270, when William de Sutton held part of a knight's fee from Robert de Everingham (Testa, 324). Sutton appears to have been part of the fee held from Robert de Everingham and the see of York by Thomas Neville of Rigsby and Sutton (Testa, 331). John de Neville was father of the latter, and was also named John ' de Rigsby '; and the above William de Sutton was son of Geoffry de Sutton living 1270; who was probably brother of John de Neville or Rigsby. This was one of the nu-

merous Lincolnshire branches of the Nevilles of Normandy.

Swait, for SWEET.

Sweet. Hubertus Dulcis, mentioned in Normandy 1195 (MRS); Roger, William, John, Adam Swet in England c. 1272 (RH).

Sweett. *See* SWEET.

Swinborn. *See* SWINBURNE.

Swinborne. *See* SWINBURNE.

Swinburn. *See* SWINBURNE.

Swinburne, or Hairun. In the 13th cent. William Herun held a barony in Northumberland, including Swinburne, which John de Wircester held from him by ancient enfeoffment (Testa). Ralph de Wircester had held the same barony 1165, as had Paganus de W. a quarter of a fee from him (Swinburne). The family of Wircester, of which Swinburne was a branch, appears to have been the same as that of Heron or Hairun. *See* HERON.

Sword. Radulphus Espée, Normandy 1180–95 and 1198 (MRS); John de Espey, Engl. c. 1272 (RH).

Swords, for SWORD.

Sydney, for SIDNEY.

Syer, for SAYER.

Syer, for SEYER.

Syers, for SYER.

Sylvester, for SILVESTER.

Syme. In 1221 Philip Augustus granted lands at Heudboville, Normandy, to Richard Syme (Mem. Soc. Ant. Norm. v. 159); Adam Symie, Engl. t. John (Hardy, Rot. de Libert.)

Symes, for SYME.

Symes. *See* SYME.

Symmons. *See* SIMONDS.

Symonds, for SIMONDS.

Symons, for SIMONDS.

Syms, for SYMES.

Synnott. *See* SINNETT.

Syres, for SAYERS.

Tabberer. *See* TABER.

Taber. Robert Tabare, Normandy 1180–95; Raginald Taboer, 1198 (MRS); John and Richard le Taborer, Engl. c. 1272 (RH).

Taborer. *See* TABER.

Tabor. *See* TABER.

Tabrar, for TABERER.

Tacey. Robert Taisie or Tessy, and Gervase, Normandy 1180–95 (MRS); John Tassi, Engl. c. 1272 (RH).

Tacy. Rualen de Tissie, Normandy 1180–95 (MRS); and in 1198 (Ib.); Symon Tyse, Engl. c. 1272 (RH).

Taffrell, for Taunfrenel. *See* TUFFNELL.

Tagg. Radulphus Tac, Normandy 1180–95 (MRS); Richard Tagg, Engl. c. 1272 (RH).

Tait. *See* TATE.

Taite. *See* TATE.

Talbot, or D'Eu, a baronial name. Bartholomew, Robert, Quintin, Hugh Talbot, Talebot, or Thalebot, Normandy 1180–95 (MRS); Geoffry, Hugh, Robert T. 1198 (Ib.). This family originally bore, bendy of ten, the arms of the Cornets of Eu, being barry of ten; and descends from Hugh Taleboth, probably younger son of William first Count of Eu (son of Richard I. of Normandy). He, c. 1035, granted a charter in favour of Trinité du Mont, Rouen, which was witnessed by his brother Count Gilbert of Eu (Forester's Ordericus, iii. 452). William Talebot his son was mentioned in the foundation charter of Treport, Eu, by his cousin Robert Count of Eu; and was a benefactor

to that abbey (Gall. Christ. xi. 15, Instr.). This William T. came to England 1066, and had, 1. Richard; 2. Geoffry, ancestor of Lord Talbot of Malahide. Richard in 1086 held in Bedford from Walter Giffard, Baron of Bolbec (Domesd.). He had Hugh Talebot, Castellan of Plessis, Normandy, 1119 (Ord. Vit. 815), who m. a sister of Robert Fitz-Hamon, Baron of Creuilly, Gloucester, and Glamorgan; and of Hamo Dapifer; and had, 1. Richard; 2. Hugh, Baron of Cliville, Normandy, by m. with the dau. of Hugh de C., before 1130 (Rot. Pip. 31 Hen. I.). His son Hugh m. a sister of Geoffry de Mandeville, Earl of Essex; and his descendants continued in Normandy.

Richard, the elder son, obtained 1156 a grant of Linton and Wilton, Hereford; and in 1165 held two fees from Giffard Earl of Bucks; also a baronial fief in Normandy (Lib. Niger, Feod. Norm. Duchesne). Gilbert, his son and heir, in 1165 held the Herefordshire estate (Lib. Niger). Richard, his son, was father of Gilbert t. Henry III., Constable of Grosmont, Skenfrith, and other castles in the Welsh marches. From him descended the Lords Talbot of Blackmere and Goderich, summoned by writ 1387, and the famous John Talbot Earl of Shrewsbury; also the Lord Chancellor Talbot, ancestor of the Earls of Shrewsbury and Talbot.

The Lords Talbot of Malahide descend from Geoffry T. (*See* above), who 1086 held lands in Essex (Domesd.), and was a benefactor to the church of Rochester (Mon. i. 30). In 1130 Geoffry, his son, paid 200 marks for his father's estates Kent (Rot. Pip.). William T., his son, was governor of Hereford 1139, and soon after was granted Gainsborough, Lincoln; and was ancestor of the Talbots of Bashall and Thornton, York (Banks, Dorm. and Ext. Bar. i. 179). He had, 1. William Talebot, living 1186 (Mon. ii. 506), ancestor of the T.s of Bashall; 2. Richard; 3. Walter.

Richard Talbot accompanied Henry II. to Ireland, and obtained grants in Ulster and in Fingal and Malahide near Dublin. The latter was confirmed to him by King John in 1199, as appears by the extant charter. He gave the church of Malahide to his brother Walter; and had issue, 1. Robert; 2. Reginald; 3. Adam. Robert T. had great possessions in Ulster and in Fingal. In 1215 the estate of Irewe and Castle of Carrickfergus were restored to him, after his rebellion (Hardy, Rot. Claus. i. 233); also the estate of Brakenburgh given to him by De Lacy (241). In 1241 his estates were seized (Ib. ii. 32); and the rent payable from Fingal by his brother Reginald de Fingal was granted away (Ib. 40); but he subsequently recovered his estates (Ib. 60). He is mentioned in Yorkshire as Robert de Tolebu, who granted lands to Gisburne, and directed his body to be buried there (Burton, Mon. Ebor. 354). He and Reginald probably died s. p.

Adam, the younger brother, inherited the barony of Malahide, which his descendants have always since retained. Hence the Barons Talbot, summoned by writ 1361, the

Earls and Dukes of Tyrconnell, and the Lords Talbot of Malahide.

Talbott, for TALBOT.

Talbut, for TALBOT.

Talfer, or Taillefer. *See* TELFER.

Talford, for TALFOR.

Tall, for Taille. *See* TRALE.

Tall. Ugo Tale, Normandy 1180–95 (MRS); John Tail, Engl. c. 1272 (RH).

Tallboy or Taillebois, a baronial name. Geoffry Taillebois, Normandy 1180–95 (MRS); Turstin, Walchelin, William T. 1198 (Ib.). *See* PRESTON.

Tallett, for Tallard. Ralph Teillart, Normandy 1180; Hugh Tallart 1198 (MRS); Ralph Talliard, Engl. c. 1272 (RH).

Tamblin, for Tombelaine, from Tomblain in Lorraine.

Tamlin. *See* TAMBLIN.

Tamlyn. *See* TAMBLIN.

Tamplin. *See* TAMBLIN.

Tancred. Thomas Thancard with Helias Giffard, Robert de Mowbray, &c., witness to a charter of Kelso 1153 (Kelso Chartulary). He was probably of foreign origin.

Tann, a baronial name. Rainald de Tan, Than, Taon, or Taun, Normandy 1180 (MRS); John de T. 1195 (Ib.); Ralph, Richard, Simon de Tahon 1198 (Ib.).

Tanner. Hugh de Tanur made grants to the Abbey of Culture, Normandy 1082 (Gall. Christ. xi. 107 Instr.).

Tanner. Robert, Albert, Norman, Ingulf Taneor, Normandy 1180–95; Heudebert, Ingulf, Ralph, William Tanator 1198 (MRS); William Tannator and Jordan Tanur, Engl. 1194 (RCR).

Tanqueray. Radulphus, Robert Tankeré, Normandy 1198 (MRS).

Tant. *See* TENT.

Tanton. Adam, William Tanetun or Tanetin, Normandy 1180–95 (MRS); Adam 1198 (Ib.); William de Tanton 1202 Engl. (Rot. Canc.). The name is in some cases from an English locality.

Taperel. *See* TAFFRELL.

Taperell, for TAFFRELL.

Taplin. Roger Topelin, and Philip, Normandy 1180–95 (MRS); Robert Topeline 1198 (Ib.); Hugh Tuplin, Engl. c. 1272 (RH).

Tapling, for TAPLIN.

Tappin. *See* TOPPIN.

Tapping. *See* TAPPIN.

Taprell. *See* TAFFRELL.

Tapson, for D'Abison. *See* ABSON.

Tarbox. *See* TARBUCK.

Tarbuck. John de Torbaco, Normandy, temp. Philip Augustus (Mem. Soc. Ant. Norm. v. 183).

Tarn. William Taurne, Normandy 1180–95 (MRS); Hubert Tarun, Alice and Hugh Thorne, Engl. c. 1272 (RH).

Tarner, for TURNER.

Tarran, for TARN.

Tarry, for TORRE. *See* TORR.

Tarsey, for DARCY.

Tart. *See* TARTE.

Tarte, or Tort. Roger Tortus or Torto, Normandy 1180–95 (MRS); Richer 1198 (Ib.); Thomas Turt, Engl. c. 1272 (RH).

Tasker. Bernart Taskier, Normandy 1180–95 (MRS); Gilbert, Hugh Tasker, Engl. c. 1272 (RH).

Tassel. *See* TASSELL.

Tassell. Richard Tosel or Tossel and Ralph, Normandy 1180–95 (MRS); Wymond de Taissel, Bedford 1086 (Domesday); Adeliza, William, Walter de Taissel or Tessel, and the parish of St. German de Tassel, Norm. 1180–95 (MRS).

414

Tatchell, for Tateshall, or TATTERSHALL.

Tate, or Tête. Robert Teste, Normandy 1180–95 (MRS); Nicholas Tate, Engl. c. 1272 (RH).

Tattersall. *See* TATTERSHALL.

Tattershall, a baronial name, derived from Eudo Fitz-Spirwic or Fitz-Spirwin, probably of Breton origin, who came to England 1066, and obtained Tateshall, Lincoln, and other estates in Lincoln, Norfolk, and Suffolk, which he held in barony 1086. From him descended the Barons of Tateshall and the family of that name, also the family of Denton. *See* Banks (Dorm. and Ext. Bar.).

Tattersill. *See* TATTERSHALL.

Tatton, of Tatton, Cheshire, identified armorially with the family of MASSY, and apparently a branch of it (Ormerod, Cheshire, iii. 314, 315).

Tavener. *See* TAVERNER.

Taverner. Robert le Tavernier, Normandy 1180–95 (MRS); Richard le T., Engl. c. 1272 (RH).

Tavner. Ralph de Taberna, Ralph Tabernarius, and Maria, Normandy 1180–95 (MRS), also 1198 (Ib.); Eustace, William Tabernar, Engl. c. 1272 (RH).

Tawell. Augustus Tavel, Normandy 1180 (MRS); Unfrid and William T., 1198 (Ib.).

Tawney, or Tany, a baronial name. Alan de Taneo, Samson, John, Eudo de Tany, and the Castle of T., Normandy 1180–95 (MRS). Walchelin de T. occurs in Normandy 1110 (Ord. Vit. 856); Theodeline de Tani 1050 (Forester's Ordericus, iii. 473); Hasculf de T., Essex 1130; Gilbert de T., Essex 1158.

Tawse. John, Robert, Thomas, Aitard, William Tose, Normandy

1180–95 (MRS); Walter and John Tuss or Tuse, Engl. c. 1272 (RH).

Tay, or Tye. Hugo de Toie, Norm. 1198 (MRS); Hugo de la Tye, Engl. o. 1272 (RH).

Tayfeld, for Tavel. *See* TA-WELL.

Tayler. Matthew, Geoffry, William, Lambert, Ralph, Hugo, Ansketel Telarius, Normandy 1180–95 (MRS); Richard and Walter Telarius, Engl. 1202 (Rot. Canc.). The name in England no doubt comprised Normans. Bishop Jeremy Taylor was a descendant.

Tayleur, for TAYLER.

Taylor. *See* TAYLER.

Taylour. Hugo, Rainald Taillor, Taillour, or Talleor, Normandy 1180–95 (MRS); Rener Talliator 1198 (Ib.); Radulphus Talliator 1180–95 (Ib.). Ricardus Talliator held a tenement from the King at Winchester 1110 (Wint. Domesd.). In 1130 Geoffry Talleator had a pardon in Hants. (Rot. Pip.). Temp. Henry II., Henry Taillard witnessed a charter of Shireburne Abbey, Hants. (Mon. i. 578). C. 1200 William Tallator had a grant at Southampton; and also in Kent from King John (Testa 236, 215). The family then became seated in Kent and Sussex. In 1307 Henry le Taillur was of Sussex (PPW), and in 1324 William Taylor was M.P. for Bramber, as was Richard T. in 1379 (Dallaway, ii. 54). Thomas Taylor of Ringmere, Sussex, who d. 1629 possessed of considerable estates, was collateral ancestor of the Taylours, Marquises of Headfort, and Lords Langford.

Teakle, for TIKELL.

Teal, for TEALE.

Teale. Hugo de la Taille, Nor-

mandy 1180–95 (MRS); John Tail, Engl. c. 1272 (RH).

Teall, for TEALE.

Teasell, for TASSELL.

Teat, for TATE.

Tebbitts. *See* TEBBUT.

Tebbut. Robert Tebout held lands Normandy c. 1200 (Mem. Soc. Ant. Norm. v. 191); Henry, Odo, Ralph, Robert Tiebout, Normandy 1198 (MRS); Richard Tebaud, Engl. c. 1272 (RII).

Tebbutt. *See* TEBBUT.

Tedd, for TADD.

Tee, for TAY.

Teede, for Tete, or TATE.

Tegg, for TAGG.

Tekell. *See* TIKELL.

Telbin, for ST. ALBIN, ST. AUBYN.

Telfer. William, Fulco, Robert Taillefer or Tallefer, Normandy 1180–95 (MRS); Ralph Taillefer, Engl. 1202 (Rot. Canc.).

Telford, for TELFER: hence the eminent engineer Telford.

Teller, or TAYLER.

Tellier, Telarius, or TAYLER.

Telling, for Tellon, or Tallena. Ranulph and John de Talance, Normandy 1180 (MRS).

Temple, from Temple, near Caen, Normandy. This family came to England at the Conquest. Paganus de Templo witnessed a charter in Essex 1136 (Mon. i. 460); Robert in York 1150 (Mon. ii. 816). William held lands at Winchester 1148 (Wint. Domesd.). In 13th cent. Fulco de Temple held lands in Lincoln (Testa); and his descendants settled in Leicester, where Richard de T. held lands in 1279 (Nicholls, Leic. iv. 936): hence the Temples of Temple Hall, ancestors of the historical house of Temple, Viscounts Palmerston. The descent of this family from the Earls of Mercia is purely mythic.

Tennant, or Tanant, mentioned c. 1198 (RCR), is probably foreign.

Tennent, for TENNANT.

Tent. Robert Tent-grue, Normandy 1180–95 (MRS); Robert Tentegue 1198 (Ib.); Richard Tanet, Engl. c. 1198 (RCR).

Terrell, for TIRRELL.

Terrill, for TIRRELL.

Testar, for TESTER.

Tester. William Testard, Normandy 1180–95 (MRS); William and Philip Testard, Engl. c. 1198 (RCR).

Tett. See TITE.

Tewson or Tuson, armorially identified with TYSON.

Thackeray, for Thankeray, or TANQUERAY: hence the eminent novelist Thackeray.

Thackery, for THACKERAY.

Thackrah, for THACKERAY.

Thackray, for THACKERAY.

Thackrey, for THACKERAY.

Thackwray, for THACKERAY.

Thain, for Than, or TANN.

Thaine. See THAIN.

Thane. See TANN.

Tharp. William and Richard de Torp or Torpes, Normandy 1180–95 (MRS). Alan and Geoffry de Torp, Engl. 1189 (Rot. Pip.). In some cases the name of Torp was from English localities. Robert de Torp was of Normandy 1050 (Ord. Vit. 465). See EDEN, LAMBTON.

Theobald, or Tiebaud. See TEBBUTT.

Thickell. See TIKELL.

Thies, for Tyes, a baronial name. The family of Teutonicus, or Tyes, is frequently mentioned both in Normandy and England. It may possibly have been descended from

Baldric Teutonicus, ancestor of the Courcys and Nevilles. Everard Teutonicus, or Tyes, was in 1244 the husband of Ramet le Vicount, Baroness of Emilden, Northumberland (Dugd. i. 643). Henry de Tyes was a baron by writ 1293.

Thin, for THYNNE.

Thing, for THIN.

Thirkettle. William Fitz-Turquetil, Normandy 1180 (MRS). Walter Turketil 1204, Normandy. Richard Turketill, Engl. c. 1198 (RCR).

Thorn. See THARN.

Thorne. See THARN.

Thorne. See TARN.

Thornely. See TURNLEY.

Thornes, for THORNE.

Thorold. Hamo, Ranulph, William Toroude or Torolde, Normandy 1198 (MRS). Petrus Torold, Engl. c. 1272 (RH).

Thorold, baronets. The first person bearing this name in Lincoln lived t. Richard II., which disposes of the imaginary descent from Toraldus de Buckenhall 1052. This family is a branch of the De Vers, from Ver, near Bayeux, of whom Alberic de Ver witnessed a Breton charter 1058 (Gall. Christ.). He had: 1. Alberic de Ver, ancestor of the Earls of Oxford; 2. Erneis de Ver, who acquired lands in Holderness from the Earl of Albemarle, and in Lincoln from de Aincourt. He had issue: 1. Wido de Ver, living 1130 (Rot. Pip.; Mon. i. 374), whose son, Wido, held a barony in York 1165 (Lib. Niger). 2. Robert de Gousla, or Fitz-Erneis, who gave Gousla Church to Bridlington Priory (Burton, Mon. Ebor. 230). His descendants and the De Vers of Lincoln bore the same arms, viz., barry of six, a canton. Robert de G. had issue Adam, father of Walter de Ver, or Gousla, who is mentioned 1205 as son of Adam, son of Robert (Hardy, Obl. et Fin. 324). Walter had issue: 1. Simon de Gousla or Gousell. 2. Giles de Gousla. 3. Ralph de Gousell, who is mentioned 1284 as brother of Giles (Roberts, Cal. Geneal., 370). He held a fief from D'Aincourt, Lincoln (Testa), and gave lands in Holderness and at Gousell to Bridlington Priory (Burton, 241, 230). He had issue Thorold, who gave lands at Gousell or Gousla to Bridlington Priory (Ib. 230). His son, Robert Fitz-Thorold or Gousell, was of Merston, Lincoln, and d. 1306 (Inq. p. m.). John de Merston, his son, appears 1376 as John Thorold, and was the ancestor of the Thorolds, baronets. *See* WARHAM.

Thorp. *See* THARP.

Thorpe. 1. Wido Angevin or of Anjou, of Massingham, Norfolk, was ancestor of the Thorpes of Thorpe Ashwell, Norfolk (Blomefield, Norfolk, ix. 14). 2. Torp, in Normandy, derived its name from Denmark or Sweden in 912. Rodbert de Torp witnessed the charter of St. Evroult c. 1050 (Ord. Vit. 465). Another Robert de T. was living c. 1080 (Gall. Christ. xi. 227). His descendants in 1165 held estates in Lincoln, York, and Norfolk (Lib. Niger). William de T., who was of Lincoln, held Torpe, and a fief of the Honour of Grentmesnil, in Normandy (Feod. Norm. Duchesne).

Thorns, for THORN.

Throp, for THORP.

Thrupp, for THORP.

Thrussell, or Trussell, a baronial family. Guido Trussel was a distinguished Crusader 1096 (Ord. Vitalis). He was Lord of Montcheri, and Seneschal of France. Osbert Trussel in 1165 held a fief from the Earl of Warwick, and Fulco de Trussel one in Norfolk from the see of Ely (Lib. Niger). William T., son of Osbert, was a benefactor to Sulby Abbey, Northants (Mon. ii. 630); and Sir William Trussel was living c. 1300 (PPW). He was summoned to Parliament by writ as a baron 1293, as was William Trussel in 1341.

Thurlow, a branch of De Clare or De Brionne, whose arms, three chevrons, it bears. Robert de Clare, second son of Richard Fitz-Gilbert (descended from Richard I. of Normandy), obtained the barony of Baynard's Castle on the forfeiture of its owner (*See* BEAUMONT). He had: 1. Walter, ancestor of the Lords Fitz-Walter, who bore a fesse between two chevrons. 2. Hamon Peché, or Peccatum, ancestor of the barons of Brunne, who bore the arms of Fitz-Walter; 3. Simon; 4. Ralph Peché; 5. Robert Peché, Bishop of Ely. Simon Peché or Peccatum Fitz-Robert possessed estates in Suffolk and Essex 1130 (Rot. Pip.), including probably Trillawe, Suffolk, which had belonged to Richard Fitz-Gilbert, his ancestor, in 1086. He was Baron of Daventry by his father's gift (Dugdale), and had: 1. Robert Fitz-Simon, ancestor of the Fitz-Walters of Daventry, barons by writ 1292; 2. Gilbert Peché, who possessed estates in Suffolk, of which Trillawe being the chief, it gave name to the family. In 1199 he is mentioned as Gilbert de Trillawe (ROR. i. 229). His grandson

Gilbert Peché (brother of Richard Trillawe, living 1280) settled his son John in the lordship of Plechden, Essex, 1274 (Morant, ii. 569); and d. 1292, seized of Plechden and Trillawe (Inq. p. m.). John Peché, or de Trillawe, his son, had: 1. Gilbert Peché, who d. 1322 seized of Plechden; 2. John de Trillaw, or Thyrlow, from whom descended the Thurlows of Burnham, Norfolk, ancestors of Lord Chancellor Thurlow, and of the Lords Thurlow.

Thurn, for THORN.

Thurnham, for TURNHAM, a branch of the house of De Garlande, France. Robert de Turnham paid a fine to the Crown in Kent 1156 (Rot. Pip.), and Robert de Turnham held three fees in Kent 1165, and Michael de T. in Surrey (Lib. Niger). This Robert de Turnham (or his son of the same name) accompanied Richard I. to Palestine, and was in command of the fleet at Cyprus. Stephen de T., his brother, was Viscount of Wilts, and Seneschal of Anjou.

Thurston, or Turstan. *See* TUSTIN.

Thyne, for THYNNE.

Thynne, or Goyon, a branch of the Breton house of the barons of Roche-Goyon, Marquises of Lonray. William Goyon c. 1070 witnessed the charters of John and Gelduin de Dol to St. Florent, Saumur. Eudes or Hugh Goyon, his son, attested a charter of St. Michel 1075 (Des Bois). This Eudes Goyon, or his son Alan, came to England, and was provided for in Salop by Alan Fitz-Flaald, who also came from the same locality (*See* STUART). Alan Goyon held Upton, Salop, from Fitz-Alan in 1138 (Eyton, i. 140, 141). He had: 1.

Adam de Upton, living 1165, a tenant of Fitz-Alan, whose son, William de Upton, was living 1180; 2. John de Upton, who was father of Walter Fitz-John, who occurs in 1190. His son, William Fitz-Walter, in 1200 claimed land in Botesfield, or Botevile, Salop, against the Templars, by a writ of Mort d'ancestre, his mother having been an heiress, from whom he claimed (Eyton). He appears to have recovered this estate; for William and Gregory de Botesfield, his sons, are mentioned 1234–1255 as involved in disputes with the Templars of Botesfield (Stemmata Bottevilliana, 19). From this time the family of De Botfield, or Botevyle, is constantly mentioned in Salop, and bore barry of ten, the Goyons of Bretagne bearing barry of eight (Lobineau, Hist. Bret. ii. plates). The name was changed by popular use to 'Del Inne,' the name of the family mansion near Church Stretton; some branches, however, continuing to bear the name of Botfield. Hence the Thynnes, Marquises of Bath, and Barons Carteret.

Tibbalds, for THEOBALD.

Tibbatts, for TEBBUTT.

Tibbetts, for TEBBUTT.

Tibbitts, for TEBBUTT.

Tibbles, for TIBBALDS.

Tibbutt. *See* TEBBUTT.

Tibeaude, or Tibouto, a baronial name. Walter and John Tiboutot, Normandy 1180–95 (MRS). Thiboutot was in the Caux, and John de T. is mentioned 1107 (Des Bois). Hence descended the Tibetots, barons by writ 1307, and the Tiptofts, Earls of Worcester.

Tickell, or Tickhill, descended from a branch of the De Buislis,

Barons of Tickhill, York, t. William I. *See* BINGHAM.

Tickle, for TICKELL.

Tidd, for TADD.

Tigg. William Tike, Normandy 1198 (MRS). William Tig, Engl. c. 1272 (RH).

Tighe. *See* TYE.

Tiley, for TILLY.

Till, for THALE.

Tilleard. *See* TELLART.

Tiller. *See* TILLARD.

Tillett. *See* TULLETT.

Tillett, for TULLETT.

Tilley, for TILLY.

Tillie, for TILLY.

Tilling, for TELLING.

Tillotson. John Tillotson, Archbishop of Canterbury, was a scion of the Tillotsons, or Tilstons, of Tilston, Cheshire, which estate was the possession of the family of St. Pierre, from St. Pierre near Avranches. (*See* De Gerville, Anc. Chateaux.) Tilston was held as a fief from St. Pierre by the Tilston family, who from that circumstance, and from bearing the arms of St. Pierre (a bend), with the differences of a younger branch, appear to have been St. Pierres.

Tilly, a baronial name. William, William Fitz-John, Henry, Ralph, Dionysia, Robert de Tilly, and the Castle and Barony of Tilly, Normandy 1180–95 (MRS). Tilly was near Caen, of which the family were Castellans. (La Roque, Mais. Harcourt, ii. 1662, 1994, 1999.) Henry de Tilly held the Castle 1165 (Feod. Norm.). Ralph de T. held lands in Devon 1083 (Exon. Domesday). Haymon de Telleia occurs in Normandy 960 (Neustria Pia, 98). *See* WORDSWORTH.

Tillyard. *See* TILLARD.

Tillyer. *See* TILLARD.

Tilston. *See* TILLOTSON.

Timberlake, for Timberlain, or Tombelaine. *See* TAMBLIN.

Tirrel. Tustin Tirrel, Normandy 1198 (MRS).

Tippett, for TIPPETTS.

Tippetts, for TIBBETTS.

Tippitt. *See* TIPPETT.

Tiptaft, or Tibetot. (*See* TIBEAUDO.) The Castle of Thiboutot was between Fécamp and Havre, and this family long remained in Normandy. In 1165 Radulfus de Toboltot or Toboutot held a fief in Suffolk from De Clare (Lib. Niger). Robert de Tibetot witnessed a charter of Edward I. (Mon. i. 300); and in 1277 sat in Parliament as a baron, from whom descended the barons Tibetot. John de Tiptoft, of a younger branch, was summoned to Parliament by writ 1425, and was created Earl of Worcester 1448.

Tirebuck, for TARBUCK.

Tirrell. *See* TYRRELL.

Tison, for TYSON.

Tisoun, for Tesson, or TYSON.

Tite. Anketil Tiet, Normandy 1180–95 (MRS). Michael Titte, Engl. c. 1272 (RH).

Titt. *See* TITE.

Tissard. Richard and Robert Tesard, or Tesart, Normandy 1180–95 (MRS).

Tobin. *See* TOBYN.

Tobitt. *See* TEBBUTT.

Tobut. *See* TEBBUTT.

Tobutt, for TEBBUTT.

Toby, for TOBYN.

Tobyn, for ST. AUBYN (Lower).

Tod, for TADD.

Tod. Richard Tad, Normandy 1180–95 (MRS). Adam, Real Tod, Engl. c. 1272 (RH). Also a Celtic name.

Todd, for TOD.

Tofield, for Tavel. *See* TAWELL.

Toghill, for TAWELL.

Togwell, or TOKEVILLE. Hugh de Touqueville held a fief in 1165 in the bailifry of Lizieux, Normandy (Feod. Norm. Duchesne).

Toland. Alveredus Tolan, Normandy 1198 (MRS). Hence the infidel writer Toland.

Toler, or De Toulouse, a princely name. The Counts of Toulouse descended from Fulcoald, Count of Rodez 837, whose son Fridolind became Count of Toulouse 849 (L'Art de Vérif. les Dates), and was ancestor of that Sovereign house, whose services in the Crusades, and whose ruin in the Albigensian wars, occupy so important a place in history. A branch of this illustrious house, bearing the name and arms, settled in England at the Conquest (the arms were a cross fleury voided, commonly called the 'Cross of Toulouse'). Hugh de Toulouse obtained grants from Richard Fitz-Gilbert in Surrey. His grandson Peter de Thalews (Tolouse) held more than two fees there in 1165 from the house of De Clare (Lib. Niger). William de T. paid a fine in Northants 1189, and 1201 in Lancashire. The family becomes widely extended, under the names of Toulouse, Tolus, Tolous, Tollar, Towler, Toler, retaining however the arms of Tolouse. Henry Tolouse was Lord of Brookley, Hants, 1316 (PPW). The name occurs in Norfolk 16th cent. as Tollar and Toler (Blomefield), and from that county a branch migrated to Ireland, from which descended the eminent statesman and jurist John Toler, Lord Chief Justice and first Earl of Norbury.

420

Toll. Osbert Thol, Normandy 1180–95 (MRS).

Toll. *See* TULL.

Toller, for TOLER. Armorially identified.

Tollett. Osbert de Toleta, Normandy 1180 (MRS); Henry and Robert Tullet, Engl. c. 1272 (RH).

Tollitt. *See* TOLLETT.

Tolmie. Alan de Thelomeio, Normandy 1180–95 (MRS).

Tomalin, for Tombelaine. *See* TAMBLIN.

Tomblin, for TAMBLIN.

Tombling, for TOMBLIN.

Tomblins, for TOMBLIN.

Tomelin, for TOMBELAINE. *See* TAMBLIN.

Tomlin, for TAMBLIN.

Tomline. *See* TOMLIN.

Tomlins, for TOMLIN.

Tomlyn, for TOMLIN.

Tomson, or Thomaston, descended from Robert, Lord of Tomaston, Norfolk 1286, whose father William de Thomaston was living before 1250. The latter, as William de Monasteriis or de Moutiers, conveyed part of Thomaston to G. Crowe 1247 (Blomefield, Norfolk, ii. 366, 371). The descendants of the Thomastons bear the arms of De Moutiers, viz. a lion passant guardant, with slight differences. This was a branch of the Norman house of Moutiers or MUSTERS, of Notts.

Toner, or Tonerre. Milo was Count of Tonerre, France, c. 980, from whom descended the Counts of Tonerre (Anselme, iii. 200). Walter Tonitruum (De Tonerres) held lands 1083 in Dorset (Exon. Domesday); William Tonitruum in Norfolk, &c. 1130 (Rot. Pip.). Alured Tonare, of Dorset, occurs 1165, and William de Tonor, of Stafford (Lib. Niger).

Henry T. was M.P. for Dorset in 1297 (PPW).

Tonson. Radulphus Tunçon held lands from Philip Augustus, Normandy c. 1200 (Mem. Soc. Ant. Norm. v. 187).

Took, for TOOKE.

Tooke, or De Toques, from the Castle and Lordship of Touques, Normandy. The Sire de T. was present at Hastings 1066 (Wace, ii. 235). Jordan, Robert, Roger, and Henry de Touques came to England. Roger de T. occurs in Hants 1130 (Rot. Pip.); Humphrey in Derby, William in Derby, Roger in Dorset 1165 (Lib. Niger). Sir Walter Touk was of Notts and Derby c. 1300, and bore sable billetée or, a quarter ermine. Sir Robert Touk at the same time was of Cambridge, and bore barry of six. Reginald Thukes t. Stephen gave Hanworth to Gloucester Abbey (Mon. i. 116). This name appears as Tooke, Toke, &c.

Tooley. See TULLY.

Toomer. Osbert Toulemer, Tollemer, or Tolemer, Normandy 1180–95 (MRS).

Toppin. Robert, Ernald Topin, Normandy 1180–95 (MRS); Robert T. 1198 (Ib.); Richard Topin, Engl. c. 1272 (RH).

Topping. See TOPPIN.

Torr. Roger de Turre, Normandy 1180–95 (MRS); Richard and Roger de Turre 1198 (Ib.).

Torry, a baronial name. Henry and Richard de Tury, Turi, or Turri, Normandy 1180–95, and the Castle and Barony of Turry (MRS); Jordan and Simon de Turri, Engl. 1189 (Rot. Pip.).

Tory. See TORRY.

Tosar. See TIZZARD.

Tosh. William de Tosca, Nor-

mandy 1198 (MRS); Ralph le Tock, Engl. c. 1272 (RH).

Tossell. See TUSSELL.

Touray, for Towry, and TORRY.

Tourle. See TURLE.

Toussaint, from Toussaints, between Yvetot and Fécamp, Normandy. Roger de Omnibus Sanctis in 1165 held two fees in Devon (Lib. Niger). In 1194 a suit in Cambridge against Joscelin de Omnibus Sanctis was appointed to be decided by duel (RCR). Roger de O. SS. mentioned in Essex 1199 (Ibid.); Hugh de Omnibus SS., Devon, made a payment to the Crown 1205 (Hardy, Obl. et Fin. 283). The name failed in Devon t. Henry II. (Pole, Devon).

Tovell, for Tavel. See TAWELL.

Towell, for TAWELL.

Towill, for TOWELL.

Towle, for TOWELL.

Tower. See TURR.

Towers, or De Tours, descended from the Umfrevilles of Normandy, Barons of Prudhoe. Stephen de Tours occurs in Lincoln 1130, where the family were long of great consequence. See UMFREVILLE.

Towers, for TOWER.

Towersey, or Towersey, for Torcy. Robert de Torcy, and the fief and honour of Torcy, Normandy c. 1200.

Towill, for TOWELL.

Towle. See TULL.

Towler. See TOLER.

Towlers, armorially identified with TOLER.

Townley, a branch of the family of VENABLES (see Ormerod, Cheshire).

Townsend. See TOWNSHEND. The name included various families, and was local.

Townshend, or Baynard, descends from Osbert de Bellomont, son of

Geoffry Baynard (*see* MARSHAM, BEAUMONT), and father of Roscelin de B. and Alexander de Draiton. The latter had — 1. Hermer de Draiton, whose descendant Geoffry de Bellomont owned Taverham and Drayton t. Edward I.; 2. Baldric de Taverham, father of William Fitz-Baldric, named De Taverham or Ad Caput Villæ, who in 1200 divided his lands at Taverham with Geoffry de Bellomont, his brother (RCR. ii. 171). He was father of Thomas ad Caput Villæ or Townsend living t. Henry III., who bore the arms still used, which are derived from those of Baynard or Bellomont (a chevron). His son William Townshend was father of Thomas of Snoring Magna 1377, whose son, John Townshend, held part of a fee at Rainham from the honour of Clare. His son, Sir Roger, was seated at Rainham c. 1400 (Blomefield, vii. 141): hence the Marquises Townshend and Viscounts Sydney.

Townson. *See* TONSON.

Towrey. *See* TORRY.

Towse, for DOWSE.

Toy, for TYE.

Toye, for TYE.

Tozer. *See* TOSAR.

Tracey, for TRACY.

Tracy, a baronial name. William de Tracy, Normandy 1180–95 (MRS); Turgis, Oliver, Reginald, William de T. 1198 (Ib.). The Castle and Barony of Tracy were near Vire, Normandy. William de Tracy came to England 1066, and is mentioned by Wace as at the battle of Hastings (ii. 244). The family possessed two baronies in Devon 1165, and also estates in Gloucester and Normandy. (*See* Dugdale, Banks.) The Viscounts Tracy were a branch.

Trafford, or De Villiers, descended from Paganus de Villars, of Normandy, Baron of Warrington, who t. Henry I. enfeoffed Alan de Villiers, his son, in Trafford, which lordship was held by Robert de Villers in the 13th cent. (Testa). In the same century Henry de Trafford, evidently a younger son, held lands in thanage and from the family of De Charlton, Lancashire (Ibid.): hence the Baronets Trafford, for whom an Anglo-Saxon descent has been imagined. *See* VILLIERS.

Traggett, for Tregot or Tregots, a baronial name. Robert de Tregots or Tregoz and the fief of T., Normandy 1180–95 (MRS). Tregoz was a castle near St. Lo, in the Cotentin. The Lord of T. is mentioned by Wace 1066. The family became seated in Hereford at the Conquest (Testa). Its name was frequently written Tregot: hence the Barons Tregoz, by writ 1260.

Traine. Petrus Traine, Normandy 1180 (MRS); William T. 1198 (Ib.); Simon Trane, Engl. c. 1272 (RH).

Travers, or De Trevieres, from Trevieres, near Bayeux and Caen. Robert de Travers or Estrevers t. Will. I. m. a daughter of Ranulph Meschin, sister of Ranulph, Viscount of Bayeux, Earl of Chester. He had issue only a dau., his heir, but collaterals existed, of whom in 1165 was Ralph Travers, who held from the See of Worcester, while Bertram and Paganus Travers held from Evesham Abbey, and Robert T. from Henry Lupel in Somerset (Lib. Niger). The name continued in Normandy, where Ranulph de Clinchamp after 1138 assumed the name of Travers.

Of this family was the celebrated *Waiter* Puritan preacher Robert Travers t. Elizabeth.

Traverse, for TRAVERS.

Traves, for TRAVERS.

Travis, for TRAVERS.

Trawin, for TRONE. Girard Trone and Richard T., Normandy 1180-98 (MRS); John de Tron, Engl. c. 1272 (RH).

Trayler. Richard Treveler, Normandy 1180-95 (MRS).

Treacy, for TRACY.

Trebeck. *See* Terbuck, or TARBUCK.

Treble. Richard Trepel, Normandy 1180-95 (MRS); Robert Tripel, Engl. c. 1272 (RH).

Tree, for TRY.

Trego. *See* TRAGGETT.

Trelawney. The origin of Cornish families is a matter of difficulty, from the deficiency of records. However, in 1325 William de Trelouny was M.P. for Launceston (PPW). In the preceding century Reginald Walensis and Henry de Tredraet held three fees in Tredameton, Tredraet, and Trelowyn (Trelawney) from the Earl of Cornwall (*see* Testa, p. 201). The name of Trelawney was not then borne. We find the name of Wallensis before this in Cornwall. Richard W. occurs there 1202 (Rot. Canc.). On examining the fiefs of the Earl of Cornwall in 1165 only two cases of persons occur holding three fiefs each, viz. Henry de Pomeraye, and Hoel and Jordan joint tenants (Lib. Nig.). It will be observed that the three fees were held from the Earl of Cornwall in the 13th cent. by joint tenants also. The name Hoel indicates a Welsh origin, which also connects it with the name 'Wallensis.' It

is presumed that this family descends from Hamelin de Balaon, son of Dru de Balaon, Baron of Abergavenny, who had vast grants in Cornwall. He had a brother Wynebald (Mon. Angl. i. 590), who appears to have obtained either from his brother or the earl the three fees of Trehampton, Tredrea, and Trelawney, and coming from Wales would be styled 'Wallensis.' His sons would be—Roger de Trehampton (seated in Lincoln), Hoel of Trelawney, and Jordan of Tredrea. In t. Richard I. Richard Wallensis (probably son of Hoel) paid scutage for two fees in Cornwall (Trehampton and Trelawney ?), and Ralph de Treat or Tredraet for one (Carew, Survey, 45). The Castle of Balaon, Normandy, was garrisoned by William Rufus 1088 (Ord. Vitalis). (*See* Dugdale and Banks.) The Hamelin who held Treloan 1086 is, according to Lysons (Cornwall), of unknown origin.

Treminet, from Tremenech, Bretagne. William de Tribus Minetis witness to a charter of Alan, Earl of Cornwall and Richmond 1140 (Mon. ii. 902). The family long remained in Devon and Cornwall.

Tremlett, for TREMINET.

Trenchard. Richard Trenchart, Normandy 1198 (MRS); Pain Trenchard (Rot. Pip.) occurs in Hants 1130, and was ancestor of the Trenchards of Dorset (Wiffen, Hist. Russell, i. 172, 3).

Trevallion. *See* TREVELYAN.

Trevers. *See* TRAVERS.

Treves. *See* TREVERS.

Trevillion. *See* TREVELYAN.

Trew, from Trou, Normandy. Hugh and Richard Troue, 1198 (MRS); Gerard de la Truwe, Engl. c. 1272 (RH).

Trevelyan. The name of this family first occurs in the 13th cent. In 1273 Felicia, wife of William de Bodrugan, confirmed to (her son) Andrew, Trevelyan and Cumi, and to Nicholas de Trevelyan her son, Polran. She had been the wife of Nicholas de Trevelyan deceased (Collins, Baronetage). Trevelien was 1086 part of the great barony held by Offels from the Earl of Cornwall. This barony was granted t. Henry II. to Richard de Lucy. Several new families were enfeoffed by him, as Fitz-Walter, Fitz-William, &c. From the arms borne by the family (three bars wavy, in chief a demi-horse issant) it seems not improbable that it was a branch of Tregoz, introduced by Richard de Lucy, which family certainly was settled in Cornwall, and bore three bars, a lion passant in chief.

Trickett. This family came to England 1066. Radulphus Trichet paid a fine 1130 for his father's land in Middlesex (Rot. Pip.). In 13th cent. Ida Triket held Brembeley, Middlesex, by service of holding a towel for the king's hands at the Coronation (Testa).

Trill, for TERRILL.

Triquet. See TRICKETT.

Tristin, or TRISTRAM.

Tristram. Reginald Tristan had a grant of lands Normandy from Philip Augustus, and John Tristan was chamberlain to the king. Henry and Robert Tristrem, Engl. c. 1272 (RH).

Trivass, for TREVERS.

Troll. William Troel, Normandy 1180–95 (MRS); N. Trolle, Engl. c. 1272 (RH).

Trorey, for DRURY.

Trower. Hubert, Geoffry Turgis,

424

Hugh de Troarz or Troarn, Normandy 1180–95 (MRS). There was an abbey at Troarn, Normandy.

Trowell. See TRUELL.

Troy, for TRY.

Truell. See DRUELL.

Trudgett, for TRAGGETT.

Trustrum, for TRISTRAM.

Try. John de Tria, Ralph de Triée, Normandy 1180–95 (MRS). The Lords of Trie in the Vexin were a branch of the house of Chaumont, which was of high rank. An account is found in La Roque (Maison de Harcourt, i. 130).

Trye. See TRY.

Tuch. Richard Toka or Tocha, Normandy 1180–95 (MRS); Adam Tuche, Engl. c. 1272 (RH).

Tuck, for TOOKE.

Tuckett, or Touchet, a baronial name from Touchet, near Mortaine, Normandy. In 1082 Ursinus de T. granted lands to the Church of St. William, Mortaine (Gerville, Anc. Chateaux). The name still remains in Normandy. (See Mem. Soc. Ant. Norm. xii. 23.) Joceline T. was seated in Cheshire t. William I., and was father of Henry, father of Henry to whom Ralph Gernons, Earl of Chester, gave Tatenhall (Ormerod, ii. 393). Hence the Touchets, Lords Audley, Earls of Castlehaven.

Tuckfield. See TUCKWELL.

Tuckwell, for TOKEVILLE. Hugh de Tokevilla, Normandy 1180 (MRS); Mainer, Nicholas, Robert de T. 1198.

Tudge, for TUCH.

Tuely. Robert Tuelou, Normandy 1180–95 (MRS); Richard le Tulye, Engl. c. 1272 (RH).

Tuer, for Tour, or TORR.

Tuffield, for TOVILLE. Wiard de Toville, Normandy 1180 - 95 (MRS).

Tuffil, for TUFFIELD.

Tuffnell. Robert Tafernel, Normandy 1180–95 (MRS); Adam and John Taunfrenel, Engl. c. 1272 (RH), abbreviated to Tuffnell.

Tugwell. *See* TUCKWELL.

Tuit, a baronial name, from Tuit, Normandy. Ranulph de Tuit Bernard, Normandy 1180–95 (MRS); Radulphus de Tuit 1198 (Ib.). The name occurs 1076 in the foundation charter of Belvoir Abbey, amongst the feudal tenants of Berenger de Toeny (Mon. Angl.). Hugh de Tuit held one fief in Norfolk 1165, and William de T. estates in the Viscounty of Rouen. Richard Tuit obtained the Barony of Moyashull, Ireland, 1172. His descendant sat in parliament as a baron 1374, and hence derive the Baronets Tuite.

Tuke, for TOOK.

Tull, probably from Tull-Noelant, Normandy (MRS); Nicholas Tolle, Joanna Toul, Engl. c. 1272 (RH).

Tullett. *See* TOLLETT.

Tullett, for TOLLETT.

Tulley. *See* TULLY.

Tully. *See* TULLY.

Tunny, Tony, or Toeni. *See* LINDSAY.

Tur. *See* TORR.

Turbefield, for TURBEVILLE.

Turberville. *See* TURBEVILLE.

Turbyfield, for TURBEVILLE.

Turbeville, or Troubleville. William de Troublevilla, Normandy 1180–95 (MRS). Richard and Ralph de T. were of Normandy t. John (Mem. Soc. Ant. Norm. v. 122). Turbeville was near Pont-Audemer. Payne de T. witnessed the foundation charter of Neath Abbey t.

Henry I. Hence the Turbervilles of Glamorgan and Brecon. William de T. was of Dorset 1130, and in 1165 there were branches in Norfolk, York, Dorset, and Wilts.

Turck. *See* TURK.

Turk, or Turks. Durandus Turkeis, Normandy 1198 (MRS); John, Richard Turgis, Engl. c. 1272 (RH).

Turle, for TURRELL.

Turnbull, for Tornebu, or Turnebu, a baronial name. Simon, Thomas, Amauri de Turnebu, Normandy 1180–95 (MRS). The heir of Amauri de Turnebu is mentioned in Hants 1202 (Rot. Canc.). Tournebu was a barony near Falaise. William de Turnebu accompanied the Conqueror 1066 (MSAN, 1867, p. 181, &c.). King John granted to Geoffry de Neville, Chereberge, Dorset, which had belonged to Richard Tornebue (Testa, 163). The Barony of Tornebu held by Thomas de T. 1165 consisted of twenty fees (Feod. Norm. ap. Duchesne).

Turnebull. *See* TURNBULL.

Turnell. Roger Tornel, Normandy 1180–95 (MRS).

Turner. In some cases, perhaps, from the ville of Torneor, Normandy: usually, however, from Le Turnur, an employment which included Norman and other families.

Turney, for TOURNAY.

Turnham. Gilbert, Lord of Garlande, in Brie, t. William I., had issue Ansel de Garlande, Seneschal of France 1108, and Gilbert de Garlande, Butler of France; the latter of whom had issue Guy, who purchased Turnham, and went to Palestine in 1147 (Des Bois). He had issue Robert de Turnham, of Kent,

1156, 1165, and Michael de T., of Surrey, 1165. Stephen de Turnham was a Baron t. Henry II. and Richard I., and he is mentioned in Normandy 1180–95 (MRS). Stephen de T. held in Salop 13th cent. (Testa).

Turney, or Tournay. Robert de Tornaio or Torney, Alberic, Gervase, Ralph, and Robert de Tornai, Normandy 1180–98 (MRS). Tornai was in Normandy. Walter de Torni held it 1165 by Castle-guard (Feod. Norm.). Goisfrid de Tornai held a fief in Lincoln 1086 (Domesd.). William de T. was Viscount of Lincoln before 1130 (Rot. Pip.). The name is frequently mentioned thenceforth in England.

Turnley. Richard Tornelvie, Normandy 1180–95 (MRS).

Turpin, or Torpin. William Torpin, Normandy 1180–95, and the fief of Turpin au Bois (MRS); William T. and the Estate of T., 1198 (Ib.); Stephen Turpin, of Engl., 1194–1200 (RCR); Walter T., of Dorset, 1202; William, of Gloucester and Oxford, 1282 (Rot. Canc.).

Turrall. See TURRELL.

Turrell. Radulphus Turel, Normandy (MSAN, v. 196); Peter and Bernard Torel, Normandy 1180–95 (MRS); John, Robert, Roger T., 1198 (Ib.). The family of Torell or Torrell was seated in Essex.

Turrill. See TURRELL.

Tuson. See TEWSON.

Tussell. See TASSELL.

Tustian, for Tustain or TUSTIN.

Tustin. Geoffry, Robert, Nigel, Unfrid Fitz-Tustin, Normandy 1180–95 (MRS); Robert and Roger Tustin, 1198 (Ib.); Robert Thurstein, Engl. c. 1272 (RH).

426

Tutin, for TUSTIN.

Tutt, for Tot. William, John, Hugh, Robert de Tot, and the fief of T., Normandy 1180–95 (MRS); Matilda Tut, Engl. c. 1272 (RH).

Tween, for TWINE.

Twin. See TWINE.

Twine. William Tuine, Normandy 1180–95 (MRS); Nicholas, Richard Twin, Engl. c. 1272 (RH).

Twinn, for TWINE.

Twiss, for TWIST.

Twist, the English form of Tortus or Torto. Roger Tortus or De Torto, Robert and Richer, Normandy 1180–95 (MRS). See TARTE.

Twitchett, for TUCHETT.

Twite, for TUITE.

Twoart, for Tort, or TARTE.

Twort, for Tort, or TARTE.

Tyars, for TYAS.

Tye. See THIES.

Tyer, or TYERS. Walter Tier or Tiers, and William, Normandy 1180–95 (MRS).

Tyers. See TYER.

Tyas, or Tyes, a baronial name. Terric, Theodorus, Richard Teutonicus or Tyes, Normandy, t. John (MSAN). See THIES.

Tyes. See THIES.

Tylee. See TILLY.

Tyler, from the fief and Castle of Tilers or Tillers, Normandy. Gialebert de Teliares and Gillo, 1180–98 (MRS); Ralph de Tilere, Engl. c. 1272 (RH).

Tyliard, for Teillart, or Tilleard.

Tylor. See TYLER.

Tyley. Albercia and Robert de Tylia or Tilia, Normandy, t. Hen. II. (MSAN, v. 130); John Tille, Engl. c. 1272 (RH).

Tynte, for TENT.

Tyrer. Stephen, Robert Terrer or Terrier, Normandy 1180–95 (MRS).

Tyres, for TYERS.

Tyrrell, a baronial family. William and Baldwin Tirel, or Tirell, Normandy 1180–95 (MRS), and the fiefs of Tirel; also William, Roger, Ralph Tyrel, 1198 (Ib.). Walter T. occurs in a charter of Henry I. to Dive Abbey, Normandy, 1124 (Gall. Christ. xi. 159). Walter Tirel, Castellan of Pontoise and Lord of Poix, was living in the Vexin 1091. The death of Rufus was attributed to him (Forester's Ordericus, iii. 263, 264). Walter Tiralde, 1086, was of Essex, whence the Tyrrells of Essex, Baronets. Hugh Tyrrel was granted Castle Knock, Ireland, 1172, of which his family long remained barons.

Tysall, for Tosell. *See* TASSELL.

Tyser. *See* TIZZARD.

Tyson, or Tisson, a baronial name. The Tessons were commonly said to have possessed a third of Normandy. The name of this family was originally Ticio, and it is stated to have been seated in the vicinity of Angoulême (whence its Gothic origin may be inferred), and to have been distinguished in war against the Saracens, c. 725 (Des Bois, Art. Achard). The Tessons were afterwards seated in Anjou (Vaultrier, apud Mem. Soc. Ant. Norm. x. 78). Radulphus Taxo, of Angers, in 1028 witnessed a charter regarding the Abbey of Coulombs (Gall. Christ. viii. 297, Instr.). Ralph T. led 120 knights of his barony to the aid of Duke William at the battle of Val des Dunes, 1047, and was created Viscount of the Cotentin. He founded the Abbey of Fontenay, near Caen; and from him descended the powerful family of Tesson in Normandy. Gilbert Tyson or Tesson, his brother, obtained the Barony of Alnwick from Edward the Confessor, and fell at the battle of Hastings. William, his son, had a dau. who m. Ivo de Vesci. Gilbert Tyson, another son, held great estates in York, Lincoln, and Notts 1086 (Domesd.). Adam Tyson granted lands in Notts to the Hospitallers, t. Rich. I. (Mon. ii.), and to Thurgarton Priory (Ib. 93). In the 13th cent. Warin Fitzgerold held lands late the fee of Ralph Tesun (Testa, 77). This family appears also to have been the origin of those of PERCY, MARMION, and BYRON.

Tyte. *See* TITE.

U

Udale. *See* UDALL.

Udall, or Uvedale. Ansgot de Ouvedale, Normandy 1180–95 (MRS); Walder de Hudal, 1198 (Ib.). Peter de Uvedale was a baron by writ 1331.

Udell, for UDALL.

Uffell, for OFFELL.

Ullman, for ALLMAN.

Umfrewill, for Umfreville, a Norman baronial name. The original seat was at Amfreville, in the viscounty of Evreux, which was held by the service of two knights (Feod. Norm. Duchesne). This family came to England at the Conquest, and Robert de Umfreville received from the Conqueror a grant of the baronies of Redesdale and Prudhoe, Northumberland, 1076 (Hodgson, Northumb. i. II. 6). From him descended the De Umfrevilles, Barons of Prudhoe, of whom Robert occurs 1110 as witness to the foundation of Kelso Abbey (Kelso Chartular. Ed. Bannatyne), and Odonel was grandfather of Richard de Umfreville of Northumberland 1161–1182 (Hodgson). Gilbert de U., Baron of Prudhoe in 1243, m. the dau. of Malcolm, Earl of Angus, and his son was Earl of Angus 1296, and as such sat in the English Parliament. Robert de Umfraville had witnessed the foundation charter of Neath Abbey, Glamorgan, t. Henry I. (Mon. i. 719), and from him descended a branch seated in that county. His descendant Henry de Humfreville held five knights' fees of the honour of Gloucester 1201 (Hardy, Obl. et Fin. 134). A branch also remained in Normandy, descended from Walter de Umfreville, who was at the battle of Gisors 1097 (Ord. Vitalis, 767). Robert de U. received at the Con-

quest a grant of the barony of Redesdale, Northumberland, and had, 1. Robert; 2. Gilbert, who joined in the Conquest of Glamorgan 1091; 3. Odonel, Baron of Redesdale and Prudhoe. Hence the Barons Umfreville, Earls of Angus.

Upton, Adam and Barnard de Upton held U. 13th cent. from the Honour of Totness (Testa). They were probably descended from Ralph Fitz-Stephen, t. Henry II., and from the arms appear to have been a branch of De la Folie of Normandy, seated in Wilts. *See* FOLEY. Hence the Viscounts Templetown.

Urch, for ARCH.

Ure, for EURE.

Usher, or Neville. James U. the celebrated Archbishop of Armagh, was a son of A. Usher, one of the six clerks in Chancery, descended from a branch of the Norman family of De Neville, which assumed the name of Le Uschere or Le Huissier, from the office of Ostiarius granted to them by King John. Of this family was the gallant Admiral Sir Thomas Usher.

V

Vacher. William and Gilbert Vacarius, Normandy 1180–95 (MRS); Clement, Hugh, John Vaccarius, Engl. c. 1272 (RH).

Vade. *See* WADE.

Vail. *See* VEAL.

Vaile. *See* VEAL.

Vaisey. *See* VAIZEY.

Vaizey. Philip, Eudo, Hugo de Vaaceio, or Waaceio, Normandy, 1180–95. Juliana de Vaacy held 5

fees in barony, Normandy 1165 (Duchesne, Feod. Norm.). Guitbert de Guaceio is mentioned in Normandy c. 960 (Neustria Pia, 93).

Valantine. *See* VALENTINE.

Vale, a baronial name. Roger de la Vale, Normandy 1180 (MRS); Hugh de la Val, Engl. c. 1272. In 1065 John de Laval witnessed a charter in Normandy. Hugh de Laval occurs in York t. Henry I.

(Mon. ii. 34); Wido, t. Henry II. (ii. 554); and Gilbert 1165. The latter was a baron in Northumberland (Lib. Niger).

Valder. Geoffry Valdare, Hugh de Valdore, Normandy 1180–95 (MRS).

Valens, for Valence. *See* VALLANCE.

Valery, for St. Valery, a baronial name, from St. Valery, Normandy. Gilbert, Advocate or Protector of St. Valery, c. 990, m. a dau. of Richard Duke of Normandy, by whom he had Bernard, father of Walter de St. Valery, and Richard de Hugleville (who supported Duke William against the rebellion of William of Arques, 1053). Walter de St. Valery had extensive grants in England t. William I. The family remained in Berks and Hants 13th cent. (PPW).

Valentine. William Valentinus of Normandy, t. Philip Augustus (MSAN, v. 172). John and Henry Valentin, Engl. c. 1272 (RH). Hence probably the names Ballantine and Bannatyne.

Valentiny, for VALENTINE.

Vales, for VALE.

Vallance, from Valence, Normandy. William and Richard de V. and the fief of Valence, Normandy 1180–95 (MRS); Richard de Valencie 1198 (Ib.). William de Balance granted lands to Bordesley Abbey, Worcester, confirmed by Richard I. 1189 (Mon. i. 804). A land e Valence was a Baron in Bucks 1165 (Rot. Pip.). This was a Norman family, different from that of Valence Earl of Pembroke; and appears in Battle Abbey Roll. Its insertion there has been supposed to determine the interpolated character

of that document, but the name does not there bear any relation to the Valences Earls of Pembroke, who came to England in the thirteenth century.

Vallancey. William de Walencio, Normandy 1198 (MRS). *See* VALLANCE. General Vallancey, an able writer on Irish history.

Vallentin, for VALENTINE.

Vallentine, for VALENTINE.

Valler. The fief of Valeres, Normandy, was held by John of Gisors, t. Philip-Augustus. Geoffry de Valier, Herbert Waler, Normandy 1180–1200 (MRS). Roger le Walur 1189, of Norfolk (Rot. Pip.). *See* WALLER.

Valles, for VALLIS.

Vallis. William de Valz, Normandy 1180 (MRS); Sibil de Valeise, Engl. c. 1272 (RH).

Vallings, for VALOGNE.

Valogne, a baronial name, from Valognes, in the Cotentin, Normandy. Peter de V., with his brothers, came to England 1066, and 1086 held 41 lordships in barony in the Eastern Counties. Walter de V. occurs t. Rufus (Raine, North Durham, App. 2). The family became widely spread in England, Scotland, and Ireland.

Vance, or Vans, a form of VAUX.

Vanier. *See* VANNER.

Vann. *See* VENN.

Vanner. Richard Vanier, Robert de Vanario, Normandy 1180 (MRS); Walter le Vanner, Engl. c. 1272 (RH).

Vant, for FAUNT.

Varden. *See* VARDON.

Vardon. Durand Vardon, Normandy 1198 (MRS), armorially identified with VERDON.

Varley. Robert de Verlie, Normandy 1180–95 (MRS). Robert

de Verli held in Norfolk 1086;
Torald de V. gave lands to Salop
Abbey, c. 1100 (Mon. i. 378). In
1086 Hugh and William de V. held
in Essex and York.

Varnell, for Verneuil. *See* VER-
NALL.

Varney, or Verney. Wigen de
Verigny, or De Verincio, and Walter
de V. Normandy 1180–95 (MRS);
also in 1198 (Ib.).

Varty, for FERTÉ. *See* BROWNE.

Varville, for Vireville, from that
place in Normandy. Walter de
Waraville, Normandy 1180–95
(MRS); Baldwin de Verevale,
Kent, 13th cent. (Testa).

Vasey, for VESEY.

Vass, for Wasse, or WACE.

Vasser, an abbreviation of VA-
VASOUR.

Vassie. *See* VAIZEY.

Vastie, or Vestie. Walter Vesdie,
John V., Normandy 1180–95 (MRS).
Robert de Vesduit, Engl. c. 1272
(RH).

Vaters, for WATERS.

Vaus. *See* VAUX.

Vause. *See* VAUX.

Vaux, a Norman and baronial
name. Robert de Vallibus, Ralph,
William, Stephen, Richard de V.,
William de Vals, Normandy 1180–
95 (MRS). The Castle of Vaux, or
de Vallibus, is mentioned by Ordericus Vitalis (775). In 1080 Robert
de Vals, or Vaux, gave his tithes to
St. Evroult (Ib. 576). Robert held
fiefs 1086 in the Eastern Counties,
and by gift of Ranulph Meschin,
Dalston, Cumberland (Mon. i. 400).
Hubert de V., his brother, by gift of
the same, held Gillesland, from
whom descended the Lords Vaux of
G. Another brother, Aitard de V.,

430

held in Norfolk in 1086; and
Ranulph de Vaux in Cumberland.

Vavasour. John, Ralph, Richard,
Peter, Geoffry, William Vavassor,
Normandy 1180–95. Alexander,
Gervase, Richard, Robert, Walter,
William, 1198 (Ib.). Of these
Robert occurs in Cambridge, Lin-
coln, and Notts; William in York
and the North. This family has
always remained in Yorkshire.
William V. occurs in York 1165
as a considerable landholder (Lib.
Niger).

Vavasseur, for VAVASOUR.

Vavasor. *See* VAVASOUR.

Vawdrey, or Vaudré. Geoffry Val-
daré, or Vaudaré, Normandy 1180–
95 (MRS). Richard de Valdairie,
or Vaudairie, 1198 (Ib.). Robert de
Valdari, of Hunts 1154 (Rot. Pip.).

Vaxey. *See* VAIZEY.

Veal, a Norman and baronial
name. Peter de Vetula, Normandy
1180–95 (MRS). Robert de Vetula
1198 (Ib.). Robert Viel (Ib.).
Richard, William Viel, Engl. 1189
(Rot. Pip.). Richard, Roger de
Vetula 1202 (Rot. Canc.). The
family was formerly of great consequence, and Peter le Veel or de
Veel was summoned by writ 1341
as a baron.

Veale. *See* VEAL.

Vear. *See* VERR.

Veare. *See* VERR.

Vears, for VEAR.

Veary. Ranulph de Viry had a
grant in Normandy from King John
(MSAN, v. 121). Drogo de Virrie
1198 (MRS). John Viry, Engl. c.
1272 (RH).

Venable, for VENABLES.

Venables, a baronial name, from
Venables, near Evreux, Normandy.

The family does not appear under this name in Normandy, its proper name being le Venour, or Venator. Arnulph, Gialebert, Gaufridus, Hugh, Richard Venator, Normandy 1180-95 (MRS). Richard V. 1198 (Ib.). Gialebert Venator, or De Venables, held the barony of Kinderton, Cheshire, 1086, from whom descended the V.s, barons of Kinderton, and many other families. *See* LEIGH, TOWNELEY. *See* also GROS-VENOR.

Vener, or le Venur. *See* VEN-ABLES.

Veness, for Venus, or De Venoix. William Marescallus de Venoix, or Venoia, held from Philip Augustus in Normandy (MSAN, v. 176). *See* HASTINGS. Robert de Venuiz occurs in Wilts 1130. Leonard de V. held a barony in Essex 1165 (Lib. Niger).

Venn. John de Vein, Normandy 1198. Geoffry de Venis (Ib.). Rualen de Vein 1180-95 (Ib.). Ralph and Thomas de Vein, Engl. c. 1198 (RCR).

Vennell. *See* FENNELL.

Venner. *See* VANNER.

Ventem, for Vendome. *See* FINCH.

Venter, for Venator. *See* VEN-ABLES.

Venters. Ralph Ventras, or Vintras, Normandy 1180-95 (MRS). Ralph de Vintyr, Engl. c. 1272 (RH).

Ventham, for Vendome. *See* VENTOM.

Ventris, or Ventras. *See* VEN-TERS.

Venus. *See* VENESS.

Verden, for VERDON.

Verdin, for VERDON.

Vercoe. *See* VIRGO.

Verden, or De Verdun, a Norman baronial name. Robert, and Robin, Ralph, Thomas, Ranulph, Richard de Verdun, Normandy 1180-95 (MRS). Thomas, Robert de Verdon 1198 (Ib.). Verdun was near Avranches. Bertram de V. came to England 1066, and 1086 held as a baron in Bucks (Domesd.). In 1165 Bertram and Walter de V. held baronies in Stafford and Oxford. Hence the Barons de V. by writ 1295, 1332.

Vere, a Norman baronial name. Henry de Ver, Normandy 1180-95 (MRS). The name is derived from Ver, near Bayeux and Caen. Ver was part of the ducal demesne 1026, when it was included in the dowry of the duchess Judith. It was afterwards granted to this family, of whom Alberic de Ver occurs 1058 (Gall. Christ. xi. 108). He had issue: 1. Alberic de Ver, Chamberlain, a baron 1086, ancestor of the Earls of Oxford (*See* Dugdale); 2. Humphry Fitz-Alberic, a baron in Norfolk and Suffolk 1086, ancestor probably of the Barons Hunting-field; 3. Erneis de Ver, of Holdernesse and Lincoln, ancestor of the families of De Ver, Gousell, and THOROLD. *See* MANDEVILLE.

Verey. *See* VRARY.

Verge, or Vierge, a foreign name, of which the Latin form VIRGO remains also, but which has not been identified.

Verinder, or Warrender—perhaps a form of Warenger. N. Warenger, Normandy 1180-95 (MRS). Henry Varencer, or le Warencer, Engl. c. 1272 (RH). Hence the baronets Warrender.

Verity, for Feritate, or Ferté. *See* BROWNE.

Vernall, for Vernoil or Verneuil.

Tustin de Vernol, Normandy 1180 (MRS). Verneuil was near Evreux. King John confirmed to Nun-Appleton Priory, York, the gift of Henry Fitz-Henry de Vernoil (Mon. i. 909). Henry de Vernoil was one of the 'fideles' and principal men of Ireland 1301 (PPW).

Verney. Ranulph, and Roger de Vernai, and the Forest of Vernai, Normandy 1180–95 (MRS). Philippus Vernei 1195 (Ib.). Vernai was near Bayeux, Normandy. Gerelinus de V. c. 1080 granted lands to St. Peter Conches (Gall. Christ. xi. 132, Instr.); and Ralph de V. about the same time held, jointly with Ralph de Toeni, lands at Bois-Raillate (Ibid.). Walter de V. occurs in Cambridge 1158, Richard de V. in Stafford t. Richard I. Hence the Earls of Fermanagh, and Lords Willoughby de Broke.

Vernham, for VERNUM.

Vernon, a Norman baronial name. William, Richard, Gervin, Ralph, de Vernon, Normandy 1180–95 (MRS). Roger was Baron of Vernon c. 1030, about which time his dau. Blithildis was married. She in 1082 granted to Trinity, Caen, the lands at Vernon given to her by her father Roger. The grant was made with consent of William, her nephew, then Lord of Vernon (Gall. Christ. xi. 70, Instr.). This William recovered Vernon (which had been granted to Count Guy of Burgundy); and from him descended the Barons of Vernon, who held sixty-one knights' fees in barony; and of whom William de V. founded the Collegiate Church at Vernon in 1160 (Gall. Christ. xi. 583). William I. had several brothers who came to England 1066, viz., 1. Richard; 2.

Walter of Cheshire 1086, d. s. p.; 3. Alured of Suffolk, living 1086. Richard held sixteen lordships in barony in Cheshire 1086, and is said to have been heir of his brother Walter. Hugh, his son, had Walter, father of Warin, father of Richard, barons of Shipbroke. The latter had: 1. Warin, ancestor of the Vernons, barons and earls of Shipbroke; 2. William, Chief Justice of Chester, ancestor of the Vernons of Haddon, and of the Lords Vernon.

Vernum, for VERNON.

Vero. Simon Verot, Normandy 1180–95 (MRS).

Verral, for VERRALL.

Verrall. Richard and Baldwin Verol, Normandy 1180 (MRS).

Verralls. *See* VERRALL.

Verrell. *See* VERRALL.

Verrey. *See* VEREY.

Verrier, for FERRIER.

Verrill, for VERRELL.

Verrinder. *See* VERINDER.

Verry, for VEREY.

Versey, for Farsi, or FURSE.

Vertue. *See* VIRTUE.

Very. *See* VEREY.

Vesey, or De Vesci, a baronial name. The elder branch of the family of De Burgh. Serlo de Pembroke, or de Burgh, who appears to have been one of those who accompanied Arnulph de Montgomery to the conquest of Pembroke c. 1090, was high in favour with Henry I., and held from him Burgh and Knardesburgh, Yorkshire (Rot. Pip. 31 Hen. I.; Mon. i. 743). He had a son, Osbert, who was d. before 1130 (Rot. Pip.), when Eustace, son of John, brother of Serlo, was constituted his heir. Osbert, his nephew, had been justiciary with him in York before 1130 (Rot. Pip.). He was probably ancestor of the Lords Pons, or Poyntz, of Gloucester. It appears that Serlo and John his brother, and a third brother (the father of Osbert), were sons of Osbert Fitz-Pons, or De Pons, who is mentioned t. William I. *See* CLIFFORD.

Eustace Fitz-John above mentioned m. the heiress of Vesci, and acquired with her the barony of Alnwick. His son assumed the name of Vesci. It is needless to state the details of the history of this family, which appear in Dugdale and Banks. On the extinction of the direct male line 1295, the next heir male was descended from William de Vesci, brother of Eustace II. and of Warin (whose descendant in the female line, John de Aton, inherited the estates). William paid a fine 1199 in Northumberland (Hodgson, iii., iii., 65); and occurs again there in 1200 (Ib. 74). In 1348 Alicia was widow of William de Vesci (Ib. i., iii., 76). In 1340 Robert Vesey occurs (Ib. iii., ii., 316); and in 1421 Agnes Vescy (iii., ii. 316). We next find the family in Durham; John Veysey being of Coniscliffe 1436, where the family bore the arms of De Vesci (Surtees, iii. 379). Another branch was of Newlands, Durham, c. 1500, from which descend the Viscounts de Vesci (Durham Visit. 1615).

Vesper. *See* VOSPER.

Vessel, or Vassall. Robert de Wacellis, Roger Wasel, Normandy 1180–95 (MRS). Stephen Vassel, Engl. c. 1272 (RH).

Vessey. *See* VESEY.

Vezard. *See* FESSART.

Vezey, for VESEY.

Vial, or Vyell. *See* VEAL.

Vialls, or De Vielles, from Vielles,

Normandy. Humphrey de Vetulis, or Vielles, 11th cent., ancestor of the house of Beaumont, Earls of Leicester and Mellent. This was probably a younger branch.

Vian. Tustin and William de Viana, Normandy 1198 (MRS). The Umfrevilles were Lords of Tours and Vian, Normandy, of whom this was probably a branch.

Vicarey. *See* VICARY.

Vicars. *See* VICKERS.

Vicary. William de la Vacherie, Normandy, was granted the estate of his uncle William de la V. in Normandy by King John (MSAN, v. 115). Richard de Vickery, Engl. c. 1272 (RH).

Vick, from the fief of Vic, Normandy (MRS). Robert de Vico, Engl. c. 1272 (RH).

Vickers, or Vicker, for Vaccar. *See* VACHER.

Vickery. *See* VICARY.

Vickress. *See* VICKERS.

Victor, or St. Victor, a Norman baronial name, the family being a branch of Mortimer. Gilbert St. Victoris, Normandy 1180 (MRS), and the fief and Abbey of St. V. The Abbey of St. Victor in the Caux 1074 was founded by Roger Mortimer. Simon Victor held in Northampton 13th cent. (Testa); and in 1275 James de St. Victor was assessor of aids in Essex and Herts (PPW).

Victors, for VICTOR.

Videon. Henry Vidion, Normandy 1180–95 (MRS); Roger Widding, Engl. c. 1272 (RH).

Vidler, armorially identified with Vidlow, or Vis de Lu. *See* FIDLER. Humphry Vis de Lou held a barony in Berks 1086 (Domesd.). He also held as mesne lord in Berks and Hants (Ibid.); and Ralph Vis-de-lew, his brother, held lands in Norfolk (Ibid.). From the Berkshire line descended Walkelin Vis-de-leu, who returned his barony in Berks 1165 as held by the service of one knight (Lib. Niger), and Sir William Vis-de-lou, of Berks, who c. 1300 bore three wolves' heads (Palg. P. Writs). Of the Norfolk line descended from Ralph, William de Vis-de-lou was Lord of 'Visdelieus' in Shelfhanger in 1170 (Blomefield, i. 114–117). In 1300 William Vis-de-lou was living. His son Sir Thomas left two daughters, his heirs. A branch was seated for seven generations at Shotley, Suffolk, and bore three wolves' heads (Ibid.). In 13th cent. Winemar V. held Stotel, Suffolk, and Walchelin V. a fief at Shotley (Testa de Neville). In 1329 Sir William de Vis-de-lew presented to the Rectory of Santon, Norfolk, and in 1374 John Jernagan m. the dau. of Sir Thomas Vis-de-low (Blomefield, ii. 157, 415).

Viel. *See* VIALLS.

Vigers, for VIGOR.

Vigne, for Vine, or VIAN.

Vignes, for VIANS.

Vigo, or De Vico. *See* VECK.

Vigor. Richard de St. Vigor, and William Anglicus de St. Vigor, Normandy 1198 (MRS); Thomas de St. Vigor, Essex 1199 (RCR). St. V. was near Evreux. Drogo de S. V. witness 1066 to a charter Normandy (Gall. Christ., xi. 60). Humphry de S. V. a baron in Wilts 1165 (Lib. Niger). Thomas de S. V. 1283 summoned to a council at Shrewsbury (PPW).

Vigurs, for VIGOR.

Vile, for VAILE.

Villars. *See* VILLIERS.

Villiers. Roscelin, Robert, Wil-

liam, Richard, Geoffry, Cecalia, Gilbert de Vilers or Villers, Normandy 1180–95 (MRS); Almaric, Esmale, Geoffry, Nicholas, Richard, William de Vilers, Normandy 1198 (Ib.). These seem to have belonged to different families, there being several places so named in Normandy; and there are five different coats belonging to these families in England.

Roger de Vilers is mentioned 1066 as one of the barons who attended the Council of William I. before the Conquest (Wace, ii. 127). He had Galferius de V., who accompanied the Conqueror 1066, and witnessed a charter of St. Ebrulf 1081 (Nicholls, Leic. iii. 189). He had a son, from whom descended the Villierses of Gloucester, who bore a cross, as did the rest of the family; also Paganus de V., who obtained the barony of Warrington from Roger de Poitou t. William I. (Baines). Paganus was also Lord of Crosby, Lancashire, and had possessions in Notts and York (Nicholls, Leic., iii. 189, 197). He had issue— 1. William; 2. Arnold (Mon. ii. 369, d. s. p.); 3. Alan, of Trafford, ancestor of the Baronets Trafford. William de Villiers, Baron of Warrington, was father of Paganus de V., who had issue—1. Matthew, whose d. and heir carried the barony to the family of Le Botiler; 2. William, of Notts, ancestor of the Villierses of Brokesby, Dukes of Buckingham, Viscounts Purbeck, Earls of Jersey and of Grandison.

Villinger, for Warenger. *See* VERINDER.

Vines. Herbert de Vinas, Normandy 1198 (MRS).

Vincett, for VINCENT.

Vine. *See* VEIN.

Vinen. Robert de Veinions, Normandy 1198 (MRS); Hugh and John de Vinon, Engl. c. 1272 (RH).

Vincent. N. Vincent, Thomas V., Harvey Fitz-V., William V., Normandy 1180-95 (MRS); Robert Fitz-V., Engl. c. 1198 (RCR); John, Robert, Thomas V., Engl. c. 1272 (RH): hence the Baronets Vincent.

Viney, from Vignie, Normandy. Alberic de la Vignie held lands from Philip Augustus (MSAN, v.). Matilda la Vine, Engl. c. 1272 (RH).

Vinis, for Fynes. *See* FINNIS.

Vinn, for VENN.

Vinson, for VINCENT.

Vinsum, for VINCENT.

Vinter. *See* VENTERS.

Vinton, for Venton, or FENTON.

Vipan, or De Vieuxpont, a Norman baronial name. Fulco de Veteriponte, Robert, Osbert, Gislebert, William, Normandy 1180-95 (MRS); Fulco, Robert, William de V. P., 1198 (Ib.). William de Veteriponte or Vezpont was at the battle of Hastings (Wace, ii. 230). The family was of great importance in Normandy, and in England acquired the barony of Westmoreland. (*See* Dugdale, Banks.)

Virge. *See* VERGE, or Vierge.

Virgoe. *See* VIRGO.

Virtue. Ranulph (de) la Vertu, Normandy 1180-95 (MRS). The arms of Virtue of Berks are preserved by Robson.

Vise. *See* WYSE.

Visick. *See* PHYSICK.

Vivian. Denis Vivian, Normandy 1180-95; N. de Viviano (Ib.); Ralph Vivianus or Vivien, 1198 (Ib.); John Vivyan, Engl. c. 1272 (RH). Gilbert and Hugh Fitz-Vivien occur in Suffolk and Berks 1194 (RCR); Henry V. in Cambridge 1226 (Hardy, Rot. Claus.). The name of Vyell occurs in Essex, Vivian in Suffolk (Rot. Hundr.), and Sir Vyell Vivian was seated in Cornwall, probably by marriage (Lysons). He was father of Ralph, father of Richard, father of William, M.P. 1325, ancestor of the V's. of Trelowarren, baronets, and Vivian of Trenowth, Lords Vivian.

Vizard. *See* FESSART.

Vise. *See* WYSE.

Vizer, for VIZARD.

Voak, for VOKES.

Veake, for VOKES.

Voile, for Viel. *See* VEAL.

Voke. *See* VOKES.

Vokes, for VAUX.

Volke, for VOKES.

Vorley. *See* VARLEY.

Vose, for VAUX.

Vosper, for Waspre, or Guaspre, of Normandy. Osmund de Waspria witnessed a charter of the De Clares t. Henry I. (Mon. i. 246). Ralph de Waspre, Robert, and William W. occur in Wilts 13th cent. (Testa).

Vosper. *See* VESPER.

Voss, for Foss.

Voules. *See* VOWLES.

Vowler. *See* FOWLER.

Vowles, for Fowell. *See* FOWLE

Vyse. *See* VISE.

Vyvyan. *See* VIVIAN.

Wace. Radulphus Wace, Normandy 1180-95 (MRS); Hugh de Wasa, 1198 (Ib.); William Wace, Eng. c. 1272 (RH).

Wack, for Wac, or WAKE.

Wacick, for WAKE.

Waeland. See WAYLAND.

Waddell. Walchelin Vaduil, Normandy 1180-95 (MRS); Walter de Wedull, Eng. c. 1272 (RH).

Waddilove, for Vadelou, Wadlow, or Visdelou. See VIDLER.

Wade. William, Humphry, Matthew de Vado, Normandy 1180-95 (MRS); Adam, Andrew, &c. de Wade, Eng. c. 1272 (RH).

Waddy. See WADEY.

Wadey. Henricus de Vada, Normandy 1180-95 (MRS).

Wadie. See WADEY.

Wadlaw. See WADDILOVE.

Wadsworth or De Tilly. See WORDSWORTH.

Waggett. Radulphus Faget, Normandy 1180-95 (MRS). The name was probably changed to Vaget, and then Waget by pronunciation.

Wagland, for Wayland.

Waigh, for WAIGHT.

Waight, for WAIT.

Wain, for WANE.

Waine, for WANE.

Wait. Robert La Waite, Normandy 1180 (MRS); William La Waite, Eng. 1199 (RCR); Adam La Wayte, &c., Eng. c. 1272 (RH).

Waistell, for WASTELL.

Waite. See WAIT.

Waites. See WAITE.

Waits. See WAIT.

Wake, a baronial name. William and Baldwin de Wac, Normandy, t. Philip Augustus (MSAN, v.); Wil-

liam and Gilbert Vaca, or de la Wac, 1180 (MRS); Baldvinus Wac, Normandy 1198 (Ib.). In England the name was sometimes translated into 'Vigil,' as in 1130 John Vigil had pardons in Oxford (Rot. Pip.). Hugh Wac, probably his son, acquired estates in Lincoln by m. with the heir of Richard de Rullos, and is mentioned 1156, 1165. At the same time Simon W. and Ymfrid W. held fees respectively in Lincoln and Wilts. William Wace or Wake was of Oxford 13th cent., and the heirs of Reginald W., of the same county, held lands in Wilts. The Baronets Wake, the Lords Wake of Lydall, and Archbishop Wake were of this family.

Wakelin. N. and Robert Valchelinus, or Walchelinus, Normandy 1180-95 (MRS); Richard Walclin, Engl. c. 1272 (RH).

Wakeling. Alan, William Waukelin, Normandy 1198 (MRS).

Waland, for WAYLAND.

Waldegrave, or De Maloure, of Bretagne. Maloures or Malesoures was near St. Brieux, Bretagne. Durand de Malesoures lived c. 1040. He had two sons, who came to England 1066. 1. Adam FitzDurand, who held in Essex 1086; and 2. Fulcher de Maloure, whose barony was in Rutland, and who held in Northants from Countess Judith 1086, Walgrave (Bridges, Northants, ii. 127). Henry Malesoures, t. Henry II., held Waldgrave from David King of Scots, successor of Countess Judith. Walter Malesoures, by a fine levied 1235, conveyed a knight's fee in Waldgrave to Geoffry M. Richard de M. in 1295 held

Waldgrave of the honour of Huntingdon (Countess Judith's). His nephew John, son of Walter de Waldgrave, held W. (Testa). Hence the family of Waldegrave, who bore per pale or per pale indented, as did Maloure, or Malesoures, or Malory. Hence the Earls of Waldegrave, the gallant Admiral, Lord Radstock.

Wale, for VALE.

Wales, for WALE.

Waley, for VALEY.

Walker, or Walcher. *See* WALLIKER.

Wall. Nicholas and Odo de Muro, Normandy 1180 (MRS); Gilbert de Walle, John de la Walle, Engl. c. 1272 (RH); Robert de Vallo, Warwick 1165 (Rot. Pip.).

Wall, or de Valle. Ralph, Henry, Robert, Warin, Goscelin, Saifred, William, Richard de Valle, Normandy 1189–95 (MRS); Robert de Valle, Ralph and Richard de Valeia, Engl. c. 1198 (RCR).

Wallace. Roger, Hugh, Ralph, William Le Waleis, Normandy 1180–95 (MRS). The name of Le Walleis or Wallensis was frequent in the English records.

Wallace, or de Corcelle, of Normandy. According to Chalmers (Cal. i. 577), the ancestors of Sir William Wallace, Regent of Scotland, were an Anglo-Norman race, who settled in Ayr and Renfrew under Walter Fitz-Alan, the first Steward of Scotland (*see* STUART). The family of Walensis, originally de Corcelle, derived from William Walensis, who c. 1160 granted lands to Melrose Abbey, sealing with an eagle (probably a device). (H. Laing, Scottish Seals, 139.) Richard Walensis, his son, witnessed

charters of Walter Fitz-Alan; and granted lands to Melrose Abbey (Chart. Mailros.; Laing, 140). Sir Richard Walensis, his son, in 1220 bore a lion rampant surmounted by a bendlet, the family arms, as appears by 'his seal. From him descended Wallace of Craigie and Riccartoun. Henry W., brother of the first Richard Walensis (Chart. Paisley), was father of Sir Malcolm, father of the great Sir William Wallace.

This family came from Salop with the Fitz-Alans. Blakeway remarks on the name in the Fitz-Alan charters, as an evidence of the Shropshire origin of the latter (Sheriffs of Shropshire); and Eyton observes the name of Walensis as from Shropshire (Hist. Salop, vii. 225). The family of W. were tenants of the Fitz-Alans of Salop, for Roger W. in 1165 held from them (Lib. Niger).

In 1086 Roger de Corcelle, a Baron of Wilts, &c., held nine lordships in Salop from Hugh Earl of Salop. Richard de Corcelle or Pincerna, and other members of the family were also settled in Salop, where Richard, with his brother Robert Pincerna, witnessed a charter of Picot de Say to Salop Abbey, c. 1090. The family of Corcelle took part with Robert of Normandy, and lost their estates. Richard Pincerna or De Corcelle and his sons took refuge in Wales. After some time the heir of Roger de Corcelle was granted the hundred of Frome, Somerset; and Richard Walensis (or de Corcelle), returning from Wales, obtained from the Fitz-Alans the fief of Tasseley, Salop, which had belonged to his father. He in 1120-26 witnessed a charter of Ranulph, E.

of Chester (Mon. i. 260). Richard W., his son, is mentioned (Mon. i. 461) as witnessing a charter of Beatrix de Say. William Walensis, his brother, founded the Scottish family. *See* CHURCHILL.

The remarkable fact with regard to the two branches of the Corcelle family in Somerset and Salop is, that while the latter (as appears from the arms borne by Walensis in Scotland) bore a lion rampant debruised by a bendlet, the former (as appears by the arms which descended to the great Duke of Marlborough) bore the very same arms; merely varied in tincture. The two branches thus seem to have been armorially identified in the 12th century.

Wallbank, for MALBANK. *See* MILBANK.

Waller, or Valers, one of those families of VILLIERS which bore a bend or a fesse. Valers and Waller bore the same. Alexander de Waller held from Earl Bigod 1165 (Rot. Pip.). Robert de Willers of York 1194, and Robert de Walur of Essex 1198, were probably the same person (RCR). Michael de Valers or Vilers was summoned from Gloucester in 1300 for military service in Scotland (PPW). From Walers or Valers, of the Eastern Counties, probably descended the Kentish family of Waller, who bore three leaves on a bend voided. Of this family were Sir William Waller, the Parliamentary General; and Edmond Waller, the poet.

Wallett, for WILLETT.

Walliker. Richard Wilekier, Normandy 1180–95 (MRS).

Wallis. Secane Wallis, Normandy 1180–95 (MRS); John de Walles, Engl. c. 1272 (RH).

Wallis. *See* WALLACE.

Wallop, or Peverel. The family of Peverel of Normandy appears to have been possessed of Tenchebrai, in the Duchy. Ranulph P. m. Maude Fitz-Ingelric, who had been a concubine of Duke William, and became ancestor by her of the powerful baronial families of Peveril of Notts, Peveril of London, Peveril of Dover, Peveril of Brunne, Peveril of Essex, and Peveril of Salop. William Peverel, brother of Ranulph, witnessed in 1075 the Foundation Charter by William de Braiose of Sele Abbey, Sussex (Mon. i. 581). He and his descendants held four knight's fees in Sompting and Ewhurst from the Barons of Braiose (Testa, 222). In 1086 he also held Hovestone, Hants, from the See of Winchester (Domesd.). William Peverel, his son, held a knight's fee from the See of Winchester, which he appears to have alienated on obtaining Berton, Hants (Lib. Niger). Robert Peverel, his son, 1165 with Norman de Normanville (*see* BASSETT) held a fee in Sussex in barony, also Berton and other lands in Hants by ancient enfeoffment in barony (Lib. Niger). His son, Robert Peverel, had—1. Andrew, who had livery of Berton, &c., Hants 1226 (Roberts, Excerpta, i. 162), had writs of military summons in 1241 and 1260, and was ancestor of the great family of Peverel, of Sussex, Hants, and Dorset; 2. Peter Peverel, or De Berton, who t. Henry III. m. Alice, dau. and heir of Robert, Lord of Wallop, Hants, by whom he obtained large estates in that county, whence the name and arms of Wallop were assumed by his descendants, of whom Sir Oliver Wallop, a gallant commander at the battle of Mussel-burgh, was ancestor of the Earls of Portsmouth.

Walls, for WALLIS.

Walper, for WALPOLE.

Walpole, appears to have been a branch of Baynard or BEAUMONT, of Maine, bearing their arms with a slight difference. Reginald de W. t. Henry I. held from the See of Ely (Blomefield, Norfolk, vii. 105), and had Richard, who t. Stephen m. the d. and heir of Houton. Ralph Fitz-Richard, his son, who held from the See of Ely 1165 (Lib. Niger), occurs as Ralph de Bellomont t. Henry II. (Blomefield, x. 76). He had Josce-line, living 1199, ancestor of the Earls of Orford, and of the cele-brated minister Sir Robert Walpole.

Walrond, a baronial name. Geoffry, Hamo Waleran, Normandy 1180–95 (MRS). Walter Waleran held a barony of 25 fees in England 1165, and 1216 Robert Waleran was Baron of Kilpec.

Walsh. *See* BENN-WALSH.

Walsh, or Waleys. *See* WALLACE.

Walsingham, or De Clare, from Walsingham, Norfolk. Blomefield states that Sir Francis Walsingham, Queen Elizabeth's great minister, descended from Thomas W., who removed from Norfolk to Kent, and d. c. 1456 (vii. 270), whose ancestor Sir Richard W., of Norfolk, t. Ed-ward III. was son of Thomas, son of Sir Richard, a Justiciary in Norfolk 1304, whose father, Richard, had lived t. Henry III. The latter was probably a son of William de Clare, who died seized of Walsingham 1257, and brother of Richard, Earl of Clare (father of Thomas and Gilbert). William de C. also ap-pears as 'De Walsingham' (Roberts, Excerpta, ii. 308). This descent of the Walsinghams is inferred from the surname, the possession of the estate of Walsingham, and the similarity of Christian names. The family of De Clare had long possessed an estate at W., for on the founda-tion of Walsingham Abbey in the 12th century, the grants of Geoffry de Faverches at W. were confirmed by Roger, Earl of Clare. The estate of W. was granted to William de C. by his brother, Earl Richard.

Walter. Robert, Drogo, William, Hugh Walter, Normandy 1180–95 (MRS); Osbert, Robert, William W. 1198 (Ib.); Hugh Walter, Essex, 1194 (RCR); John, Richard, Wil-liam Walter, Engl. c. 1272 (RH).

Walters. *See* WALTER. Ar-morially identified.

Walther, for WALTER.

Walton, or De Cramaville, from Cramaville, near Evreux, Normandy. The family held a fief in Essex from the barony of Peverel from the Con-quest (Testa, 268). Osbert de C. held lands in Essex 1165 (Lib. Niger); Roger and Henry de C. in the 13th cent. A branch was early seated in Yorkshire, of which Robert de Cramaville gave lands at Walton to Fountains Abbey (Burton, Mon. Ebor. 200). His descendants, who bore the name of 'De Walton,' were also benefactors to Fountains and Bridlington. John de Wauton had free warren on his lands in York t. Henry III. In 1316 the heirs of Gilbert de W. were landowners in York, and 1324 Sir Robert de W. was made prisoner at the battle of Boroughbridge (PPW). After this the family lost its consequence, but still continued in the same vicinity, where its descendant, the learned Brian Walton, Bishop of Chester, and author of the 'Polyglott,' was born.

Walwin. Arnulphus Wauvain or Walvain, Normandy 1198 (MRS); Robert de Valuinis, England c. 1198 (RCR). The name of Walwyn flourished in Hereford.

Walwyn. Geoffry Wawein, Normandy 1198 (MRS).

Wand, for GAND.

Wane. Robertus Huan, Normandy 1180–95 (MRS); John Huene, England c. 1272 (RH).

Wanner. Richard Vanier, Normandy 1180 (MRS); Walter le Vanner, Engl. c. 1272 (RH).

Wansey. Robert de Wancy, Wancie, or Wansie, Normandy 1180–95 (MRS), also 1198 (Ib.). Hugh and Osberne de Wanceio held fiefs in Suffolk 1086 (Domesd.). The family afterwards appears in Wilts, Northants, Rutland, Berks, Devon, Suffolk.

Waple, or Waspail. Henry Wapul held his lands in Normandy by serjeantry at the Castle of Rouen t. Philip Augustus (MSAN, v. 171). Henry, Roger Waspail, Normandy 1198 (MRS); Roger Waspail, Wilts 1130 (Rot. Pip.). Roger W. 1165 held five fees from the Earl of Gloucester (Lib. Niger). Sir Roger Aspal was of Suffolk in 1300 (PPW).

Waples, for WAPLE.

Warbey, for WARBOYS.

Warboys, from Verbois, near Rouen, Normandy (Lower). Walter Wardebois, Engl. 1194 (RCR).

Warburton. *See* SPENCER.

Warby. *See* WARBOYS.

Ward, from Gar or Garde, near
440

Corbeil, Isle of France. Ingelram de Warda occurs in Northants 1130, and Ralph de Gar in Norfolk t. Henry II. (Blomefield, ix. 5). John de Warda of Norfolk occurs 1194 (RCR). In 1286 and 1290 Stephen de Ware and Thomas de W. are mentioned as holding fiefs there (Ibid. 359, 360). From the latter descended the Lords of Tottington, Pickenham, and Dudlington, of whom John Ward 14th cent. acquired Kirkby-Beadon, and from him lineally descended the first Lord Ward and the Earls of Dudley.

The Viscounts Bangor descend from a branch seated in Yorkshire, where Robert de la Gar 12th cent. gave lands to Selby Abbey (Burton, Mon. Ebor. 396), after which Simon Warde held a knight's fee in York 1165 (Lib. Nig.), and with William, his son, gave lands to Esholt Priory (Ibid. 139). Robert de la Warde was summoned by writ as a baron 1299. A branch settled in Ireland t. Elizabeth, from which descend the Viscounts Bangor.

Warde, for WARD.

Wardell. *See* FARDELL.

Wardill. *See* WARDELL.

Wardle. *See* WARDELL.

Warden, or Wardein, for De Gardino, or Garden.

Ware. *See* WARRE.

Warham, or De Vere. Of this name was William Warham, Archbishop of Canterbury. This is a branch of the house of De Vere, descended from Erneis, probably a brother of Alberic de Ver, who accompanied the Conqueror. His descendants possessed Gousell, Lincoln, and were thence named De Gousell. (*See* THOROLD.) Robert Fitz-Erneis, his son, had a grant of Warham,

Norfolk, from Henry I., and had issue—Eudo, who had lands at Gousell (Burton, Mon. Ebor. 230), father of William, father of Robert Fitz-Erneis, who preferred to retain his Norman estates, whereupon Warham was given to the De Clares. Peter de Warham (mentioned 1199), probably son of William Fitz-Eudo, and Walter de Warham occur t. John, and Robert de W., Bishop of Chichester, was of the family. The Warhams bore the arms of Gousell (a fesse), adding in chief one or three goats' heads (a branch of the Gousells still bears three goats. *See* Thorold) and three escallops in base. The Gousells bore three martlets in chief and three in base.

Warin. Robert, John, Ralph, Clapion Warin, Normandy 1180-95 (MRS); Richard Warin, Engl. c. 1198 (RCR); Geoffry, Henry, &c., Warin or Fitz-Warin, Engl. c. 1272 (RH).

Waring, for Warin.

Warlters, for Walters.

Warn, for Warren.

Warne, for Warren (Lower).

Warner. Richard, Hubert, William Warnerus, Normandy 1180-95 (MRS); Hubert Warnier, 1198 (Ib.); Geoffry, Robert, John Warnerius, Warnir, le Warner, Engl. c. 1272 (RH).

Warnes, for Warne.

Warnier. *See* Warner.

Warr. *See* Ward.

Warre, for War, or Gar. *See* Ward.

Warren. 1. for Warin; 2. for Warrenne.

Warren. William de Warenna or Warennes, Earl of Surrey t. William I. The history of this family is recorded by Dugdale and Banks.

See also Mortimer. Ralph Sire de Garenne, so called from a place in Normandy, afterwards named Bellencombre, where a magnificent castle long remained, was father of William de Warenne, who accompanied the Conqueror 1066 (Wace, ii. 241), and had vast grants in England. He was Great Justiciary of England, and in 1089 was created Earl of Surrey, a dignity which long descended in his family. The family of Bellencombre appears to have been a branch.

Warrender. *See* Verinder.

Warrick. *See* Warwick.

Warrilow. Gerold de Watetot, Normandy 1180-95 (MRS); Geoffry and William de Wautitot, 1198 (Ib.).

Warring, for Warin.

Warry or Werry, for Gerry or Geary.

Warville, for Varville.

Warwick, for Warroc. Clemens de Warrok, Normandy 1180 (MRS); Roger Waroc, 1198 (Ib.).

Wase. *See* Wace.

Washington. Jared Sparks (Life of Washington, App. No. I.) derives the family of Washington from William de Hertburn, who came into possession of Wessington (Washington), Durham, prior to the compilation of Boldon Book 1183 (Hutchinson, Durham, ii. 489; Surtees, ii. 40). The family soon after assumed the name of Washington.

Hertburn, in the wapentake of Sadberge, Durham, was granted by Richard I. to the See of Durham, including, amongst others, 'the service (or fief) of the son of Godfrey Baard for two parts of a knight's fee in Middleton and Hertburn' (Surtees, iii. 265), and as late as 1364 the Baards or Barts had lands there (iii. 221).

William de Hertburn appears to have been a son of Godfrey Baard or Bayard. The family of Baird or Bayard in Scotland is the same, and originally the arms of that family were a fesse, in chief three mullets, the same arms as those of the De Washingtons, to which the Bairds added a boar passant, by way of difference (Geneal. Coll. regarding the name of Baird, by W. Baird, Esq., 2nd ed. 1870).

Godfrey Bayard or Baiard, above named, held a barony in Northumberland in 1165 (Lib. Niger), and was descended from a Norman family, mentioned amongst the Conqueror's companions as 'Barte.' Jordan Baard occurs in Essex and Hertf. 1130 (Rot. Pip.), and from him descended William B., who in 1165 held two fees from the See of London, and was the probable ancestor of Bard, Viscount Bellamont. Another branch was seated in Lincoln in 1165, when Richard B. held lands there from Earl Simon de Senlis. Of this family Dodo Bard granted his manor of Folingham to Blancheland Abbey, Normandy (Mon. Angl. ii. 1015), and with Hugh and Hamelin B. witnessed the charter of Richard de la Haye to the same house (Ibid.). The ancestor of this family, Raoul Baiart, of Normandy c. 1050, granted lands in Fontenay to Barberie Abbey (MSAN, vii. 144).

Wason. Geoffry de Vaçon and John de V. held fiefs in Normandy t. Philip Augustus (MSAN, v. 169, 170); Simon Wasin, Engl. c. 1272 (RH).

Wass, for WASH.

442

Wasselin, for Gascelin. Samson Wascelin, Normandy 1180–95 (MRS); Roger Wascelin, 1198 (Ib.); Geoffry Wascelin, Engl. c. 1272 (RH).

Wassell. Roger Wasel, Normandy 1180–95 (MRS); Stephen Vassel, Engl. c. 1272 (RH).

Wastall. See WASTELL.

Wastell. Roger, Hugh Wastel, Normandy 1180 (MRS); Ralph, Richard Wastel, Engl. c. 1272 (RH).

Waterall. Gervasius Waterel, Normandy 1180–95 (MRS); John de Waterhulle, Eng. c. 1272 (RH).

Waterer, for Vautrier or Veltrier, from V., near Cambray, Flanders. William de Veltrier held three fiefs from Albini, in Norfolk, 1165 (Lib. Niger).

Waterfall, for WATERFIELD.

Waterfield, for Waterville or Wateville, a Norman baronial name. Waleran de Watevilla or Wartevilla; N. Alexander, Durand, Richard, and the Manor and Forest of Wateville, Normandy 1180–95 (MRS); Robert de Waterville, summoned to Parliament as a Baron 1326.

Waterhouse, for Wastheose. Alan Wastehose, or Wastheose, Normandy 1180–95 (MRS); Alan W. 1198 (Ib.); Roger de Wateruse, Engl. c. 1198 (RCR); Alan Wasthose, Engl. 1189 (Rot. Pip.); Ralph, Richard Wasthouse, Engl. c. 1272 (RH).

Waterlow, for Wadlow, or WADLAW.

Waters, for WALTERS; also a local name.

Watt, for Wate (or WAIT), of Normandy, armorially identified. Hence Watt, the celebrated inventor of the Steam Engine.

Watters, for WATERS.

Watts. Robert de Wauz, Normandy 1198 (MRS).

Watts, for WATT.

Waud. William de Wauda, Normandy 1180-95 (MRS); Thomas de la Waude, Engl. c. 1272 (RH).

Wavell. Robert de Wauville, and the Estate of W. Normandy, 1180-95 (MRS); Richard, William de Vauville (Ib.). From Vauville, near Valognes, Normandy, where there was a castle. The Vauvilles were also Lords of Septvents, near Caumont (Gerville, Anc. Chateaux). William de Vauville occurs 1050 (Gall. Christ. xi. 229). The family was a branch of the Barons of Briquebec (Wiffen, Hist. Russell, i. 6). *See* BERTRAM.

Wayland. Simon Fitz-Osbert de Wailun held lands in Normandy, which King John granted to another (MSAN, v. 120). The family was of importance in Suffolk, Sir Nicholas being M.P. for that county 1290-1305. William de W. had been escheator of the King 13th cent. The name Wayland was a form of Watlande, which manor in Kent was held t. Edward III. by Richard Weyland, and from him by John de Evering, or Avranches (Hasted). It was part of the Barony of Avranches, and the probability is that the Weylands were a branch of that family, for they bore a cross, which was also borne by a branch of the Avranches. *See* AVERANCH.

Waylat, for WILLETT.

Waylen, for WAYLAND.

Waylett, for WILLETT.

Waymark, for WYMARK.

Wayne, for WANE.

Wayre. Roger Vasier, Normandy 1180-95 (MRS).

Wayt, for WAIT.

Wayte, for WAIT.

Weaire, for WAYRE.

Weale, for WALE.

Weall. *See* WEALE.

Wear, for WAYRE.

Weare, for WAYRE.

Wearing, for WARING.

Wearne, for WARNE.

Wears. *See* WEAR.

Weathers. *See* WITHERS.

Weaver. Hubert de Wevre, Normandy 1198 (MRS); Robert, Hugh, Ernald, Oger, Serlo, William, Gerard, Gauffrid Textor, Normandy 1180-95 (MRS); Godfrey T., Engl. c. 1198 (RCR); Ralph T. 1189 (Rot. Pip.). The last possessed estates in Lincoln 1202.

Webb. *See* GIBB.

Webbe. *See* WEBB.

Wedd, for WADE.

Wedde, for WEDD.

Weddel. *See* WADDELL.

Weddell, for WADDELL.

Weed, for WADE.

Weede, for WADE.

Weet, for WAIT.

Weight, for WAIT.

Weir, for WERE.

Weise, for WISE.

Welbank. *See* WALBANK.

Welbore, for Wellebo. Landri and Stephen de Wellebo, Normandy 1198 (MRS); the Estate of Wellebue, and Robert de Wellebuef, 1180-95 (Ib.); Hugh and William de Wellebof, Engl. c. 1198 (RCR).

Welch, or Waleys, for WALLACE.

Weld, for WILD.

Wellard, for WILLARD.

Wellborne. *See* WILBORN.

Weller, for WILLER.

Welles. *See* WILLIS.

Wellesley. *See* COLLEY-WELLESLEY.

443

Welling. Ralph, Richard, Robert, Roger Hueline, Normandy 1198 (MRS); William Welin, Engl. c. 1272 (RH).

Wellman. *See* WILMIN.

Wellmin. *See* WILMIN.

Welman, for WILMIN.

Welsh, for WALSH.

Welton, for WALTON.

Wengefield, for WINGFIELD.

Wenn, for WANR.

Wentworth, or De Oissy, or De Cambray. This family has been, without any proof, stated to be Anglo-Saxon. It was Flemish, and derived from the ancient Castellans of Cambray, of whom Walter de Lens is mentioned in the Chronicle of Baldric of Noyon, c. 950. Walter II., his son, was Castellan of Cambray c. 990, and had Walter, who was succeeded by his nephew, Walter D'Oissy, Castellan in 1049. He had issue Hugh, father of Hugh II., who was Viscount of Meaux, and was living 1096 (Des Bois). Walter, a younger son of this house, accompanied the Conqueror in 1066. His descendants bore three crescents instead of one, as borne by the Castellans of Cambray. Walter (surnamed Flandrensis) obtained the Barony of Wahull, Bedford, which he held 1086. He had issue, 1. Simon, from whom descended the Barons de Wahull, by writ 1295; 2. William, father of Reiner; 3. Walter, who appears in York 1120 (Mon. ii. 101). Reiner Flandrensis, the son of William, founded Kirkby Priory, York, one of the witnesses being another Walter F. (Mon. i. 487). Reiner held in 1165 two fees of the Honour of Skipton (Lib. Niger). William Flandrensis, his son, granted

444

lands at Wentworth to Fountains Abbey (Burton, Mon. Ebor. 119). William, son of William de Wentworth, occurs 13th cent. (Ib. 99). Henry de W. was father of Hugh, who gave lands to Arden (Ib. 98). From William de Wentworth, who m. the heiress of Woodhouse, the descent of this family is well known. Hence came the great and unfortunate Earl of Strafford.

Were, for VERE.

Werner, for WARNER.

Wessels. Robert Wissel, Normandy 1180 (MRS). *See* VASSELL.

Wesley. *See* WESTLEY. Hence the celebrated John Wesley.

Wesson. *See* WASON.

Wescott, for WESTCOTT.

West. Robert de West, William de West, Normandy 1198 (MRS).

West, or De Gaste, probably a branch of the Meurdracs, Barons of St. Denis-de-Gaste, in the Cotentin. Robert de Gaste or Waste, t. William I., gave his tithes in Hunts to Bec Abbey, Normandy; and his wife's father is mentioned, William Fitz-Geroie, one of the Geroies, Barons of Escalfoy (Mon. ii. 877). Nigel de Gaste, his son, held from Nigel de Albini in Bedford in 1086. Ralph de G. was father of Everard; and John Fitz-Everard de G., t. John, made grants to Waltham Abbey (Mon. i. 18). In 1216 Fulco Waste and Gilbert le Gros (one of the family of Geroie) held a fief in Oxford (Testa). Thomas West, of Oxfordshire, occurs t. Edward I. (Rot. Hundr.). Sir Thomas West was bailsman in Oxford for Peter de Scudamore and others when pardoned (PPW); was M.P. for Warwick 1322; m. Alianore de Cantelupe; and was summoned by writ as a Baron 1342. From him descend the Earls Delawarr and Barons Buckhurst.

Westacott, or Westcote. *See* LYTTELTON.

Westale, for WESTALL.

Westall, for WASTELL.

Westcoatt, for Westcote. *See* LYTTELTON.

Westcott. *See* WESTCOAT.

Westell, for WASTELL.

Westfall. *See* WESTPHAL.

Westle, for WESTELL.

Westley. Walter Wasteleie, Normandy 1180–95 (MRS) ; Roger Wastelai, 1198 (Ib.) ; William de Westle, Engl. c. 1272 (RH).

Westphal. *See* WAPLE or Waspail.

Wever. *See* WEAVER.

Whait, for WAITE.

Whaite, for WAITE.

Whale, for WALE.

Whales, for WHALE.

Whall, for WALL.

Whealler, for WHEELER.

Wheals, for WEALE.

Wheat, for WAITE.

Wheate, for WAITE.

Wheeler. Osmondus Huielor, Normandy 1198 ; William and Roger Huelier, 1180–95 (MRS) ; Hugh le Welere, Engl. c. 1272 (RH).

Wheeller. *See* WHEELER.

Wheelright. Alexander Fitz-Huielrat, Normandy 1180–95 (MRS) ; William Walraed, Engl. c. 1272 (RH).

Wheeley, for WILLY.

Wheelock. *See* WILLOCK.

Wheen, for WANE.

Wheller, for WHEELER.

Whellock, for WILLOCK.

Whenn, for WAYNE.

Whewell, for Hewel, Huel, or Hoel. *See* HOILE. Hence the emi-

nent philosopher, Whewell, Master of Trinity College, Cambridge.

Whicker, for WHICKER.

Whicker, for VICAR.

Whillier, for Huilor, or WHEELER.

Whiskard, or Wiscard, for GUISCARD. Garinus Guischart, Normandy 1198 (MRS) ; Nicholas Wiscard, Engl. c. 1272 (RH).

Whisker, for Guiscard or WHISCARD.

Whisler. *See* WHISTLER.

Whistler, or Whisler, for OSLER or Oiselur.

Whitbread. The English form of Blancpain, a foreign name, which, however, does not appear in the Rolls of the Exchequer of Normandy, and may have come from another province. Hugo Blancpain and William de Reini agreed regarding lands in Bucks 1202 (Rot. Canc.). In 1268 Ralph Fitz-Walter Whitbread paid a fine in Bedfordshire (Roberts, Excerpta, ii.).

Whitby. Ernaldus Kitebue, Normandy 1180–95 (MRS) ; William Withbid, Engl. c. 1272 (RH).

Whitcher. *See* WHICHER.

White. Matthew and Hubert le Blanc, Normandy 1180–95 ; Richard and Robert L., 1198 (MRS) ; Godefrid Albus, Engl. 1189 (Rot. Pip.) ; Dionysia, Gilbert, &c., le Wite ; Henry Blanche, Engl. c. 1272 (RH). The name doubtless includes families not of Norman origin.

Whitefoot. Richard Blancpie, Engl. 1202 (Rot. Canc.). Evidently a foreign name, translated into Whitefoot.

Whitehand. Robert Blanchesmains, Normandy 1180–95 (MRS) and 1198 ; Stephen Blanmong, Engl. c. 1272 (RH).

Whitgift, or Painel, of Normandy. John, Archbishop of Canterbury, was grandson of John W., Lord of Whitgift, York. In 1308 John, son of Adam de W., gave lands to St. Mary's, York (Strype, Life of W., i. 4; Surrey Archæol. Collect., ii. 202). Whitgift was held from Drax, the barony of the Paganels or Painels, with Airmine (Drake, Eboracum), and in 13th century Adam bore these two names (Whitgift and Airmine) indifferently. He had—Adam, ancestor of the Airmines, baronets; and John de Whitgift, a benefactor to St. Mary's, York (Burton, Mon. Ebor. 100). The elder, Adam, in the 13th cent., held as 'Adam Painel' one fee in Lincoln (Testa de Neville, 345), which had been held in 1165 by Fulco Painel from William Painel or Paganel, of Drax (Lib. Nig.). The Whitgifts bore the arms of Paganel or Painel, a cross flory or moline. The Paganels were a great baronial family in Normandy.

Whiting. Robert Vitenc, Normandy 1180-95 (MRS); Richard Witing or Witine (Ib.); Thomas de Whitene, Engl. c. 1272 (RH); Gerin, Ralph Wyting (Ib.).

Whitlark, or Whitler. Richard Wetlere, Normandy 1180-95 (MRS).

Whitear. Robert Witer, Normandy 1180 (MRS); Henry, John Wyther, Engl. c. 1272 (RH).

Whiteing. See WHITING.

Whitrod, for Witerol. Rainald Witerol, Gervase, Roger, William Witerel, Normandy 1180-95 (MRS).

Whitt. See WHEATE.

Whittome, for WHITTON.

Whitten. See WHITTON.

Whitting. See WHITING.

Whitton. Robert Witon, Nor-

mandy 1180-95 (MRS); Rob. de Witone, 1198 (Ib.); Robert de Witton, Engl. c. 1272 (RH).

Whowell, for WHEWELL.

Whybrew, or Wybrew, for Wibue. Ralph and Richard Wybue, Normandy 1180-95 (MRS); Rich. and Will. de Wibo, 1198 (Ib.).

Whyle, for HOILE.

Whyte. See WHITE.

Wibrew, for Wibue. See WHYBREW.

Wickens. See WIGAN.

Wicker, for VICARS.

Wicker. See VICARS.

Wickers, for VICARS.

Wicking, for Wickin, or WICKENS.

Wickings. See WIGAN.

Wickins, or Wiggins. See WIGAN.

Widger, for WICHER.

Widdow, for Wido, or Guido. See GUY.

Widdows, for WIDDOW.

Wieland, for WAYLAND.

Wier. See WAYRE.

Wigan, or Guigan. Radulphus Wigan, Richard Wiguen, Normandy 1198 (MRS); Henry Wygeyn, Engl. c. 1272.

Wigans, for WIGAN.

Wigfield, for WINGFIELD.

Wigg, for WEGG.

Wiggett, for BIGOT. See LYTTON-BULWER.

Wiggin, for WIGAN.

Wiggins. See WIGAN.

Wigney, or Vigny, from Vigny, near Pontoise, Normandy. Simon de Vigneio held one fee in Passey, Normandy 1165 (Feod. Norm.). Roger de Wignai, of Bedfordshire, 1198 (RCR).

Wight, for WHITE, WAIGHT.

Wilbourn. Philip de Wilde-

brene and Ranulph, Normandy 1180
(MRS); Thomas de Wellbrun,
Engl. 1194 (RCR).

Wilbraham, descends from Odo,
Chamberlain to Alan, Earl of Richmond, whose son Robert gave lands
at Wilbraham to Denny Abbey,
Cambridge, witnessed by Walter
Pilet (Mon. ii. 883). Picot and
Peter Pilet had grants at Wilbraham 1157 (Rot. Pip.). It seems
probable that this was the Norman
name of the lords of Wilbraham,
usually styled Camerarius or De
Wilburgham. Conan, son of Peter
Pilet, of Rouen, 1090 supported the
cause of Duke Robert (Ord. Vit.
689), and Raimond Pilate was a
chief leader in the Crusade 1096
(Roger Wend., ii. 120, 136).

Wild, or Le Sauvage. Unfrid
Salvage and Walter S., Normandy
1180-95 (MRS); Ralph, Ranulph
Sauvage 1198 (Ib.); Geoffry Sal-
vage, Engl. 1189 (Rot. Pip.); Wal-
ter, William le Wilde, Engl. c. 1272
(RH): hence the Lords Truro and
Penzance.

Wildbore, for WELBORE.
Wilde. See WILD.
Wilding, for WALDING, WALDIN.
Wiles, for Wailes, or WALE.
Wiley, for WILLY.
Will, for Waile, or WALE.
Willan. Hamelin Willan, Nor-
mandy 1180 (MRS); Bernard,
Hamelin de Willon 1198 (Ib.);
Richard Willam, Engl. c. 1272.

Willans, for WILLAN.
Willard. Robert le Guillart,
Normandy 1198 (MRS); Ranulph
and Ralph Wislart, 1180-95 (Ib.).

Willats, for WILLETT.
Willborn. See WILBOURN.
Willement. See WILMIN.
Willemite, for WILMOT.

Willer. See WILLARD.
Willes, or Welles. Gislebert,
Hugh, Robert de Wellis, Nor-
mandy 1198 (MRS); Effric de
Welles, and the fief of Wellis, Nor-
mandy 1180 (Ib.); John de Welles,
Richard Wellis, Eng. c. 1272 (RH).

Willett. See GILLETT.
Willey, for WILLY.
Willies. See WILLES.
Willimott. See WILMOT.
Willin. See WELLING.
Willing. See WILLIN.
Willings, for WILLAN.
Willings. See WILLING.
Willion, for WILLAN.
Willis, for WILLES.
Willits, for WILLETT.
Willman, for WILMIN.
Willmett, for WILMOT.
Willmote. See WILMOT.
Willmott, for WILMOT.
Willock. Elriche, Roger Wal-
loche, Normandy 1180-95 (MRS).

Willomatt, for WILMOT.
Willott, for WILLETT.
Willoughby, or De Muscamp,
from Muscamp, Normandy, which
was held by a branch of DE TILLY
(MSAN, xv. 175). This family
settled at the Conquest in the north
of England. In 1130 Reginald was
of Northumberland (Rot. Pip.).
Hugh de M., t. Henry I., gave lands
to Nostel Priory, York (Mon. ii. 35)
and 1165 Thomas was of Notts, and
Hugh of Lincoln and York (Lib.
Niger). Roger held Wilgebi, Lincoln, 1086. Robert de Muscam, his
son, Seneschal to Gilbert de Gand,
had issue Robert (Mon. i. 963),
whose son Hugh de M. has been
mentioned. His nephew, Ralph de
Wilebi, occurs 1199 and 1208
(RCR, Hardy, Obl. et fin. 408).
His great grandson, Sir William de

Willoughby, m. the heiress of De Bec, Baron of Eresby; and hence sprang the Lords Willoughby of Eresby, so renowned in the French wars, and the Lords Middleton, Willoughby de Broke, and W. of Parham.

Wills, for WILLIS.

Willey. Petrus and Richard de Velly, and the fief of V. Normandy, t. Philip Augustus (MSAN, v.); Adam, John Willy, Engl. c. 1272 (RH).

Wilmin. Richard Willemin, Normandy 1180–95 (MRS) and 1198; Simon Wileman, Engl. c. 1272 (RH).

Wilmot. Galterus de Villa Mota held lands in Normandy t. Philip Augustus (MSAN, v. 181). His lands of Villa Mota or Villa Monta occur, 182. Henry Wilmot, Engl. c. 1272 (RH). Hence Wilmot, Lord Chief Justice, and the Baronets Wilmot.

Willmott. *See* WILMOT.

Windebank. Richard de Onnebank, Normandy 1198 (MRS); William, Richard, John de O., and the parish of Onnebanc (MSAN, v. 200, 208, 208). Secretary Windebank, t. Charles I., was one of this family.

Windibank. *See* WINDEBANK.

Windsor, a baronial name. *See* FITZGERALD.

Winfield, for WINGFIELD.

Wingfield, or De Braiose, a branch of the baronial house of Braiose of Normandy. William de Braiose came to England 1066, and was a great baron in Sussex 1086. His great grandson, William de B., m. a dau. and coheir of Milo, Earl of Hereford, and had, 1. William, ancestor of the Barons B. of Bramber, summoned by writ 1293; 2. Giles, Bishop of Here-

448

ford; 3. Reginald, Baron of Brecknock; 4. Roger. The last-mentioned received grants of Wingfield and other lordships in Suffolk and Norfolk, then in possession of the Crown, as part of the honour of Eye. In 1205 he paid a fine in Hants (Hardy, Rot. Claus. 26), and had custody of the forest of Mauling (58), and was in the king's service 1207, 1214 (97, 142). He had Roger de Breouse, mentioned 1256 (Blomefield, Norf. vi. 242), whose son, Sir Richard de Brews, was Lord of Wingfield and Stradbroke 1274 (Rot. Hundr. ii. 186). He d. 1296, leaving, 1. Sir Giles de Breuse, ancestor of the B.s of Norfolk; 2. Sir Roger de Breuse, who had a writ of military summons 1312, and was sometimes styled 'De Wingfield' (Blomefield, viii. 345, v. 185); 3. Richard; 4. Thomas de Wingfield, living 1318. Richard de Breuse bore the name of 'Wingfield;' was joint Lord of Wingfield 1316 (PPW), and in 1324 was summoned as a man-at-arms of Suffolk (PPW). He and his descendants adopted a pair of wings for arms, in allusion to the name of Wingfield. His son Sir John, Lord of Wingfield, was living 1360 (Blomefield, vii. 70). His brother Sir Thomas was ancestor of the W.s of Letheringham, and their branch the Wingfields, Viscounts Powerscourt.

Winkfield, for WINGFIELD.

Winn. William Win, Normandy 1180–95 (MRS); John, William, Wine, Engl. c. 1272 (RH). Some families of the name are Cambro-Celtic.

Winser, for WINDSOR.

Winsor, for WINDSOR.

Winter. *See* VINTER.

Wintere, for VINTER.

Winters, for WINTER.

Wire, for WAYRE.

Wise. Richard Sapiens, Normandy 1180; Vigor Sapience, 1180-96 (MRS); John, Ranulph, Roger, William S. 1198 (MRS); Robert Sapiens, Engl. c. 1198 (RCR).

Wiseman. Wisman, of Falaise, Normandy, occurs t. William I. (MSAN, xv. 174). Ranulph Wisman witnessed a charter of Beatrix de Say, c. 1140, in favour of Waltham Abbey, Essex (Mon. i. 401). Reginald Wisman, of Essex, 1194 (RCR). Hence the Baronets Wiseman.

Wisker. See WHISKER.

Wiss, for WISE.

Withers. Robert Witer, Normandy 1180 (MRS); Samuel Wither, Engl. c. 1272 (RH).

Witt, for WAITE.

Witte, for WITT.

Witten, for WHITTON.

Witton, for WHITTON.

Witts, for WITT.

Woollis, for WILLIS.

Wolf, for Lu, Loup. See LOWE.

Wolfe. See WOLF.

Wolff. See WOLF.

Wollen. See WALWYN.

Wolter, for WALTER.

Wolvine. See WALWYN.

Wood, generally local English, but in some cases a translation from De Bosco or Boys, of Normandy.

Woodall, or DE WAHUL. See WENTWORTH.

Woodard, or Wadard. Wadard came to England with the Conqueror 1066, and 1086 held estates under Odo of Bayeux in several counties (Ellis, Intr. Domesd. ii. 404). Henry and Simon Wadard, 1278, in Sussex, were distrained to compel them to be knighted (PPW).

Woodfall, for WOODFIELD.

Woodfield, for Woodville, of Normandy. See WYVILLE.

Woodfield, for Woodville. See WYVILLE.

Woodin. Ranulph Waudin, Normandy 1198 (MRS); Henry de Wadon, Engl. c. 1272 (RH).

Wooding. See WOODIN.

Woods. See WOOD.

Woodville. See WYVILLE.

Woodwell. See WOODVILLE.

Woolard. See WILLARD.

Woollard. See WILLARD.

Woollatt, for WOLLARD.

Woollett, for WOOLLATT.

Wooley. See WILLY.

Woolf. See WOLF.

Woolfe. See WOLF.

Woolhouse, for Walhouse or WALLIS.

Woolman, for WILMAN.

Woolven. See WALWYN.

Woolvine. See WALWYN.

Worboyes, for WARBOYS.

Worboys, for WARBOYS.

Wordsworth, or De Tilly. The family of Wordsworth has been traced to the time of Edward III., when it became seated at Peniston, York, through marriage with an heiress (Hunter, South Yorkshire, ii. 334). It is considered impossible to trace it higher (Ib.). The difficulty in the case, however, arises only from the changes of orthography. The records produced clearly show that the name was spelt Wordisworth, Wardysworth, and Wadysworth. The latter, i.e., Wadsworth, was the original form. The lordship so named was in the West Riding, and the family of De Wadworth bore the arms of De Tilly (three fleur de lys), reversing the tinctures. This latter family (see TILLY) was Norman and baronial, being from T., near

Caen. Odo de Tilly, who granted lands to Troarn Abbey, Normandy, t. Henry I., appears to have obtained fiefs in York, where his family long continued. Godfrey de Wadworth, t. Stephen (Burton, Mon. Ebor. 323), was father of Eudo or Otto de Tilly, who is also called Eudo 'de Wadeworth.' This Eudo de Tilly in 1165 held lands from the Barony of Pontefract (Lib. Niger); and in 1180 Urban III. confirmed the grants of Eudo de Wadworth, son of Godfrey, to Roche Abbey, York. In 1179 Hugh de Wadworth was Abbot of Roche. His brother Henry was father of Peter de Wadworth. Eudo de W. occurs about the same time. In 1245 William de W. witnessed a charter of Roche Abbey (Burton, Mon. Ebor. 320). From this family, which was very numerous, and had many branches in York and the adjoining counties, descended William Wordsworth, the Poet.

Worrall. *See* WORRELL.

Worrell. William Werel, Normandy 1180–95 (MRS); Robert, Stephen W. 1198 (Ib.); H. Werle, Engl. c. 1272 (RH).

Worrill. *See* WORRELL.

Woulfe. *See* WOLF.

Wrake, for RAKE.

Wray, for RAY.

Wrenulds. *See* REYNOLDS.

Writer. Rainbald Scriber, or Scriptor, Normandy 1180–95 (MRS); Richard Wrythere, Engl. c. 1272 (RH).

Wroe, for ROE.

Wulf. *See* WOLF.

Wyand, for WYON.

Wyard. *See* WYATT.

Wyatt, for Wyard perhaps. Ralph, Roger Wiardus, Normandy 1198 (MRS).

Wycliffe, John, or Musard, the great reformer, was born at Wycliffe, N.R. Yorkshire, which had belonged to his ancestors from soon after the Conquest. They were descended from a younger son of Enisand Musard of Bretagne (*see* BURTON and CONYNGHAM), who obtained from his father Cleseby, near Richmond, part of his demesne in 1086 (Domesd. i. 309b). Witcliffe (Wycliffe), Torp, and Gerlington were granted to the family by Alan, Earl of Richmond, by the service of one knight. Hasculph de Cleseby was succeeded by his nephew Hasculph, t. Stephen (Mon. i. 838). Temp. Henry III. Hasculph de Cleseby held Wycliffe, Thorp, and Gerlington from the Honour of Richmond (Gale). In the following reign Cleseby, or Cleasby, passed to a younger branch, which assumed the name. Wycliffe, &c. passed to Robert de Wycliffe (Gale, Registr. Richm. 50), who witnessed a charter of the Earl of Richmond in 1278 (Mon. ii. 197). He was succeeded by his brother Alan de Momby, of M., Lincoln (where the Earls of Richmond had large possessions), where he resided. Roger de Wycliffe, his son, was living 1319, and was father of William Wycliffe, who m. a dau. of Sir Robert Bellasis (Whitaker, Richm. i. 200). John Wycliffe, the reformer, was a brother or first cousin of the latter, as the name of Wycliffe had not been borne in the family for more than two generations.

The arms of the Musards of Stavely were two chevrons; those of the Constables of Richmond (descendants of Enisand Musard) a cross fleury. The ancient arms of the Wycliffes in W. Church combined these, being two chevrons between three crosses fleury. The family of Momby bore the cross fleury in a canton on a field fretty; that of Cleasby exchanged the two chevrons of Musard for two bends. *See* RICHMOND, BURTON, CLEASBY.

Wyett, for WYATT.

Wyld, for WILD.

Wylde, for WILD.

Wylie, for WILLY.

Wyllie, for WILLY.

Wymar. Martin Wimar, Normandy 1180–95 (MRS); Peter, Tustin Wimare, 1198 (Ib.); John, Richard, William Wimarc or Wimar, Engl. c. 1272 (RH).

Wymark, for WYMAR.

Wymer. *See* WYMAR.

Wynter, for WINTER.

Wyon. Gaufrid, Islebert, and Ralph Vion, Normandy 1180 (MRS).

Wyre, for WAYRE.

Wyse. *See* WISE.

Wyville, or Widville. Ascelin, Alexander, Francus, John, Polet, Raginald, Richard, Thomas de Wiville, Normandy 1198, &c. (MRS). The earlier part of the Wyville pedigree in Collins is fabulous. Widville, Guidoville, or Viville was held from the De Toesnis in Nor-

mandy. Hugh de Guidville came to England 1066, and 1086 held in Northants and Leicester (Domesd.). Robert, his son, t. Henry I., granted the tithes of Guidoville to Conches Abbey, with consent of Ralph de Toesni (Gall. Christ. xi. 182, Instr.); and in 1130 held the estates of Roger de Mowbray in farm from the Crown (Rot. Pip.). He also held the forest of Pickering, York, from the Crown (Rot. Pip.). He had, 1. Ralph, father of Robert de Withville, whose brother, William de Widville, of Northants, 1165 (Lib. Niger), was ancestor of the Earls Rivers; 2. William, whose son, Richard de Withville, held five knight's fees in York from Mowbray, and half a fee in capite (Lib. Niger). He was a benefactor to Byland Abbey (Burton, Mon. Ebor.). Walter de Widville occurs t. Richard I. (Mon. ii. 984); and William, son of William de Wyville, in 1299 confirmed his ancestor's gifts to Byland Abbey (Ib.). From this line descend the Baronets Wyville. The gallant Earl Rivers, t. Edward IV., and his sister Elizabeth Widville, Queen of that monarch, are conspicuous in history.

Y

Yarnold, for ARNOLD.

Yarrell, for Yarle, or EARLE.

Yarrow, for ARROW.

Yates, for GATES.

Yeames, for Hiesmes or AMES.

Yeates. *See* YATES.

Yeats. *See* YATES.

Yetts, for YATES.

Yemma, for YEAMES.

Yeulett, for HEWLETT.

Yewd, for JUDE.

Yolland, for HOLLAND.

Yonge, for YOUNG.

Youatt, for JEWITT.

Youd, for JUDE.

Youell, for YOULE.

Youens, for HUAN.

Youill. *See* YOUELL.

Youle. *See* YOUELL.

Youles. *See* YOULE.

Young. William Juven or Juvenis, and Robert, Normandy 1180-95 (MRS); Hubert Jouvin, 1198 (Ib.); Adam, Gilbert, &c. Juvenis, Engl. c. 1272. Hence the Baronets Young and Lords Lisgar.

Younge. *See* YOUNG.

Youngs, for YOUNG.

Yuill. *See* YOUILL.

Yuille. *See* YOUILL.

Yule, for YOUILL.

Yull, for YULE.

Z

Zealey, for SEALEY.

Zeall, for SELE.

Zissell, for Sissel. *See* CECIL.

Zouche. *See* SUCHE. A branch of the Counts of Bretagne who had been settled in England from the Conquest. *See* Dugdale and Banks. Hence the Lords Zouche.

APPENDIX.

NORMAN NAMES FROM A A TO A L L, TAKEN FROM THE OFFICIAL LISTS, SOMERSET HOUSE.

** Names already noticed in the Alphabetical Series are in Italics, new names in Roman character.

Aastley, for Astley.
Aba. *See* Abbott.
Abadam. *See* Aberdeen.
Abba. *See* Abbay.
Abbatt. *See* Abbott.
Abbery. *See* Aubrey.
Abbey.
Abbiss.
Abbley. *See* Abley.
Abbis. *See* Abbiss.
Abbitt.
Abbot.
Abbots. *See* Abbot.
Abbotson, for Abson.
Abbott.
Abby, for Abbey.
Abdon, for Abadon or Aberdeen.
Abe, for Abbey.
Abel.
Abele, for Abel.
Abell. *See* Abel.
Aberdeen.

Aberdein.
Aberson, for Abison, or Abson.
Abery. *See* Aubrey.
Abey. *See* Abbey.
Ablard, for Abillard. William Abillard witness to a charter of William de Onnebank, Normandy 1196 (MSAN.v.201). *See* Windebank.
Ablart. *See* Ablard.
Able. *See* Abel.
Ableson, for Abison, or Abson.
Abley.
Ablin. *See* Abelon.
Ablett.
Ablitt.
Abree, for Aubrey.
Abrey. *See* Aubrey.
Absalom.
Absalon.

Absell. *See* Absolom.
Absolom. *See* Absalom.
Absolon. *See* Absalon.
Abson, from Abison in Aquitaine. In 1213 King John gave directions to the Viscount of Abison regarding affairs at Limoges (Hardy, Rot. Claus.). In 1270 Petrus de Abescun was of Salop (Rot. Hundr.).
Absone, for Abson.
Acasan, for Acason.
Acason, perhaps for Algazon, a Norman name, mentioned by Ordericus Vitalis t. Henry I.
Ackeny. *See* Dakin.

Ackland.
Acland.
Aclin. N. Acelin, of Normandy 1195 (MRS). W. Acelin took the oaths to King John in France 1214 (Hardy, Rot. Claus.). Hugh Acelin, Oxfordshire c. 1270 (Rot. Hundr.).
Ackling. *See* Aclin.
Acouley, perhaps for Acoulon.
Acoulon.
A'Court.
Ackrall. *See* Ackrell.
Acrel. *See* Ackrell.
Acrell.
Action.
Acktom.
Acton.
Acut, for Agut. *See* Ague.
Adan, for Haddan.

Adde, for Addy.

Addearley, for Adderley.

Adden, for Haddan.

Ades, for Ardes.

Addey, for Atty.

Addie, for Addy.

Addington.

Addis, for Ardes.

Addinsell, or De Odingseles, from Flanders, formerly Barons of Maxtoke, Warwick. *See* Dugdale, Banks.

Addiss. *See* Ades.

Adds. *See* Ades.

Addy, for Atty.

Adey, for Addy.

Adie, for Addy.

Adin, for Haddan.

Adis, for Ardes.

Adlard, for Allard.

Adnitt.

Adran, for Adron.

Adrey. *See* Audrey.

Adrian. *See* Adrain.

Adron.

Adye, for Addy.

Aebe, for Abbey.

Aedy, for Addy.

Afey, or Haffie, from Auffay, near Rouen, Normandy. Richard and Gerard de Alfay or Aufay, Normandy 1180–95(MRS). John de Aufay, Somerset, c. 1272 (RH).

Affield, for Haffield or Haville. *See* Hovell.

Affials, for Affreils, from Arfeuilles, near Moulins, France. Wassal de Af-

froillbus had a writ of military summons to pass into Bretagne 1243.

Affron, for Avranches.

Agace.

Agard, for Apegard. *See* Apcar.

Agass. *See* Agace.

Agate.

Agee, for De Augo. *See* Agg.

Aget. *See* Agate.

Agett. *See* Agate.

Agg.

Aggard, for Agard.

Aggas.

Aggass. *See* Agga.

Aggett. *See* Achet.

Aggis, for Aggs.

Aggiss.

Aggs.

Aggus, for Aggs.

Agland.

Agnes. *See* Aina.

Agnew.

Agnis.

Agus. *See* Agga.

Agness. *See* Aina.

Aguaw, for Agnew.

Agney, for Agnis.

Aheary, for Airey.

Ahranes, for Arenes.

Aickin, for Aikin.

Aigen, for Aikin.

Aiken. *See* Dakin.

Aikens. *See* Dakins.

Aikin.

Ailes, for Iles.

Ailion, for Helion, a baronial family, from Hillion, near St. Brieux, Bretagne. Hervey de Helion held in capite in Devon 1086 (Domes.). The Helions Lords

of Asseriston, and Credy-Helion, Devon, long continued there. *See* Pole, Devon.

Ailing, for Ailion.

Aime. *See* Ames.

Aimers, for Hamars or Dormer.

Aimes, for Ames.

Aingel. *See* Angell.

Aingell.

Ainger.

Aingier. *See* Anger.

Ainscough, for Ayscough, or Askew.

Airay. *See* Airey.

Aireton. *See* Ayrton.

Airton, for Ayrton.

Airy.

Airzee, for Areci or Darcy.

Aisbell. *See* Isabel.

Aked. *See* Achett.

Aken. *See* Dakin.

Akerill. *See* Acrell.

Akeyn. *See* Dakin.

Akines. *See* Dakin.

Akins, for Akin.

Akney, for Akeny. *See* Dakin.

Akrill.

Alabaster.

Alard. *See* Allard.

Alatt. *See* Alet.

Alban, for Albany.

Albany, or De Albini. *See* Daubeny.

Albee, for Alby.

Alben. *See* Albon.

Alber, for Albert.

Albers, for Alber.

Albert.

Albery, for Aubrey.

Alberry. *See* Aubrey.

Albeury, for Aubrey.

Albin.

Albion. *See* Albon.

Alblaster. *See* Alabaster.

Albon.

Albra, for Albray.

Albray, for Aubrey.

Alburt, for Albert.

Albutt, for Albert.

Alce. *See* Alcy.

Alcey, for Alcy.

Alcy, or Halsey, from Aucy, in the Cotentin, Normandy. Galfridus de Aucie, Normandy 1195, 1198 (MRS); Alice and John Alsy or Aucy in England c. 1272 (Rot. Hundr.).

Aldmound, or Almont. N. Aumont (Almont), of Normandy 1195 (MRS).

Aldworth.

Alebon. *See* Albon.

Alee. *See* Aley.

Alenson. *See* Alison.

Aley, from Ailly, near Evreux, Normandy. Walter Allie, and Simon de Allies, Normandy 1180–95 (MRS); Walter Allye and Geoffry D'Alli, of England c. 1272 (Rot. Hundr.).

Alfin. Robert Alvine, of Normandy 1195 (MRS); Ralph and Richard Alwin, England c. 1272 (RH).

Alfrey.

Ahbone. *See* Albon.

Alice.

Alison.

Aliston, for Alison.

Alistone, for Alison.

Alivers. *See* Alivers.

Allad, for Allatt.

Allan.

Allar, for Allard.

Allard.

Allars, for Allar.

Allart, for Allard.

Allason. *See* Alison.

Allass, for Alice.

Allberry, for Aubrey.

Allbery, for Aubrey.

Allblaster. *See* Alabaster.

Allbon, for Albon.

Allbones. *See* Allebone. [brey.

Allbuary, for Aubrey.

Allday, from Haliday. Haliday, in Normandy, was granted by Philip Augustus

to Robert de Los 1219 (MSAN, v. 159); Reginald and Philip de Halidai occur in England 1199 (RCR).

Allden. *See* Alden.

Alldin, for Alden.

Allebone.

Allee. *See* Aley.

INDEX

OF

MEDIÆVAL SURNAMES

IN THIS WORK.

———◆———

INDEX.

461

INDEX.

INDEX.

474

INDEX.

477

INDEX.

Spottiswoode & Co., Printers, New-street Square, London.

Lightning Source UK Ltd.
Milton Keynes UK
14 December 2010

164371UK00005B/34/P